JEAN ANDREWS, PhD

Jump Right In!

Essential
Computer Skills
Using Microsoft®
Office 2010

PEARSON

1 Lake Street, Upper Saddle River, NJ 07458

Handwritten notes:

Room-327
Comp. Lit.

Username:
Chekeeperbf
password
March 13, 1986

Course
ID: CRSKLZLL-

Mozilla
Frcbx 8019448
& that's
webbrowser.
Install google
chrome.

nhorton@bcc.edu

Look under
Student resources
is where you
will find the
answers

questions will be on
blackboard

type in
word and email
to teacher

URL-
uniform
Resource
Locator

Homework:
Began chapter 3

Simulation
Chapter 3
Due next
thurs Oct 10, 2013

MY IT lab
.com

Chapter
11 due
next
week.

Oct 17, 2013
1st test/Quiz
need to be on
time (5:30)
test on
Chapter 3

Jump Right In! Essential Computer Skills Using Microsoft Office 2010

ISBN-13: 978-0-13-297570-4
ISBN-10: 0-13-297570-X

Library of Congress Cataloging-in-Publication data is on file.

Printed in the United States on America

First Printing: December 2011

Trademarks

Warning and Disclaimer

Associate Publisher
Dave Dusthimer

Executive Editor
Mary Beth Ray

Executive Editor, Higher Education Group
Jenifer Niles

Development Editor
Dayna Isley

Managing Editor
Sandra Schroeder

Senior Project Editor
Tonya Simpson

Copy Editor
Chuck Hutchinson

Indexer
Brad Herriman

Proofreader
Sheri Cain

Technical Editors
Jeri L. Burkhart
Julie Sharf-Craig
Gary Marrer

Publishing Coordinator
Vanessa Evans

Multimedia Developers
John Herrin
Dan Scherf
Christopher Cleveland

Book Designer
Gary Adair

Composition
Studio Galou

Graphics
Tammy Graham

Illustrator
Laura Robbins

Contents at a Glance

Contents of the DVD

Glossary

Sample Files

About the CompTIA Strata Exam

Videos

Contents

Contents of the DVD

About the Author

Jean Andrews, PhD, has more than 30 years of experience in the computer industry, including more than 13 years in the college classroom and 3 years in public schools. She has worked in a wide variety of businesses and corporations designing, writing, and supporting applications software; managing a PC repair help desk; and troubleshooting wide area networks. She has written a variety of books on software, hardware, and the Internet. She lives in northeast Georgia.

Dedication

This book is dedicated to the glory of God.

Acknowledgments

Thank you to the wonderful people at Pearson who put so much creativity, innovation, and hard work into this book. Dayna Isley, Mary Beth Ray, and Dave Dusthimer, your contributions have made this book what it is. As Dave said, "We'll take your ideas and make them better." That's precisely what you did, and I appreciate that more than words can say. You certainly make a creative and impressive team!

Thank you, Gary Marrer, Jeri Lyn Burkhart, and Julie Craig, who carefully reviewed every word in the book. Your comments and ideas coming from extensive classroom experiences have helped to shape each chapter. You'll see your hands in the results.

Thank you to Joy Dark and Anne Marie Francis, who helped with the writing process. Joy and I spent many late nights working together, and I'm sure Anne Marie worked late nights as well. Without you both, this book would not have happened.

Thank you to the many other reviewers, editors, designers, and managers who gave so much to make a book we can all be proud of. It was truly a team effort and a delight working with each of you.

About the Reviewers

Jeri L. Burkhart has been involved in higher education as an instructor and administrator throughout her career at various state universities and private universities. Most recently, she has been an Adjunct Associate Professor for Ivy Tech Community College for over 16 years and an Enrollment Manager for Indiana Institute of Technology. She holds a master's degree in Public Affairs with a Public Management concentration from Indiana University. She also completed postgraduate work at Indiana University in Public Policy and Public Management.

Gary Marrer has taught a variety of technology classes for the past 10 years at Glendale Community College in Glendale, Arizona. Mr. Marrer worked in private industry in various technology positions for almost 20 years before becoming a computer instructor. He enjoys working with new computer programming students but also likes working with students in improving their computer literacy.

Julie Sharf-Craig is an adjunct faculty member in the Business and Computer Information Systems Department at Scottsdale Community College in Scottsdale, Arizona. She teaches and develops curriculum for Microsoft Office applications, computer concepts, terminology, and the role of computers in business and society. She teaches both online and face-to-face classes at Scottsdale Community College. She holds a bachelor's degree in Liberal Arts in Psychology from the University of Nevada, Las Vegas, and a master's degree in Arts in Organizational Management from the University of Phoenix. Before joining Scottsdale Community College, Ms. Sharf-Craig spent 10 years selling computers, networks, and computer services and managing technical help desks at MicroAge and Gateway Computers.

We Want to Hear from You!

As the reader of this book, *you* are our most important critic and commentator. We value your opinion and want to know what we're doing right, what we could do better, what areas you'd like to see us publish in, and any other words of wisdom you're willing to pass our way.

As an executive editor for Pearson, I welcome your comments. You can email or write me directly to let me know what you did or didn't like about this book—as well as what we can do to make our books better.

Please note that I cannot help you with technical problems related to the topic of this book. We do have a User Services group, however, where I will forward specific technical questions related to the book.

When you write, please be sure to include this book's title and author as well as your name, email address, and phone number. I will carefully review your comments and share them with the author and editors who worked on the book.

Email: jenifer.niles@pearson.com

Mail: Jenifer Niles
Executive Editor
Pearson
75 Arlington Street
Boston, MA 02116

Reader Services

Visit our website and register this book at http://www.pearsonhighered.com/jump/ for convenient access to any updates, downloads, or errata that might be available for this book.

Introduction

Jump Right In! Essential Computer Skills Using Microsoft Office 2010 was written to be the best tool in the market today to prepare you to be a skilled and knowledgeable computer user. Computers are everywhere, and we all need to know how to use them, how to take care of them, how to buy one, and what to do when they don't work.

Microsoft Office 2010 is the most popular personal productivity software on the market today. It is a suite of applications including Microsoft Word, PowerPoint, Excel, Access, OneNote, and Outlook. This book teaches you how to use these applications to help you perform the most common personal and business tasks. You learn to use Word to create documents including a flyer, business letter, résumé, and research paper. OneNote is used to collect and organize your research notes. You use PowerPoint to create dynamite presentations. Excel is a great tool to manage tables of text, numbers, and calculations. Outlook is used to manage email, and Access can be used to manage a database. Each project you work on is one that you actually might encounter in the real world. You learn not only how to use the application, but also how the application can help you solve a problem in your personal, academic, or professional career.

Knowing how to take care of a computer to keep it secure and running well and knowing what to do when things go wrong are just as important as knowing how to use a computer. Several chapters in the book are devoted to help you become a confident computer owner. You learn all the technical knowledge you need to make the best buying or upgrading decisions and how to secure your computer and keep it maintained and running smoothly. You learn how to fix the most common computer problems, such as an Internet connection that doesn't work, a virus infection, or a missing or corrupted data file. By the end of this course, expect your family and friends to be impressed at how confident you are at solving common computer problems.

Although these are all important computer skills, the most important computer skill of all is now to teach yourself a computer skill. Computer hardware and software are constantly changing and improving. In the computer world, what you learn today won't carry you through tomorrow. This book is designed to help you teach yourself a computer skill. Rather than provide the step-by-step, paint-by-number approach to learning a computer skill, this book encourages you to tinker, poke around, and explore on your own with minimum direction. You learn to teach yourself using the web or help tools that each application or Windows makes available to you. The more you can figure out on your own, the better prepared you will be to teach yourself a computer skill after you complete this course. However, know that each activity in the chapter has a complete step-by-step solution available *if you need or want it.*

A Note to Instructors

As instructors, we are always looking for the best tools to help our students. This book is designed to be just that because it allows you to teach the way you want to teach and allows students to learn the way they want to learn.

You can easily tailor this book and the accompanying materials to each student's needs. Some students might need to step through each solution to each On Your Own activity. Other students need more of a challenge. For these students, you can encourage them to skip directly to the Chapter Mastery Project. After they have completed the projects at the end of the chapter, they can use any extra time to tutor slower students in your class. Most students will fall somewhere in the middle: They might be able to skip directly to the Chapter Mastery Project on some chapters but not others. They will rely on the solutions occasionally but will not always need them. They might start the Chapter Mastery Project, get stuck, and turn back to the chapter to complete the tasks there. Because students can use a variety of methods as they choose, everyone can work at the pace she is comfortable and the entire class can be successful. Your guidance to help each student find the method that works best for her will be crucial to her success.

The freedom to try, explore, make mistakes, and try again is one of the best learning experiences we can provide our students. This learning style is more in keeping with the real world and what our students will most certainly encounter when they leave our classrooms. The very best experience we can provide them in this course is this process of learning to teach themselves a computer skill.

Skills Learned in This Book

In reexamining the computer skills needed for the 21st century, it becomes evident that change is needed. We need less of the history of computing and details about Microsoft Office and more about other related computer skills, such as using the Windows operating system; exploring the Internet; and buying, maintaining, and securing a personal computer. The content in this book is about a 50-50 split between Microsoft Office applications and these other valuable hands-on computer skills.

Hardware, Software, and Internet Requirements

To successfully complete the activities in this book, you need access to the following equipment and software:

- ▶ A personal computer using Windows 7 and Microsoft Office 2010
- ▶ Internet access, using either a wired or wireless connection
- ▶ A DVD drive
- ▶ A USB port on the computer
- ▶ A USB flash drive is desirable but not required
- ▶ A printer is desirable but not required

Strata IT Fundamentals Certificate by CompTIA

If you are interested in a career in IT or just want to better understand the technology you learned about in a chapter, read the "Going Deeper with a Strata Certificate" document provided on the DVD. On the companion website you will find the Quick Reference to the Strata IT Fundamentals certificate by CompTIA (www.comptia.org).

Jump Right In
and Learn How to Teach Yourself Computer Skills!

One main goal of this book is to prove to you that you really don't need a textbook to learn a computer skill. It is our hope that after working through a few chapters, you will agree. Think of this book as a diving board. It's a jumping-off point to a lifetime of teaching yourself how to use, maintain, buy, and fix computers.

Explore, experiment, and follow the path that works for you.

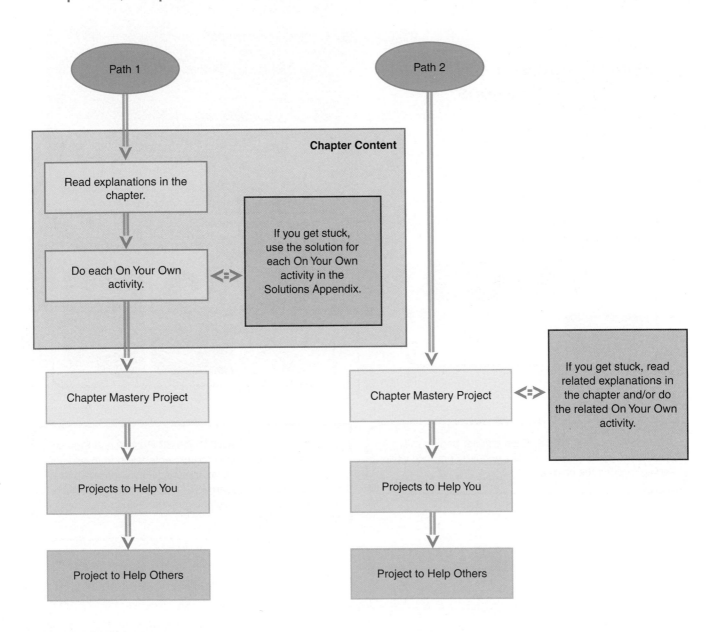

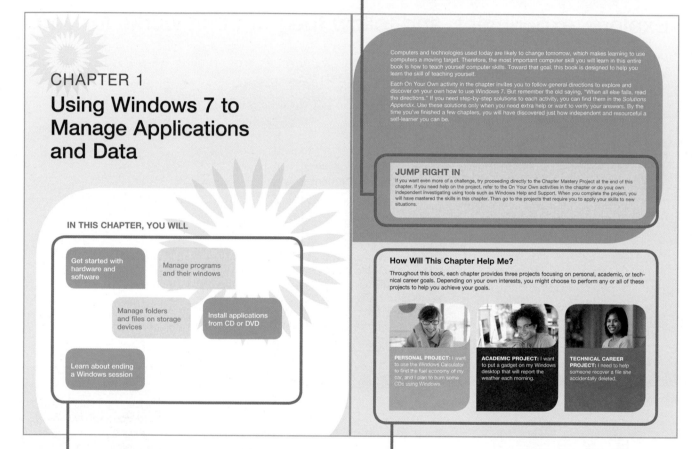

JUMP RIGHT IN: If you already know the material in a chapter or want to test the waters as an independent investigator and learner, you are encouraged to jump directly to the Chapter Mastery Project.

CHAPTER 1
Using Windows 7 to Manage Applications and Data

Computers and technologies used today are likely to change tomorrow, which makes learning to use computers a moving target. Therefore, the most important computer skill you will learn in this entire book is how to teach yourself computer skills. Toward that goal, this book is designed to help you learn the skill of teaching yourself.

Each On Your Own activity in the chapter invites you to follow general directions to explore and discover on your own how to use Windows 7. But remember the old saying, "When all else fails, read the directions." If you need step-by-step solutions to each activity, you can find them in the *Solutions Appendix*. Use these solutions only when you need extra help or want to verify your answers. By the time you've finished a few chapters, you will have discovered just how independent and resourceful a self-learner you can be.

JUMP RIGHT IN

If you want even more of a challenge, try proceeding directly to the Chapter Mastery Project at the end of this chapter. If you need help on the project, refer to the On Your Own activities in the chapter or do your own independent investigating using tools such as Windows Help and Support. When you complete the project, you will have mastered the skills in this chapter. Then go to the projects that require you to apply your skills to new situations.

IN THIS CHAPTER, YOU WILL

Get started with hardware and software

Manage programs and their windows

Manage folders and files on storage devices

Install applications from CD or DVD

Learn about ending a Windows session

How Will This Chapter Help Me?

Throughout this book, each chapter provides three projects focusing on personal, academic, or technical career goals. Depending on your own interests, you might choose to perform any or all of these projects to help you achieve your goals.

PERSONAL PROJECT: I want to use the Windows Calculator to find the fuel economy of my car, and I plan to burn some CDs using Windows.

ACADEMIC PROJECT: I want to put a gadget on my Windows desktop that will report the weather each morning.

TECHNICAL CAREER PROJECT: I need to help someone recover a file she accidentally deleted.

CHAPTER OBJECTIVES: Each chapter begins with a list of concepts you will learn or tasks you will complete while reading through the chapter.

HOW WILL THIS CHAPTER HELP ME? and Projects to Help You: Three real-world projects taken from personal life, academic, or technical careers give you experience in applying what you've learned in these areas. The projects are introduced at the beginning of the chapter and completed at the end.

On Your Own

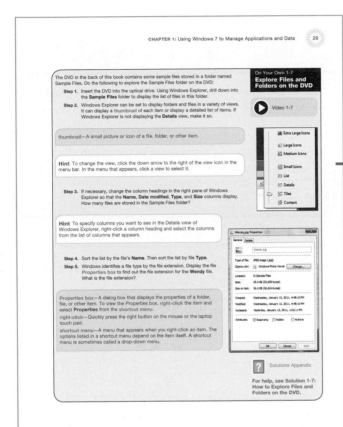

ON YOUR OWN: More than 120 On Your Own projects give you hands-on practice to apply what you are learning.

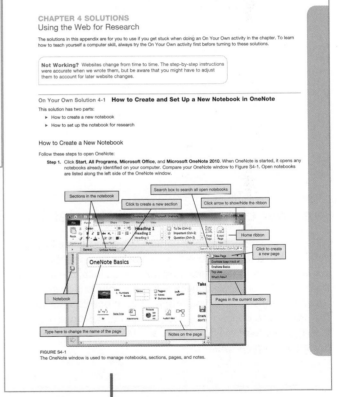

SOLUTIONS APPENDIX: Try to do each On Your Own activity with the minimal directions given in the activity. If you need help, turn to the step-by-step solution for the activity in the *Solutions Appendix*.

Chapter Mastery Projects

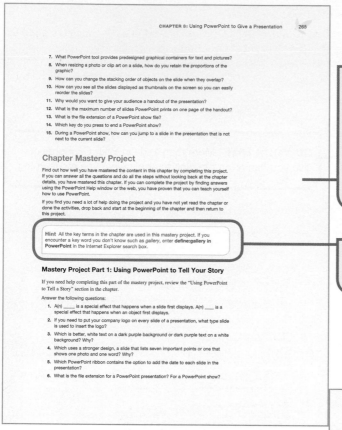

CHAPTER MASTERY PROJECT: This project helps you pull together all your new skills. Complete this project to find out whether you have mastered the chapter. All the key terms, concepts, and skills covered in the chapter are covered in the Chapter Mastery Project. You can start the chapter by attempting to complete this project. If you get stuck, go back and read the chapter and do the On Your Own activities.

HINTS: A hint gives just enough information to get you going when you might be stuck.

Are Your Learning to Teach Yourself?

After you successfully complete the Chapter Mastery Project, you are asked to rate yourself as to how independent a learner you are. Rate yourself by how much help you needed from the On Your Own activities and the solutions in the *Solutions Appendix*. As you progress from one chapter to the next, try to depend less and less on the solutions so that toward the end of the book you can truly say, "I can teach myself a computer skill!"

INDEPENDENT LEARNER sections help you get better at learning about computers.

Projects to Help You and Others

At the end of each chapter are three "Projects to Help You" in your personal, academic, and technical careers. Depending on what you want to accomplish, you might want to complete one or all of these projects.

No matter what you are doing in your life, always look for opportunities to give back. The last project in each chapter is a project to help another. Find an apprentice who wants to learn about computers—perhaps a neighbor, younger brother, uncle, grand-mother, or friend. The best learning happens as you teach someone else. Help this person learn what you have learned in the chapter. For the best experience, teach someone older or younger than you and encourage this person to stick it out with you through the entire course.

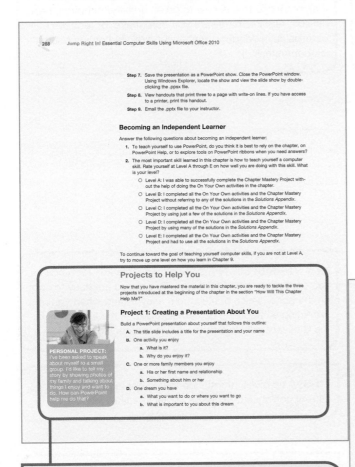

PROJECTS TO HELP YOU enable you to achieve personal, academic, or technical career goals.

PROJECTS TO HELP OTHERS encourage you to mentor others using the skills you've learned.

Help Along the Way

SKILL-BASED SIMULATIONS available through myITLab give you the opportunity to practice a skill that might require permission in Windows that is not available on your school lab computer. For more information, visit http://www.myitlab.com.

 Video #

INSTRUCTIONAL VIDEOS by the author are on the DVD in the back of the book and on the accompanying myITLab. Watch a video to see how to do an activity that might be difficult, requires hardware you don't have, or requires a permission in Windows that is not available on your school lab computer.

---

50   Jump Right In! Essential Computer Skills Using Microsoft Office 2010

Getting News on the Web

The web is a great way to get news. In the past, news came to us by town criers, newspapers, radio, and television. But when we use the web to get our news, we can also voice our opinions about news and easily share it with others.

The Internet is made up of many computers all over the world connected to each other. The news comes to us over the Internet from computers serving up the news in web pages. A web page is a document that contains text and perhaps graphics, sound, animation, or video, to be displayed on a computer screen by a browser. The collection of all web pages available on the Internet is called the World Wide Web, also called the web.

> **Internet**—Many computers over the world connected to each other. This global network of computers is used to receive and serve up untold amounts of data and provides us powerful ways to communicate with others. When you use a computer connected to the Internet, know that your computer is also part of the Internet.
>
> **browser**—A program that searches or browses web pages from the web.
>
> **web page**—A document that can include text, graphics, sound, animation, and video. The document is constructed using a group of rules collectively called the Hypertext Markup Language (HTML). The document is called a hypertext document and is designed to be displayed by a browser.
>
> **World Wide Web or web**—A collection of web pages made available by computers connected to the Internet. The World Wide Web is one of many applications that the Internet supports.

> **Tip** The Internet and the web are similar to a transportation system that supports the delivery of cargo. For example, the road system (the Internet) in our country is used by the postal system (World Wide Web) to deliver the mail (web pages).

Introduction to Internet Explorer

If your computer is connected to the Internet, you can use Internet Explorer (IE) to find information on the Internet. Recall from Chapter 1, "Using Windows 7 to Manage Applications and Data," that Internet Explorer, Version 8, is the browser included in Windows 7.

> **Not Working?** This chapter assumes that the computer you are using is a Windows 7 computer connected to the Internet. If you have a problem with the connection, know that Chapter 12, "Connecting to the Internet and Securing a Computer," and Chapters 13, "Maintaining a Computer and Fixing Computer Problems," cover how to connect a computer to the Internet and what to do when the connection fails.
>
> Windows 7 comes with Internet Explorer version 8 and can be upgraded to Internet Explorer version 9. The instructions and figures used in this chapter are for Windows 7 and Internet Explorer 8. To find out what version of IE you have, click the Help button in the Internet Explorer window, and then click **About Internet Explorer.** If you have IE version 9 installed, know that some IE features described in the chapter might work differently on your computer.

KEY TERMS: Key terms are defined in a key term box as you encounter them in the text. The boxes are easy to spot on the page, which makes them easy to find when you're skimming a chapter. You can also find all the key terms in the Glossary.pdf file on the DVD in the back of the book.

TIPS: A tip gives information that is not necessary for the current activity but might be useful in a later situation.

NOT WORKING?: These boxes tell you what to check or try when something is not working.

Wrapping Up the Chapter

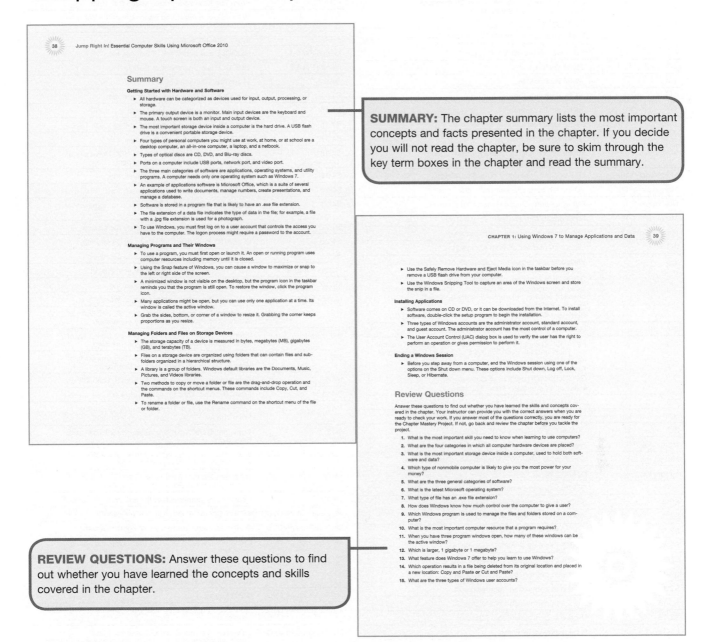

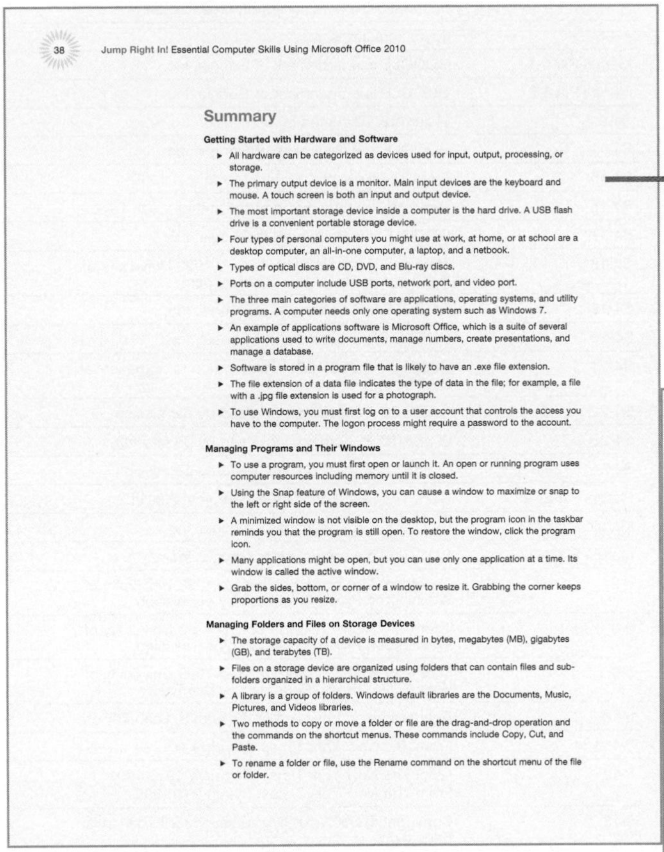
38 Jump Right In! Essential Computer Skills Using Microsoft Office 2010

Summary

Getting Started with Hardware and Software

- All hardware can be categorized as devices used for input, output, processing, or storage.
- The primary output device is a monitor. Main input devices are the keyboard and mouse. A touch screen is both an input and output device.
- The most important storage device inside a computer is the hard drive. A USB flash drive is a convenient portable storage device.
- Four types of personal computers you might use at work, at home, or at school are a desktop computer, an all-in-one computer, a laptop, and a netbook.
- Types of optical discs are CD, DVD, and Blu-ray discs.
- Ports on a computer include USB ports, network port, and video port.
- The three main categories of software are applications, operating systems, and utility programs. A computer needs only one operating system such as Windows 7.
- An example of applications software is Microsoft Office, which is a suite of several applications used to write documents, manage numbers, create presentations, and manage a database.
- Software is stored in a program file that is likely to have an .exe file extension.
- The file extension of a data file indicates the type of data in the file; for example, a file with a .jpg file extension is used for a photograph.
- To use Windows, you must first log on to a user account that controls the access you have to the computer. The logon process might require a password to the account.

Managing Programs and Their Windows

- To use a program, you must first open or launch it. An open or running program uses computer resources including memory until it is closed.
- Using the Snap feature of Windows, you can cause a window to maximize or snap to the left or right side of the screen.
- A minimized window is not visible on the desktop, but the program icon in the taskbar reminds you that the program is still open. To restore the window, click the program icon.
- Many applications might be open, but you can use only one application at a time. Its window is called the active window.
- Grab the sides, bottom, or corner of a window to resize it. Grabbing the corner keeps proportions as you resize.

Managing Folders and Files on Storage Devices

- The storage capacity of a device is measured in bytes, megabytes (MB), gigabytes (GB), and terabytes (TB).
- Files on a storage device are organized using folders that can contain files and subfolders organized in a hierarchical structure.
- A library is a group of folders. Windows default libraries are the Documents, Music, Pictures, and Videos libraries.
- Two methods to copy or move a folder or file are the drag-and-drop operation and the commands on the shortcut menus. These commands include Copy, Cut, and Paste.
- To rename a folder or file, use the Rename command on the shortcut menu of the file or folder.

SUMMARY: The chapter summary lists the most important concepts and facts presented in the chapter. If you decide you will not read the chapter, be sure to skim through the key term boxes in the chapter and read the summary.

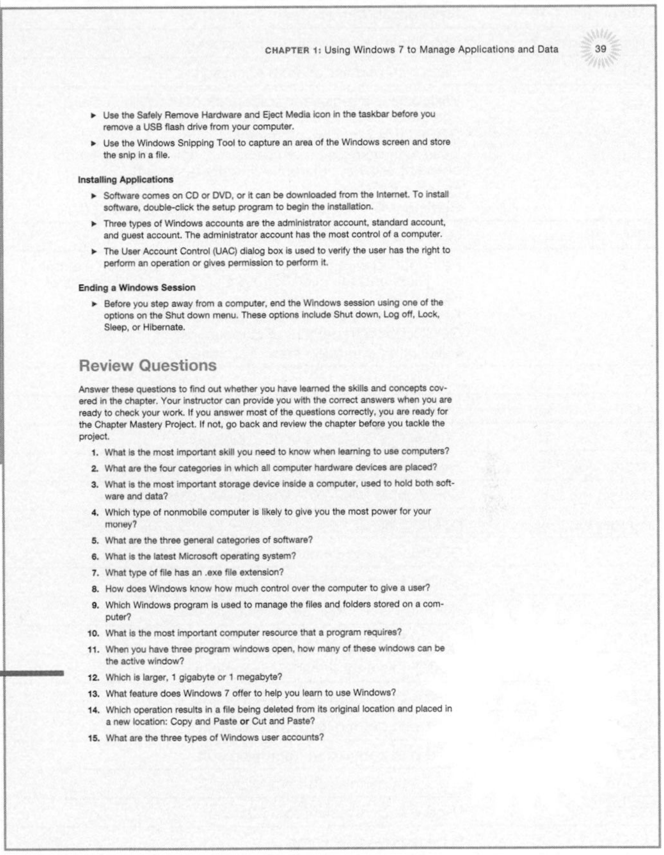
CHAPTER 1: Using Windows 7 to Manage Applications and Data 39

- Use the Safely Remove Hardware and Eject Media icon in the taskbar before you remove a USB flash drive from your computer.
- Use the Windows Snipping Tool to capture an area of the Windows screen and store the snip in a file.

Installing Applications

- Software comes on CD or DVD, or it can be downloaded from the Internet. To install software, double-click the setup program to begin the installation.
- Three types of Windows accounts are the administrator account, standard account, and guest account. The administrator account has the most control of a computer.
- The User Account Control (UAC) dialog box is used to verify the user has the right to perform an operation or gives permission to perform it.

Ending a Windows Session

- Before you step away from a computer, end the Windows session using one of the options on the Shut down menu. These options include Shut down, Log off, Lock, Sleep, or Hibernate.

Review Questions

Answer these questions to find out whether you have learned the skills and concepts covered in the chapter. Your instructor can provide you with the correct answers when you are ready to check your work. If you answer most of the questions correctly, you are ready for the Chapter Mastery Project. If not, go back and review the chapter before you tackle the project.

1. What is the most important skill you need to know when learning to use computers?
2. What are the four categories in which all computer hardware devices are placed?
3. What is the most important storage device inside a computer, used to hold both software and data?
4. Which type of nonmobile computer is likely to give you the most power for your money?
5. What are the three general categories of software?
6. What is the latest Microsoft operating system?
7. What type of file has an .exe file extension?
8. How does Windows know how much control over the computer to give a user?
9. Which Windows program is used to manage the files and folders stored on a computer?
10. What is the most important computer resource that a program requires?
11. When you have three program windows open, how many of these windows can be the active window?
12. Which is larger, 1 gigabyte or 1 megabyte?
13. What feature does Windows 7 offer to help you learn to use Windows?
14. Which operation results in a file being deleted from its original location and placed in a new location: Copy and Paste **or** Cut and Paste?
15. What are the three types of Windows user accounts?

REVIEW QUESTIONS: Answer these questions to find out whether you have learned the concepts and skills covered in the chapter.

Companion Website

Visit our website and register this book at **http://www.pearsonhighered.com/jump/** for convenient access to any updates, downloads, or errata that might be available for this book. You will also find the Quick Reference to the Strata IT Fundamentals certificate by CompTIA (www.comptia.org).

PHOTO CREDITS

Figure	Credit Line
Chapter-opening photos	David Lees/Digital Vision/Getty Images Goodluz/Shutterstock Pius Lee/Shuttertock
1-1	Keyboard: Borodaev/Shutterstock Mouse: janprchal/Shutterstock Processor: Lipowski Milan/Shutterstock Hard drive: Kitch Bain/Shutterstock Memory modules: Norman Chan/Shutterstock Monitor: Kitch Bain/Shutterstock Printer: Shutterstock
1-2	Desktop computer: karam Miri/Shutterstock CPU: Ivan Montero Martinez/Shutterstock CD player: Fotocrisis/Shutterstock
1-3	Joyful Ventures, Inc.
1-4	Joyful Ventures, Inc.
1-5	Joyful Ventures, Inc.
1-7	Joyful Ventures, Inc.
1-10	Joyful Ventures, Inc.
1-19	alxpin/istockphoto.com
Margin pic 1-9	Touch screen: arindambanerjee/Shutterstock Touch pad: INSAGO/Shutterstock
Margin pic 1-10	USB and network ports: hfng/Shutterstock
Margin pic 1-14	VGA video port: carroteater/Shutterstock
Margin pic 1-15	DVI video port: Charlie Hutton/Shutterstock
Margin pic 1-16	Flash drive: Norman Chan/Shutterstock
Margin pic 1-17	Dog: Dmitry Kalinovsky/Shutterstock
2-1	Used with permission from Microsoft.
2-3	Wikipedia is a registered trademark of the Wikimedia Foundation, Inc., a non-profit organization. GOOGLE is a trademark of Google, Inc. Used with permission of About Inc., which can be found online at www.about.com. All rights reserved. Facebook © 2011. Copyright © 1995-2011 eBay, Inc. All rights reserved.
2-4	GOOGLE is a trademark of Google, Inc.
2-5	Reproduced with permission of Yahoo! Inc. ©2011 Yahoo! Inc. Flickr and the Flickr logo are registered trademarks of Yahoo! Inc. Reproduced by permission of Shutterfly, Inc. GOOGLE is a trademark of Google, Inc. Used with permission from Microsoft.
2-6	Buy.com
S2-1	Used with permission from Microsoft.
2-7	GOOGLE is a trademark of Google, Inc.
Margin Pic 2-1	From *The New York Times*, March 25, © 2011
Margin Pic 2-5	Copyright © 1999-2011 PayPal. All rights reserved.
Margin Pic 2-6	© 2011 Dell.
S2-5	GOOGLE is a trademark of Google, Inc.
S2-6	GOOGLE is a trademark of Google, Inc.
S2-7	GOOGLE is a trademark of Google, Inc.
S2-8	GOOGLE is a trademark of Google, Inc.
S2-10	GOOGLE is a trademark of Google, Inc.
S2-12	Used with permission from Microsoft.
S2-13	Used with permission from Microsoft.
S2-14	Used with permission from Microsoft.
S2-15	Used with permission from Microsoft.
S2-16	Used with permission from Microsoft.
S2-17	Provided by Wells Fargo.
S2-19	Used with permission from Microsoft.
S2-22	Used with permission from Microsoft.
S2-23	Used with permission from Microsoft.
Margin Pic S2-1	Used with permission from Microsoft.
Margin Pic S2-3	GOOGLE is a trademark of Google, Inc.
Margin Pic S2-4	GOOGLE is a trademark of Google, Inc.
Margin Pic S2-5	Used with permission from Microsoft.
Margin Pic S2-6	GOOGLE is a trademark of Google, Inc.
Margin Pic S2-7	GOOGLE is a trademark of Google, Inc.
Margin Pic S2-9	Used with permission from Microsoft.
3-17	GOOGLE is a trademark of Google, Inc.
4-6	Wikipedia is a registered trademark of the Wikimedia Foundation, Inc., a non-profit organization.
4-7	GOOGLE is a trademark of Google, Inc.

Figure	Credit Line
4-9	Courtesy of Amazon.com, Inc. or its affiliates. All rights reserved.
4-10	Wikipedia is a registered trademark of the Wikimedia Foundation, Inc., a non-profit organization.
4-11	NewspaperArchive.com. Reprinted by permission. From *The New York Times*, January 27 © 2011
4-12	From *The New York Times*, March 9 © 1999
4-13	Wikipedia is a registered trademark of the Wikimedia Foundation, Inc., a non-profit organization.
4-14	Joyful Industries, Inc.
Margin Pic 4-1	GOOGLE is a trademark of Google, Inc.
Margin Pic 4-2	GOOGLE is a trademark of Google, Inc.
S4-9	© carrot2. Reprinted by permission.
S4-11	GOOGLE is a trademark of Google, Inc.
S4-15	From *The New York Times*, March 9 © 1999
S4-16	Reprinted by permission of the author, Leah Taylor.
S4-17	GOOGLE is a trademark of Google, Inc.
S4-18	Thomsen, Moritz. *Living Poor*. © 1990 University of Washington Press. Reprinted by permission.
S4-19	GOOGLE is a trademark of Google, Inc.
S4-20	GOOGLE is a trademark of Google, Inc.
S4-21	Copyright © 2007-2011 Association for Experiential Education.
S4-22	© EBSCO Publishing, Inc. Used by permission.
S4-23	© EBSCO Publishing, Inc. Used by permission.
S4-24	© EBSCO Publishing, Inc. Used by permission.
Margin Pic S4-6	From *The New York Times*, February © 2011
Margin Pic S4-7	GOOGLE is a trademark of Google, Inc.
Margin Pic S4-8	GOOGLE is a trademark of Google, Inc.
5-2	Thomsen, Moritz. *Living Poor*. © 1990 University of Washington Press. Reprinted by permission.
5-3	Thomsen, Moritz. *Living Poor*. © 1990 University of Washington Press. Reprinted by permission.
5-9	Thomsen, Moritz. *Living Poor*. © 1990 University of Washington Press. Reprinted by permission.
5-10	Reprinted by permission of the author, Leah Taylor.
5-11	From *The New York Times*, March 9 © 1999
5-12	From *The New York Times*, February 19 © 1991 From *The New York Times*, March 9 © 1999
5-13	Copyright © 2007-2011 Association for Experiential Education.
My Research on DVD	Wikipedia is a registered trademark of the Wikimedia Foundation, Inc., a non-profit organization.
S5-8	Thomsen, Moritz. *Living Poor*. © 1990 University of Washington Press. Reprinted by permission.
S5-10	Reprinted by permission of the author, Leah Taylor.
My Research on DVD	© 2011 CompTIA, Inc. All rights reserved.
My Research on DVD	© 2011 Demand Media, Inc. All rights reserved.
My Research on DVD	Copyright © 2009 MediaTec Publishing, Inc. All rights reserved.
My Research on DVD	© 2011 Steven Niznik (http://jobsearchtech.about.com). Used with permission of About Inc., which can be found online at www.about.com. All rights reserved.
My Research on DVD	© 2011 Cisco
My Research on DVD	From Sage Publications, Inc., Vol. 32, Issue 3. Reprinted by permission.
My Research on DVD	University of South Carolina College of Mass Communications and Information Studies Mentor Program. © USC Communications Alumni Society.
My Research on DVD	Kate Schrauth: Reprinted by permission of the author.
My Research on DVD	Reprinted with permission from Axzo Press LLC.
My Research on DVD	Wikipedia is a registered trademark of the Wikimedia Foundation, Inc., a non-profit organization.
My Research on DVD	GOOGLE is a trademark of Google, Inc.
My Research on DVD	From *The New York Times*, March 9 © 1999
My Research on DVD	Reprinted by permission of the author, Leah Taylor.
My Research on DVD	© EBSCO Publishing, Inc. Used by permission.
My Research on DVD	© carrot2. Reprinted by permission.
My Research on DVD	From *News and Tribune*, March 22, 2010. Reprinted by permission.
My Research on DVD	Career Builder, August 24, 2009. Reprinted by permission.
My Research on DVD	*Online social networking on campus: understanding what matters in student culture* by Martínez Alemán, Ana M. © 2008 Reproduced with permission of TAYLOR & FRANCIS GROUP LLC - BOOKS in the format Textbook via Copyright Clearance Center.

PHOTO CREDITS

Figure	Credit Line
My Research on DVD	*Saving Facebook* by James Grimmelmann, 94 Iowa L. Rev. 1137 (2009).
My Research on DVD	© News Limited, November 1, 2011.
6-7	Facebook © 2011. Photos reprinted with permission from Jennifer Dark, Julie Cherolis, Lucinda Dark, and Mike West.
6-9	Facebook © 2011.
6-10	Facebook © 2011. Photos reprinted with permission from Julie Cherolis, Joy Dark, Jennifer Dark, Lucinda Dark, and Mike West
6-11	Facebook © 2011.
6-13	Facebook © 2011. Photos reprinted with permission from Julie Cherolis, Jennifer Dark, and Mike West.
6-14	Facebook © 2011.
6-15	Facebook © 2011.
6-16	© 2011 Twitter.
6-17	LinkedIn and the LinkedIn logo are registered trademarks of LinkedIn Corporation, Inc., in the United States and/or other countries. All rights reserved. Photos reprinted with permission from Amanda Brodkin and Miles Anthony Smith (http://www.linkedin.com/in/milesanthonysmith).
6-18	LinkedIn and the LinkedIn logo are registered trademarks of LinkedIn Corporation, Inc., in the United States and/or other countries. All rights reserved. Photo reprinted with permission from Sarah Sambol.
6-19	LinkedIn and the LinkedIn logo are registered trademarks of LinkedIn Corporation, Inc., in the United States and/or other countries. All rights reserved. Photos reprinted with permission from Sarah Sambol and Nadar Allan.
6-20	Marc and Angel Hack Life (blog). Reprinted by permission.
6-21	carlosseller/Shutterstock
6-22	GOOGLE is a trademark of Google, Inc.
6-23	GOOGLE is a trademark of Google, Inc.
Margin Pic 6-3	Facebook © 2011. Photo reprinted with permission from David Dusthimer.
Margin Pic 6-4	Facebook © 2011. Photo reprinted with permission from Joy Dark.
Margin Pic 6-5	Facebook © 2011. Photo reprinted with permission from Joy Dark.
Margin Pic 6-6	© 2011 Twitter.
Margin Pic 6-7	Joyful Industries, Inc.
Margin Pic 6-8	Denis Dryashkin/Shutterstock
S6-11	© 2011 Twitter.
S6-12	© 2011 Twitter.
S6-13	© 2011 Twitter
7-1	Copyright © 2011 craigslist, inc. Reprinted by permission.
7-10	Joyful Industries, Inc.
8-1	Joyful Industries, Inc.
9-6	iStockPhoto
9-16	iStockPhoto
9-17	iStockPhoto
9-18	iStockPhoto
Margin pic 12-1	tuanyick/Shutterstock
Margin pic 12-2	Coprid/Shutterstock
Margin pic 12-6	Oshvintsev Alexander/Shutterstock
12-6	Joyful Industries, Inc.
Margin pic 12-7	Joyful Industries, Inc.
12-7	© Panera Bread
12-8	Natthawat Wongrat/Shutterstock
Margin pic 12-8	Joyful Industries, Inc.
Margin pic 12-9	Charles B. Ming Onn/Shutterstock
Margin pic 12-10	Olivier Vanbiervliet/Shutterstock
12-11	Joyful Industries, Inc.
12-16	Joyful Industries, Inc.
Margin pic 13-3	Joyful Industries, Inc.
Margin pic 13-4	Joyful Industries, Inc.
Margin pic 13-5	bubamarac/Shutterstock
Margin pic 13-6	Joyful Industries, Inc.
14-2	Joyful Industries, Inc.
14-3	bouzou/Shutterstock
14-4	Joyful Industries, Inc.
Margin pic 14-1; 14-14	Joyful Industries, Inc.

Figure	Credit Line
14-5	Joyful Industries, Inc.
14-9	Joyful Industries, Inc.
14-10	Tablet PC: Alexirius/Shutterstock Apple iPad: Courtesy of www.istockphoto.com Touchscreen smartphone: Courtesy of www.istockphoto.com
14-11	Copyright © 2011 Hewlett-Packard Development Company, L.P. Reproduced with permission.
14-12	© 2011 Dell
14-13	Copyright © 2011 Hewlett-Packard Development Company, L.P. Reproduced with permission.
14-15	© 2011 Dell.
14-16	© 2011 Dell.
14-17	Joyful Industries, Inc.; Denis Dryashkin/Shutterstock
14-18	© 2011 Dell.
14-19	Joyful Industries, Inc.
14-20	Joyful Industries, Inc.
Margin pic 14-9	Joyful Industries, Inc.
Margin pic 14-10	Joyful Industries, Inc.
14-21	Copyright © 2011 Hewlett-Packard Development Company, L.P. Reproduced with permission.
14-23	Joyful Industries, Inc.
14-24	© 2011 Dell.
14-25	© 2011 CompUSA.com, Inc. All rights reserved. CompUSA and CompUSA.com are registered trademarks of New CompUSA Corp.
14-26	luchschen/Shutterstock
Margin pic 14-11	jcjgphotography/Shutterstock
S14-1	Copyright © 1995-2011 eBay, Inc. All rights reserved.
S14-2	Copyright © 1995-2011 eBay, Inc. All rights reserved.
S14-3	Copyright © 2011 craigslist, Inc. Reprinted by permission.
S14-4	Courtesy of Intel Corporation.
S14-5	© 2011 CompUSA.com, Inc. All rights reserved. CompUSA and CompUSA.com are registered trademarks of New CompUSA Corp.
S14-6	© 2011 CompUSA.com, Inc. All rights reserved. CompUSA and CompUSA.com are registered trademarks of New CompUSA Corp.
S14-7	© 2011 Dell.
S14-8	GOOGLE is a trademark of Google, Inc.
S14-9	© A1 Assets. Reprinted by permission.
S14-10	Courtesy of Amazon.com, Inc. or its affiliates. All rights reserved.
S14-11	Courtesy of Amazon.com, Inc. or its affiliates. All rights reserved.
S14-12	© 2011 Dell.
Margin Pic S14-1	Courtesy of Intel Corporation.
W-2	Copyright © 2003–2011 AWARDSPACE.COM. Owned by AttractSoft GmbH & Zetta Hosting Solutions, Ltd. All rights reserved.
W-3	Copyright © 2003–2011 AWARDSPACE.COM. Owned by AttractSoft GmbH & Zetta Hosting Solutions, Ltd. All rights reserved.
W-4	Copyright © 2003–2011 AWARDSPACE.COM. Owned by AttractSoft GmbH & Zetta Hosting Solutions, Ltd. All rights reserved.
W-11	Photo reprinted with permission from Julie Cherolis and Mike West.
W-12	Copyright © 2003–2011 AWARDSPACE.COM. Owned by AttractSoft GmbH & Zetta Hosting Solutions, Ltd. All rights reserved.
W-13	Photo reprinted with permission from Mike West.
W-14	Photo reprinted with permission from Julie Cherolis and Mike West.
W-17	Photo reprinted with permission from Julie Cherolis.
W-18	Photo reprinted with permission from Julie Cherolis and Mike West.
SW-2	Copyright © 2003–2011 AWARDSPACE.COM. Owned by AttractSoft GmbH & Zetta Hosting Solutions, Ltd. All rights reserved.
SW-3	Copyright © 2003–2011 AWARDSPACE.COM. Owned by AttractSoft GmbH & Zetta Hosting Solutions, Ltd. All rights reserved.
SW-11	Copyright © 2003–2011 AWARDSPACE.COM. Owned by AttractSoft GmbH & Zetta Hosting Solutions, Ltd. All rights reserved.

CHAPTER 1

Using Windows 7 to Manage Applications and Data

IN THIS CHAPTER, YOU WILL

Get started with hardware and software

Manage programs and their windows

Manage folders and files on storage devices

Install applications from CD or DVD

Learn about ending a Windows session

Computers and technologies used today are likely to change tomorrow, which makes learning to use computers a moving target. Therefore, the most important computer skill you will learn in this entire book is how to teach yourself computer skills. Toward that goal, this book is designed to help you learn the skill of teaching yourself.

Each On Your Own activity in the chapter invites you to follow general directions to explore and discover on your own how to use Windows 7. But remember the old saying, "When all else fails, read the directions." If you need step-by-step solutions to each activity, you can find them in the *Solutions Appendix*. Use these solutions only when you need extra help or want to verify your answers. By the time you've finished a few chapters, you will have discovered just how independent and resourceful a self-learner you can be.

JUMP RIGHT IN

If you want even more of a challenge, try proceeding directly to the Chapter Mastery Project at the end of this chapter. If you need help on the project, refer to the On Your Own activities in the chapter or do your own independent investigating using tools such as Windows Help and Support. When you complete the project, you will have mastered the skills in this chapter. Then go to the projects that require you to apply your skills to new situations.

How Will This Chapter Help Me?

Throughout this book, each chapter provides three projects focusing on personal, academic, or technical career goals. Depending on your own interests, you might choose to perform any or all of these projects to help you achieve your goals.

PERSONAL PROJECT: I want to use the Windows Calculator to find the fuel economy of my car, and I plan to burn some CDs using Windows.

ACADEMIC PROJECT: I want to put a gadget on my Windows desktop that will report the weather each morning.

TECHNICAL CAREER PROJECT: I need to help someone recover a file she accidentally deleted.

Getting Started with Hardware and Software

All hardware can be categorized as devices used for input, output, processing, or storage (see Figure 1-1). In this part of the chapter, you learn about several types of computers and common input, output, and storage devices. In Chapter 14, "Buying Your Own Personal Computer," you learn about the central processing unit (CPU), which is the main device used for processing.

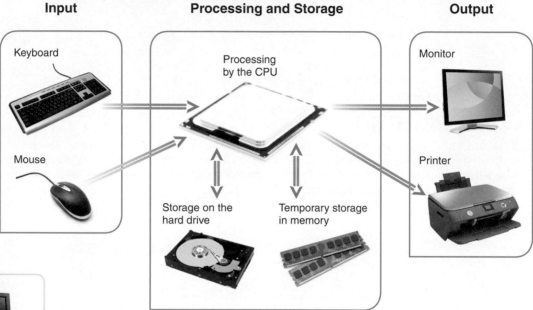

FIGURE 1-1
Computer devices are used for input, output, processing, or storage.

In this book, a key term box like the following provides an easy and quick reference to new computer terms.

monitor

keyboard

mouse

hard drive

monitor—The primary output device for a computer.

keyboard—The primary input device for a computer.

mouse—An input device used to move a pointer on the computer screen and to perform other operations.

hard drive—The most important storage device inside a computer, used to store both software and data until you need them.

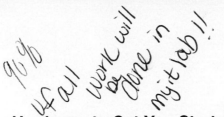

Hardware to Get You Started

Four types of personal computers you might use at work, home, or school are a **desktop computer**, an **all-in-one computer**, a **laptop**, and a **netbook**.

> **desktop computer**—A computer that sits on or under a desk with an attached monitor, keyboard, and mouse.
>
> **laptop**—A portable computer small enough to hold in your lap. Sometimes called a notebook.
>
> **netbook**—A small, light, inexpensive portable computer that is powerful enough for only general computer use.
>
> **all-in-one computer**—A computer that sits on a desk and has the monitor and computer case built together. A keyboard and mouse are attached. Some all-in-one computers have a touch screen.

Look at Figures 1-2 through 1-5 and take note of each labeled device. Locate each device on the computer you plan to use with this course. In later chapters, you learn about many other hardware devices, but these are enough to get started.

desktop computer

laptop

netbook

all-in-one computer

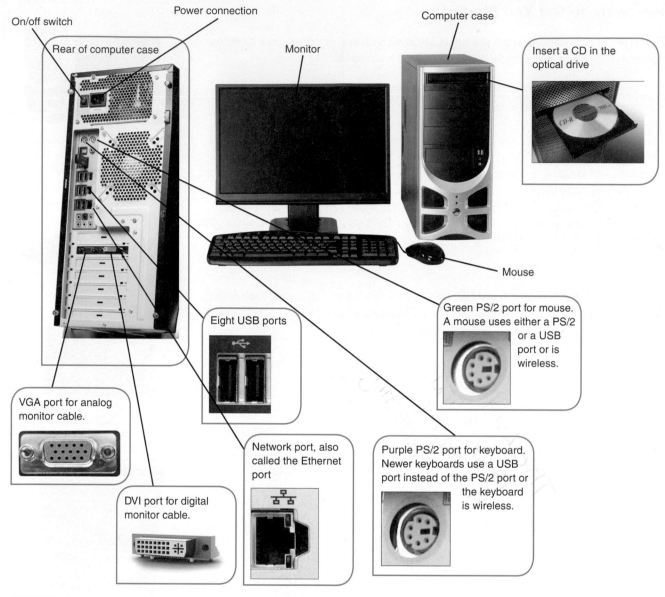

FIGURE 1-2
A desktop computer has input and output devices attached to ports and an optical drive.

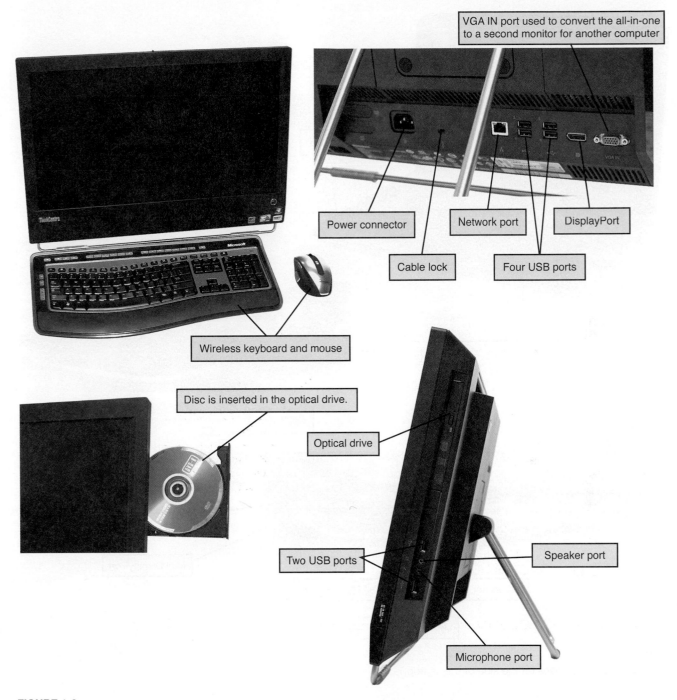

FIGURE 1-3
An all-in-one computer might have multitouch display and a wireless mouse and keyboard.

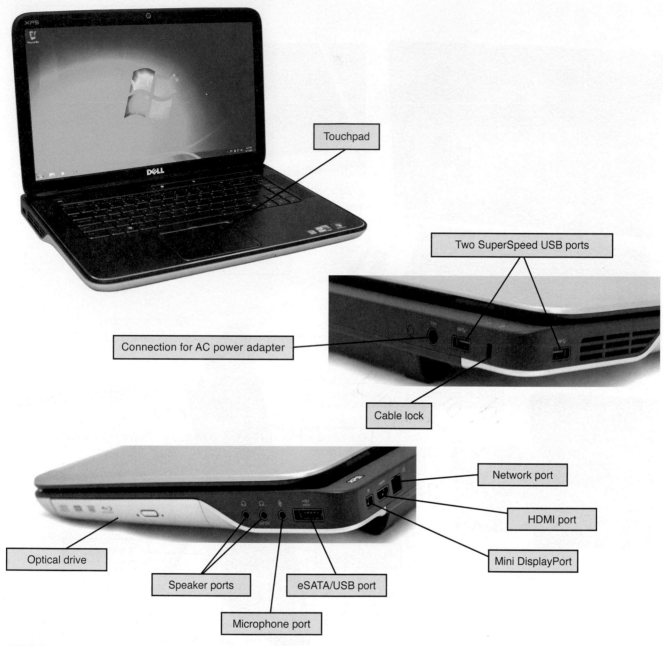

FIGURE 1-4
A Blu-ray/DVD drive opens on the side of this laptop.

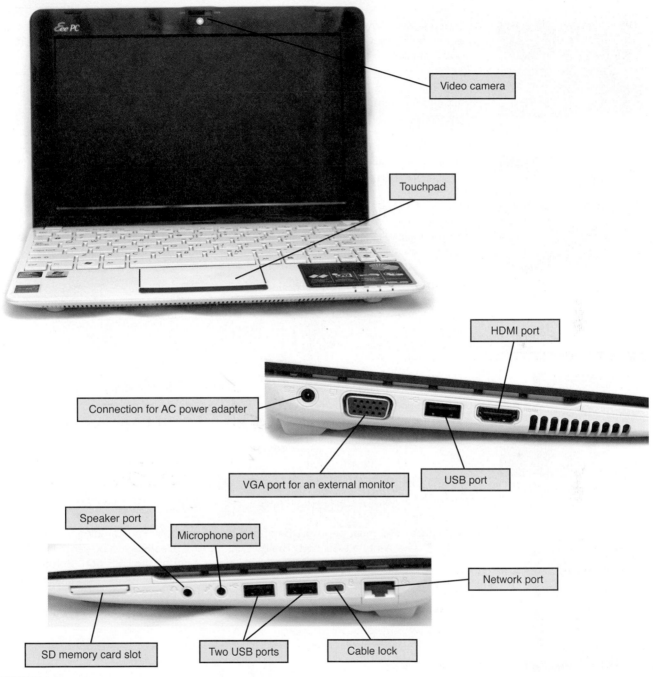

FIGURE 1-5
A netbook computer has a smaller screen size than a laptop and no optical drive. It might have a touch screen.

All computers need a keyboard for input and a monitor for displaying output. Desktop and all-in-one computers use a mouse, which you use to move the pointer on the monitor screen and select items on the screen. Laptops and netbooks use a **touch pad** for the same purposes. If you don't like to use a touch pad, you can connect a USB or wireless mouse to your laptop or netbook.

touch screen

touch screen—A monitor screen that receives touch input. You can control the computer by moving your fingers over the screen. A touch screen is both an output and input device and is used on netbooks, laptops, and all-in-one computers.

touch pad—The small pad with two buttons near the keypad on a laptop or netbook. You use the pad to move a pointer on the monitor screen, and you use the left and right buttons to perform other operations.

touch pad

A desktop computer has a heavy **computer case** and is the least portable of all computers. A desktop is also the best buy to get the most power.

computer case—The large box of a computer that contains the main components. Components installed inside the computer case are called internal components. Components outside the case are called external components or peripherals.

optical drive—A type of drive that can read an optical disc. Most drives can also write on a disc. Optical discs include CD, DVD, and Blu-ray discs. The three discs look the same, but a Blu-ray disc holds more data than a DVD, which holds more data than a CD.

optical drive

Notice the **ports** labeled on the photos of all four computers. Not all ports are labeled—only the important ones you need in this course. Look at your own computer and find each port labeled in the photos. Identify the cables connected to these ports and explore where the other end of the cable is attached.

port—A socket or connection on a computer used to connect a cable or external device.

USB port—The most popular type of port on a computer. You can plug a USB cable or USB device into a USB port. The port can provide electricity to power the device. For example, a USB keyboard receives its power through the USB port. Some USB devices, such as a printer, require much more electricity and use an additional power cord.

network port—A port used for a network cable to connect to a wired network.

USB port

network port

network cable—The cable that connects a computer to a wired network.

VGA video port—An analog video port used to connect a monitor to the computer. The port is slower than the newer DVI video port.

DVI video port—A digital video port, which is faster than the older analog or VGA video port.

VGA video port

DVI video port

A **USB flash drive** is a popular small device used for storage. You can store music, photos, documents, and other data on a USB flash drive. These devices are popular because they are small, inexpensive, and easily moved from one computer to another.

USB flash drive—A small storage device that plugs into a USB port. Some USB flash drives use a password to protect their data.

USB flash drive

Software to Get You Started

Software is a group of instructions a computer can follow to do a job. Software is also called a **program**. The three main categories of software are **applications**, operating systems, and **utilities**.

software—A group of instructions that a computer can follow to do a job. Three general types of software are operating systems, applications, and utility programs.

program—Another name for software.

application—A type of software designed with a specific purpose in mind, such as drawing pictures, editing video, creating documents, or playing a game. Examples of applications software include Microsoft Office, QuickBooks (used by accountants and bookkeepers), and AutoCAD (used by architects).

utility program—A program that helps the operating system and might not need user interaction to work. An example of a utility program is software used to back up important data.

In this course, you learn to use **Microsoft Office** applications. These applications include Microsoft Word, OneNote, Outlook, PowerPoint, Excel, and Access (see Figure 1-6).

Microsoft Office—Personal productivity software including software for creating and editing documents, notes, email, presentations, worksheets, and databases.

Tip In the key terms, notice some initials such as USB and VGA. USB stands for Universal Serial Bus, and VGA stands for Video Graphics Adapter. To keep things simple in this book, we're not explaining the meanings of initials unless the meaning is really important. If you want to know the meanings, see the Glossary on the DVD in the back of the book.

 On the DVD

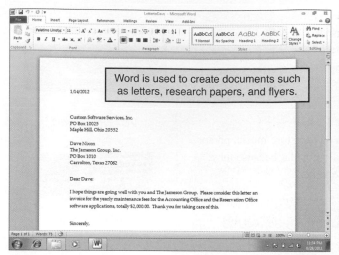

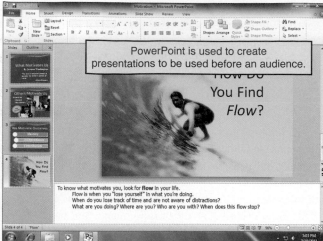

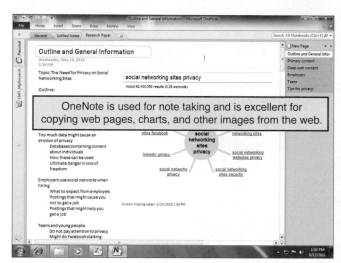

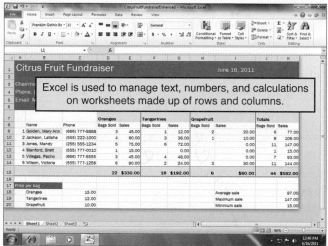

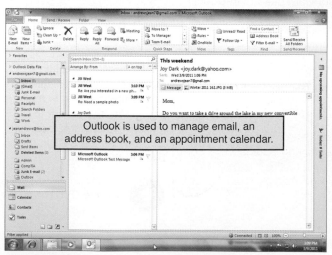

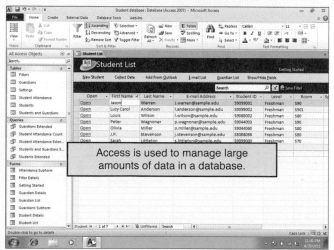

FIGURE 1-6

The Microsoft Office suite includes several personal productivity applications.

An **operating system**, such as Windows 7, is the most important software installed on a computer because the operating system controls everything the computer does. It controls all the hardware devices, all the applications, and all the data. When you want the computer to do something, such as print a letter, you must tell the operating system what you want, and it sees that the job gets done. Because all the work you do with a computer is done by way of the operating system, it is important that you understand how to use the operating system. That's why learning to use **Windows 7** is the first thing covered in this book.

> **operating system (OS)**—Software that manages a computer. It controls other software, hardware, and data and receives user input.
>
> **Windows 7**—The latest computer operating system sold by Microsoft. A computer can have many applications installed on it, but it needs only one operating system.

Software such as the Windows 7 operating system and the Microsoft Office applications are installed in a computer on the hard drive. The hard drive permanently holds both software and data until you need them. Figure 1-7 shows a 3.5-inch hard drive used inside a desktop computer and a smaller 2.5-inch hard drive used inside a laptop. The storage capacity of a hard drive determines how much software you can install on the computer. You learn about the storage capacity of hard drives later in the chapter.

FIGURE 1-7
A 3.5-inch hard drive is used in a desktop computer, and a smaller 2.5-inch hard drive is used in a laptop.

Data or software is stored in a file, and the file is assigned a name such as MyData.txt. A file that holds data is called a **data file**, and a file that stores software is called a **program file**.

> **file**—A collection of data or software in a computer stored under a single name. Two general types of files are program files and data files.
>
> **data file**—A file that contains data, which is a record kept of something. Examples of data files are files that contain a photograph, business letter, list of names and addresses, or video.
>
> **program file**—A file that contains a program. Complex software such as Windows 7 and Microsoft Office 2010 uses many program files to hold all the software.

Two examples of program files are

▶ The file **OneNote.exe** holds the OneNote application, which is one of the Microsoft Office applications and is used for taking notes.

▶ The file **WordPad.exe** holds the WordPad application, which is used to create documents.

Notice the period in the name of each file. The letters to the left of the period are called the filename (OneNote and WordPad). The period and the letters to the right of the period are called the file extension. Both upper- and lowercase letters are used in filenames and file extensions.

The file extension tells you something about what type of data or program is contained in the file. A file extension of .exe identifies the file as a program file.

> **file extension**—The part of a filename including the last period and the letters following the last period that identifies what kind of program or data is contained in the file.

Here are two examples of data files:

▶ The file **Wendy.jpg** holds a photograph of a dog.

▶ The file **LetterToDave.docx** holds the letter I wrote last week to a business associate.

The .jpg file extension identifies the file as a file containing a photo. The .docx file extension identifies the file as a document file created by Microsoft Word.

Now that you know a little about hardware, software, and files, you are ready to use Windows 7.

Start a Windows 7 Session

As you read about using Windows, follow along at your computer. To get started, you might need to turn on your computer and log on to Windows with a user account and password. This **user account** was previously created when Windows 7 was installed or created later by the person responsible for the computer. If only one user account is set up on the computer and this account does not require a password, Windows skips the logon screen and automatically logs you in to that account.

> **user account**—Information that tells Windows what degree of control a user has over a computer, including what **folders** on the hard drive the user can access and the user's preferences such as the screen background.
>
> **folder**—A location on a storage media (for example, a hard drive or USB flash drive) that can contain files or other folders called subfolders.

On Your Own 1-1
Turn on Your Computer

Power up your computer and log on to Windows 7. You might be required to enter a user account and/or password on the Windows logon screen shown in Figure 1-8. If you don't know the Windows password in your computer lab, ask your instructor. After logon, the Windows desktop appears (see Figure 1-9). The **desktop** is the place where you do all your work in Windows.

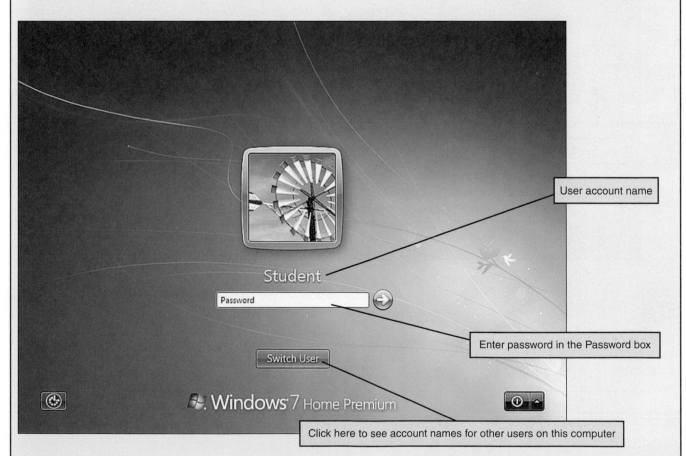

FIGURE 1-8
The Windows logon screen determines which user account is in use.

On Your Own 1-1
Turn on Your Computer

Not Working? If you don't see your user account, try using both hands to press three keys at the same time: **Ctrl**, **Alt**, and **Delete** (also written as **Ctrl-Alt-Delete**). You might need to enter your user account in the box that appears. When you are using a lab computer, ask your instructor for specific directions for logging on.

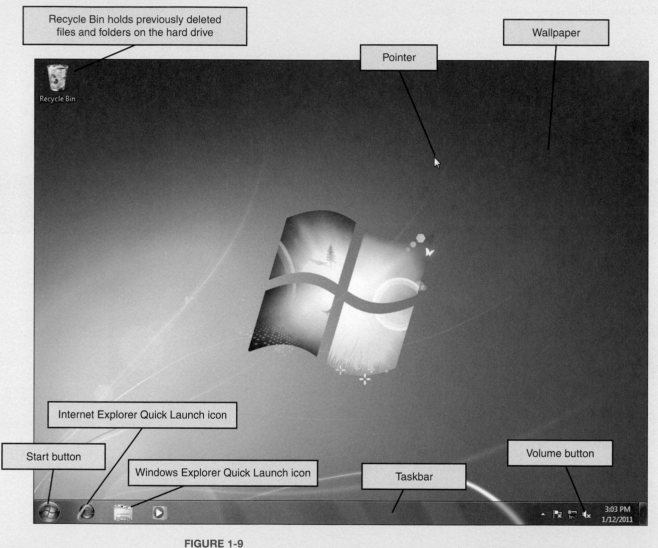

Recycle Bin holds previously deleted files and folders on the hard drive

Pointer

Wallpaper

Internet Explorer Quick Launch icon

Start button

Windows Explorer Quick Launch icon

Taskbar

Volume button

FIGURE 1-9
The Windows desktop is the place where you do your work in Windows.

? Solutions Appendix

For help, see Solution 1-1: How to Turn on Your Computer.

Not Working? Try to do each On Your Own activity without help. But remember, the *Solutions Appendix* has the step-by-steps if you need them.

Compare all the items labeled in Figure 1-9 to your computer's desktop. Here is the list of computer terms you need to identify on the desktop:

desktop—The Windows screen where you work.

wallpaper—The color or pattern on the desktop. You learn later in the book how to change the wallpaper to suit your own tastes.

taskbar—The bar at the bottom of the screen that includes the Start button and program icons.

Start button—The button or circle 🔵 on the far left of the taskbar. Use it to start programs. It contains the Windows logo.

Quick Launch icon—A small square on the left side of the taskbar used to start a program that you use often. The two Quick Launch icons that normally appear in the taskbar are Internet Explorer 🔵 and Windows Explorer. 🔲

Internet Explorer—A program called a browser that is used to display web pages from the Internet.

Windows Explorer—A program used to manage the files and folders stored on your computer.

volume icon—The icon in the taskbar used to control sound. Click it and then move the bar up and down to control the volume.

Recycle Bin—The Windows trashcan in the upper-left corner of the desktop. Deleted files are stored in the Recycle Bin in case you change your mind and want them back.

Before you move on, practice using your mouse to move the **pointer** around the desktop.

pointer—The movable icon ⍺ on the desktop that allows you to point to a position on the screen or to a command. When you move the mouse or move your finger over the touch pad on a laptop, the pointer moves on the screen. The shape of the pointer can change to indicate what work is currently in progress. The pointer is sometimes called the **cursor**.

cursor—Another name for the pointer.

Now that you're familiar with starting a Windows session and the Windows desktop, let's learn to use some applications and their windows.

Managing Programs and Their Windows

To use any program, including an application, you must first start it. When you start a program, the operating system assigns to the program the resources the program needs to do its work. Starting a program is sometimes called *launching the program*, and a program that has been started is called an **open program**.

open program—A program that has been started. Open programs need computer resources to work, and these resources are assigned to the program when it starts. An open program is also called a running program.

The most important computer resource a program requires is memory. **Memory**, also called **RAM**, is temporary storage a program uses to do its work. A computer's memory is kept on small boards inside the computer case. Figure 1-10 shows one board (called a memory module) that fits in a desktop and a smaller module that fits in a laptop. The amount of memory a computer has determines how many applications you can have open at the same time. If you don't have much memory installed, opening three or four applications at one time can cause your computer to run slower.

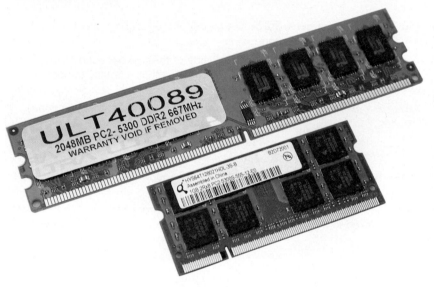

FIGURE 1-10
A memory module used in a desktop and a smaller module used in a laptop hold the computer's memory.

---

memory—The temporary storage used by programs when they are running. Also called *RAM*.

RAM (random access memory)—Another name for memory.

Manage an Application Window

If a program allows user input, the program creates a **window** for user interaction when it first starts.

---

window—A rectangle on the desktop that Windows has assigned to a program. You can use the window to work with the program. You can change the size of a window.

What goes inside a window is determined by the program. But every window has some common elements that Windows 7 determines. In the instructions that follow, you start Paint, a freehand drawing program. The goal here is not to learn to use Paint, but to learn to use Windows 7 to manage a program window. The skills you learn here can be applied to any window, not just the Paint window.

To open the Paint program, **click** **Start**, 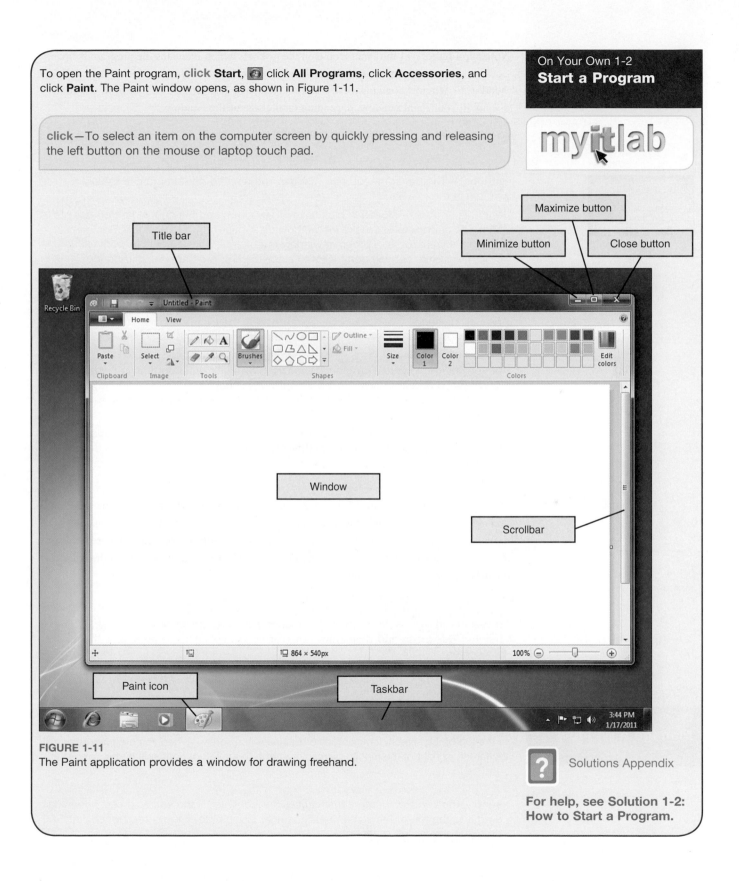 click **All Programs**, click **Accessories**, and click **Paint**. The Paint window opens, as shown in Figure 1-11.

click—To select an item on the computer screen by quickly pressing and releasing the left button on the mouse or laptop touch pad.

On Your Own 1-2
Start a Program

myitlab

FIGURE 1-11
The Paint application provides a window for drawing freehand.

Solutions Appendix

For help, see Solution 1-2: How to Start a Program.

Notice in Figure 1-11 the Paint icon is in the taskbar, which indicates the program is open. Look at Figure 1-11 and find the items labeled in the figure on your computer screen. Every Windows 7 window contains these common elements. The scrollbar might or might not display in your Paint window, depending on the size of the window.

New terms used in the figure are explained here:

title bar—The bar at the top of a window. The name of the program is usually written in the title bar.

Minimize button—Most title bars have three buttons on the right side. You use the Minimize button ▭ to make the window disappear from the desktop. Sometimes you might want to get a program window out of your way so you can work with other programs, but you don't want to close the first program. Minimizing the window gets it off the desktop, but the program is still open.

Maximize button—One of the three buttons on the right side of the title bar. Use the Maximize button ▢ to make the window fill the entire screen (except the taskbar can still be seen). When a window is maximized, the button changes to the Restore button ▣. Use the Restore button to return the window to its original size.

close button—One of the buttons on the right side of the title bar. Use the close button ✕ to close a program. When you finish using a program, you close it. When a program closes, it releases back to the computer the memory it was using to hold data. All data that was not saved to a storage device is lost when the program is closed.

scrollbar—A vertical or horizontal bar on the right side or bottom of a window or pane used to scroll through the window or pane.

A program window has a lot of other text, buttons, and other tools specific to the program you are using. The Paint window that you now have open is a great tool for freehand drawing. If you like, take a few moments to experiment with this program. To draw in the Paint window, **press and drag** your pointer. Have some fun playing with the colors, brushes, and shapes in the Paint window.

press and drag—Hold down the left mouse button at the same time you drag the pointer. This press-and-drag action enables you to select items and move them on the screen.

On Your Own 1-3
Manage a Window

You can change the size and position of a window on the screen. When you drag a window to the top of the screen, it maximizes or fills the entire screen. When you drag a window to the far left or right of the monitor screen, it **snaps** to the left or right side of the screen.

snap—The Windows feature that causes a window to fill the entire screen when you drag it to the top of the screen or fill the right or left side of the screen when you drag it to the far left or far right.

Manage the Paint window by doing the following:

Step 1. Maximize the window by dragging the window to the top of the screen.

> **Hint** To drag a window, position your pointer in the title bar at the top of the window. Then press and drag the title bar.

Step 2. Restore the window to its original size by dragging it downward on the screen.

Step 3. Snap the window to the right side of the screen by dragging it to the right.

Step 4. Snap the window to the left side of the screen by dragging it to the left.

Step 5. Click the **Minimize** button to minimize the window.

Step 6. Notice the Paint icon is still in the taskbar. When you see the Paint icon, you know the application is still open even if the window is not visible. Click the **Paint** icon in the taskbar to restore the window.

 Solutions Appendix

For help, see Solution 1-3: How to Manage a Window.

You can resize a window by pressing and dragging the side, bottom, or corner of a window.

> **resize**—Change the size of a window.

Do the following to resize and close the Paint window:

Step 1. Practice resizing the window by changing first the height and then the width of the window. Then change both the height and width at the same time.

> **Hint** When your pointer is on the side or bottom of a window, it changes to a double arrow.

Step 2. Resize the Paint window so that a scrollbar appears on the right side of the window. Use the scrollbar to scroll through the window.

Step 3. To close the **Paint** window, click the red **X** in the upper-right corner of the window. If you have drawn on the window, Paint asks whether you want to save your work. Click **Don't Save**. The Paint window closes. When you close a window, you are closing the program.

 Solutions Appendix

For help, see Solution 1-4: How to Resize and Close a Window.

You have learned how to open a program using the Windows 7 Start menu, to manage a program window, and to close a program.

Manage Multiple Windows

Sometimes you might want to work with two or more open windows at the same time. You may have many windows open, but only one is the **active window**. When a program is running, you see the program icon in the taskbar.

> **active window**—The window you are currently using. When using the normal Windows display settings, the active window always has a red X close button. ![x close button]
>
> **program icon**—A small picture that represents a program. When a program is open, the program icon appears in the taskbar. When you click a program icon, the window it represents becomes the active window.

On Your Own 1-5

Manage Multiple Windows

 Solutions Appendix

For help, see Solution 1-5: How to Manage Multiple Windows.

Do the following to practice managing multiple open windows:

Step 1. Using the Start menu, open the **Paint** program. Use the Quick Launch icon in the taskbar to open **Windows Explorer.**

Step 2. Move the windows so that the Windows Explorer window overlaps the Paint window. Then click anywhere on the Paint window to make it the active window, causing it to come to the foreground. Notice that the active window always has a red close button.

Step 3. Use the taskbar to make the Windows Explorer window the active window.

Step 4. Close both windows.

> **Tip** We all like to have more than one program open at the same time. Just don't overdo it unless you have a lot of memory installed on your computer.

You now know how to handle multiple program windows. Be aware, however, that an open program uses memory, a computer resource. The more programs you have open, the more memory you have tied up. Having many programs open at the same time can slow down a computer because Windows doesn't have all the memory it needs to work.

Minimizing the windows of open programs doesn't solve the problem of a slow computer. Even when a window is minimized, the program is still tying up memory. To free up memory, you must close the program window.

Managing Folders and Files on Storage Devices

Suppose you use your computer to write a business letter. The letter you type is stored as data in a data file. Two popular places to store data files in a computer are on the hard drive and on a USB flash drive. In this part of the chapter, you learn to use both devices to store files using your local computer. In the next chapter, you learn how to store your files on computers on the Internet.

A hard drive installed inside the computer case is called a **local disk**. Some computers have more than one local disk. A local disk holds the Windows 7 operating system and all the applications software installed on the computer. In most cases, there's still plenty of extra room for data files.

> **local disk**—A hard drive installed inside the computer case.

How much software and data can you store on a hard drive? The storage capacity for a hard drive is measured in **gigabytes** or **terabytes**. Here are the units used to measure storage capacity:

> **byte**—One unit of storage that can store one letter, number, or other character. For example, the word "hello" needs 5 bytes to store it.
>
> **megabyte (MB)**—About 1 million bytes.
>
> **gigabyte (GB)**—Roughly 1,000 megabytes or about 1 billion bytes.
>
> **terabyte (TB)**—Roughly 1,000 gigabytes or about 1 trillion bytes.

Tip To do all the activities in this part of the chapter, you need a USB flash drive. Some schools and colleges don't allow USB flash drives to be used with lab computers. If you are working in a lab, ask your instructor whether using flash drives is allowed. If you are not able to use flash drives in the lab, you can still use them with your home computer.

The hard drive on the four-year-old computer I'm now using has a capacity of 141GB. That's small by today's standards. Newer hard drives hold about 500GB upward to 2TB. A USB flash drive has much less storage capacity—for example, 2GB to 64GB. But a USB flash drive is much easier to move from computer to computer.

So where on a hard drive or USB flash drive will you put that data file holding your business letter? A file on a drive is stored in a folder, and the folders are organized like branches on an upside-down tree. A folder can contain files and other folders, called subfolders. The top level of a storage device is called the **root** and can contain both folders and files.

> **root**—In Windows, the top level of the folder tree on a storage device. The root contains folders and files.

Figure 1-12 shows Windows Explorer displaying the folders and subfolders on a USB flash drive and a diagram of the folder tree on the drive.

In Windows Explorer, you can use the left pane, called the *navigation pane*, to find drives and folders. Click a white triangle beside a drive or folder to show its details. Click the black triangle to hide the details.

A **library** is a group of one or more folders. Windows 7 provides four libraries named Documents, Music, Pictures, and Videos on the hard drive. You can also create your own libraries. Figure 1-13 shows these four libraries, which display when you first open Windows Explorer. Notice in the figure the elements of the Windows Explorer window that you can use to manage libraries, folders, and files.

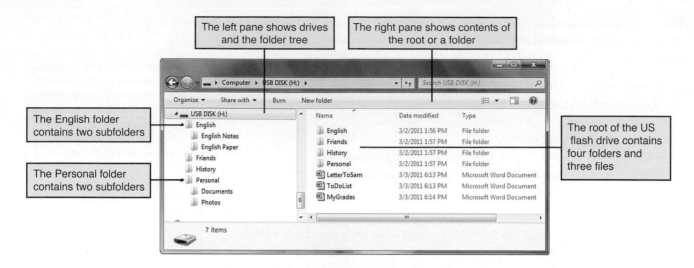

The left pane shows drives and the folder tree

The right pane shows contents of the root or a folder

The English folder contains two subfolders

The Personal folder contains two subfolders

The root of the US flash drive contains four folders and three files

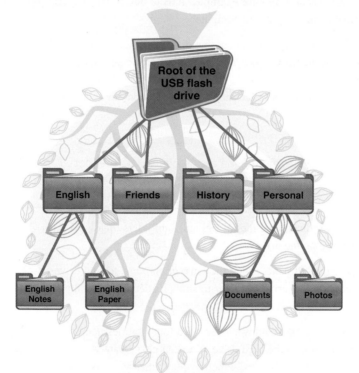

FIGURE 1-12
On a storage device, the root, each folder, and subfolder can contain files.

> **library**—A group of one or more folders. Windows 7 provides four libraries named Documents, Music, Pictures, and Videos to store these types of data on the hard drive.

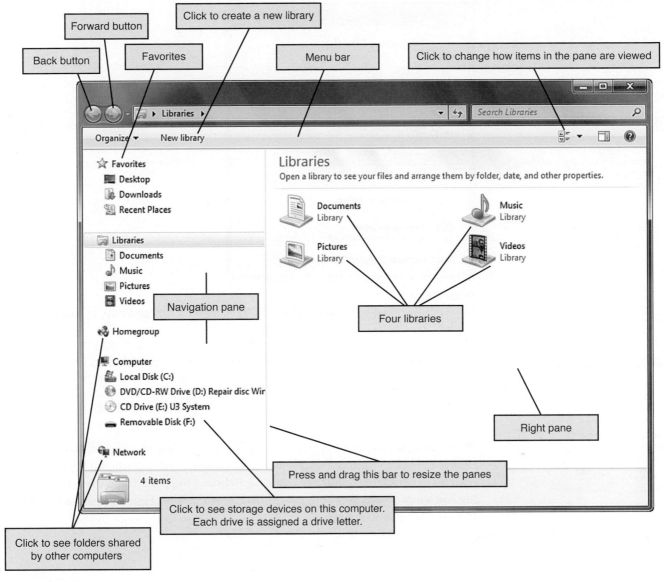

FIGURE 1-13
Using Windows Explorer, you can manage libraries, folders, and files on your computer.

Each hard drive, flash drive, optical drive, or other drive installed in a computer is assigned a drive letter. You can see the drive letter followed by a colon listed in the Computer group of Windows Explorer. For example, in Figure 1-13, the installed drives are C:, D:, E:, and F:. When you first insert a flash drive in a USB port or a CD or DVD in the optical drive, Windows 7 might display the AutoPlay **dialog box**, like the one in Figure 1-14. If so, close the dialog box.

FIGURE 1-14
The AutoPlay dialog box appears when you first connect a storage device to your computer.

> **dialog box**—A rectangle used to display information and provide menu choices. The difference between a dialog box and window is that a window can be resized and a dialog box has only one size.

When you're learning to use any software, look for a help feature in the software that you can use to get help when you need it. Windows 7 offers Windows Help and Support. To open this program, click **Start** and then click **Help and Support**. The Windows Help and Support window opens (see Figure 1-15). To find information, type words in the Search Help text box and press **Enter**.

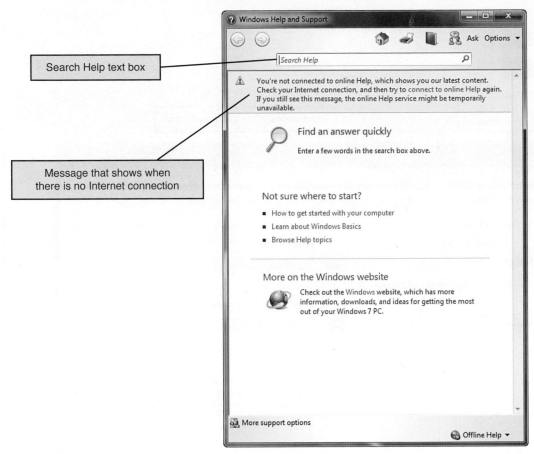

Search Help text box

Message that shows when there is no Internet connection

FIGURE 1-15
Use Windows Help and Support to teach yourself about Windows 7.

On Your Own 1-6
Explore Files, Folders, and Libraries on the Hard Drive

Do the following to explore the files, folders, and libraries on your hard drive:

Step 1. Click the **Windows Explorer** icon 📁 in the taskbar. Windows Explorer opens (refer to Figure 1-13). What are the four libraries Windows provides for your data? The menu bar shows commands that you can perform to manage libraries. The commands on the menu bar change depending on what is displayed in the Windows Explorer window.

Step 2. **Double-click** the **Documents** library so that you can drill down to see its contents. Then use the **back button** 🔙 to move back up one level in the folder tree so you can see all the libraries.

double-click—Press the left mouse button twice very quickly.

Step 3. Use the **Computer** view of Windows Explorer to identify all the drives installed on this computer and the drive letters assigned to these drives. Figure 1-16 shows the drives on one computer, but yours might look different. For most computers, Windows is installed on the local disk identified as drive C:. What is the storage capacity of drive C: on your computer? How much free space does the drive have?

On Your Own 1-6
Explore Files, Folders, and Libraries on the Hard Drive

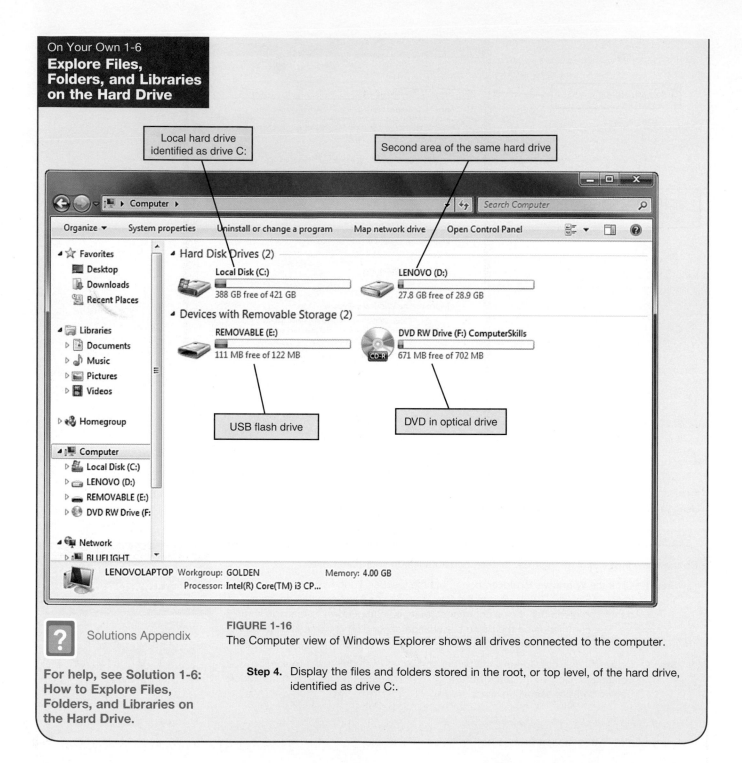

Local hard drive identified as drive C:

Second area of the same hard drive

USB flash drive

DVD in optical drive

FIGURE 1-16
The Computer view of Windows Explorer shows all drives connected to the computer.

Solutions Appendix

For help, see Solution 1-6: How to Explore Files, Folders, and Libraries on the Hard Drive.

Step 4. Display the files and folders stored in the root, or top level, of the hard drive, identified as drive C:.

The DVD in the back of this book contains some sample files stored in a folder named Sample Files. Do the following to explore the Sample Files folder on the DVD:

Step 1. Insert the DVD into the optical drive. Using Windows Explorer, drill down into the **Sample Files** folder to display the list of files in this folder.

Step 2. Windows Explorer can be set to display folders and files in a variety of views. It can display a **thumbnail** of each item or display a detailed list of items. If Windows Explorer is not displaying the **Details** view, make it so.

 Video 1-7

thumbnail—A small picture or icon of a file, folder, or other item.

Hint To change the view, click the down arrow to the right of the view icon in the menu bar. In the menu that appears, click a view to select it.

Step 3. If necessary, change the column headings in the right pane of Windows Explorer so that the **Name**, **Date modified**, **Type**, and **Size** columns display. How many files are stored in the Sample Files folder?

Hint To specify columns you want to see in the Details view of Windows Explorer, right-click a column heading and select the columns from the list of columns that appears.

Step 4. Sort the list by the file's **Name**. Then sort the list by file **Type**.

Step 5. Windows identifies a file type by the file extension. Display the file **Properties box** to find out the file extension for the **Wendy** file. What is the file extension?

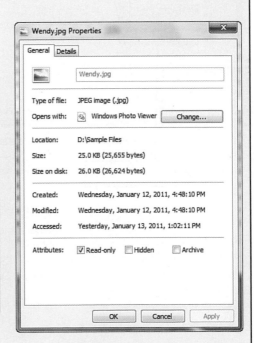

Properties box—A dialog box that displays the properties of a folder, file, or other item. To view the Properties box, **right-click** the item and select **Properties** from the **shortcut menu**.

right-click—Quickly press the right button on the mouse or the laptop touch pad.

shortcut menu—A menu that appears when you right-click an item. The options listed in a shortcut menu depend on the item itself. A shortcut menu is sometimes called a drop-down menu.

 Solutions Appendix

For help, see Solution 1-7: How to Explore Files and Folders on the DVD.

Tips for Working with Folders and Files

When you first insert a USB flash drive in a USB port, Windows recognizes the drive and adds it to the list of installed storage devices. The drive might be listed as a removable disk or USB disk. You can then use Windows Explorer to display the drive contents and manage folders and files on the drive. Figure 1-17 shows the Windows Explorer window displaying the contents of a USB flash drive that contains folders and files. The figure also shows a shortcut menu that appears when you right-click a file.

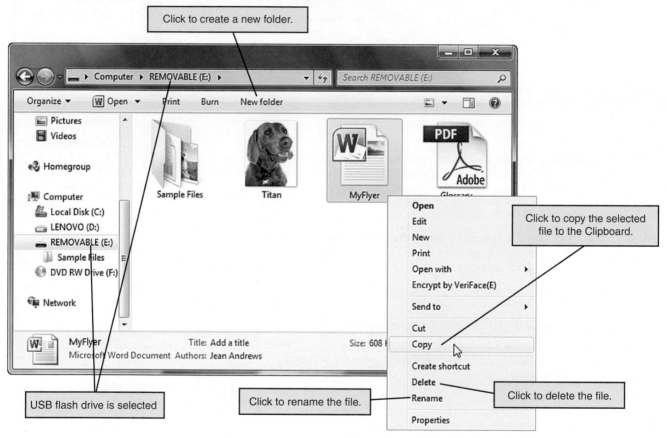

FIGURE 1-17
Folders and files can be managed using the Windows Explorer menu or a folder or file shortcut menu.

Here are some useful tips when working with folders and files on a storage device:

▶ To create a folder, use the **New folder** button in the Windows Explorer menu bar. See Figure 1-17. The folder is created in the currently displayed folder. It is named New folder, but the name is selected so you can type a new name.

▶ To copy a folder or file, right-click the item and click **Copy** on the folder or file's shortcut menu (see Figure 1-17). Windows temporarily places the item and its contents in the Windows Clipboard. Then right-click the device or folder where you want to place the item and select **Paste** from the shortcut menu.

Clipboard—A temporary storage area used by Windows to transfer data (folders, files, text, or other data) from one location to another. The copy and paste operations use the Clipboard.

copy and paste—The operation of copying a folder, file, or other item in a new location without deleting it from the original location.

▶ To move a folder or file, use the **Cut** option on the item's shortcut menu. Then right-click the device or folder where you want to place the item and select **Paste** from the shortcut menu.

cut and paste—The operation of moving a folder, file, or other item from one location to another. The item is deleted from the original location. Cut and Paste are commands on the shortcut menus for a file or folder.

▶ To delete a folder or file, select the item and press the **Delete** key. You can also use the **Cut** command or the **Delete** command on the folder or file's shortcut menu.

▶ Another way to copy or move a folder or file is to **drag and drop** the item to its new location. This method works well when you have two Windows Explorer windows open. When you drag and drop a folder or file to another location on the same storage media, Windows moves the item. When you drag and drop the item from one storage device to another, Windows copies the item.

drag and drop—The operation of moving a folder, file, or other item from one location to another by holding down and releasing the left mouse button.

▶ To rename a folder or file, use the **Rename** command on the item's shortcut menu.

Manage Folders

Folders are a great way to organize files on a removable storage device, such as a USB flash drive. For example, you might want to keep your files in three folders on your flash drive: Computer Class, English Class, and Sample Files.

On Your Own 1-8

Manage Folders on a USB Flash Drive

 Video 1-8

 Solutions Appendix

Do the following to practice creating, deleting, renaming, and copying folders:

Step 1. Create a folder named **Computer Class** on your USB flash drive.

Step 2. Create a subfolder named **Data** in the Computer Class folder. Then delete the **Data** folder.

Step 3. Create a folder named **History Class** at the root level of the USB flash drive. Rename the **History Class** folder to **English Class**.

Step 4. Using two Windows Explorer windows, drag and drop the **Sample Files** folder on the DVD in the back of this book to the root of your USB drive.

For help, see Solution 1-8: How to Manage Folders on a USB Flash Drive.

Manage Files

One way to open a file is to double-click it in Windows Explorer. When you open a data file, you view its contents. The program used to create the file is normally used to open the file, but this is not always the case. For example, when you open a photograph file, Windows opens a picture viewer so you can view the file.

On Your Own 1-9

Open, Copy, Move, and Delete a File

 Video 1-9

 Solutions Appendix

Use the same USB flash drive you used in On Your Own 1-8. Do the following to practice opening, copying, moving, and deleting files:

Step 1. In the **Sample Files** folder on your USB flash drive, open the **Wendy** file to view this photograph.

Step 2. Copy the Wendy file from the **Sample Files** folder to the **Computer Class** folder on your USB flash drive. Verify the file is now stored at two locations on the drive.

Step 3. Move the **Wendy** file from the **Computer Class** folder to the **English Class** folder. Verify the file is no longer in the Computer Class folder.

Step 4. Rename the **Wendy** file to **YourDog**.

Step 5. Delete the **YourDog** file from the **English Class** folder.

For help, see Solution 1-9: How to Open, Copy, Move, and Delete a File.

You now know how to copy, move, delete, and rename folders and files. Here are two more tips when you want to copy and paste multiple files:

▶ If you want to copy multiple files in a list, click the first file in the list to select it. Hold down your **Shift** key and click the last file in the list. All the files in the list are selected. Then right-click anywhere in the list and select **Copy** from the shortcut menu (see Figure 1-18). All files selected are copied to the Clipboard. You can now use one **Paste** command to copy all the files to a new location.

▶ If you want to copy multiple files that are not together in the same list, click one file to select it. Then hold down your **Ctrl** key while you click other files.

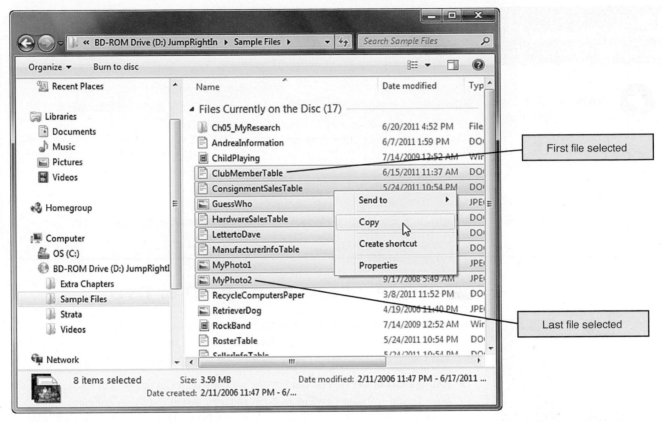

FIGURE 1-18
Multiple selected files can be copied to the Clipboard.

Safely Remove Hardware and Eject Media

After you write files to your USB flash drive, don't unplug the drive immediately because the write operation might not be finished. To be certain it is safe to unplug the flash drive, click the up arrow on the right side of the Windows taskbar and click the **Safely Remove Hardware and Eject Media** icon.

In the list that appears, click the item to eject your USB flash drive. It is now safe to unplug the flash drive from the USB port.

The Windows Snipping Tool

All editions of Windows 7, except the Windows 7 Starter edition, offer the Snipping Tool. You can use the tool to capture a screenshot or **snip** of your screen. The tool can be useful when you need to document your work in Windows. Your instructor might ask you to create a snip of your Windows screen to show you have done the work as assigned. You can store a snip in a file.

> **snip**—A capture of part or all of a Windows screen that can be stored in a file. You can use the Windows Snipping Tool to take a snip.

On Your Own 1-10
Use the Windows Snipping Tool

Take a snip of part of your Windows screen. Save the snip to your USB flash drive or another location specified by your instructor. Name the file **MySnip1**. By default, Windows uses the **PNG file** format to save the file.

▶ Video 1-10

> default—The choice made by software that applies until someone changes it.
>
> PNG file—A file with a .png file extension that contains a graphic. The file has a smaller file size than other types of graphics files.

 Solutions Appendix   **For help, see Solution 1-10: How to Use the Windows Snipping Tool.**

Installing Applications from CD or DVD

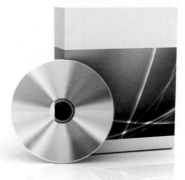

FIGURE 1-19
Software purchased on CD or DVD is called boxed software.

Software must be installed on your computer before you can use it. Windows 7 includes several applications such as Internet Explorer, and you can install other applications such as Microsoft Office 2010. Software can be installed on your computer in two ways:

▶ **Using a CD or DVD.** You can buy the software on a CD or DVD in a box, called boxed retail software (see Figure 1-19) and then install it on your computer. This method works well if your computer has a DVD or CD drive, but boxed retail software usually costs a little more than the same software downloaded from the Internet.

▶ **Downloading the software from the Internet.** You can download the software from the Internet and then install it on your computer. This method requires an Internet connection and is good when you're using a netbook computer that does not have a CD or DVD drive. You learn how to buy and download software in Chapter 2, "Finding and Using Information on the Web."

Recall that when you first start Windows, you need a user account to log on. The type of user account determines how much control the user has over the computer. The three levels of control are

▶ An **administrator account** has full control over the computer.

▶ A **standard account** has less control and cannot install software.

▶ A **guest account** has very little control over the computer.

If Windows skips the logon screen when you first start Windows, taking you directly to the Windows desktop, the computer has only one user account set up, and that account is an administrator account. In this situation, you have full control of the computer.

> administrator account—A type of Windows user account that has the most control over a computer.
>
> standard account—A type of Windows user account that has limited control over a computer.
>
> guest account—A type of Windows user account that has the least control over a computer.

If you log on to Windows using an account that is not an administrator account, you can still install software. However, you must provide the password for an administrator account at the beginning of the installation process. When you begin the installation, Windows displays a **User Account Control dialog box**, such as the two shown in Figure 1-20:

▶ The box on the top appears when the user is logged on with an administrator account. To continue the installation, click **Yes**.

▶ The box on the bottom appears when the user is logged on with a standard account. To continue, type the password for an administrator account and click **Yes**.

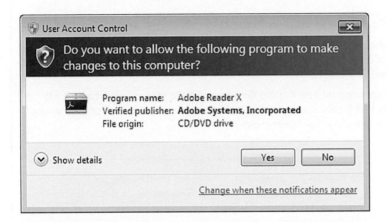

A standard user can enter an administrator's password to continue the operation.

FIGURE 1-20
The User Account Control dialog box protects against unauthorized software installations (top) when the user is an administrator and (bottom) when the user is a standard user.

User Account Control (UAC) dialog box—A dialog box used to verify the user has the right to perform a Windows operation and gives the user the opportunity to stop the operation.

On Your Own 1-11
Install Software from DVD

Video **1-11**

The DVD in the back of this book contains the Adobe Reader program used to read a file that has a .pdf file extension. Several files on the DVD are **PDF files**.

> **PDF file**—A type of file first created by Adobe Systems used to distribute documents over the Internet and on CD or DVD. Because a PDF file can be read by many applications, it is said to have a universal file format. PDF stands for Portable Document Format.

To install and use the software, do the following:

Step 1. Launch the **AdbeRdr1000_en_US.exe** program on the DVD and then follow directions onscreen to install the software. During the installation, you are asked to respond to the UAC box.

Step 2. Test the software by opening the **Glossary.pdf** file stored in the root of the DVD. The first time you use the software, you are asked to accept the terms of the **Software License Agreement**.

Hint To launch a program using Windows Explorer, double-click the program filename.

 Solutions Appendix

For help, see Solution 1-11: How to Install Software from DVD.

> **Software License Agreement**—An agreement that gives permission for someone other than the owner of software to use the software. The owner of the software retains the copyright, which is the right to copy it.

Ending a Windows Session

When you finish using a computer, you have options as to what you do before you step away. These options are shown in Figure 1-21, and several of them are listed in the key terms that follow.

FIGURE 1-21
Shut down menu on a laptop shows hibernation as an option.

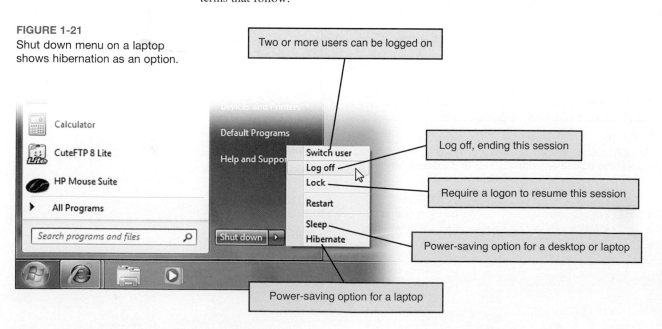

Two or more users can be logged on

Log off, ending this session

Require a logon to resume this session

Power-saving option for a desktop or laptop

Power-saving option for a laptop

shut down—To completely stop all computer operations. All windows are closed, and the computer is powered down. If you plan to be away from your computer for at least until the next day, you should shut down Windows and turn off the power to the computer.

log off—To close all your open programs and then close access to your user account in Windows.

lock—Close access to your user account in Windows without closing the open programs. Use this option if you are stepping away from your computer for just a few moments and don't want other people to see the work on your desktop while you are away. To unlock your computer, you have to log back on.

restart—To log off your account and any other users who also might be logged on and close Windows. Windows then loads again, and you can log back on the system. Some program installations require you to restart the system before the installation completes.

sleep state—To save all work and put the computer in a power-saving mode. Any open windows remain open. If you plan to be away from your computer for more than a few minutes but not all day, you can put the computer in a sleep state. Later, when you press a key on the keyboard or move the mouse, the computer resumes just where you left off.

hibernation—To save your current Windows session and all your work to the hard drive and then power down the system. Later when you press the power button, Windows reloads any open applications and documents. Hibernation is used on laptop and netbook computers to conserve power. When a laptop computer is put in sleep state for a long time and the battery is getting low, the laptop automatically goes into hibernation. Desktop computers don't normally show the hibernation option on the Shut down menu.

Before you step away from a computer, you need to end the Windows session. Practice each of these methods:

Step 1. To close all open windows and close access to your user account, using the Windows **Shut down** menu, select the **Log off** option to log off the computer. How do you log back on?

Step 2. Put the computer in **Sleep** mode to conserve power. How do you wake up the computer?

Step 3. Using the **Shut down** button, shut down the computer, stopping all computer operations in an orderly manner.

Step 4. If you are using a laptop or netbook, cause the computer to **Hibernate**. How do you wake up the computer?

On Your Own 1-12
End a Windows Session

 Video **1-12**

 Solutions Appendix

For help, see Solution 1-12: How to End a Windows Session.

Summary

Getting Started with Hardware and Software

▶ All hardware can be categorized as devices used for input, output, processing, or storage.

▶ The primary output device is a monitor. Main input devices are the keyboard and mouse. A touch screen is both an input and output device.

▶ The most important storage device inside a computer is the hard drive. A USB flash drive is a convenient portable storage device.

▶ Four types of personal computers you might use at work, at home, or at school are a desktop computer, an all-in-one computer, a laptop, and a netbook.

▶ Types of optical discs are CD, DVD, and Blu-ray discs.

▶ Ports on a computer include USB ports, network port, and video port.

▶ The three main categories of software are applications, operating systems, and utility programs. A computer needs only one operating system such as Windows 7.

▶ An example of applications software is Microsoft Office, which is a suite of several applications used to write documents, manage numbers, create presentations, and manage a database.

▶ Software is stored in a program file that is likely to have an .exe file extension.

▶ The file extension of a data file indicates the type of data in the file; for example, a file with a .jpg file extension is used for a photograph.

▶ To use Windows, you must first log on to a user account that controls the access you have to the computer. The logon process might require a password to the account.

Managing Programs and Their Windows

▶ To use a program, you must first open or launch it. An open or running program uses computer resources including memory until it is closed.

▶ Using the Snap feature of Windows, you can cause a window to maximize or snap to the left or right side of the screen.

▶ A minimized window is not visible on the desktop, but the program icon in the taskbar reminds you that the program is still open. To restore the window, click the program icon.

▶ Many applications might be open, but you can use only one application at a time. Its window is called the active window.

▶ Grab the sides, bottom, or corner of a window to resize it. Grabbing the corner keeps proportions as you resize.

Managing Folders and Files on Storage Devices

▶ The storage capacity of a device is measured in bytes, megabytes (MB), gigabytes (GB), and terabytes (TB).

▶ Files on a storage device are organized using folders that can contain files and sub-folders organized in a hierarchical structure.

▶ A library is a group of folders. Windows default libraries are the Documents, Music, Pictures, and Videos libraries.

▶ Two methods to copy or move a folder or file are the drag-and-drop operation and the commands on the shortcut menus. These commands include Copy, Cut, and Paste.

▶ To rename a folder or file, use the Rename command on the shortcut menu of the file or folder.

▶ Use the Safely Remove Hardware and Eject Media icon in the taskbar before you remove a USB flash drive from your computer.

▶ Use the Windows Snipping Tool to capture an area of the Windows screen and store the snip in a file.

Installing Applications

▶ Software comes on CD or DVD, or it can be downloaded from the Internet. To install software, double-click the setup program to begin the installation.

▶ Three types of Windows accounts are the administrator account, standard account, and guest account. The administrator account has the most control of a computer.

▶ The User Account Control (UAC) dialog box is used to verify the user has the right to perform an operation or gives permission to perform it.

Ending a Windows Session

▶ Before you step away from a computer, end the Windows session using one of the options on the Shut down menu. These options include Shut down, Log off, Lock, Sleep, or Hibernate.

Review Questions

Answer these questions to find out whether you have learned the skills and concepts covered in the chapter. Your instructor can provide you with the correct answers when you are ready to check your work. If you answer most of the questions correctly, you are ready for the Chapter Mastery Project. If not, go back and review the chapter before you tackle the project.

1. What is the most important skill you need to know when learning to use computers?

2. What are the four categories in which all computer hardware devices are placed?

3. What is the most important storage device inside a computer, used to hold both software and data?

4. Which type of nonmobile computer is likely to give you the most power for your money?

5. What are the three general categories of software?

6. What is the latest Microsoft operating system?

7. What type of file has an .exe file extension?

8. How does Windows know how much control over the computer to give a user?

9. Which Windows program is used to manage the files and folders stored on a computer?

10. What is the most important computer resource that a program requires?

11. When you have three program windows open, how many of these windows can be the active window?

12. Which is larger, 1 gigabyte or 1 megabyte?

13. What feature does Windows 7 offer to help you learn to use Windows?

14. Which operation results in a file being deleted from its original location and placed in a new location: Copy and Paste **or** Cut and Paste?

15. What are the three types of Windows user accounts?

Chapter Mastery Project

Find out how well you have mastered the content in this chapter by completing this project. If you can answer all the questions and do all the steps without looking back at the chapter details or using Windows Help and Support, you have mastered this chapter. If you can complete the project by only using Windows Help and Support and not referring to the chapter content, you have proven that you are well on your way to teaching yourself essential computer skills.

If you find you need a lot of help doing the project and you have not yet read the chapter or done the activities, drop back and start at the beginning of the chapter and then return to this project.

> **Hint** All the key terms in the chapter are used in this mastery project. If you find a word you don't know, glance through the chapter and find that key term.

Mastery Project Part 1: Getting Started with Hardware and Software

If you need help completing this part of the mastery project, please review the "Getting Started with Hardware and Software" section in the chapter.

Answer the following questions about hardware devices, software, and data files:

1. Are you using a desktop, laptop, netbook, or all-in-one computer? Does your computer have a touch screen?

2. If you are using a laptop, how many buttons are near your touch pad? Are you using a mouse or touch pad? If you are using a mouse, what type of port is your mouse using?

3. Does your computer use an embedded or external keyboard?

4. A component installed outside the computer case is called a(n) ____ component.

5. Does your computer have a network port? Is a network cable plugged into the port?

6. Does your computer have an optical drive?

7. Does your computer have an analog video port? Digital video port? How many video ports does your computer have?

8. Do you have a USB flash drive to use for this course?

9. How many USB ports does your computer have?

10. Of the three general types of software, which type is the Paint program?

11. Which operating system will we use in this course?

12. What storage device holds the operating system used by a computer?

13. Which file is a program file, Write.exe or Wendy.jpg?

14. Which file is a data file, OneNote.exe or LetterToDave.docx?

Follow these steps to start a Windows 7 session:

Step 1. Power up your computer and log on. What is your Windows 7 screen called? What is your screen background called? What is the purpose of the Recycle Bin?

Step 2. List the Quick Launch icons showing in your taskbar. What program is represented by the big blue letter *e* Quick Launch icon? Which icon in the taskbar is used to adjust sound?

Mastery Project Part 2: Managing Programs and Their Windows

If you need help completing this part of the mastery project, please review the "Managing Programs and Their Windows" section in the chapter.

Follow these steps to manage programs and their windows:

Step 1. Open the **Paint** program. What was the first button you clicked to open the Paint program? An open program is also called a _____ program.

Step 2. Maximize the **Paint** window by using Snap and the press and drag action. Then restore the window to its original size. What button could you have used to maximize the window if you had not used Snap and press and drag?

Step 3. Move the **Paint** window so that it snaps to the right side of your monitor screen. Now snap the window to the left side of the screen. Where do you need to position your pointer or cursor to move a window?

Step 4. Minimize the **Paint** window, and then restore it. What did you click to minimize the window?

Step 5. Resize the **Paint** window by changing first the height and then the width of the window. Then change the height and width at the same time.

Step 6. Close the **Paint** window by using the close button.

Step 7. Open the **Paint** window and the **Windows Explorer** window. Practice making each window the active window. How do you know which window is the active window? Describe how you can use the program icon in the taskbar to make a window the active window.

Step 8. Close both windows. A program uses portions of RAM when it is running. What might happen to your computer performance if you have several windows open at the same time?

Mastery Project Part 3: Managing Folders and Files on Storage Devices

If you need help completing this part of the mastery project, please review the "Managing Folders and Files on Storage Devices" section in the chapter. Answer these questions about managing storage devices, folders, and files:

1. In the Computer window, what is the hard drive called that holds Windows 7?

2. What are four units of measure used to measure the capacity of a storage device? Which unit is large enough to hold only a single character?

3. Which capacity is larger, 500GB or 0.5TB?

4. What is the major advantage a USB flash drive has over a hard drive?

Follow these steps to manage folders and files:

Step 1. Using **Windows Explorer**, display the contents of your **Documents** library. What is one folder in the Documents library that contains a subfolder? What are three other libraries on your hard drive?

Step 2. Using **Windows Explorer**, list the drives installed on your computer. What is the drive letter and storage capacity of the hard drive? How much free space does the drive have? What happens if you double-click drive C:? What is this action called?

Step 3. Insert the DVD from the back of this book into the optical drive and drill down to the **Sample Files** folder. If necessary, change the view in Windows Explorer to **Details**. Display only the **Name**, **Date modified**, **Type**, and **Size** columns in Explorer. How many files are stored in the **Sample Files** folder? Sort the list of files by **Size** ordered from smallest file size to largest.

Step 4. Display the file **Properties** box of the **MyPhoto1** file. What is the file extension of this file?

Step 5. Resize the Windows Explorer window so that a scrollbar appears. Practice using the scrollbar.

Follow these steps to use your USB flash drive:

Step 1. Insert a USB flash drive in your computer. Create a folder named **Computer Class** on the drive. In the Computer Class folder, create a subfolder named **Data**. What happens when you right-click in the whitespace of the right pane of Windows Explorer?

Step 2. Create a folder named **History Class** at the root of the USB flash drive. Rename the History Class folder to **English Class**.

Step 3. Using two Windows Explorer windows, drag and drop the **Sample Files** folder on the DVD to the USB flash drive.

Step 4. In the Sample Files folder on the USB flash drive, open the **MyPhoto1** file.

Step 5. Close the **MyPhoto1** file.

Step 6. Copy the **MyPhoto1** file to the **Computer Class** folder on the flash drive using a copy and paste operation. When you copy the file, where is it temporarily stored?

Step 7. Move the **MyPhoto1** file from the **Computer Class** folder to the **English Class** folder using a cut-and-paste operation.

Step 8. In the English Class folder, rename the **MyPhoto1** file to **MyFriend**. Then delete the **MyFriend** file.

Step 9. Sort the files in the **Sample Files** folder on your USB drive by **Name** in ascending order.

Step 10. Copy the first five files in the **Sample Files** folder into the **Computer Class** folder using only a single drag-and-drop operation.

Step 11. Delete the **Data** folder in the Computer Class folder.

Step 12. Use the Windows Snipping Tool to take a capture of the Windows Explorer window and save the snip to the USB flash drive or another location given by your instructor. Name the snip file **MySnip2**. Before you can safely remove a USB flash drive that you have written on, what should you do?

Mastery Project Part 4: Installing Applications from CD or DVD

If you need help completing this part of the mastery project, please review the "Installing Applications from CD or DVD" section in the chapter.

Follow these steps to install software:

Step 1. The DVD in the back of this book contains the Adobe Reader software used to read PDF files. What is a PDF file? Launch the **AdbeRdr1000_en_US.exe** program on the DVD.

Step 2. Follow directions onscreen to install the software on your computer. Installing software requires administrator rights. Are you logged on to Windows using an administrator account? Were you required to enter an administrator password in the UAC box when you installed the software?

Step 3. Test the software by opening the **Glossary.pdf** file on the DVD. What window appears before Adobe Reader displays the Glossary.pdf file?

Mastery Project Part 5: Ending a Windows Session

If you need help completing this part of the mastery project, please review the "Ending a Windows Session" section in the chapter.

Follow these steps to practice ending a Windows session:

Step 1. **Lock** your computer so that a logon is required to use it. Then unlock your computer using your password.

Step 2. **Log off** and log back on to your computer.

Step 3. Put your computer in a **sleep** state. Return the computer from sleep state.

Step 4. **Restart** your computer using the Shut down menu.

Becoming an Independent Learner

Answer the following questions about becoming an independent learner:

1. To teach yourself to use Windows 7, do you think it is best to rely on the chapter or on Windows Help and Support when you need answers?

2. In Question 1, why one or the other?

3. The most important skill learned in this chapter is how to teach yourself a computer skill. Rate yourself at Level A through E on how well you are doing with this skill. What is your level?

   ○ Level A: I was able to successfully complete the Mastery Project without the help of doing the On Your Own activities in the chapter.

   ○ Level B: I completed all the On Your Own activities and the Mastery Project without referring to any of the solutions in the *Solutions Appendix*.

   ○ Level C: I completed all the On Your Own activities and the Mastery Project by using just a few of the solutions in the *Solutions Appendix*.

   ○ Level D: I completed all the On Your Own activities and the Mastery Project by using many of the solutions in the *Solutions Appendix*.

   ○ Level E: I completed all the On Your Own activities and the Mastery Project and had to use all of the solutions in the *Solutions Appendix*.

Regardless of how you did it, the good news is you completed the work. Congratulations! Continue toward the goal of teaching yourself computer skills. If you are not at Level A, try to move up one level on how you learn in Chapter 2.

Projects to Help You

Now that you have mastered the material in this chapter, you are ready to tackle the three projects introduced at the beginning of the chapter in the section "How Will This Chapter Help Me?"

Project 1: Windows in Your Personal Life

Learning to use computers in your personal life is a moving target because what you want to do with a computer changes as your needs change. In addition, hardware and software are constantly changing. To keep up with all this change, you need to learn to teach yourself computer skills. Do the following to learn to use some features of Windows that were not covered in the chapter:

Step 1. Windows offers the Calculator program, which you can use to convert numbers and dates and do calculations. Open the **Calculator** program, which you can find in the **Start**, **All Programs**, **Accessories** group.

PERSONAL PROJECT: I want to use the Windows Calculator to find the fuel economy of my car, and I plan to burn some CDs using Windows.

Step 2. Use Windows Help and Support to learn about the Calculator. To open the Windows Help and Support window, click **Start** and then click **Help and Support**. The Windows Help and Support window opens.

Step 3. Type **Calculator** in the search box near the top of the Help and Support window and press **Enter**. Using information provided by Windows Help and Support, answer these questions using the Calculator:

    a. How do you set the Calculator to perform Unit conversion? What is 29 degrees Celsius converted to degrees Fahrenheit?

    b. How do you perform a Date calculation? How many days are there from August 10, 2012, to January 1, 2013?

    c. Which option on the View menu is used to calculate fuel economy (mpg)? If your car used 12 gallons to travel 220 miles, what is the fuel economy (mpg)?

    d. You are considering buying a house. The purchase price is $155,000. The down payment is $17,000. Use the Calculator to find out your monthly payments over 30 years at 5% interest.

    e. Set the Calculator for basic calculations. What is 55.6 * 72 / 45?

    f. What is 55% of 783?

Step 4. Windows Help and Support can give you solutions to problems and help with Windows. Using Windows Help and Support, answer these questions:

    a. In the search box in the Windows Help and Support window, type **problems with sound** and press **Enter**. What are three things you can do to solve a problem with sound?

    b. You want to burn a CD using Windows Explorer. In the search box, type **Burn a CD in Windows Explorer** and press **Enter**. What two disc formats does Windows use when it burns a CD?

    c. Which disc format should you use if you want to burn a CD to be used with other Windows 7 computers?

Project 2: Windows in Your Academic Career

In the process of getting a degree or a certification or taking a few classes, you are certain to need a computer for much of your work. Being able to teach yourself computer skills will make your computer work less stressful. Do the following to teach yourself about some features of Windows that were not covered in the chapter:

ACADEMIC PROJECT:
I want to put a gadget on my Windows desktop that will report the weather each morning.

1. Desktop gadgets are icons placed on the Windows desktop that you can use to get the date and time, news, and weather. To see the available gadgets, right-click anywhere on the desktop and click **Gadgets** in the shortcut menu. The available gadgets appear in a small window. Press and drag the **Clock** gadget and place it anywhere on your desktop.

2. Use Windows Help and Support to learn about Windows. To open the Windows Help and Support window, click **Start** and then click **Help and Support.** The Windows Help and Support window opens.

3. Type **Gadgets** in the search box near the top of the Help and Support window and press **Enter**. Using information provided by Windows Help and Support, answer these questions:

    a. Briefly describe how the Slide Show gadget works.

    b. Briefly describe how the Feed Headlines gadget works.

    c. How do you remove a gadget from your desktop?

4. Place the **Weather** gadget on your desktop and change the location to your city.

5. Windows 7 comes in several editions, including Windows 7 Home Premium and Windows 7 Professional. In the search box of Windows Help and Support, type **which edition of Windows 7** and press **Enter**. What edition of Windows 7 is installed on your computer? Which window gave you this information?

6. Windows 7 Peek can be used to clear your desktop. Using the Help and Support window, answer these questions about Peek:

    a. How do you use Peek to minimize all the windows on the desktop?

    b. How do you use Peek to restore the minimized windows?

Project 3: Windows in Your Technical Career

TECHNICAL CAREER PROJECT: I need to help someone recover a file she accidentally deleted.

If you are planning a career in technology, you will constantly learn about new technologies as they arise. Knowing how to teach yourself computer skills is essential for keeping up with all these new technologies. Do the following to teach yourself about some features of Windows that were not covered in the chapter:

1. When you delete a folder or file on your hard drive, Windows moves the item to the Recycle Bin. Double-click the **Recycle Bin** icon on your desktop. Does it contain any files or folders?

2. Use Windows Help and Support to teach yourself about Windows. To open the Windows Help and Support window, click **Start** and then click **Help and Support**. The Windows Help and Support window opens.

3. Type **Recycle Bin** in the search box near the top of the Help and Support window and press **Enter**. Using information provided by Windows Help and Support, answer these questions:

    a. List the steps to recover a file that has been deleted and you can see is in the Recycle Bin.

    b. When you delete a file from your USB flash drive, why is the file not moved to the Recycle Bin?

    c. List the steps to empty the Recycle Bin. Emptying the Recycle Bin can free up some space on your hard drive.

4. Windows 7 Shake can be used to manage windows. Using the Help and Support window, answer these questions about Shake:

    a. How do you use Shake to minimize windows on the desktop?

    b. How do you use Shake to restore the minimized windows?

5. Recall that the Windows Snipping Tool can be used to capture a screenshot or snip of your screen. The tool can be extremely useful when writing instructions to users on how to use software. Using Windows Help and Support, find out how to annotate a snip.

6. Take a snip of part of your Windows screen. Use the highlighter tool to highlight an area of the snip. Use the red pen to write on the snip. Save the snip to your USB flash drive, naming the file **MySnip3**.

7. Using Windows Explorer, create a new folder named **Snips** on your USB flash drive. Move the MySnip3 file to this new folder.

Project to Help Others

One of the best ways to learn is to teach someone else. And, in teaching someone else, you are making a contribution into that person's life. As part of each chapter's work, you are encouraged to teach someone else a skill you have learned. In this case, you help your apprentice learn to use Windows. Who is your apprentice? A parent, younger sibling, neighbor, or friend? For the best experience, this person should be someone much older or younger than you and should really want to learn to use a computer. Find that person! What is your apprentice's name? _____

It is hoped your apprentice will receive your help for the entire course, but if you need to switch to another person, be sure to let your instructor know.

Working with your apprentice, do the following:

Step 1. Ask your apprentice how he expects to use a computer and what he would like to learn. Do your best to help this person meet these goals as you move forward to other chapters. What are the goals of your apprentice?

Step 2. Show your apprentice how to start a computer and log on. Then point out the items on the Windows desktop. Show him how to open program windows and manage these windows. How quickly did the apprentice learn these skills?

Step 3. Explain the purpose of Windows Explorer to manage folders and files. Make sure your apprentice understands the purpose of

  ▶ Windows Explorer

  ▶ Folder

  ▶ File

  ▶ Storage devices including the hard drive, a USB flash drive, and an optical drive

  ▶ How well do you think your apprentice understands the purpose of each item?

Step 4. Ask your apprentice to copy a folder or file from the DVD in the back of this book to his USB flash drive. Watch and coach as he works. Don't do it for him.

Step 5. Show him how to use Windows Help and Support so he can teach himself. Based on the goals of your apprentice, what other skills in this chapter do you think would be useful to him? List these skills.

Step 6. Help your apprentice learn each one, but try to coach him to discover on his own rather than doing it for him. Remind him that teaching himself a computer skill is the most important computer skill to know.

Step 7. Ask your apprentice to evaluate how the tutoring session went. Briefly describe his response.

CHAPTER 2
Finding and Using Information on the Web

IN THIS CHAPTER, YOU WILL

Get the news on the web

Search for other information on the web

Use applications and store data in the cloud

Learn to safely do business on the web

Because the Internet and the web are constantly changing, what you learn today is likely to change tomorrow. Remember the most important computer skill is to know how to teach yourself a new computer skill. Therefore, this chapter is designed to help you teach yourself about using the web. Try to do each On Your Own activity without any help. If you find that you need help, you can always refer to the solutions in the *Solutions Appendix*.

JUMP RIGHT IN

If you want even more of a challenge, try proceeding directly to the Chapter Mastery Project at the end of this chapter. If you need help on the project, refer to the On Your Own activities in the chapter or do your own independent investigating by searching the web for what you need to know. When you complete the project, you will have mastered the skills in this chapter. Then go to Projects to Help You that require you to apply your skills to new situations.

How Will This Chapter Help Me?

Throughout this book, each chapter provides three projects focusing on personal, academic, or technical career goals. Depending on your own interests, you might choose to perform any or all of these projects to help you achieve your goals.

PERSONAL PROJECT: I'm planning a trip to Niagara Falls, Canada. I need to find out about sites to visit along the way, driving directions, hotels, restaurants, tours, and currency exchange in Canada. I also need to buy a digital camera and share my photos with friends. Can I do all that online?

ACADEMIC PROJECT: I want to find out about nursing careers, and I need to research questions in my history, chemistry, and literature classes. I also need to buy and download the Academic Edition of Microsoft Office and install it on my laptop.

TECHNICAL CAREER PROJECT: My boss is asking me questions about cell phone technologies I don't understand. Users I support keep getting error messages that I don't recognize. Also, a manager has asked me to help her find and buy some software. The laser printer needs toner, and I don't know how to change the toner cartridge. Can the web give me all these answers?

Getting News on the Web

The web is a great way to get news. In the past, news came to us by town criers, newspapers, radio, and television. But when we use the web to get our news, we can also voice our opinions about news and easily share it with others.

The **Internet** is made up of many computers all over the world connected to each other. The news comes to us over the Internet from computers serving up the news in web pages. A **web page** is a document that contains text and perhaps graphics, sound, animation, or video, to be displayed on a computer screen by a **browser.** The collection of all web pages available on the Internet is called the **World Wide Web**, also called the **web.**

> **Internet**—Many computers over the world connected to each other. This global network of computers is used to receive and serve up untold amounts of data and provides us powerful ways to communicate with others. When you use a computer connected to the Internet, know that your computer is also part of the Internet.
>
> **browser**—A program that searches or browses web pages from the web.
>
> **web page**—A document that can include text, graphics, sound, animation, and video. The document is constructed using a group of rules collectively called the Hypertext Markup Language (HTML). The document is called a hypertext document and is designed to be displayed by a browser.
>
> **World Wide Web** or **web**—A collection of web pages made available by computers connected to the Internet. The World Wide Web is one of many applications that the Internet supports.

> **Tip** The Internet and the web are similar to a transportation system that supports the delivery of cargo. For example, the road system (the Internet) in our country is used by the postal system (World Wide Web) to deliver the mail (web pages).

Introduction to Internet Explorer

If your computer is connected to the Internet, you can use Internet Explorer (IE) to find information on the Internet. Recall from Chapter 1, "Using Windows 7 to Manage Applications and Data," that Internet Explorer, Version 8, is the browser included in Windows 7.

> **Not Working?** This chapter assumes that the computer you are using is a Windows 7 computer connected to the Internet. If you have a problem with the connection, know that Chapter 12, "Connecting to the Internet and Securing a Computer," and Chapters 13, "Maintaining a Computer and Fixing Computer Problems," cover how to connect a computer to the Internet and what to do when the connection fails.
>
> Windows 7 comes with Internet Explorer version 8 and can be upgraded to Internet Explorer version 9. The instructions and figures used in this chapter are for Windows 7 and Internet Explorer 8. To find out what version of IE you have, click the Help button in the Internet Explorer window, and then click **About Internet Explorer**. If you have IE version 9 installed, know that some IE features described in the chapter might work differently on your computer.

Do the following to get the news using Internet Explorer:

Step 1. Open **Internet Explorer** (see Figure 2-1). What web page does IE use as your **home page**?

home page—The web page that appears when you first open a browser.

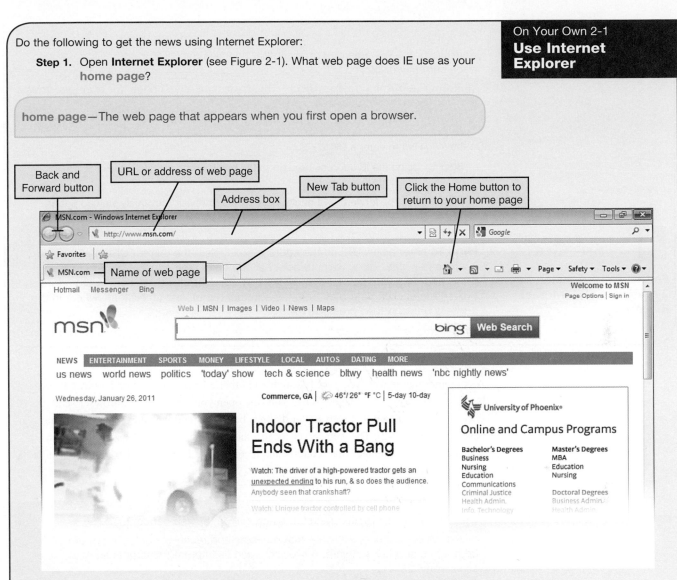

FIGURE 2-1
The home page is the first page that displays when you open your browser.

Step 2. Click a **link** on your home page to drill down to another web page. Click a link on the new page that displays.

link—Text or graphic on a web page that points to another web page. When you mouse over a link, the pointer changes to a hand. 🖑 When you click the link, the browser requests and displays the other web page. A link is also called a hyperlink.

Step 3. Use the **Home** button 🏠 to return to your home page.

You can type the address of a web page in the **address box** of Internet Explorer. The address of a web page is called the **Uniform Resource Locator (URL)**.

On Your Own 2-1
Use Internet Explorer

address box—The area of a browser that contains the URL or address of the web page currently displayed.

Uniform Resource Locator (URL)—The address of a web page, for example, www. cnn.com or cnn.com/business.

Do the following to enter a URL:

Step 1. Using the IE address box, go to the **www.cnn.com** news site. Click a link on that page.

Step 2. Use the forward and backward buttons to revisit previously viewed pages.

    Solutions Appendix

For help, see Solution 2-1: How to Use Internet Explorer.

Hint To enter a new URL in the address box, select the current URL and replace it with a new one. Three ways to select all the text in the address bar are to (a) press and drag your pointer over all the text, (b) right-click anywhere in the address box and then click **Select all** from the shortcut menu, and (c) click anywhere in the address box and then press **Ctrl-A**.

A computer that makes web pages available to other computers is called a **web server** because it serves up web pages. When you first open your browser, the browser sends a URL over the Internet to a web server that has been assigned the address of your home page (see Figure 2-2). The web server locates the requested page and sends the page to your browser. A computer that requests and receives a web page or other content is called a client computer or just a **client**.

web server—A computer that stores and serves up web pages.

client—A computer or software that requests and receives content from other computers or other software. A browser such as Internet Explorer is an example of client software.

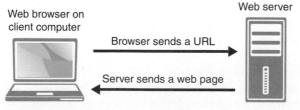

FIGURE 2-2
A client computer sends a URL to a web server, which returns the requested web page.

The collection of web pages that one web server makes available is called a **website**. For most websites, entering the www is not required. Earlier you visited the CNN news website at www.cnn.com. You could have entered only cnn.com in your address box and the browser would still find the CNN site.

> **website**—All the web pages that one web server stores and makes available to the web.

Every computer on the Internet has a name, and that name is called the **domain name**. The domain name can have several parts, each separated by a period as in www.cnn.com. The last part of the domain name is called the **top-level domain name**.

> **domain name**—The name of a computer on the Internet, which consists of letters and periods.
>
> **top-level domain name**—The ending of a domain name that identifies the type of organization that owns the domain name. Common top-level domain names are .com (commercial), .edu (educational), .org (nonprofit), .gov (government), .info (information), and .museum (museums).

Suppose your browser sends out the URL of www.cnn.com. The CNN server receives the request and serves up its home page (also called the default page) at the server because no specific page was requested. To request a specific page on a server, the browser adds a slash and the name of the requested page following the domain name of the server. For example, if the browser sends the URL www.cnn.com/business, the CNN server responds with the web page on the server named business.

News and More News

Let's explore some other news sites. As you do, you'll learn a few tricks about Internet Explorer that can make surfing the web easier.

On Your Own 2-2
Manage Multiple Web Pages

Do the following to explore several news sites and manage multiple web pages:

Step 1. Navigate to The New York Times site at **nytimes.com**. Open a new tab and go to **news.yahoo.com**. Open a third tab and go to **news.google.com**. Open a fourth tab and go to **cnn.com**. Practice moving from one open tab to another.

Step 2. Use the **Quick Tabs** button to view all pages. Select the **Google News** page and then close that tab.

Not Working? Internet Explorer version 8 has the Quick Tabs button, but IE version 9 does not. In IE version 9, press Ctrl+Q instead.

For help, see Solution 2-2: How to Manage Multiple Web Pages.

 Solutions Appendix

You now know about four popular news sites: cnn.com, news.yahoo.com, news.google. com, and nytimes.com. In the process, you have learned how to use the basic features of Internet Explorer.

Save a Favorite Site

During an Internet Explorer session, you can use the backward and forward buttons to step through pages you just visited. If you want to save a web page address so that you can easily return to it even have you have closed Internet Explorer or restarted your computer, add the web page address to your **Favorites**.

> **Favorites**—A list of web page addresses saved by Internet Explorer so you can easily revisit the page.

On Your Own 2-3
Save a Web Page to Your Favorites

Using Internet Explorer, navigate to the **news.google.com** site. Add the site to your Favorites list. Revisit the Google News site by using your Favorites list.

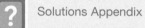 Solutions Appendix

For help, see Solution 2-3: How to Save a Web Page to Your Favorites.

Searching for Other Information on the Web

So what other information can you find on the web? Let's do a little exploring (also known as surfing). Follow along at your computer and feel free to explore on your own. Surfing the web can be a lot of fun.

The easiest way to find information on the web is to use a **search engine**. Google.com and Bing.com are the two most popular search engines, and Google is more popular than Bing.

> **search engine**—A website that finds information on the web. The two most popular search engines are Google (www.google.com) and Bing (www.bing.com).

To make it easier for you to use a search engine, Internet Explorer provides a search box in the upper-right corner of the IE window. Unless you change it, the bing.com search engine is used.

Two ways to use a search engine are to use the Internet Explorer address box and search box. Use both methods to find information on the web:

Step 1. Using the IE address box, visit **google.com**. To find out the weather in Seattle, Washington, enter **seattle weather** as the search string. If the instant search feature of Google is on, results appear even as you type. Use the autosuggest feature of Google to select **seattle weather** to get the weather in Seattle, Washington.

> **search string**—The text you type in the search box of a search engine website such as Google.com or Bing.com. The text is not case sensitive, meaning that you can type either lowercase or uppercase letters and get the same results.
>
> **autosuggest**—A search engine feature that offers search strings that might be similar to the one you are typing. Also called *autocomplete*.

Step 2. View previews of pages in the hit list that appears. Drill down to one of these web pages found by Google.

> **hit list**—The list of web pages found by a search engine.

> **Hint** When you click the magnifying glass icon in a hit, a preview of the page appears.

Step 3. Practice using the Internet Explorer search box by searching for how to change the oil in a car. Which search engine is used by your IE search box?

For help, see Solution 2-4: How to Use a Search Engine.   [?] Solutions Appendix

Popular Websites

As you use a search engine, you will notice a few sites that tend to reappear frequently depending on the type of information you are searching. Figure 2-3 shows some familiar and popular sites.

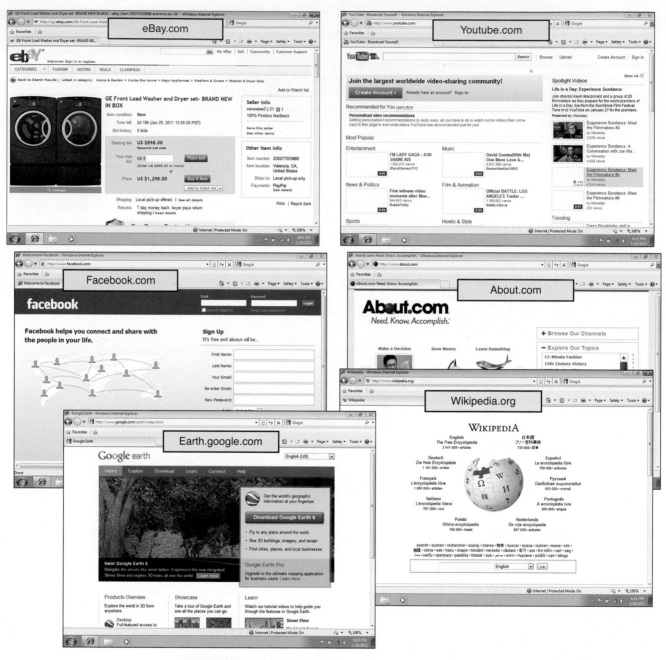

FIGURE 2-3
Get familiar with these popular websites.

The following list describes each of the sites shown:

▶ **wikipedia.org** contains more than 17 million articles written by volunteers around the world on all kinds of topics. It is the most popular **wiki** on the web. Wikipedia gets its name from wiki and encyclopedia.

> **wiki**—A website where many people freely contribute and collaborate about a topic of common interest.

▶ **earth.google.com** gives geographic information. Find cities, places, and local businesses and see 3D images of terrain, buildings, and streets. Tour the moon and the stars. Explore any location on planet earth.

▶ **about.com, ehow.com, wisegeek.com,** and **howstuffworks.com** frequently pop up when you search on how to do something, how something works, or what something is.

▶ **eBay.com** and **craigslist.org** are the two most popular sites individuals use to sell goods and services online.

▶ **facebook.com** is a **social networking** site where you can keep up with your friends and let them know what is happening in your life. Google and Facebook are the two most popular websites on the web. Facebook is often used by businesses, public figures, and organizations. When you search on a person's name, his Facebook page might appear in the hit list.

> **Tip** Notice that craigslist.org ends with .org rather than .com, which is used by commercial sites. Craigslist is a nonprofit organization, and nonprofit sites use the .org name.

> **social networking**—Interaction between people who share a common interest. Facebook.com and twitter.com are the two most popular social networking websites.

▶ **youtube.com** is the most popular website for sharing videos. To share your own videos, first click **Create Account**. Then click **Upload** to upload a video to the site.

Other popular websites are

▶ **maps.google.com** and **mapquest.com**, the two most popular sites for finding driving directions and maps.

▶ **blogger.com** and **wordpress.com**, popular blogging websites where you can post a **blog**.

> **blog**—Short for *weblog* and is an online diary or journal used to express your thoughts, opinions, and activities.

Want to know the current most popular websites on the web? Do a Google search using the search string **most popular websites on the web**.

More Advanced Google Searches

Google, Bing, and other search engines present web page hits to you ordered according to how well the search engine determines the page matches your search string. This order is called the **page rank**. In addition, a website can pay Google to put its pages first. These paid-for hits are called **sponsored links**. In Google, sponsored links are marked with the word *Ads* (see Figure 2-4).

> **page rank**—The order of importance assigned to a list of pages found in a search by a search engine.
>
> **sponsored link**—A link displayed at the top of a search engine hit list because the owner of the web page has paid for this favored position. Sponsored links provide income for Google and other search engine sites.

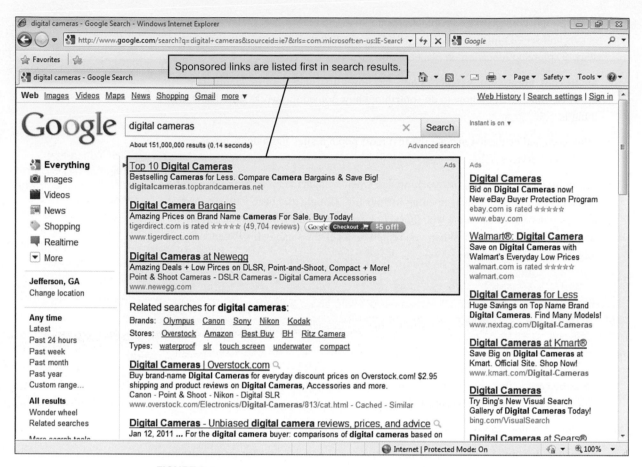

FIGURE 2-4
Sponsored links are listed at the top of the hit list or in the right column.

A search engine can find and list millions of hits. Fortunately, you are likely to find what you are looking for on the first page or two of hits because of how well the search engine orders the results. However, you can limit the number of hits, called the **hit count**, to help zero in on what you need by performing more advanced searches.

> **hit count**—The number of hits resulting from a search by a search engine.

The goals of using advanced searches are to reduce the hit count and to cause the most important hits to appear near the top in page rank. Advanced searches can be formed to

▶ Search for specific words or groups of words or exclude certain words

▶ Limit the search by how recently the page was last updated

▶ Limit the country where the web page is stored

▶ Limit the search to specific websites or exclude specific websites

Google and Bing both offer tips and tutorials for building advanced searches. On Google's home page at **google.com**, click **Advanced search** to find these tools.

Use the Google search engine to perform the following advanced searches:

On Your Own 2-5
Perform Google Advanced Searches

Step 1. Search for information on how a search engine works, limiting the search only to the **wikipedia.org** site. Next, limit the results of the preceding search to content updated in the past 24 hours.

Hint Use the **site:** option in the search string.

Step 2. Try a new search for an exact group of words. To search for the exact group of words, use double quotation marks around words in the search string. Search for the exact string like this: **"who invented google earth"**.

Step 3. Next, try a search where you want to exclude a word from the results. To not include a word in a search, put a minus sign in front of the word. Search for an apartment near **Emory University** but eliminate **luxury** apartments from your search.

? Solutions Appendix

For help, see Solution 2-5: How to Perform Google Advanced Searches.

You can easily limit a search to images, videos, maps, and other types of content using the Google menus at the top of the Google search page. Do the following:

On Your Own 2-6
Find Images, Videos, Directions, and Translations

Step 1. Find images about the 2010 gulf oil spill.

Step 2. Find videos showing you how to make a homemade pizza.

Step 3. Find driving directions from Baltimore, Maryland, to Newark, New Jersey.

Step 4. Find a translation into Spanish for the text, "Good morning. Welcome to my home."

For help, see Solution 2-6: How to Find Images, Videos, Driving Directions, and Translations

? Solutions Appendix

Customize Your Browser

You can customize Internet Explorer. One setting you can change is the home page that IE uses when you first launch the browser.

Change your home page to your favorite website. For example, if you want to get the latest sports scores each time you open your browser, change your home page in Internet Explorer to **espn.go.com**.

On Your Own 2-7
Change Your Home Page

Hint To change many Internet Explorer settings, click **Tools** in the menu bar and then click **Internet Options**.

 Video **2-7**

For help, see Solution 2-7: How to Change Your Home Page.

? Solutions Appendix

Using Applications and Storing Data in the Cloud

cloud computing— Applications and data stored on remote computers on the Internet made available through a browser.

In the last chapter, you learned how to install and use an application on your computer. You also learned to store data files to local storage devices such as a USB flash drive or the hard drive. With **cloud computing**, the application is installed on a computer somewhere on the Internet and the data files are also stored on a remote computer on the Internet (in the cloud). You use your browser to access both the application and your data.

The advantages of cloud computing are that you don't need to buy the application and the data is always available from whatever computer you use so long as that computer has access to the Internet. It's also easy to share the data with other users on the Internet.

Websites That Provide Free Cloud Computing

Figure 2-5 shows several examples of websites that provide free cloud computing.

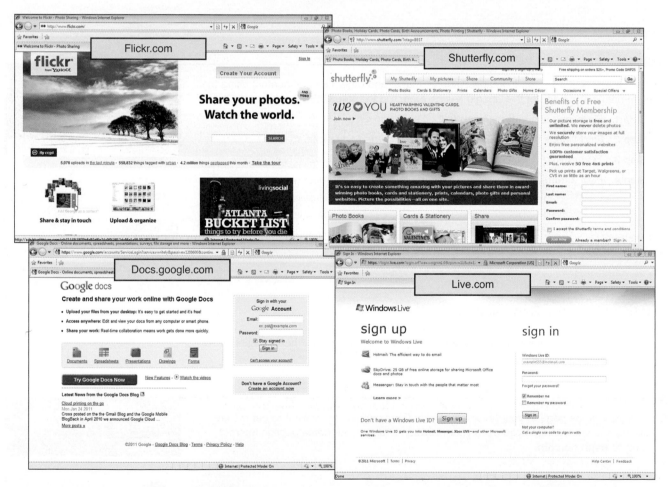

FIGURE 2-5
Flickr.com, shutterfly.com, docs.google.com, and live.com all provide free cloud computing applications and data storage.

The following list describes each of the sites shown:

▶ **Flickr.com** lets you store and share photos. You can use the applications on the site to crop, fix, and edit the photos; attach notes and tags to them; and print them.

▶ **Shutterfly.com** is a popular site to store and share photos. Using the applications on the site, you can make cards, stationery, calendars, and even books with your photos.

▶ **Docs.google.com** (called Google Docs) lets you upload any type file to its free file storage. Using personal software applications on the site, you can edit documents, worksheets, presentations, drawings, and forms. You can also work with a team as several people contribute to a work.

▶ **Live.com** (called Windows Live) is similar to Google Docs. It includes **SkyDrive**, a storage location for files, and scaled-down versions of Microsoft Office personal applications. These applications include Word (for creating documents and forms), Excel (for managing text and numbers in columns and row), PowerPoint (for creating presentations), and OneNote (for note taking).

> **SkyDrive**—A personal storage location on the live.com website where you can upload and save any type of file.

Use a SkyDrive

A SkyDrive, available on live.com, is a quick and easy way to store a file in the cloud and share it with others. Some instructors prefer that you send your homework to them by posting your file on your SkyDrive and giving your instructor access to your SkyDrive.

Do the following to set up your personal SkyDrive and post a photo to your SkyDrive:

Step 1. Using the **live.com** site, create a SkyDrive account using your email address. If you don't have an email address, sign up for one using the live.com site. What is the maximum storage capacity of your SkyDrive?

Step 2. Post a photo of yourself to the Public folder of your SkyDrive. If you don't have a photo, use this one that is included on the DVD with this book: **\Sample Files\MyPhoto1.jpg**. What is the name of the photo file you posted to your SkyDrive?

Step 3. Your instructor might want access to your SkyDrive so you can post homework files there. If requested by your instructor, share the My Documents folder on your SkyDrive with your instructor using his email address. Have Windows Live send a notification to your instructor that contains a link to the SkyDrive folder.

On Your Own 2-8
Set Up and Use a SkyDrive

 Solutions Appendix

For help, see Solution 2-8: How to Set Up and Use a SkyDrive.

Doing Business Safely on the Web

Doing business on the web is convenient and can save you time. In this section, you learn how to stay safe while doing business on the web and how to purchase, download, and install software from the web.

Stay Safe on the Web

The web is a great tool, but it can also be dangerous. Stay safe as you do business on the web by following these safety precautions:

▶ **Do business only with trustworthy sites.** Never give personal information such as your date of birth or credit card information to a website unless you trust that site. If you are not sure if the site is trustworthy, you can use Google to search for reviews about the site. For example, to find reviews about www.buy.com, enter **www.buy. com reviews** in the Google search box and press **Enter**.

▶ **Download free data or software only from sites you trust.** Some sites offer free music, videos, games, or other software just so they can install **adware** or other malicious software on your computer during the download. Before you download anything from a website, read some reviews about the site.

> **adware**—Software that runs on your computer to display pop-up ads when you surf the web. Adware can be annoying and slow down a system.

▶ **Use only secured transmissions.** Before you enter personal information on a website, make sure the site is using **HTTPS** to protect your information when it is in route from your computer to the web server.

> **HTTPS (Hypertext Transfer Protocol Secure)**—A group of rules (called a protocol) used to transfer data securely to a website. The data is coded (said to be encrypted) so that it cannot be read if intercepted by thieves.

You know the data is protected if you see the padlock to the right of the address bar. Also notice the http:// that usually appears to the left of the web page address, is written as https://. See Figure 2-6.

FIGURE 2-6
Notice the padlock and https://, which both indicate your personal data is protected during transmission to this secured website.

▶ **Use a strong password to each online account.** Before you can pay a bill online to your utility company or manage your bank account online, you must set up an online account at the company's website. Most retail sites require you set up an account before you can buy online. Use a **strong password** for each online account. If you write down the password, keep it in a safe place.

> **Tip** To protect your online accounts, use a different password for each online account.

> **strong password**—A password that is not easy to guess. Strong passwords include a mix of uppercase and lowercase letters and numbers that are not easy to guess. Don't include the name of your pet or child or your date of birth in a password. Examples of strong passwords are UtPp93ej and dUh427Yq.

▶ **Keep a record of important transactions.** When you do banking or business, you need a record of the transaction in case the bank or business makes a mistake and overcharges or charges you for something you did not buy. Many retail sites email you a receipt. Just in case that email doesn't arrive, you might want to save or print the web page showing the transaction so you have a record of it.

Saving a web page to your USB flash drive, SkyDrive, or hard drive is more convenient than printing the page. By default, Internet Explorer saves a web page to a file using the **MHT file format**, which uses the .mht file extension.

> **MHT (Multipurpose HyperText) file format**—A web archive file format by Microsoft used to save and email web pages. The file has an .mht file extension and is viewed using Internet Explorer.

▶ **Use antispyware.** To protect against **spyware**, install and run **antispyware** software on your computer.

> **spyware**—Software running on your computer without your knowledge that is trying to steal personal information you type on your computer.
>
> **antispyware**—Software designed to catch and prevent spyware from stealing your personal data.

▶ **Use antivirus software.** Besides spyware, another type of malicious software is a **virus**. Every computer needs **antivirus software** running on it to protect it from viruses and other types of malicious software. Later in the chapter, you learn how to download, install, and run Microsoft Security Essentials, which is antispyware and antivirus software.

> **virus**—Software running on your computer without your knowledge that is trying to corrupt Windows, applications, or your data installed on your computer.
>
> **antivirus software**—Software designed to discover and remove a virus that might have infected your computer. Most antivirus software also searches for spyware.

PayPal

> **PayPal**—An online money account at paypal.com used for shopping and paying bills online without having to share your banking information with a retail or business site.

▶ **Use PayPal, which is a convenient and safe way to pay for purchases online.** You set up a PayPal account at www.paypal.com and connect the account to your bank account, debit card, or credit card. Then when you make an online purchase, you enter the PayPal account and password rather than give the retail site your banking or credit card information. Then PayPal charges the transaction to your bank account, debit card, or credit card. You can also put money directly into your PayPal account.

▶ **Compare prices and read online reviews about products or services before you make a buying decision.** To compare prices, enter a product in the Google search box and click **Shopping**. You can then sort the list by price (see Figure 2-7). To find online reviews about a product, enter the product followed by the word **reviews** in the Google search box.

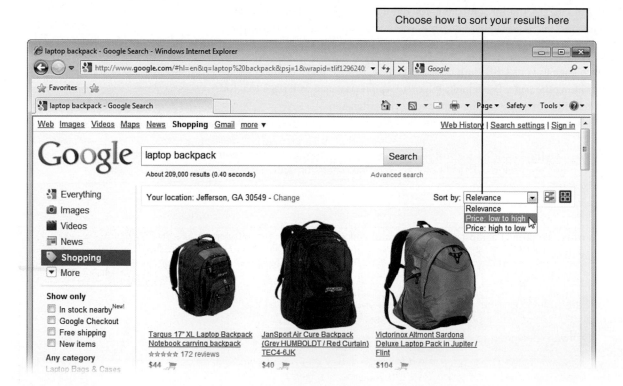

FIGURE 2-7
Google Shopping results show images and prices.

Tip Some sites specialize in product reviews, such as epinions.com, consumersearch.com, and shopping.yahoo.com. Amazon.com also keeps reviews about its products. Many customers post videos about a product on youtube.com.

▶ **Learn to identify an authoritative source.** As you search for reviews about a product, know that some reviews might give wrong information about a product. The website of the product manufacturer is considered the **authoritative source** about its own products.

authoritative source—A source that is considered the final word on a matter. For example, the authoritative website about an MP3 player is the website of the manufacturer. A website that reviews the MP3 player is not considered authoritative.

Tip In Chapter 12, you learn even more ways to stay safe and secure your computer and its data.

Some companies offer online chat sessions to help customers with their questions. For example, as you browse the Dell.com website looking for a new computer, the *Have a question?* box might pop up. Click **Chat Now** to begin a **chat** session online with a customer service representative. This person can answer your questions.

chat—An Internet service that allows two or more people to communicate in text online.

It's a good idea to keep a record of all your online business or banking transactions. To practice printing a web page and saving it to your USB flash drive or another place given by your instructor, do the following to print and save the wellsfargo.com home page:

Step 1. Go to **wellsfargo.com** and print this web page. If you don't have access to a printer, display the **Print preview** of the page. A page might be disorganized when it prints, but all the important text does print.

Step 2. Save the page as a data file to your USB flash drive or other location given by your instructor. To verify you have saved the page, close your browser and then display the saved web page. Where did you save the file?

Not Working? You cannot save a web page directly to a SkyDrive unless you have set up Windows 7 to do the job. If your computer lab does not give you permission to save to a USB flash drive or the hard drive, you might not be able to complete this activity.

On Your Own 2-9
Print and Save a Web Page

? Solutions Appendix

For help, see Solution 2-9: How to Print and Save a Web Page.

Buy Software Online

Recall from Chapter 1 that software can come on CD or DVD or you can download it from the Internet. Software can be purchased (called commercial software), can be free (called **freeware**), or might be offered on a trial basis without cost or for a small donation (called **shareware**).

> **freeware**—Software that is free.
>
> **shareware**—(1) Software that is offered free on a trial basis. If you decide to continue using the software after the trial period is over, you must purchase the software. (2) Software provided by the owner for a small donation.

Freeware and shareware are usually downloaded from a website. Shareware that is downloaded on a trial basis locks itself when the trial period expires so that you cannot use it. After you purchase the software, it unlocks. Buying commercial software online usually costs less, but you don't have the CD or DVD for backup.

When you purchase software, you do not actually own the software. You own a license to use the software according to the agreed-to terms of use. This agreement includes the number of computers on which you can install the software. Installing the software on more computers than you have agreed to is called **software piracy**.

> **software piracy**—Installing and using software in a way that violates the agreement you made with the owner of the software.

When you first install new software on your computer, make sure you have the **documentation** available so you can get your questions answered when learning to use the software.

> **documentation**—The directions and help for using a product, which can be provided in a printed booklet, in a file on CD or DVD, or online.

> **Tip** Computers in school labs might be configured so that you cannot install software and you will not be able to complete the following activity. In this situation, know that you can watch Video 2-10 to see the installation. If you don't already have antivirus software installed on your home computer, install Microsoft Security Essentials on it to help protect it.

Microsoft Security Essentials is freeware and protects a computer against spyware, viruses, and other types of **malware**. When you're using the Internet, it's important that your computer be running antivirus software so it is protected.

Microsoft Security Essentials—Free antivirus and antispyware software available from Microsoft that protects a computer against viruses and spyware.

malware—Malicious software that intends harm such as a virus, spyware, or adware.

It is best to have only one antivirus program running on a computer. If you do not already have antivirus software installed on your computer, do the following to install Microsoft Security Essentials:

Step 1. Go to the **www.microsoft.com/security_essentials** website. What is the link on this page that gives you access to the software documentation?

Not Working? Websites and links sometimes change. If the URL in Step 1 doesn't work, try going to www.microsoft.com and drilling down to Security and then Microsoft Security Essentials.

Step 2. Download **Security Essentials** to your computer. Save the file to your Windows desktop. What is the name of the file you downloaded?

Step 3. Install the Security Essentials software.

Step 4. To clean up your desktop, delete the downloaded file.

Step 5. Verify that **Real time protection** is turned on so that the antivirus software is always running in the background to constantly protect your computer.

Step 6. Verify that the software is scheduled to scan your computer either weekly or daily to check for malware. What is the name of the window that allows you to change these two settings?

 Video **2-10**

For help, see Solution 2-10: How to Download, Install, and Run Microsoft Security Essentials.

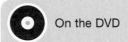 Solutions Appendix

Tip In this chapter, you have learned how to find and use websites. You might like to know how websites are created. Look in the Extra Chapters folder on the DVD in the back of the book to find Chapter W, "Authoring Your Own Website." Using this chapter, you learn how to build and publish your own website.

 On the DVD

Summary

Getting the News on the Web

▶ The Internet is a network of computers connected globally. Some of these computers make web pages available to other computers and are collectively called the World Wide Web.

▶ A web page is built using HTML and is called a hypertext document.

▶ Internet Explorer is a browser that is part of Windows 7 and is used to explore the Internet, which is called surfing the web.

▶ Every web page available on the Internet has an address called its URL.

▶ A client computer requests and receives content from a server. A web server provides web pages to clients.

▶ Every computer on the Internet has a domain name assigned to it. The ending of the domain name, called the top-level domain name, identifies the type organization that owns the domain name.

▶ Save a web page address (URL) to your Favorites to easily revisit it later.

Searching for Other Information on the Web

▶ Google.com and Bing.com are the two most popular search engines, used to find information on the web.

▶ A search string is entered into a search box on a search website to locate information. Websites that match the search are displayed in a hit list ordered by how closely the site content matches the search string.

▶ Wikipedia.org is the most popular wiki on the web. Sites that explain how things work include about.com, ehow.com, wisegeek.com, and howstuffworks.com. Two popular sites for finding driving directions and maps are maps.google.com and mapquest.com.

▶ Facebook.com is the most popular social networking site on the web. Youtube.com is the most popular site for distributing videos. A blog site such as blogger.com and wordpress.com is used for personal journaling that you can share with family and friends.

▶ One measure of performance for a search engine is how well it orders the pages in the hit list so that close matches to your search appear at the top of the list. This order is called the page rank.

▶ Use advanced searches with a search engine to reduce the hit count and zero in on your search. Advanced searches can limit the search to a certain website, exclude a site, limit the age of the content, search for exact words, and exclude words.

▶ You can use the Internet Options dialog box to change your browser's default settings including the home page.

Using Applications and Storing Data in the Cloud

▶ Cloud computing lets you use applications and storage space made available by remote computers on the web.

▶ Sites that provide cloud computing include flickr.com (for storing and editing photos), shutterfly.com (for storing photos and making documents with them), and docs.google.com and live.com for storing and editing documents, worksheets, presentations, drawings, and forms.

▶ Use a SkyDrive on live.com to store and share data files.

Doing Business Safely on the Web

▶ Do business only with trustworthy sites. Read online reviews of a site if you are not familiar with it.

▶ Download free software, music, videos, and other data only from sites you trust because some downloads might include adware and other malware.

▶ Use an HTTPS secure transmission to transmit your personal data to a web server and use strong passwords to protect your online accounts.

▶ Run antispyware and antivirus software on your computer to protect it and your identity from malware and thieves.

▶ Use shopping features of a search engine and online reviews to find the best products and prices online.

▶ Keep a record of every online purchase in the event the site overcharges you or makes other mistakes. The record can be a web page saved to your local storage device, a printed web page, or a receipt sent to you by email.

▶ When Internet Explorer saves a web page, it uses the MHT file format.

▶ Freeware, shareware, and commercial software can be downloaded from the web. When you first download software, make sure you have access to the software documentation to help you use the software.

▶ Microsoft Security Essentials is free antivirus and antispyware software that you can download from the web to protect your computer, your data, and your identity.

Review Questions

Answer these questions to assess your skills and knowledge of the content covered in the chapter. Your instructor can provide you with the correct answers when you are ready to check your work.

1. What is the most important skill you need to know when learning to use computers?

2. All the computers connected together in the world's largest global network are called the _____. Some of these computers provide web pages for distribution and these computers and web pages are called the _____. All the web pages stored on one of these computers are called a(n) _____.

3. When you click a link on a web page, what does your browser do?

4. What are three ways to select all the text in the address bar of your browser so that you can enter another URL?

5. A computer that serves up web pages to a client is called a(n) _____.

6. How can you display a second web page in your browser without closing the first page?

7. What type of website is the best choice to use if you want to keep a journal of your six weeks' trip to Europe so that your friends and family can read about your adventures each day?

8. How does a company get its website at the top of a hit list in Google?

9. What is the purpose of the **site:** text added to a search string?

10. What dialog box is used to change your Internet Explorer home page?

11. What is the name of the personal cloud computing service offered by Windows Live? Offered by Google?

12. When doing business online, what protocol is used to assure that personal information is not stolen while in transmission from the browser to the website?

13. What is the default file format that Internet Explorer uses when saving a web page to a storage device?

14. What type of organization uses a URL that ends in .org? In .com?

15. Describe what makes a password a strong password.

Chapter Mastery Project

Find out how well you have mastered the content in this chapter by completing this project. If you can answer all the questions and do all the steps without looking back at the chapter details, you have mastered this chapter. If you can complete the project by finding answers on the web, you have proven that you understand its power and value.

If you find you need a lot of help doing the project and you have not yet read the chapter or done the activities, drop back and start at the beginning of the chapter and then return to this project.

> **Hint** All the key terms in the chapter are used in this mastery project. If you encounter a word you don't know such as *wiki*, enter **define:wiki** in the Internet Explorer search box. The word is defined in the chapter, but it's more fun to find the definition on the web.

Mastery Project Part 1: Getting the News on the Web

If you need help completing this part of the mastery project, please review the "Getting the News on the Web" section in the chapter.

Answer the following questions about the web:

1. Explain the difference between the Internet and the World Wide Web.

2. A web page is written using what set of rules?

3. What is the URL for the home page assigned to the browser on the computer you are using for this course?

4. A web page is stored and served up by a _____ to a ____ computer.

Follow these steps to get the news on the web:

Step 1. Open **Internet Explorer** and visit The Washington Post website at **www.washingtonpost.com**.

Step 2. Use the **Home** button to return to your home page. Visit the **news.yahoo.com** site. Now use your forward and backward buttons to revisit previously viewed pages.

Step 3. Open four tabs in Internet Explorer to view these websites: cnn.com, nytimes.com, news.google.com, and foxnews.com. Use the **Quick Tabs** button to view all these pages and then select the **Fox News** tab.

Step 4. Close the **Fox News** tab.

Step 5. Save the news.google.com page to your Favorites.

Mastery Project Part 2: Searching for Other Information on the Web

If you need help completing this part of the mastery project, please review the "Searching for Other Information on the Web" section in the chapter.

Answer these questions about searching for information on the web:

1. Describe how to view a preview of a web page in the hit list of a Google search.

2. What site is the most popular wiki on the web?

3. What two websites are the most popular for giving directions and maps?

4. If you wanted to let your friends know what you were doing each day in a brief sentence or two, would you most likely use Facebook.com or a blogging site?

5. What is the most popular site for distributing videos on the web?

Follow these steps to use Google.com to search for more information on the web:

Step 1. Search for information on how the Internet works, limiting the search only to the Wikipedia.org site. What is your search string? What is another search string that Google autosuggest offered as you typed? What is the hit count?

Step 2. Limit the preceding search to content updated in the past 24 hours. What is the hit count? What option on the Google menu did you use?

Step 3. Remove the time limitation from the preceding search. What is the hit count?

Step 4. Search for the exact words "how a cell phone works". What is your search string? What is the hit count?

Step 5. Search for a list of the top smartest dog breeds but exclude hits that include the word *poodle.* What is your search string?

Step 6. Find images of a border collie. What option on the Google menu did you use?

Step 7. Find videos of climbing a mountain. What option on the Google menu did you use?

Step 8. Use Google Maps to find driving directions from Los Angeles to San Francisco. How many miles is the drive?

Step 9. Use Google Translate to translate into Spanish: "The food was delicious. Thank you." Listen to the translation.

Follow these steps to customize your browser:

Step 1. Use the Internet Options dialog box to change your home page to **news.google.com**.

Step 2. Use the Internet Explorer search box to search for the definition of HTTP. What search string did you use?

Step 3. The default setting for the IE search engine is bing.com. Change your default IE search engine to **google.com**.

Mastery Project Part 3: Using Applications and Storing Data in the Cloud

If you need help completing this part of the mastery project, review the "Using Applications and Storing Data in the Cloud" section in the chapter.

Answer the following questions about cloud computing:

1. What two types of services do computers in the cloud offer?

2. What are two advantages of using cloud computing?

3. Google Docs at docs.google.com and Windows Live at live.com offer similar applications used to create and edit what type of content?

If you have not already set up a SkyDrive account, follow these steps:

Step 1. Using the live.com site, create a SkyDrive account using your email address. If you don't have an email address, get one using the live.com site. What is the maximum storage capacity of your SkyDrive?

Step 2. Post a photo of yourself to the Public folder on your SkyDrive. If you don't have a photo, use this one that is included on DVD with this book: **\Sample Files\MyPhoto2.jpg**. What is the name of the photo file you posted to your SkyDrive?

Step 3. Your instructor might want access to your SkyDrive so you can post homework files there. If requested by your instructor, share the My Documents folder on your SkyDrive with your instructor using his email address. Use the **Send a link** command to send to your instructor a link to the My Documents folder on your SkyDrive.

Mastery Project Part 4: Doing Business Safely on the Web

If you need help completing this part of the mastery project, review the "Doing Business Safely on the Web" section in the chapter.

Follow these steps to practice shopping online:

Step 1. Use the Google Shopping feature to search for a GPS navigator. What is the URL of one sponsored ad in the results? Sort the products first by relevance and then by price from low to high.

Step 2. Search for product comparisons. List three features about a GPS navigator that are likely to affect your choice.

Step 3. Select a device to review. Open a new Internet Explorer tab and find online reviews about the selected device. List three sites that focus on product reviews.

Step 4. Find a video review of the device. What site offers a video review?

Step 5. Open a third tab in IE to compare prices for the selected device. List two sites that focus on product price comparisons. Select a retail site that offers the device at a reasonable price.

Step 6. Open a fourth tab and find online reviews about this retail site so that you can decide whether the site is trustworthy. What search string did you use?

Follow these steps to print a web page, save the page to a data file, and copy the file to your SkyDrive:

Step 1. Visit the web page **target.com** and click **My Account**. Print this web page. If you don't have access to a printer, display the preview of the printed page.

Step 2. Save the page to your USB flash drive, hard drive, or another location given by your instructor. What is the name and location of the file? What file format does the file use? Close your browser and then open the saved file.

Step 3. Copy the file to your SkyDrive.

Follow these steps to pretend to purchase a product online:

Step 1. Go to **tigerdirect.com** and start the process of purchasing a GPS navigator. What model did you select? What is the total cost including shipping and handling and tax?

Step 2. Take the purchase far enough so that you can verify that TigerDirect.com is using HTTPS for secure transmission. What is the first item of personal information that TigerDirect.com requests that uses HTTPS for the transmission? Does TigerDirect.com accept payments by PayPal? Do not complete the purchase unless you really do want to buy the GPS.

A computer needs antivirus software installed to protect it when surfing the web. If antivirus software is not already installed on your computer, follow these steps to download and install Microsoft Security Essentials:

Step 1. Go to the www.microsoft.com/security_essentials website.

Step 2. Download the software, saving the downloaded file to your desktop.

Step 3. Install the software and then verify that it is configured to run in the background and scan your system either daily or weekly. Delete the file you downloaded to your desktop.

Answer these questions about doing business online and protecting your computer against malware:

1. After downloading free music from the web, you notice pop-up ads appear as you surf the web. What type of malware got installed when you downloaded the music? In the future, how can you find out whether a website is safe to use?

2. What type of software is Microsoft Security Essentials? Is the software freeware or shareware?

3. What does the Microsoft Security Essentials software documentation say about having more than one antivirus or antispyware program running on a computer at the same time?

4. Retail sites ask for personal information such as your email address and credit card number, and this information needs to be protected while in transit. What two items can you look for on the Internet Explorer window to verify the information is protected in transit? What security protocol is used to transmit the data?

5. Why is it important to print or save a record of an online transaction?

6. Before you can pay a bill online to a utility company, what must you do first?

7. Should you use the same password for every online account?

8. Is sally1972 a strong password to use for your online banking account? Why or why not?

Becoming an Independent Learner

Answer the following questions about becoming an independent learner:

1. To teach yourself to use Internet Explorer, do you think it is best to rely on the chapter or on Windows Help and Support when you need answers?

2. To teach yourself to construct advanced Google searches, do you think it is best to rely on the chapter or on the help features available on the Google website?

3. The most important skill learned in this chapter is how to teach yourself a computer skill. Rate yourself at Level A through E on how well you are doing with this skill. What is your level?

   ○ Level A: I was able to successfully complete the Chapter Mastery Project without the help of doing the On Your Own activities in the chapter.

   ○ Level B: I completed all the On Your Own activities and the Chapter Mastery Project without referring to any of the solutions in the *Solutions Manual*.

   ○ Level C: I completed all the On Your Own activities and the Chapter Mastery Project by using just a few of the solutions in the *Solutions Manual*.

   ○ Level D: I completed all the On Your Own activities and the Chapter Mastery Project by using many of the solutions in the *Solutions Manual*.

   ○ Level E: I completed all the On Your Own activities and the Chapter Mastery Project and had to use all of the solutions in the *Solutions Manual*.

Regardless of how you did it, the good news is you completed the work. Congratulations! To continue toward the goal of teaching yourself computer skills, if you are not at Level A, try to move up one level on how you learn in Chapter 3, "Creating Documents with Microsoft Word."

Projects to Help You

Now that you have mastered the material in this chapter, you are ready to tackle the three projects introduced at the beginning of the chapter in the section "How Will This Chapter Help Me?"

Project 1: Using the Web in Your Personal Life

PERSONAL PROJECT: I'm planning a trip to Niagara Falls, Canada. I need to find out about sites to visit along the way, driving directions, hotels, restaurants, tours, and currency exchange in Canada. I also need to buy a digital camera and share my photos with friends. Can I do all that online?

Untold amounts of information and services are available on the web, and the web has become an integral part of our personal lives. The web can help make vacations and road trips easier and more fun.

Do the following to find information to help plan a road trip to Niagara Falls:

Step 1. Get driving directions from your home in Hershey, Pennsylvania, to Niagara Falls, Canada. What is the total miles traveled?

Step 2. You would like to visit some parks in the Finger Lakes area on your way home. Select three parks and find directions from Niagara Falls to these parks and then back to Hershey.

Step 3. Find two hotels in the Niagara Falls area on the USA side that will accept your dog, Wendy. Find one hotel on the Canada side of the Falls that will accept a dog. What hotels did you find?

Step 4. Will you need your passport to cross over into Canada and return to the USA? Find a website that gives the authoritative answer to this question. An authoritative answer is an answer given by someone with authority. In this case, look for a website with a .gov URL, which means the site is hosted by the government. What site did you find?

Step 5. While in Canada, you want to visit Niagara-on-the-Lake, Ontario. Find an elegant restaurant with an awesome view in the Niagara-on-the-Lake area. What is the name and address of this restaurant?

Step 6. How much will it cost to take the Maid of the Mist boat ride up near the bottom of the falls? What website gave you the answer? Find a photo of the Maid of the Mist near the falls. What website has this photo?

Step 7. You plan to take $400 in U.S. currency into Canada. How much is that in Canadian currency? What website gave you the answer?

Step 8. When you are vacationing, it's interesting to know the history behind the area. Who was the first person to go over the falls and live to tell about it? What website gave you the answer?

Do the following to record and share the trip with friends and family:

1. Shop for a digital camera to use on your trip. Save a web page to your USB flash drive that shows the camera and its price on a retail site that you would trust to make the purchase. Save another web page to your flash drive that contains a review of the camera.

2. Sign up for a shutterfly.com account and post one photo to the site. Share your site on Shutterfly with a class member, friend, or family member. If you don't have your own photo to post to the site, you can use the MyPhoto1.jpg photo in the Sample Files folder on the DVD in the back of this book.

Project 2: Using the Web in Your Academic Career

You are likely to use the web in any academic class you take. You can use it to find solutions to a problem, get background information about a topic, research a topic, find a forum of people who want to discuss a topic with you, and share data with class members and your instructor.

ACADEMIC PROJECT:
I want to find out about nursing careers, and I need to research questions in my history, chemistry, and literature classes. I also need to buy and download the Academic Edition of Microsoft Office and install it on my laptop.

Do the following to explore how a forum on the web can help you in your academic career:

1. What is a forum? Find a definition on the web. What website did you use?

2. Suppose you are considering a career in nursing. Find two forums that are focused on nursing. What are the two sites? On one of these forums, find a question that a nursing student asks nurses about what life is like being a nurse. What is the question? What is one answer to the question?

3. What career are you considering? Find a forum about that career. Join the forum and post a question. What question did you post? If you have received an answer on the forum, what is that answer?

Do the following to find information that might help you in a variety of classes:

1. **History class:** Who are three people all credited with inventing peanut butter? What site or sites gave you the answer?

2. **Finance class:** How much does an ounce of gold cost today? How much did it cost on this same day last year? Two years ago? What site or sites did you use to find your answers?

3. **Chemistry class:** At what temperature in Fahrenheit does copper melt? What temperature in Celsius? What websites did you use to find your answers?

4. **Literature class:** List four compelling reasons why William Shakespeare has stood the test of time, and, after 400 years, is still studied in literature classes.

In this course, you learn to use the Microsoft Office software. Search the Microsoft.com site to answer these questions about Microsoft Office:

1. List the four applications that are included in the Home and Student edition of Microsoft Office.

2. The Home and Business edition of Microsoft office contains the Outlook application. What is the purpose of the Outlook application?

3. Which application that is included in the Professional edition of Microsoft Office is used to manage a database?

4. Define a database.

If you are using a computer in your school computer lab, the software is already installed. However, you might need to install Microsoft Office on your home computer or laptop.

The Professional Academic Edition of Microsoft Office is offered to students who have an email address assigned by their school. This address will end in .edu—for example, yourname@example.edu.

You might want to purchase, download, and install on your own computer the Academic Edition of Microsoft Office 2010 for student use. If so, follow these steps:

Step 1. Open Internet Explorer and visit **theultimatesteal.com**. The Microsoft web page displays.

Step 2. To begin the process of buying the software, click **BUY NOW**.

Step 3. On the next screen, enter your university or school email address two times and click **SUBMIT**.

Step 4. An email is sent to you. Follow directions in the email to complete the purchase and download and install the software.

After you install software, do the following to verify the Word application opens correctly:

Step 1. Click **Start**, **All Programs**, and **Microsoft Office**. In the list of applications installed under Microsoft Office, click **Microsoft Word 2010**. The Microsoft Word window opens.

Step 2. If the Word window opens correctly, you can assume the software installed correctly. You learn how to use the Word window in Chapter 3. For now, close the window.

Project 3: Using the Web in Your Technical Career

TECHNICAL CAREER PROJECT: My boss is asking me questions about cell phone technologies I don't understand. Users I support keep getting error messages that I don't recognize. Also, a manager has asked me to help her find and buy some software. The laser printer needs toner, and I don't know how to change the toner cartridge. Can the web give me all these answers?

If you are planning a career in technology, you will constantly learn about new technologies as they arise. Knowing how to teach yourself and others computer skills is essential for technicians.

Technology is always changing. Find answers to these questions about current and future technologies:

1. The latest advance in cell phone use is called 4G, which gives even greater performance than its predecessor, 3G. What is 4G and what website did you use to find your answer?

2. Two major technology systems are competing technologies used by 4G. What are these two technology systems? Which system does Verizon back? What websites gave you this information?

3. Define the word *broadband* as it is used when speaking of cell phone technologies. What website gave you the definition?

Microsoft.com is the authoritative site about Microsoft products including Windows 7 and Microsoft Office. Find answers to these questions, searching only the Microsoft.com site:

1. A user, Fernanda, gets this error message while browsing the web: "Internet Explorer cannot display the webpage." This message can be caused by a variety of problems. Find an article on the support.microsoft.com website that lists multiple things a user can do to solve the problem. What is the Article ID? What search string did you use to find the article? What are the first two methods the article suggests to fix the problem?

2. A user, Janice, gets this error message when trying to install Microsoft Office: "Error 25004. The product key you entered cannot be used on this machine." What caused the error and how does she fix the problem?

3. Frank, another user, gets this error message while trying to install Office: "Error 1920. Service 'Office Software Protection Platform' (osppsvc) failed to start. Verify that you have sufficient privileges to start system services." What caused the error and how does he fix the problem?

Find the following useful information when supporting users and their computer equipment:

1. A user has asked you to help her prepare marketing material for new technologies. She wants to include web pages in her documentation and needs to convert several web pages to PDF files. Research software that you can purchase and download that will convert web pages to PDF files. Find two products. What are the two products and their prices? What website offers each product?

2. You are responsible for supporting an HP P2035 laser printer, which is printing faintly and you suspect is running low on toner. What model toner cartridge does this printer use? What is one retail site that sells this toner cartridge? How much does the cartridge cost? Find a review of this retail site. What website offered the review?

3. You have purchased the toner cartridge online and are now ready to install it, but discover that the user manual for the HP P2035 printer that explains how to replace the cartridge is missing. (Missing manuals is a common problem for technicians.) Go to the **hp.com** website and find the directions for replacing the print cartridge. Print these directions or save them to your USB flash drive.

Project to Help Others

One of the best ways to learn is to teach someone else. And, in teaching someone else, you are making a contribution into that person's life.

As part of each chapter's work, you are encouraged to teach someone else a skill you have learned. In this case, you help your apprentice learn to use the web.

Who is your apprentice? _____

Working with your apprentice, do the following:

Step 1. Ask your apprentice how he expects to use the web to find information, shop, do banking, or pay bills. Describe what your apprentice wants to learn. Do your best to help this person meet these goals.

Step 2. Coach your apprentice as he uses Internet Explorer to surf the news on a news website. Try not to touch the keyboard or mouse. Let the apprentice do all the work.

Step 3. Help your apprentice set his home page to a site that interests him. What is that site? If he does not have a specific site in mind, use Google.com as the home page.

Step 4. Coach your apprentice to find images and videos of a topic that interests him. What topic did you use?

Step 5. Ask your apprentice about something he would like to understand better, such as how something works. Coach him to find that information. What topic did you use?

Step 6. Coach your apprentice to do a Google search on his own name and that of his close friends and family. What information about himself and others did he find?

Step 7. Ask your apprentice what service or product he might need. Coach him how to find that online. If he does not have ideas, use these:

    a. Find an auto mechanic in his area that gets good reviews.

    b. Find a restaurant in his area that gets good reviews and that he has not yet tried.

    c. Shop for a new television, office desk, or patio furniture.

Step 8. Ask your apprentice to evaluate how the tutoring session went. Briefly describe his response.

Step 9. How do you think the session went? How would you like to improve it next time?

CHAPTER 3
Creating Documents with Microsoft Word

IN THIS CHAPTER, YOU WILL

Enter and edit text and save the document

Format text

Add graphics to a document

Finish a document and print it

Use text boxes, shapes, and WordArt in a document

Use templates as great shortcuts to making creative documents

From inviting friends to a birthday party to posting a flyer in the school hallways about an upcoming club meeting, most of us find it necessary to make short and simple documents. These documents contain little text, an attention-grabbing photo or graphic, and background color for impact.

In this chapter, you see how to use Microsoft Word to make one-page documents with text, graphics, and color. In the chapter, you create three documents: a checklist for a camping trip, an announcement about a jazz concert, and an invitation to a party.

As always, remember the most important computer skill is how to teach yourself a computer skill. Therefore, this chapter is designed to help you teach yourself how to create documents. Try to do each On Your Own activity without any help. But remember, if you need help, you can always refer to the solutions in the *Solutions Appendix*.

JUMP RIGHT IN

If you want even more of a challenge, try proceeding directly to the Chapter Mastery Project at the end of this chapter. If you need help on the project, refer to the On Your Own activities in the chapter or do your own independent investigating using Word Help or searching the web for answers. When you complete the project, you have mastered the skills in this chapter. Then go to the projects that require you to apply your skills to new situations.

How Will This Chapter Help Me?

Throughout this book, each chapter provides three projects focusing on personal, academic, or technical career goals. Depending on your own interests, you might choose to complete any or all of these projects to help you achieve your goals.

PERSONAL PROJECT: I'm starting up a pet-sitting business. I want to post a flyer in the neighborhood park where people walk their dogs.

ACADEMIC PROJECT: I need to create a calendar that shows my class schedule and all the due dates for important assignments.

TECHNICAL CAREER PROJECT: Users keep jamming paper in the network printer. My boss has asked me to create a document to post over the printer about how to load paper in the printer.

Entering Text and Saving the Document

Microsoft Word is a popular word processing program that allows you to enter text and add graphics to documents. Using Word, you can easily format the text and change the layout of the text and graphics to make the document look nice. After you create a document, you can save the document for later use, print the document, and modify it.

> **Tip** In this chapter, you create three documents, all designed to show you different features of Word. Don't worry about getting the details of each document perfect. To get the most out of the chapter, focus on learning to use the tools.

> **Microsoft Word**—One of the applications included in the Microsoft Office suite of applications. Word is used to create documents that can include text, color, pictures, drawings, and other graphics. Several editions of Microsoft Office have been published. This book uses Microsoft Office 2010.

Follow along on your computer to create the document. As you work, don't be afraid to experiment with the tools explained in this chapter or to try other tools you see at the top of the Word window.

On Your Own 3-1
Use the Word Window

Video **3-1**

Do the following to learn about the Word window:

Step 1. Open **Microsoft Word 2010**. Maximize the window. When you open Word, you start with a new blank document.

Step 2. Compare Figure 3-1 to your Word window and identify all the items labeled in Figure 3-1 on your Word window. As you mouse over a button, a bubble appears describing the tool.

> **Not Working?** More than one version of Microsoft Word exists. In this book, we are using Word 2010. If you are using a different version, such as Word 2007, your window might not look the same as the one shown.

Step 3. Make sure the rulers above the document area and along the left side of the document are displayed.

Step 4. Make sure the **Print Layout** view is selected.

> **Hint** Word has a built-in Help window that gives directions to use all the Word features. You access Help by clicking the **Microsoft Word Help** button 🔲 in the top-right corner. As an independent learner, you can use this Help feature to teach yourself about Word.

Step 5. Locate the **insertion point**, which shows where your text will appear when you start typing.

> **insertion point**—The blinking vertical bar 🔲 that marks where characters will appear when you type.

Step 6. Use the Word Help window to find out what is the Backstage view.

On Your Own 3-1
Use the Word Window

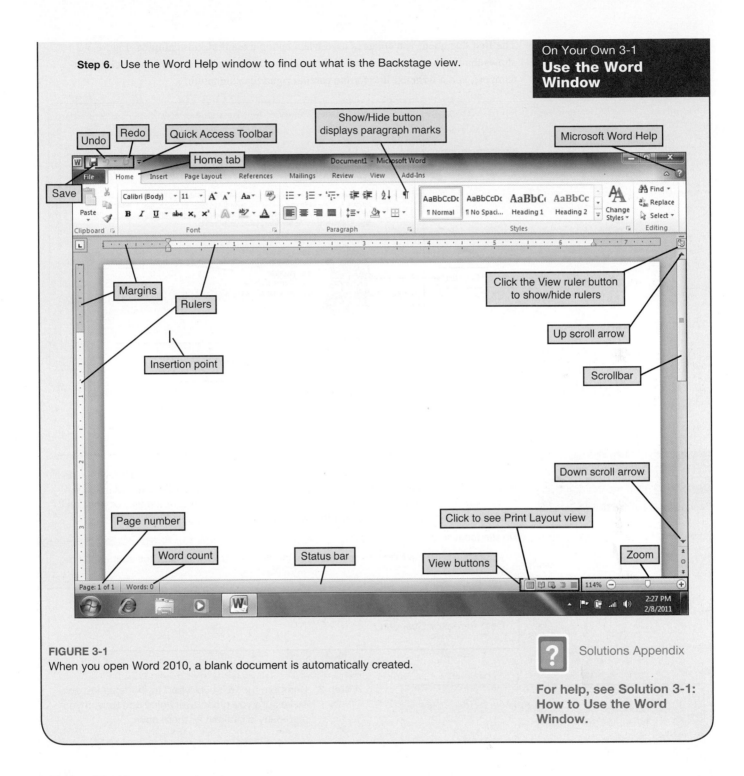

FIGURE 3-1
When you open Word 2010, a blank document is automatically created.

Solutions Appendix

For help, see Solution 3-1: How to Use the Word Window.

Enter Text

The first step to creating a document is to enter text. If you aren't an expert at typing, don't worry. Word makes it easy to edit what you type and correct any errors. As you read through this section, follow along on your computer. Don't be afraid to experiment as you are introduced to new features of Word.

The first document you create is used when taking a team of kids camping. Figure 3-2 shows the finished document, which includes a graphic (called clip art), a checklist for campers, and a write-on line for the parent or guardian signature.

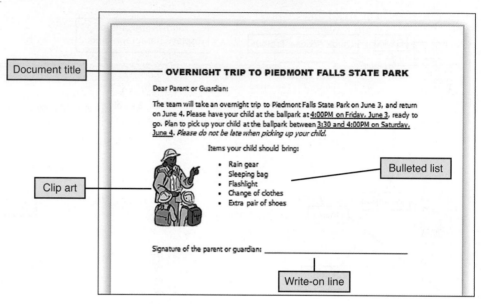

FIGURE 3-2
This document uses a bulleted list and clip art.

In this activity, you type the first lines of text into the document. If you make a mistake as you enter information, use the **Backspace** key to delete the unwanted text and make the correction. To advance to a new line, press **Enter**. Don't worry about the size or position of the text on the page; you will format the text later.

Do the following:

> **Step 1.** Type the following text in the blank document, pressing **Enter** after each line:

> Overnight Trip to Piedmont Falls State Park
>
> Dear Parent or Guardian:

Step 2. Compare the text you typed to the text here and make sure you typed everything correctly. If you made any mistakes, fix them now.

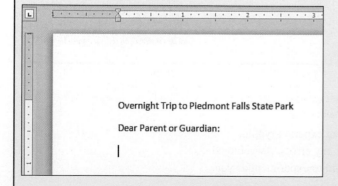

On Your Own 3-2
Enter and Edit Text

Hint Microsoft Word flags a word that it thinks is misspelled by drawing a curvy red line under the word. Right-click a word that has a red line to see a shortcut menu with spelling suggestions. Click the suggestion, and Word replaces the misspelled word with the correct spelling. Click **Ignore** to tell Word not to flag the word.

Step 3. The next part of the document is a paragraph. When typing a paragraph, don't press Enter as you type. As one line is filled, the text automatically spills to the next line. This feature is called **word wrap**. Type the following text. Do not press Enter until you finish typing the entire paragraph. Then press **Enter**.

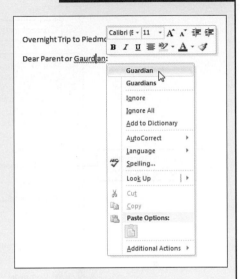

The team will take an overnight trip to Piedmont Falls State Park on June 3, and return on June 4. Please have your child at the ballpark at 4:00PM on Friday, June 3, ready to go. Plan to pick up your child at the ballpark between 3:30 and 4:00PM on Saturday, June 4. Please do not be late when picking up your child.

word wrap—A feature of Word that automatically causes text to flow to a new line when a line is full.

 Solutions Appendix

For help, see Solution 3-2: How to Enter and Edit Text.

You now have part of the text entered into the document. Before you spend more time on the document, let's stop and save the document.

Save the Document File

After you invest your time in a document, it's important to save that file even before you are finished. Be sure to save every few minutes and after you make any major changes. The first time you save it, you must specify the name of the document and the location to be saved. In Word 2010, the default file extension of a document file is **docx**.

docx—The file extension that Word 2010 uses for document files.

On Your Own 3-3
Save, Close, and Open a Document

As you work on a document, save it about every five minutes and after any major change. You can save the document on the computer's hard drive; a USB flash drive; the SkyDrive that you set up in Chapter 2, "Finding and Using Information on the Web"; or another location given by your instructor.

Hint Your instructor might require a specific location to save your files such as a server in the computer lab. If so, follow her instructions to save the file.

 Video **3-3**

Do the following to save the document to a USB flash drive or the computer's hard drive:

Step 1. With the document still open, click the **File** tab and click **Save**. Because this is the first time you have saved the document, the Save As dialog box appears (see Figure 3-3).

On Your Own 3-3
Save, Close, and Open a Document

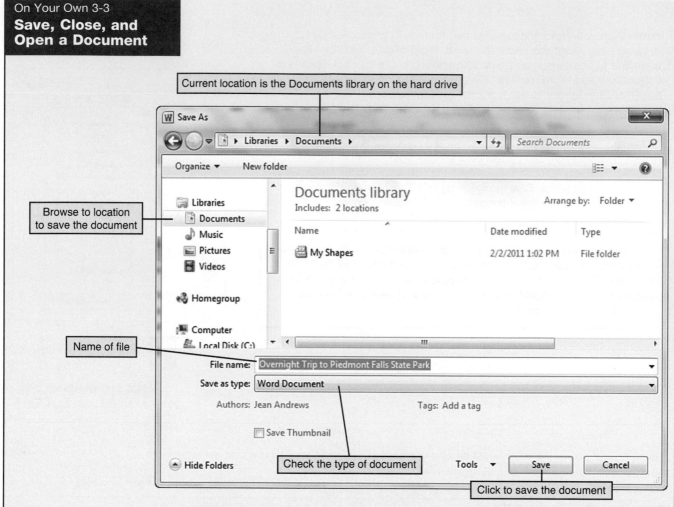

FIGURE 3-3
The Save As box allows you to enter the name, location, and file type for the document you are saving.

> **Step 2.** Word suggests a filename and location for your document. Point to the location where you want to save. Change the filename to **CheckList**. Do not change the file type. Click **Save**.

Do the following to save the document to your SkyDrive on the web:

> **Step 1.** Click the **File** tab, click **Save & Send**, and click **Save to Web**.
>
> **Step 2.** Name the document **CheckList**. You might need to sign in with your Windows Live ID.

After you save a document the first time, Word does not require you to give the document name or save location again. Instead, the document is saved with the original name and in the same location.

You can use any one of the following three methods to save a document after it has been saved the first time. Do the following to practice resaving the document:

> **Step 1.** Click the **File** tab and click **Save**. The document saves again.
>
> **Step 2.** Press **Ctrl-S**. The document saves again.

Step 3. Click the **Save** button 🖫 on the **Quick Access Toolbar**. The document saves again.

> **Quick Access Toolbar**—In Office applications, a group of commands in the title bar that include Save and Undo.

On Your Own 3-3
Save, Close, and Open a Document

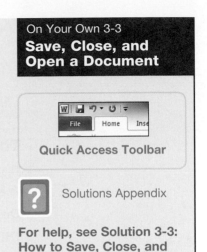

Quick Access Toolbar

Solutions Appendix

For help, see Solution 3-3: How to Save, Close, and Open a Document.

As you work, use one of the preceding three methods to save your document about every five minutes or after making significant changes.

To practice closing and reopening your document, do the following:

Step 1. Close the **Word** window.

Step 2. Open the **CheckList** document again.

Before you finish typing the rest of the text in the document, let's pause to format the existing text.

Formatting Text

When formatting text, you can change the size, color, and font of the text. The **font** used determines the shape of each letter. The size of text is measured in a unit called a **point**. Word 2010 gives you many options for fonts, text size, colors, and other special features.

> **font**—The style of text used to determine the shape of each character.
> **point**—A unit of measure used to measure font size; 72 points equal 1 inch.

Word 2010 offers four methods to format text and all four methods can be found on the Home **ribbon** (see Figure 3-4).

> **ribbon**—In Office applications, the area across the top of the application window that contains groups of commands. Click a tab above the ribbon to switch to a new ribbon.

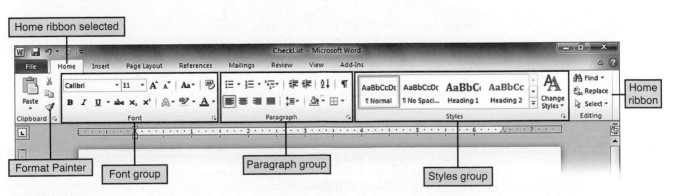

FIGURE 3-4
Text formatting is done using the tools on the Home ribbon.

The four methods are

> ▶ **Font group.** Use tools in the Font group to format selected text. Tools in the Font group allow you to change the size and font of text. You can also underline, bold, italicize, and strikethrough your text. You can change the color of text and apply other special features. Figure 3-5 shows some formatting that was done using the Font group.

The font and size of this text is Arial Black 14 point.

The font and size of this text is Times New Roman 10 point.

The color of this text is red.

This text is highlighted in yellow.

THIS SENTENCE USES UPPERCASE, AN OPTION UNDER CHANGE CASE.

This <u>word</u> is underlined. This ~~word~~ has strikethrough applied.

THIS SENTENCE USES TEXT EFFECTS.

Water can be written as H_2O and needs a subscript, which is a small character below the baseline.

FIGURE 3-5
Font, size, and other formatting features available in the Font group are applied to selected text.

> ▶ **Paragraph group.** Select one or more paragraphs and use the Paragraph tools to format the selected paragraphs. You can **left-justify**, **right-justify**, **justify**, center, create a bulleted or numbered list, and sort or indent paragraphs.

> **left-justify**—To align text with the left side of the document. Left-justify is the default setting for text in Word.
>
> **right-justify**—To align text with the right side of the document.
>
> **justify**—To align text with both the left and right sides of the document.

> ▶ **Styles.** Select the text and apply a style. A **style** is a shortcut for formatting. Examples of style names are Heading 1 and Heading 2. When you apply a style to selected text, all the formatting features assigned to that style are applied.

> **style**—A predetermined set of formatting features that have been assigned a name and can be applied to text.

> ▶ **Format Painter.** Use the Format Painter tool 🖌 to duplicate formatting already applied to other text in the document.

> **Format Painter**—A tool used in Office applications to duplicate text formatting already applied in the document. The tool is handy when applying the same formatting to different parts of a document.

In this chapter, you learn to use the Font and Paragraph tools and the Format Painter. Styles are covered in Chapter 5, "Writing Papers Using Microsoft Word Templates and Tools." Let's begin with the Font tools.

Format Text with the Font Tools

All the Font tools on the Home ribbon are labeled in Figure 3-6. To format text using the Font tools, first select the text and then use a Font tool to format the selected text. As you move your mouse over a tool, a bubble appears describing the tool.

> **Hint** As you format text, to undo what you have just done, click the Undo button found on the Quick Access Toolbar.

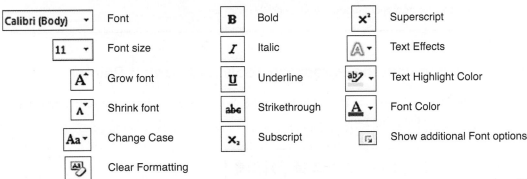

Calibri (Body) ▼	Font	**B**	Bold	x^2	Superscript
11 ▼	Font size	*I*	Italic	𝐴 ▼	Text Effects
A^	Grow font	U̲	Underline	ab✐ ▼	Text Highlight Color
Aᵥ	Shrink font	a̶b̶c̶	Strikethrough	**A** ▼	Font Color
Aa ▼	Change Case	x₂	Subscript	⌐	Show additional Font options
	Clear Formatting				

FIGURE 3-6
The tools in the Font group are used to format text.

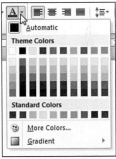

A down arrow ⓐ▾ beside a tool indicates you have options within the tool that you can select. For example, when you click the down arrow next to the Color Font tool, a palette of colors appears from which you can choose.

Do the following to format the text that you have entered so far in the document:

Step 1. Format all the text in the document in **Tahoma, 12 point**. A good size for text in the body of a document is 12 point.

> **Hint** To select all the text in a document, press the **Ctrl** key and **A** at the same time.

Step 2. Select the title and format it as **Arial Black**, **14** points, **Uppercase**.

Step 3. Underline the text **4:00PM on Friday, June 3**.

Step 4. Underline the text **3:30 and 4:00PM on Saturday, June 4**.

Step 5. Format the last sentence in the paragraph in **italic**.

Step 6. The document should now look like that in Figure 3-7. Check the document for errors and save it.

OVERNIGHT TRIP TO PIEDMONT FALLS STATE PARK

Dear Parent or Guardian:

The team will take an overnight trip to Piedmont Falls State Park on June 3, and return on June 4. Please have your child at the ballpark at <u>4:00PM on Friday, June 3</u>, ready to go. Plan to pick up your child at the ballpark between <u>3:30 and 4:00PM on Saturday, June 4</u>. *Please do not be late when picking up your child.*

FIGURE 3-7
Text in the document is formatted using the Font tools.

Format with the Paragraph Tools and Format Painter

The Paragraph tools are labeled in Figure 3-8. When you use a Paragraph tool, formatting is applied to the entire paragraph.

Bullets	Sort a list or paragraphs	Justify
Numbering	Show/Hide	Line and Paragraph Spacing
Multilevel List	Align Text Left	Shading to color background
Decrease Indent	Center	Borders around paragraphs or tables
Increase Indent	Align Text Right	Show more Paragraph options

FIGURE 3-8
Tools in the Paragraph group apply formatting to the entire paragraph.

Tip By default, Word places more space between paragraphs than it does between the lines within a paragraph. You can control the spacing between lines and paragraphs using the Line and Paragraph Spacing tool in the Paragraph group.

How do you know where one paragraph ends and the next paragraph begins? A paragraph ends when you press the Enter key as you type. The special character created when you pressed the Enter key is called a **hard return**. The positions of hard returns in a document are displayed using a **paragraph mark**. If you want to see where the hard returns are in a document, display the paragraph marks by clicking the Show/Hide button in the Paragraph group. Click the button again to hide the marks.

hard return—The nonprinting character created in a document when you press the Enter key that marks the end of a paragraph. Hard returns are indicated by the paragraph mark.

paragraph mark—A nonprinting character ¶ that can be displayed in a document to show the hard returns which mark the ends of paragraphs.

On Your Own 3-5
Format Text and Create a Bulleted List

In this activity, you use the Center paragraph tool, create a bulleted list, and use the Format Painter. When the activity is completed, the document looks like that in Figure 3-9.

OVERNIGHT TRIP TO PIEDMONT FALLS STATE PARK

Dear Parent or Guardian:

The team will take an overnight trip to Piedmont Falls State Park on June 3, and return on June 4. Please have your child at the ballpark at 4:00PM on Friday, June 3, ready to go. Plan to pick up your child at the ballpark between 3:30 and 4:00PM on Saturday, June 4. *Please do not be late when picking up your child.*

Items your child should bring:

- Rain gear
- Sleeping bag
- Flashlight
- Change of clothes
- Extra pair of shoes

Signature of the parent or guardian: _____

FIGURE 3-9
The document title is centered and a bulleted list and signature line are added.

Do the following:

Step 1. Center the document title.

Step 2. Position your insertion point at the end of the document. Type the following text, pressing **Enter** after each line of text:

Items your child should bring:

Rain gear

Sleeping bag

Flashlight

Change of clothes

Extra pair of shoes

Step 3. Use the **Format Painter** to format this new text in **Tahoma, 12 point**.

Step 4. Change the last five lines of text to a bulleted list by using the **Bullets** button in the Paragraph group.

Hint Use the Format Painter to copy formatting from one place in a document to another place. First, select text, a paragraph, or a graphic that has the formatting you want to copy. Then click the **Format Painter**. ⌁ The pointer changes to a paint brush. ⌁ Whatever text you select next will be formatted the same as the original text.

On Your Own 3-5
**Format Text and
Create a Bulleted
List**

    Solutions Appendix

**For help, see Solution 3-5:
How to Format Text and
Create a Bulleted List.**

Step 5. To complete the text in the document, at the end of the document, drop down two lines and add the signature write-on line, formatting it as **Tahoma, 12 point**.

Signature of parent or guardian: _____

Step 6. The text in the document is now finished. Save the document.

Adding Graphics to a Document

Graphics, including photographs, shapes, and clip art, can add impact to a document. In this section, we add **clip art** to the document.

> **clip art**—A cartoon or other drawing that can be inserted into a document. Microsoft Office provides much clip art for documents. You can also add your own clip art to a document.

Word inserts graphics, including clip art, into a document using one of two methods:

▶ An **inline graphic** is tied to text and moves with the text if the text changes position. When the text moves, so does the picture. This method is the default method for Word.

▶ A **floating graphic** stays where you put it on the page and text flows around it. To change an inline graphic to a floating graphic, use the Format ribbon or the graphic's shortcut menu. On the Format ribbon, use either the Position command or the Wrap Text command.

> **inline graphic**—A graphic that moves with the text as the text changes position.
> **floating graphic**—A graphic that stays in a fixed position on the page even when the text around it is changed.

When Microsoft Word is installed, some clip art is also installed and, if you are connected to the Internet, Word finds other clip art on the Office.com website. When inserting clip art into a document, you first use the Insert ribbon to insert the clip art. Then you might need to move, resize, or format it. Do the following to insert a clip art of campers into the document:

Step 1. Position your insertion point at the beginning of the line **Items your child should bring:**.

Step 2. On the Insert ribbon, click **Clip Art**. The Clip Art pane opens on the right side of the Word window. In the *Search for* box, type **campers** and click **Go**.

Step 3. In the list of clip art that appears, click the clip art of three campers shown earlier in Figure 3-2. The clip art is inserted at your insertion point. Don't worry about its exact position.

> **Hint** Office provides some clip art that is installed with Word on the hard drive. If *Include Office.com content* is checked in the Clip Art pane, clip art downloaded from the Office.com website is also available.

Step 4. The clip art is inserted as an inline graphic. Use the **Wrap Text** button on the Format ribbon to change the graphic to a floating graphic. The **Square** selection works well.

> **Hint** When you select a graphic, the Format tab shows up on the Word window. Click the **Format** tab to format a graphic. You can use tools on this ribbon to change a graphic from inline to floating, add shadow effects, change the graphic's brightness or contrast, or recolor a graphic.

Step 5. Resize and/or move the graphic so that it is below the paragraph and to the left of the bulleted list, as shown earlier in Figure 3-2.

> **Hint** To move an object, first select it. With your pointer showing four-directional arrows, ⊹ press and drag the object to move it.
>
> When an object is selected, you can see the sizing handles. Press and drag a **sizing handle** to resize the object.

sizing handle—In Office applications, a white circle or square on the boundaries of a clip art, shape, or other object that is used to resize the object. To resize an object without changing its proportions, use a corner sizing handle.

Step 6. Save the document.

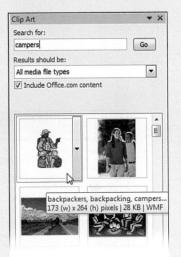
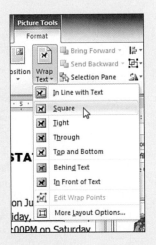

Finishing Up and Printing Your Document

Word keeps up with who is the author of a document. In this section, you verify that you are identified as the document author. Then you are ready to print the document.

Set Document Properties

Every document created in Word has certain properties. The document properties include the size of the document file, the date created, the author, and the document location. The properties can be found in the **Backstage view** when you select the File tab. See Figure 3-10.

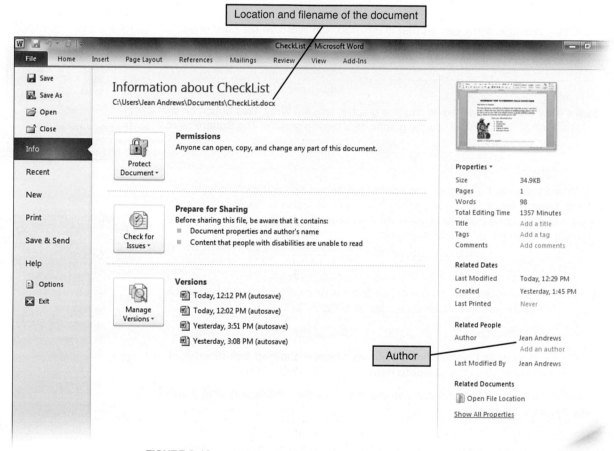

FIGURE 3-10
The Info group on the Backstage view shows the document's author.

> **Backstage view**—In Office applications, the window that appears when the File tab is selected. Use it to manage files. The Info group in the Backstage view shows the file properties including the filename, location, and author of the document.

Your instructor is likely to require you to submit your work electronically instead of printing it. If you are asked to email a document to your instructor or post it to a SkyDrive or other location, be sure to verify that you are listed as the document author. Do the following:

Step 1. Use the **Backstage view** to display the document properties. Who is listed as the author of the document?

Step 2. If you are not the author, make it so. Then save the document.

> **Hint** To change the document author, begin by right-clicking the name of the author.

On Your Own 3-7
Change Document Properties

 Solutions Appendix

For help, see Solution 3-7: How to Change Document Properties.

Print the Document

When you print a document, you decide the number of copies to print, which printer to use, what pages to print, and other printing settings. A printout of a document is also called a **hard copy**.

> **hard copy**—Another name for a printout.

On Your Own 3-8
Print a Document

 Video **3-8**

Do the following to print your document:

Step 1. The document should have only one page. Look in the bottom-left corner of the Word window for the page number including the total number of pages in the document. If the document has more than one page, make the necessary corrections so the document is a one-page document.

> **Not Working?** If you cannot see the page number on the status bar at the bottom of the Word window, right-click the status bar and check **Page Number**.

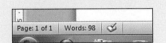

> **Hint** If your document has more than one page, you need to go back and fix the problem. Perhaps text or a blank line has spilled over to a second page. Use the paragraph marks to make sure you don't have extra lines.

Step 2. Save the document. You should get in the habit of always saving the document before printing it.

Step 3. Click the **File** tab and click **Print**. The Print group appears (see Figure 3-11). Using this window you can select the number of copies, the printer, and the pages to print, as well as other print settings. Select your printer and click **Print**.

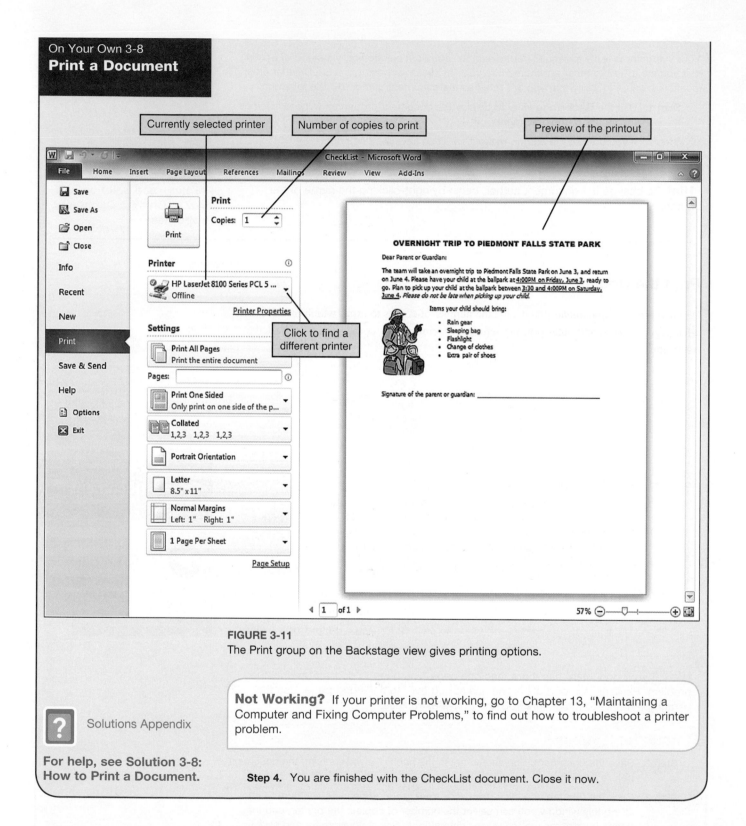

On Your Own 3-8
Print a Document

FIGURE 3-11
The Print group on the Backstage view gives printing options.

Solutions Appendix

For help, see Solution 3-8: How to Print a Document.

Not Working? If your printer is not working, go to Chapter 13, "Maintaining a Computer and Fixing Computer Problems," to find out how to troubleshoot a printer problem.

Step 4. You are finished with the CheckList document. Close it now.

Using Page Color, Text Boxes, Shapes, and WordArt

When creating documents in Word, you might want to have more control over where text is placed on the page and add special effects such as decorative letters, shapes, and color. In this section, you learn how to create text boxes, apply WordArt effects, and create shapes. As you read, follow along at your computer. Together, we'll make the document shown in Figure 3-12.

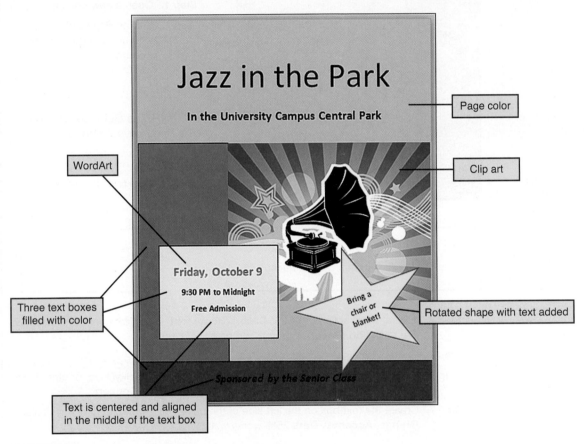

FIGURE 3-12
This "Jazz in the Park" document uses three text boxes, page color, WordArt, clip art, and a shape.

This document is an ad about a jazz concert that is intended to be included in a mass email sent to all students and faculty. Because we don't intend to print the ad, we are free to use background color. Background color doesn't print well but can greatly improve an email message.

Create Text Boxes

Text boxes are used to keep text together and to give you more control over where text is placed on a page. The *Jazz in the Park* document in Figure 3-12 uses text boxes to position color and text on the page.

When creating a text box, first you insert the text box and then you add text and formatting. After the text box is created, you can format, move, resize, or rotate the box and add text inside the box.

On Your Own 3-9
Add Page Color and Text Boxes

Jazz in the Park

In the University Campus Central Park

Sponsored by the Senior Class

FIGURE 3-13
The Jazz in the Park ad has page color, text, and two text boxes.

Tip When a document is printed, page color does not print, but fill color in a text box or shape does print.

? Solutions Appendix

For help, see Solution 3-9: How to Add Page Color and Text Boxes.

To build the flyer shown in Figure 3-12, we first add the title, subtitle, and page color. Then we add two text boxes to put more color on the page. When this activity is completed, the document should look like that in Figure 3-13.

Do the following:

Step 1. Open a new document.

Step 2. Set the Page Color to a medium orange. **Orange, Accent 6, Lighter 40%** works well.

Hint The Page Color command is on the Page Layout ribbon.

Step 3. Type two lines of text:

Jazz in the Park

In the University Campus Central Park

Step 4. Format the first line of text to **Calibri (Body) font, 72 point**. Format the second line to **Calibri (Body)**, **26 point**, and **bold**.

Step 5. Center both lines on the page.

Step 6. Save the document to your USB flash drive, hard drive, SkyDrive, or other location given by your instructor. Name the document **JazzConcert**.

Step 7. Create the text box on the left side of the page. Fill it with a dark orange color. **Orange, Accent 6, Dark 25%** works well.

Hint To insert a text box in a document, on the **Insert** ribbon, click **Text Box** and click **Draw Text Box**. Draw the box in the document. You can then add text in the box and move, resize, and format the box.

Step 8. Create a second text box, positioning it along the bottom of the page. Fill it with a red color.

Step 9. In this red text box, enter this text:

Sponsored by the Senior Class

Step 10. Format this text as **Calibri (Body)** font, **24 point**, **bold** and **italic**. **Center** the text in the text box. **Align** the text in the text box in the middle of the box.

Step 11. Save the document.

We're now ready to add the gramophone clip art to the document. The colors and shapes in this clip art were the inspirations that led to the overall design of the Jazz in the Park ad.

Tip When designing an ad or other document, start with a great graphic. Then design the entire document around the graphic.

On Your Own 3-10
Add Clip Art to a Document

In this activity, you add the gramophone clip art to the document. At the end of this activity, the document looks like that in Figure 3-14.

Do the following:

Step 1. Use the **Insert** ribbon to insert **Clip Art**. In the *Search for* box, enter **gramophone**. Select the gramophone clip art, as shown in Figure 3-14.

Not working? The gramophone clip art is downloaded from the Office.com site. To see it listed in the Clip Art pane, check **Include Office.com content**. You need to be connected to the Internet.

FIGURE 3-14
The Jazz in the Park ad has clip art inserted and positioned.

? Solutions Appendix

Step 2. Format the clip art as a floating graphic. Move and resize the clip art so that it is aligned at the top of the vertical text box, as shown in Figure 3-14. Save your document.

For help, see Solution 3-10: How to Add Clip Art to a Document.

Add a Shape to a Document

The star in the Jazz in the Park ad is one of many shapes that Word offers. After you insert a shape, you can move, resize, and rotate it. You can also format the shape and add text inside the shape. Here are some tips to help you when using a shape in a document:

▶ Hold down the Shift key as you resize a shape to keep it in proportion.

▶ To rotate a shape or other object, select it and then press and drag the **rotation handle**.

▶ To add text inside a shape, right-click it and click **Add Text** in the shortcut menu that appears.

▶ To format a shape with color or other special effects, use the Format ribbon, which shows up when a shape is selected.

> **rotation handle**—In Office applications, a green circle on the boundary of a picture, shape, or text box that is used to rotate the object. Drag the rotation handle in the direction you want to rotate the object.

On Your Own 3-11
Add a Shape to a Document

 Video **3-11**

Tip If a shape or text box is rotated, it returns to the original, upright position when you add or edit the text. Don't worry because when you click off the object, it returns to the rotated position.

? Solutions Appendix

Do the following to insert a star and format it, adding text inside the star:

Step 1. On the Insert ribbon, in the Shapes group, select a **star**. Your pointer changes to a cross. **+** Press and drag to draw the star on the document.

Step 2. If necessary, move the star to the correct position (refer to Figure 3-12). Rotate the star so that it points to the upper left of the document.

Step 3. Add the following text inside the star:

> Bring a chair or blanket!

Step 4. Make the font color of this text **black**. Size the text **18 point**.

Step 5. Change the fill color of the star to **yellow**.

Step 6. Save your document.

For help, see Solution 3-11: How to Add a Shape to a Document.

As you layer text boxes, clip art, and shapes in a document, the object on top is the one that displays. Here are some tips to help you change the layering order and select objects:

▶ To change the layering order of objects, click an object to select it. Then click the **Format** tab. Click **Bring Forward** to bring the object forward one layer. Click **Send Backward** to send the object behind an object. If you have several objects layered, you might have to click **Bring Forward** several times to bring an object to the front of several layered objects.

▶ If you are having trouble selecting an object, on the Format ribbon, click **Selection Pane**. A list of shapes in the document appears. Select one from the list.

Use WordArt

WordArt is used to add special effects to text. For the most impact, don't overdo WordArt. Use a little WordArt in a document to add emphasis to only the most important text.

Do the following to add a text box with WordArt to the document:

Step 1. Look back at Figure 3-12 and create the text box shown in the ad to hold the date and time information about the concert. Fill the text box with a light orange. **Orange Accent 6, Lighter 80%** works well.

Step 2. Enter the following text in the text box:

> Friday, October 9
>
> 9:30 PM to Midnight
>
> Free Admission

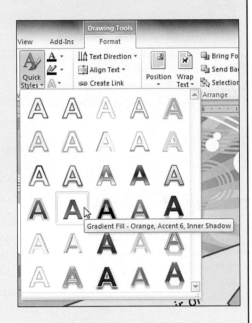

Step 3. Format the first line of text as **WordArt. Gradient Fill – Orange, Accent 6, Inner Shadow** works well. Increase the size of the text so as to add emphasis, but not so large as to cause word wrap. For this ad, **26 point** works well.

Step 4. Format the last two lines of text in **Calibri (Body), 18 point**, **bold**.

Step 5. Center all the text in the text box. Align the text in the middle of the text box.

Step 6. The document is finished. Take a moment to look back at Figure 3-12. Correct any problems you see with your work and save the document.

For help, see Solution 3-12: How to Add WordArt to a Document.

Solutions Appendix

Save a Document as a PDF File

Your instructor expects you to post or send your documents as Word documents so that she can view and edit them using Microsoft Word. However, if you are sending a document to your friends or posting it to a website, you might want to save the document using the PDF file format.

Most computers have software installed to read a PDF file, and if they don't, the reading software can be downloaded free. The software allows the PDF file to be read, but others cannot edit the document without additional software.

The *Jazz in the Park* document needs to be saved as a PDF file so that it can be emailed to the person responsible for sending it out to all students and faculty in a mass email. In Chapter 6, "Communicating with Others Using the Internet," you learn how to send a PDF file in an email message.

For now, do the following to save the document as a Word document and also as a PDF file:

Step 1. Save the document as usual. Then save the document again, this time as a PDF file. Save the file to the same location you previously saved the Word document file.

 Video **3-13**

Hint To save a document using a different file type, use the Save As command and change the file type in the *Save as type* field on the Save As dialog box.

Step 2. Close all windows.

Step 3. If you saved the files to the hard drive, USB flash drive, or other local storage device, open **Windows Explorer** and verify you have saved two files: the Word document file and the PDF file. Open the PDF file. Can you edit this file?

Step 4. If you saved the files to your SkyDrive, open **Internet Explorer** and verify both files are saved to your SkyDrive folder.

Templates as Shortcuts to Great Documents

template—In Office applications, a document designed for a specific purpose that already has elements included and places for you to add your own content.

It's good to know the mechanics of building a document step by step, but knowing some shortcuts can save time and also produce some dazzling results.

A template is a great shortcut to a great document. A **template** is a document that already has the look and feel you want and includes places where you can add your own text and graphics. Microsoft Word offers many templates for a variety of purposes such as business cards, calendars, certificates, and invitations. The templates can be downloaded from the Office.com website. Figure 3-15 shows you a sample of the templates offered in Word.

FIGURE 3-15
Word gives a variety of templates to fit a wide range of document types and uses.

In this activity, you use a template to create a party invitation. The completed document is shown in Figure 3-16.

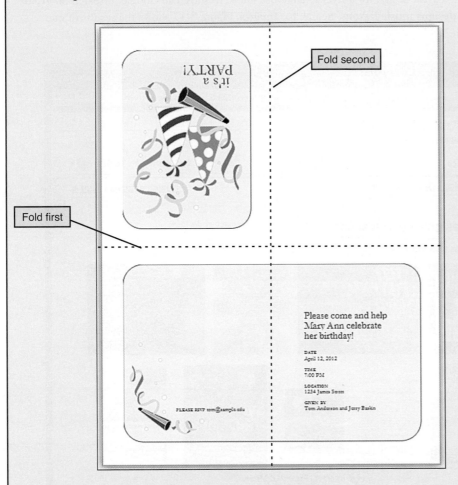

Fold second

Fold first

it's a
PARTY!

Please come and help
Mary Ann celebrate
her birthday!

DATE
April 12, 2012

TIME
7:00 PM

LOCATION
1234 James Street

GIVEN BY
Tom Anderson and Jerry Baskin

PLEASE RSVP tom@sample.edu

FIGURE 3-16
A Word template is used to
create a birthday party invitation.

To use a template, you start by selecting the template. Do the following:

Step 1. Click the **File** tab and open a new document to view a list of templates. Drill down into the **Invitations** group and then **Party invitations**. In the list of templates that display, select and download the **Birthday party invitation**.

Step 2. In the new document, type the text for the invitation. Use this text or make up your own:

Name of person: Mary Ann

Date: April 12, 2012

Time: 7:00 PM

Location: 1234 James Street

Given by: Tom Anderson and Jerry Baskin

RSVP to: tom@sample.edu

 Solutions Appendix

Step 3. Verify the author name for your Word document is correct. Save the document, naming it **Party**. Print the document. Fold the printed page so the document looks like a party invitation card.

**For help, see Solution
3-14: How to Use a Party
Invitation Template.**

Sometimes you cannot find a template to meet your needs, and you must design your own documents. To find sample designs for a document, try searching the web. For example, to find a great design for a flyer to advertise music lessons, use Google to search on **great flyer designs music lessons**. Search for **Images**. Figure 3-17 shows the results of one search.

FIGURE 3-17
Use a Google search for images to get ideas for document designs.

Document designs generally are not protected by **copyright**, and you can use these ideas to design your own documents. But the graphics and photos used in a document might be copyrighted. Honor the rights of others; don't copy their work and distribute it to others without the permission of the owner.

> **copyright**—The right to copy a work, which belongs to the creator of the work or to someone the creator has given the right.

Summary

Entering Text and Saving the Document

▶ Microsoft Word is a word processing program that allows you to enter text, format text, and insert graphics into a document.

▶ Word's help feature is a good way to research Word's features and to solve problems when you get stuck while using Word.

▶ The insertion point in Word shows where text will be entered when you type.

▶ Use the press and drag action to select text. Selected text is highlighted and can be deleted, replaced, or formatted.

▶ The Quick Access Toolbar has commonly used commands such as save, redo, and undo.

▶ Word automatically wraps text to the next line so you don't have to worry about typing off the page. This feature is called word wrap.

▶ You should save your work every five minutes or so to avoid losing information.

▶ Three ways to save a document are click **File**, **Save**; press **Ctrl-S**; and click the **Save** button in the Quick Access Toolbar. When first saving a document to a SkyDrive, on the Backstage view, click **Save & Send**.

▶ The first time you save a document you must specify the filename and location. When you save the document again, Word automatically uses the same name and location.

▶ The Insert ribbon of Word is used to insert elements into the document. Some of these elements include shapes, photos, WordArt, and Clip Art.

Formatting Text

▶ The Home ribbon provides access to many formatting commands. Formatting changes the size, color, and font of text.

▶ The font used determines the shape of each character typed.

▶ The size of the font is measured in points; there are 72 points in an inch.

▶ Formatting in Word can be done to selected text or an entire paragraph.

▶ The four types of formatting tools available on the Home ribbon or the Font group, the Paragraph group, the Style group, and the Format Painter.

▶ The Format Painter makes it easy to copy formatting from one part of a document to another.

▶ A style is a predetermined set of formatting that has been assigned a name and is a shortcut method to formatting.

▶ The Show/Hide button is used to toggle between showing and hiding the hard returns and other nonprinting characters in a document.

Adding Graphics to a Document

▶ A graphic in a document can be inline or floating. An inline graphic moves with the text, and a floating graphic stays put on the page.

▶ When an object is selected, sizing handles and a rotation handle appear. Use them to resize and rotate the object. Press and drag an object to move it.

Finishing Up and Printing Your Document

▶ The document properties can be viewed in the Info group in the Backstage view. The properties include the name and location of the document, the document author, and the date and time created and modified.

▶ Print a document using the **Print** command on the Backstage view. The printer used and printer settings can also be controlled in this window.

Using Page Color, Text Boxes, Shapes, and WordArt

▶ Page color adds impact to a document and is useful when the document is not printed.

▶ A text box can be positioned anywhere and can contain text, fill color, borders, and graphics.

▶ Shapes are inserted using the Insert ribbon and can be resized, reshaped, moved, rotated, and filled with color and text.

▶ Graphics and text can be layered in a document. Use the **Bring Forward** and **Send Backward** commands to change the layering order.

▶ WordArt is a fun way to add special effects to text. For the most impact, don't use too much WordArt in a document.

▶ Word files can be saved as PDF files using the Save As command in the Backstage view.

▶ PDF files save the formatting of the original document and are useful when emailing documents to others or posting them on the web.

Templates as Shortcuts to Great Documents

▶ Templates are good shortcuts to well-designed documents, and Word offers many templates downloaded from the Office.com site.

▶ When designing a document, search the web for great document designs, but don't copy the works of others.

Review Questions

Answer these questions to assess your skills and knowledge of the content covered in the chapter. Your instructor can provide you with the correct answers when you are ready to check your work.

1. What is the Backstage view in Word?

2. What is the icon for Help in Word?

3. What keys do you press to quickly save a Word document that has been saved before?

4. What group on the Home ribbon has the formatting command to make text bold?

5. When referring to formatting, what is a style?

6. Where is the Quick Access Toolbar located?

7. What is word wrap?

8. What key do you press to end a paragraph?

9. What is the difference between an inline graphic and a floating graphic?

10. How do you find the sizing handles on an object?

11. On what ribbon of the Word window can you find Page Color?

12. What tab on the Word window do you click to change the author of a document?

13. What file format should be used to email a document to someone who might not have Microsoft Word installed on her computer?

14. When you add a graphic into a document, when do you need to use Send Backward?

15. Where does Word store most of its templates?

Chapter Mastery Project

Find out how well you have mastered the content in this chapter by completing this project. If you can answer all the questions and do all the steps without looking back at the chapter details, you have mastered this chapter. If you can complete the project by finding answers using the Word Help window, you have proven that you can teach yourself Microsoft Word.

> **Hint** All the key terms in the chapter are used in this mastery project. If you encounter a key word you don't know such as *font*, enter **define:font** in the Internet Explorer search box. You can also search for the word using the Word Help window.

If you find you need a lot of help doing the project and you have not yet read the chapter or done the activities, drop back and start at the beginning of the chapter and then return to this project.

By following the steps in this mastery project, you create the document shown in Figure 3-18.

FIGURE 3-18
This document uses text, a text box, a bulleted list, a shape, and clip art.

Mastery Project Part 1: Entering Text and Saving the Document

If you need help completing this part of the mastery project, please review the "Entering Text and Saving the Document" section in the chapter.

Follow these steps to enter text in a document:

Step 1. Open **Word**. On the Page Layout ribbon, click **Orientation** and click **Landscape**. The document is now oriented in Landscape view.

Step 2. Type the following four lines of text:

Want to play guitar?

Jamie Jackson can help.

B.S. degree in Music Education

Private lessons at $45/hour

Step 3. Use the **Backstage** view to save the document. Save the document file to your USB flash drive, hard drive, SkyDrive, or other location given by your instructor. Name the document **GuitarLessons**.

Mastery Project Part 2: Formatting Text

If you need help completing this part of the mastery project, please review the "Formatting Text" section in the chapter.

Follow these steps to format the text you have already typed into the document:

Step 1. Right-justify all the text in the document and format the text as **Bookman Old Style**.

Step 2. Format the first line of text as **48 point**, **bold**.

Step 3. Use the **Format Painter** to copy the formatting of the first line to the second line. Then change the point size of the second line to **36 point**.

Step 4. Format **Jamie Jackson** in the second line in **italics**.

Step 5. Format the last two lines of text in **26 point**, **bold**.

Step 6. Save the document using the **Save** button in the Quick Access Toolbar.

Mastery Project Part 3: Adding Graphics to a Document

If you need help completing this part of the mastery project, please review the "Adding Graphics to a Document" section in the chapter.

Do the following to add clip art to the document:

Step 1. Insert the clip art of a guitar player into the document. Change the graphic to a floating graphic.

Step 2. Position the clip art as shown earlier in Figure 3-18. Use sizing handles to resize the graphic to about the size shown in the figure. The exact position and size are not important.

Step 3. Save the document using **Ctrl-S**.

Mastery Project Part 4: Using Page Color, Text Boxes, Shapes, and WordArt

If you need help completing this part of the mastery project, please review the "Using Page Color, Text Boxes, Shapes, and WordArt" section in the chapter.

Do the following to add page color, a text box, and a shape to the document:

Step 1. Make the page color of the document a gray color. **White, Background 1, Darker 25%** works well. Format all the text in the document as **White**.

Step 2. Insert a text box to the right of the clip art, as shown in Figure 3-18. Make the shape fill color a light purple. **Purple, Accent 4, Lighter 80%** works well.

Step 3. Type the following text into the text box:

Call or email Jamie:

Cell: 555-234-1234

Email: jamie@sample.com

Step 4. Format the text in the text box as **Bookman Old Style**, **18 point**, **bold**. Make the last two lines in the text box a bulleted list. The text in the text box is left-justified.

Step 5. Insert a Horizontal Scroll shape into the table. Make the shape fill color a medium purple. **Purple, Accent 4, Lighter 60%** works well.

Step 6. Use the rotation handle to rotate the scroll as shown in Figure 3-18.

Step 7. Type the following text into the scroll:

First lesson is free!

Step 8. Format the scroll text as **Bookman Old Style**, **26 point**. Center the text in the scroll.

Step 9. Format the word **free** using **Text Effects**, using a dark purple. **Gradient Fill – Purple, Accent 4, Reflection** works well.

Step 10. Make sure the scroll is layered on top of the text box, not beneath it. If necessary, use the **Bring Forward** or **Send Backward** commands to change the layering of the objects.

Step 11. Save the document using the Backstage view.

Mastery Project Part 5: Finishing Up and Printing Your Document

If you need help completing this part of the mastery project, please review the "Finishing Up and Printing Your Document" section in the chapter.

Do the following to finish up the document and save it as a PDF:

Step 1. Verify the document is a one-page document. If the document has more than one page, fix the problem. Use the paragraph marks to make sure you don't have extra lines.

Step 2. Verify the document properties show you as the author of the document. If necessary, change the document author to your name.

Step 3. Save the document as a Word document.

Step 4. Save the document as a PDF file.

Step 5. This document is not designed to be printed. Display a Print Preview of the document. Why would printing the document present a problem?

Answer the following questions about creating the GuitarLessons document:

1. In creating the document, you did not use the word wrap feature of Word. Why was the feature not used?

2. What file extension did Word assign to the GuitarLessons document file?

3. What keys do you press to select all the text in a document?

4. If you are having trouble selecting an object in a document, how can you get a list of objects from which you can select one?

Mastery Project Part 6: Templates as Shortcuts to Great Documents

If you need help completing this part of the mastery project, please review the "Templates as Shortcuts to Great Documents" section in the chapter.

Do the following to create a document showing your family tree:

Step 1. Open a new document to view a list of templates. Drill down into **Charts and diagrams** and then **Business charts**. In the list of templates that display, select and download **Family tree (3 generations)**.

Step 2. Fill in the information for your own family tree.

Step 3. Save the document as **MyFamilyTree**. Print the document.

Answer the following questions:

1. If you cannot find a template that you can use for a document design, what is one way to find great designs you can use?

2. Sometimes you might find a great photo or graphic that you want to use in a document you create. Why should you not use a photo or other graphics that you find on the web in a document you plan to distribute to others?

Becoming an Independent Learner

Answer the following questions about becoming an independent learner:

1. To teach yourself to use Microsoft Word, do you think it is best to rely on the chapter or on Word Help when you need answers?

2. The most important skill learned in this chapter is how to teach yourself a computer skill. Rate yourself at Level A through E on how well you are doing with this skill. What is your level?

   ○ Level A: I was able to successfully complete the Chapter Mastery Project without the help of doing the On Your Own activities in the chapter.

   ○ Level B: I completed all the On Your Own activities and the Chapter Mastery Project without referring to any of the solutions in the *Solutions Appendix*.

   ○ Level C: I completed all the On Your Own activities and the Chapter Mastery Project by using just a few of the solutions in the *Solutions Appendix*.

   ○ Level D: I completed all the On Your Own activities and the Chapter Mastery Project by using many of the solutions in the *Solutions Appendix*.

   ○ Level E: I completed all the On Your Own activities and the Chapter Mastery Project and had to use all of the solutions in the *Solutions Appendix*.

To continue toward the goal of teaching yourself computer skills, if you are not at Level A, try to move up one level on how you learn in Chapter 4, "Using the Web for Research."

Projects to Help You

Now that you have mastered the material in this chapter, you are ready to tackle the three projects introduced at the beginning of the chapter in the section "How Will This Chapter Help Me?"

Project 1: Using Word in Your Personal Life

PERSONAL PROJECT:
I'm starting up a pet-sitting business. I want to post a flyer in the neighborhood park where people walk their dogs.

The most important computer skill is how to teach yourself a computer skill. Microsoft Word has many features not covered in the chapter. In this project, create a one-page document advertising a business you are starting. The business can be for anything you like, perhaps a hobby or business you enjoy. Business ideas might be golf lessons, tutoring, pet sitting, or babysitting. Don't forget to put your contact information in the document.

Include these features and elements in the document:

▶ Text that uses Text Effects, WordArt, or SmartArt.

> **Hint** Text Effects is found in the Font group on the Home ribbon. WordArt and SmartArt are found on the Insert ribbon.

▶ A photo, which can be a picture of yourself or any other photo that can help advertise your business. If you don't have a photo, use the MyPhoto1.jpg photo in the Sample Files folder on the DVD in the back of the textbook.

> **Hint** To insert a photo in a document, click **Picture** on the Insert ribbon. In the Insert Picture dialog box that appears, locate the photo and then click **Insert**.

Name the document **MyBusiness**. After you finish the document, print it.

ACADEMIC PROJECT: I need to create a calendar that shows my class schedule and all the due dates for important assignments.

Project 2: Word in Your Academic Career

Word offers several templates that can help you plan your schedule, homework assignments, or events. To see these templates, open a new document in Word. Then drill down into the **Planners** templates. Select a template that can be useful to you in your academic career. Download the template and fill it in. Name the document **MyPlanner**. After you finish the document, print it.

Project 3: Word in Your Technical Career

You are working part time for a small business providing desk-side technical support for employees. All employees share a laser printer on the network that accommodates several sizes and types of paper and envelopes. The paper keeps jamming in the printer because users don't know how to load the paper correctly. Your boss has asked you to create a document to post over the printer about a coffee timeout to learn about loading the paper and freeing up a paper jam.

TECHNICAL CAREER PROJECT: Users keep jamming paper in the network printer. My boss has asked me to create a document to post over the printer about how to load paper in the printer.

The document might say something like "Tired of paper jams? Come Friday morning at 10:00 AM with a cup of joe and an open mind. In ten minutes, we'll cover everything you need to know to load paper and free up a jam."

Get creative with the document using clever text, clip art, and shapes. Name the document **PrinterTraining**. After you finish the document, print it.

Project to Help Others

One of the best ways to learn is to teach someone else. And, in teaching someone else, you are making a contribution into that person's life. As part of each chapter's work, you are encouraged to teach someone a skill you have learned. In this case, help your apprentice learn to use Microsoft Word.

Who is your apprentice? _____

When helping others learn, don't do the work for them. Coach and instruct. Show them how to find information for themselves. Help them be as independent a learner as possible.

Working with your apprentice, do the following:

Step 1. Ask your apprentice what type of one-page document he might like to create. Examples are a flyer, business card, certificate, invitation, ad to be posted on craigslist.org, meeting agenda, permission slip, or organizational chart.

Step 2. Help your apprentice create the document. Will a template help? If you can find a template that suits your purpose, show your apprentice how to download and use the template. If you cannot find a template, help your apprentice create the document from a blank new document.

Step 3. Ask your apprentice to evaluate how the tutoring session went. Briefly describe his response.

Step 4. Think about the mentoring session. How do you think it went? How would you like to improve it next time?

Step 5. Print the document that your apprentice created and bring it to class.

CHAPTER 4
Using the Web for Research

IN THIS CHAPTER, YOU WILL

Prepare to take research notes and select your research topic

Find general information and subtopics about the topic

Find authoritative and scholarly research

Evaluate your research and organize your research notes

The web has changed the way we research. Because the web offers many credible and authoritative works including books and professional journals, it is possible to do all of your scholarly or academic research on a topic without ever walking through the doors of a library. If you know about the many shortcuts discussed in this chapter, you can find the best works quickly, saving much time.

As always, remember the most important computer skill to learn is how to teach yourself a computer skill. Therefore, this chapter is designed to help you teach yourself how to research on the web. Try to do each On Your Own activity without any help. But remember, if you need help, you can always refer to the solutions in the *Solutions Appendix*.

JUMP RIGHT IN

If you want even more of a challenge, try proceeding directly to the Chapter Mastery Project at the end of this chapter. If you need help on the project, refer to the On Your Own activities in the chapter or do your own independent investigating by searching the web or by using the OneNote Help feature. When you complete the project, you will have mastered the skills in this chapter. Then go to the Projects to Help You that require you apply your skills to new situations.

How Will This Chapter Help Me?

Throughout this book, each chapter provides three projects focusing on personal, academic, or technical career goals. Depending on your own interests, you might choose to perform any or all of these projects to help you achieve your goals.

PERSONAL PROJECT: My brother and his wife are considering adopting a child. They've asked me to help them research domestic and international adoptions and find a good book on the topic. They want to know what problems an adopted child might have later in life. I need to use the web to do this research.

ACADEMIC PROJECT: I'm majoring in law enforcement and my English Composition teacher has assigned a research paper. My law enforcement advisor has suggested I write the paper on INTERPOL. I have to find websites, books, journal articles, and newspaper articles about INTERPOL. Can I do all that research on the web?

TECHNICAL CAREER PROJECT: I want a job in IT, and I've noticed that job postings are asking for IT certifications. What are these certifications, when do I need them, and who offers them? What are people saying about which certifications are the best to have? How can I find all these answers on the web?

Preparing to Take Research Notes and Selecting Your Research Topic

Researching and reporting on a topic are important skills used by students and employees. For example, suppose you hold a part-time job working for your school counselor. One day he says:

> *Many students are asking about the Peace Corps. I need you to research it and tell me what are the requirements and benefits and how does someone apply. Include what to expect when serving in the Peace Corps. Put everything in writing and be sure to include your sources. I'll give your paper to whomever comes into the office asking about the Peace Corps.*

This work assignment requires you to find credible information on the Peace Corps, maintain organized notes from your research, and compose a paper from that information.

In this chapter, you learn how to use the web to research this and other topics. In Chapter 5, "Writing Papers Using Microsoft Word Templates and Tools," you learn how to use Microsoft Word to create a research paper.

An expert researcher uses a four-phase process when researching a topic:

Phase 1. Explore general information about the topic.

Phase 2. Go deeper to find the best works.

Phase 3. Evaluate where the research is taking you and ask penetrating questions.

Phase 4. Organize the research notes.

Each of these research phases is explored in this chapter. First, we need to get our tools for note taking in place and see how the web can help you when you are asked to select your own research topic. Microsoft Office OneNote is a great tool for taking notes because it is easy to grab content from your browser into OneNote.

Use OneNote for Taking Research Notes

Microsoft Office includes the **OneNote** application, which is designed to receive notes taken from the web and other sources and to keep notes organized. Notes are kept in notebooks. Just as with physical notebooks, a OneNote notebook has sections and each section has pages, as shown in Figure 4-1.

> **OneNote**—A Microsoft Office application used to hold and organize notes, including content taken from the web. OneNote keeps content in notebooks. Notebooks are divided into sections. Sections can have one or more pages.

> **Tip** In this chapter, we don't cover many of the features of OneNote. However, you can use the Help feature of OneNote to learn more about the application.

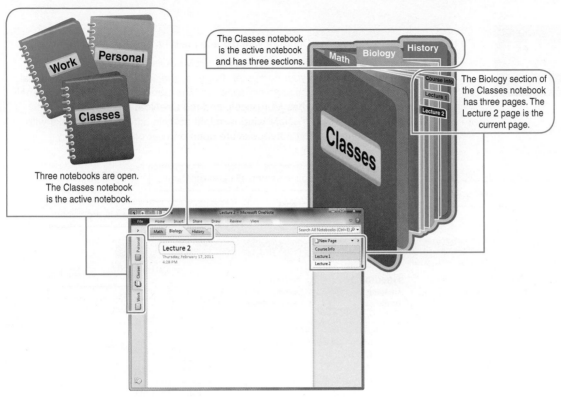

FIGURE 4-1

A OneNote notebook is organized like a physical notebook: A notebook has sections, and each section has pages.

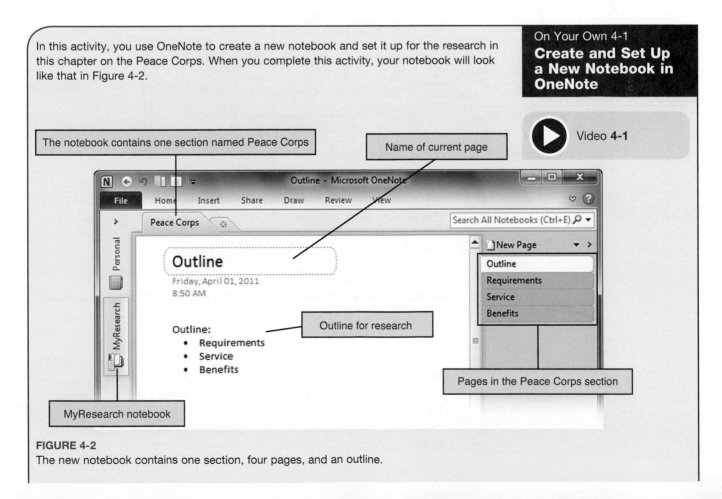

In this activity, you use OneNote to create a new notebook and set it up for the research in this chapter on the Peace Corps. When you complete this activity, your notebook will look like that in Figure 4-2.

On Your Own 4-1
Create and Set Up a New Notebook in OneNote

Video **4-1**

The notebook contains one section named Peace Corps

Name of current page

Outline for research

Pages in the Peace Corps section

MyResearch notebook

FIGURE 4-2

The new notebook contains one section, four pages, and an outline.

On Your Own 4-1
Create and Set Up a New Notebook in OneNote

Do the following to examine the OneNote window and create a new OneNote notebook:

Step 1. Open **OneNote**. When the OneNote window opens, it loads any notebooks already identified on your computer. For example, in Figure 4-3, the Personal notebook is open. It has two sections, and the General section is the current section. This section has four pages, and the OneNote Basics page is the current page. Your OneNote window might contain different notebooks with different content. What notebooks are open on your computer?

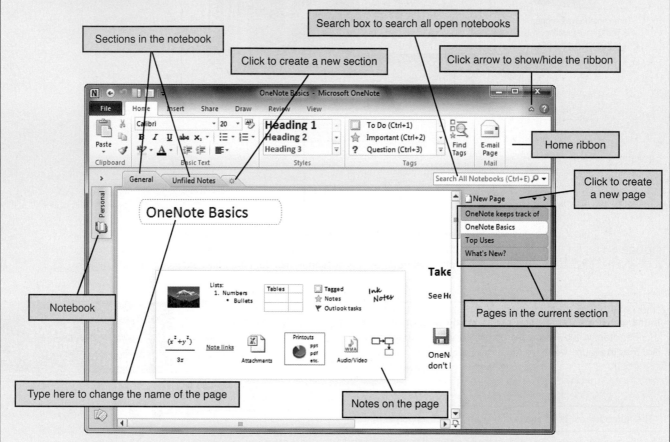

FIGURE 4-3
The OneNote window is used to manage notebooks, sections, pages, and notes.

Step 2. Create a new notebook, naming the notebook **MyResearch**. Save it to your USB flash drive, hard drive, SkyDrive, or another location given by your instructor.

> **Hint** To create a new notebook, start by clicking the **File** tab and then clicking **New**.

As you work, OneNote automatically saves your notebook to this device each time you make changes in the notebook. Do the following to set up your new notebook for research in this chapter:

Step 1. The notebook has only one section named *New Section 1*. Rename the section **Peace Corps**.

Step 2. The first page of this section is named *Untitled page.* Rename the page **Outline**.

Hint To rename a page, type the name of the page in the text bubble at the top left of the page. The name showing in the page tab changes as you type.

Step 3. Research about each subtopic can be kept on its own subtopic page. Create three new pages, naming them **Requirements**, **Service**, and **Benefits**. If you later identify other subtopics, you can add new pages as needed. As you research, keep your research notes organized by putting research about a particular subtopic on its page.

Hint To add a new page, click **New Page** on the right side of the OneNote window.

Step 4. Return to the Outline page and type an outline that has three subtopics: **Requirements**, **Service**, and **Benefits**. Figure 4-2 shows the completed outline.

Hint To type on a page, click an insertion point and start typing.

Solutions Appendix

For help, see Solution 4-1: How to Create and Set Up a New Notebook in OneNote.

Step 5. Leave OneNote open. As you search the web using Internet Explorer, you can switch back and forth between OneNote and IE by clicking the program icons in the taskbar.

OneNote keeps each notebook you create in a separate folder. The name of the folder is the name of the notebook. Each section in a notebook is kept in its own file that has a .one file extension. For example, your MyRescarch notebook has the Peace Corps section. That means there is a folder named MyResearch, which has the Peace Corps.one file in it, as shown in Figure 4-4. In the figure, the Properties box for the Peace Corps file is open so you can see the file extension, which is .one.

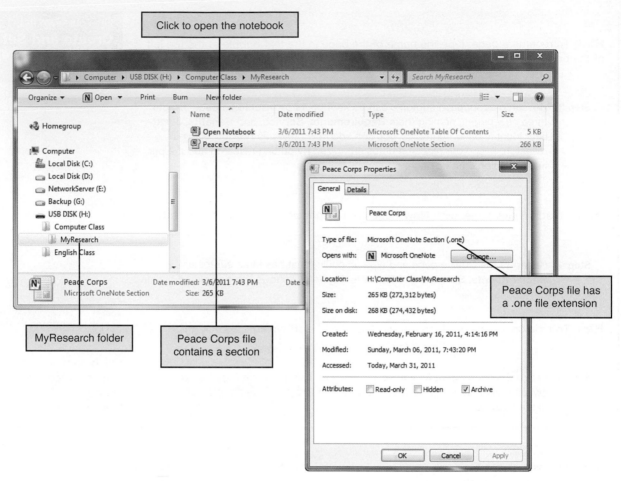

FIGURE 4-4
A OneNote notebook is a folder, and a section is a .one file.

One way to open a notebook is to double-click the **Open Notebook** file, which is showing in Figure 4-4.

Find a Research Topic for an Assigned Research Paper

Learning to research and write a research paper is an important skill in your academic career. Sometimes an instructor asks you to select the research topic. Suppose an English instructor gives you the research and writing assignment shown in Figure 4-5. In Chapter 5, you learn about typing and formatting the research paper. For now, let's focus on selecting the topic so that it fits the criteria given in the assignment.

Notice the instructor asks you to include at least one **primary source** in your sources.

primary source—In research, a source that provides first-hand content by someone who is directly involved in an activity or event. In comparison, a secondary source provides content from someone not directly involved. For example, a letter written by a soldier in a battle is a primary source, but an analysis of the battle written by a general who was not involved in the battle is a secondary source.

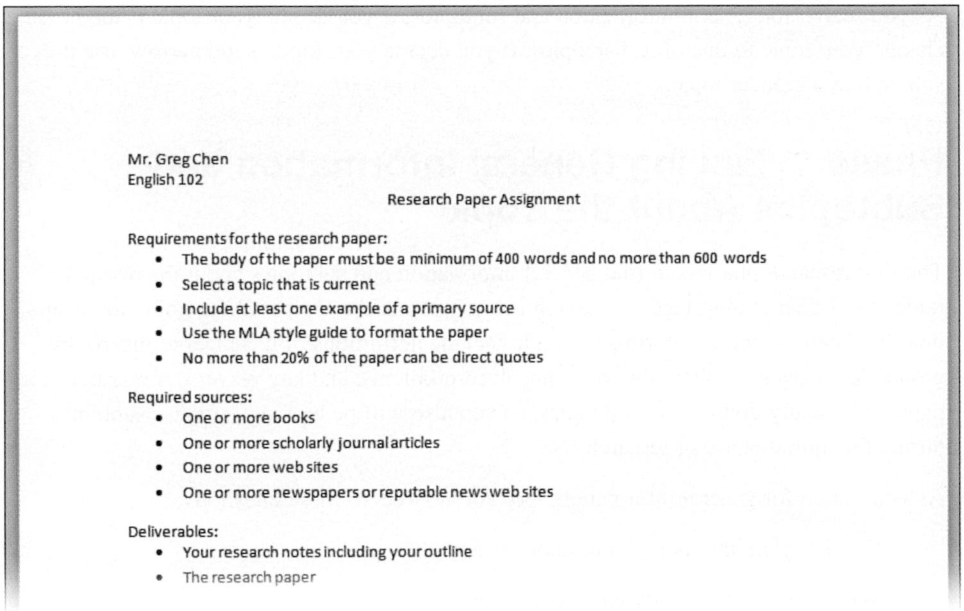

Mr. Greg Chen
English 102

Research Paper Assignment

Requirements for the research paper:
- The body of the paper must be a minimum of 400 words and no more than 600 words
- Select a topic that is current
- Include at least one example of a primary source
- Use the MLA style guide to format the paper
- No more than 20% of the paper can be direct quotes

Required sources:
- One or more books
- One or more scholarly journal articles
- One or more web sites
- One or more newspapers or reputable news web sites

Deliverables:
- Your research notes including your outline
- The research paper

FIGURE 4-5
This research paper assignment lists required types of sources and allows you to select the topic.

When deciding on a good topic for a research paper, keep these tips in mind:

▶ The topic should be of interest to you. Pick a hot topic that is exciting and you want to learn about it.

▶ The topic gives you the opportunity to offer your own opinions or solutions.

▶ The paper offers a solution to a problem or helps someone.

▶ The topic lends itself well to the source requirements. For example, books come out about two years after an event. If you must use a book as a source, recent events will not work unless you can include historical or background information about the event, which you can find in a book.

▶ The topic is not so obscure or narrow that you will not find enough sources.

▶ The topic is not so broad that the number of sources will overwhelm you or you cannot adequately cover it in the number of required pages.

▶ Your instructor likes the topic and approves it.

The web can help you find a good topic. Here are some tips:

▶ Do a Google search on "research topics."

▶ Get more specific. For example, search for "political research topics" or "autism research topics."

Don't settle for the first ideas you find. Browse a bit until you find a topic that truly sparks your interest and fits the criteria given earlier.

Tip As you search the web for research topics, you might find a paper mill site. This type of site offers to write a research paper for you or offers research papers for sale. Avoid **plagiarism**! Most schools have an academic code of honor that says you will not present other works as your own and you will not do others' work for them. Breaking the honor code can lead to failing a class or being expelled from school.

plagiarism—Presenting someone else's ideas or words as your own.

As you search for general information and subtopics, if you decide your topic is too broad, change your topic to one of its subtopics. If you decide your topic is too narrow, use it as a subtopic in a broader topic.

Phase 1: Finding General Information and Subtopics About the Topic

The first research phase is to find general information and subtopics about the research topic. Your goal at this stage of research is to scope out the topic without going too deep into the details. General information might include definitions of technical terms, background, controversies about the topic, unsolved problems, and key players. A research paper is typically divided into subtopics, so you also will be looking for these subtopics during this initial phase of research.

As you search for general information, look for answers to these questions:

> ▶ Can I explain the topic in one short paragraph?
>
> ▶ What are the issues and who are the experts?
>
> ▶ When and where did important events happen?
>
> ▶ What are people saying who are directly involved?
>
> ▶ What are people saying who are analyzing the topic?
>
> ▶ What problems are not yet solved?
>
> ▶ Who is responsible for solving these problems?

Tip At this stage of research, don't pay too much attention to the sources of information. If you do find something interesting, however, be sure to bookmark it so you can return to the website later. In the next phase of research, you focus on finding authoritative and credible sources that you can use in your research paper.

Websites can help you find general information and subtopics:

> ▶ Use Google.com *autosuggest* to find subtopics. Google *related searches* can help you broaden a topic. A Google *Timeline* can give a historical perspective about a topic. You learn to use all these tools in On Your Own activities in this part of the chapter.
>
> ▶ Use a **clustering search engine** to find subtopics.

clustering search engine—A search engine that specializes in sorting hits by subtopics. Examples are carrot2.org, yippy.com, and www.webclust.com.

> ▶ Use Wikipedia.org to find general information, subtopics, an outline, and links to other content.

Tip Wikipedia.org articles are written by anyone who wants to contribute to them. Because the articles are not always written by recognized experts, most instructors do not allow Wikipedia.org to be cited as a source for a research paper. However, Wikipedia.org is a great place to look for general information about a topic for the first phase of your research. The site can also lead you to authoritative sources you'll need for the second phase of research.

Do the following to use Google autosuggest and Google related searches to find ideas for subtopics or ideas to broaden a topic that is too narrow:

Step 1. Use Google.com to search on the phrase **peace corps**. What are four subtopics that Google autosuggest offers to complete the search string?

Step 2. The related searches or Something Different list on the Google results page can help you broaden a topic if your current topic is too narrow. What might be a research topic that includes the Peace Corps and the other topics listed under related searches?

Do the following to use Wikipedia.org to find general information and subtopics about the Peace Corps:

Step 1. Search for information about the Peace Corps, limiting your Google search only to the **Wikipedia.org** site.

Step 2. Find an article on the Peace Corps and a paragraph in that article that gives a good overview and definition of the Peace Corps. Bookmark the article in Internet Explorer **Favorites**.

Step 3. Copy the paragraph onto the Outline page of the Peace Corps section of your OneNote notebook.

Tip You could use the search utility on the Wikipedia.org site rather than a Google search, but a Google search usually gives better results.

Hint To copy a paragraph in your browser into OneNote, press and drag to select the paragraph. Right-click on the selection. In the shortcut menu that appears, click **Send to OneNote**, as shown in Figure 4-6. The Select Location in OneNote dialog box appears. Select the OneNote page to receive the paragraph and click **OK**.

FIGURE 4-6
Selected text in Wikipedia.org is ready to be copied into OneNote.

On Your Own 4-2
Use Google.com and Wikipedia.org for Preliminary Research

 Solutions Appendix

For help, see Solution 4-2: How to Use Google.com and Wikipedia.org for Preliminary Research.

Step 4. Notice that OneNote inserts the URL of the paragraph below the text. Use the highlighting feature of OneNote to highlight an important sentence in this paragraph.

> typically with a college degree, who works abroad for a period of training. Volunteers work with governments, schools, non-profit organizations, and entrepreneurs in education, hunger, business, and the environment.
>
> Inserted from <http://en.wikipedia.org/wiki/Peace_Corps>

Step 5. Most Wikipedia articles include an outline, and this outline can help you make sure you've not overlooked an important subtopic. Find the outline in the Peace Corps article. Besides the three subtopics we have already identified, what are two other subtopics that could be added to the paper?

On Your Own 4-3
Find Subtopics Using a Clustering Search Engine

A clustering search engine can help you find subtopics about a topic.

Use the site carrot2.org to search for information about the Peace Corps. What are some subtopics that the search identified?

> **Tip** If you find a good source, don't forget to bookmark it. If content looks really good, you can go ahead and copy it into OneNote.

 Solutions Appendix

For help, see Solution 4-3: How to Find Subtopics Using a Clustering Search Engine.

Google can display hits in a graphical timeline showing when the articles were written or when the event took place. A timeline about a topic can help with your research in these ways:

▶ By clicking older hits, you can get a historical perspective about a topic. By clicking the latest hits, you can find recent information or news.

▶ Peaks in the timeline can help you find important breakthroughs about a topic.

▶ A timeline can tell you how hot the topic is. If hits are increasing over time, the topic is still hot. If hits are decreasing or have already peaked, the topic is no longer hot.

On Your Own 4-4
Use a Google Timeline

 Video **4-4**

Do the following to view and use a Google Timeline:

Step 1. Use Google to display a Google Timeline about the Peace Corps. Figure 4-7 shows one example. Yours might look different.

Step 2. Copy the timeline into the Outline page in your OneNote notebook using the OneNote Screen Clipping tool.

Hint The OneNote Screen Clipping tool is useful for copying graphics into OneNote. To use the tool, click the **Insert** tab in OneNote. Then click **Screen Clipping**. The OneNote window goes away. Press and drag across the area of your screen you want to capture. The clipping is copied into OneNote onto your current OneNote page.

Click here to find peak interest

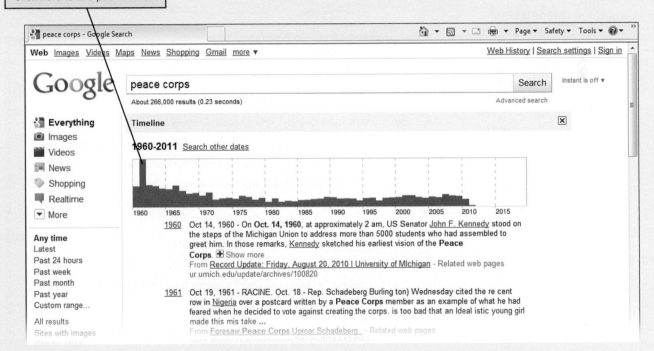

FIGURE 4-7
A Google Timeline gives you a picture of hits over time.

Step 3. Based on the timeline, it appears interest in the Peace Corps remains steady since its beginning. In what month and year was the most interest in the Peace Corps? To find hits at this peak, drill down into the timeline. What event regarding the Peace Corps caused this heightened interest?

 Solutions Appendix

For help, see Solution 4-4: How to Use a Google Timeline.

As you find general information and subtopics about a topic, develop your outline on the Outline page of OneNote. Don't forget to bookmark the sites that offer useful information.

Phase 2: Finding Authoritative and Scholarly Research

After you are familiar with a topic and have an outline, you are ready to dig deeper. The next step is to find authoritative and scholarly research about the topic.

When you use information in your research paper from any source, that source must be listed in the **Works Cited** list of the paper. Figure 4-8 shows an example of a Works Cited page. The information about the source in a Works Cited list should be enough for others to find the source if they want to verify what you've written or they want to learn more about the topic.

> **Works Cited**—The list of all sources used to write a research paper. The Works Cited list is at the end of the paper and is also called the Bibliography or References. List all sources even if you don't include a direct quote from the source.

Witt 3

Works Cited

Peace Corps. n.d. Web. 15 February 2011 <http://www.peacecorps.gov>.

Plante, Thomas G., Katy Lackey, and Hwang Jeong Yeon. "The Impact of Immersion Trips on Development of Compassion Among College Students." *Journal of Experiential Education* 32.1 (2009): 28-43. *EBSCO.* Web. 14 Feb. 2011.

Stickney, Benjamin D. "Nigerians Speak Warmly of the Peace Corps." *The New York Times* 9 March 1991. Web. 15 Feb. 2011.

Taylor, Leah. *Lntaylor's Weblog.* 5 July 2010. Web. 15 February 2011 <http://lntaylor.wordpress.com/>.

Thomsen, Moritz. *Living Poor: A Peace Corps Chronicle.* Seattle: University of Washington Press, 1969. *Google Book Search.* Web. 15 Feb. 2011.

FIGURE 4-8
This sample Works Cited page lists all sources used in the research paper.

Table 4-1 lists the information you need for each type of source. If you find a book or article online rather than in print, in addition to the information listed in Table 4-1, include this information about the online source:

- ▶ Name of website or online database
- ▶ URL of the website
- ▶ Date you accessed the website

As you find sources, record the citation information in OneNote. Later, you will use it to build your Works Cited list. In Chapter 5, you learn how to arrange and format a Works Cited list.

TABLE 4-1 Information About a Source Needed for a Works Cited List

Type of Source	Required Citation Information
Book	Author or authors (up to four authors). If the book has an editor, be sure to make that clear.
	Title, including subtitle
	Publisher
	City of publication (only one city required)
	Latest copyright year (year published)
	Volume number (might not apply)
	Type of source: Book
Journal or magazine article	Author or authors (up to four authors)
	Article title
	Journal or magazine title
	Volume and issue number
	Date published (month, day, year)
	Pages that the article spans (for example, 72–73) or first page of the article if it jumps pages (for example, 72+)
	Type of source: Journal or magazine
Newspaper article	Author or authors (up to four and might be omitted)
	Article title
	Newspaper title
	Newspaper edition (optional, for example, "Late edition")
	Date published (month, day, year)
	Pages that the article spans or first page of article if it jumps pages
	Type of source: Newspaper
Website content, including text and image	Author or authors (up to four and might not be available)
	Title of work (might not be available)
	Title of website
	Date of publication of the work (if known)
	Date you accessed the source
	URL
	Type of source: Electronic book, article, blog, or other
Interview	Name of person interviewed
	Date of interview
	Type of source: Interview

A researcher is responsible for deciding whether a website, book, magazine article, or other work is credible. Let's look at how to decide whether a source is credible.

Decide Whether Content Is Credible

As you research, you will find websites, books, and journal articles that might not be credible sources. A good researcher knows how to weed out bad sources from the good ones.

Some websites present false information or facts that are not verified, and a website might be intentionally lying. When searching the web, you must decide whether the content you find is credible.

When deciding whether content is credible, consider the following questions:

▶ What is the type of website and who owns it?

▶ What are others saying about the source?

▶ Is the author of a work credible?

▶ Are there opposing views?

The next sections explain the reasons behind each question.

What Is the Type of Website and Who Owns It?

Websites that have a top-level domain name of .gov or .edu belong to the government or to educational institutions. Content from these sites is considered credible and appropriate for research papers.

The owner of a website is usually listed at the bottom of its home page. If you want to find out more, go to the website **whois.net** and enter the domain name of the website in the search box. Whois.net returns the person or organization that owns the domain name unless the owner's name is blocked for privacy. If you don't recognize the owner's name, do a Google search to find out more about the owner.

What Are Others Saying About the Source?

Use Google to search for reviews about the source. For example, to find reviews about the website soyouwanna.com, use this search string in Google:

soyouwanna.com website reviews

To limit the hits to sites other than soyouwanna.com, use this search string:

soyouwanna.com website reviews –site:soyouwanna.com

You can also search for reviews about magazines, books, or journals. Amazon.com is a great place to look for reviews about a book. For example, Figure 4-9 shows a book on the Amazon.com site. From this page, you can read customer reviews, a biography of the author, and some pages in the book.

> **Tip** When you are researching a project in a class, your instructor might prefer you use only your school library's website because the library attempts to use only credible resources.

FIGURE 4-9
Amazon.com presents book reviews written by customers and a biography of the author.

Is the Author of a Work Credible?

You can find information about the author on the web. Ask these questions about the author:

- What are others saying about the author? To find out, enter the name of the author in a Google search box and follow some links.

- Is the author considered an expert on the topic? What are the author's credentials?

- Does the author's name appear with the website? Does the author not want to be associated with the website? If so, suspect the credibility of the work.

- Is contact information about the author published? If not, the author might be trying to avoid confrontation or honest discussion about a topic.

- Do others quote the author in their own works?

Are There Opposing Views?

Many websites take sides on an issue and fail to present opposing views. Ask these questions when considering how the author handles opposing views:

- Is a website presenting only one side of an issue? If so, the site might be biased. A biased site sometimes presents the facts in a slanted way so as to make a point. What are the opposing views?

- Is the site giving opinions without backing these opinions with facts?

- Are there glaring omissions that indicate the author does not want you to consider other facts or opinions?

- Is the site attacking the character of those who disagree with its position? Biased authors tend to do that.

As you search for authoritative content about your topic, be sure to ask yourself if each source you are about to use is credible.

Wikipedia.org Can Lead You to the Experts

Although Wikipedia.org is not an authoritative site, it can lead you to the experts and authoritative sources. Wikipedia.org articles sometimes include sections titled References, Books, and External links. These sections can provide links to authoritative sources.

On Your Own 4-5
Use Wikipedia.org to Locate Authoritative Content

Do the following to use Wikipedia.org to find authoritative sources and content:

Step 1. Return to the Peace Corps article in Wikipedia.org that you bookmarked earlier. Does the article contain sections titled Books or References?

Step 2. Look near the bottom of the article to find a list of **External links**. See Figure 4-10.

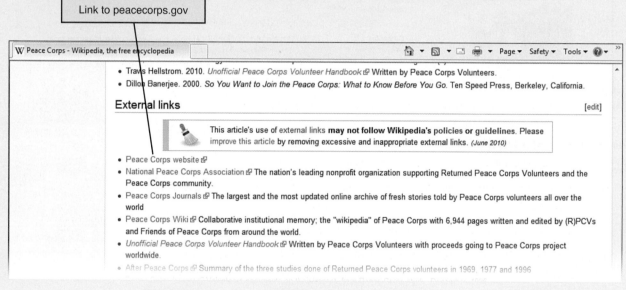

Link to peacecorps.gov

FIGURE 4-10
The External links section of a Wikipedia.org article can lead you to authoritative sources and content.

Step 3. The first item listed in the External links section shown in Figure 4-10 is *Peace Corps website*. Go to **www.peacecorps.gov** and bookmark this site. What does the top-level domain name of .gov tell you about the Peace Corps?

Step 4. Browse the **peacecorps.gov** site to find answers to the following questions. When you find what you need, copy the text into the Requirements page of OneNote and highlight the most important parts of that text:

a. Who is eligible to serve in the Peace Corps? How long is the commitment? What type of jobs might a volunteer perform?

b. How long does the application process take? What all is involved in the application process?

Hint Government websites have a .gov top-level domain name.

 Solutions Appendix

For help, see Solution 4-5: How to Use Wikipedia.org to Locate Authoritative Content.

Step 5. Make sure you have the information in OneNote that you will later need to cite the source in your Works Cited list of your research paper. Information needed for a website includes the title of the website, the URL, and date you accessed the site.

Find Online Newspapers, Blogs, and Other Primary Sources

Blogs can be excellent sources when you are searching for first-hand information about a topic. And newspapers can give excellent insight into how people view an event or activity. Many newspapers offer news websites. These sites often keep records of old newspapers many years back (called *archives*). Newspaper articles sometimes quote people involved in an event, and these quotes can be great primary sources.

When you browse the web for news sites, be sure to verify the news site is reputable. If you are not sure the site is reputable, do a Google search to get reviews of the site. Two websites that are reputable news sites and hold newspaper archives are shown in Figure 4-11.

newspaperarchive.com holds a database of 200 years of historical newspaper articles.

nytimes.com by *The New York Times* archives many old news articles.

FIGURE 4-11
Two examples of websites that can be counted on for reputable newspaper articles.

Suppose you want to find newspaper articles about how Peace Corps volunteers have made a difference in other countries. Do the following:

Step 1. Go to the *New York Times* site at **nytimes.com**. Search for an article about how Peace Corps volunteers have made a difference. What search string did you use that located a good article? Figure 4-12 shows one article that fits the criteria. The article is named *Nigerians Speak Warmly of the Peace Corps*. What is the title of the article you found?

FIGURE 4-12
Newspaper articles can give valuable insight as to how people view an event or activity.

Step 2. Copy a paragraph from the article you found into OneNote. Put the text on the Service page in OneNote. Highlight text in the paragraph that you think is most useful. If you find a quote by someone directly involved, that quote can serve as a primary source.

Step 3. Include on the page in OneNote all the information you need to cite the article later in your Works Cited list. For an online newspaper article, you need the author, article title, newspaper title, date published, URL, and date you accessed the site.

Step 4. Find a blog written by someone in the Peace Corps in the past year. Copy text into the Benefits or Service page of OneNote and make sure you have all the citation information you need.

[?] Solutions Appendix

For help, see Solution 4-6: How to Find Newspaper Articles and Blogs.

As you search the archives of newspaper sites, you might find an article that cannot be viewed unless you pay a fee or subscribe to the site. Perhaps your school library or a public library near you subscribes to the site. Later in the chapter in the section "Use Your School Library's Website," you learn about accessing information paid for by your school.

Find Books Online

Most instructors require you use at least one book for a research source. Recall that some Wikipedia.org articles have a Books section where you can find books about the topic. Google Books (books.google.com) is a powerful tool used to locate books on any topic. The site offers online pages of many books so that you can use content from the book without having to locate the book in a library.

Sometimes Google Books presents a book that appears to be useful for your research, but the pages in the book are not available. In this situation, you can

▶ Search other websites for the book pages online. Amazon.com often includes pages in a book that you can search.

▶ Search the Worldcat.org website, which contains a catalog of almost all the books ever printed. Use it to find a library near you that has the book. Google Books contains links to the Worldcat.org site.

On Your Own 4-7
Find Books Using Wikipedia.org, Google Books, and Worldcat.org

Do the following to use Wikipedia.org, Google Books, and Worldcat.org to find a book:

Step 1. Return to the Wikipedia.org article about the Peace Corps that you book-marked. Look in the **Books** section and find a book written by someone that served in the Peace Corps. Figure 4-13 shows one book, *Living Poor*, by Moritz Thomsen.

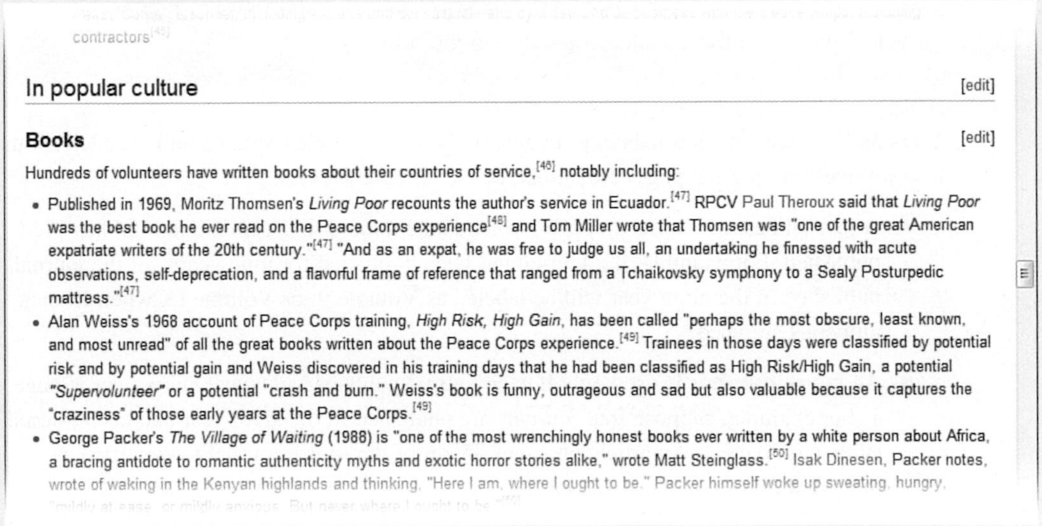

contractors[45]

In popular culture   [edit]

Books   [edit]

Hundreds of volunteers have written books about their countries of service,[46] notably including:

• Published in 1969, Moritz Thomsen's *Living Poor* recounts the author's service in Ecuador.[47] RPCV Paul Theroux said that *Living Poor* was the best book he ever read on the Peace Corps experience[48] and Tom Miller wrote that Thomsen was "one of the great American expatriate writers of the 20th century."[47] "And as an expat, he was free to judge us all, an undertaking he finessed with acute observations, self-deprecation, and a flavorful frame of reference that ranged from a Tchaikovsky symphony to a Sealy Posturpedic mattress."[47]
• Alan Weiss's 1968 account of Peace Corps training, *High Risk, High Gain*, has been called "perhaps the most obscure, least known, and most unread" of all the great books written about the Peace Corps experience.[49] Trainees in those days were classified by potential risk and by potential gain and Weiss discovered in his training days that he had been classified as High Risk/High Gain, a potential *"Supervolunteer"* or a potential "crash and burn." Weiss's book is funny, outrageous and sad but also valuable because it captures the "craziness" of those early years at the Peace Corps.[49]
• George Packer's *The Village of Waiting* (1988) is "one of the most wrenchingly honest books ever written by a white person about Africa, a bracing antidote to romantic authenticity myths and exotic horror stories alike," wrote Matt Steinglass.[50] Isak Dinesen, Packer notes, wrote of waking in the Kenyan highlands and thinking, "Here I am, where I ought to be." Packer himself woke up sweating, hungry,

FIGURE 4-13
The Books section of a Wikipedia.org article can lead you to good books about the topic.

Step 2. Use **Google Books** to search for the book. Copy into OneNote some text from the book that gives a first-hand account of Peace Corps service.

Step 3. Include the citation information for the book in OneNote. Include the author, title, publisher, city of publication, and year of copyright.

Step 4. Use the **Worldcat.org** website to find a library near you that holds the book, *Living Poor,* by Moritz Thomsen. Which library did you find?

 Solutions Appendix

For help, see Solution 4-7: How to Find Books Using Wikipedia.org, Google Books, and Worldcat.org.

Find Scholarly Journal Articles

Google Scholar (scholar.google.com) is a great shortcut for web research. Google Scholar returns hits for scholarly research including books and articles in **scholarly journals**. By clicking these links, you can sometimes find enough scholarly research so that you don't need to go to a library searching for printed books and journals.

> **scholarly journal**—A publication that is published periodically (for example, monthly) and written by experts. The publication is addressed to other experts and professionals. Articles in a scholarly journal are **peer reviewed** and are considered among the best types of sources when doing academic research. An article in a scholarly journal often begins with an **abstract** of the article. Some scholarly journals can be found online.
>
> **peer reviewed**—When people with a similar background and knowledge about a subject read a work and verify the work is accurate. This review by peers happens before the work is published.
>
> **abstract**—An overview of a journal article that can be used to find out what the article covers and the conclusions made in the article.

You can find scholarly journals in print and on the web. A little explanation is needed about how journals and journal pages are numbered (see Figure 4-14):

▶ A journal has a **volume number**, which is the number of years the journal has been published. For example, if a journal has been published for nine years, all the journals published in the ninth year will be labeled as Volume 9, or Volume IX when Roman numerals are used.

▶ An **issue number** is used only if each journal published in a year starts over at page 1. For example, suppose four journals are published in the sixth year and each journal starts with page 1. An article on pages 45–46 of the fourth journal is identified as Volume 6, Issue 4, Pages 45–46.

> **volume number**—The number of years a journal has been published. Roman numerals are sometimes used for volume numbers.
>
> **issue number**—The number assigned a journal when each journal published in a single year restarts at page 1.

▶ If the pages in the journals don't start over at page 1 during the year, no issue number is needed. For example, if an article is found on pages 756–757 in the fourth journal of the sixth year, the article is identified as Volume 6, Pages 756–757. In this case, an issue number is not needed to locate the article.

Volume and Issue numbers

Volume 65 • Issue 4

August 2010 • Volume 65 • Issue 4

FIGURE 4-14
A journal has a volume number and might have an issue number.

Do the following to use Google Scholar to find a journal article about the Peace Corps:

Step 1. Use **Google Scholar** to search on **Peace Corps volunteer benefits**. Locate one journal article about the topic. Copy the abstract of the article into the Benefits page of OneNote.

Step 2. Include in OneNote all information you need to cite the article in the Works Cited list of your research paper. Citation information for a journal article includes the author, title of the article, journal title, volume and issue number, date published, and the pages the article spans or first page if the article jumps pages.

Step 3. Some websites allow you to view the abstract free, but you must pay to see the full article. Can you view the full article without paying a fee?

Sometimes an abstract of an article is all you need. If you need to see the full article, know that your school pays for subscriptions to many journals. Rather than pay for the article yourself, use your school library website to locate and view the article.

On Your Own 4-8
Use Google Scholar to Find a Journal Article

 Solutions Appendix

For help, see Solution 4-8: How to Use Google Scholar to Find a Journal Article.

Hint Content in scholarly journals is likely to be too technical for most research projects. To save time, use only the required minimum of journal articles. A good shortcut is to take most of your research from reliable and authoritative websites.

Use Your School Library's Website

Content that search engines can locate on the web is called the *free web*. The **deep web** includes content on the web that you cannot find by using search engines.

> **deep web**—Content on the web that cannot be found by search engines. Most content on the web is in the deep web and includes content that can be accessed only when you pay for the service.

Your school pays for subscriptions to many **databases** that hold scholarly research and makes that research available to you through the school library website. The school provides access to this data to students, faculty, and other patrons.

> **database**—A collection of data about a topic that is organized so the data can be searched and retrieved quickly.

As a student, you are assigned a user ID and password that you can use to access the school library website. If the library has paid for access to databases, they are available to you after you have logged in.

On Your Own 4-9
Explore Your School Library's Website

When you become a student at a school or university, you are assigned a user ID and password that you can use to access the library's website.

> **Not Working?** If you are not a student, you can apply for a library card at a public library in your area. This card gives you a user ID and password that you can use to access the public library's website and its holdings.

? Solutions Appendix

For help, see Solution 4-9: How to Explore Your School Library's Website.

Do the following to use your school library website:

Step 1. Log on to your school's website using the user ID and password assigned by your school. If you are not sure of the website or your login information, ask your instructor.

Step 2. Explore the online databases that your library provides. Try to find the journal article you found using Google Scholar earlier in the chapter. Can you find the article? Can you view the full text of the article?

Step 3. Some journal databases give you the citation information for an article. If you can find the article, does the website give you this citation information already prepared for a Works Cited list? If so, copy this information into OneNote on the same page as the article abstract.

Table 4-2 lists several websites that provide excellent content for research on various topics. Some of these sites hold content that is not free. You might be able to access this content through your school library's website. Follow links on your school library's site that will take you to the other sites. When you arrive at the other site, you will have access to the content your school has subscribed to.

TABLE 4-2   Websites That Hold Specialized Databases Useful for Research

Website	Description
www.eric.ed.gov	The Education Resources Information Center (ERIC) database, owned by the Department of Education, contains scholarly articles about education.
www.apa.org/pubs/databases	American Psychological Association (APA) databases are about behavioral sciences.
www.nlm.nih.gov	Several databases, including the popular PubMed/MEDLINE database, are owned by the U.S. National Library of Medicine (NLM) and are about medicine and health care.
www.oyez.org	The Oyez database, owned by the Oyez Project, is about the U.S. Supreme Court and its work.
www.fedstats.gov	This federal website contains statistics from more than 100 federal agencies.
www.government-records.com	This site is a large database of public records.
www.usa.gov	This site provides general government data and statistics.
www.bls.gov	U.S. Bureau of Labor Statistics (BLS) provides economic data, tools, and calculators.
www.bls.gov/bls/other.htm	This BLS webpage lists links to websites of international statistical agencies.
infomine.ucr.edu	INFOMINE, owned by the Regents of the University of California, contains scholarly research on a variety of topics.
www.ipl2.org	Internet Public Library (IPL), a public service site hosted by Drexel University and other colleges and universities, holds works on many topics. A chat service is manned by volunteers.
www.worldcat.org	WorldCat is the world's largest library catalog; use it to find almost any library holdings on the planet.

Not Working? If you are not able to access one of these sites using a school computer lab, your school might have blocked the website.

Phases 3 and 4: Evaluating Your Research and Organizing Your Research Notes

Before you consider your research complete, verify you have found all your required sources and perhaps a few extra. It is always better to have extra research than not to have enough research. After you have found the required sources, you are ready for the third and fourth phases of research.

Evaluate Your Research by Asking Important Questions

The third phase of research is to pause and ask yourself these questions:

- ▶ What have I learned from my research?
- ▶ Where is my research taking me?
- ▶ What are my lingering questions?
- ▶ Will my research satisfy my reader?

As you consider these questions, you might want to change your outline for your research paper. Or you might find that you need to do additional research on one subtopic. Perhaps you have discovered a new direction that you want to explore and you still have questions unanswered. Keep researching until your questions are answered and you believe your research will satisfy your reader.

After your research is finished, take time to organize your research notes before you start writing your research paper.

Use OneNote to Organize Your Notes

Organizing research notes in OneNote is easy. Using OneNote, you can move content from one page to another, and you can move, rename, and delete pages.

Your instructor might require a digital version of your research notes. If your instructor has OneNote installed on her computer, you can give her the .one file. Recall that an .one file contains one section of a OneNote notebook. Your instructor can double-click the file to open it.

Your instructor in another class might not have OneNote. In this case, you can **export** the data from OneNote to an .mht file containing all the pages in a section. Recall from Chapter 2, "Finding and Using Information on the Web," that an .mht file is a web page file that can be viewed in Internet Explorer.

> **export**—To copy data used by a program such as OneNote into a file format that can be used by another program, such as Internet Explorer.

Do the following to organize, print, and export your research in OneNote:

Step 1. Make sure your outline in OneNote is complete and organized. This outline will guide you when you are writing your research paper. Add several lines to your outline based on your research about the Peace Corps in this chapter.

Step 2. Practice copying or moving a note container from one page to another page in OneNote.

 Video **4-10**

> **Hint** OneNote stores all notes in note containers. Click a container to select it. Right-click a container to see a shortcut menu to copy, cut, paste, or delete the container.

Step 3. If you have access to a printer, print the entire Peace Corps section of your OneNote notebook.

> **Hint** To print a section in OneNote, click the **File** tab and use the **Print** command in the Backstage view. Be sure to print the entire section.

Step 4. Create an .mht file containing all the pages in the Peace Corps section of your OneNote notebook.

? Solutions Appendix

For help, see Solution 4-10: How to Organize, Print, and Export Your Research in OneNote.

> **Hint** To create an .mht file with OneNote, select the **File** tab, click **Save As**, and then click **Section**. In the Select Format area, click **Single File Web Page (*.mht)**.

Summary

Preparing to Take Research Notes and Selecting Your Research Topic

▶ The four phases of research are to (1) explore general information about the topic, (2) go deeper to find the best works, (3) evaluate where the research is going and ask penetrating questions, and (4) organize the research notes.

▶ OneNote is a Microsoft Office application designed to hold and organize notes including content taken from the web. OneNote keeps notes in notebooks, sections, and pages.

▶ Create a section in a OneNote notebook for each research topic. Keep each subtopic on its own page in the section.

Phase 1: Finding General Information and Subtopics About the Topic

▶ Wikipedia.org is a great place to start to find general information about a topic.

▶ A clustering search engine can help you find subtopics about a topic.

▶ A Google Timeline can help you find historical and current information and show you trends over time about a topic.

Phase 2: Finding Authoritative and Scholarly Research

▶ Each source you use to write a research paper must be cited in the paper. The citation includes enough information for someone to locate the work.

▶ When you are deciding whether content is credible, ask these questions: What is the type of website and who owns it? What are others saying about the source? Is the author of a work credible? Are there opposing views?

▶ Although Wikipedia.org is not considered an authoritative source, a Wikipedia article can lead you to authoritative information and sources.

▶ The government uses the .gov top-level domain name and educational institutions use the .edu top-level domain name. These sources are generally considered to be authoritative and credible.

▶ The OneNote Screen Clipping tool is used to copy graphics into OneNote.

▶ Newspapers can give insights into how people view an event or activity. Blogs can be excellent primary sources if written by people directly involved in an event or activity.

▶ Wikipedia.org, Google Books, Amazon.com, and Worldcat.org are useful websites when searching for books.

▶ A peer-reviewed scholarly journal is one of the best sources for authoritative research. Abstracts of journal articles can be found online free.

▶ Your school library subscribes to many databases containing scholarly research. You can access this information through your school library's website.

Phases 3 and 4: Evaluating Your Research and Organizing Your Research Notes

▶ Before your research is done, evaluate where your research is going and ask yourself if you have unanswered questions or if your reader might have unanswered questions.

▶ Use OneNote to organize research by building an outline and making sure all research notes are placed on the right pages of OneNote according to the subtopics being researched.

Review Questions

Answer these questions to assess your skills and knowledge of the content covered in the chapter. Your instructor can provide you with the correct answers when you are ready to check your work.

1. What is the most important skill you need to know when learning to use computers?

2. What are the four phases of research?

3. Why is OneNote a good application to use when taking research notes? Give two reasons.

4. How does OneNote store a notebook, in a file or in a folder?

5. If a research topic is kept in a section of a OneNote notebook, where should each subtopic be kept?

6. How can a clustering search engine such as carrot2.org help you research a topic?

7. Why is Wikipedia.org not considered an authoritative source on a research topic?

8. What tool on the Google site is useful when you need a historical perspective about a topic?

9. What are three names for the page(s) in a research paper that lists the sources used in the paper?

10. Which is the best choice to find a primary source about the 2010 gulf oil spill: a blog or Wikipedia.org?

11. Which website can help you find a library near you that holds a book you need?

12. What is the advantage of a peer review of a journal article?

13. What is an overview of a journal article called?

14. If a journal has printed on its front Volume 8, Issue 3, how many years has the journal been published?

15. If you have answered all your questions about a topic during your research, what one last question should you ask before your research is done?

Chapter Mastery Project

Find out how well you have mastered the content in this chapter by completing this project. If you can answer all the questions and do all the steps without looking back at the chapter details, you have mastered the chapter.

If you find you need a lot of help doing the project and you have not yet read the chapter or done the activities, drop back and start at the beginning of the chapter and then return to this project.

> **Hint** All the key terms in the chapter are used in this mastery project. If you encounter a word you don't know such as *primary source,* enter **define:primary source** in the Internet Explorer search box. The word is defined in the chapter, but it's more fun to find the definition on the web.

Mastery Project Part 1: Preparing to Take Research Notes and Selecting Your Research Topic

If you need help completing this part of the mastery project, please review the "Preparing to Take Research Notes and Selecting Your Research Topic" section in the chapter.

Suppose your instructor gives you this research and reporting assignment:

> *Find out about mentoring. What are some best practices when being mentored or being a mentor? What should a mentee know and practice to get the most out of the experience? What are the benefits of mentoring? Put your research in writing and be sure to include your sources.*

Answer the following questions about researching:

1. In which of the first two phases of research is it acceptable to use content taken from Wikipedia.org? In which of the first two phases is it not acceptable to use Wikipedia content? Explain your answer.

2. As you use the web to search for ideas for a research topic, you might stumble onto a paper mill site. What is the purpose of a paper mill site and why are papers sold on these sites considered plagiarism?

To prepare to research this topic, do the following to create a notebook in OneNote and set it up for research:

Step 1. Open **OneNote**. If you have not already created a notebook named **MyResearch**, do so now. Save the notebook to your USB flash drive, hard drive, SkyDrive, or other location given by your instructor.

Step 2. Create a new section in the notebook named **Mentoring**. Create four pages in this section named **Outline**, **Mentee Tips**, **Mentoring Benefits**, and **Best Practices**.

Step 3. Create the following outline on the **Outline** page of OneNote:

Outline:

- Tips to maximize being mentored
- Benefits of being a mentor
- Best practices of mentoring

Mastery Project Part 2: Phase 1: Finding General Information and Subtopics About the Topic

If you need help completing this part of the mastery project, please review the "Phase 1: Finding General Information and Subtopics About the Topic" section in the chapter.

Follow these steps to find general information and subtopics about mentoring:

Step 1. Find three topics that Google autosuggest offers that might be considered additional subtopics to the mentoring topic.

Step 2. Find two topics that Google Something Different offers that might broaden the mentoring topic.

Step 3. Create a search string in Google that searches for information about mentoring and limits the search to the Wikipedia.org site. What search string did you use?

Step 4. Find a good Wikipedia article about mentoring. Bookmark the article in Internet Explorer Favorites. Copy one paragraph of the article into the Outline page of the Mentoring section of OneNote. In OneNote, use the highlighting tool to highlight an important sentence in this paragraph.

Step 5. Does the Wikipedia article have an outline? If so, what ideas for subtopics to mentoring does the outline offer?

Step 6. Use a clustering search engine such as **carrot2.org** to find subtopics and general information about mentoring.

Step 7. Display in your browser a Google Timeline about mentoring. Based on the timeline, is interest in mentoring increasing or decreasing? Click some links to find the latest news about mentoring. Find another link that describes what mentoring might have looked like in the 1700s.

Mastery Project Part 3: Phase 2: Finding Authoritative and Scholarly Research

If you need help completing this part of the mastery project, please review the "Phase 2: Finding Authoritative and Scholarly Research" section in the chapter.

As you search for authoritative and scholarly research, keep in mind you must keep a record of each source you plan to use in your research paper so that you can build a Works Cited list at the end of your paper. Follow these steps to find authoritative content:

Step 1. Return to the Wikipedia article on mentoring that you bookmarked earlier or find another Wikipedia article about mentoring. Look in the **External links** section of the article and search for a website that list tips for the mentee. Bookmark the website.

Step 2. Copy the tips into the Mentee Tips page of OneNote. In OneNote, highlight important text. Include in OneNote the information you need for the Works Cited list.

Step 3. To decide whether the website you used in Step 2 is credible, answer these questions about the site:

   a. What is the top-level domain name of the site?

   b. Who owns the website?

   c. Does the website list an author? If so, who is the author? What are others saying about this author?

   d. Try to find a review about this website on another site. What search string did you use to search for this review?

Step 4. Find a newspaper or magazine article online about the benefits of mentoring. Copy text in the article into the Mentoring Benefits page of OneNote. Highlight text in OneNote that you think is important. Include on the page in OneNote all the information you need to cite the article later in your Works Cited list. See Table 4-1 for a list of citation information.

Step 5. To make sure you have a primary source in your research, find a blog written by a mentee or a mentor about her mentoring experiences. Copy the text into the Mentoring Benefits page of OneNote. Highlight important text and include the information you will later need to cite the source.

Step 6. Using Google Books, find a book about best practices in a mentoring relationship. View the pages of the book. Find one paragraph that describes a best practice. Copy the paragraph into the Best Practices page of OneNote. Highlight an important sentence in the paragraph. Include the citation information for the book in OneNote. See Table 4-1 for a list of citation information.

Step 7. Use Worldcat.org to find a library near you that has the book. What library did you find?

Step 8. Use Google Scholar to find a peer-reviewed article in a scholarly journal about any subtopic on mentoring. Copy the abstract of the article into the appropriate page of OneNote.

Step 9. Include in OneNote all information you need to cite the article in the Works Cited list of your research paper. See Table 4-1 for a list of citation information.

Step 10. Can you read the full text of the article? Some websites provide the article abstract free and charge a fee to read the full article.

Do the following to use your school library website to search the deep web for scholarly works about mentoring:

Step 1. What is the URL of your school's website? Sign on to the site using your school user ID and password. Explore the online databases provided by your library. List two or three databases provided by your library.

Step 2. Try to find the journal article about mentoring that you found using Google Scholar. Does the library site provide the article? Can you read the full text of the article?

Step 3. Does the site give you the citation information for the article? If so, copy the citation information into OneNote on the same page as the article abstract.

Mastery Project Part 4: Phases 3 and 4: Evaluating Your Research and Organizing Your Research Notes

If you need help completing this part of the mastery project, please review the "Phases 3 and 4: Evaluating Your Research and Organizing Your Research Notes" section in the chapter.

Answer the following questions:

1. What four questions should a researcher ask that indicate the research is compete?

2. What is the final phase of research that should happen before you start writing?

Follow these steps to use OneNote to organize, print, and export your research:

Step 1. On the Outline page of OneNote, expand your outline so that it better reflects what you have learned from your research about mentoring.

Step 2. If you have access to a printer, print the **Mentoring** section of your OneNote notebook.

Step 3. Create an .mht file of your research about mentoring. View the file using Internet Explorer.

Becoming an Independent Learner

Answer the following questions about becoming an independent learner:

1. To teach yourself to research using the web, do you think it is best to rely on the chapter or on the web when you need answers?

2. To teach yourself to use OneNote, do you think it's best to rely on the chapter or on the OneNote Help feature?

3. The most important skill learned in this chapter is how to teach yourself a computer skill. Rate yourself at Level A through E on how well you are doing with this skill. What is your level?

   ○ Level A: I was able to successfully complete the Chapter Mastery Project without the help of doing the On Your Own activities in the chapter.

   ○ Level B: I completed all the On Your Own activities and the Chapter Mastery Project without referring to any of the solutions in the *Solutions Appendix*.

   ○ Level C: I completed all the On Your Own activities and the Chapter Mastery Project by using just a few of the solutions in the *Solutions Appendix*.

   ○ Level D: I completed all the On Your Own activities and the Chapter Mastery Project by using many of the solutions in the *Solutions Appendix*.

   ○ Level E: I completed all the On Your Own activities and the Chapter Mastery Project and had to use all of the solutions in the *Solutions Appendix*.

To continue toward the goal of teaching yourself computer skills, if you are not at Level A, try to move up one level on how you learn in Chapter 5.

Projects to Help You

Now that you have mastered the material in this chapter, you are ready to tackle the three projects introduced at the beginning of the chapter in the section, "How Will This Chapter Help Me?"

Project 1: Research in Your Personal Life

Using the web for research can apply to many areas of your life. Suppose, for example, you or a close family member is considering adopting a child. You might have these questions:

▶ Is it best to do a domestic adoption or an international adoption? What are the pros and cons of each? What countries offer children for adoption and which countries are the best to use?

▶ How long will an adoption take and about how much will it cost?

▶ What emotional or social problems might an adopted child have later in life and what can the adoptive parents do to help overcome these problems?

Using the web, research answers to these questions and other questions that might arise during your research. Save your research in your **MyResearch** notebook in OneNote. Create a new section for the research, naming the section **Adoption**. Include these sources:

▶ One or more websites that give credible content

▶ One or more books

▶ One or more scholarly journal articles

▶ One or more newspapers, reputable news websites, or blogs

Include in OneNote all the citation information you need to prepare a Works Cited list for a research paper.

PERSONAL PROJECT: My brother and his wife are considering adopting a child. They've asked me to help them research domestic and international adoptions and find a good book on the topic. They want to know what problems an adopted child might have later in life. I need to use the web to do this research.

ACADEMIC PROJECT: I'm majoring in law enforcement and my English Composition teacher has assigned a research paper. My law enforcement advisor has suggested I write the paper on INTERPOL. I have to find websites, books, journal articles, and newspaper articles about INTERPOL. Can I do all that research on the web?

Project 2: Research in Your Academic Career

You can rely heavily on the web for the research you will do during your academic career. Suppose, for example, you are majoring in law enforcement and you need to understand the functions of INTERPOL, not the rock band, but the International Criminal Police Organization. You might have these questions:

▶ What is the INTERPOL organization? When and why was it formed, and who manages and regulates it?

▶ What does INTERPOL do? In what areas does it assist local, state, federal, and foreign law enforcement agencies?

▶ What are the limitations and constraints of INTERPOL?

Using the web, research answers to these questions and other questions that might arise during your research. Save your research in your **MyResearch** notebook in OneNote. Create a new section for the research, naming the section **INTERPOL**. Include these sources:

▶ One or more websites that give credible content

▶ One or more books

▶ One or more scholarly journal articles

▶ One or more newspapers, reputable news websites, or blogs

Include in OneNote all the citation information you need to prepare a Works Cited list for a research paper.

Project 3: Research in Your Technical Career

When preparing for a career in computer technologies, recognize that employers are looking for three general qualifications: degrees, certifications, and experience. Certifications in Information Technology (IT) are provided by several organizations. Three major organizations that offer IT certifications are Microsoft, CompTIA, and Cisco.

TECHNICAL CAREER PROJECT: I want a job in IT, and I've noticed that job postings are asking for IT certifications. What are these certifications, when do I need them, and who offers them? What are people saying about which certifications are the best to have? How can I find all these answers on the web?

Use the web to answer these questions about IT certifications offered by Microsoft, CompTIA, and Cisco:

▶ How valuable are certifications in the IT industry?

▶ What are two entry-level certifications offered by Microsoft that a person might need when supporting Windows 7 and Microsoft Office applications at a small business?

▶ What is the most popular CompTIA certification? Describe what the certification covers and what types of IT jobs might require this certification.

▶ What types of certifications does Cisco offer? What is the entry-level certification offered by Cisco? What types of IT jobs might require Cisco certifications?

▶ If someone is planning a career in IT and wants to start out as a desktop support technician, what are the two most important certifications you would recommend?

Using the web, research answers to these questions and other questions that might arise during your research. Save your research in your **MyResearch** notebook in OneNote. Create a new section for the research, naming the section **IT Certifications**. Include these sources found on the web:

▶ One or more websites that give credible content

▶ One or more books

▶ One or more magazine articles

▶ One or more newspapers, reputable news websites, or blogs

Include in OneNote all the citation information you need to prepare a Works Cited list for a research paper.

Project to Help Others

One of the best ways to learn is to teach someone else. And, in teaching someone else, you are making a contribution into that person's life. As part of each chapter's work, you are encouraged to teach someone a skill you have learned. In this case, you help your apprentice research a topic using the web.

Who is your apprentice? _____

Working with your apprentice, do the following:

Step 1. Ask your apprentice what topic interests him that he would like to know more about. If he does not have a research topic, suggest one. What is the research topic?

Step 2. Show your apprentice how to set up a new OneNote notebook for his research and create a section for the research topic.

Step 3. Coach your apprentice to use Google autosuggest, Google Something Different, and a Google Timeline to learn about the topic. Encourage your apprentice to find links to the topic and to bookmark these links.

Step 4. Find one website such as Wikipedia.org that gives general information about the topic. Show your apprentice how to copy content into OneNote from this website.

Step 5. Watch and coach as your apprentice continues his research on the topic to find authoritative and credible sources. Be sure to point out how to use Google Books to view pages in a book and to use Google search strings to find blogs, newspaper articles, and magazine articles about the topic.

Step 6. Help your apprentice decide whether each source is credible.

Step 7. Ask your apprentice if he is satisfied with the research. What lingering questions does he still have? Help him find answers to these questions.

CHAPTER 5

Writing Papers Using Microsoft Word Templates and Tools

IN THIS CHAPTER, YOU WILL

Prepare to write a paper

Type and format the paper

Create the Works Cited page

Proof and revise the paper

In Chapter 4, you learned to use the web for research. After the research is done, you might be required to report that research in a paper. Microsoft Word has many tools to help you when writing a paper. In this chapter, you learn to use these tools to organize and format your paper.

When learning to use any application such as Microsoft Word, realize you will always be learning something new. It is impossible to cover all the features of Word in this book, and Microsoft occasionally updates Microsoft Office applications. For both reasons, you need to know how to teach yourself to use an application. Therefore, this chapter is designed to help you teach yourself about using Word. Try to do each On Your Own activity without any help. But remember, if you need help, you can always refer to the *Solutions Appendix*.

JUMP RIGHT IN

If you want even more of a challenge, try proceeding directly to the Chapter Mastery Project at the end of this chapter. If you need help on the project, refer to the On Your Own activities in the chapter or do your own independent investigating by searching the Word Help feature or the web. When you complete the project, you will have mastered the skills in this chapter. Then proceed to the other projects that require you to apply your skills to new situations.

How Will This Chapter Help Me?

Each chapter provides three projects focusing on personal, academic, or technical career goals. Depending on your own interests, you might choose to perform any or all of these projects to help you achieve your goals.

PERSONAL PROJECT: I want to convince my friends they need to protect their privacy when using social networking sites like Facebook. If I put everything in writing, I think my paper might persuade them.

ACADEMIC PROJECT: My English teacher has asked me to help her grade research papers presented to her as Word documents. She wants me to make sure MLA guidelines are followed.

TECHNICAL CAREER PROJECT: I'm planning my career in IT. I've read that getting a certification in IT might help me land a great part-time job while I work toward a degree. I need to document what I've found.

Preparing to Write Your Paper

In your academic or professional career, you might be called on to write a paper. Examples of the types of papers you might write are

- **A research paper to report your findings about a topic.** A research paper starts with an introduction to the topic, includes research findings, and ends with the author's conclusions regarding the research. All the sources used to write the paper are listed at the end of the paper.

- **A white paper to educate readers about an issue, product, service, or solution to a problem.** White papers are sometimes written by manufacturers to introduce a new product or by the government to announce a new government policy. A white paper always begins with an abstract, which summarizes the entire paper. Sources might be included to help readers learn more.

- **A Request for Proposals (RFP) to invite individuals or companies to respond to a need.** A large corporation or the government might release an RFP because it wants to contract with someone to provide a service or product. Individuals and organizations respond with proposals describing their offering.

- **A proposal to offer a service or product.** Sales and marketing departments within a large corporation might write a proposal to present to a future customer. If the proposal is in response to an RFP, it must contain all the information requested in the RFP. An individual might submit a proposal to a customer to perform a job such as lawn maintenance or roof repair.

- **A business plan to define business goals.** Banks and other investors often require a business plan before they will consider investing in a new or growing business.

> **Tip** When writing papers, know that Microsoft Word includes templates for many types of papers (see Figure 5-1). Try using one of Word's templates to help you structure and format the paper. If you can't find a Word template, search the web for good examples of the type of paper you are writing and copy the general structure and style of the paper.

In this chapter, we focus on creating a research paper. But know that the skills you learn in the chapter can be applied to all the types of papers listed.

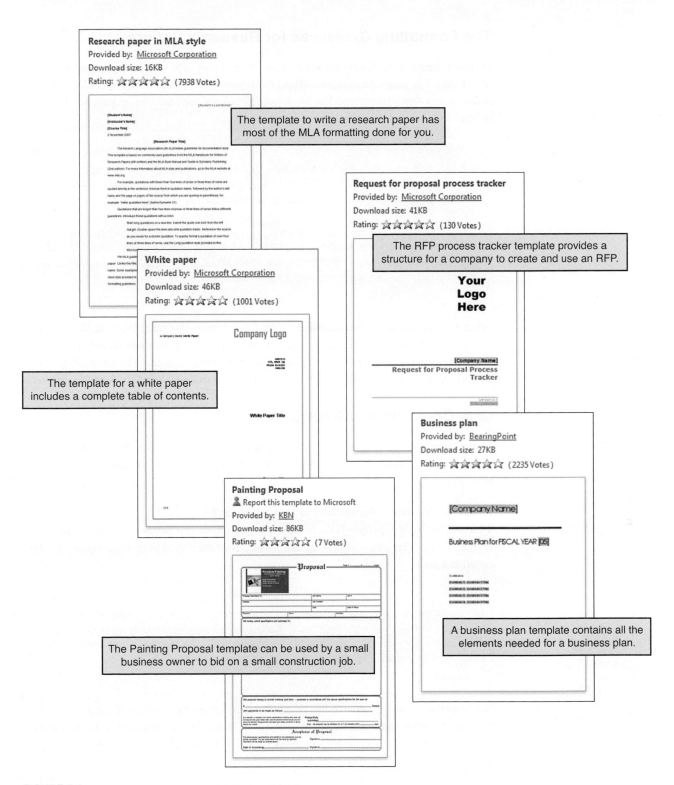

FIGURE 5-1
Templates offered by Word can be great writing shortcuts.

The Formatting Guidelines for Research Papers

Several formatting guidelines are used for research papers. The two most popular are the Modern Language Association (MLA) guidelines and the American Psychological Association (APA) guidelines. The **MLA guidelines** are used for literary papers. The **APA guidelines** are used for scientific or technical papers.

> **MLA guidelines**—The rules for formatting a research paper developed by the Modern Language Association (MLA). The MLA guidelines, also called the MLA style, are used primarily in literary, philosophy, and history papers. See www.mla.org for details.
>
> **APA guidelines**—The rules for formatting a research paper developed by the American Psychological Association (APA). The APA guidelines, also called the APA style, are used primarily in social science, education, political science, technical, and scientific papers. See www.apastyle.org for details.

> **Tip** When writing a paper for another class, know that the instructor for that class might require formatting that varies from the MLA guidelines covered in this chapter. Always follow the guidelines given by your instructor.

When you are writing a research paper for an English composition class, most likely your instructor will require the MLA guidelines. In this chapter, we use these guidelines. The MLA guidelines include rules for page margins, paragraph formatting, heading information, a Works Cited page, and many more formatting details that you learn about in this chapter.

Give Credit Where Credit Is Due

As you learn to write papers, keep in mind you must avoid plagiarism. Recognize another author owns the copyright to his works. When you use another's work, always give that person credit.

When Do You Need Permission to Use a Source?

To avoid breaking copyright laws, never copy, publish, or sell another person's work without first getting permission from that person. However, there is an exception to this law called **fair use**.

> **fair use**—When using another person's work in your own work is considered fair and not a violation of copyright laws. According to the copyright laws posted at www.copyright.gov, fair use includes "reproduction by a teacher or student of a small part of a work to illustrate a lesson."

Fair use includes using a source in a research paper written by a student if you only present that paper to your instructor and do not publish it. In this limited situation, you don't need to ask permission from an author to use his works. You are still required, however, to give the author credit for his work.

When and How to Document a Source

If you use information from a website, journal, book, or other source in your paper, you must document the source in two ways:

▶ **In a citation.** Include a citation following the sentence or paragraph in your paper where you use information from the source. A **citation** is enclosed in parentheses and includes enough information that the reader can identify the source in the Works Cited list. You learn to create citations later in the chapter in the section "Typing and Formatting the Paper."

▶ **On the Works Cited page.** The Works Cited page gives enough details about your sources so the reader can locate a source. You build a Works Cited list later in the chapter in the section "Creating the Works Cited Page."

citation—Brief text inside parentheses within the body of a research paper that gives credit to another source. If the source uses page numbering, include the page or pages where you found the information. Also called *parenthetical documentation*.

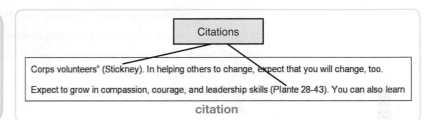

Citations

Corps volunteers" (Stickney). In helping others to change, expect that you will change, too.

Expect to grow in compassion, courage, and leadership skills (Plante 28-43). You can also learn

citation

Document all sources even if you don't use a direct quotation from a source.

How to Handle Direct Quotations

Your paper can include a small amount of **direct quotations**, but don't overdo them.

direct quotation—A repetition of someone's exact words. In research papers, always give credit to a person you quote.

A research paper can handle direct quotations in two ways (see Figure 5-2):

▶ A quotation that is four or fewer lines is written in the text inside quotation marks.

▶ A quotation five lines or more starts on a new line and is indented one inch from the left margin.

Always include where the quotation came from by putting a citation at the end of the sentence. Figure 5-2 shows a short and long quotation. The first quotation was taken from a website and the second from a book.

expenses are also covered by the Corps. To find out more about what it is like to serve in Peace Corps, search the Web for blogs written by Peace Corps volunteers.[1]

So why join the Peace Corps? Volunteer because you want to make a contribution and help others change for the better. Entire nations can change. For example, a Nigerian newspaper publisher, Bukar Zarma, said, "Most of Nigeria's leaders today were taught by Peace Corps volunteers" (Strickney). In helping others to change, expect that you will change, too. Expect to grow in compassion, courage, and leadership skills (Plante 28-43). You can also learn the language and culture of another country. When you come home, you are likely to find these global skills to be in demand by corporations that do business in a global community.

> A short quotation is written in the text inside quotation marks.

> The citation for a short quotation follows the quotation and is placed before the last punctuation mark.

> A long quotation is set in its own indented paragraph.

During your first three months in the Peace Corps, you are immersed in cultural training and might receive intense training to learn the language of your host country. Moritz Thomsen had this to say about his three months of training:

> Peace Corps training is like no other training in the world, having something in common with college life, officer's training, Marine basic training, and a ninety-day jail sentence. What makes it paradoxical is that everything is voluntary; the schedule exists for you to follow if you wish....Our schedule began at 5:45 each morning and lasted until 9:30 at night. After that, if we so desired, our Spanish instructors were available to work with us. (Thomsen 4)

> The citation for a long quotation follows the last punctuation mark in the quotation.

FIGURE 5-2
A direct quotation can be in line with the text or set off as an indented paragraph.

Tip Many schools use websites such as www.turnitin.com to scan research papers for copied works that are not cited.

Learn to Paraphrase Text

As a writer, you need to learn to **paraphrase**. By writing information in your own words, you avoid too many direct quotations in your papers.

paraphrase—To rewrite text written by another in your own words.

Here are some steps you can follow to learn to paraphrase:

Step 1. Carefully read the text written by another.

Step 2. Cover up the source so you cannot see the text.

Step 3. Write the information in your own words without peeking at the source.

Step 4. After you finish writing in your own words, look back at the source to verify you have all the facts correct.

Tip Even though you might not use a direct quotation, you still need to cite the source you used for your paraphrased text.

Use Research Notes Taken in OneNote

In this chapter, we organize and format a research paper about the Peace Corps using the research notes from Chapter 4, "Using the Web for Research." The completed paper is shown in Figure 5-3.

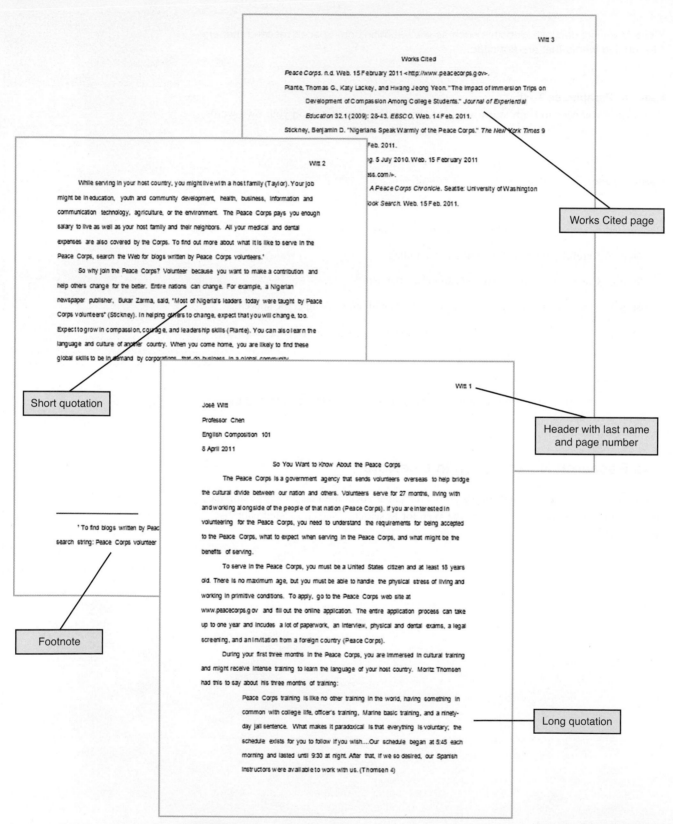

FIGURE 5-3

The completed paper on the Peace Corps includes short and long quotations, a header, a footnote, and a Works Cited page.

Normally, you would open your own OneNote notebook, but to make things easier in this chapter, we provided a notebook with research notes in the Ch05_MyResearch subfolder in the Sample Files folder on the DVD in the back of this book.

Using the DVD in the back of the book, double-click the **Peace Corps** file in the CH05_ MyResearch folder. The OneNote notebook opens with the Peace Corps section selected. To save you typing time, we created the text for the research paper for you. You can find the text on the Text for Research Paper page, as shown in Figure 5-4.

On Your Own 5-1

Open the OneNote Notebook to View Research Notes

▶ Video **5-1**

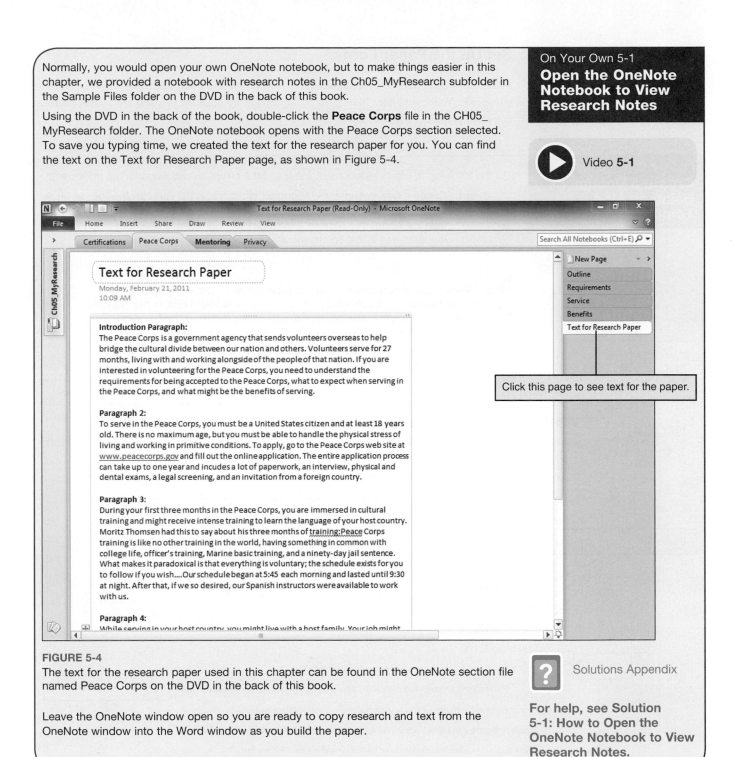

Click this page to see text for the paper.

FIGURE 5-4

The text for the research paper used in this chapter can be found in the OneNote section file named Peace Corps on the DVD in the back of this book.

Leave the OneNote window open so you are ready to copy research and text from the OneNote window into the Word window as you build the paper.

? Solutions Appendix

For help, see Solution 5-1: How to Open the OneNote Notebook to View Research Notes.

Note Normally, you create text for a research paper by paraphrasing the research you have put in OneNote. The details of this creative writing stage of making a research paper are not covered in this chapter.

Set Up the Paper Format

Microsoft Word offers several templates for research papers using either the MLA or APA guidelines. These templates have most of the formatting done for you and are a great short-cut when preparing a research paper.

On Your Own 5-2
Create a Document Using an MLA Template

Do the following to create a document using an MLA template and examine the document:

Step 1. Create a new document in Microsoft Word, using the **Research paper in MLA style** template. Under **Office.com Templates**, look in the **Reports** group and then the **Academic papers and reports** group. Identify on your screen the items labeled in the document shown in Figure 5-5.

Not Working? If you cannot find the MLA research paper template in the Office.com templates, a substitute document is available. Look in the Sample Files folder on the DVD in the back of the book for the Word document named MLA_Research_Paper. Double-click the file to open it in Word.

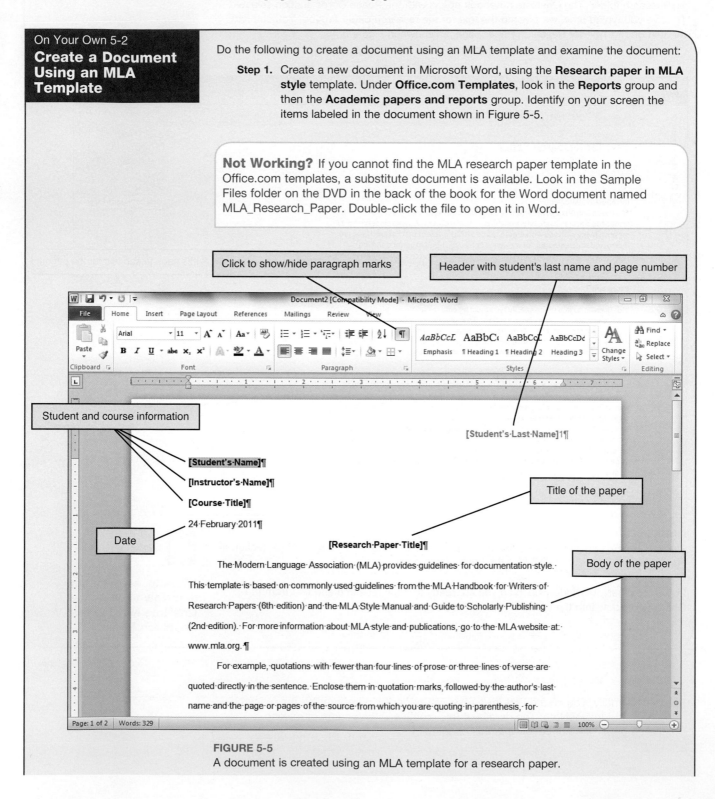

FIGURE 5-5
A document is created using an MLA template for a research paper.

On Your Own 5-2
Create a Document Using an MLA Template

Tip When to use a hard return is important in MLA guidelines. Displaying the paragraph marks as you edit the document can help you get the hard returns right.

MLA guidelines require specific formatting for the paper, and much of this formatting has been done for you using custom-made styles and other Word settings applied to the template. If you were not using the template, you would have to manually make these settings. MLA requirements for formatting already done in the template include

▶ A **header** that contains the student's last name and page number. Put one space between the name and the page number. Right-align the header.

Tip Recall that a style in Word is a predetermined set of formatting that has been assigned a name and can be applied to text.

header—The area at the top of a page in a Word document. Text inserted in the header repeats on every page in the document.

▶ The header, student and course information, date, and title of the paper must be double-spaced with no bold, italics, quotation marks, or underlining.

▶ Left-align the student and course information and the date. Center the title.

▶ The current date is required below the course title. The Date & Time command on the Insert ribbon has been used in the template. It is set to automatically update whenever you open the document.

▶ Page margins are 1 inch on the top, left, bottom, and right sides of the page.

▶ Custom styles have been created for all elements in the paper and set for MLA guidelines. For example, the *Research paper contents* style can be used to format a paragraph in the body of the paper. The style is set for a paragraph to be aligned left, double-spaced, and no extra spacing before or after the paragraph. The first line of the paragraph is indented 0.5 inches.

Step 2. Use the Styles box to view the custom-made styles. Verify the first paragraph has the **Research paper contents** style applied. Verify this style uses the MLA guidelines for paragraph formatting.

Hint To view the Styles box, click the down arrow under Change Styles on the Home ribbon. To apply a style, select the text and then click the style in the Styles box. To view or modify a style, right-click it and select **Modify** from the shortcut menu.

? Solutions Appendix

Step 3. Save the document to your USB flash drive, hard drive, SkyDrive, or other location given by your instructor. Name the document **PeaceCorpsPaper**.

As you work on your paper, don't forget to save often.

For help, see Solution 5-2: How to Create a Document Using an MLA Template.

Now that you have your research notes ready and your research paper document prepared, you are ready to start writing your paper.

Typing and Formatting the Paper

Tip The Word template we are using already has page numbers inserted. However, if you need to insert page numbers in a document, click the **Insert** tab and click **Page Number**.

A research paper using the MLA guidelines begins with a header, student and course information, and title of the paper, as shown in Figure 5-6. Your date will be different from the one shown in the figure.

Use one space in the header following the last name.

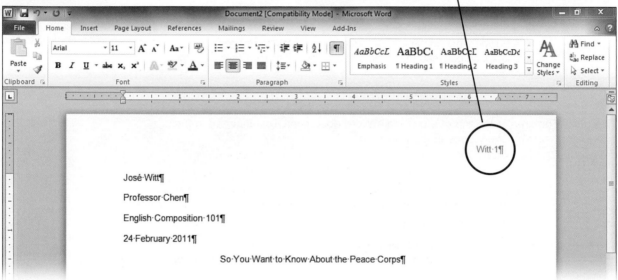

Witt·1¶

José·Witt¶

Professor·Chen¶

English·Composition·101¶

24·February·2011¶

So·You·Want·to·Know·About·the·Peace·Corps¶

FIGURE 5-6
The research paper begins with a header, student and course information, and the title of the paper.

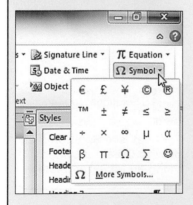

On Your Own 5-3
Enter Header, Student and Course Information, and Paper Title

According to the MLA guidelines, all information in the header, student and course information, and title of the paper should not use bold, italics, underlining, quotation marks, or all capital letters (also called all caps). Do the following:

Step 1. Enter the information shown in Figure 5-6. The paper is by José Witt, written for Professor Chen's English Composition 101 class. The title of the paper is "So You Want to Know About the Peace Corps." Use your current date for the paper.

Hint To edit an existing header, double-click it. To return to the document, double-click somewhere in the document. If you need to create a new header in a document, click the **Insert** tab and click **Header**.

Hint To insert the Latin letter **é** in José Witt, use the **Symbol** command on the Insert ribbon.

Step 2. Delete all the text in the paper following the title down through the end of the paper including the Works Cited page and save the document.

? Solutions Appendix   **For help, see Solution 5-3: How to Enter Header, Student and Course Information, and Paper Title.**

You are now ready to build the body of the paper.

Enter the First Paragraph and Create a Citation

In this activity, you enter the first paragraph and insert a citation in that paragraph. When the activity is completed, the paragraph should look like that in Figure 5-7 when paragraph marks are displayed.

Tip MLA guidelines require one space following each sentence in a paragraph.

▶ Video **5-4**

Citation goes before the period

Witt·1¶

José·Witt¶

Professor·Chen¶

English·Composition·101¶

24·February·2011¶

So·You·Want·to·Know·About·the·Peace·Corps¶

The·Peace·Corps·is·a·government·agency·that·sends·volunteers·overseas·to·help·bridge· the·cultural·divide·between·our·nation·and·others.·Volunteers·serve·for·27·months,·living·with· and·working·alongside·of·the·people·of·that·nation·(Peace·Corps).·If·you·are·interested·in· volunteering·for·the·Peace·Corps,·you·need·to·understand·the·requirements·for·being·accepted· to·the·Peace·Corps,·what·to·expect·when·serving·in·the·Peace·Corps,·and·what·might·be·the· benefits·of·serving.¶

FIGURE 5-7
The first paragraph is inserted and formatted and a citation added.

To save you time in this chapter, we have done all the writing for you. To enter the first paragraph, do the following:

Step 1. Copy the Introduction Paragraph from the Text for Research Paper page in OneNote into the Word document. Apply the **Research paper contents** style to the paragraph as shown in Figure 5-7.

Step 2. Following the second sentence in the paragraph, insert a citation from the Peace Corps website. Insert the citation before the period at the end of this sentence. The citation information can be found in OneNote on the Requirements page. To cite this website, you need the name of the website, the date the site was accessed, and the URL. Include **http://** at the beginning of the URL.

Hint To insert a citation, position the insertion point and click the **References** tab. Verify the **MLA Sixth Edition** style is selected in the Citations & Bibliography section. Then click **Insert Citation**.

For help, see Solution 5-4: How to Enter the First Paragraph and Create a Citation.

 Solutions Appendix

In the previous activity, you created a citation and its source. If you use the same source for another citation later in the paper, you don't have to enter the source information again.

> **Hint** If you find a mistake in the information you entered for a source, click a citation in the body of the paper that uses that source. Then click the down arrow on the right side of the citation box. Click **Edit Source** from the drop-down menu that appears. In the Edit Source box, make your changes and click **OK**.

On Your Own 5-5
Enter the Second Paragraph and a Citation

In this activity, you enter the second paragraph and a citation. When the activity is completed, the paragraph should look like that in Figure 5-8.

Copy Paragraph 2 from the Text for Research Paper page in OneNote into the Word document. Apply the **Research paper contents** style to the paragraph. Add a citation for the Peace Corps website at the end of this paragraph.

To·serve·in·the·Peace·Corps,·you·must·be·a·United·States·citizen·and·at·least·18·years·old.·There·is·no·maximum·age,·but·you·must·be·able·to·handle·the·physical·stress·of·living·and·working·in·primitive·conditions.·To·apply,·go·to·the·Peace·Corps·web·site·at·www.peacecorps.gov·and·fill·out·the·online·application.·The·entire·application·process·can·take·up·to·one·year·and·incudes·a·lot·of·paperwork,·an·interview,·physical·and·dental·exams,·a·legal·screening,·and·an·invitation·from·a·foreign·country·(Peace·Corps).¶

Citation goes before the period

FIGURE 5-8
The second paragraph has a citation at the end of the paragraph.

? Solutions Appendix   **For help, see Solution 5-5: How to Enter the Second Paragraph and a Citation.**

In the next four activities, you create citations for a book, blog, newspaper article, and journal article. The book, newspaper article, and journal article were published first in print and then posted online. Cite these works as though they are printed works. Later, when you create the Works Cited page, you add the additional facts that the works were found online.

In this activity, you enter the third paragraph, format a long quotation, and add a citation for a book. When the activity is completed, the third paragraph and the indented long quotation should look like that in Figure 5-9.

A colon usually introduces a long quotation.

During·your·first·three·months·in·the·Peace·Corps,·you·are·immersed·in·cultural·training·and·might·receive·intense·training·to·learn·the·language·of·your·host·country.·Moritz·Thomsen·had·this·to·say·about·his·three·months·of·training:¶

Long quotation

Peace·Corps·training·is·like·no·other·training·in·the·world,·having·something·in·common·with·college·life,·officer's·training,·Marine·basic·training,·and·a·ninety-day·jail·sentence.·What·makes·it·paradoxical·is·that·everything·is·voluntary;·the·schedule·exists·for·you·to·follow·if·you·wish....Our·schedule·began·at·5:45·each·morning·and·lasted·until·9:30·at·night.·After·that,·if·we·so·desired,·our·Spanish·instructors·were·available·to·work·with·us.·(Thomsen·4)¶

The book citation follows the period and includes a page number.

FIGURE 5-9
The third paragraph uses a long quotation from a book. The long quotation must be set in its own indented paragraph.

Do the following:

Step 1. Copy Paragraph 3 from the Text for Research Paper page in OneNote into the Word document. Apply the **Research paper contents** style to the paragraph.

Step 2. The paragraph contains a long quotation that needs to be set in its own indented paragraph. Insert a hard return following the colon in the text **Moritz Thomsen had this to say about his three months of training:**

Step 3. Format the quotation using the **Long quotation** style.

Step 4. Following the quotation, insert the citation from the book *Living Poor: A Peace Corps Chronicle*. You can find the citation information for the book on the Requirements page of OneNote. Don't forget to include the page number in the citation.

Hint When entering the author's name in a citation, enter his last name first, followed by a comma, and then his first name.

Hint A citation for a long quotation is inserted at the end of the quotation following the last punctuation mark in the quotation.

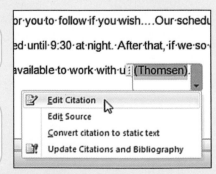

or·you·to·follow·if·you·wish....Our·schedu
ed·until·9:30·at·night.·After·that,·if·we·so·
available·to·work·with·u   (Thomsen).

	Edit Citation
	Edit Source
	Convert citation to static text
	Update Citations and Bibliography

Hint A book citation requires a page number. First, insert the citation without the page number. Then select the citation, click the down arrow beside the citation box, and click **Edit Citation**. You can then add the page number to the citation.

For help, see Solution 5-6: How to Enter More Text, a Long Quotation, and a Book Citation.

? Solutions Appendix

A **footnote** in a paper can be used to add extra information that does not fit into the body of the paper. In the following activity, you create a footnote. Word automatically assigns a number to each footnote in a document and places a footnote in the page **footer**.

> _____
> ¹ To find blogs written by Peace Corps volunteers, use Google.com and the following
> search string: Peace Corps volunteer blogs.
>
> **footnote**

footnote—Text placed at the bottom of the page that contains comments about the main text. To insert a footnote, click the **References** tab and click **Insert Footnote**. Word places the footnote in the page footer area.

footer—The area at the bottom of a page in a Word document. The footer might contain footnotes, a page number, and other information.

On Your Own 5-7
Enter More Text, a Blog Citation, and a Footnote

In this activity, you enter the fourth paragraph, a citation for a blog, and a footnote. When this activity is completed, the paragraph and the footnote should look like that in Figure 5-10. This figure does not display paragraph marks so that you can better see the footnote details.

Do the following:

Step 1. Copy Paragraph 4 from the Text for Research Paper page in OneNote into the Word document. Apply the **Research paper contents** style to the paragraph.

Step 2. Following the first sentence of the paragraph, add a citation for Lntaylor's Weblog. Taylor's entry was made on July 5, 2010. You can find the details for the citation information on the Service page of OneNote.

Step 3. Add a footnote at the end of the paragraph. Enter this text for the footnote:

> To find blogs written by Peace Corps volunteers, use Google.com and the following search string: Peace Corps volunteer blogs.

On Your Own 5-7
Enter More Text, a Blog Citation, and a Footnote

Step 4. Apply the **Research paper contents** style to the footnote.

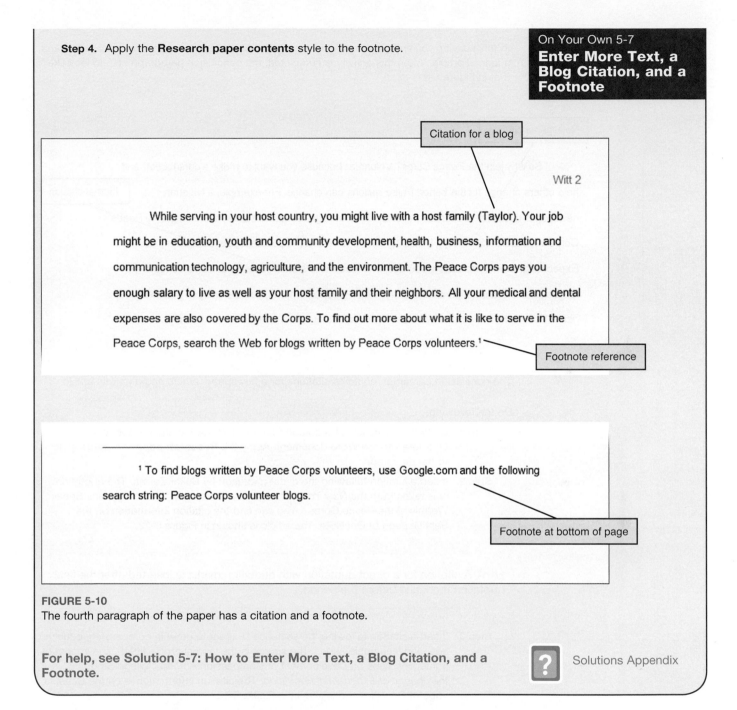

Citation for a blog

Witt 2

While serving in your host country, you might live with a host family (Taylor). Your job might be in education, youth and community development, health, business, information and communication technology, agriculture, and the environment. The Peace Corps pays you enough salary to live as well as your host family and their neighbors. All your medical and dental expenses are also covered by the Corps. To find out more about what it is like to serve in the Peace Corps, search the Web for blogs written by Peace Corps volunteers.[1]

Footnote reference

[1] To find blogs written by Peace Corps volunteers, use Google.com and the following search string: Peace Corps volunteer blogs.

Footnote at bottom of page

FIGURE 5-10
The fourth paragraph of the paper has a citation and a footnote.

For help, see Solution 5-7: How to Enter More Text, a Blog Citation, and a Footnote.

Solutions Appendix

On Your Own 5-8
Enter the Conclusion Paragraph and Two More Citations

In this activity, you enter the conclusion paragraph and citations for a newspaper article and a journal article. When this activity is completed, the conclusion paragraph should look like that in Figure 5-11.

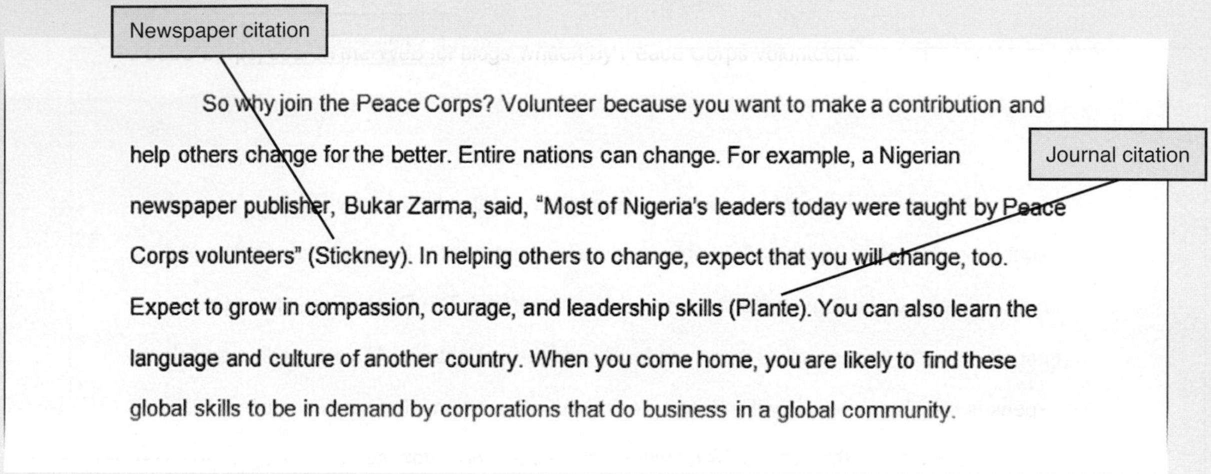

Newspaper citation

Journal citation

So why join the Peace Corps? Volunteer because you want to make a contribution and help others change for the better. Entire nations can change. For example, a Nigerian newspaper publisher, Bukar Zarma, said, "Most of Nigeria's leaders today were taught by Peace Corps volunteers" (Stickney). In helping others to change, expect that you will change, too. Expect to grow in compassion, courage, and leadership skills (Plante). You can also learn the language and culture of another country. When you come home, you are likely to find these global skills to be in demand by corporations that do business in a global community.

FIGURE 5-11
The conclusion paragraph contains citations for a newspaper article and a journal article.

Do the following:

Step 1. Copy the Conclusion Paragraph from the Text for Research Paper page in OneNote into the Word document. Apply the **Research paper contents** style to the paragraph.

Step 2. Insert a citation following the direct quotation by Bukar Zarma. The quotation was taken from the *New York Times* newspaper article titled "Nigerians Speak Warmly of the Peace Corps." You can find the citation information on the Service page of OneNote. The article is shown in Figure 5-12.

> **Hint** A citation for a direct quotation with quotation marks is inserted after the final quotation mark and before the period.

Step 3. Insert a citation following the sentence "Expect to grow in compassion, courage, and leadership skills." The source is the journal article titled "The Impact of Immersion Trips on Development of Compassion Among College Students" in the *Journal of Experiential Education*. The citation information is on the Benefits page of OneNote and is shown in Figure 5-13.

> **Hint** When a work has more than one author, enter the primary author's name with last name first, followed by first name. Other authors follow with first name first and separated by a comma. For example: Stone, Tammy D., Elizabeth Anderson, Rachel Davis.

On Your Own 5-8
Enter the Conclusion Paragraph and Two More Citations

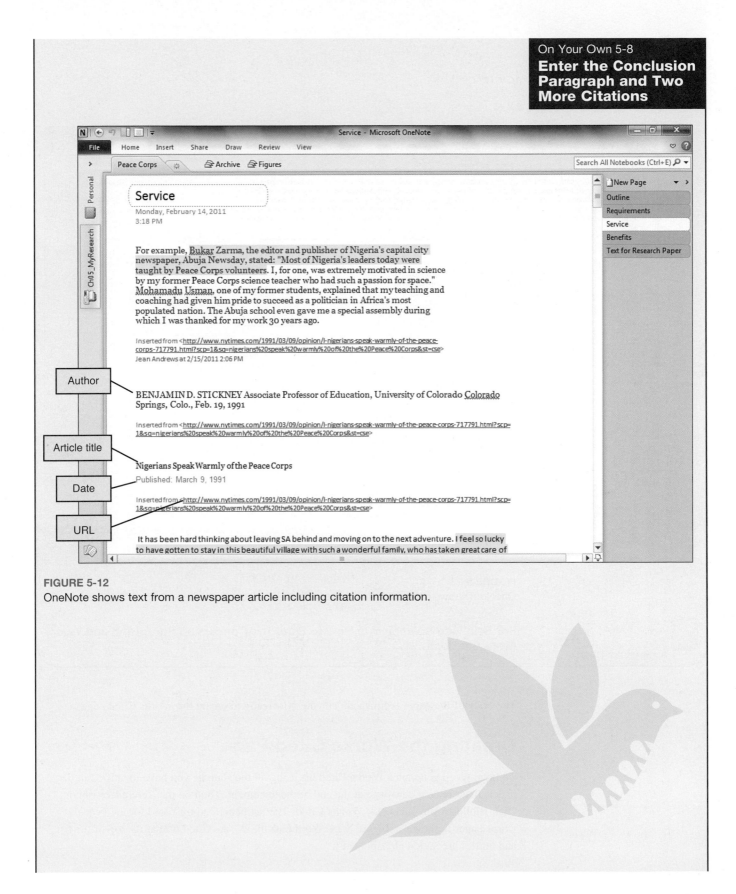

FIGURE 5-12
OneNote shows text from a newspaper article including citation information.

On Your Own 5-8
Enter the Conclusion Paragraph and Two More Citations

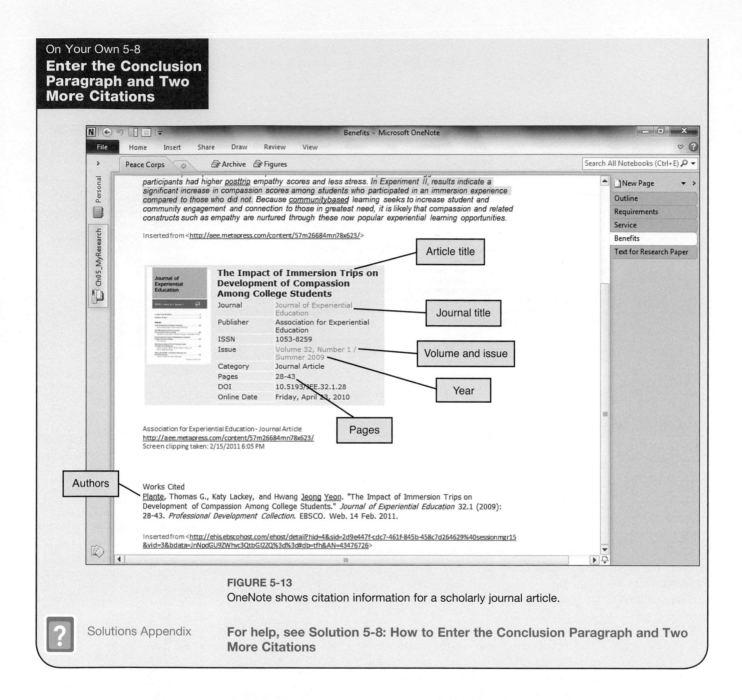

FIGURE 5-13
OneNote shows citation information for a scholarly journal article.

Solutions Appendix   **For help, see Solution 5-8: How to Enter the Conclusion Paragraph and Two More Citations**

The body of the paper is finished. You are now ready to create the Works Cited page.

Creating the Works Cited Page

To have Word generate a Works Cited list using all the sources you have identified in the paper, first create a new page at the end of the document. Then on the References ribbon, click **Bibliography** and click **Works Cited**. The list generated by Word for the Peace Corps paper is shown in Figure 5-14. Word puts the Works Cited title at the top of the list and entries are sorted alphabetically.

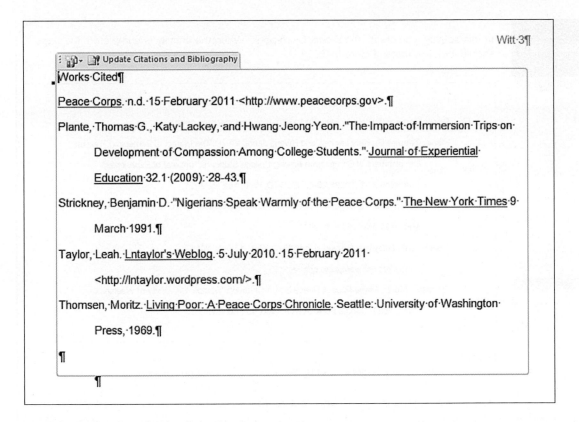

Witt·3¶

Update Citations and Bibliography

Works·Cited¶

Peace·Corps.·n.d.·15·February·2011·<http://www.peacecorps.gov>.¶

Plante,·Thomas·G.,·Katy·Lackey,·and·Hwang·Jeong·Yeon.·"The·Impact·of·Immersion·Trips·on·
Development·of·Compassion·Among·College·Students."·Journal·of·Experiential·
Education·32.1·(2009):·28-43.¶

Strickney,·Benjamin·D.·"Nigerians·Speak·Warmly·of·the·Peace·Corps."·The·New·York·Times·9·
March·1991.¶

Taylor,·Leah.·Lntaylor's·Weblog.·5·July·2010.·15·February·2011·
<http://lntaylor.wordpress.com/>.¶

Thomsen,·Moritz.·Living·Poor:·A·Peace·Corps·Chronicle.·Seattle:·University·of·Washington·
Press,·1969.¶

¶

¶

FIGURE 5-14
The Works Cited page generated by Word needs editing.

Unfortunately, the list does not completely follow MLA guidelines and needs editing. Here are the MLA guidelines that apply to the Works Cited list shown:

▶ The Works Cited title is centered on the page.

▶ Titles of works including websites, books, magazines, journals, and newspapers should be in italics and not underlined. Where Word has used underlining for titles, replace that formatting with italics. For example, change **The New York Times** to *The New York Times*.

▶ Months should be spelled out in the text but are abbreviated in the Works Cited list except for May, June, and July. Always use a period following the abbreviation. For example, change **15 February 2011** to **15 Feb. 2011**.

▶ When a printed work is found on the web, add to the end of the Works Cited entry the following:

    ▶ The title of an online database set in italics and followed by a period (if the title is not available, it can be omitted).

    ▶ The word **Web** followed by a period.

    ▶ The date accessed followed by a period.

▶ When any other work is found on the web, insert before the date accessed the word **Web** followed by a period.

Hint The Works Cited list is inserted in a document inside a container box. To have Word regenerate the list, select the container and click **Update Citations and Bibliography** at the top of the container. But be aware that any changes you have made to the list are lost when Word updates it.

Tip MLA guidelines have recently changed so that URLs are no longer required in the Works Cited list. Some instructors still require them. For complete MLA guidelines that apply to a Works Cited list, see www.mla.org or ask your instructor or librarian.

On Your Own 5-9
Create a Works Cited Page

 Video **5-9**

In this activity, you create the Works Cited page. When the activity is completed, the page should look like that in Figure 5-15.

Works Cited

Peace Corps. n.d. Web. 15 Feb. 2011 <http://www.peacecorps.gov>.

Plante, Thomas G., Katy Lackey, and Hwang Jeong Yeon. "The Impact of Immersion Trips on Development of Compassion Among College Students." *Journal of Experiential Education* 32.1 (2009): 28-43. *EBSCO*. Web. 14 Feb. 2011.

Strickney, Benjamin D. "Nigerians Speak Warmly of the Peace Corps." *The New York Times* 9 Mar. 1991. Web. 15 Feb. 2011.

Taylor, Leah. *Lntaylor's Weblog*. 5 July 2010. Web. 15 Feb. 2011 <http://lntaylor.wordpress.com/>.

Thomsen, Moritz. *Living Poor: A Peace Corps Chronicle*. Seattle: University of Washington Press, 1969. *Google Book Search*. Web. 15 Feb. 2011.

FIGURE 5-15
The Works Cited page is generated by Word and then changes were made.

Do the following to create a Works Cited page:

Step 1. Create a page break following the last paragraph in the document. Insert a Works Cited list. Correct any problems with underlining and the format used for dates.

Hint If you find a mistake in the source information used to generate the Works Cited list, go back and find the citation in the body of the paper. Select the citation and click **Edit Source** from the drop-down menu. Correct the source information and then generate a new Works Cited page. Any edits you made to the Works Cited page are lost and must be done again.

---

page break—A mark in a document that indicates a new page. To insert the mark, click the **Page Break** button on the Insert ribbon or press **Ctrl-End**. When you click **Show/Hide**, the Page Break mark displays on the screen along with other formatting symbols.

Step 2. Three printed works in the list were found online. Make these changes:

    a. Add the following to the end of the Plante, Thomas G. entry:

> *EBSCO*. Web. 14 Feb. 2011.

    b. Add the following to the end of the Stickney, Benjamin D. entry (no database title is available):

> Web. 15 Feb. 2011.

    c. Add the following to the end of the Thomsen, Moritz entry:

> *Google Book Search*. Web. 15 Feb. 2011.

Solutions Appendix

For help, see Solution 5-9: How to Create a Works Cited Page.

Step 3. For the other two entries in the Works Cited list, insert before the date accessed the word **Web** followed by a period. Save your work.

Now that everything has been entered into the paper and formatted, it's time to check the paper for errors.

Proofing and Revising the Paper

Word offers tools to help you find mistakes and revise your writing.

Correct Grammar Errors

Word draws a curvy green line under any word or phrase that it thinks has a grammar error. If you see one of these lines, right-click the text to see a fix offered by Word in the shortcut menu (see Figure 5-16). Click the fix to make the correction. If you know the grammar is correct as it is, click **Ignore Once**.

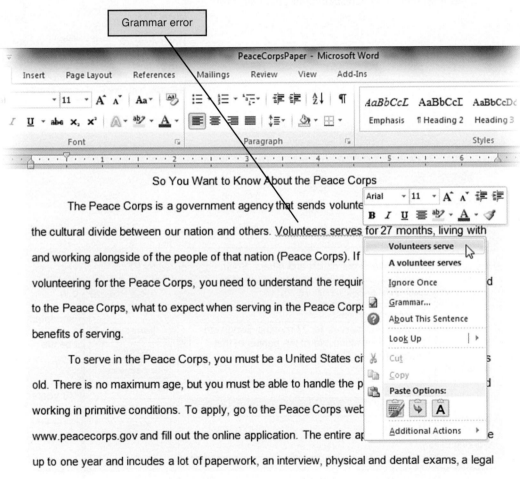

FIGURE 5-16
Word identifies a possible error in grammar and offers a fix.

Correct Spelling Errors

Recall from Chapter 3, "Creating Documents with Microsoft Word," that Word identifies misspelled or unfamiliar words with a curvy red underline. You can scroll through the paper looking for these red lines and correct any spelling errors.

Another way to check a paper for all spelling and grammar errors is to click **Spelling & Grammar** on the Review ribbon. The Spelling and Grammar box appears (see Figure 5-17). Use it to work your way through the entire document as it searches for each spelling or grammar error.

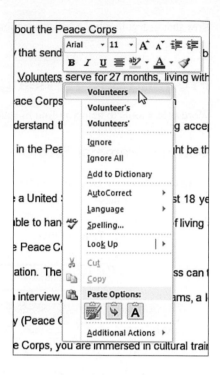

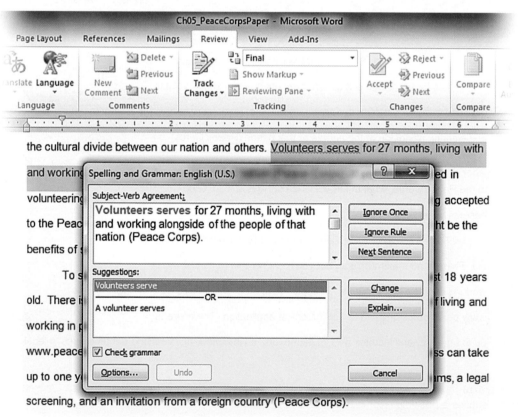

FIGURE 5-17
Use the Spelling and Grammar box to search an entire document for spelling and grammar errors.

Check the Word Count

If your instructor has assigned a minimum or maximum number of words in the paper, check the status bar at the bottom of the Word window for the number of words in the document.

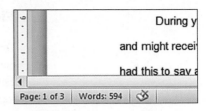

Use Synonyms

As you write, you might appreciate the built-in thesaurus offered by Word. Right-click a word and point to **Synonyms** from the shortcut menu. A list of **synonyms** appears (see Figure 5-18). Click one to substitute it for the original word. In the shortcut menu, click **Thesaurus**. The **thesaurus** shows a longer list of synonyms from which you can choose.

> **synonym**—A word similar to another word. For example, a synonym for *interesting* is *stimulating,* which is, well, a more stimulating word.
>
> **thesaurus**—A list of synonyms.

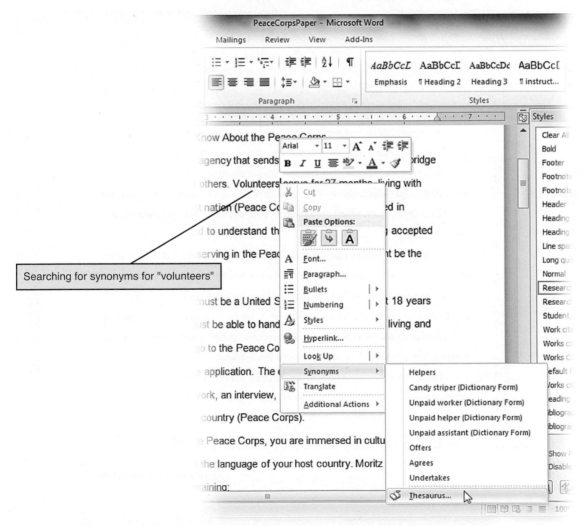

FIGURE 5-18
Word offers synonyms and access to a thesaurus with even more synonyms.

Find Text

On the Home ribbon, click **Find**. The Navigation pane appears and snaps to the left side of the window. Enter text you want to find in the search box at the top of the Navigation pane. Instances of the text are highlighted in the document and also display in a list in the Navigation pane. See Figure 5-19.

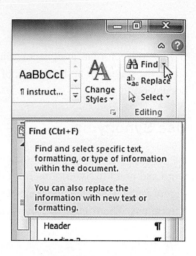

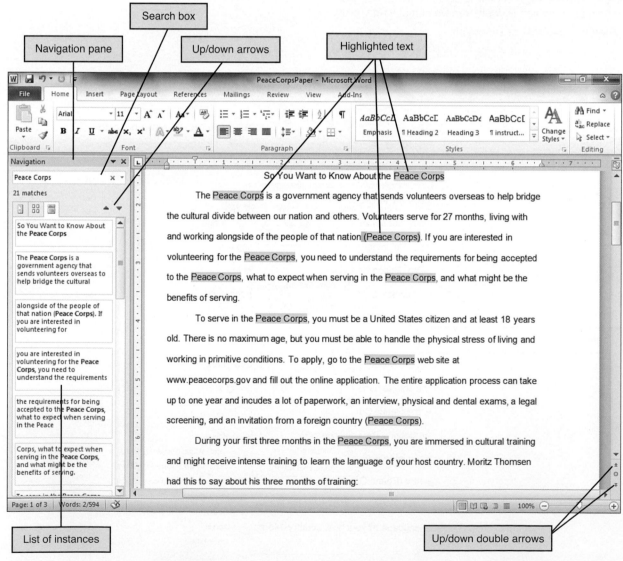

FIGURE 5-19

Search results are highlighted in the document and listed in the Navigation pane.

To move to places in the document where the text was found, you can

- ▶ Click one of the items listed in the Navigation pane.

- ▶ Click the up and down arrows above the list to step through the list.

- ▶ Click the double-up and double-down arrows at the bottom of the scrollbar to step through the list.

Find Unwanted Hard Returns

To verify you have no extra hard returns, use the Show/Hide button ¶ on the Home ribbon to display paragraph marks. Scan through the document looking for unwanted hard returns and delete them. Having two hard returns next to each other is most likely a problem.

Change the Font and Font Size

The MLA template used in this chapter uses Arial, 11 point, which is allowed in MLA. However, an instructor might require a different font or font size, such as Times New Roman, 12 point. You can press **Ctrl-A** to select all text in the document and change it to Times New Roman, 12 point. But know that when you select all, Word does not include the header and footer in the selection. You have to select these items individually to change the font and font size.

After you check the paper for errors and make revisions, don't forget to make sure the document properties show you as the author of the document. You are then ready to print the document.

Summary

Preparing to Write Your Paper

▶ Types of papers you might need to write during your academic or professional career include research papers, white papers, Requests for Proposals, proposals, and business plans. Word templates can help you construct and format all these types of papers.

▶ The two most popular guidelines for constructing and formatting research papers are MLA guidelines and APA guidelines. MLA is used for literary, philosophy, and history papers. APA is used for social science, education, political science, technical, and scientific papers. MLA guidelines are used in this chapter.

▶ In a paper, always give credit where credit is due. Copyright laws posted at copyright.gov apply to copying another person's works.

▶ An exception to copyright laws is fair use, which applies to papers written in a class and presented to an instructor.

▶ Document sources used with a citation and list the source on a Works Cited page. Direct quotations should always be cited in a paper.

Typing and Formatting the Paper

▶ Word templates that can be used to produce a research paper using MLA or APA guidelines can be found in the Office.com templates Reports group.

▶ MLA requires a header containing the student's last name and page number.

▶ According to MLA, paragraphs in the body of the paper must be double-spaced, aligned left, and no extra spacing before or after the paragraph. The first line of the paragraph must be indented 0.5 inches. One space follows each sentence in the paragraph. Other MLA guidelines can be found at **www.mla.org**.

▶ A style contains a predetermined set of formatting that can be modified.

▶ A page number can be inserted in a document using a command on the Insert ribbon.

▶ A citation is added to a paper using the Insert Citation command on the References ribbon.

▶ A footnote can be added to a paper using the Insert Footnote command on the References ribbon.

▶ The footer is the area at the bottom of a Word page and can contain footnotes, a page number, and other information.

▶ A book citation includes the author of the book and the page number in the book.

Creating the Works Cited Page

▶ Insert a page break in a document using the Page Break command on the Insert ribbon.

▶ Insert a Works Cited page in a paper using the Bibliography command on the References ribbon. You might need to edit the page to conform to MLA guidelines or to add additional information.

Proofing and Revising the Paper

▶ Use the spell checking and grammar checking features of Word to correct errors.

▶ Word features used to revise a paper include synonyms, a thesaurus, word count, and a Find command to search for text.

Review Questions

Answer these questions to find out if you have learned the skills and knowledge in the chapter. Your instructor can provide you with the correct answers when you are ready to check your work. If you answered most of the questions correctly, you are ready for the Chapter Mastery Project. If not, go back and review the chapter before you tackle the project.

1. What is the purpose of a research paper? A white paper? An RFP? A proposal? A business plan?

2. What are the two most popular guidelines for writing research papers and when is each used?

3. What are exceptions to copyright laws called that include reproducing a small part of a work in a research paper required by a teacher for a school assignment?

4. What punctuation marks are used to enclose a citation at the end of a sentence in a research paper? What is another name for a citation?

5. What determines if a direct quotation is written in line with the paragraph and enclosed in quotation marks or written in its own indented paragraph?

6. What is one website a school might use to scan research papers for plagiarism?

7. According to MLA guidelines, what information goes into the header of a paper?

8. On what ribbon of the Word window is the command to insert a citation in a document?

9. What information is included in the citation for a book shown in the body of the text?

10. On what ribbon of the Word window is the command to insert a footnote in a document?

11. When you are using a long quotation in a paper, the citation goes at the end of the quotation. Does the citation go before or after the last period at the end of the quotation?

12. According to MLA guidelines, are titles in the Works Cited page underlined or placed in italics?

13. How does Word indicate a mistake in grammar?

14. What is the name of the pane on the Word window where search items are listed?

15. When you use Ctrl-A to select all the text in a document, is text in the headers and footers included in the selection?

Chapter Mastery Project

Find out how well you have mastered the content in this chapter by completing this project. If you can answer all the questions and do all the steps without looking back at the chapter details, you have mastered this chapter. If you can complete the project by finding answers using the Word Help window or the web, you have proven that you can teach yourself how to write papers.

If you find you need a lot of help doing the project and you have not yet read the chapter or done the activities, drop back and start at the beginning of the chapter and then return to this project.

By following the steps in this mastery project, you will create a research paper about mentoring. You did the research for this paper in the Chapter Mastery Project in Chapter 4. The completed paper is shown in Figure 5-20.

> **Hint** All the key terms in the chapter are used in this mastery project. If you encounter a key word you don't know such as *citation*, enter **define:citation** in the Internet Explorer search box.

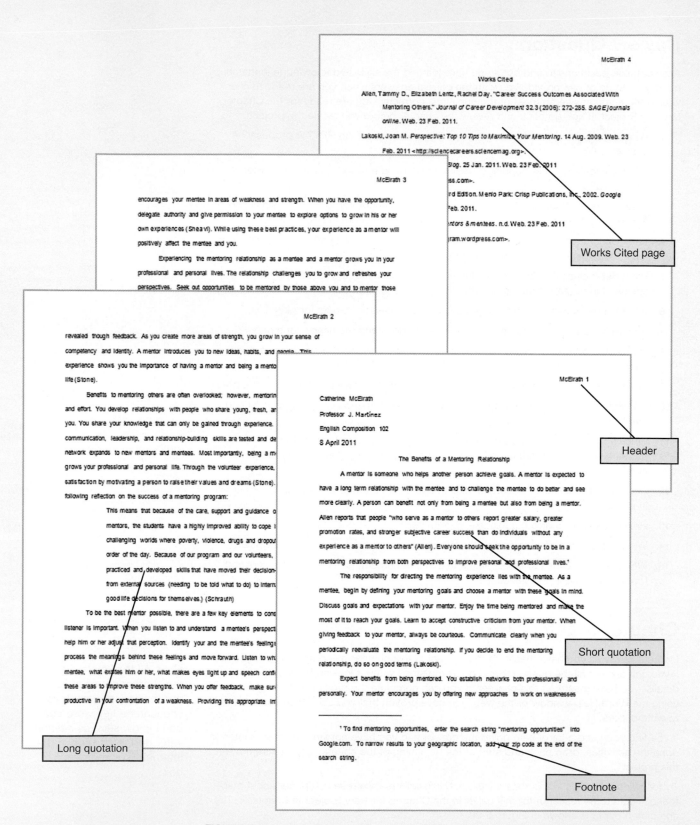

FIGURE 5-20

The completed paper on mentoring includes short and long quotations, a header, a footnote, and a Works Cited page.

Mastery Project Part 1: Preparing to Write Your Paper

If you need help completing this part of the mastery project, please review the "Preparing to Write Your Paper" section in the chapter.

Answer the following questions about writing papers:

1. When your business is describing a new technical solution to potential customers, is it appropriate to write an RFP, a white paper, or a business plan?

2. When your business needs to find a contractor to build a database and website, is it appropriate to write an RFP, a business plan, or a proposal?

3. Which guidelines—MLA or APA—are most likely to be required for a research paper in a history class? In a computer systems design class?

4. You write a paper for an English class and have the opportunity to publish the paper on your school's website. Under fair use laws, can you put the paper on the site without getting permission from the authors of the works you use in the paper? Why or why not?

5. When you use a direction quotation that is four lines long, how do you format the quotation in your paper?

6. When you put text written by another in your own words, you are _____ the text.

Do the following to prepare to write the research paper on mentoring:

Step 1. Using the DVD in the back of the book, open Windows Explorer and drill down into the **CH05_MyResearch** folder. In the folder, double-click the OneNote section file named **Mentoring**. A OneNote notebook opens with the Mentoring section selected. All the research you need for this project is found in this section.

Step 2. To save you time, we have done all the typing for the body of the paper for you. To see this text, select the **Text for Mentoring Paper** page in the Mentoring section of the notebook. Leave the OneNote window open so you are ready to copy information from OneNote into your Word document.

Step 3. Open a new document in Word using the **Research paper in MLA style** template in the **Reports** group of templates. Save the document to your USB flash drive, hard drive, SkyDrive, or another location given by your instructor. Name the document **MentoringPaper**.

Step 4. View the **Long Quotation** style. How wide is the left indent for this style? The right indent?

Answer the following questions about the MLA guidelines used in this template:

1. What are the formatting rules that apply to the header, student and course information, date, and title of the paper?

2. What are the page margins?

3. What are the MLA guidelines that apply to the custom-made style named *Research paper contents?*

Mastery Project Part 2: Typing and Formatting the Paper

If you need help completing this part of the mastery project, please review the "Typing and Formatting the Paper" section in the chapter.

Answer the following:

1. In the Word template, the page number is already inserted. If it were not inserted, how would you do it?

2. When inserting a citation following a sentence in a paragraph, where does the citation go, before or after the last punctuation mark in the paragraph?

3. When inserting a citation following a long quotation, where does the citation go, before or after the last punctuation mark in the quotation?

4. Suppose a source has two authors: Samuel Sandford and Emily Burton. How do you enter these authors' names when creating the source?

5. After you enter a citation with its source information, how can you edit the citation? How can you edit the source?

Using the MentoringPaper document you created earlier, do the following:

Step 1. Edit the header, student and course information, and title of the document. Use the following information. Be sure to use the Latin letter in the name, Martínez:

> Student's Name: Catherine McElrath
>
> Instructor's Name: Professor J. Martínez
>
> Course Title: English Composition 102
>
> Research Paper Title: The Benefits of a Mentoring Relationship

Step 2. Delete all the text in the rest of the document.

Step 3. Copy all the text on the **Text for Mentoring Paper** page in OneNote into the Word document. In Word, apply the **Research paper contents** style to this text.

Step 4. Following the fourth sentence of the first paragraph, insert a citation for the journal article by Allen, Lentz, and Day. You can find the information you need about the source highlighted in yellow on the Introduction page in OneNote.

Step 5. At the end of the first paragraph, insert the following footnote:

> To find mentoring opportunities, enter the search string **mentoring opportunities** into Google.com. To narrow results to your geographic location, add your zip code at the end of the search string.

Step 6. At the end of the second paragraph, insert a citation for the article by Lakoski published on a website. You can find the information you need about the source highlighted in yellow on the Mentee Tips page in OneNote.

Step 7. At the end of the third paragraph, insert a citation for the blog entry by Stone. You can find the information you need about the source highlighted in yellow on the Mentoring Benefits page in OneNote.

Step 8. Edit the fourth paragraph as follows:

    a. Insert a second citation for the blog website by Stone at the end of the sentence "Through the volunteer experience, you gain personal satisfaction by motivating a person to raise their values and dreams."

    b. Format the following text in the fourth paragraph as a long quotation:

> This means that because of the care, support and guidance of their online mentors, the students have a highly improved ability to cope in their very challenging worlds where poverty, violence, drugs and dropouts are the normal order of the day. Because of our program and our volunteers, our kids have practiced and developed skills that have moved their decision-making abilities from external sources (needing to be told what to do) to internal sources (making good life decisions for themselves.)

     c. At the end of this long quotation, insert the citation for the blog by Schrauth. You can find the information for the citation highlighted in yellow on the Mentoring Benefits page.

Step 9. Following the next-to-last sentence in the fifth paragraph, insert a citation for the book by Shea. You can find the citation information highlighted in yellow on the **Best Practices** page.

Mastery Project Part 3: Creating the Works Cited Page

If you need help completing this part of the mastery project, please review the "Creating the Works Cited Page" section in the chapter.

Do the following to add the Works Cited page to the paper:

Step 1. Insert a page break and then insert a Works Cited page.

Step 2. Format the Works Cited page, centering the title, replacing underlining with italics for all titles of works, and using abbreviations for dates where appropriate.

Step 3. Because the journal article and book were first published in print and then posted online, you need to add the additional web information to the Works Cited page. Make these changes:

     a. The journal article by Allen, Lentz, and Day was found on the **Web** in the **SAGE journals online** database on **Feb. 23, 2011**.

     b. The book by Shea was found on the **Web** in a **Google Book Search** on **Feb. 23, 2011**.

Step 4. Before the date accessed, insert the word **Web** followed by a period in other Works Cited entries found on the web.

Mastery Project Part 4: Proofing and Revising the Paper

If you need help completing this part of the mastery project, please review the "Proofing and Revising the Paper" section in the chapter.

Answer these questions:

1. What does a curvy green line under a word indicate? How do you fix the problem?

2. What command on the Review ribbon can help you scan a long document for spelling and grammar errors?

3. How can you find out the number of words in a document?

4. How do you use Word to find a more interesting word to use in place of *weird* in the sentence "The man had a weird look on his face"?

5. What are the steps to search for text in a document?

6. When you press **Ctrl-A** to select all the text in a document, what text is not selected?

Becoming an Independent Learner

Answer the following questions about becoming an independent learner:

1. To teach yourself to use Microsoft Word to write papers, do you think it is best to rely on the chapter or on Word Help when you need answers?

2. When you need help with the details of MLA guidelines, which source is the most authoritative, this chapter, the www.mla.org website, or a Wikipedia.org article about MLA?

3. The most important skill learned in this chapter is how to teach yourself a computer skill. Rate yourself at Level A through E on how well you are doing with this skill. What is your level?

   ○ Level A: I was able to successfully complete the Chapter Mastery Project without the help of doing the *On Your Own* activities in the chapter.

   ○ Level B: I completed all the *On Your Own* activities and the Chapter Mastery Project without referring to any of the solutions in the *Solutions Appendix*.

   ○ Level C: I completed all the *On Your Own* activities and the Chapter Mastery Project by using just a few of the solutions in the *Solutions Appendix*.

   ○ Level D: I completed all the *On Your Own* activities and the Chapter Mastery Project by using many of the solutions in the *Solutions Appendix*.

   ○ Level E: I completed all the *On Your Own* activities and the Chapter Mastery Project and had to use all the solutions in the *Solutions Appendix*.

To continue toward the goal of teaching yourself computer skills, if you are not at Level A, try to move up one level on how you learn in Chapter 6, "Communicating with Others Using the Internet."

Projects to Help You

Now that you have mastered the material in this chapter, you are ready to tackle the three projects introduced at the beginning of the chapter in the section "How Will This Chapter Help Me?"

Project 1: Writing Papers in Your Personal Life

PERSONAL PROJECT:
I want to convince my friends they need to protect their privacy when using social networking sites like Facebook. If I put everything in writing, I think my paper might persuade them.

Your friend, Emily, is posting far too much personal information on Facebook. You have tried to convince her to protect her privacy, but she's not listening. So you decide to write a paper about the topic. All the research and the text for the paper are stored in the OneNote Privacy file in the Ch05_MyResearch folder on the DVD. Use the information to construct the paper complete with citations and the Works Cited page using the MLA guidelines. The paper requires the following:

▶ **Five citations:** The position for each citation is marked and highlighted in yellow.

▶ **One footnote:** The position for the footnote is highlighted in blue.

▶ **A Works Cited page:** The page should include the five sources used for the five citations. Note that not all sources included in the OneNote Privacy section are used.

Project 2: Writing Papers in Your Academic Career

Your English professor is so impressed with your knowledge of creating research papers using MLA guidelines that she has asked you to help her grade research papers. One paper, named RecycleComputersPaper, can be found in the **Sample Files** folder on the DVD. List ten errors in the paper that fail to follow the MLA guidelines discussed in the chapter.

Project 3: Writing Papers in Your Technical Career

Format a research paper using the MLA guidelines on how certifications can help you build a career in Information Technology (IT). All the research and the text for the paper are stored in the OneNote section file named Certifications in the Ch05_MyResearch folder on the DVD. Use the information to construct the paper complete with citations and the Works Cited page. The paper requires the following:

▶ **Four citations:** The position for each citation is marked and highlighted in yellow.

▶ **One footnote:** The position for the footnote is highlighted in blue.

▶ **A Works Cited page:** The page should include the four sources used for the four citations. Note that not all sources included in OneNote are used.

ACADEMIC PROJECT: My English teacher has asked me to help her grade research papers presented to her as Word documents. She wants me to make sure MLA guidelines are followed.

Project to Help Others

One of the best ways to learn is to teach someone else. And, in teaching someone else, you are making a contribution into that person's life. As part of each chapter's work, you are encouraged to teach someone else a skill you have learned.

Who is your apprentice? _____

When helping others learn, don't do the work for them. Coach and instruct. Show them how to find information for themselves. Help them be as independent a learner as possible.

In previous chapters, you helped your apprentice learn about Word. Coach your apprentice to explore more of Word, looking for interesting tools and buttons he might like to learn about. Here are some ideas if you and your apprentice cannot come up with your own:

▶ Browse through the Word templates looking for some fun documents to make.

▶ Insert shapes in a document to build a diagram, organizational chart, or other graphic.

▶ Explore how to import a photo in a document. (On the Insert ribbon, click **Picture**.) After you insert a picture, select it and use options on the Format ribbon to jazz up the photo.

▶ Explore how to add a header or footer to a document.

What new skills using Word did you help your apprentice learn?

TECHNICAL CAREER PROJECT: I'm planning my career in IT. I've read that getting a certification in IT might help me land a great part-time job while I work toward a degree. I need to document what I've found.

CHAPTER 6

Communicating with Others Using the Internet

IN THIS CHAPTER, YOU WILL

Communicate through email

Understand and use social networking websites including Facebook, Twitter, and LinkedIn

Present yourself with blogging

Communicate in real time using text, voice, and video

The Internet has forever changed the way we communicate. Email has replaced U.S. mail and inter-office memos as the first choice for personal and business communication. The Internet also supports social networking, blogging, and instant messaging on the web and voice communication. In this chapter, you learn how to use the Internet to "get connected."

As always, remember the most important computer skill is how to teach yourself a computer skill. Therefore, this chapter is designed to help you teach yourself how to communicate using the Internet. Try to do each On Your Own activity without any help. But remember, if you need help, you can always refer to the solutions in the *Solutions Appendix*.

JUMP RIGHT IN

If you want even more of a challenge, try proceeding directly to the Chapter Mastery Project at the end of this chapter. If you need help on the project, refer to the On Your Own activities in the chapter or do your own independent investigating searching the web for answers. When you complete the project, you will have mastered the skills in this chapter. Then go to the more advanced projects that require you to apply your skills to new situations.

How Will This Chapter Help Me?

Each chapter provides three projects focusing on personal, academic, or technical career goals. Depending on your own interests, you might choose to complete any or all of these projects to help you achieve your goals.

PERSONAL PROJECT: I want to use Facebook and a blog to stay connected online with family and friends. I want to use Skype to talk for free with family members who live in another country.

ACADEMIC PROJECT: I want to see what my instructors are saying on Facebook. Also, my club wants to use Facebook to show pictures of our events and attract other members.

TECHNICAL CAREER PROJECT: The business I work for part time expects my email messages to look professional. I want to build a professional network using LinkedIn, and I want some personal advice and tips for finding a great job in IT.

Communicating Through Email

Electronic mail (email) transfers messages from one computer to another. When you sign up for an email account, the organization assigns you an email address and requires you to select a password.

An email address has two parts that are separated by an at symbol (@) as in andrewsjean7@gmail.com. The first part (andrewsjean7) identifies the account, and the second part (gmail.com) is the domain name of the mail server the account uses. Two types of **mail servers** are used to manage email messages.

> **mail server**—A computer or software used to manage email. Two types of mail servers are the sender's mail server and the mailbox server. The mailbox server holds the mail until the recipient requests it.

The process of sending and receiving email happens in three legs. Figure 6-1 shows the process when I send a message from my andrewsjean7@gmail account to my daughter Joy at joy.dark@yahoo.com:

1. My message goes from my computer to the gmail.com mail server.

2. The gmail.com mail server sends the message to the yahoo.com mailbox server.

3. The message sits on that server until Joy logs in to the mailbox server and receives the message.

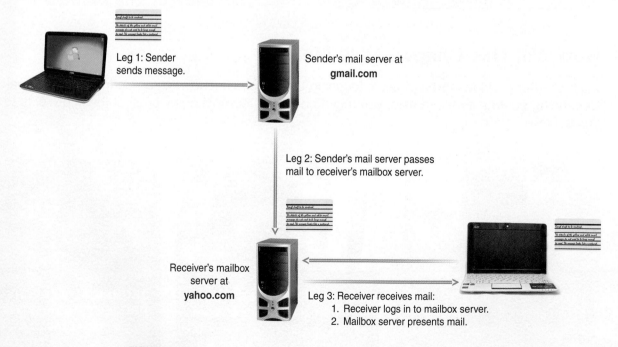

FIGURE 6-1
Sending and receiving email occurs in three legs.

When first learning about email, you need to know how to do these basic functions:

▶ Open your **inbox** and view, print, and delete messages.

inbox—A folder that contains email messages you have received.

▶ Create a new message and send it. If you start a message and are not yet ready to send it, you can save it as a draft.

▶ Send a message to multiple recipients.

▶ Reply to a message that you receive. When you receive a message that has been sent to multiple recipients, you can reply to all recipients.

▶ Include a file with a message. The file is called an **attachment**. For example, you might like to email a photo to a friend.

▶ Open an attachment you receive in a message and save the attachment to a storage location such as your USB flash drive.

Tip When you're replying to a message, the best practice is to type your response above the last message so the thread of back-and-forth replies shows the most recent reply first.

attachment—A file that is sent or received with an email message.

The two types of tools used to manage email are

▶ A website offered by your email provider

▶ Software installed on your computer, called an **email client**

email client—Software installed on a computer used to manage email. Microsoft Outlook is an email client. The software manages email messages, which can be stored on the local computer.

Let's first see how to manage email using a website and then how to use Microsoft Outlook. Then you can decide which tool you like the best to manage your email.

Email Using a Website

Companies or schools that offer email accounts provide websites where you can manage your email. The advantage of using a website to manage your email is that you can use any computer to access the website and your messages. Figure 6-2 shows the website where I can manage my email for my andrewsjean7@gmail.com account. I got the Google Mail account by signing up for it on the Google.com website.

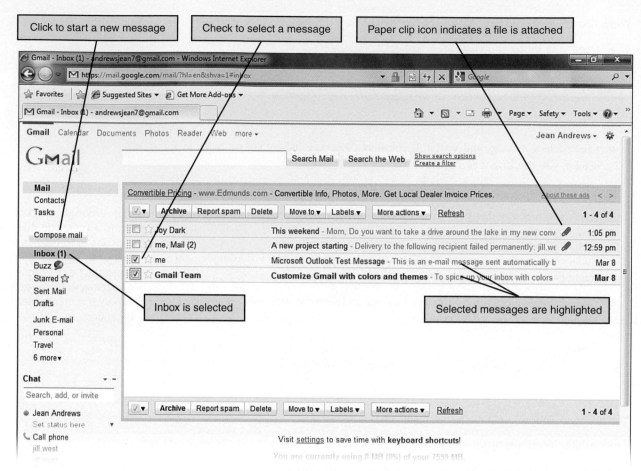

FIGURE 6-2
An email provider offers a website that can be used to manage email.

On Your Own 6-1
Manage Email Using a Website

To do this activity, you must have an email account. In Chapter 2, "Finding and Using Information on the Web," you needed an email account to set up a SkyDrive, so mostly likely, you already have an email account. If you do not, you can open a free email account at gmail.com, live.com, mail.com, or yahoo.com.

Using the email account you used in Chapter 2 or another email account, do the following to use a website to manage email:

Step 1. Open Internet Explorer and go to the website of your email provider. For example, if your email address is andrewsjean7@gmail.com, enter **gmail.com** in your browser address box. Sign in to your email account. How many messages are in your inbox?

Step 2. If you have a message in your inbox, select the message to view it. Figure 6-3 shows a message using Gmail, but yours might look different. If you have access to a printer, print the message.

Step 3. Next, write a message and send it to someone who has an email account. If you don't know someone with an email account, send the message to andrewsjean7@gmail.com or to your instructor. Verify the message is in your Sent folder.

Hint In a new message, be sure to include the email address of the receiver, a subject line, and the body of the message. Make sure the email address is entered correctly. An email message with an incorrect address might bounce back to you or end up in the wrong person's inbox.

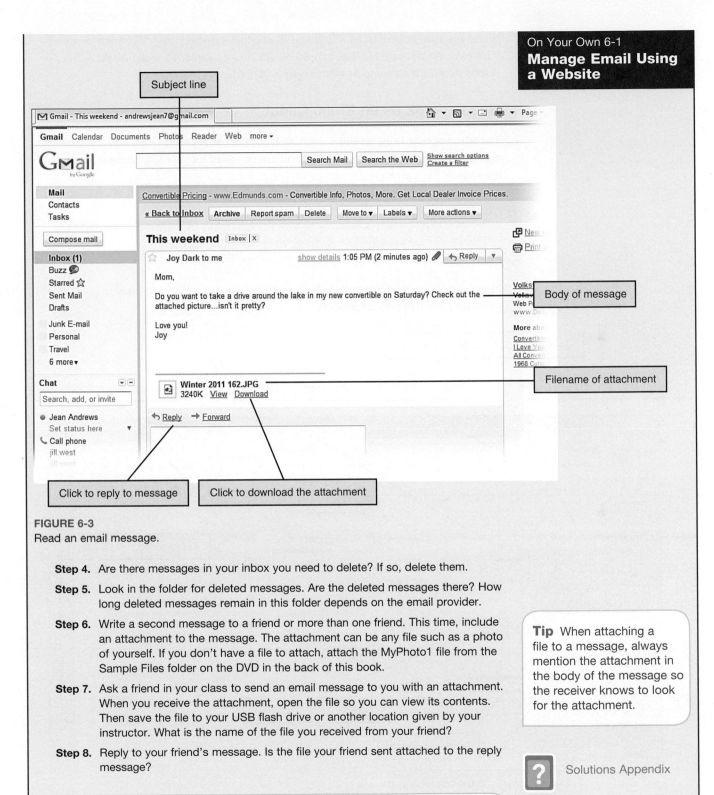

FIGURE 6-3
Read an email message.

Step 4. Are there messages in your inbox you need to delete? If so, delete them.

Step 5. Look in the folder for deleted messages. Are the deleted messages there? How long deleted messages remain in this folder depends on the email provider.

Step 6. Write a second message to a friend or more than one friend. This time, include an attachment to the message. The attachment can be any file such as a photo of yourself. If you don't have a file to attach, attach the MyPhoto1 file from the Sample Files folder on the DVD in the back of this book.

Step 7. Ask a friend in your class to send an email message to you with an attachment. When you receive the attachment, open the file so you can view its contents. Then save the file to your USB flash drive or another location given by your instructor. What is the name of the file you received from your friend?

Step 8. Reply to your friend's message. Is the file your friend sent attached to the reply message?

Tip When attaching a file to a message, always mention the attachment in the body of the message so the receiver knows to look for the attachment.

? Solutions Appendix

For help, see Solution 6-1: How to Manage Email Using a Website.

Hint When you reply to a message, attached files are not automatically included. When you forward a message, attached files are also forwarded by default.

When you attempt to open an attachment in an email message, know that your computer must have the software installed to open the file. For example, you need Adobe Reader or Adobe Acrobat installed to be able to open a PDF file.

Use Outlook as an Email Client

The advantages of using an email client such as **Microsoft Outlook** are that the client can manage multiple email addresses and email can be stored on your local computer in case the website has a problem.

> **Microsoft Outlook** —One application in the Microsoft Office suite. It is used to manage email, appointments on a calendar, and address lists.

Figure 6-4 shows the Microsoft Outlook application window set up to manage my gmail.com and live.com email accounts.

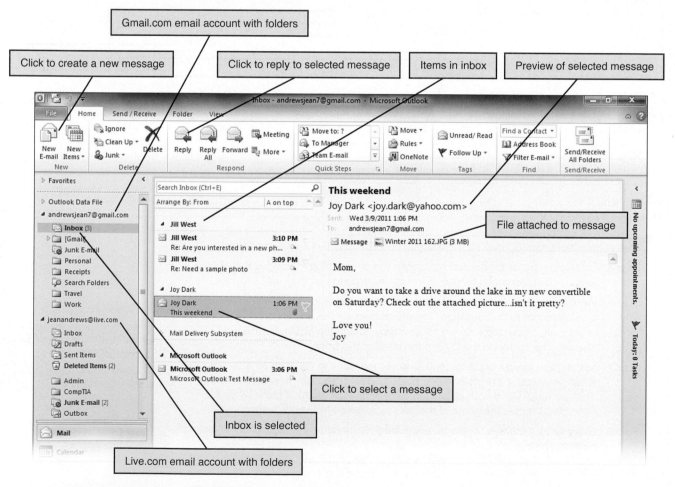

FIGURE 6-4
Outlook can be used to manage multiple email accounts.

Tip Why have more than one email account? I use one email account for business, family, and close friends. I use another account when I sign up for newsletters and other public emails so that the first account is better protected from **spam** and other abuse. Some companies assign email accounts to employees and expect these accounts not to be for personal use.

spam—Email you didn't ask for and don't want.

On Your Own 6-2
Set Up Outlook to Manage an Email Account

Before you can use Outlook to manage your email, you must tell it your email account information. This setup can happen when you open Outlook the first time, or you can set up an account later.

When you set up a hotmail.com or live.com email account, you must install extra software called the Microsoft Outlook Hotmail Connector. This software is used to sync up Outlook and the live.com website so that your email can be managed at both locations.

Do the following to set up an email account in Outlook:

Step 1. Open Microsoft Outlook 2010 and set up an email account. When the account is set up, the Outlook window shows the email account in the left pane.

Step 2. Click **Inbox** under the email account to view messages in the inbox. Your screen should look similar to that in Figure 6-4 except only one email account appears in the left pane.

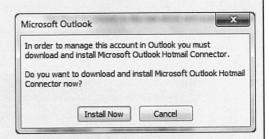

Hint To set up a hotmail.com or live.com email account, you enter your name, email address, and password and click **Next.** The Microsoft Outlook dialog box appears asking for permission to install Microsoft Outlook Hotmail Connector. Click **Install Now** to install the software. After the software is installed, close Outlook. When you reopen Outlook, it finds the software installed. You can then set up a hotmail.com or live.com account.

 Solutions Appendix

For help, see Solution 6-2: How to Set Up Outlook to Manage an Email Account.

On Your Own 6-3
Use Outlook to Manage Email

Earlier in the chapter, you used a website to manage email. You can perform the same tasks using an email client such as Outlook. Do the following:

Step 1. View the contents of your inbox. Sort messages by date. Then sort messages by sender. If you have a message in your inbox, view its contents. If you have access to a printer, print the message.

Step 2. Write a message and send it to a friend. Verify the message is in the Sent folder.

Step 3. Are there messages in your inbox you need to delete? If so, delete them. Look in the Trash or Deleted Items folder. Are the deleted messages there?

Step 4. Write a second message to your friend. This time, include an attachment to the message. The attachment can be any file such as a photo of yourself. If you don't have a file to attach, attach the MyPhoto2 file in the Sample Files folder on the DVD in the back of this book.

On Your Own 6-3
Use Outlook to Manage Email

Step 5. Ask a friend in your class to send an email message to you with an attachment. When you receive the attachment, open the attachment so you can view its contents. Then save the file to your USB flash drive. What is the name of the file you received from your friend?

Step 6. Reply to your friend's message.

?   Solutions Appendix   **For help, see Solution 6-3: How to Use Outlook to Manage Email.**

Best Practices for Email Safety and Etiquette

Here are some best practices for staying safe when using email:

▸ **Never click a link in an email message unless you know and trust the sender.** By clicking a link in an email message, you can spread a virus to your computer.

▸ **Avoid viruses in email attachments.** Don't open an attachment unless you know and trust the sender. Set your antivirus software to scan an email attachment as soon as it is downloaded. For example, Figure 6-5 shows the Microsoft Security Essentials window with real-time protection on. The software is set to scan all files and attachments as they are downloaded.

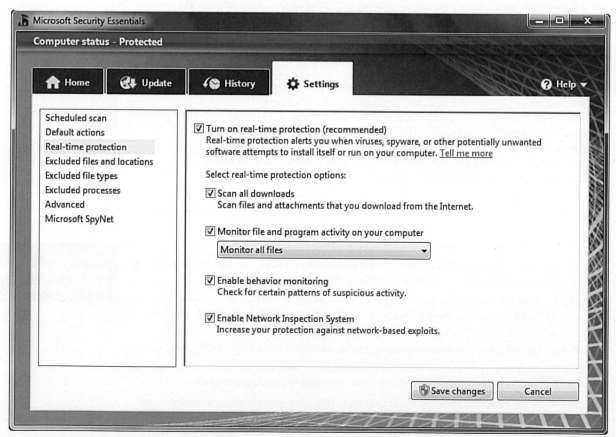

FIGURE 6-5
Microsoft Security Essentials is set to scan all downloaded files and attachments.

▶ **Never give personal information by email.** Email is not secure. Think of it like a post card that anyone can read while in route. Never put your credit card information or other personal information in an email message.

▶ **Don't take the bait when thieves go phishing.** Phishing is an attempt to lure you into a scam. For example, you might receive an email offering you lots of money if you get involved in recovering millions for a Russian oil tycoon. Don't take the bait.

phishing (pronounced "fishing")—Attempts to trick you into giving private information by lying to you.

▶ **Beware of fake websites.** For example, you receive an email that appears to have come from your bank. You are asked to click a link in the message that takes you to a fake website. There you are asked to enter your logon account and password to your online banking site. This technique is a type of **social engineering**.

social engineering—Tricking people into giving private information to thieves.

▶ **Filter out spam.** Check the website of your email provider for a spam filter you can set to control email ads and other unwanted email. For example, Gmail automatically moves email it considers to be spam out of your inbox into your spam box. You can also select any message and click the Spam button to mark it as spam (see Figure 6-6). In the future, messages from this same source are sent to your spam box.

FIGURE 6-6
Select a message and click Spam to send all messages from this source to your spam box.

▶ **Never forward chain email.** Chain email comes from a friend asking you to forward it to all your other friends. The original sender is often trying to clog up email servers and find email addresses to be spammed.

When using email, you want to present yourself well. Here are some good manners for using email:

- **Respond to email in a timely manner.** Respond to all professional and business emails within one day. Even a brief response to acknowledge that you received the message and are looking into the matter further is better than not responding or responding several days later.

- **Write professional email messages.** Use proper grammar and check your spelling. Don't use texting language such as "r u ok." Break your main thoughts into paragraphs. Always reread an email before you send it. Check for typos or bad sentence structure. Make sure your tone or attitude is positive.

- **Be polite.** Never use all caps in email, which is like shouting. Stay positive and don't express anger in an email message.

- **Use a subject line that summarizes the message.** Use short subject lines that are not too wordy or vague. Include enough information to make searching for specific emails easy.

- **Use CC and BCC features when appropriate.** The CC (carbon copy) feature allows you to send a copy of the message to someone other than the primary receivers. The BCC (blind carbon copy) is used to copy another person without others seeing that person's email address or knowing that person has been copied.

- **Protect the email addresses of your friends and coworkers.** Don't forward email messages to others that reveal the email addresses of your friends and coworkers unless you know it's okay to share that information.

- **Don't send large attachments in email.** Some email servers won't receive large files as attachments and the attachments might bog down the receiver's computer.

- **Don't email embarrassing or confidential information.** Keep private information private. Your email message might be forwarded to others you did not expect would receive it.

- **Know when email is not appropriate.** Never give bad or unpleasant news in an email. Be considerate and make a phone call instead. Also, complex conversations are best done over the phone and not by email. Email is intended to be brief and direct. If your email message is getting very long, it's probably time to pick up the phone or meet face to face.

Now let's turn our attention to social networking websites such as Facebook, Twitter, and LinkedIn.

Social Networking with Facebook, Twitter, and LinkedIn

We all have a social network of friends, family, and business associates. The people in our network have their own networks that can broaden our network. Using websites for social networking makes it easy to stay connected and share our lives with others.

In the past, the web was primarily used to provide content to those who requested it. Today, many users contribute to content on the web. This second generation of how the web is used is called **Web 2.0.** Online social networking is one example of Web 2.0.

> **Web 2.0**—The second generation of how the web is used. Content on the web is constantly changing as we all contribute to it.

The most popular **social networking sites** include

- ▶ **Facebook.com.** The most popular social networking website in the world.

- ▶ **Twitter.com.** A quick and easy way to send short messages of 140 or fewer characters to others.

- ▶ **LinkedIn.com.** Mostly used by professionals to maintain business contacts and to build a professional network.

> **social networking site**—A website designed for people and organizations to build a social network of friends, family, or business associates and share information with them.

Build a Social Network Using Facebook

Facebook offers two types of accounts: a personal account and a business account. Let's see how a personal account works.

Use a Facebook Personal Account

When you sign up for a personal account, a **Facebook profile** is created for you. Use your profile to share personal information, photos, videos, and more. Figure 6-7 shows the profile for my Facebook account.

> **Facebook profile**—The area of a Facebook personal account used to share wall posts, personal info, photos, and a network of friends.

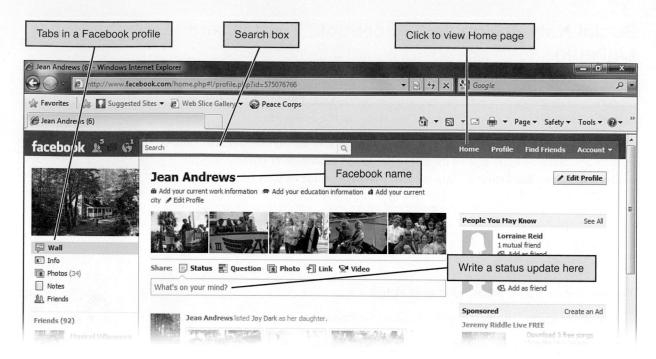

FIGURE 6-7
My Facebook profile shows the wall selected.

> **Note** Facebook is continually evolving. The organization of a Facebook page and how Facebook works change often. You might, therefore, find that current Facebook pages look different from those shown in the figures in this chapter.

The center column on the profile page can be your **wall**, the info area (information about you), a photo album, or your list of **Facebook friends**. To change the center column, click the tab on the left side of the profile window. In Figure 6-7, the wall tab is selected.

> **wall**—A column on the profile page where you and your friends can write or post photos or videos.
> **Facebook friend**—A Facebook user that you have accepted into your network.

All personal Facebook accounts are organized the same way (see Figure 6-8). You decide who is allowed to see your profile, but only you can see your Home page. From your Home page, you can manage your messages, events, and **News Feed**.

> **News Feed**—A column on your Home page that shows posts made by your Facebook friends and businesses that you follow. Facebook orders items in your News Feed by Top News or Most Recent.

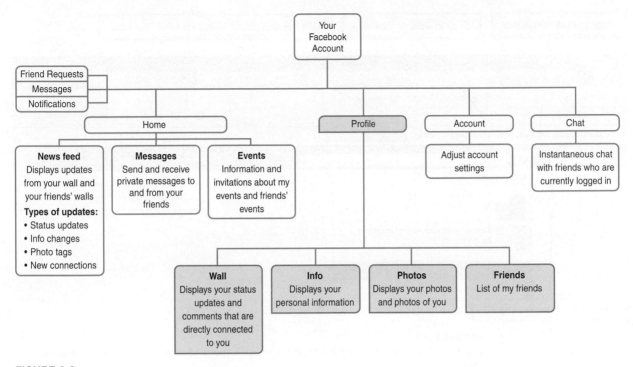

FIGURE 6-8
All personal Facebook accounts are organized the same way. The orange areas can be seen by others.

The blue menu bar at the top of the Facebook window gives you access to Friend Requests, **Facebook Messages**, **Facebook Notifications**, Home, Profile, Account, and Chat. Click an icon or link to see its contents (see Figure 6-9). Use the search box in the menu bar to search for people and content.

> **Facebook Messages**—A private message between friends, which works similar to email. You can set your Facebook account to email your messages to you. You have to sign in to Facebook to reply to the message.
>
> **Facebook Notifications**—Notices of activity in your Facebook account such as when a friend comments on a post you made to her wall or someone accepts your friend request.

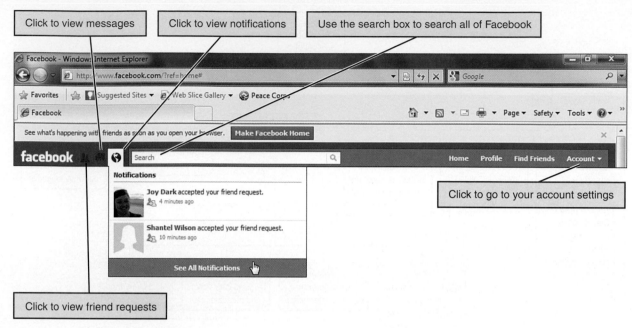

FIGURE 6-9
The menu bar at the top of the Facebook window gives access to pages in your Facebook account.

The menu bar always applies to your account even when you visit a friend's profile. For example, in Figure 6-10, when I visit Joy Dark's profile, the menu bar at the top still applies to my account and not to hers. By the way, notice the right side of the Facebook window in the figure where Facebook has displayed a group of photos that have **tags** with both our names.

> **tag**—A link on a photo or in a wall post to a Facebook user. Click the tag to see the user's profile.

Now that you know a little about how Facebook works, it's time to set up your own Facebook account. If you are already on Facebook, you can skip this activity.

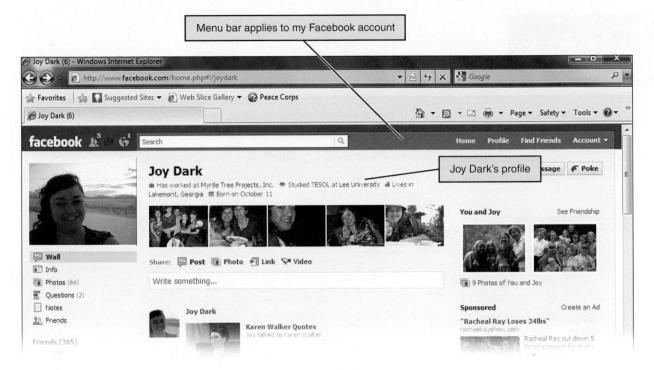

FIGURE 6-10
The menu bar contains links to my account even when I'm visiting my friend's profile.

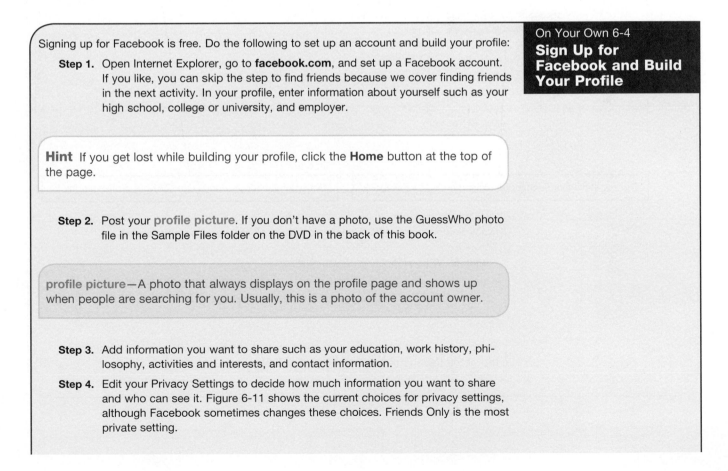

On Your Own 6-4
Sign Up for Facebook and Build Your Profile

Signing up for Facebook is free. Do the following to set up an account and build your profile:

Step 1. Open Internet Explorer, go to **facebook.com**, and set up a Facebook account. If you like, you can skip the step to find friends because we cover finding friends in the next activity. In your profile, enter information about yourself such as your high school, college or university, and employer.

Hint If you get lost while building your profile, click the **Home** button at the top of the page.

Step 2. Post your profile picture. If you don't have a photo, use the GuessWho photo file in the Sample Files folder on the DVD in the back of this book.

profile picture—A photo that always displays on the profile page and shows up when people are searching for you. Usually, this is a photo of the account owner.

Step 3. Add information you want to share such as your education, work history, philosophy, activities and interests, and contact information.

Step 4. Edit your Privacy Settings to decide how much information you want to share and who can see it. Figure 6-11 shows the current choices for privacy settings, although Facebook sometimes changes these choices. Friends Only is the most private setting.

On Your Own 6-4
Sign Up for Facebook and Build Your Profile

Everyone can see your profile information

Friends of your Facebook friends can see your profile information

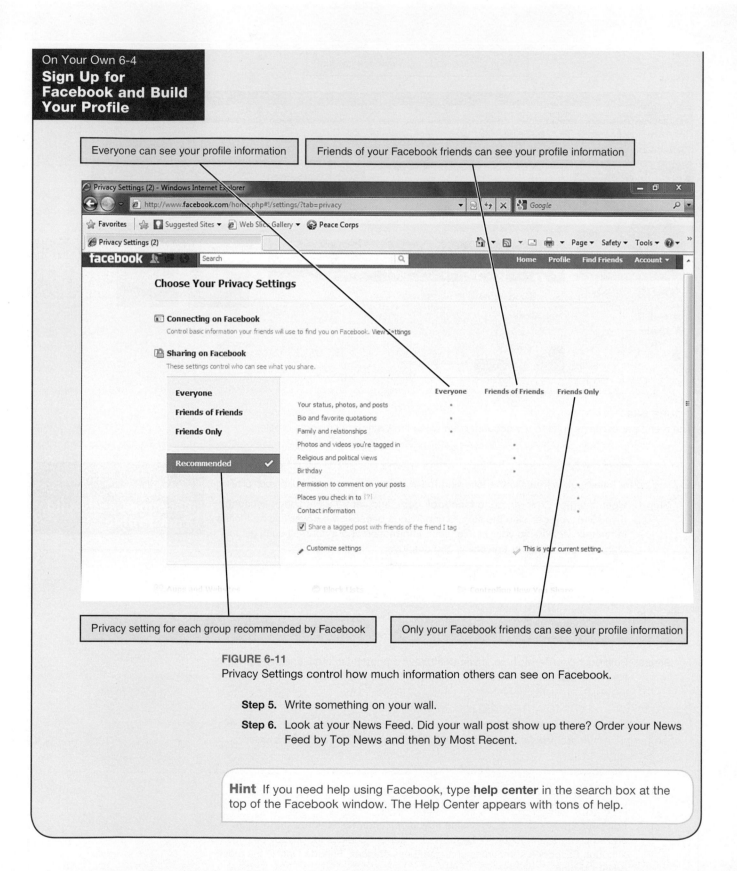

Privacy setting for each group recommended by Facebook

Only your Facebook friends can see your profile information

FIGURE 6-11
Privacy Settings control how much information others can see on Facebook.

Step 5. Write something on your wall.

Step 6. Look at your News Feed. Did your wall post show up there? Order your News Feed by Top News and then by Most Recent.

Hint If you need help using Facebook, type **help center** in the search box at the top of the Facebook window. The Help Center appears with tons of help.

As Facebook continues to evolve, so do the activities that show up on your News Feed. These activities might include

- Updates written on your wall

- Info changes

- Photo tags

- New connections with friends, businesses, and public figures

- Postings on a friend's wall

On Your Own 6-5
Find Friends on Facebook

So now you need some Facebook friends. When you find someone you know on Facebook, you send that person a Friend Request and wait until he approves the connection. Use these three methods to find friends:

- Use the search box in the menu bar to search on a person's name or email address. When you find a person you know, click **Add as Friend**. The person must respond to your Friend Request before you are friends.

Hint Information about you that everybody can always see in Facebook is your name, gender, profile picture, username, and network (list of friends). This is the information you can always count on to decide whether a person is someone you know.

- Facebook sometimes suggests people you might know based on your current connections. Look for a box in the right column on your profile page called *People You May Know*. To friend this person, click **Add as friend**. If you don't see the box, look under Find Friends in the menu bar. Or it might be that Facebook doesn't have a suggestion at this time.

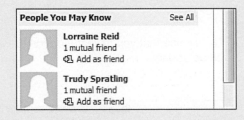

- Browse a friend's profile. Look at her list of friends. If you find a person you know, click **Add as Friend**.

Facebook offers many ways to communicate with your friends. Figure 6-12 shows some of these ways. In the figure, the green lines represent shared communication. The blue lines represent private communication between friends. The orange boxes represent pages that can be seen by others. If Privacy Settings are low, friends of friends or everybody might be able to see your profile and what you write on a friend's wall.

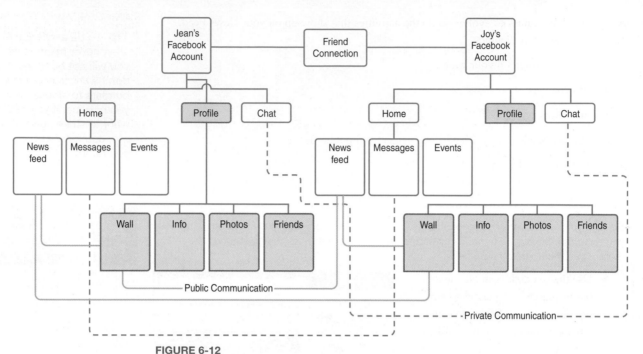

FIGURE 6-12
Content and communication on Facebook might be shared or private.

On Your Own 6-6
Build Online Relationships with Facebook Friends

To get started developing an online relationship with your friends, share on your wall what you are doing or thinking and reply to friends' updates. You can post photos in albums, tag yourself and friends in photos, and comment on photos. As you do this, you'll gradually learn more ways to interact on Facebook. Do the following:

Step 1. Visit a friend's profile and look at his photos. Click **Like** on a photo you like. This notifies your friend that you appreciate his sharing the photo. You can also unlike the photo if you change your mind.

> **Tip** Notice that you have the option to Like other items such as shared links and status updates, too.

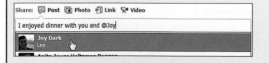

Step 2. Leave a comment on your friend's wall. Include a tag to another friend in your comment so your tagged friend will be notified that you mentioned her.

> **Hint** To tag a friend's name in a comment or status update, type @ followed by your friend's Facebook name. Select her name from the list that appears.

Step 3. While still on your friend's profile page, click **Send Message**. A box appears that you can use like email to send a message to your friend (see Figure 6-13). You can add other names in the To: field to send the message to other Facebook friends. Use the box to send a message to your friend.

FIGURE 6-13
Send a private message to a friend.

Green dot means friend is active in Facebook

Gray moon means friend is idle in Facebook

Step 4. Another way to communicate with your Facebook friends is through Chat. No matter where you are in Facebook, Chat is in the lower-right corner of your screen, as shown in Figure 6-14. Use the Chat box to chat with a Facebook friend who is currently online.

FIGURE 6-14
Use Chat to text in real time with your friends.

Tip If you don't want your friends to know you are online, in the Chat box, click **Options** and then click **Go offline**.

Businesses and Public Figures Use Facebook Pages

Individuals use a Facebook profile, but organizations and public figures use a **Facebook page** to connect with consumers and clients. Facebook pages can be seen by all Facebook users.

> **Facebook page**—A page that represents a business, organization, or public figure on Facebook. A page contains information about the subject, wall posts, photos, videos, events, discussions, and links.

When you Like a page as shown in Figure 6-15, your wall reports it. The page you Like is then listed under Activities and Interests on your Info tab. You get later updates from that page in your News Feed.

Click a page to Like it

FIGURE 6-15
To Like a page, mouse over it and then click **Like**.

On Your Own 6-7
Find and Like Facebook Pages

Browse Facebook pages and view one page about a business. Which page did you view? Find another page about a public figure. **Like** that page. Which page did you Like?

Use Twitter to Know What's Happening Now

Twitter is a quick and easy way to send short messages of 140 or fewer characters to others. Sign up for Twitter at twitter.com and select Twitter accounts to follow. Then, whenever you log on to Twitter, you can read their **Tweets** or messages. You can send Tweets to whoever is following you (see Figure 6-16).

Tweet—A short message (140 characters or less) sent to followers on Twitter.com. A Tweet can contain URL links to websites.

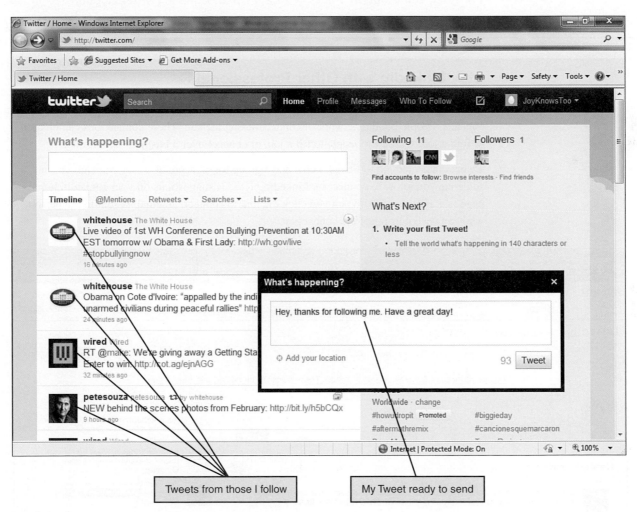

Tweets from those I follow

My Tweet ready to send

FIGURE 6-16
Send a quick Tweet to your followers about what's happening now.

Many people enjoy using Twitter on their iPhones and other smartphones. You can download an **app** from twitter.com to your phone so that you can send and receive Tweets at any time.

app—An abbreviation for *application,* which is a software program. A small program downloaded to your iPhone, Blackberry, Android, or other smartphone is called an app.

The joy of Twitter is to instantly know what your friends or those you admire are doing. The downside of Twitter is information overload. Twitter was invented by Jack Dorsey, who said the chirps of a bird are like unimportant information. That's why he decided to call his invention Twitter.

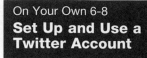
On Your Own 6-8
Set Up and Use a Twitter Account

Go to **twitter.com** and set up a Twitter account. Follow at least three organizations or celebrities. Follow at least one friend who uses Twitter and get one friend to follow you. Post at least two Tweets. What interesting Tweets did you receive?

? Solutions Appendix **For help, see Solution 6-8: How to Set Up and Use a Twitter Account.**

Stay LinkedIn with Other Professionals

LinkedIn.com is a social networking site mostly used by professionals to maintain business contacts. People build a network of connections on the site. These connections can be used to find a job, search for people to fill a job, or connect over a business opportunity.

To get connected, go to linkedin.com and sign up for an account. After you sign up, find someone you know to connect to. LinkedIn provides suggestions on your LinkedIn home page (see Figure 6-17). When you click the link to connect, an email is sent to the person, who can accept or reject the connection.

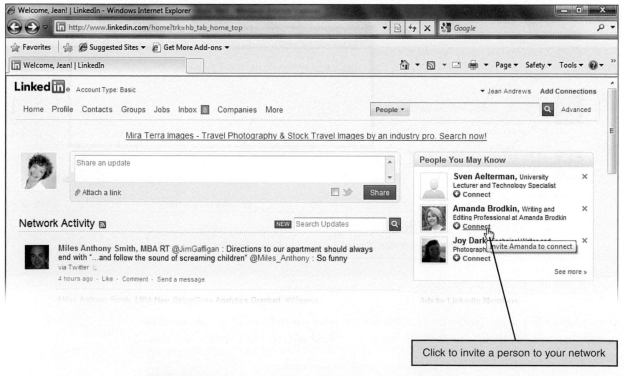

FIGURE 6-17
Make a connection in LinkedIn.

After you make the connection, that person is listed on your home page. For example, Sarah Sambol is listed on my home page with her recent updates and a link to her connections (see Figure 6-18). If I'm looking for a professional photographer to help with a project, I might find that person through Sarah's connections. By clicking the link on my page to Sarah's connections, I find a photographer listed on Sarah's page (see Figure 6-19).

FIGURE 6-18
My connections show on my LinkedIn home page.

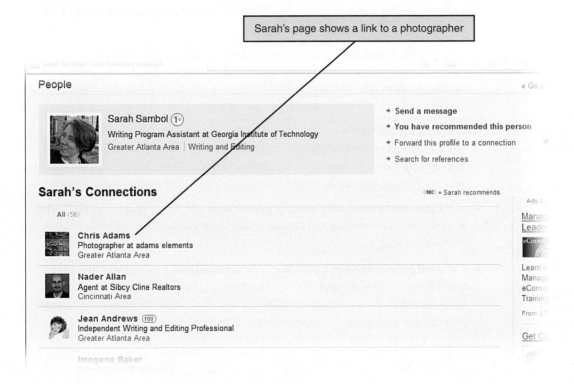

FIGURE 6-19
Find a new connection through your current connections in LinkedIn.

I can also post an update that I'm looking for a photographer, and my network of connections all see my post. The word gets out there's a project available for a photographer. And so it goes to build a network of business and professional connections.

Best Practices for Social Networking

Now that you know about Facebook, Twitter, LinkedIn, and other social networking sites, let's consider best practices when using them. Here are some tips for staying safe and presenting yourself well:

▶ **Security settings.** Understand your security settings on each social networking site you use. Protect your privacy using these settings. Check your security settings occasionally to make sure the site has not changed the rules. When a site changes its rules, you might be more exposed than you expect. For Facebook, recall that you can view and change your security settings by clicking **Account** and then clicking **Privacy Settings**.

▶ **Be kind online.** Angry confrontations don't belong online. It's okay to express disagreements on Facebook, a blog, or other site, but write professionally when you do so. Anger online only makes you appear petty and unconvincing. Kind words turn away anger. Be gracious to others.

▶ **Pay attention to what you reveal about yourself.** To protect from thieves, never post online when you will be away from home. Never make public your date of birth, mother's maiden name, or other security questions that someone might use to steel your identity.

Most potential employers search for you online when you apply for a job. If an employer finds inappropriate photos, content about drugs and drinking, negative statements about previous employers or clients, or information that showed you lied on your application, you are unlikely to get the job.

> **Tip** If someone tags you in an embarrassing photo on his site, untag yourself.

▶ **Present yourself well.** Speaking of finding a job, employers are more likely to hire you if they find online that you can communicate well, that friends respond well to you, and you generally have a positive outlook on life. Your online social networking sites are your opportunity to shine.

▶ **Use LinkedIn to focus only on your professional life.** Don't post comments about your personal life on LinkedIn. Generally limit your connections to people in your professional life.

> **Tip** Remember this rule: *What you put online is forever.* If you later remove it, someone still has a record of it somewhere.

▶ **Use good judgment when balancing your personal and professional life.** What might happen if you friended a boss, coworker, or client on Facebook? Would they know too much about your personal life that you don't want shared at work? Keeping personal and professional lives separated is difficult to do when we use social networking sites. Think before you share or connect online.

Present Yourself with Blogging

A blog, or weblog, is an online diary or journal. Many websites offer blog space. The two most popular blog sites are blogspot.com and wordpress.com.

The creator of a blog, called the blogger, posts text, photos, and links to other sites on the blog. The creator can allow comments from others on the blog. Also, a group of people can together create a blog so the blog becomes a community blog. Corporations often use blogs to connect with their customers. Figure 6-20 shows a popular blog by Marc and Angel Chernoff at marcandangel.com.

FIGURE 6-20
Marc and Angel write a blog about practical tips for productive living.

Is a blog a social networking site? Not really. A blog is a social media. People come to your blog and make comments, but blogs are not used to build a network of blogs.

> **Tip** When creating your own blog, consider the design for your blog. To see some great designs for blogs, do a Google search on "great blog designs."

On Your Own 6-9
Create a Blog and Post to It

Create a blog using blogspot.com, wordpress.com, or another free blogging site. Write on your blog an experience you had growing up that has influenced your life, a hobby you feel passionate about, or a review of your favorite movie. What is the name of your blog? What is the URL? Email the link to your blog to your instructor.

For help, see Solution 6-9: How to Create a Blog and Post to It.

? Solutions Appendix

Communicating in Real Time with Text, Voice, and Video

You can use the Internet to communicate in real time using text, voice, and video. Figure 6-21 shows a video call in progress. Instant Messaging, Internet voice, and streaming video are discussed in this part of the chapter.

FIGURE 6-21
Real-time communication can happen in voice and video.

Instant Messaging

Instant Messaging (IM), also called chat, is real-time communication in text over the Internet. Recall from Chapter 2 that businesses might offer a chat service on their websites. You can click a link on a web page to open a chat session with a customer service representative.

> **Instant Messaging (IM)**—Real-time communication in text on the Internet. Some IM software also includes the options to include voice and video. Also called chat.

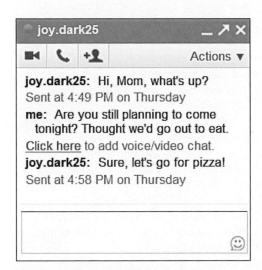

FIGURE 6-22
When no extra software or hardware is used, a chat session works only in text mode.

Many websites offer chat services including Facebook, Windows Live Messenger, Yahoo! Messenger, AIM, and Google Talk. If you have an account on these sites, you can chat with friends who have an account with the same service. Figure 6-22 shows the corner of my Gmail.com email window with a chat session open. You used Facebook Chat earlier in On Your Own 6-6.

Internet Voice using VoIP

The technology used on the Internet for voice communication is called **VoIP (Voice over Internet Protocol)**. Companies that offer VoIP services include Skype, Vonage, Google, and many others. Skype is the most popular free VoIP service.

> **VoIP (Voice over Internet Protocol)**—A technology that allows voice communication over the Internet.

To use Internet voice, go to a website that offers the service and sign up for it. A service might cost you a fee. For example, you can sign up for a Skype account at no charge, and Skype-to-Skype calls are free. But you must pay for other types of calls such as when calling land lines and cell phones. You need to download and install the Skype software.

To use Internet voice on your computer, you need a microphone and speaker. A good option for both is a **headset**.

> **headset**—A device that is both a microphone and speaker. It can use one USB port or two connectors that plug into the microphone and speaker ports on a computer.

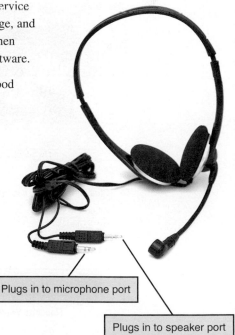

Plugs in to microphone port

Plugs in to speaker port

Streaming Video

Many websites that offer chat and Internet voice also support **streaming video**. To communicate in live streaming video, each party needs a **web cam**. You might need to first install the software that supports the web cam. This software is called a **device driver**.

web cam

streaming video—Video that flows continually to your computer as you watch the video. The video might be live or might be streamed to you from a video file stored on a server. In the second situation, you are watching the video as the data is downloaded rather than downloading the entire file and then watching it.

web cam—A video camera connected to your computer that can stream video to the Internet. Many laptops have built-in web cams, or you can plug an external web cam into a USB port.

device driver—Software that supports a hardware device such as a web cam or printer. When you purchase a device, the device drivers come on a DVD with the device and can also be downloaded from the website of the device manufacturer.

Google Chat - Chat with family and friends

Google

Check out the following ways to chat on the web and on your

Video and voice plug-in

- Chat within Gmail, iGoogle, and orkut
- All on the web
- PC and Mac

Learn more »

Install video chat plug-in

Requires Windows XP + or

Done

Tip Most external web cams use a USB port. How to install a USB device is covered in Chapter 13, "Maintaining a Computer and Fixing Computer Problems."

You also need to install the streaming video software. Figure 6-23 shows part of the page at google.com/talk where you can download chat, voice, and video software from Google.

FIGURE 6-23
A chat session can include voice and video if both parties have a speaker, microphone, web cam, and installed software.

Summary

Communicating Through Email

▶ An email address has two parts separated by an at symbol (@). The first part is the email account, and the second part is the domain name of the email server.

▶ Email is managed by a mailer server that receives incoming email and a mailbox server that holds email until the receiver requests it.

▶ When learning to use email, you need to know how to manage your inbox and to send, reply, forward, and delete messages. You also need to know how to manage email attachments.

▶ You can manage email using a website or an email client such as Microsoft Outlook.

▶ Before using Outlook to manage email, you must set up your email account in Outlook.

▶ Know how to protect your identify and your computer when using email. Avoid identity theft, viruses, phishing, spam, chain email, and other social engineering methods.

▶ When using email, respond in a timely manner, be polite, and don't include confidential or embarrassing information in email.

Social Networking with Facebook, Twitter, and LinkedIn

▶ Web 2.0 refers to the second generation of how the web is used where users both receive and post information.

▶ Social networking sites used to stay in touch with friends, family, and business associates include Facebook, Twitter, and LinkedIn.

▶ Individuals using Facebook use a Facebook profile to present themselves to and interact with other Facebook users.

▶ The wall tab on the Facebook profile is used to post text, photos, and videos. Your News Feed shows activities on your wall and on the walls of your Facebook friends.

▶ Use the Facebook menu bar to access your Facebook Home page, profile, account settings, and other parts of your Facebook account.

▶ Use Facebook privacy settings to decide how much information about yourself and your activities are revealed to others.

▶ Businesses and public figures use Facebook pages rather than Facebook profiles used by individuals.

▶ Twitter is a quick and easy way to send Tweets, which are messages of 140 or fewer characters.

▶ You need an app on your smartphone to be able to receive and send Tweets using Twitter.

▶ LinkedIn.com is a social networking site used by professionals to build a network of professional contacts.

▶ When using social networking sites, use good security settings to protect your privacy, don't reveal inappropriate or confidential information, and present yourself well.

Present Yourself with Blogging

▶ A blog, or weblog, is an online diary or journal. Others can comment on your blog posts. You can post text, graphics, and links to other sites.

Communicating in Real Time with Voice, Text, and Video

▶ Instant Messaging (IM) or chat is real-time communication in text, voice, and video on the Internet.

▶ Voice communication on the Internet uses VoIP technology. Many providers, such as Skype, offer a free limited VoIP service.

▶ To use live streaming video over the Internet, you and your friend need a web cam to stream video and software installed.

Review Questions

Answer these questions to assess your skills and knowledge of the content covered in the chapter. Your instructor can provide you with the correct answers when you are ready to check your work.

1. Which part of the email address SusieJones@sample.edu identifies the email account? The domain name of the email server?

2. Where is an email message stored until the recipient requests it?

3. When you first open an email message you have received that has an attachment, is the attachment automatically opened?

4. What two types of software tools can you use to manage email?

5. When you delete a message in your email inbox, what happens to that message?

6. Which is visible to other Facebook users, your News Feed or your Facebook profile?

7. When you find a Facebook user whom you want to be a friend, what two steps are needed to be friends on Facebook?

8. Using Facebook, a(n) _____ is when you identify a person in a photo.

9. What is the maximum length of a Tweet when using Twitter?

10. To use Twitter on your smartphone, what must you do first?

11. What is the primary purpose of LinkedIn?

12. What are the two most popular blog sites?

13. Is a blog considered a social networking site? Why or why not?

14. What technology is used by Skype, Vonage, and other services to transmit voice over the Internet?

15. What hardware device is needed to transmit video over the Internet so you can have a video chat session with a friend?

Chapter Mastery Project

Find out how well you have mastered the content in this chapter by completing this project. If you can answer all the questions and do all the steps without looking back at the chapter details, you have mastered this chapter. If you can complete the project by finding answers using the web, you have proven that you can teach yourself how to communicate with others using the web.

If you find you need a lot of help doing the project and you have not yet read the chapter or done the activities, drop back and start at the beginning of the chapter and then return to this project.

> **Hint** All the key terms in the chapter are used in this mastery project. If you encounter a key word you don't know such as *Web 2.0,* enter **define:Web 2.0** in the Internet Explorer search box.

You need an email address to complete this project. In Chapter 2, you needed an email address to sign up for a SkyDrive account. Use that email address or another address in this project.

Mastery Project Part 1: Communicating Through Email

If you need help completing this part of the mastery project, please review the "Communicating Through Email" section in the chapter.

Do the following to send and receive email using a website:

Step 1. Go to the website of your email provider and sign in to your email account. What is your account name? What is the domain name of your email server?

Step 2. How many messages are in your inbox? Open and view one message. If you have access to a printer, print the message.

Step 3. Write a message to a friend and send it. What is the email address of your friend?

Step 4. Delete the messages in your inbox you no longer need. Look in the folder for deleted messages. How many messages are there? How long will deleted messages stay in this folder?

Step 5. Write another message to a friend, this time attaching a Word document file to the message. If you don't have a file to attach, use the file LetterToDave that is provided in the Sample Files folder on the DVD in the back of the book.

Step 6. Ask a friend to send you a Word document as an attachment to an email message. When you receive the email, open the attachment. Then close the attachment and save it to your USB flash drive or another location given by your instructor. What is the name of the file you received from your friend?

Step 7. Forward your friend's message to another friend. Is the file your friend sent attached to the forwarded message?

Do the following to use Microsoft Outlook:

Step 1. Open Microsoft Outlook and set it up to use your email address to manage your email.

Step 2. Repeat the steps to use a website to manage email, this time using Outlook.

Answer these questions:

1. How can having more than one email address help prevent spam from coming to the address you use for personal communication?

2. What extra software must you install before you can set up a hotmail.com or live.com email account using Microsoft Outlook?

3. If you want to store all your email messages on your laptop, should you use a website or Outlook to manage your email? Why?

4. Why is it best not to click a link in an email message from a business or someone you don't know?

5. Why should you never include your credit card information in an email message?

6. Phishing is a type of ___ engineering. Describe phishing and explain how to avoid it.

7. When you send an attachment with an email message, does the attachment go to those who are listed under the CC feature of the message? What does CC stand for?

Mastery Project Part 2: Social Networking with Facebook, Twitter, and LinkedIn

If you need help completing this part of the mastery project, please review the "Social Networking with Facebook, Twitter, and LinkedIn" section in the chapter.

Do the following to set up and use Facebook:

Step 1. If you do not already have a Facebook account, sign up for one.

Step 2. Post a profile picture to your account. Write a status update on your wall. Check your Privacy Settings. Who can see your status, photos, and posts? Adjust your privacy settings so you feel comfortable with what is revealed to others.

Step 3. View your News Feed. Is it ordered by Top News or Most Recent? Post a comment to your News Feed.

Step 4. Post a photo. If you don't have a photo to post, use one in the Sample Files folder on the DVD in the back of the book.

Step 5. Use the search box to find a Facebook user that you know and then make a friend request.

Step 6. Go to a friend's profile and browse his list of friends. Find someone you know and make a friend request.

Step 7. Find a photo in a friend's profile. Like the photo and tag someone in the photo you know. Send a private message to your friend.

Step 8. Use Facebook Chat to chat with a friend.

Step 9. Find a public figure on Facebook and Like that person.

Do the following to use Twitter:

Step 1. If you do not already have a Twitter account, sign up for one.

Step 2. Follow a public figure and at least one friend.

Step 3. Post a Tweet.

Answer the following questions about online social networking:

1. Why is it not appropriate to post personal information on LinkedIn?

2. Why is it important not to post embarrassing or confidential information on Facebook?

Mastery Project Part 3: Present Yourself with Blogging

If you need help completing this part of the mastery project, please review the "Present Yourself with Blogging" section in the chapter.

Do the following:

Step 1. If you have not already created a blog on blogspot.com, wordpress.com, or some other blogging site, do so now. What is the name of your blog? What is the URL? Email the link to your blog to your instructor.

Step 2. Write on your blog your experiences in this course. Which project did you enjoy the most? Which project do you think could be improved? What improvements would you make to this textbook or the projects?

Step 3. If you think the author should see your suggestions for improving the textbook, post a comment on http://www.pearsonhighered.com/jump/.

Mastery Project Part 4: Communicating in Real Time with Voice, Text, and Video

If you need help completing this part of the mastery project, please review the "Communicating in Real Time with Voice, Text, and Video" section in the chapter. Answer the following questions:

1. When you watch a video posted on Youtube.com, are you using VoIP, streaming video, chat, or a downloaded video file?

2. What two input devices are used during a video phone call using Skype?

3. What output device other than the monitor is used during a video phone call?

4. What type of software must be installed before you can use a web cam with any application?

Becoming an Independent Learner

Answer the following questions about becoming an independent learner:

1. To teach yourself to use the Internet for communication, do you think it is best to rely on the chapter or on the web when you need answers? Why?

2. The most important skill learned in this chapter is how to teach yourself a computer skill. Rate yourself at Level A through E on how well you are doing with this skill. What is your level?

   ○ Level A: I was able to successfully complete the Chapter Mastery Project without the help of doing the On Your Own activities in the chapter.

   ○ Level B: I completed all the On Your Own activities and the Chapter Mastery Project without referring to any of the solutions in the *Solutions Appendix*.

   ○ Level C: I completed all the On Your Own activities and the Chapter Mastery Project by using just a few of the solutions in the *Solutions Appendix*.

   ○ Level D: I completed all the On Your Own activities and the Chapter Mastery Project by using many of the solutions in the *Solutions Appendix*.

   ○ Level E: I completed all the On Your Own activities and the Chapter Mastery Project and had to use all the solutions in the *Solutions Appendix*.

To continue toward the goal of teaching yourself computer skills, if you are not at Level A, try to move up one level on how you learn in Chapter 7, "Finding a Job Using the Web, a Résumé, and a Business Letter."

Projects to Help You

Now that you have mastered the material in this chapter, you are ready to tackle the three projects introduced at the beginning of the chapter in the section "How Will This Chapter Help Me?"

Project 1: Communicating on the Web in Your Personal Life

The web is a great way to stay in touch with extended family and friends. Use the skills you learned in this chapter to build your relationships online. Do the following:

Step 1. Encourage older family members who don't use Facebook to sign up. Help a family member set up a Facebook account and find other family members to friend. Post a family photo to Facebook and tag the photo with the names of other family members on Facebook.

Step 2. Check your privacy settings on your Facebook account. Log off your account. Then do a Google search for your name, searching on the Facebook.com site. What information can any visitors see about you even if they are not logged on

PERSONAL PROJECT: I want to use Facebook and a blog to stay connected online with family and friends. I want to use Skype to talk for free with family members who live in another country.

to Facebook? Can they see your profile picture? Your date of birth? How easy is it to find you on Facebook?

Step 3. In the chapter, you wrote a blog about an event in your childhood, a hobby, or a favorite movie. Ask a family member (spouse, sister, brother, child, grandparent, parent, aunt, or uncle) to comment on your blog. If this person does not know how to use the web and a blog, here's your chance to share what you've learned.

Step 4. Blog sites might offer privacy settings to allow everyone to access your blog, to block search engines from finding your blog, or to limit access to people you choose. What privacy settings are offered by your blog site? What settings are you currently using?

If you have a speaker, microphone, and access to a computer where you can install software, do the following to set up and use Skype:

Step 1. Go to skype.com and set up an account. You need to download and install the software on your computer.

Step 2. Find a friend or family member who has a Skype account and talk using Skype. Skype is a great way to talk with family and friends in other countries who use Skype because Skype-to-Skype calls are free.

Project 2: Communicating on the Web in Your Academic Career

Do the following to use the web for communication in your academic career:

Step 1. Select an instructor at your school that you like. Search the web for social networking sites that he uses. Does he write a blog? Does he have a profile on Facebook that is public? Is he on LinkedIn? Does he use Twitter? If he writes a blog that allows public comments, comment on his blog.

Step 2. Volunteer to build a Facebook page for a club at your school or a nonprofit organization. Do the following:

    a. Ask the leaders of the club or organization for permission and the correct information to post. Also ask for the email addresses of its members and associates and a graphic file of the logo. A photo or two will add interest to the page.

    b. Build the page and include the information, logo, and any photos you have. To find out how to set up a page for a business or other organization, search the Help Center in Facebook.

    c. Post a link to the page on your Facebook wall and invite your friends to Like the page. Send an email message to the email addresses of the members of the organization announcing the page and asking them to Like it on Facebook.

ACADEMIC PROJECT: I want to see what my instructors are saying on Facebook. Also, my club wants to use Facebook to show pictures of our events and attract other members.

Project 3: Communicating on the Web in Your Technical Career

Do the following to improve your online communication skills for your technical career:

Step 1. To improve your skill using email, do the following using the website of your email provider or using Outlook:

    a. In the chapter, you learned to attach a file to an email message. If the file contains a photo or other graphic, you can insert the file into the body of the email message. Send an email message with an inserted picture.

    b. Insert a symbol in an email message. For example, insert a happy face or a wink.

    c. Format text in an email message using bold, italic, font color, and other formatting tools.

    d. Find a stationery to use as the background for your email messages. Using Outlook, apply the stationery to an email message.

    e. Add all the email addresses you regularly use to the contact list in your email address book.

TECHNICAL CAREER PROJECT: The business I work for part time expects my email messages to look professional. I want to build a professional network using LinkedIn, and I want some personal advice and tips for finding a great job in IT.

Step 2. If you do not already have a LinkedIn account, sign up for one. Try to expand your network of professionals to instructors, employers, and other friends also building a technical career. Ask an instructor or former employer to post a recommendation on your LinkedIn page. Post an update on the page about your plans to build a career in IT.

Step 3. Search for a blog written by someone who has a job in IT similar to the job you would like to have. Post a comment on his blog and ask for advice about how to find the right job or what skills you need to know.

Project to Help Others

One of the best ways to learn is to teach someone else. And, in teaching someone else, you are making a contribution into that person's life. As part of each chapter's work, you are encouraged to teach someone else a skill you have learned.

Who is your apprentice? _____

When helping others learn, don't do the work for them. Coach and instruct. Show them how to find information for themselves. Help them be as independent a learner as possible.

Do the following to help your apprentice communicate on the web:

Step 1. If your apprentice does not already use email, help him set up an email account and use it to send and receive email. Help him learn all the email skills presented in this chapter. If he already uses email, ask him if he has questions or wants to learn more.

Step 2. If your apprentice does not already have a Facebook account, help him set one up and use it. Keep working together until he understands Facebook, has several Facebook friends, and is comfortable building a social network using Facebook.

Step 3. Show your apprentice your blog and invite him to comment on one of your blog entries. Then show him how to set up his own blog. After he has posted to his blog, make a comment on his post.

Step 4. Does your apprentice want to learn to use Skype or another free Internet voice service? If so, help him set it up and use it.

Step 5. If your apprentice has a web cam and is interested in video chat, help him set that up.

Now that your apprentice is learning to use the web for communication, be sure to encourage him to continue building his skills by sending him email messages, posting on his Facebook page, and commenting on his blog. Praise him as his skills improve.

CHAPTER 7

Finding a Job Using the Web, a Résumé, and a Business Letter

IN THIS CHAPTER, YOU WILL

Learn job-hunting strategies

Create and send a résumé

Create and send an interview follow-up letter

Most of us will find it necessary to apply for a job at some point in our career. The web and Microsoft Word can help you find a job and apply for it. In this chapter, you learn about job-hunting strategies. You use Word to manage your contacts list in a job search, and you use Word templates to make a one-page résumé and business letter.

As always, remember the most important computer skill is how to teach yourself a computer skill. Therefore, this chapter is designed to help you teach yourself how to find a job with the web and Word. Try to do each On Your Own activity without any help. But remember, if you need help, you can always refer to the solutions in the *Solutions Appendix*.

JUMP RIGHT IN

If you want even more of a challenge, try proceeding directly to the Chapter Mastery Project at the end of this chapter. If you need help on the project, refer to the On Your Own activities in the chapter or do your own independent investigating using Word Help or searching the web for answers. When you complete the project, you will have mastered the skills in this chapter. Then go to the Projects to Help You that require you apply your skills to new situations.

How Will This Chapter Help Me?

Throughout this book, each chapter provides three projects focusing on personal, academic, or technical career goals. Depending on your own interests, you might choose to complete any or all of these projects to help you achieve your goals.

PERSONAL PROJECT: I plan to apply for a job. I need to create a résumé and all the other documents that can help me land a great job.

ACADEMIC PROJECT: I love what I'm studying, and I don't want to change my major. But the job market in my field is tough. I need to find out what job options are available for me. Maybe my school can help me figure out what will work for me. What academic resources can help me?

TECHNICAL CAREER PROJECT: I want a technical job, and I love working with people. I don't want to sit in front of a computer all day. What job in IT might be right for me?

Job-Hunting Strategies

Searching for a job can be hard work, and a good strategy makes work more effective. When searching for a job, keep these ten strategies in mind:

- ▶ **Know yourself.** Know your strengths and weaknesses. Know what will make you happy and satisfied. Your school might offer career and aptitude assessments. Take advantage of these opportunities to find out more about yourself.

- ▶ **Know what job will work for you.** Know what jobs you will be good at and will enjoy. When given the opportunity, be ready to explain what makes you unique and the best candidate for the job.

- ▶ **Work at finding a job.** Don't wait for the job to come to you. Use all the strategies in this chapter, work hard, and don't give up until you find your job.

- ▶ **Network with lots of people.** Let as many people as possible know that you're looking for a job. Use social networking and professional networking sites. Tell your friends, family, neighbors, and former teachers that you're looking for a job. Most job openings are never advertised and are filled by a direct referral.

- ▶ **Communicate with real people.** Computers don't hire people; people hire people. Whenever possible, make personal contact with a real person. For example, after you post your résumé online, follow up with a personal phone call.

> **résumé**—A document summarizing job experience and education for employers to use when deciding who to interview or hire for a job. The document should be brief and to the point.

- ▶ **Go to the top.** The higher the person is in the organization you talk with, the more likely you will be hired. Do your best to reach someone with authority and influence.

- ▶ **Know what companies want.** Most employers are hiring someone because they are trying to solve a problem. Ask enough questions to uncover what is the problem to be solved. Then present yourself as the solution to the problem.

- ▶ **Be willing to settle for less.** Sometimes a temporary job that lasts only a few weeks or a part-time job is all you need to get your foot in the door. Be willing to take a job for less pay or less responsibility than you deserve. When working on this less-than-perfect job, always do your very best even when you think no one is looking. As you prove yourself, people take notice and are more likely to offer you a better or more permanent job.

- ▶ **Keep good records.** Keep a list of contacts, what you sent the contact, and when you sent it. Include follow-up information. This list helps with your current job search and also can help you with future searches.

- ▶ **Use technology effectively.** In this chapter, you learn to effectively use technology to help you find a job. You learn to create a document for tracking contacts, create a résumé and email and post the résumé online, create an interview follow-up letter, and email the letter.

You can find many job-hunting strategies on the web. For example, if you need to know how to best present yourself at a job interview, use Google.com to search the web for **tips for job interviews**.

Finding Jobs That Suit Your Skills

The web is a valuable resource when you're looking for a job. Here are a few tips and websites to consider when looking online for a job:

▶ **Job search engines.** Some job search sites are Monster.com, Indeed.com, CareerBuilder.com, Dice.com (limited to jobs in technology), LinkUp.com, and SimplyHired.com. You can search for jobs in your area, and some of these sites allow you to post your résumé to the site. Also look for jobs in the online classified ads on craigslist.org (see Figure 7-1).

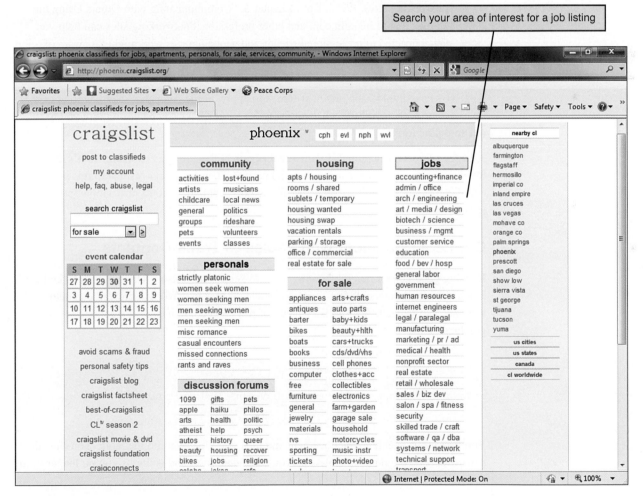

FIGURE 7-1
Craigslist.org offers job listings for specific areas.

▶ **Government jobs.** Find listings for jobs with the federal government at USAJOBS.gov. Also search your local and state government websites for job postings.

▶ **Large corporations.** Go to the websites of large corporations and look for job postings for the organization.

▶ **Local newspaper websites.** Check the classified ads sections of the website for your local newspaper for jobs in your area.

▶ **Your school or university website.** Your school might post job openings in the area on its website. If you don't find postings there, check the student and alumni service department at your school for job openings and for help finding a job.

▶ **Job fairs.** Search the web for job fairs in your city and field. For example, do a Google search on **job fairs in Baltimore**. Your school website might also post announcements about job fairs in the area.

▶ **Recruiters.** Use a recruiter to help you find a professional job. Some recruiter sites are therecruiternetwork.com, theladders.com, headhunters.com, and job-hunt.org.

▶ **Networking sites.** Recall from Chapter 6, "Communicating with Others Using the Internet," that LinkedIn.com and other professional networking sites can help you stay connected to professional friends and acquaintances who might be aware of a job that fits your needs.

> **Tip** When attending a job fair, always take several copies of your résumé with you.

After you have found a job, the next step is to apply. Some companies ask you to upload your résumé to their website when applying for a job. Other companies require you to fill out an online form.

A better approach is to connect with a real person at the company. Sometimes it's difficult, but do your best to find the name of a real person. Then send your résumé to this person by email and follow up with a phone call. Remember, computers don't hire people; people hire people.

Create a Document with Tables to Track Contacts

Keeping good notes when job hunting helps to keep you on track. These notes can be kept in a handwritten notebook or a Word document. Tables in a Word document can help keep notes organized. A **table** is made up of rows and columns that can contain text and graphics.

> **table**—An element that can be inserted into a Word document and is made up of rows and columns. Tables are used to organize text and graphics.

You first insert a table in the document and then you type text into the table. You can add new rows and columns to a table, and you can delete rows and columns you no longer need.

Create a document that uses tables to track contacts when job hunting, as shown in Figure 7-2. Use one table for each contact. The document has two contacts and a third table waiting for the next contact. Save the document to your USB flash drive, hard drive, SkyDrive, or other location given by your instructor. Name the document **MyContacts**.

Video **7-1**

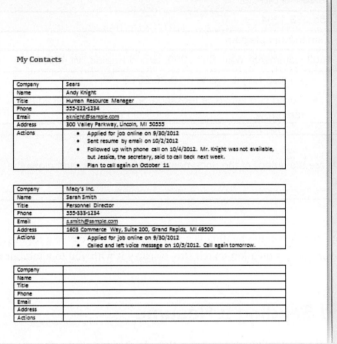

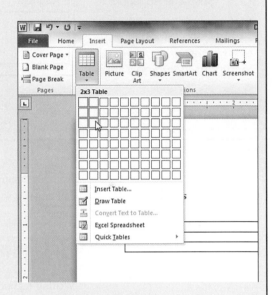

FIGURE 7-2
The contacts document uses one table for each contact.

Do the following to create the document:

Step 1. Enter the title of the document and format it using the Heading 1 style.

Step 2. Create one table with two columns. Enter the information in column one as shown in Figure 7-2 and also below. Resize the columns as shown in Figure 7-2. Make two more copies of this table in the document.

Step 3. Enter the following contact information for Andy Knight in the first table:

Hint Use the Insert ribbon to insert a table. When a table is selected or the insertion point is inside a table, the Table Tools Design tab and Layout tab show up on the Word window. Use the Layout ribbon to insert and delete rows and columns.

Company	Sears
Name	Andy Knight
Title	Human Resource Manager
Phone	555-222-1234
Email	aknight@sample.com
Address	300 Valley Parkway, Lincoln, MI 50555
Actions	• Applied for job online on 9/30/2012 • Sent résumé by email on 10/2/2012 • Followed up with phone call on 10/4/2012. Mr. Knight was not available, but Jessica, the receptionist, said to call back next week. • Plan to call again on October 11

Step 4.   Enter the following contact information for Sarah Smith in the second table:

Company	Macy's Inc.
Name	Sarah Smith
Title	Personnel Director
Phone	555-333-1234
Email	s.smith@sample.com
Address	1603 Commerce Way, Suite 200, Grand Rapids, MI 49500
Actions	• Applied for job online on 9/30/2012 • Called and left voice message on 10/5/2012. Call again tomorrow.

Step 5.   Verify you are the author of the document, save your work, and close the document.

Another document you need when job hunting is a résumé. After you create a résumé, you can email it to employers, post it on a job search site, or carry it with you to a job fair or job interview.

Creating and Sending a Résumé

Writing a good résumé is an essential job-acquiring skill. In this part of the chapter, you learn to use a résumé template to create a dynamite résumé, which can help you stand out as the best candidate for the job.

Use a Résumé Template

Although you can write your résumé without using a template, a résumé template can

▶ Provide a structure for the information in your résumé.

▶ Give your résumé an appealing format.

▶ Provide time-tested suggestions for what information to include on your résumé.

Word provides many templates for résumés. A few are shown in Figure 7-3. Choose a résumé format that looks professional without too much color or clip art. If you choose a résumé that targets the type of job you seek, the areas in the résumé are likely to work for you without a lot of changes.

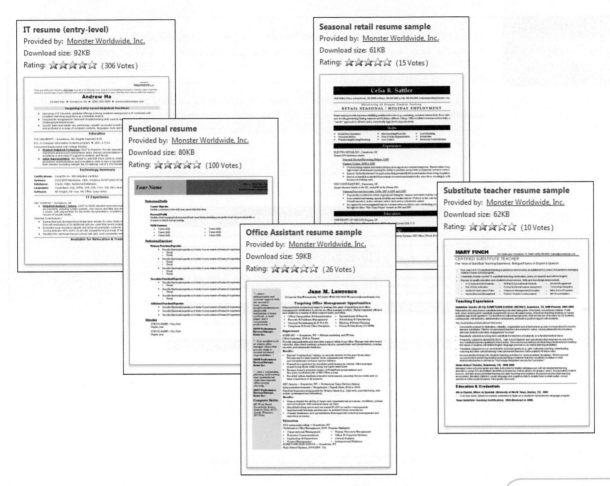

FIGURE 7-3
Templates make it easy to create professional résumés for any career.

Because employers are usually in a hurry when breezing through résumés, it's best to keep the résumé to only a single page.

Tip If you select a résumé template that uses color, don't forget to print the résumé on a color printer.

On Your Own 7-2
Create a Résumé Using a Résumé Template

Andrea Champion is looking for a seasonal retail job and has asked for your help creating a résumé. She has sent you her education and job experience in a Word document. You can find Andrea's information in the AndreaInformation file in the Sample Files folder on the DVD in the back of this book.

Using a template, create a résumé for your friend, Andrea Champion. In the **New resume samples** group of templates, select the **Seasonal retail resume sample**. Using Figure 7-4 as your guide, add the information for Andrea Champion while deleting the information that was in the résumé template.

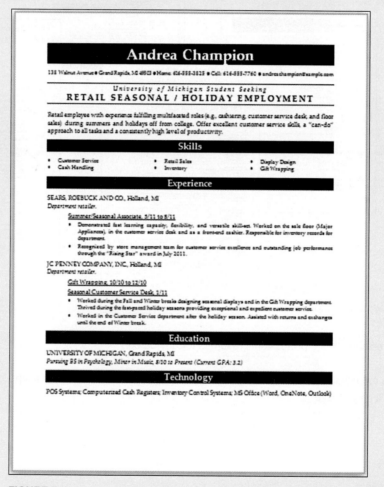

FIGURE 7-4
The completed résumé for Andrea uses the Seasonal retail resume sample template.

Save the résumé as a MS Word document and then as a PDF. Name the document and the PDF **AndreaChampionResume**.

Hint To save a document as a PDF, change the file type to PDF in the Save As dialog box.

 Solutions Appendix

For help, see Solution 7-2: How to Create a Résumé Using a Résumé Template.

Post the Résumé Online

Job search sites and corporate websites sometimes allow you to upload your résumé. For example, to upload your résumé to the indeed.com site, click **Post Your Resume** and follow directions onscreen.

If the website does not request a specific file format, use the PDF format. If a Word document is requested, use the .doc file format so the file can be opened in older editions of Microsoft Word. These and other common file formats are listed in Table 7-1.

TABLE 7-1   Common File Formats Supported by Word

File Format	File Extension	Description
Document	.docx	Current MS Word file format.
Word 97–2003 Document	.doc	Older MS Word file format.
Portable Document Format	.pdf	An image of a document that looks exactly like the print preview. Most computers have software installed to view a PDF file.
Plain Text	.txt	Text only; all formatting is lost.
Rich Text Format	.rtf	A format that can be edited by most word processors; most text formatting is preserved.
Multipurpose HyperText	.mht	A format used to save a document that is built as a single web page.

> **Tip** It is hard for a writer to catch his own errors. For this reason, always have another person carefully read your résumé, looking for errors.

> **Tip** Another computer might format or display a Word document differently than what appears on your screen. To keep the document looking exactly as you intend, use the PDF format.

In Chapter 3, "Creating Documents with Microsoft Word," you learned that you can change the file type by clicking **Save As** in the Backstage view. Then, in the Save As dialog box, change the file type. Another way to save a Word document in a new format is to click **Save & Send** in the Backstage view. Then click **Change File Type** (see Figure 7-5).

FIGURE 7-5
Save a Word document using a different file format.

Email the Résumé

If you have an email address for the human resource department or hiring manager, email your résumé to this address. In the email message, be sure to include the job you are applying for, a quick overview of your qualifications, and your contact information. In addition, you want to let the receiver know that your résumé is attached so it won't be missed.

Make sure your email is professional and does not have errors. Be sure to include a subject line. Send your résumé as a PDF file so that it can be opened on any computer and formatting does not change. Make sure the PDF filename includes your first and last name. Figure 7-6 shows an email with a résumé ready to be sent by Andrea.

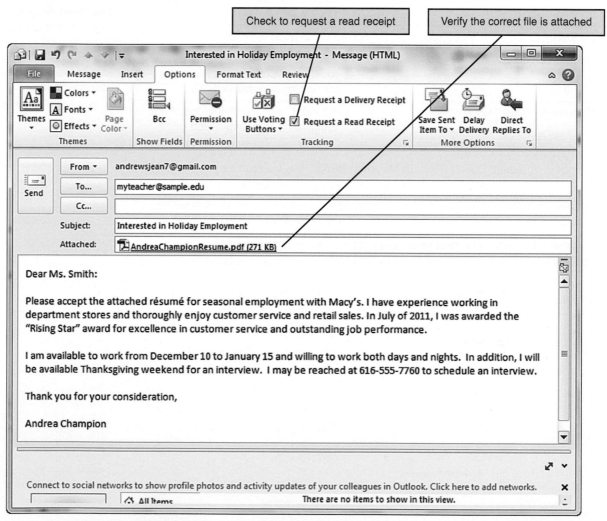

FIGURE 7-6
Make sure you send a professional email message.

Remember that you are making your first impression with the email, so it is important that it is clear and doesn't have errors.

Do the following:

Step 1. Create the email subject line and body of the message. Here is the message:

Dear Ms. Smith:

Please accept the attached résumé for seasonal employment with Macy's. I have experience working in department stores and thoroughly enjoy customer service and retail sales. In July of 2011, I was awarded the "Rising Star" award for excellence in customer service and outstanding job performance.

I am available to work from December 10 to January 15 and willing to work both days and nights. In addition, I will be available Thanksgiving weekend for an interview. I may be reached at 616-555-7760 to schedule an interview.

Thank you for your consideration,

Andrea Champion

Step 2. Verify that the email you typed is correct. Attach the résumé you created. Be sure to attach the PDF file and not the Word document file.

Hint Windows and Word identify a PDF file as an Adobe Acrobat Document file.

? Solutions Appendix

Step 3. On the Options ribbon, click **Request a Read Receipt**. The read receipt will send you a message when the receiver opens the email and agrees to send the read receipt.

For help, see Solution 7-3: How to Email a Résumé PDF.

Step 4. Send the email message with the attachment to your teacher's email address.

Creating and Sending an Interview Follow-up Letter

Based on your résumé, a company might select you for an interview. An interview can be nerve-wracking, but if you follow these tips, you can have a successful interview:

▶ **Dress professionally.** You don't have a second chance to make a first impression, so make sure you dress professionally. A man might dress in a shirt and tie or suit, and a woman might choose a skirt or dress pants and a blazer. Be sure to freshly iron your clothes.

▶ **Arrive ten minutes early.** Arriving early does more than show you are punctual; it also helps calm your nerves. You are more likely to be stressed if you must rush to get to your interview on time.

Tip In addition to emailing your résumé, also send the résumé by postal mail. This double reminder says to a potential employer that you are serious about the job.

▶ **Bring copies of your résumé.** Make sure you have several copies of your résumé to hand out to everyone at the interview. (You might be interviewed by several people.) You can also bring personal business cards that you print on your computer.

> **Hint** Business cards are easy to make using a Word Business card template. You'll need to print the cards on card stock paper that comes ten cards to a sheet.

▶ **Greet with a handshake and make eye contact.** When you first meet the person or people interviewing you, look them in the eyes, smile, and shake their hand. Don't squeeze too hard, but don't be afraid to give a firm handshake. Continue to make eye contact throughout the interview.

▶ **Get the name and contact information for the primary interviewer.** Ask the person conducting the interview for a business card. You will need the information later to follow up on the job, and it is always a good idea to have the name of the person interviewing you.

▶ **Ask questions during the interview.** Before the interview, research about the company and the position. Make sure you understand what problem the company needs solved and why it is looking to hire someone. Ask questions that show you are interested in the position and the company and are familiar with both. Make it clear that you are ready and able to solve the problem.

▶ **Ask when a decision will be made.** Don't leave the interview without finding out when the employer expects to make a hiring decision. Also ask whether it's okay if you check back later about the job.

▶ **Follow up after the interview.** Send a letter both by email and postal mail expressing your interest in the job. Sending both an email and a letter gives the interviewers two reminders of you. If they don't object, you should also call two days after the interview to thank them for the interview and to ask if they need any additional information from you.

Use Letterhead and Letter Templates

It is important that you follow up after the interview is over. A follow-up letter is another reminder of you and says you're genuinely interested in the job.

Word offers templates that can help you write great business letters. A **letterhead template** is used for the design of the letter. **Letter templates** can be used to help you write the body of the letter.

> **letterhead template**—A template used to create a design for personal or business letters.
> **letter template**—A template that helps you write the body of a letter.

As part of your job-hunting strategy, create a professional-looking personal letterhead. You can use it when writing business letters related to your job search.

Create a personal letterhead document for writing business letters. Choose a letterhead template that looks professional and reflects your taste. If your printer does not print in color, select a template that does not use color or that still looks good when printed in black and white.

In this activity, you create a letterhead document for Andrea Champion. Figure 7-7 shows the finished document.

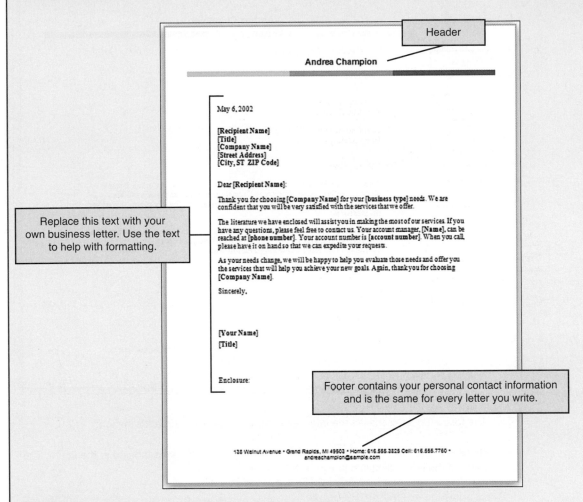

Header

Andrea Champion

May 6, 2002

[Recipient Name]
[Title]
[Company Name]
[Street Address]
[City, ST ZIP Code]

Dear [Recipient Name]:

Thank you for choosing [Company Name] for your [business type] needs. We are confident that you will be very satisfied with the services that we offer.

The literature we have enclosed will assist you in making the most of our services. If you have any questions, please feel free to contact us. Your account manager, [Name], can be reached at [phone number]. Your account number is [account number]. When you call, please have it on hand so that we can expedite your requests.

As your needs change, we will be happy to help you evaluate those needs and offer you the services that will help you achieve your new goals. Again, thank you for choosing [Company Name].

Sincerely,

[Your Name]
[Title]

Enclosure:

Replace this text with your own business letter. Use the text to help with formatting.

Footer contains your personal contact information and is the same for every letter you write.

138 Walnut Avenue • Grand Rapids, MI 49503 • Home: 616.555.3825 Cell: 616.555.7760 • andreachampion@sample.com

FIGURE 7-7
Create a personal letterhead to use for all your business letters.

Do the following to create the letterhead document:

Step 1.   Look in the Letterhead group of templates for the **Letterhead (Trendy Eclectic design)** template. This letterhead works well for a personal letterhead printed in black and white. Create a new Word document using this or another template.

Step 2.   Replace the letter heading with Andrea's name. Edit the footer to include Andrea's home number, cell number, mailing address, and email address. You can find Andrea's information in her résumé you created in the On Your Own 7-2 activity.

Step 3.   If necessary, remove the hyperlink on the email address.

Step 4.   Save the letterhead to your USB flash drive, hard drive, SkyDrive, or other location given by your instructor. Name the document **AndreaChampionLetterhead**.

When you create a letterhead, save it so that you can use it for all the letters you write.

  Solutions Appendix

**For help, see Solution 7-4:
How to Create a Personal
Letterhead for Business
Letters.**

On Your Own 7-5
Create an Interview Follow-up Letter

Using the letterhead document created in the On Your Own 7-4 activity, write a follow-up letter for Andrea Champion after her interview. She interviewed with Macy's Department Store and met with Sarah Smith. The completed follow-up letter is shown in Figure 7-8.

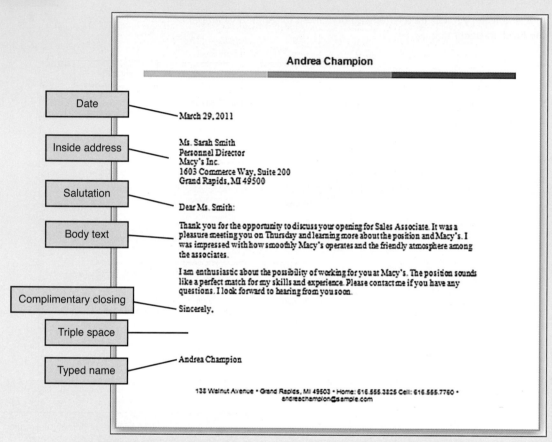

Andrea Champion

Date — March 29, 2011

Inside address — Ms. Sarah Smith
Personnel Director
Macy's Inc.
1603 Commerce Way, Suite 200
Grand Rapids, MI 49500

Salutation — Dear Ms. Smith:

Body text — Thank you for the opportunity to discuss your opening for Sales Associate. It was a pleasure meeting you on Thursday and learning more about the position and Macy's. I was impressed with how smoothly Macy's operates and the friendly atmosphere among the associates.

I am enthusiastic about the possibility of working for you at Macy's. The position sounds like a perfect match for my skills and experience. Please contact me if you have any questions. I look forward to hearing from you soon.

Complimentary closing — Sincerely,

Triple space —

Typed name — Andrea Champion

138 Walnut Avenue • Grand Rapids, MI 49503 • Home: 616.555.3825 Cell: 616.555.7760 •
andreachampion@sample.com

FIGURE 7-8
The follow-up letter thanks the interviewer for considering Andrea for the job.

Be sure to use the correct formatting and spacing for the letter as labeled in the figure. The parts of the letter identified in Figure 7-8 are defined next.

> **inside address**—The name and address of the receiver of the letter that appears a double-space below the date.
>
> **salutation**—The greeting such as Dear Mr. Jones:. Use a colon at the end of the salutation. Double-space above and below the salutation.
>
> **body text**—The reason you are writing. State your purpose in the first sentence. Always end the text with a closing call to action.
>
> **complimentary closing**—Complimentary text following the body text such as Best regards, Sincerely, or Yours truly. End the closing with a comma and a triple space.

Do the following:

Step 1. Open the **AndreaChampionLetterhead** document and save the document as **SarahSmith**. Save it to your USB flash drive, hard drive, SkyDrive, or other location given by your instructor.

Step 2. Enter today's date, and address the letter to **Ms. Sarah Smith**. You can find her address in the contacts list shown earlier in the On Your Own 7-1 activity.

Step 3. Type the salutation **Dear Ms. Smith:**

Step 4. To get ideas for writing the body of a letter, you can browse through letter templates to find a letter on your topic. Without closing the SarahSmith document, create a new document: Use the Letters group of templates, click the **Employment and resignation letters** group, **Interview letters**, and select the **Thank you for interview** template. Close the new document without saving it.

Step 5. Return to the SarahSmith letter and enter the body text. The following text was taken from the template you saw in step 4 and then adjusted for Andrea's situation:

> Thank you for the opportunity to discuss your opening for Sales Associate. It was a pleasure meeting you on Thursday and learning more about the position and Macy's. I was impressed with how smoothly Macy's operates and the friendly atmosphere among the associates.
>
> I am enthusiastic about the possibility of working for you at Macy's. The position sounds like a perfect match for my skills and experience. Please contact me if you have any questions. I look forward to hearing from you soon.

Step 6. Enter the complimentary closing and the name, **Andrea Champion**.

On Your Own 7-5
Create an Interview Follow-up Letter

 Solutions Appendix

For help, see Solution 7-5: How to Create an Interview Follow-up Letter.

Print an Envelope

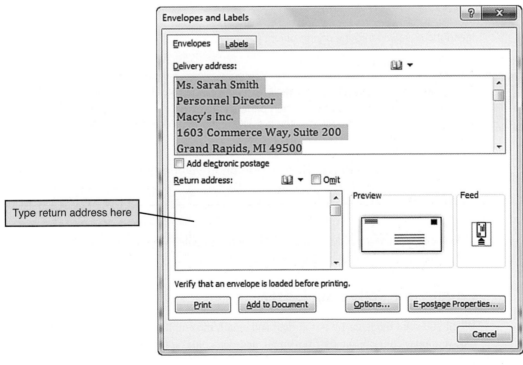

Type return address here

FIGURE 7-9
Microsoft Word makes it easy to print professional envelopes.

Word can produce a professional envelope for your business letter. To create the envelope, click **Envelopes** on the Mailings ribbon. The Envelopes and Labels dialog box appears as shown in Figure 7-9. Word uses the inside address for the envelope, but you have to type the return address.

You can save the envelope in your document or immediately print it. To save it in your document, click **Add to Document**. The envelope is created as the first page of your document. To immediately print the envelope, insert the envelope in your printer and click **Print**.

Figure 7-10 shows how to insert the envelope into a printer before printing, but your printer might work differently. Check the printer manual for directions.

FIGURE 7-10
Insert the envelope into the printer before you print.

On Your Own 7-6 **Add an Envelope to a Letter**	Add an envelope to the follow-up letter you created for Andrea. Enter Andrea's return address. If you have access to a printer, print the envelope and the letter. If you don't have access to a printer, check out the print preview of the envelope and letter to see how that will appear in print.
[?] Solutions Appendix	**For help, see Solution 7-6: How to Add an Envelope to a Letter.**

Sign your letter in blue or black ink. After you have mailed your letter, don't forget to record that action in your MyContacts document.

Email Your Follow-up Letter

When you send the letter by postal mail and email, the employer gets two reminders of you. One reminder comes instantly from email, and one comes a few days later by postal mail.

Don't attach the follow-up letter to an email message because the employer must take the extra time to open the attachment. To make it easier for the employer, copy and paste the letter into the email message.

The follow-up letter can be sent by email, as shown in Figure 7-11.

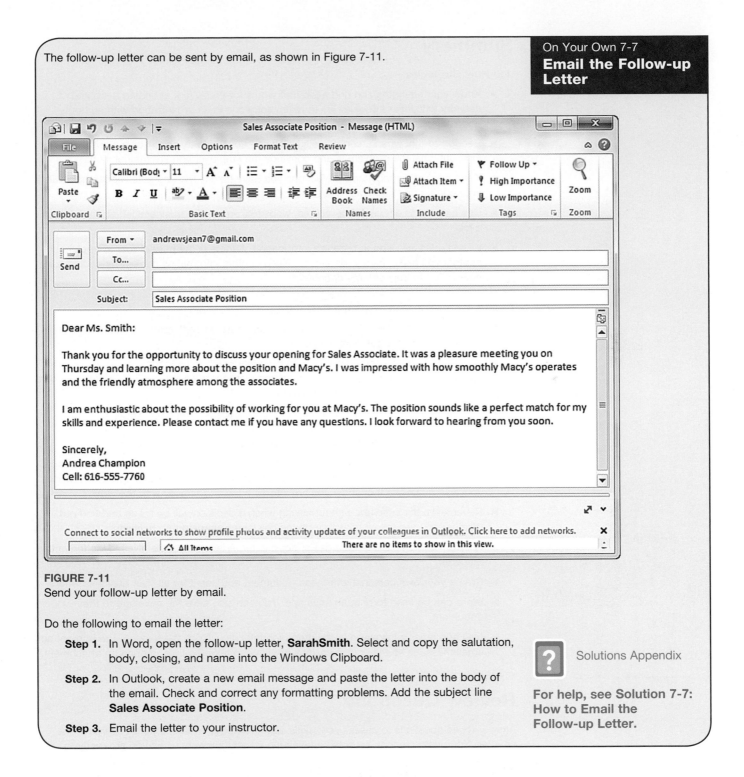

FIGURE 7-11
Send your follow-up letter by email.

Do the following to email the letter:

Step 1. In Word, open the follow-up letter, **SarahSmith**. Select and copy the salutation, body, closing, and name into the Windows Clipboard.

Step 2. In Outlook, create a new email message and paste the letter into the body of the email. Check and correct any formatting problems. Add the subject line **Sales Associate Position**.

Step 3. Email the letter to your instructor.

Solutions Appendix

For help, see Solution 7-7: How to Email the Follow-up Letter.

After you have sent the letter by email, don't forget to record that action in your MyContacts document. In addition, a few days after the interview, call the employer and ask whether a decision has been made. Make a note of the phone call in your MyContacts document.

Summary

Job Hunt Strategies

▶ Know your strengths and find a job that works for you. Work at finding a job and network with lots of people. Try to reach someone in an organization with authority and influence.

▶ Recognize that when a company is hiring someone, it is trying to solve a problem. Find out what the problem is and convince the employer you are the solution.

▶ Keep a list of contacts and the actions you have taken. The contacts list can help with your current and future job searches.

▶ Use a contacts document, a résumé, websites, email, and business letters to help find a job.

▶ Word tables are used to organize information. A table is the perfect tool to track each contact you make in your job search. Keep contact information current by adding each new action to the contacts document.

Creating, Emailing, and Posting a Résumé

▶ A résumé is an essential job-acquiring document to present your qualifications, skills, and education to a potential employer.

▶ Word offers résumé templates for a wide variety of job descriptions, experiences, and educational backgrounds. Use a résumé template to organize your information and give ideas as to what to include in the résumé.

▶ You can email a résumé, post it online, or mail it to potential employers.

Creating and Sending an Interview Follow-up Letter

▶ Dress professionally for an interview, arrive early, and bring your résumé. Greet people with a handshake, a smile, and eye contact. Get the names of the people interviewing you. Ask questions that show you are interested in and familiar with the work.

▶ Never leave the interview without asking when a decision will be made and find out whether you can follow up with a phone call later regarding that decision.

▶ A letterhead template gives a design for a letter. A letter template gives ideas for writing the letter.

▶ Create your own personal letterhead document and use it for all your business letters.

▶ Word can be used to print an envelope. You can also save the envelope to the document.

▶ Mail and email a follow-up letter after a job interview. Copy the text into the body of an email message so the employer does not have to take the time to open an attachment.

Review Questions

Answer these questions to assess your skills and knowledge of the content covered in the chapter. Your instructor can provide you with the correct answers when you are ready to check your work.

1. Why is it important to let family, friends, neighbors, and former teachers and business associates know you are looking for a job?

2. Why is it not enough to apply for a job using the web without communicating directly with people?

3. Why does a company hire someone?

4. What is the purpose of a Word table?

5. What are three reasons for using a résumé template when building your résumé?

6. Which file format is best to use when emailing a résumé to a potential employer? What are two reasons to use this format?

7. What is an Outlook read receipt?

8. What website lists job openings with the federal government?

9. What one question should you always get answered at a job interview?

10. What two contacts should you always make with a potential employer following a job interview?

11. Explain the difference between a letterhead template and a letter template.

12. Which punctuation mark is used at the end of the salutation for a business letter?

13. Which ribbon in Word is used to add an envelope to a letter?

14. Why is it not a good idea to attach a business letter to an email message?

15. After you have contacted a potential employer in any way, such as emailing an interview follow-up letter, what should you always do next?

Chapter Mastery Project

Find out how well you have mastered the content in this chapter by completing this project. If you can answer all the questions and do all the steps without looking back at the chapter details, you have mastered this chapter. If you can complete the project by finding answers using the Word Help window or the web, you have proven that you can teach yourself how to use technology to find a job.

If you find you need a lot of help doing the project and you have not yet read the chapter or done the activities, drop back and start at the beginning of the chapter and then return to this project.

> **Hint** All the key terms in the chapter are used in this mastery project. If you encounter a key word you don't know, such as *salutation,* enter **define:salutation** in the Internet Explorer search box.

Mastery Project Part 1: Job Hunt Strategies

If you need help completing this part of the mastery project, please review the "Job Hunt Strategies" section in the chapter.

Answer the following questions:

1. What are three characteristics about yourself that you need to keep in mind when searching for a job that you think you might enjoy going to each day?

2. What are three things you might do on a job that you know you would enjoy?

3. Based on your answers to the first two questions, what is one job that fits these answers?

4. Why would it be helpful to post on Facebook that you are looking for a job?

5. When you are applying for a job, why is it better to speak with someone who is influential at the company?

6. Why is it important to always do your best on a job even when no one is looking?

7. What are the benefits of keeping good records when searching for a job?

8. List three websites that provide job search engines.

Do the following:

Step 1. If you have not already done so, create the MyContacts document, shown earlier in Figure 7-2.

Step 2. Copy and paste the third table so the document has four tables. In the third table, add a new contact for Charlie Jones, who is the Personnel Manager at Cook's Dry Cleaning. His phone number is 888-555-7777, and his email address is cjones@sample.com. You don't yet know his mailing address, but you have contacted him by email to ask whether you can send him your résumé.

Step 3. You have decided to post your résumé on several job search sites. For each job search site, you need an online account and password. Create a new document with a table to keep track of this information. The table has three columns as shown:

Website	User Account	Password

Step 4. Save the document, naming it WebsiteAccounts. Because you are keeping passwords in the document, you need to password protect the document. Search Word Help to find out how to password protect a document. Then secure the document with a password.

Step 5. Close the document and open it. You must enter the password to open the document.

Step 6. To make it easier to send emails to potential employers, you can save an email address to your Outlook Address Book. To practice this skill, save the email address of your instructor to your Outlook Address Book.

> **Hint** To learn how to save addresses to the Outlook Address Book, in Outlook Help search on **address book**.

Mastery Project Part 2: Creating and Sending a Résumé

If you need help completing this part of the mastery project, please review the "Creating and Sending a Résumé" section in the chapter.

What is the next job you expect to find? Will it be a part-time job while you are in school or a job after you graduate? Search for a job using the websites identified in the chapter or other websites. Pick a job that you think you might one day want to apply for. Answer these questions:

1. What job did you pick?

2. Where did you find the job?

Do the following to create your résumé that you might use when you apply for your next job:

Step 1. Select a résumé template in Word, keeping in mind your educational background and the job you are targeting. Save the résumé document to your USB flash drive, hard drive, SkyDrive, or another location given by your instructor. Include your name in the filename—for example, **JeanAndrewsResume**.

Step 2. Enter your personal information and your education, skills, experience, and other information the résumé template suggests. Adjust the template fields and format the text as needed to fit your individual needs. Try to limit the résumé to one page.

Step 3. Save your résumé as both a Word document and a PDF.

Step 4. Create an email message with a subject line and body of the message to send the résumé to a potential employer. Pretend you are applying for the job you found earlier in this project and write an email message appropriate for that job. You can find ideas for the message in the On Your Own 7-3 activity in the chapter.

Step 5. Attach the PDF of your résumé to the email message and request a read receipt. Send the email to your instructor.

Be sure to save your résumé document so that it will be available in the future when you really are looking for a job.

Mastery Project Part 3: Creating and Sending an Interview Follow-up Letter

If you need help completing this part of the mastery project, please review the "Creating and Sending an Interview Follow-up Letter" section in the chapter.

Answer the following:

1. Why is it not appropriate to wear shorts and a t-shirt to a job interview?
2. What is the purpose of shaking hands and making eye contact when you first start the interview?
3. Why do you need the contact information of the person interviewing you?
4. Why is it important to ask questions about the job during an interview?

Do the following to create your own personal letterhead:

Step 1. Select a letterhead template in Word that looks professional and you like. Enter your personal contact information in the document.

Step 2. Save the document, naming it **MyLetterhead**. Print the document to make sure the colors look good when printed.

Pretend you have had an informational interview with a company that currently has no job openings. Do the following:

Step 1. Write an interview follow-up letter that thanks the person interviewing you and acknowledges there are no openings. As a guideline for writing the letter, search for an appropriate letter template. Which template did you use as a guide?

Step 2. Use today's date in the letter. For an inside address, make up a name, company, and address. For the salutation, don't forget to use a colon. For the closing, use **Best regards,**. Make sure you use the correct spacing and formatting in the letter.

Step 3. Save the document, naming it **MyInterviewLetter**.

Step 4. Add an envelope to the letter. Be sure to include a return address.

Step 5. Create an email message and copy the appropriate parts of the letter into the email message. Correct any problems with the text and the formatting of the message.

Step 6. Enter an appropriate subject line and send the email to your instructor. Don't forget to request a read receipt with the message.

Becoming an Independent Learner

Answer the following questions about becoming an independent learner:

1. To teach yourself to use Microsoft Word to apply for a job, do you think it is best to rely on the chapter or on Word Help when you need answers?
2. The most important skill learned in this chapter is how to teach yourself a computer skill. Rate yourself at Level A through E on how well you are doing with this skill. What is your level?

   ○ Level A: I was able to successfully complete the Chapter Mastery Project without the help of doing the On Your Own activities in the chapter.

   ○ Level B: I completed all the On Your Own activities and the Chapter Mastery Project without referring to any of the solutions in the *Solutions Appendix*.

   ○ Level C: I completed all the On Your Own activities and the Chapter Mastery Project by using just a few of the solutions in the *Solutions Appendix*.

   ○ Level D: I completed all the On Your Own activities and the Chapter Mastery Project by using many of the solutions in the *Solutions Appendix*.

   ○ Level E: I completed all the On Your Own activities and the Chapter Mastery Project and had to use all of the solutions in the *Solutions Appendix*.

To continue toward the goal of teaching yourself computer skills, if you are not at Level A, try to move up one level on how you learn in Chapter 8, "Using PowerPoint to Give a Presentation."

Projects to Help You

Now that you have mastered the material in this chapter, you are ready to tackle the three projects introduced at the beginning of the chapter in the section "How Will This Chapter Help Me?"

Project 1: Creating a Résumé Cover Letter and Personal Business Cards

PERSONAL PROJECT:
I plan to apply for a job. I need to create a résumé and all the other documents that can help me land a great job.

Besides the all-powerful résumé, two other documents that can help you land a job are a résumé cover letter and a personal business card. Do the following to create these documents:

Step 1. When mailing your résumé, a cover letter can give you the opportunity to introduce yourself, allow your personality to shine through, and say something about the company. Use these general directions to create your cover letter to apply for the job you selected in the Mastery Project Part 2:

- ○ Use the personal letterhead that you created earlier in the chapter for a business letter.
- ○ Make the cover letter short, no more than three or four paragraphs on one page.
- ○ The first paragraph explains why you are writing. The second paragraph says why you are the best candidate for the job. Avoid repeating details about yourself that are in your résumé.
- ○ The last paragraph says you will follow up later with a phone call or email.
- ○ Type **Enclosure** below your name at the bottom of the letter.
- ○ Carefully check the letter for errors. Then ask a family member or friend to proofread your letter, checking for errors.

Step 2. Select a business card template that reflects your personality and career goals, and use it to create your personal business card. A photo is a great way to help someone remember you. If you have a photo of yourself, create a business card that includes your photo. What Word template did you select?

Step 3. If you have access to a printer, print one sheet of business cards on regular paper. How many cards print to a page?

Step 4. Search the web for card stock paper that you could use to print your business cards. What website sells this paper? Is the paper intended for an inkjet printer or a laser printer? How many sheets come in a pack? How much does a pack cost?

Project 2: Using Academic Resources to Find the Right Job for You

ACADEMIC PROJECT:
I love what I'm studying, and I don't want to change my major. But the job market in my field is tough. I need to find out what job options are available for me. Maybe my school can help me figure out what will work for me. What academic resources can help me?

Knowing yourself is the first step to finding the right job for you. Check with the academic advisors office at your school and find out what resources are available to help you learn about yourself. What aptitudes do you have? What is your personality? Are you happier working on a team or working alone? Do you prefer to lead or follow? Do you like to work by a structured schedule or with plenty of freedom? Use whatever resources your school offers to learn about yourself. This information can be invaluable when deciding what job you will like the most.

Project 3: Finding a Job in Your Technical Career

Finding a great job in information technology, or IT, depends on your aptitude, skills, education, IT certifications, and experience. Suppose you are interested in becoming a computer support specialist. Use the web to find answers to these questions:

TECHNICAL CAREER PROJECT: I want a technical job, and I love working with people. I don't want to sit in front of a computer all day. What job in IT might be right for me?

1. What is a typical job description for a computer support specialist? A good website to find this answer is **www.bls.gov** by the Bureau of Labor Statistics.

2. What might a computer support specialist do each day? What website did you use to find your answer?

3. What is the median yearly wage of a computer support specialist? A good website to find this type of computational data is **wolframalpha.com**.

> **Hint** Enter **median yearly wage of a computer support specialist** in the WolframAlpha search box.

4. Are these jobs increasing or decreasing? You can find this answer on **wolframalpha.com**.

5. What skills, education, certifications, or experience does an employer typically look for when hiring a computer support specialist? What website did you use to find your answer?

6. Find four websites that have job postings for a computer support specialist. For each posting, list the website, the job title, and the city.

Project to Help Others

One of the best ways to learn is to teach someone else. And, in teaching someone else, you are making a contribution into that person's life. As part of each chapter's work, you are encouraged to teach someone else a skill you have learned. In this chapter, help someone learn to use the web and Word documents to find a job and to write letters.

Who is your apprentice? _____

When helping others learn, don't do the work for them. Coach and instruct. Show them how to find information for themselves. Help them be as independent a learner as possible.

Do the following:

Step 1. Ask your apprentice what are his job goals. If your apprentice plans to search for a job in the future, help him create his own résumé using a résumé template of his choice.

Step 2. Help your apprentice email the résumé using a professional email message. Have him email the résumé to you.

Step 3. Ask your apprentice what type of letter he might want to write in the near future. If he does not have an immediate need, suggest he write a letter of thanks to someone.

Step 4. Help your apprentice use a letterhead template and a letter template to create the letter.

CHAPTER 8
Using PowerPoint to Give a Presentation

IN THIS CHAPTER, YOU WILL

Learn to use PowerPoint to tell a story

Create a PowerPoint presentation

Revise and give a presentation

As always, remember the most important computer skill is how to teach yourself a computer skill. Therefore, this chapter is designed to help you teach yourself how to create and design a PowerPoint presentation. Try to do each On Your Own activity without any help. But remember, if you need help, you can always refer to the solutions in the *Solutions Appendix*.

JUMP RIGHT IN

If you want even more of a challenge, try proceeding directly to the Chapter Mastery Project at the end of this chapter. If you need help on the project, refer to the On Your Own activities in the chapter or do your own independent investigating using PowerPoint Help or searching the web for answers. When you complete the project, you will have mastered the skills in this chapter. Then go to the projects that require you apply your skills to new situations.

How Will This Chapter Help Me?

Recall that throughout this book, each chapter provides three projects focusing on personal, academic, or technical career goals. Depending on your own interests, you might choose to complete any or all of these projects to help you achieve your goals.

PERSONAL PROJECT: I've been asked to speak about myself to a small group. I'd like to tell my story by showing photos of my family and talking about things I enjoy and want to do. How can PowerPoint help me do that?

ACADEMIC PROJECT: An instructor in another class has asked me to speak to my class about an assigned topic. I need to send the presentation to all my classmates. How can I make a presentation using the very best designs?

TECHNICAL CAREER PROJECT: My boss has told me to make a presentation to my help desk team members. Two team members work from home. They call in on a conference line during our team meetings. How can they see my PowerPoint presentation along with the others present at the meeting?

Using PowerPoint to Tell a Story

Storytelling is one of the most effective means of communication. Microsoft **PowerPoint** is a powerful presentation tool to help you add emphasis to a story by showing key words, quotes, graphics, sound, and video. PowerPoint presentations are used by salespeople, executives, parents, children, physicians, auto mechanics, teachers, students, helpdesk technicians, and others.

> **PowerPoint**—One of the applications included in the Microsoft Office suite of applications. PowerPoint is used to create slides that can include text, color, graphics, video, and sound. A PowerPoint presentation file has a .pptx file extension. Older versions of PowerPoint created presentation files with a .ppt file extension.

A presenter tells a story to an audience while stepping through the **slides** of the PowerPoint presentation. If the audience is more than two or three people, a **projector** can be used so everyone in the room can see the presentation (see Figure 8-1).

> **slide**—The pages in a PowerPoint presentation. One slide at a time is viewed during a presentation.
>
> **projector**—A display device that projects a computer screen onto a large area.

projector

FIGURE 8-1
For a large audience, a
PowerPoint presentation can be
projected onto a large area.

First Look at PowerPoint

When you first open PowerPoint, it opens a blank presentation with one slide, the **title slide** (see Figure 8-2). To create a presentation, you enter text or objects on this slide, create new slides, and add text and objects to these new slides. A presentation can also contain **speaker notes** about each slide to help you when giving the presentation.

> **title slide**—A slide that automatically includes text boxes for the title of the presentation and the subtitle.
>
> **speaker notes**—Text to help the speaker when giving the PowerPoint presentation. These notes do not appear on the slides, so they are not visible to the audience. Notes are typed in the notes pane at the bottom of the PowerPoint window.

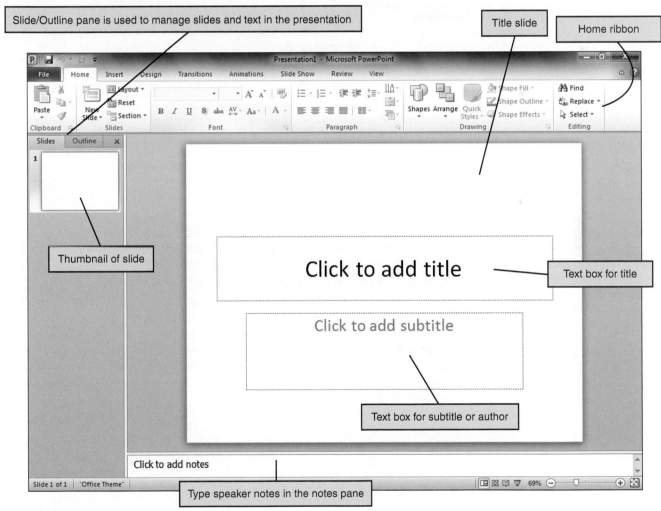

FIGURE 8-2
When you open PowerPoint, a blank presentation is created with one blank title slide.

You'll be happy to know that the PowerPoint window has many tools and ribbons that work the same as they do in the Word window. This fact makes it easy to learn a new Office application after you know how to use one Office application. Table 8-1 lists the purpose of each ribbon on the PowerPoint window.

TABLE 8-1   Main Purposes of PowerPoint Ribbons

Ribbon	Description
File	Save, print, close, or open a presentation.
Home	Insert new slides and format text.
Insert	Insert headers, footers, shapes, and other objects into an existing slide.
Design	Change the background, colors, and **theme** of the presentation.
Transitions	Add **transitions** to your presentation. Transitions are covered in Chapter 9, "Adding Action and Sound to a PowerPoint Presentation."
Animations	Add **animation** to an object on a slide. Animation is covered in Chapter 9.
Slide Show	Start or customize a slide show.
Review	Check spelling and compare two presentations.
View	View notes and **slide master**, sort slides, and control PowerPoint windows.

Tip In this chapter, you learn about the basic tools of PowerPoint. More tools are covered in the next chapter. Don't wait until then to learn the tool if you see something that interests you. If you see a tool that interests you, try it out.

theme—In Office applications, a built-in design for a Word document, Excel worksheet, Outlook message, or PowerPoint presentation that includes colors, fonts, and effects. A theme can give your work in these applications a consistent look.

transitions—A special effect as one slide changes to the next slide.

animation—A special effect that displays as an object appears or disappears on a slide.

slide master—A hidden slide. The text, color, objects, and formatting you place on this slide appear on all sides in the presentation.

When first learning about a new application, poke around in the application window and try out the tools. If you apply a change and don't like the results, use the Undo button [↻▾] on the title bar. You can use the Help feature or the web to find answers to your questions.

Do the following to learn about the PowerPoint window:

Step 1. Open **Microsoft PowerPoint 2010** and maximize the window. Compare Figure 8-2 to your PowerPoint window and identify all the items labeled in Figure 8-2 on your window. As with Microsoft Word, when you mouse over a button, a bubble appears describing the tool.

Not Working? More than one version of Microsoft PowerPoint exists. In this book, we are using PowerPoint 2010. If you are using a different version, such as PowerPoint 2007, your window might not look the same as the one shown.

Step 2. Notice the title slide has two text boxes with dotted edges where you can type text or insert objects. Also take note of the left pane, which is the Slide/Outline pane. It contains a thumbnail for this slide, which shows the slide is blank.

Step 3. Check out the two views in the Slide/Outline pane. The Slides view shows a preview of the slides in your presentation. The Outline view shows the text in your presentation as an outline. You can use the Slides view in the left pane to add new slides, select a slide, rearrange slides, copy slides, and delete slides. Use the Outline view to view and edit the text in the entire presentation.

Not Working? If you don't see the Slide/Outline pane on your window, click **Normal** on the View ribbon.

Step 4. Check out the tools on each ribbon. What are some tools you found on these ribbons that are also on the Word ribbons?

Step 5. One the Home ribbon, click **New Slide** to add a new slide. Notice the new slide has two text boxes in different positions than on the title slide. This new slide uses the Title and Content layout.

Step 6. PowerPoint offers several slide layouts to help you design slides. To see a gallery of slide layouts, click the down arrow to the right of New Slide (see Figure 8-3). Add a third slide that uses the **Comparison** layout. How many text boxes does this slide have?

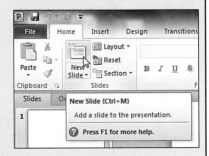

gallery—In Office applications, a list of items from which you can choose that are displayed as pictures.

On Your Own 8-1
**Explore the
PowerPoint Window**

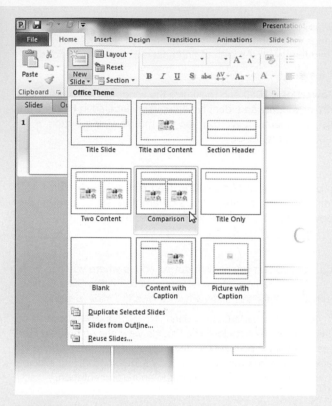

FIGURE 8-3
Choose a slide layout for a new slide.

? Solutions Appendix

**For help, see Solution 8-1:
How to Explore the
PowerPoint Window.**

Step 7. An application's Help feature can help you learn about the application. Using PowerPoint Help, answer these questions:

- How do you apply a theme to a presentation?
- How do you add a slide number to each slide in a presentation?

Step 8. Close the presentation without saving your changes.

Tips for Creating Great Presentations

When you are speaking to an audience, showing keywords and graphics on a screen helps keep you and the audience focused on the topic. Be aware that the design of the PowerPoint presentation can add to or distract from your story. Here are some tips for designing a PowerPoint presentation:

- **Keep it simple.** A busy slide can distract the audience from what you are saying. Don't overdo video, animation, or audio. (Adding video, animation, and audio to a presentation is covered in Chapter 9.)

- **Aim toward a few powerful slides.** Too many slides can overwhelm you and the audience and make you feel rushed.

- **Don't show all.** Plan to make some important points that are not on the slides. You don't want to be a robot reading from the screen. Let the slides back you up and not the other way around.

▶ **Pictures speak louder than words.** Pictures tell a story far better than words do, and people remember them longer.

▶ **Use few words.** Limit text and bullet points to no more than six words per line and no more than six lines per slide. Avoid using full sentences unless you are quoting someone.

▶ **Use simple, large fonts.** Use a simple font, such as Arial, which is easy to read from a distance. Use large fonts (at least 28 points) so people sitting in the back of the room can easily read the slides.

▶ **Use contrasting colors that are easy to read.** A light font on a dark background is easiest to read from a distance.

▶ **Put the most important points first in your presentation.** If you must make several points, put the most important points first. If you run out of time when giving the presentation, you can skip the points on the last few slides.

▶ **Start with an outline of what you want to say.** The outline helps you decide what goes on which slide and in what order. Tell your story in a logical order.

Now let's build a new presentation. As we build it, notice how we applied the tips for good design.

Creating a PowerPoint Presentation

The first step to creating a PowerPoint presentation is to make an outline, which is shown in Figure 8-4. The completed presentation that follows this outline has four slides, as shown in Figure 8-5. The rest of this section describes how to create the four slides. Follow along at your computer to create your own version.

Outline for What Motivates Us

A. What motivates us and why should we care?
    a. Title, author, and quote
    b. Motivated people tend to be happier and produce more than others

B. Others can motivate us
    a. Carrot in front of us, a stick behind us
    b. Reward
    c. Punishment

C. We can motivate ourselves from within
    a. Mastery: Opportunity to do something very well
    b. Independence: Right to make our own decisions (what, when, how, and with whom we do something)
    c. Contribution: Make a difference for others; the most significant motivator

D. How can you tell what motivates you?
    a. Look for where and when you find flow in your life
    b. Identify what type motivation you are experiencing when in this flow.

FIGURE 8-4
Use an outline to keep your presentation on track.

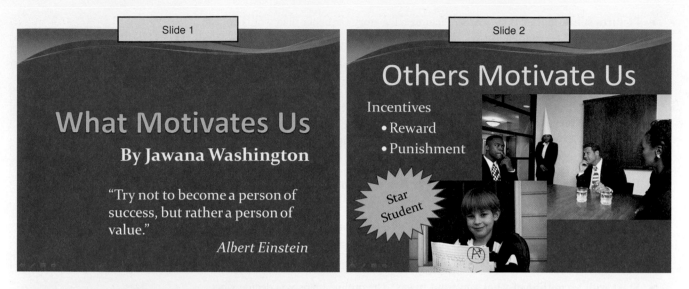

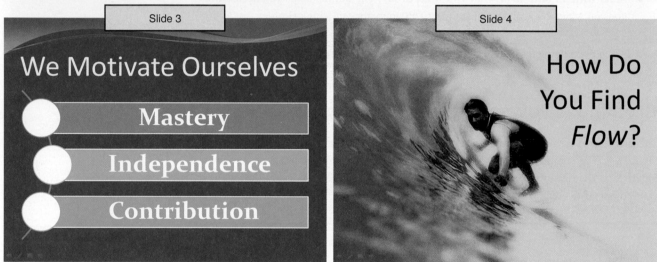

FIGURE 8-5
The presentation, "What Motivates Us," has four slides.

Select a Theme

A PowerPoint theme sets the mood for the presentation with style, graphics, color, and fonts.

Do the following to apply a theme to the presentation:

Step 1. Using PowerPoint, open a blank presentation.

Step 2. On the Design ribbon, display the gallery of themes and then choose the **Flow** theme (see Figure 8-6). This theme sets the mood for the last slide about attaining flow in our lives. Notice the applied theme appears in the status bar at the bottom of the PowerPoint window.

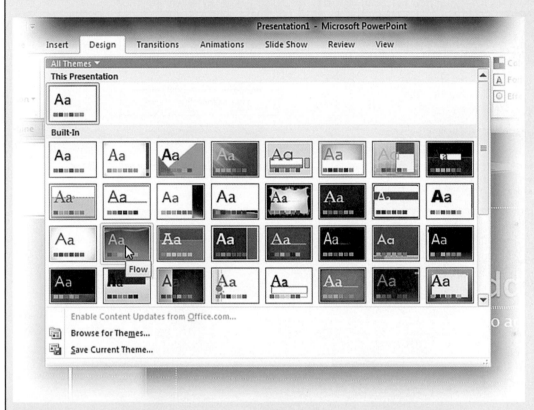

FIGURE 8-6
Select a theme for the presentation that complements the topic presented.

Step 3. After you select a theme, you can customize it. Mouse over the theme colors and see how the colors change on the title slide. Leave the theme color set to **Flow**.

Step 4. Change the Background Style to **Style 3**. This style gives us a dark background for all slides.

Step 5. PowerPoint records document properties just as Word does. Click the **File** tab and change the author to your name as you learned to do in Word.

Step 6. Save your presentation to your hard drive, USB flash drive, SkyDrive, or another location given by your instructor. Name your presentation **Motivation** and leave the file type as PowerPoint Presentation. What file extension does PowerPoint assign to your presentation file?

 Solutions Appendix

**For help, see Solution 8-2:
How to Choose a Theme.**

Create the Title Slide

A good presenter has the PowerPoint presentation set up when the audience first walks into the room. As people come in, they see the title slide displayed until you begin your presentation. Include enough information on the title slide so your audience knows the purpose of the meeting and to give them something to think about before you start presenting.

On Your Own 8-3
Create a Title Slide

Include on the title slide the topic of your presentation, your name, and possibly your school or your company. A short quote or photo can help your audience focus on the topic. Figure 8-7 shows the title slide after this activity is completed.

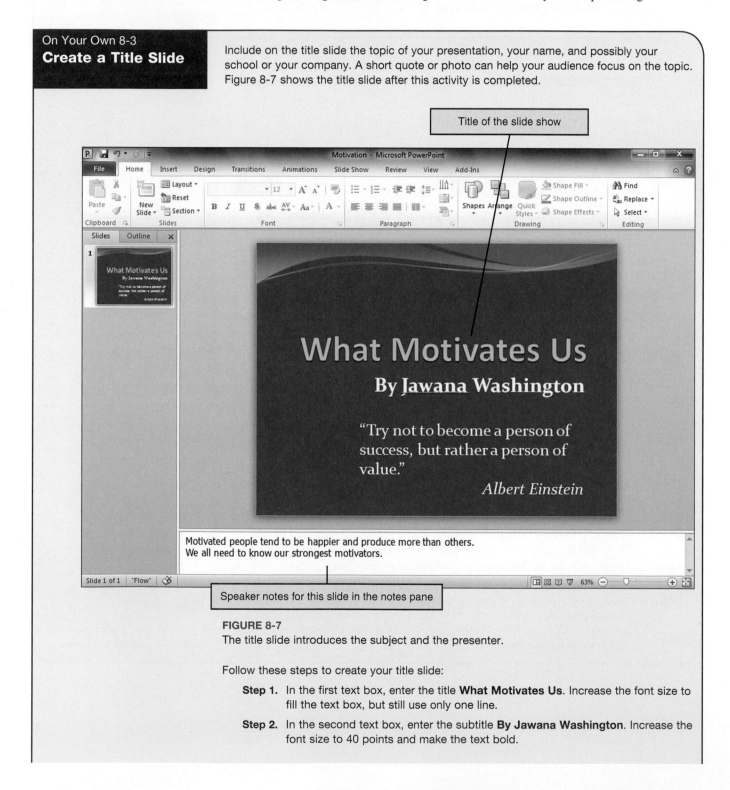

FIGURE 8-7
The title slide introduces the subject and the presenter.

Follow these steps to create your title slide:

Step 1. In the first text box, enter the title **What Motivates Us**. Increase the font size to fill the text box, but still use only one line.

Step 2. In the second text box, enter the subtitle **By Jawana Washington**. Increase the font size to 40 points and make the text bold.

Step 3. You can delete text boxes you don't need, and you can insert new text boxes. Insert a text box for a quote at the bottom of the slide and add this quote by Albert Einstein:

On Your Own 8-3
Create a Title Slide

"Try not to become a person of success, but rather a person of value."

Albert Einstein

Step 4. Increase the font size to **32** points. Right-justify and italicize Albert Einstein's name as shown in Figure 8-7.

Step 5. If necessary, move or resize the text box so the quote is positioned as shown in Figure 8-7.

Step 6. In the notes pane labeled *Click to add notes*, enter the following speaker notes to remind you to mention why the presentation is important to the audience:

Motivated people tend to be happier and produce more than others.

We all need to know our strongest motivators.

? Solutions Appendix

Step 7. View the slide as it will look in the slide show and then save your work.

For help, see Solution 8-3: How to Create a Title Slide.

Add a Slide with a Bulleted List and Graphics

The next slide has a title, bulleted list, two clip art photos, and a shape. The content follows part B of the outline (refer to Figure 8-4). Text in the outline that is not on the slide is entered as notes for this slide.

On Your Own 8-4

Add a Slide with a Bulleted List and Graphics

Create the second slide. When this activity is completed, the slide looks like that in Figure 8-8.

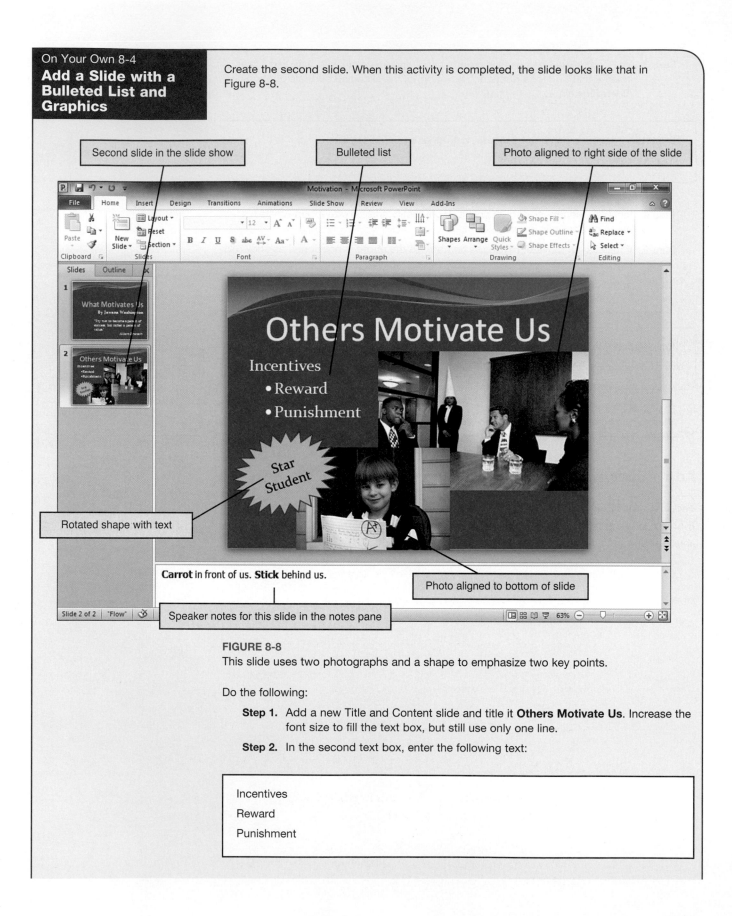

FIGURE 8-8
This slide uses two photographs and a shape to emphasize two key points.

Do the following:

Step 1. Add a new Title and Content slide and title it **Others Motivate Us**. Increase the font size to fill the text box, but still use only one line.

Step 2. In the second text box, enter the following text:

Incentives

Reward

Punishment

The text is automatically formatted as a bulleted list. Use the Increase List Level button ⊞ on the Home ribbon to indent the last two lines. Delete the bullet on the first line. Set the font size for these three lines to **32** point. To make the bullets stand out against a blue background, make the bullets white rather than blue.

> Incentives
> - Reward
> - Punishment

Step 3. Use the Insert ribbon to insert a clip art photograph that speaks of reward. Resize and move the photo as shown in Figure 8-8. Exact size and position are not important. When you're resizing the photo, be sure the photo proportions don't change.

> **Hint** When searching for clip art about how others motivate us, try searching on the text **grade A+** or **punishment** to find images that are relevant. To narrow your search results, change the file type for your search to photographs.

Step 4. Insert a clip art photograph about punishment. Resize and move the photo as shown in Figure 8-8. Keep the proportions of the photo intact as you resize it. Stack the two photos so the reward photo is in front of the punishment photo as shown in Figure 8-8.

Step 5. Insert a 24-point star shape. Change the color of the star to **Orange**.

Step 6. Add the following text to the shape. Make the text black and **28** point.

> Star Student

Step 7. If necessary, increase the size of the star so the text fits inside the shape. Then rotate the star so that it looks like that in Figure 8-8.

Step 8. In the notes pane below the slide, enter the following speaker notes:

> Carrot in front of you. Stick behind you.

 Solutions Appendix

Step 9. Bold the key words **Carrot** and **Stick** so you will see them better when you glance at your notes during your presentation.

Step 10. Save your work.

For help, see Solution 8-4: How to Add a Slide with a Bulleted List and Graphics.

Add a Slide with SmartArt

Microsoft offers **SmartArt** to help you organize text into artistic graphical containers. SmartArt is a shortcut to a professional-looking presentation.

> **SmartArt**—A feature of PowerPoint, Word, Excel, and Outlook that uses a graphical container for text and pictures.

The third slide (see Figure 8-9) uses SmartArt to present the three ways we motivate ourselves. The information in this slide comes from section C of the outline shown in Figure 8-4.

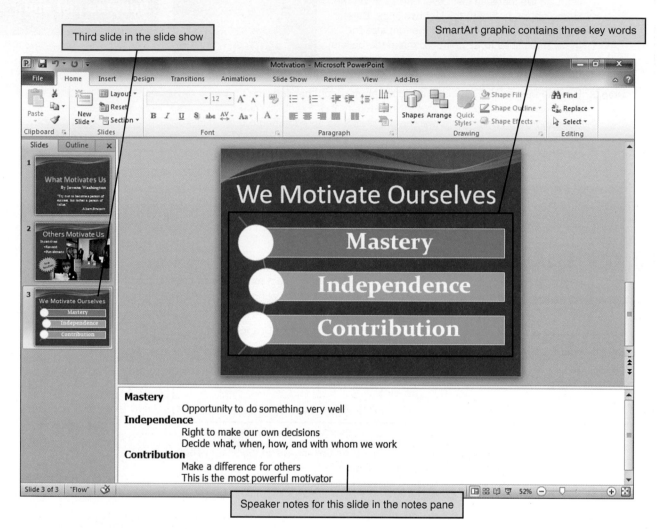

FIGURE 8-9
This slide uses SmartArt to visualize a list.

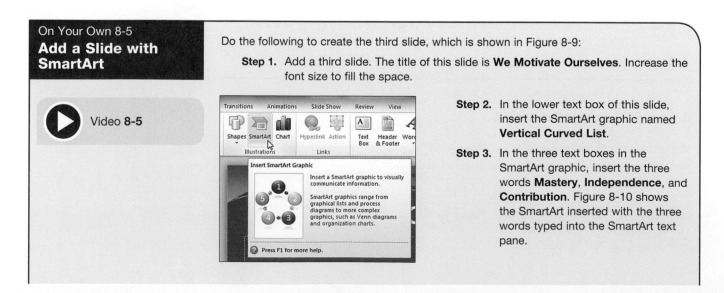

On Your Own 8-5
Add a Slide with SmartArt

Video **8-5**

Do the following to create the third slide, which is shown in Figure 8-9:

Step 1. Add a third slide. The title of this slide is **We Motivate Ourselves**. Increase the font size to fill the space.

Step 2. In the lower text box of this slide, insert the SmartArt graphic named **Vertical Curved List**.

Step 3. In the three text boxes in the SmartArt graphic, insert the three words **Mastery**, **Independence**, and **Contribution**. Figure 8-10 shows the SmartArt inserted with the three words typed into the SmartArt text pane.

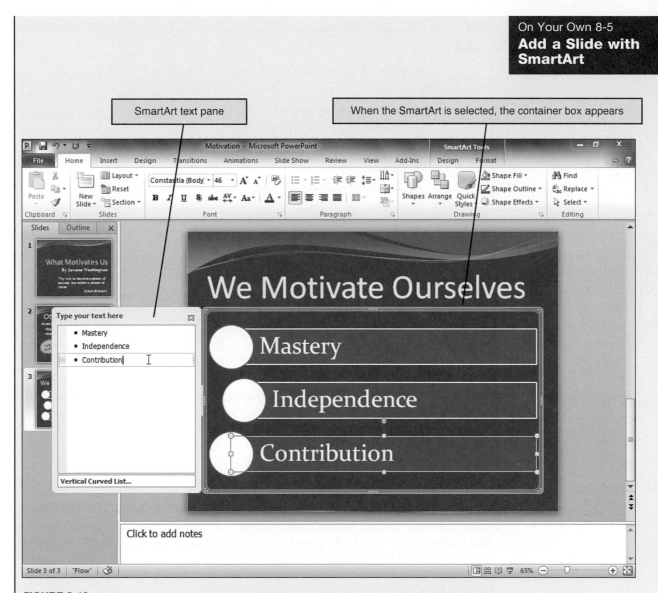

FIGURE 8-10
SmartArt provides a text pane you use to enter and format the text in the SmartArt graphic.

Step 4. It's best to use a large font size, but not larger than the font size of the slide title. Apply the following formatting to the three words in the SmartArt:

   a. Increase the font size of the three words so they fill the space but don't make them larger than the slide title.

   b. Center the three words.

Step 5. To make the colors in the SmartArt a little more interesting, first select the SmartArt container box. Then click **Change Colors** on the Design ribbon. Change the color scheme of the SmartArt to **Colorful - Accent Colors**.

Step 6. In the notes pane below the slide, add the following text to help you when giving the presentation. Make each of the motivators bold, and indent the text under each motivator to make your notes easy to scan as you are speaking.

On Your Own 8-5
Add a Slide with SmartArt

Mastery

　　　Opportunity to do something very well

Independence

　　　Right to make our own decisions

　　　Decide what, when, how, and with whom we work

Contribution

　　　Make a difference for others

　　　This is the most powerful motivator

Solutions Appendix

For help, see Solution 8-5: How to Add a Slide with SmartArt.

Hint To increase the height of the notes pane on your window, press and drag the top of the notes pane.

Tip Most SmartArt graphics have three shapes used to hold three items. After you insert the SmartArt, you can select it and use the Design ribbon to delete or add a shape. The Design ribbon shows up when SmartArt is selected.

Add the Final Slide

The final slide displays during the conclusion of your presentation and when the audience is asking questions. Because your audience might see it for several minutes, it should make a strong point. It needs to help the audience apply the presentation to their own lives.

Tip Repeat your name on the final slide in case someone came in late and missed the title slide or needs your contact information.

The information in this slide comes from section D of the outline shown in Figure 8-4.

When this activity is completed, the final slide will look like that in Figure 8-11. The slide uses a photo that has artistic effects and color to add impact and interest.

The photo fills the entire slide and has artistic effects and color applied

The text box containing the title is in front of the photo

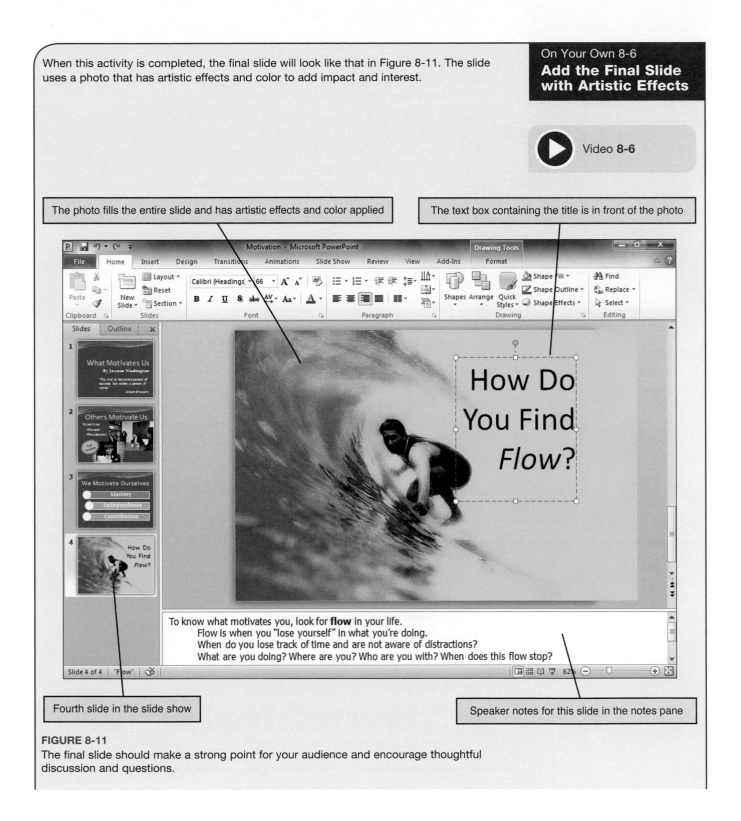

Fourth slide in the slide show

Speaker notes for this slide in the notes pane

FIGURE 8-11
The final slide should make a strong point for your audience and encourage thoughtful discussion and questions.

On Your Own 8-6
Add the Final Slide with Artistic Effects

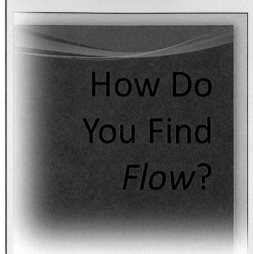

Do the following to create the slide:

Step 1. Insert a new slide using the Title Only slide layout. Add this title: **How Do You Find Flow?** Apply this formatting to the title text:

    a. Change the text color to Black. Set the word **Flow** to italic. Right-justify the text. Set the font size to **66** points.

    b. Use the Align text button 🔲▾ on the Home ribbon to align the text to the top of the text box.

    c. Resize the text box so text wrap causes the text to flow to three lines.

    d. Position the text box near the right side of the slide, as shown in Figure 8-12.

FIGURE 8-12
Position the slide title on the right side of the slide.

Step 2. Insert a clip art photograph of a surfer on a wave. You can use the words **riding a wave** in the clip art search box.

Step 3. Resize the photo so it fills the entire slide, covering even the title. Keep proportions the same as you resize and don't worry that the photo spills off the right side of the slide.

Step 4. Send the photo behind the title so that the title appears on top of the photo.

Step 5. To add interest, apply an artistic effect to the photo. The artistic effect used in Figure 8-11 is **Glow Diffused**.

> **Hint** With the photo selected, look for Artistic Effects on the Format ribbon.

Step 6. Apply a color to the photo. The color used for the photo in Figure 8-11 is **Turquoise, Accent color 3 Dark**.

> **Hint** With the photo selected, look for Color on the Format ribbon.

Step 7. The last slide invites the audience to apply the presentation to their own lives. You can ask questions to encourage thought and discussion. Enter the following notes in the notes pane for this slide:

> To know what motivates you, look for flow in your life.
> Flow is when you "lose yourself" in what you're doing.
> When do you lose track of time and are not aware of distractions?
> What are you doing? Where are you? Who are you with? When does this flow stop?

? Solutions Appendix

For help, see Solution 8-6: How to Add the Final Slide with Artistic Effects.

Step 8. Save your work.

Revising and Giving the Presentation

After you build the presentation, check it for errors. Here are some tips and tools that can help:

▶ **Check spelling.** The spell checker in PowerPoint works as it does in Word. Misspelled words are underlined in red. To fix the problem, right-click the word and select the correct spelling (see Figure 8-13). To check the spelling of all words in the presentation, click **Spelling** on the Review ribbon.

▶ **View and edit text.** Editing text works as it does in Word. You can select and replace text, click an insertion point to add text, or use the Backspace or Delete key to delete text. If you need to view or edit a lot of text in the presentation, use the **Outline** view in the left pane (see Figure 8-14).

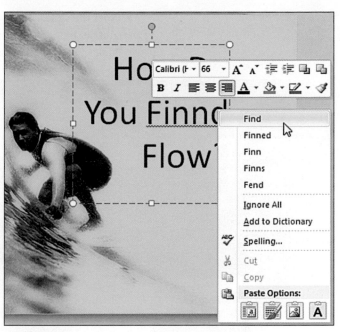

FIGURE 8-13
PowerPoint underlines a misspelled word in red.

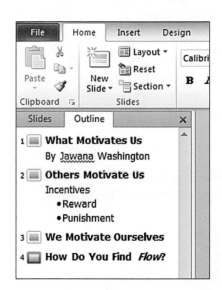

FIGURE 8-14
Use the Outline tab in the left pane to view and edit text in the presentation.

▶ **Move a slide.** You can use the Slide/Outline pane to move a slide in the presentation. Press and drag the slide to a new location.

▶ **Delete a slide.** To delete a slide, right-click the slide in the Slide/Outline pane and click **Delete Slide** from the shortcut menu (see Figure 8-15).

▶ **Insert a new slide.** To insert a slide between two existing slides, right-click a slide in the left pane and select **New Slide** from the shortcut menu. The slide is inserted below the selected slide.

FIGURE 8-15
In the Slide/Outline pane, use the shortcut menu to delete, insert, or duplicate a slide.

▶ **Sort the slides.** If you need to reorder the slides, click **Slide Sorter** on the View ribbon. In the Slide Sorter view (see Figure 8-16), press and drag thumbnails of the slides to new positions. Click **Normal** to return to Normal view.

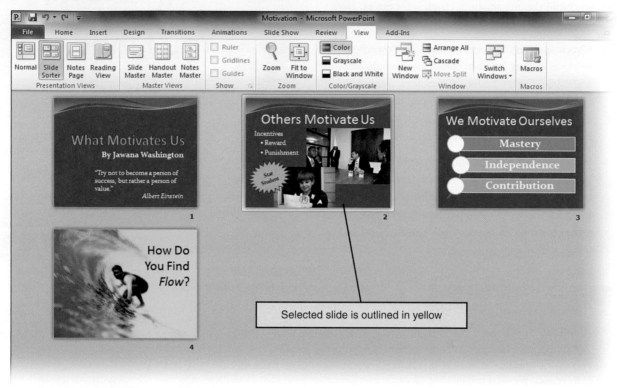

FIGURE 8-16
Use the Slide Sorter view to rearrange the order of slides.

▶ **Use the status bar buttons**. You can use the buttons in the status bar to switch quickly between Normal view, Slide Sorter view, and the Slide Show (see Figure 8-17).

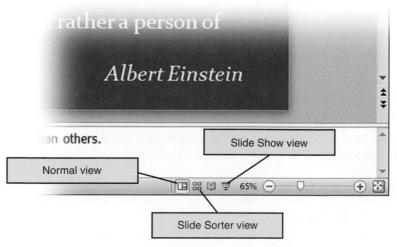

FIGURE 8-17
Use the status bar buttons to quickly switch between views.

Do the following to practice revising a presentation:

Step 1. Use the Slide/Outline pane on the left to select one slide after another and check each slide for errors. Correct any errors you find.

Step 2. Use the spelling checker to check the presentation for misspelled words and correct any misspellings.

Step 3. Use the Slide/Outline pane to practice moving a slide. For example, make the third slide the second slide in the presentation. Then return the slide to its original location.

Step 4. Go to the Slide Sorter view and practice moving a slide. Return the slide to its original location and then return to Normal view.

Step 5. Insert a new slide following slide one. Then delete this blank slide.

Step 6. Use the Notes Page view to see each slide.

Step 7. Save your work.

Step 8. Use the Slide Show button 🖵 in the status bar to view your presentation as a slide show. Use the arrow keys to step though all the slides. Verify all the slides work well when displayed in this full-screen view.

Hint If you find a problem as you view the slide show, press the **Escape** key to return to editing mode. After you make your changes, don't forget to save your work.

?   Solutions Appendix

**For help, see Solution 8-7:
How to Review and Revise
the Presentation.**

Always print your presentation so you have the notes in your hand while presenting. It's also a good practice to print handouts for your audience so your audience has a record of the presentation and place to take notes as you speak.

PowerPoint allows you to save the presentation as a **PowerPoint show**, which is the best file format to use when giving your presentation.

PowerPoint show—A file format for a PowerPoint presentation that always opens as a slide show rather than in the Normal view used for editing. Speaker notes are not included in the file. A PowerPoint show has a .ppsx file extension.

Tip When someone asks for a digital copy of your presentation, give or email the PowerPoint show file.

On Your Own 8-8
Print the Presentation and Save as a PowerPoint Show

Use the Backstage view to explore ways to print a PowerPoint presentation and answer the following questions:

Step 1. By default, slides print in black and white. Display the print preview when the slides print in **Color**. Return the print preview to **Pure Black and White**.

Step 2. You can produce handouts of the presentation for your audience. Display the print preview of the **3 Slides** option under Handouts (see Figure 8-18). What is the purpose of the lines in the right column of the handout? How many slides print to a page when using the Notes Pages option for printing slides?

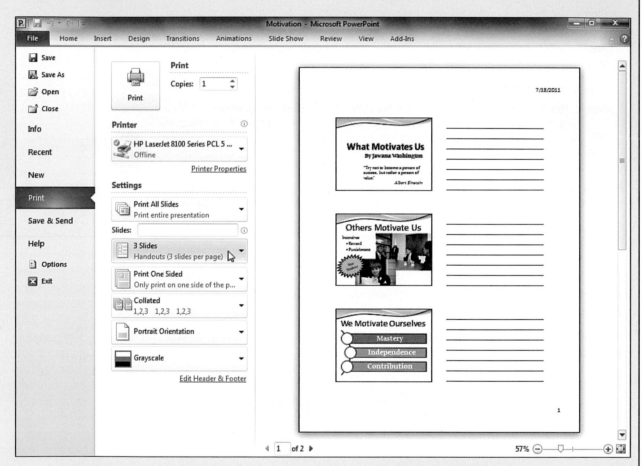

FIGURE 8-18
Three slides print to a page when you use the 3 Slides option for a handout.

Step 3. If you have access to a printer, print the notes pages and the handouts for your presentation.

Do the following to create and use a PowerPoint show:

Step 1. Click the **File** tab and use the **Save As** option to save the presentation as a PowerPoint show. Name the show **MotivationShow**. Close the PowerPoint window.

Step 2. Open Windows Explorer and double-click the file **MotivationShow**. The show starts and the title slide appears. Use the down-arrow key to step to the next slide.

Step 3. Right-click the slide and use the shortcut menu to go to another slide in the show. End the show.

? Solutions Appendix

For help, see Solution 8-8: How to Print the Presentation and Save as a PowerPoint Show.

Before giving the presentation, test it out. Here are some tips:

- ▶ If possible, set up your presentation in the same room where you will be giving it. View the slides from the back of the room and make sure people in the back can read each slide. You might need to increase the font size, change the font color, or cut some text on a slide.

- ▶ Practice your presentation using the slides and your speaker notes that you printed out in PowerPoint. Time the presentation to make sure it's about right.

- ▶ Make an extra copy of the PowerPoint file just in case something happens to the original. Bring both copies with you when you make your presentation.

When giving the presentation, keep these tips in mind:

- ▶ Don't forget to turn off your cell phone before you start. Arrive early and set up the presentation before people arrive. You might need to dim the lights in the room so the presentation can be seen.

- ▶ If appropriate, meet each person at the door, shake hands, make eye contact, smile, thank each person for coming, and give each person your handout.

- ▶ Start strong. Your opening statement needs to catch the interest of your audience. Tell the beginning, middle, and end of your story in this opening statement while the first slide is displayed.

- ▶ Don't read the slides. If necessary, you can occasionally refer to your speaker notes. Keep your eyes on the audience and try to engage them. If you forget what to say next, you can pause and ask if there are any questions.

- ▶ At the end of your talk, summarize the beginning, middle, and end. Tell the audience what you want them to do. Thank them for participating.

Summary

Using PowerPoint to Tell a Story

▶ A presenter can step through PowerPoint slides as he speaks to an audience to add key words, quotes, graphics, sound, and video to his presentation. For a large group, a projector can be used to project slides onto a large area.

▶ The PowerPoint presentation file can contain slides and speaker notes and has a .pptx file extension.

▶ Many of the tools and ribbons on the PowerPoint window are similar to those on the Word window. This similarity makes it easier to learn Office applications.

▶ When designing a PowerPoint presentation, keep to a few strong slides that use little text with simple and large fonts and make good use of graphics.

▶ When building a presentation, start with an outline to keep your slides on track and make sure you have covered all important points.

Creating a PowerPoint Presentation

▶ A PowerPoint theme sets the mode for a presentation by using consistent style, colors, and fonts.

▶ The title slide shows the title and the author and should make a strong point about the presentation.

▶ Build a slide by selecting the best slide layout and then insert text and graphics. Text boxes are used to position text on the slide. SmartArt creates a graphical container to hold text and pictures.

Revising and Giving the Presentation

▶ After you build the presentation, be sure to check it for errors, including spelling errors. You can move, delete, and insert slides and use the slide sorter to reorder slides.

▶ Handouts for your audience are printed one to nine slides to a page with and without write-on lines for note taking.

▶ The Notes Pages option for printing includes one slide to a page with speaker notes.

▶ A PowerPoint show has a .ppsx file extension and is used to view the slide show. This file is not used to edit the presentation and does not include speaker notes.

▶ When giving a presentation, tell the beginning, middle, and end of your story at the beginning of your presentation and again at the end. When you use this method, your audience is more likely to remember what you said because they heard it three times and saw the message on slides.

Review Questions

Answer these questions to assess your skills and knowledge of the content covered in the chapter. Your instructor can provide you with the correct answers when you are ready to check your work.

1. What components can PowerPoint slides add to a presentation you make?

2. What is the file extension of a PowerPoint 2010 presentation file?

3. What is the first slide in a presentation called?

4. Where on the PowerPoint window do you type speaker notes that you don't want to appear on the slides?

5. Why should text on a slide use a font size of at least 28 points?

6. Which ribbon in PowerPoint is used to add clip art to a slide?

7. What PowerPoint tool provides predesigned graphical containers for text and pictures?

8. When resizing a photo or clip art on a slide, how do you retain the proportions of the graphic?

9. How can you change the stacking order of objects on the slide when they overlap?

10. How can you see all the slides displayed as thumbnails on the screen so you can easily reorder the slides?

11. Why would you want to give your audience a handout of the presentation?

12. What is the maximum number of slides PowerPoint prints on one page of the handout?

13. What is the file extension of a PowerPoint show file?

14. Which key do you press to end a PowerPoint show?

15. During a PowerPoint show, how can you jump to a slide in the presentation that is not next to the current slide?

Chapter Mastery Project

Find out how well you have mastered the content in this chapter by completing this project. If you can answer all the questions and do all the steps without looking back at the chapter details, you have mastered this chapter. If you can complete the project by finding answers using the PowerPoint Help window or the web, you have proven that you can teach yourself how to use PowerPoint.

If you find you need a lot of help doing the project and you have not yet read the chapter or done the activities, drop back and start at the beginning of the chapter and then return to this project.

> **Hint** All the key terms in the chapter are used in this mastery project. If you encounter a key word you don't know such as *gallery*, enter **define:gallery in PowerPoint** in the Internet Explorer search box.

Mastery Project Part 1: Using PowerPoint to Tell Your Story

If you need help completing this part of the mastery project, review the "Using PowerPoint to Tell a Story" section in the chapter.

Answer the following questions:

1. A(n) _____ is a special effect that happens when a slide first displays. A(n) _____ is a special effect that happens when an object first displays.

2. If you need to put your company logo on every slide of a presentation, what type slide is used to insert the logo?

3. Which is better, white text on a dark purple background or dark purple text on a white background? Why?

4. Which uses a stronger design, a slide that lists seven important points or one that shows one photo and one word? Why?

5. Which PowerPoint ribbon contains the option to add the date to each slide in the presentation?

6. What is the file extension for a PowerPoint presentation? For a PowerPoint show?

Mastery Project Part 2: Creating a PowerPoint Presentation

If you need help completing this part of the mastery project, review the "Creating a PowerPoint Presentation" section in the chapter.

Build the four-slide presentation showing in Figure 8-19.

FIGURE 8-19
The PowerPoint presentation titled "Why Play?" has four slides.

Do the following to create the presentation:

Step 1. Use the Spring theme with the Oriel color applied to it. Name the presentation **Play** and save it to your hard drive, USB flash drive, SkyDrive, or another location given by your instructor. On the Backstage view, verify that you are listed as the author of the presentation file.

Step 2. Slide 1, the title slide, has a shape and a photo. The text in the shape is black, 32 point, italic. You can find the clip art photo when you search on **play guitar**. Be sure to increase the font size of the title and author and right-align this text.

In the notes pane, type these speaker notes for this slide:

> Play encourages imagination and innovation.
>
> Play is a great way to learn new skills.

Step 3. Slide 2 uses the Title Only layout. Increase the font size of the title to fill the space. You can find the clip art photo by searching on **play at beach**. The photo covers the entire slide and is behind the title. Apply the **Pencil Grayscale** artistic effect to the photo. You need to move the title and/or the photo so the title does not cover the heads of the people in the photo.

In the notes pane, type these speaker notes for this slide:

> Play is self-directed, open-ended, and fun.
>
> Play focuses on the process rather than the product.

Step 4. Slide 3 uses the Title Only layout. Increase the font size of the title. The three interconnected circles are created with SmartArt. You can find the clip art photo by searching for **adults at play**. To make room for the photo to fill the right side of the slide, you need to move the title a bit to the left.

In the notes pane, type these speaker notes for this slide:

> The opposite of play is depression (not work).

Step 5. Slide 4 uses the Title and Content layout. Increase the font size of the title and resize and rotate the text box. The two clip art photos can be found by searching on **family play**. Apply the **Rotated, White** picture style to each photo.

In the notes pane, type these speaker notes for this slide:

> How can you include play in learning to use computers in this course?

Mastery Project Part 3: Revising and Giving the Presentation

If you need help completing this part of the mastery project, review the "Revising and Giving the Presentation" section in the chapter.

Using the "Why Play?" presentation, do the following:

Step 1. Check the presentation for misspelled words.

Step 2. View the presentation as a slide show and correct any problems you see.

Step 3. Use the Slide/Outline pane to view the presentation as an outline. What happens when you edit text in the outline?

Step 4. Using the Slide/Outline pane, move Slide 3 before Slide 2. View the slide show. Then use the Slide Sorter to return the slide to its original position.

Step 5. Insert a new slide following the title slide. Then delete the new slide.

Step 6. On the third slide, add a fourth ring to the SmartArt and insert the text **Enjoy Life** into this ring.

Step 7. Save the presentation as a PowerPoint show. Close the PowerPoint window. Using Windows Explorer, locate the show and view the slide show by double-clicking the .ppsx file.

Step 8. View handouts that print three to a page with write-on lines. If you have access to a printer, print this handout.

Step 9. Email the .pptx file to your instructor.

Becoming an Independent Learner

Answer the following questions about becoming an independent learner:

1. To teach yourself to use PowerPoint, do you think it is best to rely on the chapter, on PowerPoint Help, or to explore tools on PowerPoint ribbons when you need answers?

2. The most important skill learned in this chapter is how to teach yourself a computer skill. Rate yourself at Level A through E on how well you are doing with this skill. What is your level?

   ○ Level A: I was able to successfully complete the Chapter Mastery Project without the help of doing the On Your Own activities in the chapter.

   ○ Level B: I completed all the On Your Own activities and the Chapter Mastery Project without referring to any of the solutions in the *Solutions Appendix*.

   ○ Level C: I completed all the On Your Own activities and the Chapter Mastery Project by using just a few of the solutions in the *Solutions Appendix*.

   ○ Level D: I completed all the On Your Own activities and the Chapter Mastery Project by using many of the solutions in the *Solutions Appendix*.

   ○ Level E: I completed all the On Your Own activities and the Chapter Mastery Project and had to use all the solutions in the *Solutions Appendix*.

To continue toward the goal of teaching yourself computer skills, if you are not at Level A, try to move up one level on how you learn in Chapter 9.

Projects to Help You

Now that you have mastered the material in this chapter, you are ready to tackle the three projects introduced at the beginning of the chapter in the section "How Will This Chapter Help Me?"

Project 1: Creating a Presentation About You

PERSONAL PROJECT:
I've been asked to speak about myself to a small group. I'd like to tell my story by showing photos of my family and talking about things I enjoy and want to do. How can PowerPoint help me do that?

Build a PowerPoint presentation about yourself that follows this outline:

   A. The title slide includes a title for the presentation and your name

   B. One activity you enjoy

      a. What is it?

      b. Why do you enjoy it?

   C. One or more family members you enjoy

      a. His or her first name and relationship

      b. Something about him or her

   D. One dream you have

      a. What you want to do or where you want to go

      b. What is important to you about this dream

The slide presentation needs to include four slides following these guidelines:

Step 1. Apply a theme to the presentation. Which theme did you use?

Step 2. On Slide 1, the title slide, include your name and a title for the presentation. What is the title of your presentation?

Step 3. Put a slide number on each slide of the presentation except the first slide.

Step 4. On Slide 2, include a shape and a clip art photograph. Use italic for at least one word on the slide.

Step 5. For Slide 3, use SmartArt. Bold at least one word on the slide.

Step 6. Slide 4 uses WordArt and a clip art photograph. Apply artistic effects, picture style, and/or color to the photo.

Step 7. Make sure you are listed as the author of the presentation file.

Step 8. Save the slides as a PowerPoint presentation and a PowerPoint show. Email the presentation file to your instructor. What is the name of the presentation file?

Project 2: Making a Presentation Using Award-Winning Designs

Search the web for great PowerPoint presentations. Find one that impresses you and identify elements on the presentation that make it stand out (design, text, color, graphics, or videos).

> **Hint** Use Google.com to search on **award-winning powerpoint presentations**.

Create a presentation that has three or four slides on a topic of your choice or a topic assigned by your instructor. Apply some of the design ideas that you found on the web to your presentation. (Do not break copyright laws by copying text or photos found in these presentations.)

On your SkyDrive, create a folder named Public and give everyone the right to view the folder. Refer to Chapter 2, "Finding and Using Information on the Web," for a refresher about using a SkyDrive.

Post your presentation to the Public folder on your SkyDrive. Email the link to the folder to your instructor.

ACADEMIC PROJECT: An instructor in another class has asked me to speak to my class about an assigned topic. I need to send the presentation to all my classmates. How can I make a presentation using the very best designs?

Project 3: Broadcasting a Presentation

Microsoft Office 2010 allows you to broadcast a PowerPoint presentation to remote viewers over the Internet. You must have a Windows Live account, which you created in Chapter 2. Broadcasting a slide show can work well if you are speaking to your audience on a conference phone line. Each member of the audience can listen on the phone and see the slide show in her web browser while you present it.

Follow these steps to broadcast a presentation to someone in your class:

Step 1. Open the presentation in PowerPoint. On the Slide Show ribbon, click **Broadcast Slide Show**. Then click **Start Broadcast**. You are required to enter your email address and password to your Windows Live account.

Step 2. PowerPoint displays a URL to your broadcast. Copy the URL into the Windows Clipboard. Paste the URL into an email message and email the message to your classmate.

Step 3. When your classmate receives the email message, he can click the link in the message. Internet Explorer displays the broadcast.

Step 4. When you are ready to start the slide show on your computer, click **Start Slide Slide**.

TECHNICAL CAREER PROJECT: My boss has told me to make a presentation to my help desk team members. Two team members work from home. They call in on a conference line during our team meetings. How can they see my PowerPoint presentation along with the others present at the meeting?

Project to Help Others

One of the best ways to learn is to teach someone else. And, in teaching someone else, you are making a contribution into that person's life. As part of each chapter's work, you are encouraged to teach someone else a skill you have learned. In this chapter, help someone learn to use PowerPoint.

Who is your apprentice? _____

When helping others learn, don't do the work for them. Coach and instruct. Show them how to find information for themselves. Help them be as independent a learner as possible.

Do the following:

Step 1. Show your apprentice how to explore the PowerPoint window and demonstrate to him some of the tools on the PowerPoint ribbons. Open a presentation you have created to show him what PowerPoint can do.

Step 2. Ask your apprentice to create his own presentation about himself, a family member, a recent vacation, a new job, or a hobby. Start by creating a short outline that lists the topics for three or four slides.

Step 3. Coach your apprentice as he builds each slide of the presentation. Encourage him to include clip art, photos, SmartArt, and other interesting elements to create well-designed and interesting slides.

Step 4. Ask your apprentice if he is satisfied with his first presentation. Was he able to present the slide show to a friend or family member?

CHAPTER 9
Adding Action and Sound to a PowerPoint Presentation

IN THIS CHAPTER, YOU WILL

Add video, audio, and animation to a presentation

Add web content to a presentation

Add transitions to a presentation

This chapter is a great one for teaching yourself a new computer skill. You already know the basics of creating a PowerPoint presentation, and now it's time to add some bells and whistles. Explore on your own and try new tools. Don't be afraid to make mistakes. Remember the all-powerful Undo button is right there if you don't like the change you just made.

Try to do each On Your Own activity without any help. But remember, if you need help, you can always refer to the solutions in the *Solutions Appendix*.

JUMP RIGHT IN

If you want even more of a challenge, try proceeding directly to the Chapter Mastery Project at the end of this chapter. If you need help on the project, refer to the On Your Own activities in the chapter or do your own independent investigating using PowerPoint Help or searching the web for answers. When you complete the project, you will have mastered the skills in this chapter. Then go to the projects that require you apply your skills to new situations.

How Will This Chapter Help Me?

Recall that throughout this book, each chapter provides three projects focusing on personal, academic, or technical career goals. Depending on your own interests, you might choose to complete any or all of these projects to help you achieve your goals.

PERSONAL PROJECT: I want to make a PowerPoint presentation to help sell my car. It needs to include sounds of a car engine, photos, and a video. I found this cool video on YouTube about my car's make and model. Can I put this video in my presentation?

ACADEMIC PROJECT: I've been asked to create a slide show to continually run on a computer in the lobby of the admin building. First, I must email it to some people for their approval. How do I do all this?

TECHNICAL CAREER PROJECT: My boss has asked me to create a PowerPoint design for all the speakers at our next conference to use. He wants all the design color, graphics, and text to go on the slide master. How do I use a slide master?

Adding Video, Audio, and Animation to a Presentation

To learn how to add action and sound to a presentation, we create a presentation to help a professional musician speak to an audience of amateurs about taking a garage band on the road. The outline used to build the presentation is shown in Figure 9-1. The completed presentation is shown in Figure 9-2 and has four slides.

How to Get a Garage Band Out of the Garage and onto the Road

- Start with the press kit
    - Band bio and a professional photo
    - List of past gigs and future schedule
    - Song list
    - Equipment list (very important)
    - Publish a professional web site and Facebook presence
    - Business cards for all members
    - Make it clear who to contact
    - Put the press kit in a colorful envelope that stands out
    - Give out your business cards at gigs
- Get exposure by playing for free
    - Open mic nights
    - Volunteer to open for another band
    - Play at town fairs, county festivals, and city concerts
    - Play at Battle of the Bands in your area
    - Play at local restaurants for tips only
    - Post videos on YouTube.com
- What to do if opportunities are not coming your way
    - Change what you're doing until you find what works for you

FIGURE 9-1
An outline keeps us on track when creating a PowerPoint presentation.

Follow along at your computer as we build the presentation. As always, remember your goal is to learn how to use PowerPoint rather than to get the details on each slide right. Have some fun with it!

We begin by using the slide master to create the design for each slide in the presentation. The design can make or break a PowerPoint presentation. If you don't like the design we're using, feel free to try out your own design ideas.

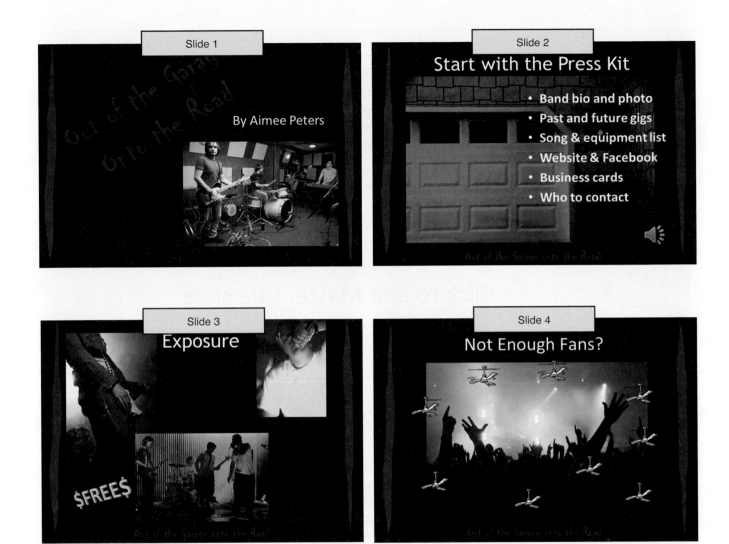

FIGURE 9-2
This presentation about garage bands has four slides and uses actions and sounds.

Use a Slide Master

Recall from Chapter 8, "Using PowerPoint to Give a Presentation," that the slide master is a hidden slide. What you put on the slide master goes on all the slides in a presentation. For example, you can use it to put a company logo or text on all slides.

To access the slide master, click **Slide Master** on the View ribbon. The Slide Master view displays, and the Slide Master ribbon is selected (see Figure 9-3). The Slide Master tab shows on the PowerPoint window as long as the Slide Master view is open. After you make your changes to the slide master, be sure to close the Slide Master view.

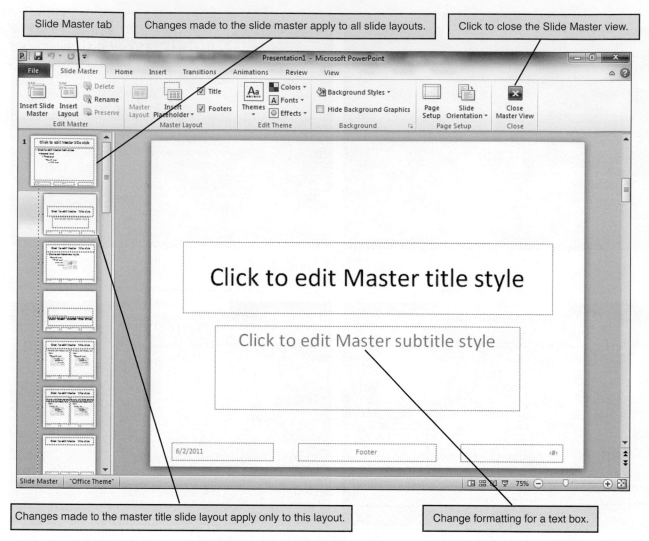

FIGURE 9-3
Changes made to the slide master apply to all slides. Changes made to a slide master layout apply only to that layout.

Here are some tips for using the slide master:

▶ Changes to the slide master apply to all slides in the presentation. Changes to a slide master layout apply only to slides that use that layout.

▶ To change formatting for text on all slides, select a text box on the slide master and change the formatting for that text box.

▶ To place text on the slide master, use the Insert ribbon to insert a new text box. Do not use an existing text box on the slide master.

If you plan to use a slide master when creating a presentation, edit the slide master first. When this activity is completed, the slide master should look like that in Figure 9-4.

On Your Own 9-1
Edit the Slide Master

▶ Video **9-1**

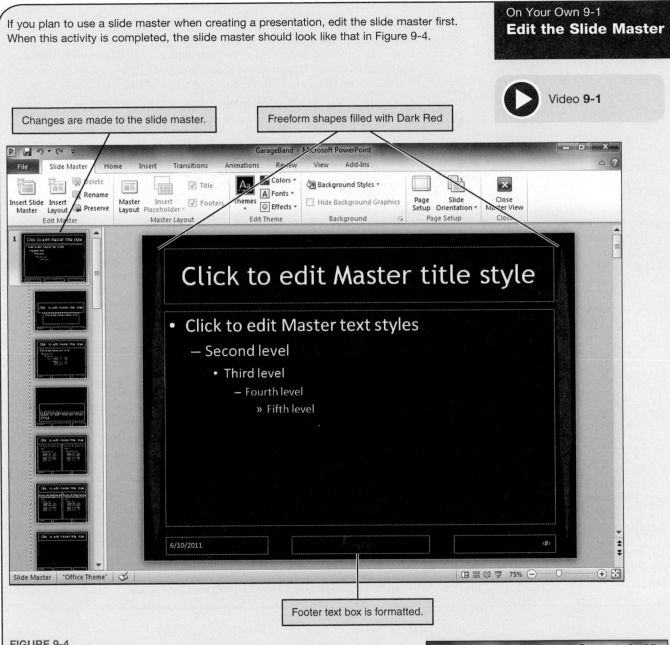

Changes are made to the slide master.

Freeform shapes filled with Dark Red

Footer text box is formatted.

FIGURE 9-4
The slide master has background color, text formatting, and two graphics that create the design for the presentation.

Open the Slide Master view and make these changes to the slide master:

Step 1. Use the **Freeform** shape to draw a jagged long shape like a flame or claw mark on each side of the master slide. Use Figure 9-4 as your guide, but feel free to be creative with these shapes. Fill the shape with **Dark Red**. Change the Line Color to **No line**.

Step 2. To make the background color black and all text white, change the Background Style to **Style 4**.

Step 3. Format the title text using the **Trebuchet MS** font, **White**, and **44** points.

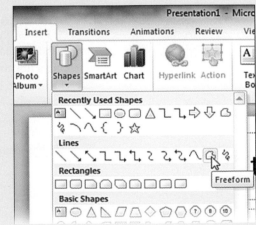

On Your Own 9-1
Edit the Slide Master

Step 4. Format the footer text using the **Chiller** font, **Dark Red**, and **32** points.

Step 5. Use the Slide Master ribbon to close the Slide Master view. On the Home ribbon, click the down arrow next to the New Slide button [New Slide▾] and verify that all slide layouts use the design on the slide master (see Figure 9-5). If this is not case, go back and correct any problems on the slide master.

Step 6. Name the presentation file **GarageBand**. Save it to your hard drive, USB flash drive, SkyDrive, or another location given by your instructor.

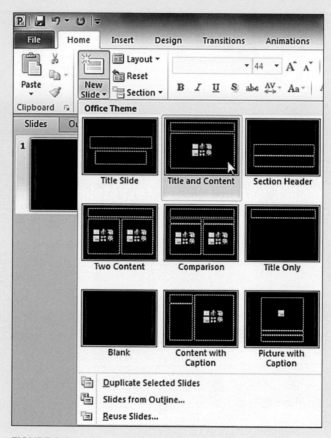

[?]   Solutions Appendix

For help, see Solution 9-1: How to Edit the Slide Master.

FIGURE 9-5
Changes to the slide master are applied to all layouts and new slides.

Add Video to a Slide

A short video, called a video clip, can be added to a slide using a **video file** or by embedding a link to an online video. In this part of the chapter, you use a video file. Later in the chapter, you learn how to embed a link to a video in a slide.

> **video file**—A file that contains audio and moving pictures. A video file might have a .mpeg, .avi, .mov, .mp4, or .wmv file extension.

When this activity is completed, the title slide should look like that in Figure 9-6 when the video clip is selected.

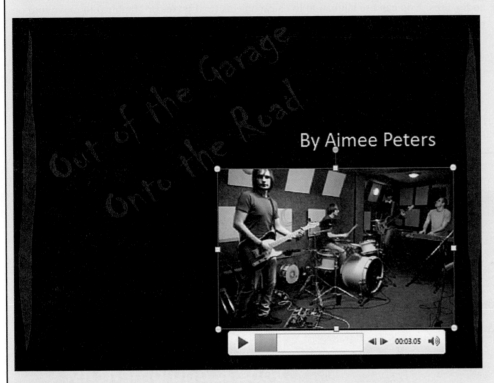

FIGURE 9-6
The title slide includes a video clip that came from a video file.

Do the following to create the title slide that contains a video:

Step 1. On the title slide, enter the title **Out of the Garage Onto the Road**. Format the text using the **Chiller** font, **80** point, **Dark Red**. Rotate and resize the text box, as shown in Figure 9-6. Text wrap causes the title to fit on two lines.

Step 2. Enter the subtitle **By Aimee Peters**. Right-justify the text and move the text box up to make room for the video box.

Step 3. A video file named **RockBand** is stored in the Sample Files folder on the DVD in the back of this book. Insert the file on the slide. Resize and position the video box as shown in Figure 9-6.

> **Hint** To insert a video file in a slide, click **Video** on the Insert ribbon.

Step 4. To test the slide and the video, view it as a slide show. With the slide show running, click the Play button to play the video.

Step 5. Save your work.

Solutions Appendix

> **Tip** The video clip is now part of the .pptx file. A long video can make a .pptx file very large. You can use Windows Explorer to find out the size of a file.

For help, see Solution 9-2: How to Add Video to the Title Slide.

Add Audio and Animation

You can add audio clips to a slide, and Microsoft Office clip art includes several short audio clips. You can use animation to cause objects (text boxes or graphics) to move into or out of a slide or fade on the slide.

On Your Own 9-3
Create the Second Slide with Audio and Animation

The second slide uses animation and an audio clip. When this activity is completed, the slide should look like that in Figure 9-7.

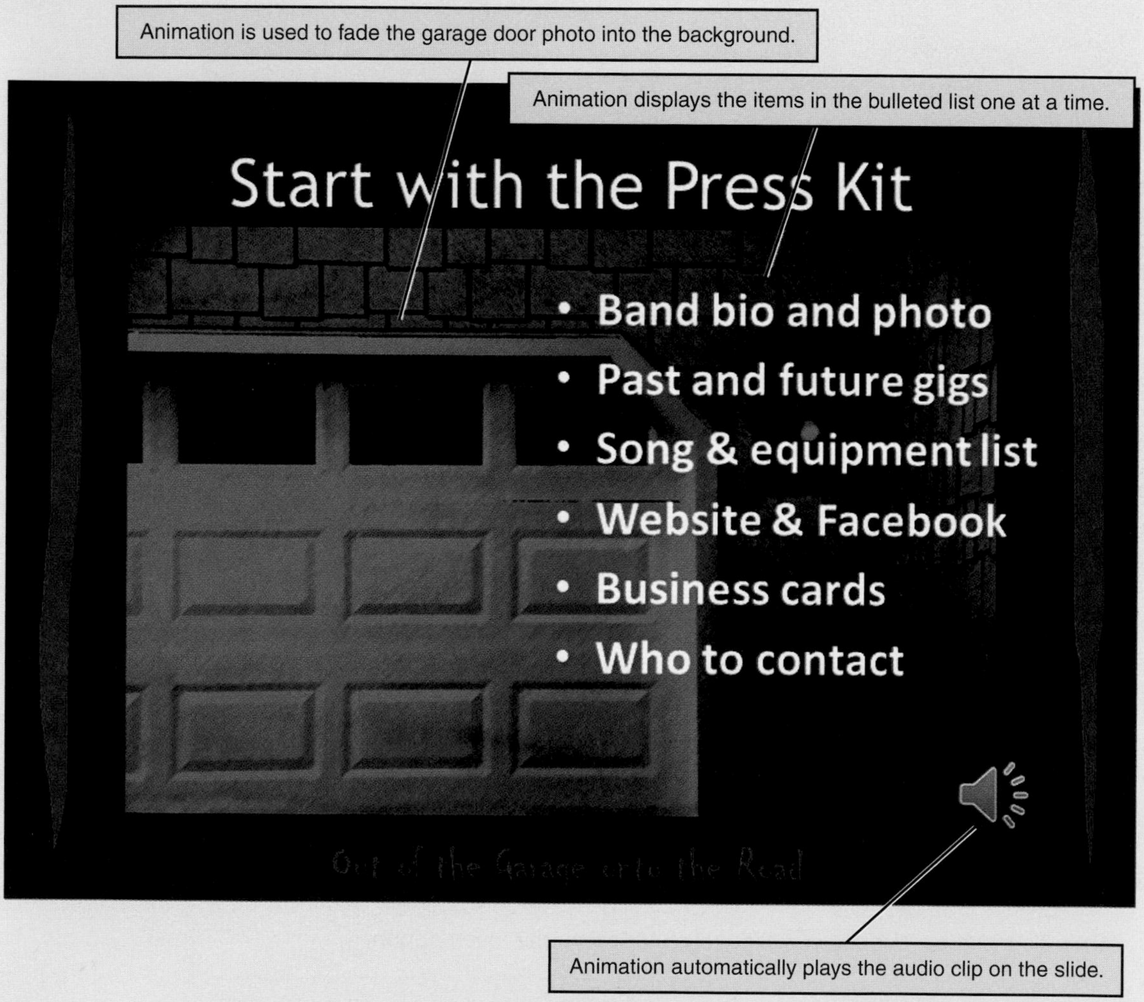

Animation is used to fade the garage door photo into the background.

Animation displays the items in the bulleted list one at a time.

Start with the Press Kit

- Band bio and photo
- Past and future gigs
- Song & equipment list
- Website & Facebook
- Business cards
- Who to contact

Out of the Garage onto the Road

Animation automatically plays the audio clip on the slide.

FIGURE 9-7
The second slide uses animated text and graphics and includes an audio clip.

Do the following to add a second slide to the presentation:

Hint To add a header or footer to a presentation, click **Header & Footer** on the Insert ribbon.

Step 1. Add a new slide using the **Two Content** slide layout. Title the slide **Start with the Press Kit**.

Step 2. Add the footer text **Out of the Garage onto the Road**. The footer goes on every slide except the title slide.

On Your Own 9-3
Create the Second Slide with Audio and Animation

Step 3. Add a bulleted list to the text box on the right using the text shown in Figure 9-7. Increase the font size to **32** points and **Bold** the text. Widen the text box so each bulleted item fits on a single line.

Step 4. Insert the clip art photo of a garage door in the slide. To search for the photo, use **garage door** in the clip art search box.

Step 5. Apply this formatting to the photo:

    a. Resize and position the photo as shown in Figure 9-7. Send the photo behind the text box.

    b. Format the photo using the **Paint Strokes** artistic effects. Change the color of the photo to **Color Saturation 0%**.

Step 6. Add an audio clip of a revving car engine to the slide.

Step 7. Display the slide as a slide show. With the slide show displayed, click the audio button to play the engine sound.

Step 8. Save your work.

Hint To reduce the search results, limit the media file type to **Photographs**.

Now let's add animation to the objects in the slide. Do the following:

Step 1. Using the animation feature of PowerPoint, you can cause an audio clip to play without having to click the Play button on the slide. With the audio clip selected, click the **Animation** tab and click **Play**.

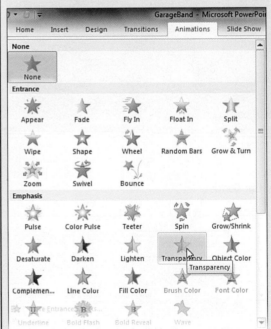

Step 2. Run the slide show again. When you press the down arrow or click anywhere on the slide, the sound plays.

Step 3. We can use animation to cause the photo to fade into the background when the bulleted list appears. With the photo selected, display the Animation gallery on the Animation ribbon. As you hover over an item, you can see how the photo is animated. Select the **Transparency** animation in the Emphasis group.

Step 4. To animate each item in the bulleted list, apply the **Grow & Turn** animation to the bulleted list.

Step 5. View the slide as a slide show. As you click, the sound, photo, and text animations happen. Keep clicking the slide until all the items display. Then return to normal view.

Hint To change the order of objects that appear on a slide, click **Animation Pane** on the Animation ribbon. Using the pane, you can change the order of animation.

Step 6. Enter these speaker notes as a bulleted list:

- Have a professional make the photo.
- Put the press kit in a large colorful envelope that stands out.
- Give your business cards out at your gigs. You never know who might receive one.

 Solutions Appendix

For help, see Solution 9-3: **How to Create the Second Slide with Audio and Animation.**

Add WordArt to a Slide

WordArt can add interest to a slide and is fun to create.

The third slide uses three photos and WordArt. When this activity is completed, the slide should look like that in Figure 9-8. Later in the chapter, you learn how to add a YouTube video to this slide.

Play for free:
- Open mic nights
- Volunteer to open for another band
- Town fairs, county festivals, city concerts, Battle of the Bands
- Play at restaurants for tips only

WordArt

Speaker notes

FIGURE 9-8
The third slide has three photos and WordArt.

Do the following to create the slide:

Step 1. Add the new slide using the **Title Only** layout. The title is **Exposure**.

Step 2. To find the photo of the guitar player, search in the clip art on **electric guitar**. Cut off or crop the photo on both its left and right sides. Resize and position it as shown in Figure 9-8.

Hint To cut off part of a photo (called cropping the photo), first select it and then click **Crop** on the Format ribbon. Cropping handles appear as shown in Figure 9-9. Press and drag cropping handles to crop the photo.

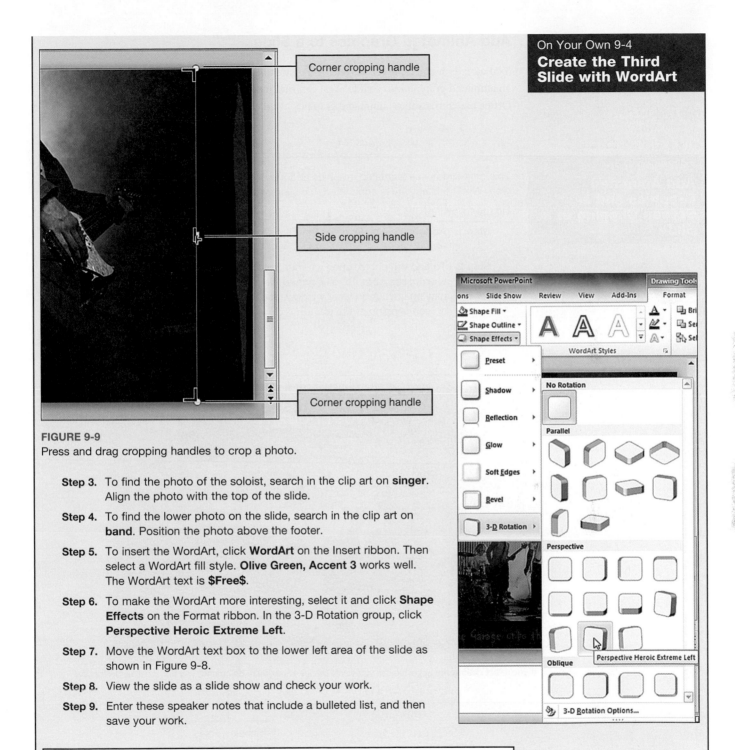

FIGURE 9-9
Press and drag cropping handles to crop a photo.

Step 3. To find the photo of the soloist, search in the clip art on **singer**. Align the photo with the top of the slide.

Step 4. To find the lower photo on the slide, search in the clip art on **band**. Position the photo above the footer.

Step 5. To insert the WordArt, click **WordArt** on the Insert ribbon. Then select a WordArt fill style. **Olive Green, Accent 3** works well. The WordArt text is **$Free$**.

Step 6. To make the WordArt more interesting, select it and click **Shape Effects** on the Format ribbon. In the 3-D Rotation group, click **Perspective Heroic Extreme Left**.

Step 7. Move the WordArt text box to the lower left area of the slide as shown in Figure 9-8.

Step 8. View the slide as a slide show and check your work.

Step 9. Enter these speaker notes that include a bulleted list, and then save your work.

Play for free:

- Open mic nights
- Volunteer to open for another band
- Town fairs, county festivals, city concerts, Battle of the Bands
- Play at restaurants for tips only

 Solutions Appendix

For help, see Solution 9-4: How to Create the Third Slide with WordArt.

Add Animated Graphics to a Slide

You already learned how to add PowerPoint animation to an object. You can also insert an animated graphic into a slide. You can find many animated graphics in Office clip art. Office categorizes these animated graphics as videos.

Add Animated Graphics and a Screen Clipping to a Slide

Video **9-5**

This next slide uses animated graphics and a screen clipping that was copied from the web. When this activity is completed, the slide should look like that in Figure 9-10.

Do the following:

Step 1. Add the new slide, using the **Title Only** layout. Add the slide title **Not Enough Fans?**

Step 2. To find the photo, open Internet Explorer and go to my blog at **lifewithjean. wordpress.com**. Scroll down to the photo on that page. With the photo displaying in your browser window, use the **Windows Snipping Tool** to take a screen clipping of the photo.

Animated clip art graphics

If you're not getting the opportunities you want, change what you're doing until you find what works for you.

Speaker notes

FIGURE 9-10
This fourth slide uses animated graphics and a screen clipping from the web.

Hint Using the Windows Snipping Tool is covered in Chapter 1, " Using Windows 7 to Manage Applications and Data." Recall the Snipping Tool is available in all Windows 7 editions except Windows 7 Starter used on netbooks.

Step 3. Return to PowerPoint and paste the photo onto the slide. Position and resize it as shown in Figure 9-10.

Step 4. To insert the fan graphic on the slide, search clip art for a **ceiling fan** and insert it on the slide. Copy and paste it multiple times over the slide.

Hint To limit the clip art search results, limit the search to the Videos media file type.

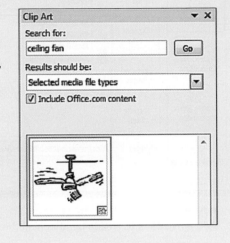

Tip Copying photos from the web into a PowerPoint presentation you create as a class assignment is covered under the fair use law and does not violate copyright laws. However, know you must have permission from the owner to publish or sell these photos.

Step 5. When you view the slide as a slide show, the fans turn. Correct any problems you see.

Step 6. Add the following speaker notes to the slide:

If you're not getting the opportunities you want, change what you're doing until you find what works for you.

Not Working? If the fans do not turn when you run the slide show, most likely you selected a graphic in clip art that is not animated. Go back and select another graphic.

Step 7. Save your work.

For help, see Solution 9-5: How to Add Animated Graphics and a Screen Clipping to a Slide.

 Solutions Appendix

Adding Web Content to a Presentation

You have already learned how you can take a screen clipping from the web and put that clipping in a presentation. In addition, PowerPoint lets you open Internet Explorer and browse the live web during a presentation, and you can also embed a link to a video in a slide.

Browse the Web During a Presentation

One way for a garage band to get exposure is to play in Battle of the Bands. Suppose you want to take your audience to the Battle of the Bands website to see where the next events are playing. PowerPoint lets you do that without interrupting your slide show.

To add a hyperlink to an object on a slide, first select the object. Click **Hyperlink** on the Format ribbon. The Insert Hyperlink box appears. Click **Existing File or Web Page**. Enter the URL in the Address box (see Figure 9-11) and click **OK**.

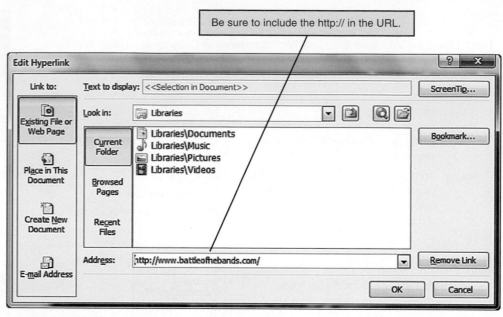

FIGURE 9-11
Add a hyperlink to a slide by attaching the hyperlink to an object already on the slide.

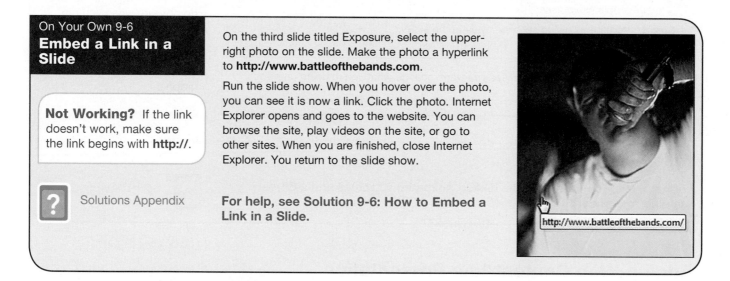

On Your Own 9-6
Embed a Link in a Slide

Not Working? If the link doesn't work, make sure the link begins with **http://**.

? Solutions Appendix

On the third slide titled Exposure, select the upper-right photo on the slide. Make the photo a hyperlink to **http://www.battleofthebands.com**.

Run the slide show. When you hover over the photo, you can see it is now a link. Click the photo. Internet Explorer opens and goes to the website. You can browse the site, play videos on the site, or go to other sites. When you are finished, close Internet Explorer. You return to the slide show.

For help, see Solution 9-6: How to Embed a Link in a Slide.

Add a Video on the Web to a Slide

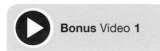

Bonus Video 1

If Adobe Flash Player is installed on your computer and the computer is connected to the Internet, you can embed a link to a video on the web in a slide. You can then watch the video during the slide show. To embed the video, you copy code into a slide. Many websites, including youtube.com, provide the code you need.

For example, we can embed a video from youtube.com on the third slide in the presentation (see Figure 9-12). The YouTube video we are using is "Song of Sixpence" by Mackenzie Chester.

Youtube.com video embedded on the slide

FIGURE 9-12
A YouTube video has been placed on the slide.

Here are the steps to embed the video:

Step 1. Using PowerPoint, select the slide that is to receive the video.

Step 2. Open Internet Explorer, go to **youtube.com**, and find a video. Below the video, click the **Share** button (see Figure 9-13). Click **Embed**. A box opens with the embed code in it. Below the box, check **Use old embed code** as shown in Figure 9-13. The code in the box changes.

Step 3. Click inside the embed code box. All the code is selected. Right-click on the code and click **Copy** from the shortcut menu. The code is copied into the Windows Clipboard.

Step 4. Return to the PowerPoint window and the third slide. On the Insert ribbon, click the down arrow under Video and click **Video from Web Site**. The Insert Video From Web Site box opens. See Figure 9-14.

Not Working? Adobe Flash Player must be installed on your computer before you can insert a link to a video on a slide. If the player is not installed, the **Video from Web Site** is gray and cannot be selected. Chapter 13, "Maintaining a Computer and Fixing Computer Problems," covers how to find out what software is installed on your computer.

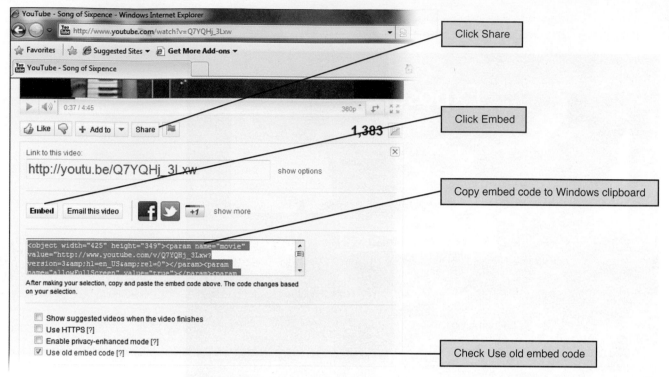

FIGURE 9-13
The code to embed the video appears in the box.

Step 5. Right-click inside the white box and select **Paste** from the shortcut menu, as shown in Figure 9-14. Click **Insert**. The box closes and the video is inserted on the slide. Double-click the video box to see the video controls. You can then play the video.

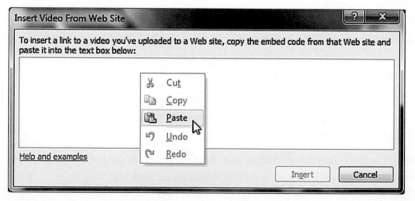

FIGURE 9-14
Paste the embed code copied from youtube.com into the white box.

Step 6. Display the slide as a slide show. Click on the video box and then play the video in the slide show. Don't forget to save your work.

So now you have learned how to include a video file in a slide and how to embed a link to a video in a slide. To decide which method to use, consider the following:

▶ Adding a video file to a presentation can make the PowerPoint file very large.

▶ While giving your presentation, you must be connected to the Internet to view a video on the web.

Adding Transitions to a Presentation

A transition is a special effect that happens when one slide changes to the next. For consistency, use the same style transition for all slides.

Before you add transitions to your presentation, view the entire slide show from beginning to end.

To add a transition to the first slide, select it and click the **Transitions** tab. Then click the down arrow to the right of the transitions. The transitions gallery appears (see Figure 9-15). Click a transition to see it. The last transition clicked is applied to the slide. Apply the same transition to all slides in the presentation.

Save your work and view the entire slide show with transitions.

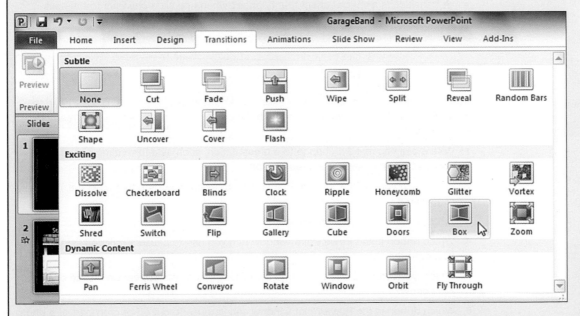

FIGURE 9-15
Transitions appear when one slide changes to the next.

Summary

Adding Video, Audio, and Animation to a Presentation

▶ Text, graphics, formatting, and color on the slide master appear on all slides in the presentation.

▶ Video added to a slide can be from a video file or from a link to a video on a website.

▶ Text and graphics can be animated so they move into or out of a slide or fade on the slide.

▶ Use the Animation pane to change the order of animation applied to objects.

▶ WordArt and the special effects applied to WordArt can add interest to a slide.

Adding Web Content to a Presentation

▶ An object on a slide can be a link to the web. When you click the link, your browser opens to find the requested website.

▶ Websites such as youtube.com provide embed code to their videos so you can embed the link to the video in a PowerPoint presentation.

▶ Know that adding a video file to a PowerPoint presentation can make the PowerPoint file very large. When you embed a video on the web in a presentation, you must have Internet access to view the video during the slide show.

Adding Transitions to a Presentation

▶ A transition is a special effect that happens when one slide changes to the next.

▶ For consistency, use only one style transition in a slide show.

Review Questions

Answer these questions to assess your skills and knowledge of the content covered in the chapter. Your instructor can provide you with the correct answers when you are ready to check your work.

1. Where can you make a change to a presentation, such as a formatting change, that applies to every slide in the presentation?

2. Where can you make a change that applies to every new slide that uses the Title Only slide layout?

3. What type file uses a .wmv file extension?

4. Which ribbon in the PowerPoint window can you use to cause a bulleted list to pop or flow onto the screen one item at a time?

5. Which pane can you use to change the order that objects appear on a slide during a slide show?

6. Which ribbon in the PowerPoint window can you use to cut off or crop part of a photo already inserted on a slide?

7. Suppose you want a photo of a race car for a PowerPoint slide you are preparing for a class assignment. You use Google to find the photo. What Windows tool can you use to copy the photo to a slide?

8. What law gives you the right to use a race car photo you found on the web in a PowerPoint assignment for a class?

9. What law is violated if you were to publish a PowerPoint presentation on the web that included photos you copied from a Google search, but you did not contact the owner?

10. Which PowerPoint ribbon is used to turn an object on a slide into a link to the web?

11. Suppose you enter a URL of www.google.com to an object so that the object becomes a link to this website. When you run the slide show, you get an error. What is wrong with this URL?

12. What software must be installed on your computer before you can embed a video on the web in a PowerPoint slide?

13. What must a website provide before you can embed a video on the site into a PowerPoint slide?

14. Suppose you insert a video file into a PowerPoint presentation. When you email the .pptx file to a friend, do you need to also email the video file? Why or why not?

15. Which PowerPoint ribbon is used to make an audio clip play automatically when you click the slide during a presentation?

Chapter Mastery Project

Find out how well you have mastered the content in this chapter by completing this project. If you can answer all the questions and do all the steps without looking back at the chapter details, you have mastered this chapter. If you can complete the project by finding answers using PowerPoint Help or the web, you have proven that you can teach yourself how to use PowerPoint.

If you find you need a lot of help doing the project and you have not yet read the chapter or done the activities, drop back and start at the beginning of the chapter and then return to this project.

Mastery Project Part 1: Adding Video, Audio, and Animation to a Presentation

If you need help completing this part of the mastery project, review the "Adding Video, Audio, and Animation to a Presentation" section in the chapter.

In this project, you build the PowerPoint presentation shown in Figure 9-16 about selecting a dog breed.

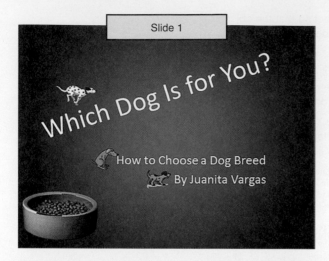

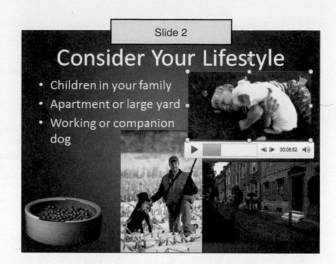

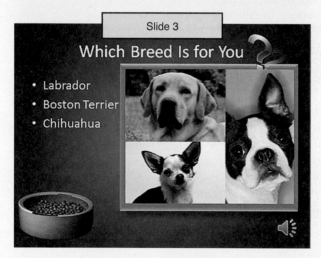

FIGURE 9-16
This presentation about selecting a dog breed has three slides and uses actions and sounds.

To build the presentation, first make these changes to the slide master:

Step 1. Insert a clip art photo of a dog bowl, which will appear on all slides. Remove the background color from the clip art.

> **Hint** Use the **Remove Background** button on the Format ribbon to remove the background color from clip art. After you save your changes, click the slide master in the left pane to return to the slide master.

Step 2. Apply **Style 11** as the Background Style for the presentation.

Step 3. Close the slide master and verify that the dog bowl appears on all slide layouts in the presentation.

Step 4. Save your work, naming the file **DogBreeds**. Save the file to your hard drive, USB drive, SkyDrive, or another location given by your instructor.

On the title slide, do the following:

Step 1. Enter the title and subtitles as shown in the first slide in Figure 9-16. Increase the font size of the title to **66** points. Rotate the title upward on the title slide. Right-justify the subtitles on the slide.

Step 2. Insert three clip art animations of dogs on the slide. Position the dogs as shown in the title slide in Figure 9-16.

Step 3. View the slide as a slide show to see the animation. Save your work.

The second slide is showing in Figure 9-17.

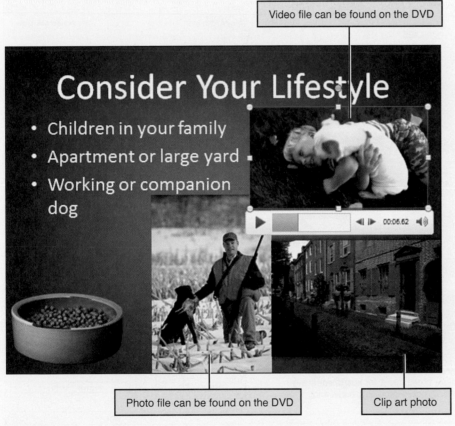

FIGURE 9-17
The second slide has two photos and a video.

To create the second slide, do the following:

Step 1. Enter the title and increase the font size of the title to fill the space.

Step 2. Enter the bulleted list and resize the bulleted list text box so it fits on the left side of the slide.

Step 3. Insert a video clip named **ChildPlaying** stored in the Sample Files folder on the DVD in the back of book. Resize and position the video box in the upper-right area of the slide.

Step 4. Insert a clip art photo of apartments. Align the photo with the right side of the slide.

Step 5. Insert the photo, **RetrieverDog**, stored in the Sample Files folder on the DVD in the back of the book. Align the photo with the bottom of the slide.

Step 6. Format the two photos using the **Center Shadow Rectangle** picture style.

Step 7. View the slide as a slide show and play the video. Save your work.

The third slide is shown in Figure 9-18. The figure shows the Animation pane open so you can see the order that objects appear on the slide.

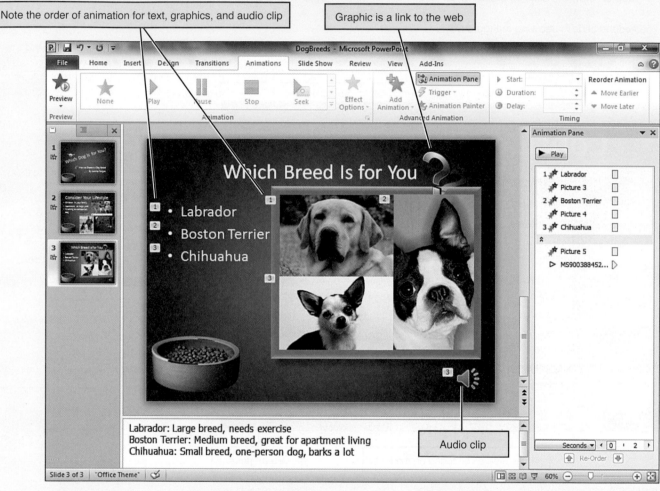

FIGURE 9-18
The third slide has three photos, audio, and a link to the web and uses animation.

To create the third slide, do the following:

Step 1. Enter the text for the slide title and the bulleted list.

Step 2. Insert a clip art of a question mark at the end of the slide title.

Step 3. Insert a **Rectangle** shape with a light blue color that will hold the three photos. Apply the **Preset 4** special effects to the shape.

Step 4. Go to my blog at **lifewithjean.wordpress.com** and take a screen clipping of the Labrador's head. Paste the clipping onto the slide. Resize, crop, and/or move the clipping so it fits in the upper-left corner of the rectangle.

Step 5. Insert a clip art photo of a Boston Terrier and position and resize the photo. The photo must be cropped on the right side to cut out the second dog in the photo.

Step 6. Insert a clip art photo of a Chihuahua and position and resize the photo.

Step 7. Insert an audio clip of a yappy dog on the bottom-right corner of the slide.

Step 8. View the slide as a slide show and correct any problems you see. Be sure to test the audio and save your work.

Step 9. Add these speaker notes to the slide:

Labrador: Large breed, needs exercise

Boston Terrier: Small breed, great for apartment living

Chihuahua: Toy breed, one-person dog, barks a lot

Do the following to add animation to the slide:

Step 1. Apply the fly-in animation to the bulleted list text box and each of the three photos.

Step 2. Apply animation to the audio clip so it plays when you click the slide.

Step 3. Test the animation by viewing the slide as a slide show.

Step 4. Using the Animation pane, change the order of animation so that the objects appear in this order:

    a. The word *Labrador,* followed by the photo of the lab.

    b. The words *Boston Terrier,* followed by the photo of the Boston Terrier.

    c. The word *Chihuahua,* followed by the photo of the Chihuahua and the yappy dog audio playing.

Step 5. Test the order of animation by viewing the slide as a slide show.

Step 6. Change the animation of each photo so it appears at the same time the breed name appears.

Step 7. Include the audio clip with the Chihuahua name and photo so all three happen together.

Step 8. Test the order of animation by viewing the slide as a slide show. Don't forget to save your work.

Mastery Project Part 2: Adding Web Content to a Presentation

If you need help completing this part of the mastery project, review the "Adding Web Content to a Presentation" section in the chapter.

Do the following to add a link to the web to the third slide:

Step 1. Make the question mark a link to the website **www.akc.org/breeds**.

Step 2. Test the slide show and make sure the link works. Save your work.

Answer the following questions:

1. What software must you have installed on your computer before you can add a you-tube.com video to a PowerPoint slide?

2. When you click the Video button on the Insert ribbon, how can you tell if this software is installed correctly?

3. Is the software installed on your computer? If so, you can add a youtube.com video to your slide show.

4. Close the DogBreeds presentation. What is the size of the DogBreeds.pptx file? How did you find your answer?

Hint When one photo is aligned with another, a dotted line appears to let you know they are aligned.

Hint To change the order of animation, press and drag an item in the Animation pane to a new position. If you don't see an item, click the down arrows in the pane.

Hint To cause two objects to appear at the same time, select an item in the Animation pane. Then click the down arrow to its right and select **Start with Previous** from the shortcut menu.

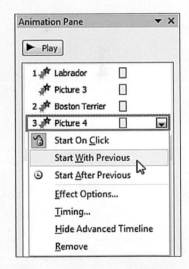

Mastery Project Part 3: Adding Transitions to a Presentation

If you need help completing this part of the mastery project, review the "Adding Transitions to a Presentation" section in the chapter.

Add the Fly Through transition to each slide. View the slide show and make sure the transitions work. Save your work.

Becoming an Independent Learner

Answer the following questions about becoming an independent learner:

1. To teach yourself to use PowerPoint, do you think it is best to rely on the chapter or on PowerPoint Help when you need answers?

2. The most important skill learned in this chapter is how to teach yourself a computer skill. Rate yourself at Level A through E on how well you are doing with this skill. What is your level?

   ○ Level A: I was able to successfully complete the Chapter Mastery Project without the help of doing the On Your Own activities in the chapter.

   ○ Level B: I completed all the On Your Own activities and the Chapter Mastery Project without referring to any of the solutions in the *Solutions Appendix*.

   ○ Level C: I completed all the On Your Own activities and the Chapter Mastery Project by using just a few of the solutions in the *Solutions Appendix*.

   ○ Level D: I completed all the On Your Own activities and the Chapter Mastery Project by using many of the solutions in the *Solutions Appendix*.

   ○ Level E: I completed all the On Your Own activities and the Chapter Mastery Project and had to use all the solutions in the *Solutions Appendix*.

To continue toward the goal of teaching yourself computer skills, if you are not at Level A, try to move up one level on how you learn in Chapter 10, "Managing Numbers and Text Using Excel."

Projects to Help You

Now that you have mastered the material in this chapter, you are ready to tackle the three projects introduced at the beginning of the chapter in the section "How Will This Chapter Help Me?:

Project 1: Using PowerPoint in Your Personal Life

Build a new PowerPoint presentation about any topic that interests you. Here are some possible topics:

▶ A car you want to sell

▶ A recent vacation or the next vacation you want to take

▶ The food you like best

▶ Who names the hurricanes

PERSONAL PROJECT: I want to make a PowerPoint presentation to help sell my car. It needs to include sounds of a car engine, photos, and a video. I found this cool video on YouTube about my car's make and model. Can I put this video in my presentation?

Follow these guidelines:

Step 1. Put a text or a graphic on the slide master that appears on every slide in the presentation.

Step 2. Include at least three slides in the presentation.

Step 3. Include animated graphics on at least one slide.

Step 4. Use transitions.

Step 5. Use animation on one slide so that several objects appear on the slide in order.

Click the **Video** button on the Insert ribbon of PowerPoint to find out if the option to insert a video from the web is available for your installation of PowerPoint. If it is, find a video on the web and insert it in your presentation.

Project 2: Using PowerPoint in Your Academic Career

Suppose you have been asked to create a PowerPoint presentation to continually run on a computer in the lobby of the admin building. You must email the presentation to others for approval. Do the following to teach yourself how to set up the presentation:

Step 1. Search the web or PowerPoint Help and find out how to make a self-running presentation continually run without user interaction. This is sometimes called kiosk mode. Test how to do this by continually running one of the presentations you created in this chapter.

Step 2. A large PowerPoint file might be difficult to send by email. You can reduce the file size by creating a PowerPoint picture presentation. Search the web or PowerPoint Help and describe what is a PowerPoint picture presentation.

Step 3. How do you create a picture presentation?

Step 4. Can the receiver of a picture presentation edit the contents of a slide in the presentation?

Step 5. Convert one of the PowerPoint presentations you have built for this chapter to a PowerPoint picture presentation and answer the following questions:

    a. Are animated graphics animated when you view the slide show from a picture presentation?

    b. Do objects that have been animated by PowerPoint to appear in order on a slide work in a picture presentation?

    c. Do transitions work in a picture presentation?

    d. Can you watch a video that was inserted in the presentation?

Step 6. Suppose the computer in the admin building lobby does not have PowerPoint installed. What free software can you download from the Microsoft.com website to view the PowerPoint presentation?

ACADEMIC PROJECT: I've been asked to create a slide show to continually run on a computer in the lobby of the admin building. First, I must email it to some people for their approval. How do I do all this?

The Office.com website offers many PowerPoint templates that you can use to quickly create a presentation. Do the following to explore these templates:

Step 1. Using the Backstage view of the PowerPoint window, click **New**. In the Available Templates and Themes pane, explore the available templates.

Step 2. Find and open a template to create a calendar.

Step 3. Find and open a template to create a certificate or award.

Step 4. When you are finished exploring the templates, close the presentations created by the templates without saving your changes.

TECHNICAL CAREER PROJECT: My boss has asked me to create a PowerPoint design for all the speakers at our next conference to use. He wants all the design color, graphics, and text to go on the slide master. How do I use a slide master?

Project 3: Using PowerPoint in Your Technical Career

Your company, Technical Help Desk Services, Inc., is planning a conference, and each speaker will make a PowerPoint presentation. Your boss wants all the presentations to have a similar look and feel and has asked you to prepare a presentation design. All the speakers will use the design to build their presentations. Follow these guidelines:

Step 1. All the changes you make to the presentation go on the slide master or the slide master layouts. Do not add slides to the presentation.

Step 2. Add a slide number to appear on each slide.

Step 3. Add the text **Copyright by THDS** to appear on each slide.

Step 4. Find a photo or an illustration on the web that represents your company—for example, a photo of a person at a help desk or a sign asking for help. Take a screen clipping of the graphic and place it in a corner of the slide master.

Step 5. Use an appropriate background style or other elements to add color to the design.

Step 6. Verify that each slide layout includes all elements in the design.

Step 7. Save the presentation, naming it **Conference**.

Project to Help Others

One of the best ways to learn is to teach someone else. And, in teaching someone else, you are making a contribution into that person's life. As part of each chapter's work, you are encouraged to teach someone else a skill you have learned. In this chapter, help someone learn to add sound and action to a PowerPoint presentation.

Who is your apprentice? _____

When helping others learn, don't do the work for them. Coach and instruct. Show them how to find information for themselves. Help them be as independent a learner as possible.

Do the following:

Step 1. Show your apprentice one of the slide shows you created in this chapter. Demonstrate animated graphics, animation added to a slide, video, audio, and transitions.

Step 2. Help your apprentice create his own PowerPoint presentation using the actions and sounds you demonstrated. What is the topic of his presentation?

CHAPTER 10

Managing Numbers and Text Using Excel

IN THIS CHAPTER, YOU WILL

Learn about Excel and how it is used

Build a worksheet with titles, headings, and data

Add calculations to a worksheet

Print a worksheet

We all find it necessary to occasionally track numbers and text. For example, you might need to keep track of money when making a budget for yourself, a business, or a club. You also might need to track scoring records for a softball team or track a list of classes and the grades you make in those classes.

Pencil and paper might be your tools for the job, or a Word table might also work. If you learn to use Excel, however, you can track numbers and text and perform calculations on those numbers.

As always, remember the most important computer skill is how to teach yourself a computer skill. Therefore, this chapter is designed to help you teach yourself how to build and use Excel worksheets. Try to do each On Your Own activity without any help. But remember, if you need help, you can always refer to the solutions in the *Solutions Appendix*.

JUMP RIGHT IN

If you want even more of a challenge, try proceeding directly to the Chapter Mastery Project at the end of this chapter. If you need help on the project, refer to the On Your Own activities in the chapter or do your own independent investigating using Excel Help or searching the web for answers. When you complete the project, you have mastered the skills in this chapter. Then go to the "Projects to Help You" that require you apply your skills to new situations.

How Will This Chapter Help Me?

Recall that each chapter provides three projects focusing on personal, academic, or technical career goals. Depending on your own interests, you might choose to complete any or all of these projects to help you achieve your goals.

PERSONAL PROJECT: I have a huge collection of music and movies on CD and DVD. I need to inventory them so I can track their values for insurance and keep track of when I loan them to friends. Can Excel help me do that?

ACADEMIC PROJECT: My instructor has asked me to help her grade some worksheets. She specifically wants me to check for errors in the formulas. What other errors do students typically make on a worksheet?

TECHNICAL CAREER PROJECT: Our help desk often gets questions about how to use an Office application. I need to learn how to help with questions about Excel. When I get a question I can't answer, how can I find the answer or help someone figure it out?

What Is Excel and How Is It Used?

Microsoft **Excel** is a **spreadsheet** program used to build a **worksheet** made up of columns and rows. An Excel data file contains one or more worksheets and is called a **workbook**.

> **Excel**—One of the applications included in Microsoft Office. It is a spreadsheet program used to manage text, numbers, and calculations in a worksheet. Excel 2010 files have an .xlsx file extension.
>
> **spreadsheet**—A type of software that builds and edits worksheets.
>
> **worksheet**—A group of columns and rows that can be used for text, numbers, graphics, and calculations. Also called a sheet.
>
> **workbook**—A spreadsheet file that contains one or more worksheets. By default, an Excel workbook contains three sheets.

When you open the Excel program, a blank workbook is created with three worksheets (see Figure 10-1).

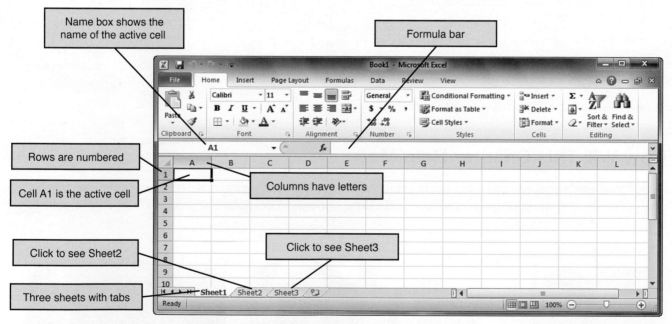

FIGURE 10-1
The Excel spreadsheet program opens a blank workbook with three worksheets.

Important items in the window are labeled and defined next.

> **column**—A column in a worksheet is labeled by a letter (A, B, C and so forth).
>
> **row**—A row in a worksheet is labeled by a number.
>
> **cell**—The box where a column and row intersect. The cell is named by the column letter and row number, for example, A5 or G3.
>
> **name box**—A box that displays the name of the selected cell.

In this activity, you get familiar with Excel without focusing on building a worksheet. Feel free to try new things and poke around. Do the following:

Step 1. Open Excel and maximize the window. Then explore the window and its tools. Click each ribbon tab and look at the items on each ribbon. The tools on several of these ribbons work about the same as they do in Word and PowerPoint.

Step 2. Go to any cell on the worksheet and start entering numbers into some cells and text into other cells. Notice that, by default, the numbers are right-aligned and the letters are left-aligned in the cell. When a cell is active, notice the cell address shows in the name box and the contents of the cell shows in the formula bar. The active cell also has a heavy black border around it.

> **Hint** To make a cell the active cell, click the cell or use your arrow keys to move to the cell. Use the **Tab** key to move to the next cell in a row. Use the **Enter** key to move down one cell.

Just as Word has templates, so does Excel. Let's look at two templates that can show you what Excel can do. Don't worry if you don't understand how these templates are built. The idea is to see what Excel worksheets can do for you. Do the following:

Step 1. On the Backstage view, click **New** and take a look at the different Excel templates. Excel is a great tool to manage your personal budget. In the **Budgets** group, open the **Home Budgets** folder and then open the **PersonalMonthlyBudget** template. A workbook is created using this template (see Figure 10-2).

On Your Own 10-1
Examine the Excel Window and Tools

 Video **10-1**

Not Working? More than one version of Microsoft Excel exists. In this book, we are using Excel 2010. If you are using a different version, such as Excel 2007, your window might not look the same as the one shown.

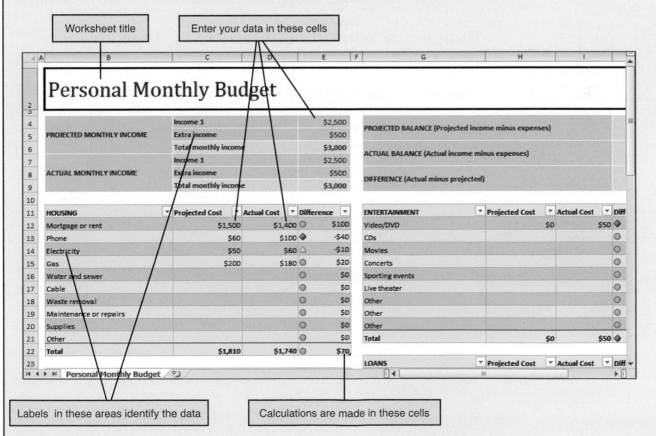

FIGURE 10-2
Enter values in a monthly budget worksheet.

On Your Own 10-1
Examine the Excel Window and Tools

Several cells hold titles, column headings, or labels. You enter your personal monthly data in some cells. Other cells are used to make calculations on that data.

Step 2. Enter numbers for the Projected Cost in column C and Actual Cost in column D for water and cable. Notice how the Difference cell in column E calculates the difference and puts a color-coded symbol in the cell. The symbol tells you if you are on or under budget, a little over budget, or very over budget.

Step 3. To see one more template that includes graphs, open the **His & Her 12 months Weight Loss chart** template. You can find the template in the **Charts and diagrams** group under **Business charts**. Enter numbers for the weights and watch how the graph and summary calculations change.

Step 4. Notice how many worksheets this workbook has. Rename one of the worksheets in this workbook. If you need help renaming a sheet, use Excel Help to find out how.

? Solutions Appendix

For help, see Solution 10-1: How to Examine the Excel Window and Tools.

Not Working? Click the **Help** button in the top-right corner of the Excel window to access Excel Help.

Step 5. Close all the workbooks you have opened without saving them.

Now let's learn how to build a new worksheet that contains text, numbers, and calculations.

Building a Worksheet with Titles, Headings, and Data

In this part of the chapter, you use Excel to create a softball roster and to track the expenses that must be collected from each team member. The finished worksheet for Coach Stevens's software team is shown in Figure 10-3. It contains a title, column and row headings, text, numbers, and calculations.

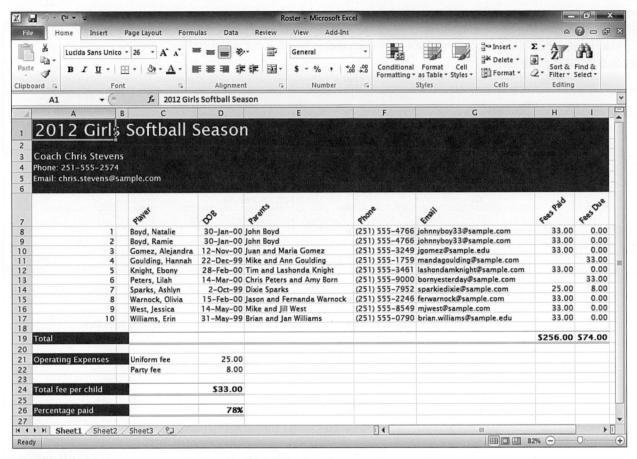

FIGURE 10-3
The Excel worksheet is used to keep a roster for a softball team.

Enter and Format Titles and Column Headings

The first step to creating the worksheet is to enter titles and column headings and format this text.

> **Tip** As you build this worksheet, remember the goal is to learn to use Excel. Don't worry about getting all the details of the worksheet correct. Focus on learning to use the tools of Excel.

On Your Own 10-2
Enter Worksheet Titles and Headings

In this activity, you enter the text for the titles and column headings. When the activity is completed, the worksheet should look like that in Figure 10-4.

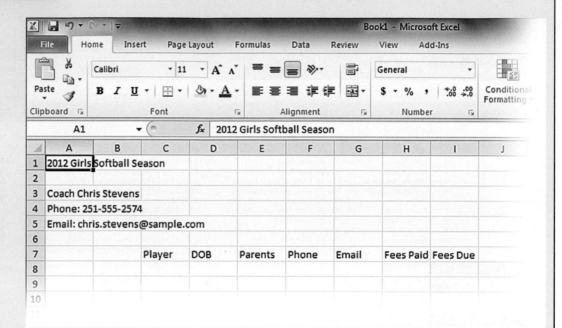

FIGURE 10-4
Titles and column headings are entered but not yet formatted.

Notice in the figure that cell A1 is the active cell. The content of cell A1 is the title **2012 Girls Softball Season**. When a cell is not wide enough to display the text in the cell, Excel handles the problem in this way:

▶ If adjacent cells to the right of the cell are empty, the displayed text spills over onto these cells. This is the case in Figure 10-4. Even though it appears that the titles are stored in more than one column, all the titles in the first five rows shown in the figure are stored in cells in column A and spill over onto adjacent empty cells.

▶ If adjacent cells to the right of the cell are not empty, Excel cuts off the text in the cell that is too narrow.

Do the following:

Step 1. Open a blank Excel workbook and enter the titles into cells in column A as shown in Figure 10-4. Enter the column headings in cells in row 7.

Step 2. Click the **File** tab and verify you are the author of this workbook file. If you are not, change it. Changing a file's author works just as it does in Word.

Step 3. Save the workbook to your hard drive, USB flash drive, SkyDrive, or other location given by your instructor. Name the workbook **Roster**.

? Solutions Appendix

For help, see Solution 10-2: How to Enter Worksheet Titles and Headings.

Hint Saving an Excel workbook file works the same way as saving a document in Word.

Formatting, styles, and themes work about the same way in Excel as they do in Word. The easiest way to format a cell or a group of cells is to use a **cell style**. Formatting can be applied before or after data is entered into the cells.

> **cell style**—Predetermined formatting that can be applied to a cell or group of cells. Cell styles are found on the Home ribbon.

In this activity, you format the titles and column headings for Coach Stevens's roster. When the activity is completed, the worksheet should look like that in Figure 10-5.

On Your Own 10-3
Format Using Styles and Themes

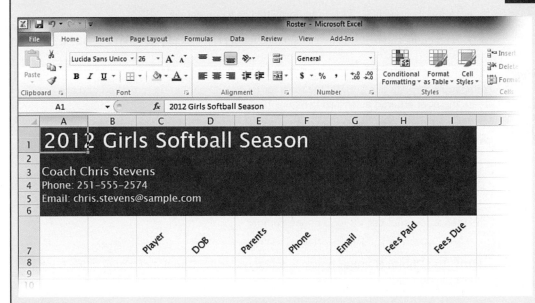

FIGURE 10-5
The softball roster has titles and column headings entered and formatted.

Do the following:

Step 1. To add background color to the top of the worksheet, apply a cell style to the block of cells A1 through I6. First, select these cells. Then, on the Home ribbon, click **Cell Styles** and select **Accent 5**.

Step 2. To make the title of the roster stand out, increase the font size for cell A1 to **26** point. Increase the font size for the cell containing the coach's name to **14** point. Increase the font size for the phone and email cells to **12** point.

Step 3. To tilt the column headings upward in row 7, select these cells and use the **Orientation** button on the Home ribbon.

Step 4. A theme applies uniform formatting to an entire workbook. On the Page Layout ribbon, mouse over the different themes and notice how the font and color on the worksheet change. Set the theme of the softball roster to **Concourse**.

Step 5. Save your work.

Hint To select a block of cells, press and drag across the cells. As you do so, your pointer is a white cross ✛ and selected cells are highlighted in a selection box.

 Solutions Appendix

For help, see Solution 10-3: How to Format Using Styles and Themes.

The worksheet is now ready to receive the data for team members.

Enter Data for Team Members

In this section, you format the cells for team data and then enter that data. For numbers and dates, it is easier to first format the cells and then enter the data into the cells. The type of formatting to apply depends on what type of data the cell will hold. Examples of formatting options are

▶ A negative number can be formatted as –1234.10, (1234.10), or 1234.10. Accountants consider a number written in parentheses or in red to be a negative number.

▶ Currency might be formatted with none or two decimal places, for example, $1,234.10 or $1,234.

▶ A date might be formatted as 14-Mar-01 or March 14, 2001.

▶ A number, such as .34, can be formatted as a percentage: 34%.

▶ Ten digits can be formatted as a phone number, for example, (888) 555-1234.

On Your Own 10-4
Format Rows for Team Data and Add One Team Member

Video **10-4**

After you complete this activity, the rows for team data should be formatted and the first team member entered as shown in Figure 10-6.

To format Coach Stevens's roster, do the following to format the first row used for data, which is row 8:

Step 1. Format cell **D8** to display the birthday as day-month-year. First, select the cell. On the Home ribbon, click **Format**. In the drop-down menu, click **Format Cells**. The Format Cells box appears. Under Category, click **Date**. Click the **14-Mar-01** format, as shown in Figure 10-7.

Step 2. Format cell **F8** for a phone number.

Hint The **Phone Number** option is found under the **Special** category in the Format Cells dialog box.

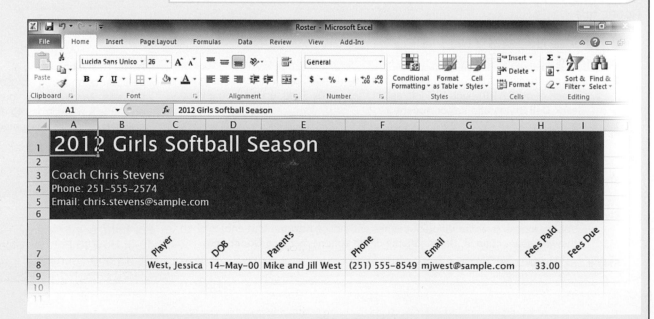

FIGURE 10-6
The rows for team data are formatted and one team member is added.

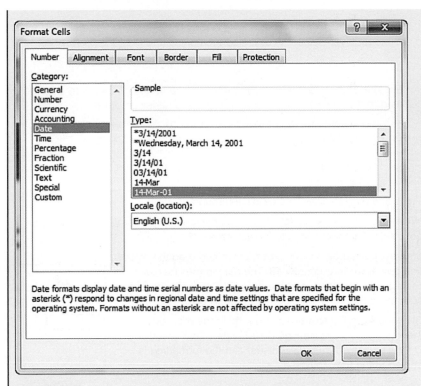

FIGURE 10-7
The Format Cells box provides options for formatting cells.

Step 3. Format cells **H8** and **I8** for a **Number** with two decimal points displayed.

Now it's time to enter data into the row. With data entered, you can check the formatting for errors and adjust the column widths. Do the following:

Step 1. Enter the following data for Jessica West into row 8.

Heading	Data
Player	West, Jessica
DOB	5/14/2000
Parents	Mike and Jill West
Phone	2515558549
Email	mjwest@sample.com
Fees Paid	33

Hint When entering a date, use a slash or hyphen to separate the month/day/year. Excel then recognizes this data as a date.

When entering numbers, don't enter the formatting symbols (for example, a comma or dollar sign). Enter only the digits and perhaps a decimal point. Excel does the rest.

Tip If you want to increase or decrease the width of a column, press and drag the vertical bar on the right side of the column letter.

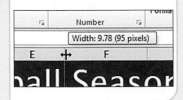

Step 2. Notice not all the data for Jessica displays because the columns are too narrow. To fix this problem, first select cells C7 through I8. Then click **Format** on the Home ribbon and click **AutoFit Column Width** on the drop-down menu.

Format Rows for Team Data and Add One Team Member

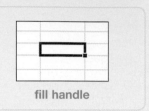

fill handle

Next, you will use the Excel Auto Fill tool to copy the formatting in row 8 to other rows for team data. To use the tool, you select the cells and then press and drag the fill handle.

> **Auto Fill**—An Excel tool that copies data, formatting, or a series of data into a range of cells. A series of data can be a series of numbers or a series of dates.
>
> **fill handle**—The small black square in the lower-right corner of a selection box. When you hover over the fill handle, your pointer changes to a black cross. ⊹

Do the following:

Step 1. Press and drag to select the cells **C8** through **I8**.

Step 2. Hover over the fill handle (black box) on the lower-right corner of the selection box. Your pointer changes to a black cross. ⊹

Step 3. With the pointer as a black cross, press and drag the selection box down through row **18**. The data in the first row fills the selected rows, and the Auto Fill Options button ⊞ appears in the lower-right corner of the fill box.

Step 4. Click the **Auto Fill Options** button. ⊞ In the drop-down menu that appears (see Figure 10-8), click **Fill Formatting Only**. The copied data disappears, and the formatting is copied to the new selection.

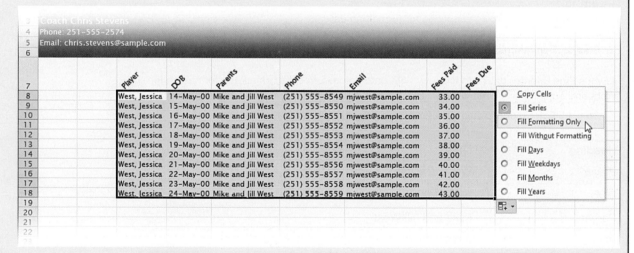

FIGURE 10-8
Use the Auto Fill tool to copy data, a series of data, or formatting to other cells.

For help, see Solution 10-4: How to Format Rows for Team Data and Add One Team Member.

> **Hint** Using the Auto Fill tool takes a little practice. If it doesn't work the first time, click the **Undo** button ⟲ in the title bar and try again.

Step 5. Save your work.

All the data for each team member can be typed into the worksheet. However, to save you typing time, this data has been stored in a Word document on the DVD in the back of the book.

In this activity, you copy the team data in a Word document into your Excel worksheet. When the activity is completed, the worksheet should look like that in Figure 10-9.

On Your Own 10-5
Copy Team Data from a Word Table and Edit the Data

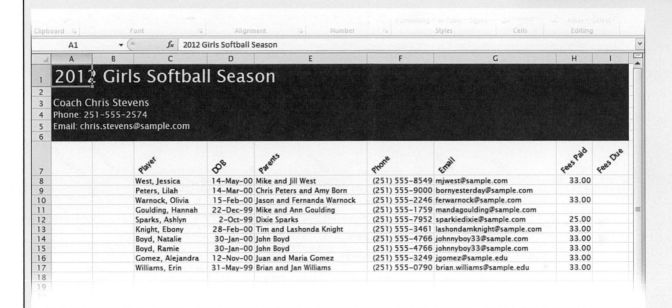

FIGURE 10-9
The Roster worksheet has team data added.

Do the following:

Step 1. Open the Word document named **RosterTable** in the **Sample Files** folder on the DVD and copy the team data into the Windows Clipboard. Paste the data into the Excel worksheet. When you paste the data, choose the option to Match Destination Formatting. By doing so, you retain the formatting in the worksheet.

Step 2. When you paste the data from the RosterTable into the worksheet, Jessica West is entered twice (one time from your data entry and one time from the table). To fix the problem, delete one of the rows containing her data.

Hint To delete a row, click somewhere in the row. Then click the drop-down arrow next to **Delete** on the Home ribbon. Click **Delete Sheet Rows**. Selected rows are deleted. Another way to delete a row is to right-click a row and select **Delete** from the shortcut menu.

Step 3. Widen the columns so that all the data displays. You can manually widen each column or use the AutoFit Column Width command.

Hint When a date or number is too wide for a column, Excel displays the hash symbol several times (######) in the cell. Widen the column to see the data.

 Solutions Appendix

For help, see Solution 10-5: How to Copy Team Data from a Word Table and Edit the Data.

Step 4. Save your work.

Sort Data and Add Row Numbers

To help organize the data, sort the team members by name. To make the roster easier to use, add counting numbers in column A. When this activity is completed, the worksheet should look like that in Figure 10-10.

		Player	DOB	Parents	Phone	Email	Fees Paid	Fees Due
8	1	Boyd, Natalie	30-Jan-00	John Boyd	(251) 555-4766	johnnyboy33@sample.com	33.00	
9	2	Boyd, Ramie	30-Jan-00	John Boyd	(251) 555-4766	johnnyboy33@sample.com	33.00	
10	3	Gomez, Alejandra	12-Nov-00	Juan and Maria Gomez	(251) 555-3249	jgomez@sample.edu	33.00	
11	4	Goulding, Hannah	22-Dec-99	Mike and Ann Goulding	(251) 555-1759	mandagoulding@sample.com		
12	5	Knight, Ebony	28-Feb-00	Tim and Lashonda Knight	(251) 555-3461	lashondamknight@sample.com	33.00	
13	6	Peters, Lilah	14-Mar-00	Chris Peters and Amy Born	(251) 555-9000	bornyesterday@sample.com		
14	7	Sparks, Ashlyn	2-Oct-99	Dixie Sparks	(251) 555-7952	sparkiedixie@sample.com	25.00	
15	8	Warnock, Olivia	15-Feb-00	Jason and Fernanda Warnock	(251) 555-2246	ferwarnock@sample.com	33.00	
16	9	West, Jessica	14-May-00	Mike and Jill West	(251) 555-8549	mjwest@sample.com	33.00	
17	10	Williams, Erin	31-May-99	Brian and Jan Williams	(251) 555-0790	brian.williams@sample.edu	33.00	

FIGURE 10-10
Players are sorted by name, and row numbers are added.

Do the following:

Tip If you need to sort by more than one column or on a column other than the first column, select the cells to sort and click **Sort** on the Data ribbon. The Sort box appears and offers more sorting options.

Step 1. To sort the rows, first select all the team data. To do so, select the block of cells **C8** through **H17**.

> **Hint** As you press and drag to select the cells, be sure not to accidentally grab the fill handle in the lower-right corner of a selection box. Doing so causes the cells to be copied, not selected.

Step 2. On the Home ribbon, click **Sort & Filter**. Then click **Sort A to Z** in the drop-down menu. The data is sorted by the first column in the range of cells.

 Solutions Appendix

Step 3. To enter counting numbers in column A, first type the number **1** in cell **A8**. You could continue typing each number, or you can let Excel do it for you. Use the Auto Fill tool to fill in counting numbers in column A down through cell **A17**.

For help, see Solution 10-6: How to Sort Data and Add Row Numbers.

Step 4. Narrow the column width of the first two columns, as shown in Figure 10-10.

Step 5. Save your work.

Adding Calculations to a Worksheet

All the information collected for the softball team roster could have been kept in a Word table. However, we can get Excel to help us with the calculations. The ability to make calculations is one advantage that Excel offers over a Word table.

The first step to including calculations is to enter the calculation labels. When this activity is completed, the worksheet should look like that in Figure 10-11.

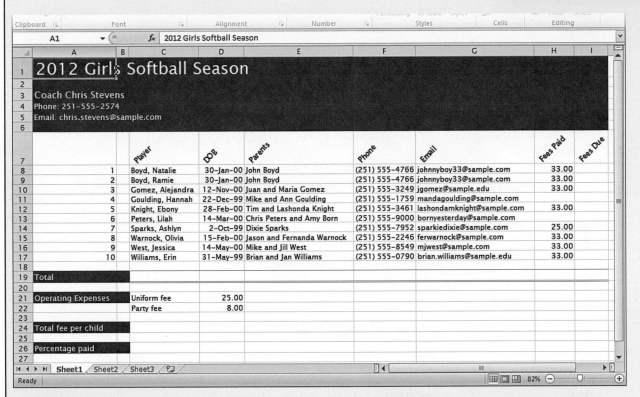

FIGURE 10-11

Labels and values for the calculations are entered.

Do the following:

Step 1. Enter the text in rows 19 through 26 as shown in Figure 10-12.

Step 2. Format the cells as follows:

▶ Use the Format Painter to copy the formatting from cell A5 to cells A19, B19, A21, B21, A24, B24, A26, and B26.

▶ Apply the **Total** cell style to row 19 in cells C19 through I19.

Step 3. Resize column A so all text is visible.

Step 4. In cell **D21**, enter **25**. In cell **D22**, enter **8**. Format both cells as numbers with two decimal places.

Step 5. Save your work.

	A	B	C	D
13		6	Peters, Lilah	14–Mar–00
14		7	Sparks, Ashlyn	2–Oct–99
15		8	Warnock, Olivia	15–Feb–00
16		9	West, Jessica	14–May–00
17		10	Williams, Erin	31–May–99
18				
19	Total			
20				
21	Operating Expenses		Uniform fee	
22			Party fee	
23				
24	Total fee per child			
25				
26	Percentage paid			
27				
28				

FIGURE 10-12

Enter the text for the calculation labels.

 Solutions Appendix

For help, see Solution 10-7: How to Enter Labels and Values for the Calculations.

Use Formulas and Functions

Excel does a calculation when you put a formula in a cell. The **formula** can use numbers or cells that contain numbers.

> **formula**—An equation in a cell used to perform a calculation or make a comparison. A formula always begins with an equal sign and can contain +, −, *, and / operators for addition, subtraction, multiplication, and division. Parenthesis can be used for grouping as in =5/(5+30). The order of operations is the same as in math.

In our Roster worksheet, cell D24 is to contain the total fee per child, which is the sum of the Uniform fee and the Party fee. Here are three ways to find this sum:

▶ **Using numbers.** Enter **=25 + 8** in cell D24. Notice in Figure 10-13 that the sum 33 displays in cell D24. The formula bar shows the formula stored in the cell.

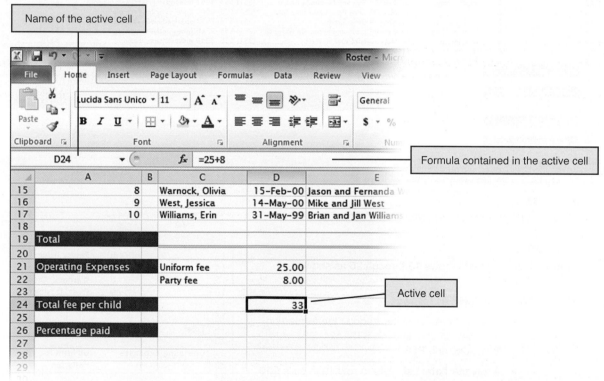

FIGURE 10-13
A formula is stored in a cell, but its calculated value displays on the worksheet.

▶ **Using cell addresses.** Enter **=D21+D22** in cell D24. This method is better than the first method. If you change the values in cells D21 or D22, the formula in cell D24 automatically calculates a new sum.

▶ **Using a function.** Enter **=SUM(D21: D22)** in cell D24. This method works not just for summing two cells but to sum an entire column of cells.

The last method uses the SUM **function**. Excel offers many functions to be used in formulas such as the **SUM**, **AVERAGE**, **MAX**, **TODAY**, and **MIN functions**.

> **function**—A tool used in a formula to enhance what the formula can do. Parentheses and a colon are used to indicate a range of cells used by the function, for example, SUM(D21:D40).
>
> **SUM function**—A function that sums a range of cells.
>
> **AVERAGE function**—A function that calculates the average for a range of cells.
>
> **MAX function**—A function that finds the largest value in a range of cells.
>
> **TODAY function**—A function that returns today's date. The date changes each day the workbook is opened. The function is written in a cell as **=TODAY( )**.
>
> **MIN function**—A function that finds the smallest value in a range of cells.

Tip To see a list of Excel functions, click **Insert Function** on the Formulas ribbon or search Excel Help on **Excel functions (by category)**.

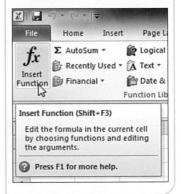

On Your Own 10-8
Enter Two Sums in the Worksheet

Video **10-8**

Accountants use a double line under a value to indicate it is the sum of a column of numbers. Excel provides a cell style named Total to format a sum in this way.

In this activity, you enter two sums in the worksheet. Do the following:

Step 1. Enter a formula in cell **D24** to calculate the sum of cells D21 and D22. Use cell addresses in the formula.

Step 2. Format cells **C24** and **D24** using the **Total** cell style. Format cell **D24** using **Currency**, **2** decimal places.

> **Not Working?** If you need to edit the formula in a cell, go to the cell. The formula appears in the formula bar. Click in the formula bar to edit the cell.

Use the SUM function in cell H19 to sum the Fees Paid column. You can type the formula in cell H19, but an easier way is to use the **AutoSum** command.

> **AutoSum**—A command on the Formulas ribbon and the Home ribbon of Excel that automatically inserts a function into a cell and defines the range of cells used in the function.

Do the following:

Step 1. Go to cell **H19**. On the Formulas ribbon, click the down arrow next to AutoSum. In the drop-down list, click **Sum**. Excel inserts a SUM function in the cell. Excel also draws a selection box around cells above H19. You can adjust the selection box as necessary.

Step 2. Hover over a top corner of the selection box until your pointer changes to a double-headed arrow. Press and drag this selection box to include all the cells in column H that are intended to contain numbers: Cells **H8** through **H18** (see Figure 10-14). Press **Enter** to enter the formula into cell H19.

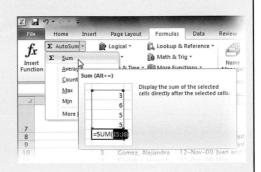

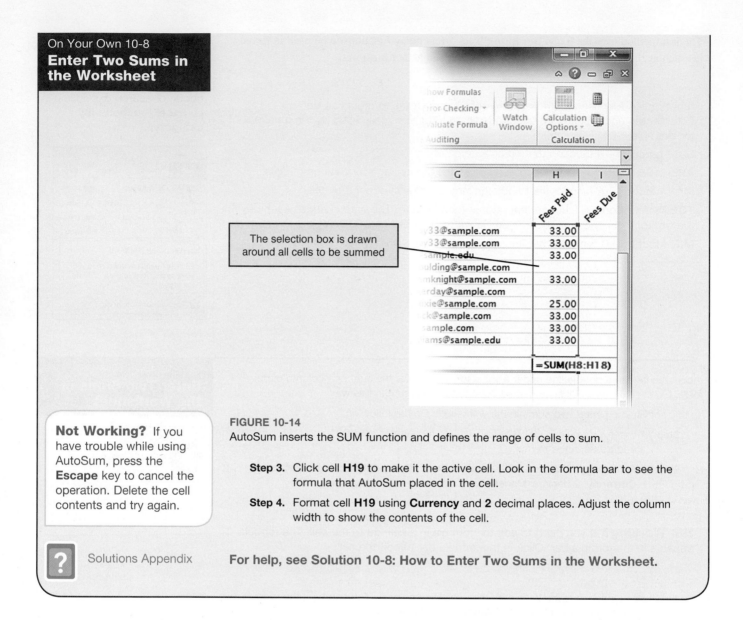

On Your Own 10-8
Enter Two Sums in the Worksheet

The selection box is drawn around all cells to be summed

=SUM(H8:H18)

FIGURE 10-14
AutoSum inserts the SUM function and defines the range of cells to sum.

Not Working? If you have trouble while using AutoSum, press the **Escape** key to cancel the operation. Delete the cell contents and try again.

Step 3. Click cell **H19** to make it the active cell. Look in the formula bar to see the formula that AutoSum placed in the cell.

Step 4. Format cell **H19** using **Currency** and **2** decimal places. Adjust the column width to show the contents of the cell.

? Solutions Appendix   **For help, see Solution 10-8: How to Enter Two Sums in the Worksheet.**

Copy a Formula Using Relative and Absolute References

Sometimes a worksheet needs a column of calculations such as the Fees Due column (column I). You can type a formula in each cell in the column. A quicker method is to type a formula in the first cell and copy this formula to other cells in the column.

When Excel copies a formula to a new cell, it automatically changes the cell addresses in the formula to adjust for the new location. This type of cell address in a formula is called a **relative reference**.

relative reference—A cell address in a formula that is relative to the location of the formula. Also called a relative address.

For example, suppose we copy the formula in cell D24 to cell F24. When we do that, the cell addresses in the new formula are relative to the new location (see Figure 10-15).

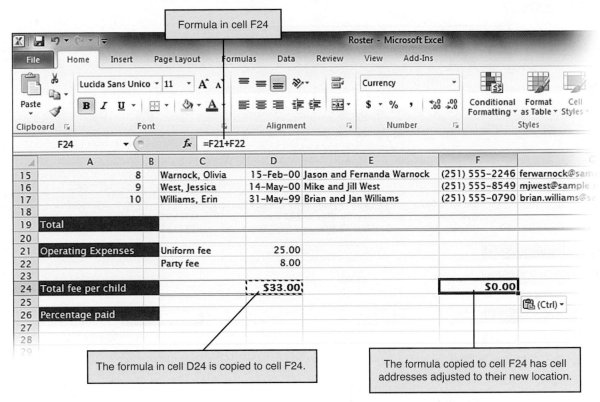

FIGURE 10-15
Using a relative reference, Excel changes a cell address in a formula when the formula is copied to a new location.

> **Hint** To copy and paste a cell or range of cells, first press and drag to select the cells to be copied. Then click **Copy** on the Home ribbon (or press **Ctrl-C**). Go to the new location and click **Paste** on the Home ribbon (or press **Ctrl-V**).

In cell D24 in Figure 10-15, the two cell addresses in the formula are above cell D24. When this formula is copied to cell F24, the two cell addresses are adjusted to be those above cell F24. The new formula, therefore, uses cells F21 and F22.

If you do not want the cell address in a formula to change when the formula is copied, you must use an **absolute reference**. To do so, type a dollar sign ($) before the column letter and row number, as in $D$21.

> **absolute reference**—A cell address in a formula that does not change when the formula is copied to a new location. Use $ in the address, for example, $D$21. Also called an absolute address.

For example, suppose a formula in cell D24 is =$D$21+D22. When this formula is copied to cell F24, the first address does not change, but the second address does change relative to its new location. The formula becomes =$D$21+F22, as shown in Figure 10-16.

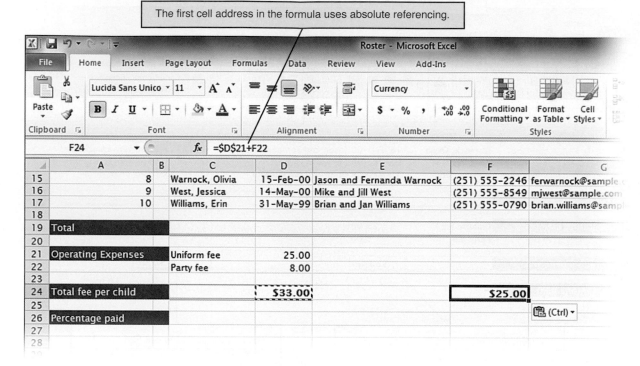

The first cell address in the formula uses absolute referencing.

FIGURE 10-16
When you use an absolute reference, Excel does not change a cell address in a formula when the formula is copied to a new location.

Tip To make typing easier when you are entering a cell address into a formula, press the F4 key to toggle the cell address from a relative address to an absolute address.

On Your Own 10-9
Calculate Fees Due

Our next task to build the worksheet is to enter formulas to calculate the Fees Due column (column I). You enter the formula for the first team member in cell I8 and then copy this formula to other cells in column I.

When this activity is completed, the worksheet should look like that in Figure 10-17.

Do the following to calculate the fees due and sum the fees due column:

Step 1. Enter a formula in cell **I8** that calculates Fees Due for the first team member. The formula is Total fees per child (cell **D24**) minus Fees Paid (cell **H8**). Use an absolute reference for cell D24 so this cell address does not change when the formula is copied. What formula did you use in this cell?

Step 2. Copy the formula into cells **I9** through **I17**.

Step 3. Use the **AutoSum** tool to put the sum of Fees Due into cell **I19**. What formula did AutoSum place in this cell?

Step 4. Use the Format Painter to copy the formatting in cell **H19** to cell **I19**.

On Your Own 10-9
Calculate Fees Due

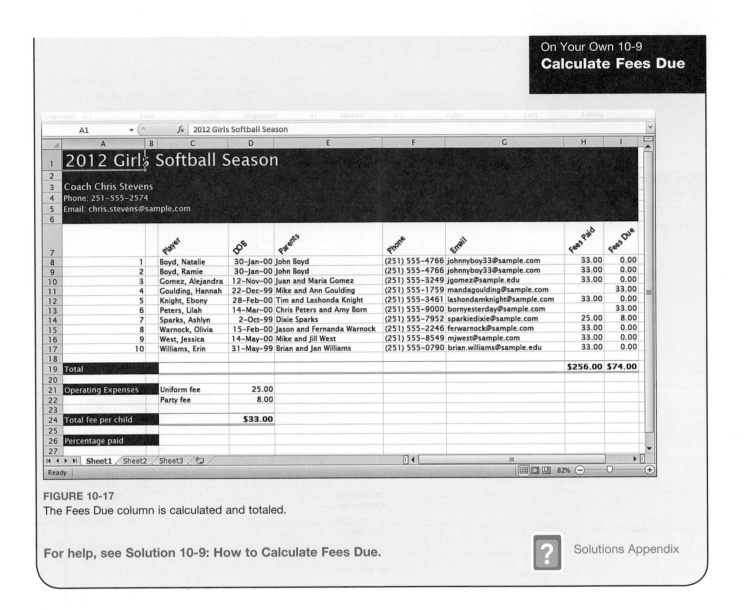

FIGURE 10-17
The Fees Due column is calculated and totaled.

For help, see Solution 10-9: How to Calculate Fees Due.   Solutions Appendix

Calculate a Percentage

The last calculation on the worksheet is the percentage of total fees that have already been paid. A percentage is a part of a whole. It is calculated by dividing the part by the whole. A percentage is a fraction, and Excel can format the fraction as a percentage.

On Your Own 10-10
Calculate the Percentage Paid

Enter a formula into cell **D26** that calculates the percentage of total fees that have been paid. The total fees paid is in cell **H19**. The total fees is the sum of cells **H19** and **I19**.

Format cells **C26** and **D26** using the **Total** cell style. Then format cell D26 using the **Percentage** cell format with no decimal points.

When you are finished with this activity, your worksheet should look like that shown earlier in Figure 10-3.

For help, see Solution 10-10: How to Calculate the Percentage Paid.   Solutions Appendix

Printing a Worksheet

> **print area**—The range of cells in a worksheet to be printed.

When you print a worksheet, Excel assumes you want to print all cells that contain information. If you want to print less of the worksheet, you must specify a **print area**.

Excel offers other print options that can be useful when printing large worksheets. These options are found on the Page Layout ribbon.

On Your Own 10-11
Print the Worksheet

To print the worksheet, click the **File** tab and click **Print**. Set the orientation to **Landscape**. To force the worksheet to print on a single page, click **No Scaling** and change to **Fit Sheet on One Page**. The print preview looks like that in Figure 10-18. If you have access to a printer, print the worksheet, which fits on a single page.

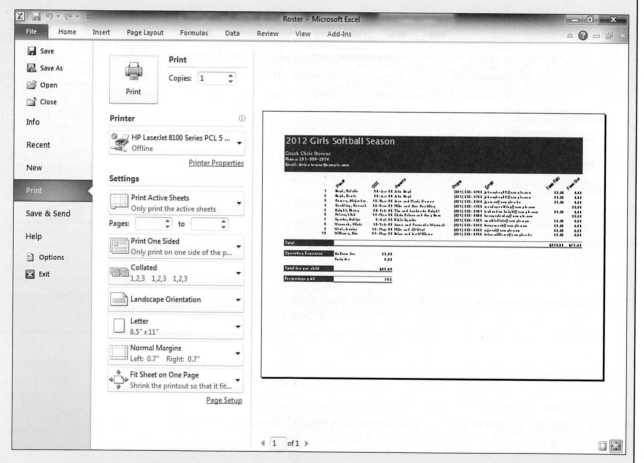

FIGURE 10-18
The worksheet prints on a single page.

? Solutions Appendix

For help, see Solution 10-11: How to Print the Worksheet.

Summary

What Is Excel and How Is It Used?

▶ Excel is a spreadsheet program used to build worksheets. Worksheets hold text, numbers, calculations, and graphs.

▶ A workbook is an Excel file that can contain one or more worksheets. Excel 2010 workbook files have an .xlsx file extension.

▶ Columns and rows in a worksheet are addressed using letters and numbers. Each cell has an address using the column letter and row number, such as A25.

▶ Excel offers many templates that can be used to create worksheets for a variety of purposes.

Building a Worksheet with Titles, Headings, and Data

▶ Begin a worksheet by entering titles and headings. Styles, themes, and other formatting can improve the appearance of a worksheet and make it easier to use.

▶ If a cell is not wide enough for text to display and adjacent cells to the right are empty, Excel allows the data to display over the adjacent empty cells. If the adjacent cells to the right contain data, Excel does not display all the text in the narrow cell.

▶ If a cell is not wide enough for a number or date to display, Excel displays the hash symbol (#) several times in the cell.

▶ For numbers and dates, it is easier to format the cells intended for data before you enter the data. The AutoFill tool can be used to copy formatting in cells to other cells.

▶ The Auto Fill tool is used to copy formatting, data, or a series of data into a range of cells. A series of data can be a series of numbers or a series of dates.

▶ Data can be sorted using the Sort & Filter command on the Home ribbon.

Adding Calculations to a Worksheet

▶ A formula in a cell is used to make a comparison or contains an equation used to make a calculation. A formula always begins with an equal symbol (=) and can contain arithmetic operators including +, −, *, /, (, and).

▶ You can use cell addresses or numbers in a formula. If you use a cell address, Excel automatically recalculates the formula when the contents of the cell address change.

▶ Functions enhance the power of a formula. Some Excel functions are SUM, AVERAGE, MAX, TODAY, and MIN functions. The (and) symbols and a colon are used by a function to indicate the range of cells used by the function.

▶ The AutoSum command on the Formulas ribbon inserts a function into a cell and defines the range of cells used by the function.

▶ Use a relative reference (also called a relative address) in a formula if you want the cell address to change when the formula is copied to a new location.

▶ Use an absolute reference (also called an absolute address) in a formula if you don't want the cell address to change when the formula is copied to a new location.

▶ A percentage is a part of the whole. To enter a percentage in a worksheet, enter in a cell the formula to calculate the fraction and format the cell as a percentage.

Printing a Worksheet

▶ When printing a worksheet, Excel prints all the cells that contain information unless you specify a print area.

▶ Options on the Print Layout ribbon can be used to print a large worksheet.

Review Questions

Answer these questions to assess your skills and knowledge of the content covered in the chapter. Your instructor can provide you with the correct answers when you are ready to check your work.

1. By default, a blank workbook contains how many worksheets?

2. What is the file extension of an Excel 2010 workbook file?

3. By default, numbers in a cell are ___-aligned and text in a cell is ___-aligned.

4. Accountants consider a number written in red on a worksheet to be a ___ number.

5. When you are entering a date into a cell, what two symbols can you use to separate the month, day, and year?

6. Which tool can be used to automatically insert counting numbers into a column?

7. What symbol does Excel display in a cell when the cell is too narrow to display a large number?

8. What symbol is always used to begin a formula in a cell?

9. What formula can you put in a cell to display today's date?

10. What command on the Formulas ribbon can be used to automatically insert a SUM function in a cell?

11. What method does an accountant use to indicate a value is the sum of a column of numbers? Which cell style uses this method?

12. The cell address $A$10 used in a formula does not change when the formula is copied to a new cell. What type of cell addressing is used?

13. Referring to question 12, how would you write the cell address if you want the address to change relative to its new location?

14. How many cells are summed in a cell that contains this formula: =SUM(A5:A7)?

15. By default, which cells in a worksheet does Excel print?

Chapter Mastery Project

Find out how well you have mastered the content in this chapter by completing this project. If you can answer all the questions and do all the steps without looking back at the chapter details, you have mastered this chapter. If you can complete the project by finding answers using Excel Help or the web, you have proven that you can teach yourself how to use Excel to build a worksheet.

If you find you need a lot of help doing the project and you have not yet read the chapter or done the activities, drop back and start at the beginning of the chapter and then return to this project.

> **Hint** All the key terms in the chapter are used in this mastery project. If you encounter a key word you don't know such as *function*, enter **define:Excel function** in the Internet Explorer search box.

Mastery Project Part 1: What Is Excel and How Is It Used?

If you need help completing this part of the mastery project, review the "What Is Excel and How Is It Used?" section in the chapter.

Do the following to use a worksheet created by a template:

Step 1. Open the Excel spreadsheet program. Open the **Loan amortization schedule** template. To find the template, look in the **Records** group and then the **Financial records** group.

Step 2. Enter the following information about a loan:

Loan amount: **120,000.00**

Annual interest rate: **5%**

Loan period in years: **30 years**

Number of payments per year: **12**

Start date of loan: **July 1, 2012**

Step 3. Answer the following questions:

a. What is the monthly payment?

b. What is the total interest paid?

c. If you make an extra optional payment of $25 per month, what is the total interest paid?

Mastery Project Part 2: Building a Worksheet with Titles, Headings, and Data

If you need help completing this part of the mastery project, review the "Building a Worksheet with Titles, Headings, and Data" section in the chapter.

In the remainder of this project, you create the worksheet shown in Figure 10-19. The worksheet tracks sales for a club fundraiser selling citrus fruit.

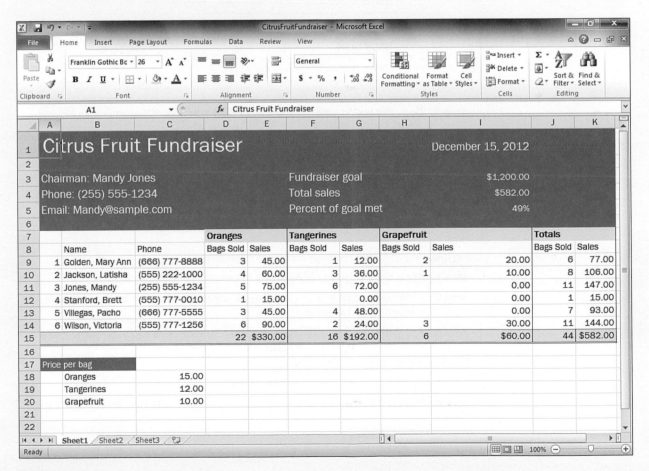

FIGURE 10-19

The worksheet tracks sales for a club fundraiser.

Do the following to enter titles and headings at the top of the worksheet and save your work:

Step 1. Open a blank workbook file and apply the **Angles** theme to the worksheet.

Step 2. Enter the titles and column headings at the top of the worksheet as follows:

Cell	Text
A1	Citrus Fruit Fundraiser
A3	Chairman: Mandy Jones
A4	Phone: (255) 555-1234
A5	Email: Mandy@sample.com
F3	Fundraiser goal
F4	Total sales
F5	Percent of goal met
D7	Oranges
F7	Tangerines
H7	Grapefruit
J7	Totals
B8	Name
C8	Phone
D8	Bags Sold
E8	Sales

Step 3. Copy the text in cells D8 and E8 to cells F8 through K8 as shown in Figure 10-19.

Step 4. Use the **Column Width** tool to adjust the column widths so that the text in rows 7 and 8 can be seen. As you build this worksheet, adjust the column widths as necessary when a cell is too narrow to display its contents.

Step 5. Make sure you are the author of the workbook file. Save the file to your USB flash drive, hard drive, SkyDrive, or another location given by your instructor. Name the workbook file **CitrusFruitFundraiser**.

Do the following to format the titles and column headings:

Step 1. Apply the Cell Styles of **Accent 2** to cells A1 through K6.

Step 2. Increase the font size of cell A1 to **26** points. Increase the font size of cells A3 through F5 to **14** points.

Step 3. Apply the Cell Styles of **20% - Accent 2** to cells D7 through K7. Bold these cells.

Do the following to add the sales data:

Step 1. Format cell C9 to hold a phone number.

Step 2. Format cells E9, G9, I9, and K9 to hold a number with two decimal places.

Hint To select nonadjacent cells, hold down the **Ctrl** key as you click the cells.

Step 3. Use the Format Painter or the AutoFill tool to copy the formatting in row 9 to rows 10 through 14.

Step 4. Club member names and phone numbers are stored in a Word document named ClubMemberTable in the Sample Files folder on the DVD in the back of this book. Open the **ClubMemberTable** document. Copy the names and phone numbers to the Windows Clipboard. Paste the data into the worksheet beginning with cell B9.

Step 5. Sort the names with phone numbers in alphabetical order.

Step 6. Enter the Bags Sold data as follows:

Cell	Number
D9	3
D10	4
D11	5
D12	1
D13	3
D14	6
F9	1
F10	3
F11	6
F13	4
F14	2
H9	2
H10	1
H14	3

Do the following to enter the Price per bag headings and data at the bottom of the worksheet:

Step 1. Enter the following headings and values:

Cell	Text or Number
A17	Price per bag
B18	Oranges
C18	15
B19	Tangerines
C19	12
B20	Grapefruit
C20	10

Step 2. Format cells A17 and B17 using Cell Styles **Accent 2**.

Step 3. Format cells C18 through C20 as numbers with two decimal places. Don't forget to save often as you work.

Mastery Project Part 3: Adding Calculations to a Worksheet

If you need help completing this part of the mastery project, review the "Adding Calculations to a Worksheet" section in the chapter.

Do the following to enter the calculations into the worksheet:

Step 1. Enter a formula in cell E9 to calculate the sales for oranges for one club member. Use cells D9 and C18 in the formula. Copy the formula to cells E10 through E14. Note that this formula uses relative and absolute referencing. What is the formula in cell E9?

Step 2. Enter a similar formula in cell G9 to calculate Tangerine sales for one club member. Copy the formula to cells G10 through G14. What is the formula in cell G9?

Step 3. Enter a similar formula in cell I9 to calculate Grapefruit sales for one club member. Copy the formula to cells I10 through I14. What is the formula in cell I9?

Step 4. Enter a formula in cell J9 to calculate the total bags sold for oranges, tangerines, and grapefruit for one club member. Copy the formula to cells J10 through J14. What is the formula in cell J9? Does the formula use absolute referencing, relative referencing, or a combination of both?

Step 5. Enter a formula in cell K9 to calculate the total sales for oranges, tangerines, and grapefruit for one club member. Copy the formula to cells K10 through K14. What is the formula in cell K9?

Do the following to enter and format the sums in row 15:

Step 1. Apply the **Totals** cell style to cells A15 through K15.

Step 2. Use the AutoSum tool to put the sum of cells D9 through D14 in cell D15. The formula uses the SUM function. What is the formula in cell D15?

Step 3. Copy the formula in cell D15 to cells E15 through K15. What is the formula in cell K15?

Step 4. Format cells D15, F15, H15, and J15 as numbers with zero decimal places.

Step 5. Format cells E15, G15, I15, and K15 as currency with two decimal places.

Step 6. Use the **TODAY** function to insert today's date in cell I1. Format the cell using the March 14, 2001 date format. What is the formula in cell I1?

Do the following to enter the summary data near the top of the worksheet:

Step 1. In cell I3, enter **1200**.

Step 2. In cell I4, enter a formula that puts whatever value is in cell K15 in cell I4. What is the formula in cell I4?

Step 3. Format cells I3 and I4 as currency with two decimal places.

Step 4. In cell I5, enter a formula that calculates the percent of goal met. Use cells I3 and I4 in the formula. What is the formula in cell I5?

Step 5. Format cell I5 as a percentage.

To make the worksheet easier to read, do the following:

Step 1. Add counting numbers in cells A9 through A14. To do so, enter a 1 in cell A9 and use the AutoFill tool to insert a series of counting numbers in cell A10 through A14.

Step 2. Narrow column A as shown in Figure 10-19.

Step 3. Select cells E7 through E15. On the Home ribbon, click the drop-down arrow beside the Borders button  and select **Right Border**. Do the same for cells G7 through G15, I7 through I15, and K7 through K15.

Mastery Project Part 4: Printing a Worksheet

If you need help completing this part of the mastery project, review the "Printing a Worksheet" section in the chapter.

Do the following to print the worksheet:

Step 1. Go to the print preview window. Change the orientation to landscape. Does the worksheet print on a single page without using the scaling option on this window?

Step 2. If you have access to a printer, print the worksheet on a single page.

Becoming an Independent Learner

Answer the following questions about becoming an independent learner:

1. To teach yourself to use Microsoft Excel, do you think it is best to rely on the chapter or on Excel Help when you need answers?

2. The most important skill learned in this chapter is how to teach yourself a computer skill. Rate yourself at Level A through E on how well you are doing with this skill. What is your level?

   ○ Level A: I was able to successfully complete the Chapter Mastery Project without the help of doing the On Your Own activities in the chapter.

   ○ Level B: I completed all the On Your Own activities and the Chapter Mastery Project without referring to any of the solutions in the *Solutions Appendix*.

   ○ Level C: I completed all the On Your Own activities and the Chapter Mastery Project by using just a few of the solutions in the *Solutions Appendix*.

   ○ Level D: I completed all the On Your Own activities and the Chapter Mastery Project by using many of the solutions in the *Solutions Appendix*.

   ○ Level E: I completed all the On Your Own activities and the Chapter Mastery Project and had to use all the solutions in the *Solutions Appendix*.

To continue toward the goal of teaching yourself computer skills, if you are not at Level A, try to move up one level on how you learn in Chapter 11, "Organizing Data Using Excel."

Projects to Help You

Now that you have mastered the material in this chapter, you are ready to tackle the three projects introduced at the beginning of the chapter in the section "How Will This Chapter Help Me?"

Project 1: Excel in Your Personal Life

Excel worksheets can be used to track a monthly budget, manage the money for a home improvement project, or record names and addresses of friends and family. Excel offers many templates that you can use just as they are or revise for your purposes. Browse through the Excel templates and select one that you find useful in your personal life. Examples you might consider are

▶ A personal budget template in the Budgets group

▶ An address book template in the Books group

▶ A calendar template in the Calendars group

▶ A home contents inventory template in the Inventories group

PERSONAL PROJECT: I have a huge collection of music and movies on CD and DVD. I need to inventory them so I can track their values for insurance and keep track of when I loan them to friends. Can Excel help me do that?

Create a worksheet using one of these or another template. If necessary, revise the worksheet to adjust to your needs. For example, you might use a template designed to track home contents inventory and revise it to inventory your music and movie CDs and DVDs.

Enter your personal data in the worksheet. Save and print the worksheet.

Project 2: Using Excel in Your Academic Career

ACADEMIC PROJECT:
My instructor has asked me to help her grade some worksheets. She specifically wants me to check for errors in the formulas. What other errors do students typically make on a worksheet?

Your instructor has asked for your help in checking some worksheets created by other students. In the Sample Files folder on the DVD in the back of the book, open the **Student01_Roster** workbook file. Find and list the eight errors on this worksheet.

> **Hint** To check the formulas used in the worksheet, you can point to each cell or use the **Show Formulas** command on the Formulas ribbon.

Project 3: Using Excel in Your Technical Career

TECHNICAL CAREER PROJECT: Our help desk often gets questions about how to use an Office application. I need to learn how to help with questions about Excel. When I get a question I can't answer, how can I find the answer or help someone figure it out?

Friends, family, customers, and coworkers often ask a technical person to help them figure out how to use an application. You might not know the answer to every question, but you can use the web or other tools to find answers. In this project, you enhance the CitrusFruitFundraiser worksheet you created in the Mastery Project. When this project is completed, the worksheet should look like that in Figure 10-20.

Do the following:

Step 1. Open the **CitrusFruitFundraiser** worksheet you created earlier in the Mastery Project.

Step 2. Increase the height of rows 7 and 15 so these rows stand out.

Step 3. Enter the labels for sales statistics in cells I18, I19, and I20.

Step 4. Enter formulas to calculate the average sale, maximum sale, and minimum sale in cells K18, K19, and K20.

Step 5. Suppose club members are expected to meet a minimum quota of $100 in sales. Use the Conditional Formatting feature of Excel to highlight in yellow the name of any club member who has not yet reached his quota.

> **Hint** Select the cells to format and click **Conditional Formatting** on the Home ribbon. Under Highlight Cells Rules, click **More Rules**. Use a formula to determine which cells to format. In the formula, use the less than operator (<).

Step 6. Someone asks you to explain the formulas used in this worksheet. Change the display of the worksheet so the formulas display in cells rather than the calculated values.

Step 7. Someone asks you how to display in the Excel window only the cells that contain information. You can see an example of this technique in the **Obama Bingo** template in the **Projects** group, **Games** subgroup. Display the CitrusFruitFundraiser worksheet with only cells A1 through K20 showing (see Figure 10-20).

> **Hint** To find out how, try a Google search on **limit display cells Excel**. The idea is to select all the rows or columns you want to hide and then use the Format command on the Home ribbon to hide these rows or columns.

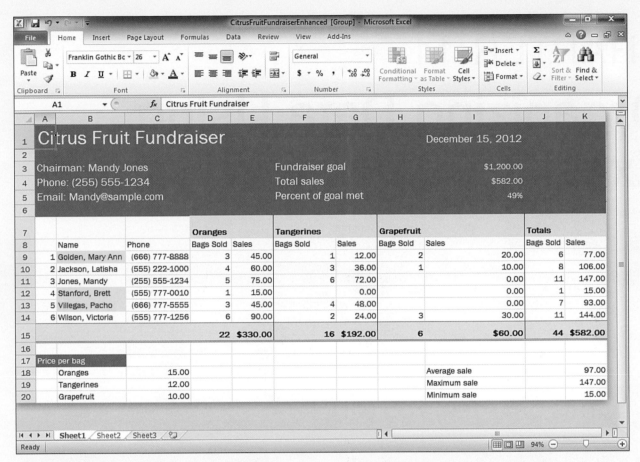

FIGURE 10-20
The fundraiser worksheet has enhancements.

Project to Help Others

One of the best ways to learn is to teach someone else. And, in teaching someone else, you are making a contribution in that person's life. As part of each chapter's work, you are encouraged to teach someone a skill you have learned. In this chapter, help someone learn to use Excel.

Who is your apprentice? _____

When helping others learn, don't do the work for them. Coach and instruct. Show them how to find information for themselves. Help them be as independent a learner as possible.

Do the following:

Step 1. Show your apprentice the worksheets you created in this chapter. Explain the elements on the Excel window and how the worksheet is built.

Step 2. Show him the templates that Excel offers.

Step 3. Help your apprentice find a template that he finds useful. Show him how to enter data in the worksheet and save the worksheet.

Step 4. If your apprentice is interested in building his own worksheet, help him design and create a worksheet of his choosing.

CHAPTER 11
Organizing Data Using Excel

IN THIS CHAPTER, YOU WILL

Use a table to manage data

Use multiple worksheets

Add a chart to a worksheet

Learn about Excel macros and Microsoft Access

In this chapter, you learn how Excel can help you track, organize, and summarize large amounts of data. The worksheets you create in this chapter use Excel tables. An Excel table offers many short-cuts for managing data. Several tasks you learned to do manually in Chapter 10, "Managing Numbers and Text Using Excel," are more automatic when using a table. In this chapter, you also learn to use several functions and to create charts that can visually summarize data.

Keep in mind the most important skill you can learn about Excel is how to teach yourself Excel. Try to do each On Your Own activity without any help. But remember, if you need help, you can always refer to the solutions in the *Solutions Appendix*.

JUMP RIGHT IN

If you want even more of a challenge, try proceeding directly to the Chapter Mastery Project at the end of this chapter. If you need help on the project, refer to the On Your Own activities in the chapter or do your own inde-pendent investigating using Excel Help or searching the web for answers. When you complete the project, you will have mastered the skills in this chapter. Then go to the projects that require you apply your skills to new situations.

How Will This Chapter Help Me?

Recall that throughout this book, each chapter provides three projects focusing on personal, academic, or technical career goals. Depending on your own interests, you might choose to complete any or all of these projects to help you achieve your goals.

PERSONAL PROJECT: I need to build an Excel worksheet that uses conditional formatting. I also want to dress up my work-sheets with clip art. And I need to adjust print settings to make large worksheets easier to read when they are printed.

ACADEMIC PROJECT: My instructor has asked me to help her grade some worksheets. She specifically wants me to check for errors using tables and formulas in these tables. What types of errors do students typically make in these cases?

TECHNICAL CAREER PROJECT: I want to take my knowledge of Excel a step further and learn to record and use a macro. Can I create a macro without using a program-ming language? Will Excel write the program for me?

Using a Table to Manage Data

In this chapter, we build a workbook for the Gently Used Consignment Shop. People bring furniture, books, clothing, and other items to the shop to sell, and the shop charges a commission for selling an item. Each month, the shopkeeper, Sarah Engels, writes a check to each seller for the money he is due for all items sold that month. The data is managed using four worksheets shown in Figure 11-1.

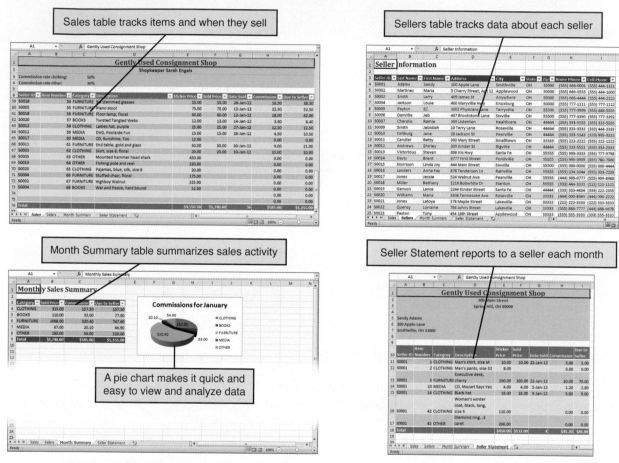

FIGURE 11-1

The Sales and Sellers worksheets track the shop activity. The Month Summary and Seller Statement worksheets summarize and process that activity.

The first three worksheets use Excel tables to manage the data. To use a table, you first define an area of a worksheet as an Excel table. Then you can quickly filter and sort the data in the table and create formulas and summary information using the data.

Enter Titles, Headings, and Data in the Sales Worksheet

The first worksheet shown in Figure 11-1, named the Sales worksheet, tracks items placed in the consignment shop by a seller and when the item sells. In this part of the chapter, you enter the titles and column headings on the Sales worksheet and then add the data.

When this activity is completed, the Sales worksheet should look like that in Figure 11-2. The worksheet title and subtitle in cells A1 and A2 use the **Merge & Center** command to cause these titles to span several columns.

On Your Own 11-1

Enter Titles, Headings, and Data on the Sales Worksheet

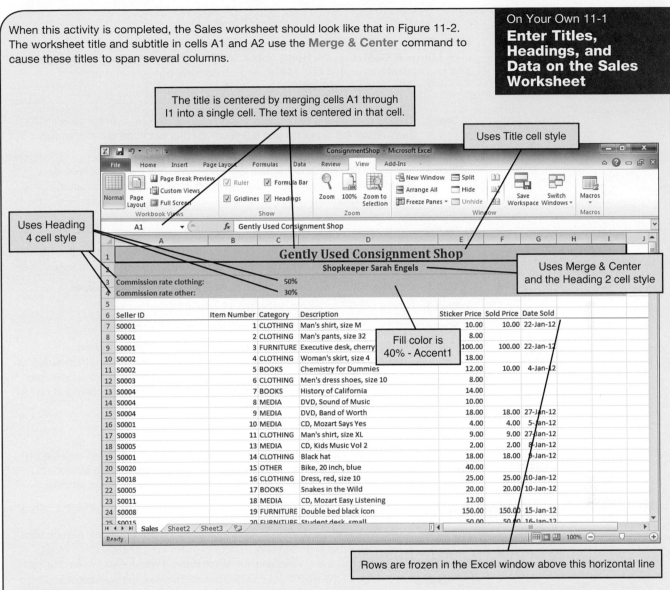

The title is centered by merging cells A1 through I1 into a single cell. The text is centered in that cell.

Uses Title cell style

Uses Heading 4 cell style

Uses Merge & Center and the Heading 2 cell style

Fill color is 40% - Accent1

Rows are frozen in the Excel window above this horizontal line

FIGURE 11-2
The Sales worksheet has titles, column headings, and data added.

Merge & Center—A command on the Home ribbon in the Alignment group that is used to cause one cell to span across multiple columns. Use it to center a title or column heading across several columns.

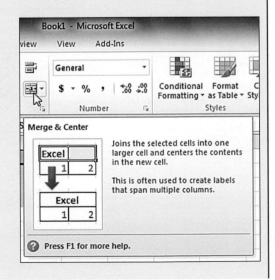

Do the following to enter and format the items in the first four rows of the worksheet:

Step 1.   Enter the titles and labels in cells A1 through A4, as shown in Figure 11-2, and format the cells as indicated in the figure.

On Your Own 11-1
Enter Titles, Headings, and Data on the Sales Worksheet

Hint To center a title or heading in a range of cells, select the range of cells and click **Merge & Center** on the Home ribbon. All the cells are merged into a single cell and text is centered in that cell. Merge and center only one row at a time.

Step 2. The shop charges a higher commission rate for clothing than for other items. Enter **0.5** in cell C3 and **0.3** in cell C4. Format these cells as shown in Figure 11-2.

Step 3. Name this first worksheet **Sales**. Save the workbook file to your hard drive, USB flash drive, SkyDrive, or another location given by your instructor. Name the file **ConsignmentShop**.

Do the following to enter column headings and data into the worksheet:

Step 1. Enter the column headings in row 6, as shown in Figure 11-2. Don't worry about the formatting or column width of this row. You handle both later.

Step 2. Format cells E7, F7, H7, and I7 as numbers with two decimal places.

Step 3. Format cell G7 as a date, using the **14-Mar-01** date format.

Step 4. Copy the formatting in row 7 down through row 72 or beyond.

Step 5. The data for the worksheet is stored in the Word document named **ConsignmentSalesTable** in the Sample Files folder on the DVD in the back of the book. Open the document in Word. Copy the data in the Word table into the Windows Clipboard. Paste the data into the worksheet beginning at cell **A7**. Use the Paste option that matches the destination formatting.

Tip When you use Windows Explorer to locate the ConsignmentSalesTable file on the DVD, the Type column in Windows Explorer reports the file to be a Microsoft Word Document file. When you double-click the file, it opens in a Word window.

Step 6. Adjust the column widths so all data and labels on the worksheet can be read.

When a large worksheet has many rows and you scroll down through these rows, the column headings at the top of the worksheet can disappear. To make the worksheet easier to use, you can freeze the title and column headings so they remain in view even when you scroll down through many rows of data. Do the following:

Step 1. Make cell **A7** the active cell. On the View ribbon, click **Freeze Panes**. Then click **Freeze Panes** in the drop-down menu. All the rows above row 7 are frozen on the window. A horizontal line appears on the worksheet to indicate which rows are frozen.

Step 2. To test the frozen rows, use your arrow keys to move down the rows. No matter how far you go down the worksheet, the first six rows stay in view.

Step 3. Save your work.

[?] Solutions Appendix

For help, see Solution 11-1: How to Enter Titles, Headings, and Data on the Sales Worksheet.

Convert the Data to an Excel Table and Add a Total Row

After the column headings and some data are on the worksheet, you can define the area as an Excel table. Here are some advantages to using an Excel table to manage data:

▶ Rows in a table can easily be sorted.

▶ Rows can be filtered so that only rows that match a criterion display.

▶ A total row can be added to the bottom of a table. This total row can contain various summary calculations for each column in the table. Excel uses the SUBTOTAL function to automatically produce these calculations.

▶ Each column in a table automatically receives a name, which is the same as the column heading. These names make it easy to build formulas using the table data.

In the following activities, you learn to use all these features of an Excel table.

In this activity, you convert the data to a table. When the activity is completed, the worksheet should look like that in Figure 11-3.

On Your Own 11-2
Convert the Data to an Excel Table

Video **11-2**

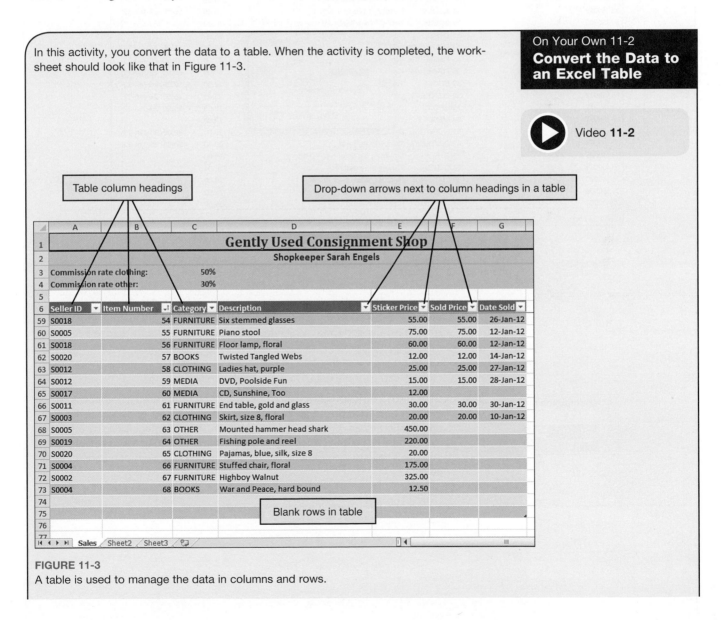

FIGURE 11-3
A table is used to manage the data in columns and rows.

Convert the Data to an Excel Table

Do the following to convert the data to a table:

Step 1. Click anywhere in the data. On the Home ribbon, click **Format as Table**. In the list of table styles, select **Table Style Medium 9**. The Format As Table box appears (see Figure 11-4).

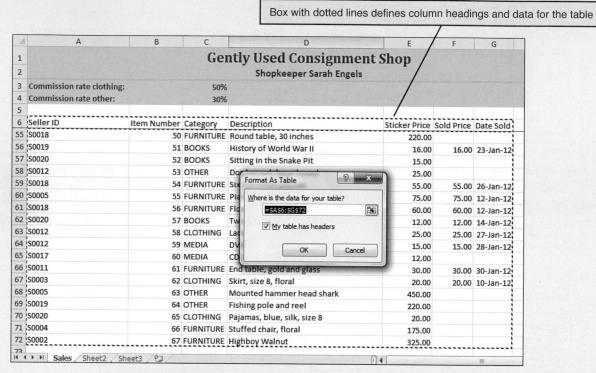

Box with dotted lines defines column headings and data for the table

FIGURE 11-4
When creating a table, Excel automatically selects the area for the table and assigns column headings to the table.

Step 2. Make sure **My table has headers** is checked and click **OK**. The table is created using the selected table style. This style uses alternating colors for each row (called banded rows), which makes it easier to read data across a long row.

Notice the drop-down arrows to the right of each column header. You can use these drop-down arrows to sort and filter the data. Do the following to find out how:

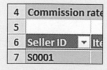

Step 1. Click the drop-down arrow next to Seller ID. The drop-down list appears (see Figure 11-5). Click **Sort A to Z**. All the data in the table is sorted by Seller ID, and the Sort icon shows next to Seller ID. The advantage of using a table to sort data rather than selecting a range of rows and columns to sort is that you don't have to worry about making sure you have the correct range of cells selected.

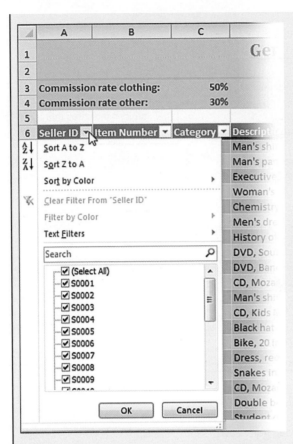

FIGURE 11-5
Excel can automatically sort or filter all data in a table.

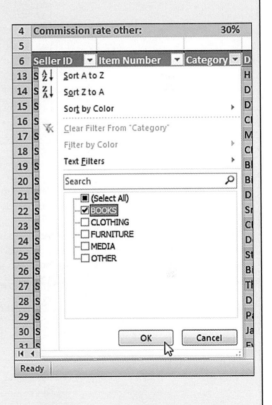

Step 2. Click the drop-down arrow next to Category. In the drop-down list, uncheck **(Select All)** and check **BOOKS**. Click **OK**. Only rows in the BOOKS category display (see Figure 11-6). The other rows are hidden, and the Filter icon ⏚ shows next to Category.

Step 3. To unhide the rows, click the drop-down arrow next to Category and check **(Select All)**. Click **OK**. All the rows of data display.

Step 4. Sort the data by **Item Number** from smallest to largest.

On Your Own 11-2

Convert the Data to an Excel Table

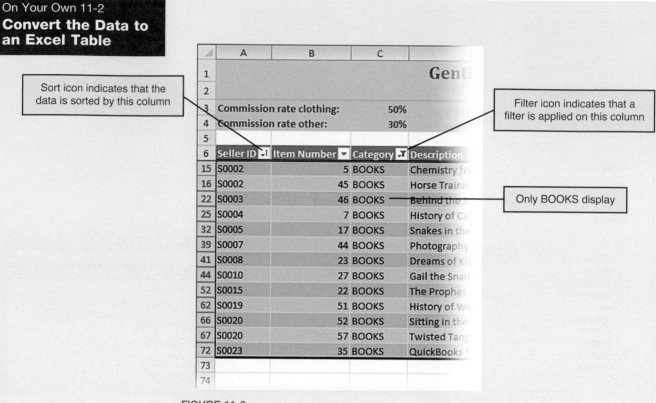

Sort icon indicates that the data is sorted by this column

Filter icon indicates that a filter is applied on this column

Only BOOKS display

FIGURE 11-6
A filter causes rows in a table to be hidden from view.

When you add new rows for data, Excel automatically includes these new rows in the table. You can also add blank rows to the bottom of the table, insert rows and columns, and delete rows and columns.

Do the following:

Step 1. Add the following row of data to the bottom of the table in row 73. Notice as you enter data into a cell, Excel automatically formats that data as part of the table.

Cell	Text or Number
A73	S0004
B73	68
C73	BOOKS
D73	War and Peace, hard bound
E73	12.50

Step 2. Use the grabber handle at the bottom right of the table to insert two new blank rows to the bottom of the table. Save your work.

When working with data in a table, you can tell whether the data has been filtered by using one of these methods:

▶ Look for missing row numbers on the left side of the Excel window. These missing row numbers indicate the rows are hidden. Excel displays adjacent row numbers in blue to indicate hidden rows are nearby.

▶ Look for the Filter icon to the right of a column heading. The icon indicates a filter is applied to this column. To clear a filter, click the drop-down arrow next to the column heading, click **Clear Filter From**, and click **OK**.

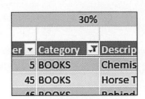

Here are two tips that can help you prevent typo errors as you type new data:

▶ Right-click a blank cell in the Seller ID column or the Category column. In the shortcut menu, click **Pick From Drop-down List**. A drop-down list appears with entries already in this column. Click an entry to select it.

▶ Type the first letter of the data. Excel completes the cell entry. Press **Enter** or **Tab** to accept the entry.

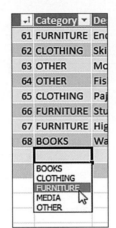

Excel can quickly put formulas at the bottom of the table in a Total row. When this activity is completed, the Total row should look like that in Figure 11-7.

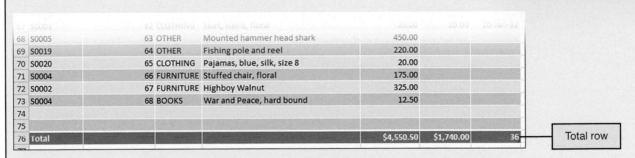

FIGURE 11-7
A Total row is easy to add to a table.

Do the following:

Step 1. Click anywhere in the table. The Design tab appears whenever a table is active. On the Design ribbon, check **Total Row**. A total row is created.

On Your Own 11-3

Add a Total Row to the Table

Step 2. Click the cell in column E of the total row. A drop-down arrow appears in the cell. Click the drop-down arrow to see a list of functions that Excel can use in the total row (see Figure 11-8).

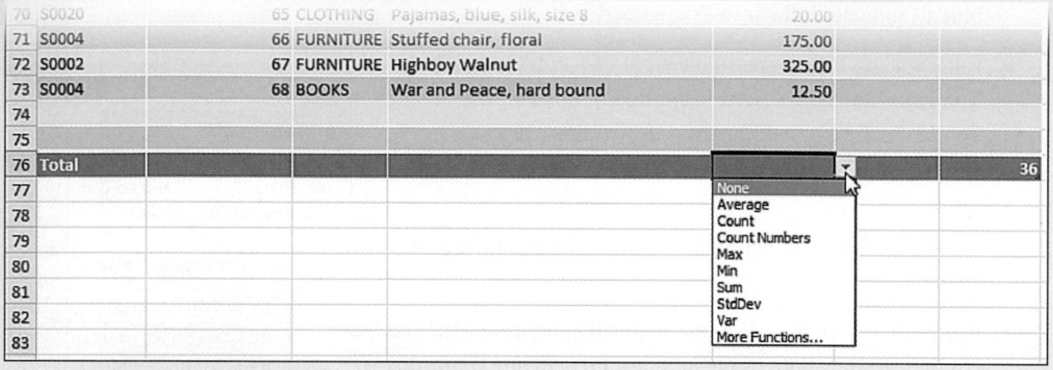

70	S0020	65 CLOTHING	Pajamas, blue, silk, size 8		20.00	
71	S0004	66 FURNITURE	Stuffed chair, floral		175.00	
72	S0002	67 FURNITURE	Highboy Walnut		325.00	
73	S0004	68 BOOKS	War and Peace, hard bound		12.50	
74						
75						
76	Total				▼	36
77				None		
78				Average		
79				Count		
80				Count Numbers		
81				Max		
82				Min		
83				Sum		
				StdDev		
				Var		
				More Functions…		

FIGURE 11-8
Excel can insert a function in the Total row of a table.

Step 3. In the list, click **Sum**. The sum of the Sticker Price column is inserted. You don't need to select the range for the sum because Excel automatically uses the entire column E in the table.

Step 4. Insert a **Sum** in the total row for the Sold Price column. Also notice Excel automatically inserted a **Count** in the Date Sold column.

Step 5. Format cells E76 and F76 as **Currency** with **2** decimal places. Save your work.

> **Tip** If you don't want to use a table that you have created, click somewhere in the table and then click **Convert to Range** on the Design ribbon. The table formatting is retained, but Excel no longer recognizes the table.

Click in cell E76 and notice the formula that Excel entered into this cell (see Figure 11-9).

Excel could have used the SUM function that you learned about in Chapter 10, but it uses the SUBTOTAL function instead. The **SUBTOTAL function** is more versatile than the SUM function. It's really several functions in one. The actual function used depends on the function number. The 109 you see in Figure 11-9 says to sum the range and do not include **hidden cells**.

SUBTOTAL function—An Excel function that is several functions in one, including an average, sum, count, maximum, and minimum. The function can be set to include or ignore hidden cells. To learn more about the function, look up **SUBTOTAL function** in Excel Help.

hidden cell—A cell that is part of a row or column that is hidden. Excel can hide or unhide a row or column using the Hide & Unhide command under the Format command on the Home ribbon. In addition, filtering rows in a table can hide or unhide a row.

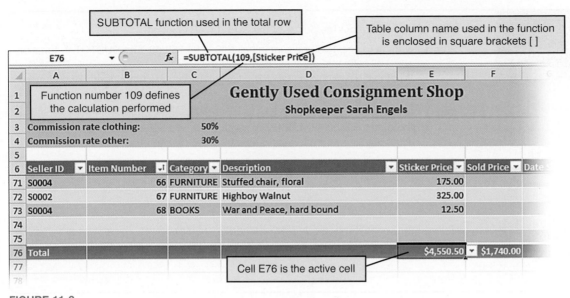

FIGURE 11-9
Excel uses the SUBTOTAL function to calculate the sum.

The SUBTOTAL function has two parts or **arguments**: the function number and a cell range. A few more examples of the SUBTOTAL function are listed in Table 11-1.

> **argument**—In an Excel function, the parts of the function inside parentheses following the function name. Also called a parameter.

TABLE 11-1 The SUBTOTAL Function Number Determines the Calculation It Performs on a Range of Cells

Function Number	Description	Example
109	SUM function: Finds the sum and ignores hidden values	SUBTOTAL(109,A1:A10)
9	SUM function: Finds the sum and includes hidden values	SUBTOTAL(9,A1:A10)
101	AVERAGE function: Finds the average and ignores hidden values	SUBTOTAL(101,A1:A10)
1	AVERAGE function: Finds the average and includes hidden values	SUBTOTAL(1,A1:A10)
103	COUNTA function: Counts cells that are not empty and ignores hidden cells	SUBTOTAL(103,A1:A10)
3	COUNTA function: Counts cells that are not empty and includes hidden cells	SUBTOTAL(3,A1:A10)

Notice in Figure 11-9 the name [Sticker Price] is used for the cell range. Excel automatically named column E in the table as [Sticker Price]. When building formulas, you can use this name rather than defining a range of cells. Square brackets [ ] around a name indicate the name is a column heading name in a table.

On Your Own 11-4

Explore the SUBTOTAL Function in a Table

  Solutions Appendix

For help, see Solution 11-4: How to Explore the SUBTOTAL Function in a Table.

Do the following to explore the power of the SUBTOTAL function:

Step 1. Note in Figure 11-7 the sum in cell E76 is $4,550.50. The SUBTOTAL function sums all cells that are unhidden. Filter the Category to display only **BOOKS**. What is the new sum in cell E76? Only cells that are not hidden are summed by the SUBTOTAL function.

Step 2. Change the formula in cell E76 to find the **Average** rather than the sum. Filter the data to display only **MEDIA**. What is the average sticker price for Media? What function number does the SUBTOTAL function use in cell E76?

Step 3. Unhide all the data in the table. Change the formula in cell E76 to find the **Sum**. Save your work.

Tip In a large worksheet, some rows might not display on the screen as you scroll through the data. These rows are still included in the SUBTOTAL calculations if they are not hidden rows.

Use Cell Names and the IF Function

Names are easier to use in formulas than cell addresses. Excel automatically gives names to columns in a table. In addition, you can manually assign a name to a cell, range of cells, or an entire table:

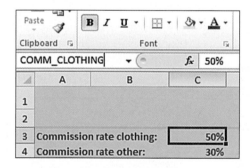

▶ To name a cell or range of cells, select the cell or range of cells and type a name in the name box. Then press **Enter**. The name can be used in a formula in place of the absolute address of the cell or range of cells.

▶ Excel automatically assigns a name to a table. To change the default name, first click anywhere in the table. On the Design ribbon, enter the new table name in the Table Name box.

Tip Excel names can include letters, numbers, periods, and underscores. The first character in the name cannot be a period. The first character can be a backslash, but you cannot use a backslash in the remaining characters.

If a cell has been assigned a name, its name appears in the name box when the cell is the active cell. To see a list of all names on the worksheet, click **Name Manager** on the Formulas ribbon. The Name Manager box opens (see Figure 11-10). In this box, you can delete, edit, or add a name.

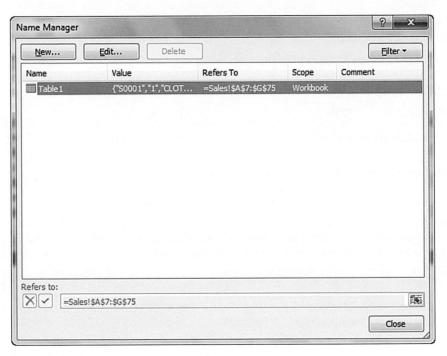

FIGURE 11-10
Use the Name Manager box to view, delete, edit, and create new names.

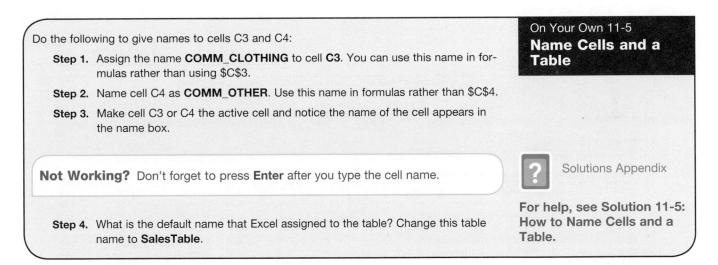

On Your Own 11-5
Name Cells and a Table

Do the following to give names to cells C3 and C4:

Step 1. Assign the name **COMM_CLOTHING** to cell **C3**. You can use this name in formulas rather than using $C$3.

Step 2. Name cell C4 as **COMM_OTHER**. Use this name in formulas rather than $C$4.

Step 3. Make cell C3 or C4 the active cell and notice the name of the cell appears in the name box.

Not Working? Don't forget to press **Enter** after you type the cell name.

Step 4. What is the default name that Excel assigned to the table? Change this table name to **SalesTable**.

? Solutions Appendix

For help, see Solution 11-5: **How to Name Cells and a Table.**

Our next step is to use the IF function to calculate the commission column. The **IF function** has three parts or arguments:

IF(*logical_test, value_if_true, value_if_false*)

IF function—A function that checks if a condition is met and returns one value if true and another value if false.

The following IF function would not work in an Excel worksheet, but it does explain the concepts used by the function:

`IF (Weather=raining, Umbrella, No umbrella)`

- *Logical_test*: Weather = raining
- *Value_if_true*: Umbrella
- *Value_if_false*: No umbrella

So now let's use the IF function to calculate commission.

On Your Own 11-6

Use the IF Function to Calculate the Commission Column and the Due to Seller Column

▶ Video **11-6**

Commission is a percentage of the sold price; the commission belongs to the consignment shop. The seller gets the sold price less the commission. Calculations for the commission and due to seller are in columns H and I on the Sales worksheet.

When you complete this activity, the Sales worksheet should look like that shown in Figure 11-11.

Begin by adding the following column headings. Notice that when you enter the text, Excel automatically includes columns H and I in the table.

Cell	Text
H6	Commission
I6	Due to Seller

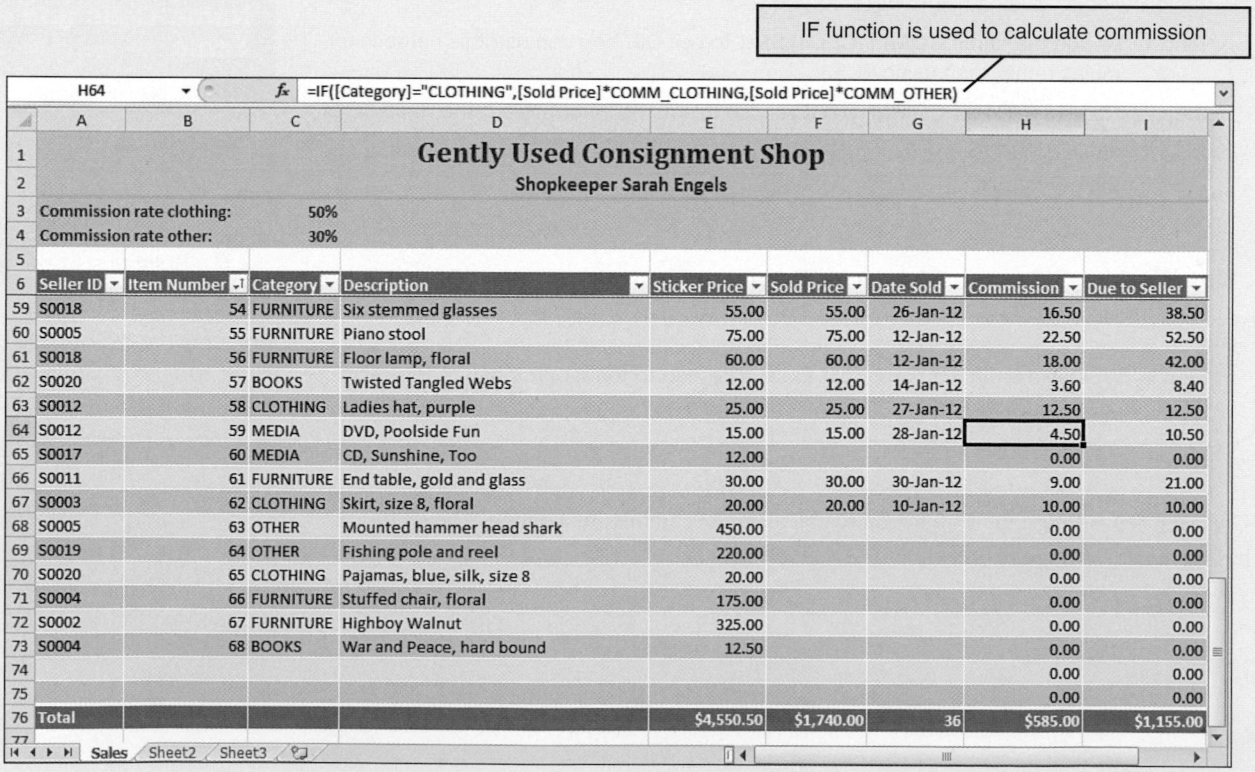

IF function is used to calculate commission

H64 = `=IF([Category]="CLOTHING",[Sold Price]*COMM_CLOTHING,[Sold Price]*COMM_OTHER)`

Gently Used Consignment Shop
Shopkeeper Sarah Engels

Commission rate clothing: 50%
Commission rate other: 30%

Seller ID	Item Number	Category	Description	Sticker Price	Sold Price	Date Sold	Commission	Due to Seller
S0018	54	FURNITURE	Six stemmed glasses	55.00	55.00	26-Jan-12	16.50	38.50
S0005	55	FURNITURE	Piano stool	75.00	75.00	12-Jan-12	22.50	52.50
S0018	56	FURNITURE	Floor lamp, floral	60.00	60.00	12-Jan-12	18.00	42.00
S0020	57	BOOKS	Twisted Tangled Webs	12.00	12.00	14-Jan-12	3.60	8.40
S0012	58	CLOTHING	Ladies hat, purple	25.00	25.00	27-Jan-12	12.50	12.50
S0012	59	MEDIA	DVD, Poolside Fun	15.00	15.00	28-Jan-12	4.50	10.50
S0017	60	MEDIA	CD, Sunshine, Too	12.00			0.00	0.00
S0011	61	FURNITURE	End table, gold and glass	30.00	30.00	30-Jan-12	9.00	21.00
S0003	62	CLOTHING	Skirt, size 8, floral	20.00	20.00	10-Jan-12	10.00	10.00
S0005	63	OTHER	Mounted hammer head shark	450.00			0.00	0.00
S0019	64	OTHER	Fishing pole and reel	220.00			0.00	0.00
S0020	65	CLOTHING	Pajamas, blue, silk, size 8	20.00			0.00	0.00
S0004	66	FURNITURE	Stuffed chair, floral	175.00			0.00	0.00
S0002	67	FURNITURE	Highboy Walnut	325.00			0.00	0.00
S0004	68	BOOKS	War and Peace, hard bound	12.50			0.00	0.00
							0.00	0.00
							0.00	0.00
Total				$4,550.50	$1,740.00	36	$585.00	$1,155.00

Sales / Sheet2 / Sheet3

FIGURE 11-11
The last two columns in the table on the Sales worksheet are calculated.

The shop charges a higher commission for CLOTHING than for other categories. Therefore, the formula to calculate the commission for CLOTHING is different than it is for other categories. The IF function is used to decide which formula to use. The completed formula is shown in Figure 11-12.

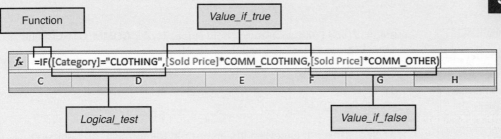

FIGURE 11-12
The IF function calculates commission after testing the Category.

You could just type what you see in the figure, but let's take it one step at a time and see how Excel can help you build an IF function with names. Do the following:

Step 1. Go to cell **H7**. Type **=IF(**. When you type the =, Excel knows you are building a formula. When you type IF(, Excel knows you are using the IF function and responds by showing the three parts (or arguments) of the function. Each argument is separated by a comma.

Step 2. Type **[**. When you type the [, Excel knows you want to see a list of column names in the table. A drop-down list of names appears (see Figure 11-13). Double-click **Category**.

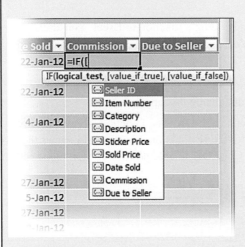

FIGURE 11-13
Excel provides a list of names in the table to be used in the formula.

Step 3. Type **]** to complete the column name. Type **="CLOTHING",** (don't forget the comma) to complete the *logical_test* part of the IF function.

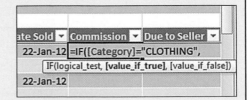

> **Hint** When typing text in a formula, include double quotation marks around the text.

Step 4. Type **[** and double-click **Sold Price**. Type **]*COMM_CLOTHING,** (don't forget the comma) to complete the *value_if_true* part of the IF function.

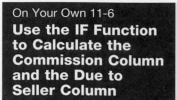

On Your Own 11-6

Use the IF Function to Calculate the Commission Column and the Due to Seller Column

Tip As you complete a column name in a formula, notice that Excel assigns a color to the name. This color is also drawn around the column in the table.

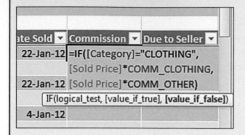

Step 5. Type **[** and double-click **Sold Price**. Type **]*COMM_OTHER)** and press **Enter** to complete the function.

Step 6. Press **Enter** to complete the formula. If other cells in the column are empty, Excel automatically copies the formula into the entire column.

Not Working? If Excel reports an error in the formula, go back and check the formula comparing it to Figure 11-12.

? Solutions Appendix

For help, see Solution 11-6: How to Use the IF Function to Calculate Commission Column and the Due to Seller Column.

Do the following to complete the table:

Step 1. The Due to Seller column is the Sold Price less Commission. Enter the formula into this column.

Step 2. Enter the sums of the Commission column and the Due to Seller column in the total row at the bottom of the table. Format these totals as Currency with 2 decimal places.

Step 3. Save your work.

It's good to know more than one method when building a function in Excel. You already learned how to type the IF function in a cell. You can also use the Formulas ribbon. Here is how it's done:

Step 1. Select the cell to contain the IF function and click **Insert Function** on the Formulas ribbon. The Insert Function dialog box appears.

Step 2. Under *Select a function*, click **IF** and click **OK**. The Function Arguments box opens. Enter the three arguments for the **IF** function. Figure 11-14 shows the box with the three arguments entered. Click **OK** to enter the IF function in the cell.

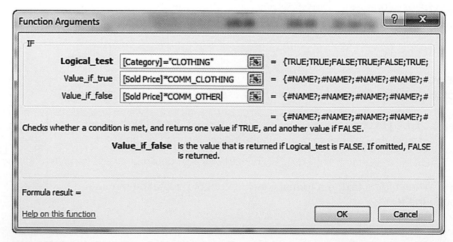

FIGURE 11-14
You can use the Function Arguments dialog box to build the IF function.

The Sales worksheet is completed. Because of the amount of data we are tracking, it is easier to organize the data if we put some of it on other worksheets.

Using Multiple Worksheets

Notice on the Sales worksheet that the seller is identified by a Seller ID. We must track other information about the seller including the seller name, address, and phone number. It's awkward to repeat that information in each row of the Sales worksheet. Seller information is kept on the Sellers worksheet, and we can use the Seller ID to find this seller information.

<table>
<tr><td colspan="3">When this activity is completed, the Sellers worksheet should look like that in Figure 11-15.</td><td>On Your Own 11-7
Build the Sellers Worksheet</td></tr>
</table>

Uses the Title cell style

The drop-down arrows indicate the data is formatted as a table

Two columns formatted as phone numbers

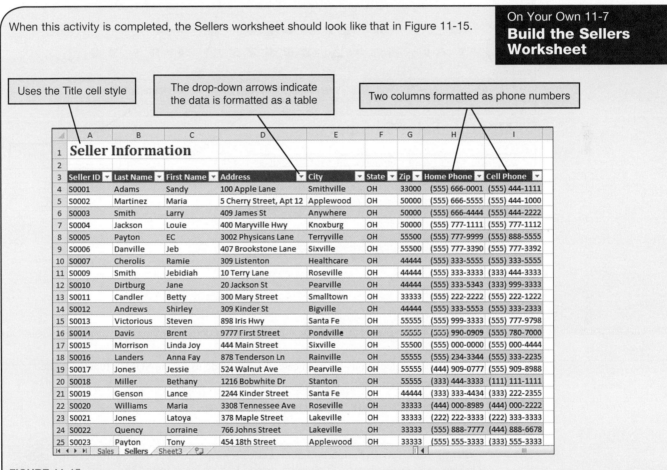

	A	B	C	D	E	F	G	H	I
1	**Seller Information**								
2									
3	Seller ID	Last Name	First Name	Address	City	State	Zip	Home Phone	Cell Phone
4	S0001	Adams	Sandy	100 Apple Lane	Smithville	OH	33000	(555) 666-0001	(555) 444-1111
5	S0002	Martinez	Maria	5 Cherry Street, Apt 12	Applewood	OH	50000	(555) 666-5555	(555) 444-1000
6	S0003	Smith	Larry	409 James St	Anywhere	OH	50000	(555) 666-4444	(555) 444-2222
7	S0004	Jackson	Louie	400 Maryville Hwy	Knoxburg	OH	50000	(555) 777-1111	(555) 777-1112
8	S0005	Payton	EC	3002 Physicans Lane	Terryville	OH	55500	(555) 777-9999	(555) 888-5555
9	S0006	Danville	Jeb	407 Brookstone Lane	Sixville	OH	55500	(555) 777-3390	(555) 777-3392
10	S0007	Cherolis	Ramie	309 Listenton	Healthcare	OH	44444	(555) 333-5555	(555) 333-5555
11	S0009	Smith	Jebidiah	10 Terry Lane	Roseville	OH	44444	(555) 333-3333	(333) 444-3333
12	S0010	Dirtburg	Jane	20 Jackson St	Pearville	OH	44444	(555) 333-5343	(333) 999-3333
13	S0011	Candler	Betty	300 Mary Street	Smalltown	OH	33333	(555) 222-2222	(555) 222-1222
14	S0012	Andrews	Shirley	309 Kinder St	Bigville	OH	44444	(555) 333-5553	(555) 333-2333
15	S0013	Victorious	Steven	898 Iris Hwy	Santa Fe	OH	55555	(555) 999-3333	(555) 777-9798
16	S0014	Davis	Brent	9777 First Street	Pondville	OH	55555	(555) 990-0909	(555) 780-7000
17	S0015	Morrison	Linda Joy	444 Main Street	Sixville	OH	55500	(555) 000-0000	(555) 000-4444
18	S0016	Landers	Anna Fay	878 Tenderson Ln	Rainville	OH	55555	(555) 234-3344	(555) 333-2235
19	S0017	Jones	Jessie	524 Walnut Ave	Pearville	OH	55555	(444) 909-0777	(555) 909-8988
20	S0018	Miller	Bethany	1216 Bobwhite Dr	Stanton	OH	55555	(333) 444-3333	(111) 111-1111
21	S0019	Genson	Lance	2244 Kinder Street	Santa Fe	OH	44444	(333) 333-4434	(333) 222-2355
22	S0020	Williams	Maria	3308 Tennessee Ave	Roseville	OH	33333	(444) 000-8989	(444) 000-2222
23	S0021	Jones	Latoya	378 Maple Street	Lakeville	OH	33333	(222) 222-3333	(222) 333-3333
24	S0022	Quency	Lorraine	766 Johns Street	Lakeville	OH	33333	(555) 888-7777	(444) 888-6678
25	S0023	Payton	Tony	454 18th Street	Applewood	OH	33333	(555) 555-3333	(333) 555-3333

Sales | **Sellers** | Sheet3

FIGURE 11-15
The Sellers worksheet tracks information about each seller.

Do the following to build the Sellers worksheet:

Step 1. Name the second worksheet **Sellers**. Enter the title and format it as indicated in Figure 11-15.

Step 2. Open the Word document **SellerInfoTable** in the Sample Files folder on the DVD in the back of the book. Copy and paste the column headings and data in the Word table into the Sellers worksheet, beginning with cell A3. Use the Paste option that matches the destination formatting.

Step 3. Convert the seller information to a table using the **Table Style Medium 3**.

Step 4. Format columns H and I as phone numbers.

Step 5. Use **AutoFit Column Width** to adjust column widths as necessary.

Step 6. Name the table **SellerInfo**. Save your work.

Solutions Appendix

For help, see Solution 11-7: How to Build the Sellers Worksheet.

Use the SUMIF Function to Create a Monthly Summary

The Month Summary worksheet holds summary data for the month using data taken from the Sales worksheet. The Month Summary worksheet with summary information added is shown in Figure 11-16.

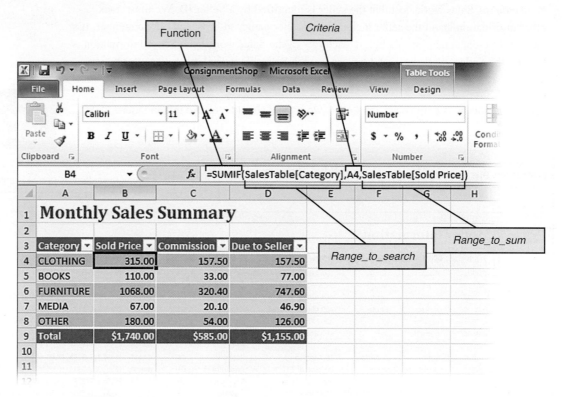

FIGURE 11-16
Summary information for the month is created using data from the Sales worksheet.

The summary calculations for each category are made using the SUMIF function. The **SUMIF function** has three arguments:

SUMIF(*range_to_search, criteria, range_to_sum*)

> **SUMIF function**—A function that searches a range of cells. If a cell meets the criteria given, a corresponding cell in the range to sum is added to the sum.

In Figure 11-16, the formula in cell B4 uses the SUMIF function to total the sold price for the "CLOTHING" category. The three arguments of the function are

- *Range-to-search*: The Category column of the SalesTable

- C*riteria:* Cell A4 on the Month Summary worksheet. Cell A4 contains the text "CLOTHING." Therefore, the SUMIF function searches the Category column in the SalesTable for the text "CLOTHING."

- *Range_to_sum*: The Sold Price column in the SalesTable. If "CLOTHING" is found in the Category column, the value in the Sold Price column is added to the sum.

With this understanding in hand, you are now ready to build the formulas for the monthly summary information.

Do the following to enter the title and text on the Month Summary worksheet:

Step 1. Name the third worksheet **Month Summary**. Enter and format the worksheet title as shown in Figure 11-17.

Use the Title cell style

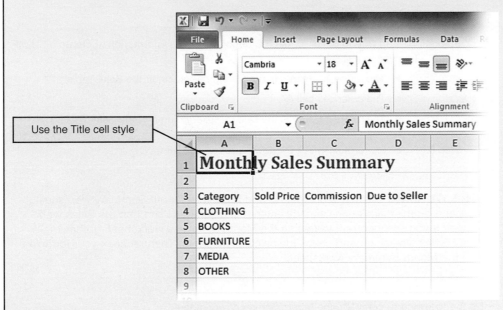

FIGURE 11-17
The Month Summary worksheet has the title, column headings, and first column entered.

Step 2. Enter the column headings in row 3 and text in column A as shown in Figure 11-17.

You are now ready to enter the SUMIF function in column B to sum the Sold Price column in the SalesTable for each category. The function searches the Category column in the SalesTable. If a cell in this column matches the criteria in column A on the Month Summary worksheet, the value in the Sold Price column of the SalesTable is added to the sum.

Do the following:

Step 1. Go to cell B4 and enter the SUMIF function either by using the Formulas ribbon or typing the function directly in the cell. Use this information for the three arguments of the function:

▶ The *range_to_search* is the Category column in the SalesTable: **SalesTable[Category]**.

▶ The *criteria* is cell **A4**.

▶ The *range to sum* is the Sold Price column in the SalesTable: **SalesTable[Sold Price]**.

Step 2. Copy the formula down the column through cell B8.

On Your Own 11-8
**Calculate Sales
Totals for One Month**

Do the following to enter similar SUMIF functions in columns C and D:

Step 3. To sum Commission for each Category, use this information to create a SUMIF function in cell C4:

▶ The *range_to_search* is the Category column in the SalesTable.

▶ The *criteria* is cell A4.

▶ The *range_to_sum* is the Commission column in the SalesTable.

Step 4. Copy the formula in cell C4 down through cell C8.

Step 5. To sum Due to Seller for each Category, use this information to create a SUMIF function in cell D4:

▶ The *range_to_search* is the Category column in the SalesTable.

▶ The *criteria* is cell A4.

▶ The *range_to_sum* is the Due to Seller column in the SalesTable.

Step 6. Copy the formula in cell D4 down through cell D8.

> **Not Working?** Values in columns C and D on your Month Summary worksheet depend on the calculations already entered in columns H and I on the Sales worksheet. If you see incorrect values on the Month Summary worksheet, go back to your Sales worksheet and check the calculations there. Then recheck your formulas on the Month Summary worksheet.

Do the following to complete the Month Summary worksheet:

Step 1. Convert the data to a table using the **Table Style Medium 12**. Add a Total row at the bottom of the table.

Step 2. Add sums to the total row and format these cells as shown earlier in Figure 11-16.

The summary calculations on the Month Summary worksheet should match up with totals and subtotals on the Sales worksheet. Do the following to spot-check the totals:

Step 1. Use filtering to find out the Sold Price for the OTHER category on the Sales worksheet. Does this value match the Sold Price for the OTHER category on the Month Summary worksheet? What is this value?

Step 2. Use filtering to find out the Due to Seller for the FURNITURE category on the Sales worksheet. Does this value match the Due to Seller for the FURNITURE category on the Month Summary worksheet? What is this value?

 Solutions Appendix

For help, see Solution 11-8: How to Calculate Sales Totals for One Month.

> **Tip** Comparing values created by different calculations in a workbook is an excellent practice to help you know you have not made mistakes in the formulas.

Create a Seller Statement

The Seller Statement worksheet shows the money due to one seller at the end of a month. This statement can be printed and mailed as a report to accompany the check sent to the seller. Figure 11-18 shows the Seller Statement worksheet for the Seller ID S0001.

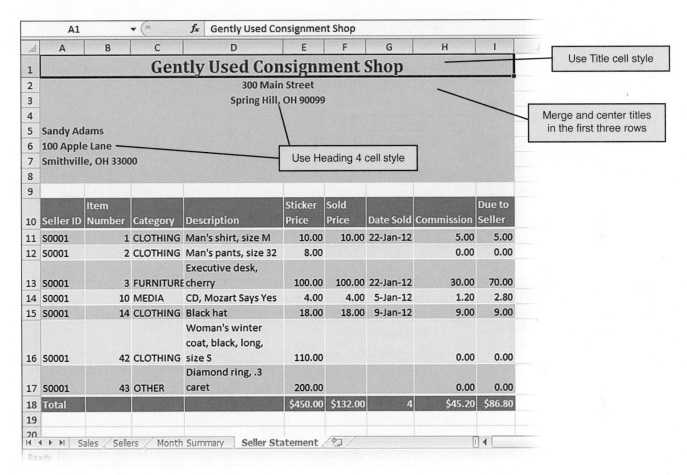

FIGURE 11-18
The seller statement can be mailed to the seller along with a check for money owed the seller.

You use the CONCATENATE function to build the name and address lines of the seller by using data on the Sellers worksheet. The CONCATENATE function can have as many parts as you need. Each part is a cell that contains text or text enclosed in quotation marks. Figure 11-19 shows an example of the function.

> CONCATENATE function—A function that joins text together into one cell. The word "concatenate" means to connect items together in a chain.

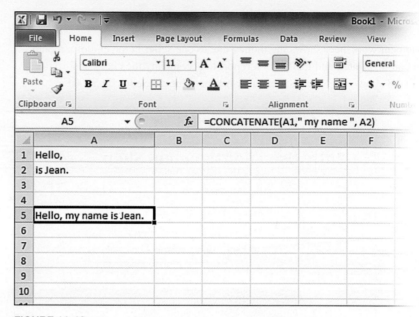

FIGURE 11-19
Use the CONCATENATE function to join text together into a cell.

On Your Own 11-9
Enter Titles and Seller Name and Address on the Seller Statement

Do the following to create and format the Seller Statement worksheet:

Step 1. Add a new worksheet to the workbook and name the worksheet **Seller Statement**.

Step 2. Apply the **40% - Accent1** cell style to cells A1 through I8. Enter and format the titles in the first three rows of the worksheet as shown earlier in Figure 11-18.

The name and address for Seller ID S0001 comes from row 4 on the Sellers worksheet (see Figure 11-20).

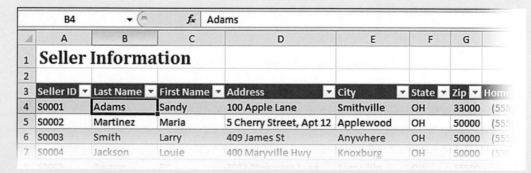

FIGURE 11-20
Use cells in row 4 to create the name and address lines on the Seller Statement.

Do the following to enter the name and address lines for Seller ID S0001:

Step 1. On the Seller Statement worksheet, go to cell A5. Use the **CONCATENATE** function to join together cells C4 and B4 on the Sellers worksheet into cell A5. Don't forget the space between the names.

On Your Own 11-9
Enter Titles and Seller Name and Address on the Seller Statement

Hint When you are creating a formula and need to refer to a cell address on a different worksheet, enter the name of the worksheet followed by the exclamation symbol (!) and then the cell address. For example, **Sellers!C4**.

Step 2. Go to cell A6. Enter cell D4 on the Sellers worksheet into this cell.

Step 3. Go to cell A7. Use the **CONCATENATE** function to join together cells E4, F4, and G4 on the Sellers worksheet to create the city, state, and zip mailing address line in cell A7. Don't forget the spaces and comma needed in the address line.

Not Working? If you are having problems with the CONCATENATE function, try entering it without including the comma and spaces between city, state, and zip. After it works with just the city, state, and zip, add the space between state and zip. Finally, add the space and comma between the city and state.

Step 4. Format the three-line name and address using the **Header 4** cell style. Save your work.

4	
5	Sandy Adams
6	100 Apple Lane
7	Smithville, OH 33000
8	
9	

? Solutions Appendix

For help, see Solution 11-9: How to Enter Titles and Seller Name and Address on the Seller Statement.

The remainder of the seller statement is created by copying data from the SalesTable. When you paste the data on the Seller Statement worksheet, you paste only the values and the formatting, not the formulas.

On Your Own 11-10
Copy Table Values to the Seller Statement

Go to the Sales worksheet and filter the data to select only Seller ID S0001. Copy the table including the column headings and total row. Paste the copied items into the Seller Statement worksheet beginning with cell A10. When you paste the copied items, use the Paste Values option, **Values & Source Formatting** (see Figure 11-21).

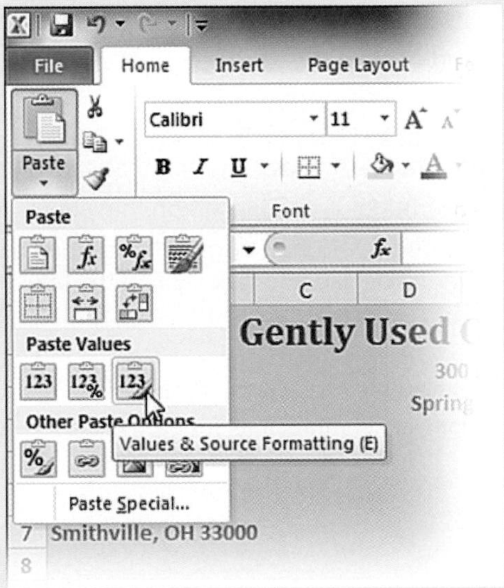

FIGURE 11-21
Paste values and source formatting into the Seller Statement worksheet.

On Your Own 11-10
Copy Table Values to the Seller Statement

Sometimes you might want to print a worksheet on a single sheet of paper without scaling down the font size. **Text wrap** can help by causing text in a cell to display on multiple lines.

> **text wrap**—All text in a cell displays on multiple lines. To turn on text wrap, select the cell or range of cells and click the **Wrap Text** button 📄 on the Home ribbon.

When you complete this activity, the worksheet should look like that shown earlier in Figure 11-18. Do the following to adjust column widths and text wrap so the statement can print on one page without reducing font size:

Step 1. Apply AutoFit Column Width to the table.

Step 2. Apply text wrap to column D and row 10.

> **Hint** To select an entire row or column, click the row number or column letter in the row or column bars on the edges of the Excel worksheet area.

Step 3. Adjust page orientation and column widths so the worksheet prints on a single page without reducing font size. To see where page breaks appear on the worksheet, click **Page Break Preview** on the View ribbon.

? Solutions Appendix

For help, see Solution 11-10: How to Copy Table Values to the Seller Statement.

> **Not Working?** As you adjust a column width, you might need to turn text wrap off and back on to cause the text to wrap in a cell.

Adding a Chart to a Worksheet

A chart is a quick and easy way to view data and can help you make sense of data or analyze the data. Excel offers several types of charts including a **pie chart**, **line chart**, and **bar chart**.

> **pie chart**—A chart or graph that shows the parts of a whole.
>
> **line chart**—A chart or graph that shows trends over time.
>
> **bar chart**—A chart or graph best used to compare values and can also show trends over time. Use it to quickly find the largest and smallest values.

The three types of charts are shown in Figure 11-22. The bar chart or pie chart makes it easy to compare commissions for each category. A line chart is not as useful for this purpose.

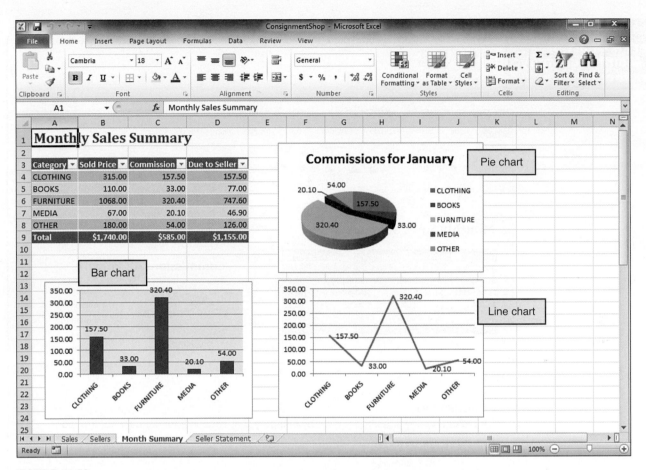

FIGURE 11-22
Excel offers a variety of chart types. Select the type that helps you best visualize the data.

To insert a chart in a worksheet, first select the data used to build the chart and then select a chart type on the Insert ribbon. After the chart is inserted, you can enhance the chart with a title, **legend**, and labels.

> **legend**—A list that tells you what each bar or slice in a chart represents.

On Your Own 11-11

Insert a Chart in the Month Summary Worksheet

When this activity is completed, the Month Summary worksheet should look like that in Figure 11-23.

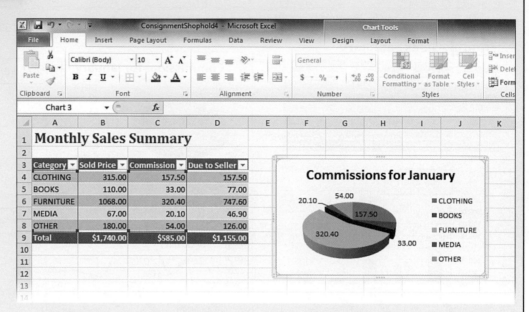

FIGURE 11-23
A pie chart shows the breakdown by category that accounts for January commissions.

Do the following:

Step 1. Go to the Month Summary worksheet and select the Category and Commission data. Insert a **Pie in 3-D** chart using that data.

> **Hint** To select nonadjacent cells, hold down the **Ctrl** key as you press and drag.

Step 2. Add the title, **Commissions for January**, to the chart as shown in Figure 11-23. Add labels to show the commission values for each slice in the pie chart. Move the FURNITURE slice outward to set it apart from the other pie slices.

Step 3. Save your work.

? Solutions Appendix

For help, see Solution 11-11: How to Insert a Chart in the Month Summary Worksheet.

Introducing Excel Macros and Microsoft Access

Excel and Microsoft Access offer more advanced tools used to manage large amounts of data. This part of the chapter gives a quick overview of a few of these tools.

Use Excel Macros to Do Repetitive Tasks

Whenever you find yourself repeating the same actions many times in a worksheet, know that you can use an Excel **macro** to automate the process.

> **macro**—A program embedded in a Word document, Excel workbook, or Access database that can perform instructions or steps that the programmer has previously recorded.

For example, look back at the Seller Statement worksheet in Figure 11-18. You learned how to build a seller statement for one seller. If you needed to build statements for each seller, you would find yourself repeating the same steps over and over for each seller. A macro can help. Here's how a macro works that writes the titles on a worksheet and formats these title rows:

Step 1. On the View ribbon, click **Macros** and click **Use Relative References**. The macros you record now work anywhere on a worksheet. Go to the cell where you want the first title. On the View ribbon, click **Macros** and click **Record Macro** to start recording a macro. You are asked to name the macro.

Step 2. Type the titles and format the title rows. When you are done, click **Stop Recording** in the Macros drop-down menu on the View ribbon. Excel creates the macro.

Step 3. Move to a new row on the worksheet. To run the macro, click **Macros** and click **View Macros**. Select the macro and click **Run**. The titles are created and formatted at the new location.

> **Tip** To learn more about recording and using macros, search Excel Help using the search string **creating and running macros**. The link in Excel Help leads you to a video about macros that you can watch on the office.microsoft.com website.

Excel uses the Visual Basic programming language to record each step in a macro. You can edit or write a macro using **Visual Basic for Applications (VBA)**. To learn more about writing macros and using VBA, consider taking an advanced course about Excel.

> **Visual Basic for Applications (VBA)**—A programming language embedded within Office applications used to write short programs to enhance the application. VBA is a subset of the Visual Basic programming language. Visual Basic is a standalone language and more powerful than VBA.

Use Microsoft Access to Manage Large Quantities of Data

Excel is useful when managing lists, calculations, and tables. If the amount of data becomes too much to view and manage easily on one or more worksheets, consider moving to a more powerful tool, the **Microsoft Access** application.

> **Microsoft Access**—One of the applications included in Microsoft Office. Access is a database management application. You can use it to create and edit a database and to build forms and reports that use the database.

Access manages data in a database using one or more database tables (see Figure 11-24). Each table is made up of rows and columns similar to Excel tables. A row is called a record. A column is called a field and has a field name.

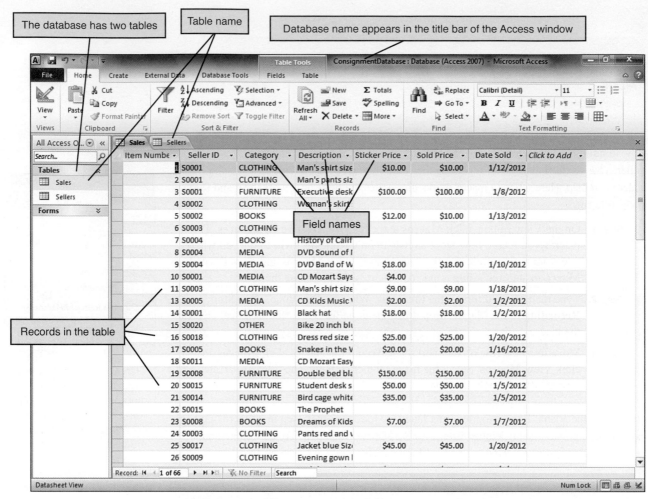

The database has two tables

Table name

Database name appears in the title bar of the Access window

Field names

Records in the table

FIGURE 11-24
A table in an Access database is made up of records (rows) and fields (columns).

Tip Notice in Figure 11-24 the title bar shows Access 2007. Access 2010 uses the .accdb file extension and format for a database that was first introduced with Access 2007. The title bar reminds us of this fact.

Normally, Access keeps only **raw data** in a database. Calculations using the raw data are created and displayed by a **query**, **Access form**, or **Access report**.

> **raw data**—Data recorded by a user. The data is not created by a calculation.
>
> **query**—A view of the data in an Access database that has selected fields and records and can include calculations.
>
> **Access form**—A screen built by Access that is used to view and edit the data in a database. The form controls what you can see and do with the data and helps to protect the integrity of the data.
>
> **Access report**—Data, calculations about the data, charts, and other information presented in a visually pleasing way appropriate for printing.

Here are a few brief differences between how Excel manages data and how Access does it:

▶ Excel keeps the data, calculations, and charts in worksheets. Access keeps data in database tables. A database might have more than one table, and the data in one table connects or relates to data in another table by way of a field they have in common. See Figure 11-25.

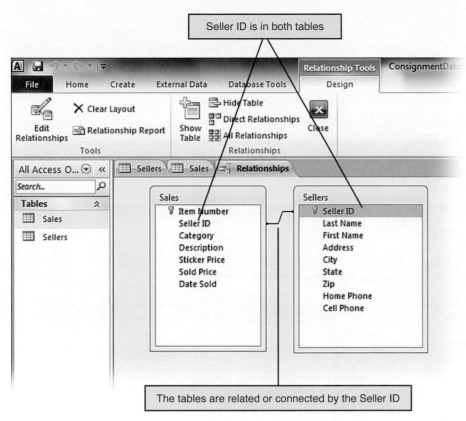

FIGURE 11-25
Two tables in an Access database relate to each other by way of the Seller ID field they have in common.

▶ You can edit an Excel worksheet by changing the contents of cells. Using Access, you use forms to edit the data. The form displays on the screen and controls exactly what you can see or edit in the table. You do not usually see the actual table. Figure 11-26 shows a form being built that will be used to edit the Sales table of Figure 11-24.

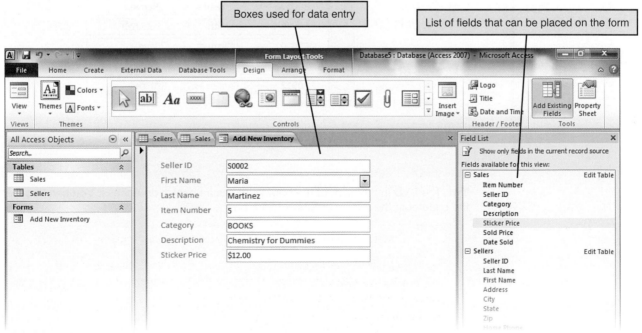

FIGURE 11-26
An Access form is used to edit a database.

▶ Access is better at protecting the integrity of the data than is Excel. For example, an Access form can make sure that all phone numbers have ten digits and zip codes are valid for a particular city and state. In addition, it can prevent duplicate data such as a duplicate Social Security number in a list of employees.

▶ Excel can create calculations and summary information anywhere on a worksheet. Summary calculations are often kept in a total row at the bottom of an Excel table. Using Access, a query displays data and calculations onscreen. An Access report can be used to view and print data and calculations. See Figure 11-27.

FIGURE 11-27
An Access report is used to view or print data and can include calculations on the data.

> **Tip** The DVD in the back of the book contains a chapter on Access. You can find the chapter in the **Extra Chapters** folder on the DVD.

Summary

Using a Table to Manage Data

▶ An Excel table makes it easier to filter and sort data and to create formulas and summary information about the data.

▶ To define an area of a worksheet as a table, click somewhere in the area and click Format as Table on the Home ribbon.

▶ To cause a title, label, or heading to span multiple columns, use the Merge & Center command on the Home ribbon. All cells in the range are merged into a single cell and text is centered in that cell.

▶ Freezing rows or columns used for titles and headings can make it easier to identify the data on a large worksheet. These frozen rows and columns stay in view as you scroll through a large worksheet.

▶ Use the drop-down menus in the column heading row of a table to sort and filter the data in the table.

▶ The Filter icon appears in the column heading cell when a filter is applied to this column. Rows that are not included in the filter are hidden.

▶ The Sort icon appears in the column heading cell when this column is used for sorting the data in the table.

▶ You can insert a total row at the bottom of the table and then insert a summary function into that row.

▶ Functions available in the total row of a table include Sum, Count, Average, Max, and Min. These functions are produced using the versatile SUBTOTAL function. This function can ignore values in hidden cells.

▶ To convert a table back to a normal range of cells, use the Convert to Range command on the Design ribbon.

▶ Excel automatically assigns column headings and column names to a table and a table name. You can manually assign a name to a cell or range of cells or change the default name of a table. Using names in formulas is easier than using absolute cell addresses.

▶ The Name Manager command on the Formulas ribbon can be used to display the Name Manager box. Use this box to manage the names used in a workbook.

▶ The IF function is used to check a condition. If the condition is met, one value is returned. If the condition is not met, another value is returned.

Using Multiple Worksheets

▶ Multiple worksheets are useful when organizing a large amount of data. Give each worksheet used a name that describes the purpose of the worksheet.

▶ The SUMIF function has three parts or arguments: a range to search, criteria, and a range to sum. The function searches the range of cells. If a cell meets the criteria given, a corresponding cell in a range to sum is added to the sum.

▶ A good practice for building error-free worksheets is to create summary information using more than one method and to compare results to make sure they are the same.

▶ The CONCATENATE function joins text together into one cell. This text can be enclosed in quotation marks, or the function can refer to cells that contain text.

▶ When writing a formula on one worksheet, you can identify a cell on another worksheet by preceding the cell address with its worksheet name and an explanation point—for example, Sheet2!C4.

▶ When copying to a new location, you can copy either the formulas or the values to the new location. You can also include source formatting in the copy.

▶ Text wrap causes all text in a cell to display on multiple lines.

Adding a Chart to a Worksheet

▶ Excel offers several types of charts used to visually represent data including the pie chart, line chart, and bar chart. Use the type chart that best represents the way you want to interpret the data.

▶ A pie chart shows the parts of a whole. A line chart shows trends over time. A bar chart compares values and can show trends over time.

▶ Use the Insert ribbon to insert a chart on a worksheet. After the chart is inserted, you can add a title, legend, and labels.

Introducing Excel Macros and Microsoft Access

▶ An Excel macro is a program embedded in an Excel workbook that can perform instructions that the programmer has previously recorded.

▶ A macro is best used to perform a task that the developer or user of the workbook does repetitively.

▶ Microsoft Access is better at handling large quantities of data than is Excel. Access manages data using a database and is one of the applications in the Microsoft Office suite of applications.

▶ A database contains rows and columns similar to a worksheet. In Access, a row is called a record and a column is called a field and has a field name.

▶ Access forms are created that display onscreen and provide a way for users to enter, view, and edit data in the database.

▶ Access reports are used to view data, generate calculations on the data, and generate summary information about the data. Reports can be viewed onscreen or printed.

Review Questions

Answer these questions to assess your skills and knowledge of the content covered in the chapter. Your instructor can provide you with the correct answers when you are ready to check your work.

1. What command on the Home ribbon can you use to cause a heading to span two columns on a worksheet?

2. What command on the View ribbon can you use to cause the first three rows of a worksheet to display as you scroll down through a long list of rows?

3. What command on the Home ribbon can you use to convert a range of cells to a table?

4. Data in a table can be sorted or filtered using drop-down menus for the data. What button do you click to see one of these drop-down menus?

5. What are two ways you can tell whether data in a table has been filtered?

6. How do you add a total row to a table?

7. What Excel function is used to insert a sum, average, or other summary information in a total row of a table?

8. What can you do to see a list of all names applied to cells or ranges of cells in a workbook?

9. Suppose cell A1 contains this formula: =IF(C3=D5, E10,F7). What value is displayed in cell A1 if cell C3 contains 25 and cell D5 contains 26?

10. When creating a formula on Sheet1, suppose you need to use cell A5 on Sheet3. How do you write this cell in the formula?

11. Suppose cell A10 contains this formula: =SUMIF(B10:B25, 13, C10:C25). No cells in column B contain 13. What value displays in cell A10?

12. Suppose cell A15 contains this formula: =CONCATENATE(E1,E2). Cell E1 contains "Fat." Cell E2 contains "Cat." What text displays in cell A15?

13. In question 12, what CONCATENATE formula is needed so that a space displays between the two words in cell A15?

14. Which type chart (pie, line, or bar) is *not* appropriate to show your weight gain or loss over one month?

15. Microsoft Access keeps data in a _____ file. The data is edited using an Access _____. Data is printed using an Access _____.

Chapter Mastery Project

Find out how well you have mastered the content in this chapter by completing this project. If you can answer all the questions and do all the steps without looking back at the chapter details, you have mastered this chapter. If you can complete the project by finding answers using the Excel Help window or the web, you have proven that you can teach yourself how to use Excel.

If you find you need a lot of help doing the project and you have not yet read the chapter or done the activities, drop back and start at the beginning of the chapter and then return to this project.

In this Mastery Project, you create the worksheets used by Adams Hardware to manage inventory purchases. The four worksheets are shown in Figure 11-28.

> **Hint** Several Excel functions are used in this mastery project. If you encounter a function you don't know about, such as SUMIF, enter the function name in the Excel Help search box.

Inventory table tracks hardware inventory

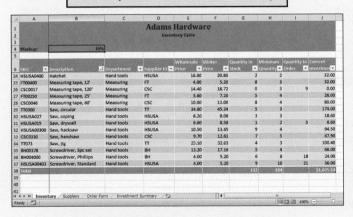

Suppliers table keeps data about suppliers

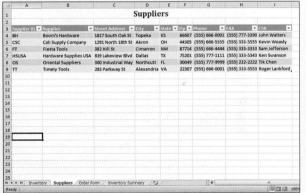

Order form is sent to supplier to order more inventory

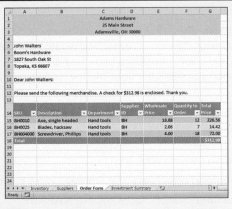

Inventory Summary shows inventory by supplier

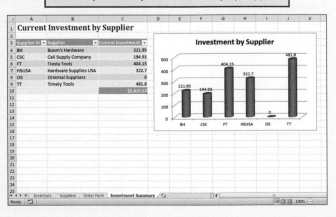

FIGURE 11-28
Adams Hardware uses four worksheets to manage inventory purchases.

Mastery Project Part 1: Using a Table to Manage Data

If you need help completing this part of the mastery project, review the "Using a Table to Manage Data" section in the chapter.

The Inventory worksheet for Adams Hardware is shown in Figure 11-29. Each type of stock item is assigned a SKU. Each supplier is assigned a Supplier ID.

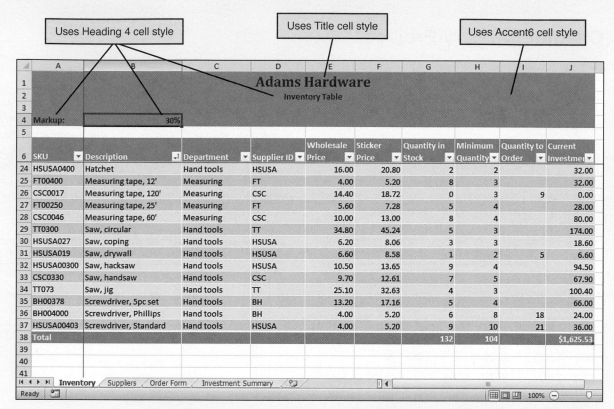

FIGURE 11-29
The Inventory worksheet tracks items in inventory and when it is time to order more items.

Tip SKU stands for Stock-Keeping Unit. The SKU uniquely identifies a type of item in stock.

Do the following to enter titles, column headings, and data in the worksheet:

Step 1. Enter and format the first four rows of the worksheet as shown in Figure 11-29. Use the Merge & Center command to center the titles in the first two rows.

Step 2. Cell B4 contains the markup value, which is 30%.

Step 3. The inventory data is stored in a Word document in the Sample Files folder on the DVD in the back of the book. The file is named **HardwareInventoryTable**. Copy and paste the data and column headings from the file into the worksheet beginning with cell A6. When you paste the data into the worksheet, match the destination formatting.

Step 4. Convert the data to an Excel table using the **Table Style Medium 14**.

Step 5. Format the Wholesale Price column as numbers with two decimal places.

Do the following to apply names and save the workbook file:

Step 1. Name the Excel table **InventoryTable**. Name this first worksheet **Inventory**.

Step 2. Cell B4 contains the percentage markup. Name the cell **MARKUP**.

Step 3. Save the workbook file to your hard drive, USB flash drive, SkyDrive, or another location given by your instructor. Name the file **HardwareStore**.

Do the following to adjust how the worksheet is viewed and add a total row:

Step 1. Apply text wrap to row 6.

Step 2. Adjust the column widths so all data and labels on the worksheet can be viewed.

Step 3. Apply **Freeze Panes** so that column A and rows 1 through 6 stay in view when you scroll down through rows or across through columns on the right.

Step 4. Add a total row to the table. In this row, add a sum for the Quantity in Stock column.

Do the following to work with the table data:

Step 1. Add a new row to the table using this data:

Column	Data
SKU	HSUSA00403
Description	Screwdriver, Standard
Department	Hand tools
Supplier ID	HSUSA
Wholesale Price	4.00
Quantity on Hand	9
Minimum Quantity	10

Step 2. Sort the rows in the table alphabetically by the Description column.

Step 3. Filter the data so that only **Hand tools** display.

Answer the following questions:

1. What is the total number Quantity in Stock?

2. What is the formula that Excel inserted into the total row to calculate this sum?

3. This formula contains the function number 109. What is the purpose of the 109 function number? What would happen if the value 109 were changed to 9?

Do the following to add columns for calculations to the table:

Step 1. Remove the filter on the data so that all rows display.

Step 2. Insert a new column in the table to the left of the **Quantity in Stock** column. Name the new column heading **Sticker Price**.

Step 3. Enter a formula in this column that calculates the sticker price. The calculated value is the **Wholesale Price** multiplied by the **MARKUP** plus **100%**. Be sure to use the column heading name Wholesale Price and the cell name MARKUP in the formula. What is the formula?

> **Tip** When data is converted to an Excel table, the column headings of the table can be used in formulas to refer to that column.

Step 4. Format the column as numbers with two decimal places.

Step 5. Add column I to the table. Name the column heading **Quantity to Order**.

Step 6. Use the IF function in the formula to calculate Quantity to Order. Use these three arguments for the IF function:

 ▶ *Logical_test:* The Quantity in Stock is less than the Minimum Quantity.

 ▶ *Value_if_true:* The Quantity to Order is three times the Minimum Quantity less the Quantity in Stock.

 ▶ *Value_if_false:* Enter a space in the cell.

What is the formula?

Step 7. Verify the formula is correct by checking row 37. Quantity in Stock is 9. Minimum Quantity is 10. Therefore, the Quantity to Order is 10*3–9=21. Cell I37 should display the value 21.

Step 8. Open the Name Manager box. How many names are listed in the box? What are these names?

Step 9. Add column J to the table. Name the column heading **Current Investment**. Enter the formula in the column for the calculation. The Current Investment is the **Wholesale Price** times the **Quantity in Stock**. Format the column using a number with two decimal places.

Step 10. Add a sum in the total row for Current Investment. Format this sum using **Currency**, **2** decimal places.

Step 11. Adjust column widths as needed so you can view the headings and data. The Inventory worksheet is complete. Don't forget to save your work often.

Mastery Project Part 2: Using Multiple Worksheets

If you need help completing this part of the mastery project, review the "Using Multiple Worksheets" section in the chapter.

The second worksheet is named Suppliers and contains a list of suppliers in a table. The completed worksheet is shown in Figure 11-30.

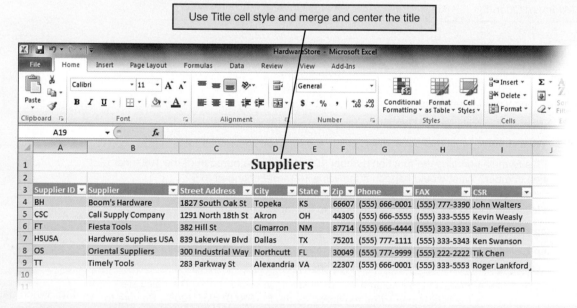

FIGURE 11-30
The Suppliers worksheet tracks information about each supplier.

Do the following to create the Suppliers worksheet:

Step 1. Name the second worksheet **Suppliers**.

Step 2. Enter the worksheet title **Suppliers** and format it as indicated in Figure 11-30.

Step 3. Open the Word document file **HardwareSuppliersTable** in the Sample Files folder on the DVD in the back of book. Copy the entire table into the Suppliers worksheet beginning with cell A3.

Step 4. Format the data as a table using the **Medium 6** table style. Name the table **SuppliersTable**.

Step 5. Format the Phone and FAX columns as phone numbers. Adjust column widths as necessary.

The third worksheet is named Order Form and is used to create a printed order to send to a supplier. The completed worksheet is shown in Figure 11-31.

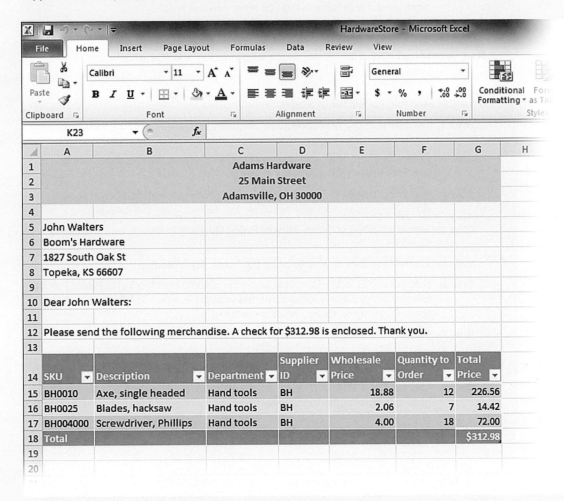

FIGURE 11-31
The Order Form worksheet is used to mail an order and check to a supplier.

Do the following to create the Order Form worksheet for the current order to Boom's Hardware:

Step 1. Name the third worksheet **Order Form**.

Step 2. Enter the three-row titles at the top of the worksheet. Center and format the titles as shown in Figure 11-31 using **40% - Accent6** and **Heading 4** cell styles.

Step 3. Enter a formula in cell A5 to copy the CSR into the cell. The CSR can be found in cell I4 on the Suppliers worksheet shown in Figure 11-30. What formula did you enter into cell A5?

Step 4. Enter a formula in cell A6 to copy the Supplier into the cell. The Supplier name can be found in cell B4 on the Suppliers worksheet shown in Figure 11-30. What formula did you enter into cell A6?

Step 5. Put a similar formula into cell A7 for the Street Address. What formula did you enter into cell A7?

Step 6. Use the CONCATENATE function to enter a formula into cell A8 to build the city, state, and zip address line. Use cells C4, D4, and E4 on the Suppliers worksheet. What formula did you enter into cell A8?

Step 7. Use the CONCATENATE function to enter a formula into cell A10 to build the Salutation line. Include in the formula the text "Dear " and cell I4 on the Supplier worksheet. What formula did you enter into cell A10?

> **Not Working?** Don't forget the space following the text "Dear".

Do the following to enter the list of orders:

Step 1. On the Inventory worksheet, filter the table to display inventory that is supplied by Boom's Hardware and Quantity to Order is greater than zero.

Step 2. Select and copy the table including the column headings through column I. Do not include the total row in the selection.

Step 3. Return to the Order Form worksheet and paste the selection beginning with cell A14. Copy values with source formatting. Do not copy the formulas.

Step 4. Delete the three columns **Sticker Price**, **Quantity in Stock**, and **Minimum Quantity**.

Step 5. Convert the data to a table using the **Table Style Medium 14**.

Step 6. Add column G to the table and name the column heading **Total Price**. Put a formula in the column to calculate the total price, which is **Wholesale Price** times **Quantity to Order**. What is the formula?

Step 7. Format column G in the table using numbers with two decimal places.

Step 8. Add a total row and make sure the sum appears in the total row for the Total Price column. Format this sum as currency with two decimal places.

Step 9. Use the CONCATENATE function to enter a formula into cell A12 to build a line of text. Include in the formula the text shown in Figure 11-31 and the cell on the current worksheet that has the total price for the order. What formula did you enter into cell A12?

> **Not Working?** If you are having problems with the CONCATENATE function, pay close attention to the double quotation marks. Make sure you have matching pairs.

Step 10. Apply text wrap to row 14 and adjust the column widths as necessary. Adjust the first three rows of the worksheet so the store name and address and the background color line up correctly over the table.

Step 11. Don't forget to save your work.

Mastery Project Part 3: Adding a Chart to a Worksheet

If you need help completing this part of the mastery project, review the "Adding a Chart to a Worksheet" section in the chapter.

The owner of Adams Hardware wants to know how much he has invested in inventory for each supplier. That information is shown in the Inventory Summary worksheet (see Figure 11-32).

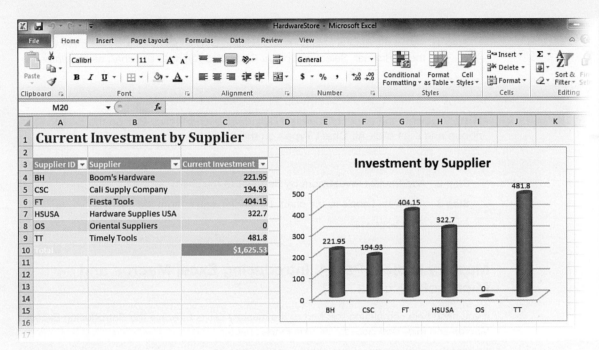

FIGURE 11-32
The Inventory Summary worksheet shows investments to supplier.

Do the following to create the Inventory Summary worksheet and add a chart:

Step 1. Create a fourth worksheet and name it **Inventory Summary**. Enter the worksheet title and format it using the Title cell style.

Step 2. Copy cells A3 through B9 in the SupplierTable on the Suppliers worksheet to the Inventory Summary worksheet beginning with cell A3.

Step 3. Convert the data on the Inventory Summary worksheet to a table using the **Table Style Medium 13**.

Step 4. Add a third column to the table naming the column heading **Current Investment**.

Step 5. Use the SUMIF function to enter a formula in the column to calculate the current investment. The SUMIF function has three arguments:

    a. *Range_to_search:* The Supplier ID column in the InventoryTable.

    b. *Criteria:* Cell A4, which identifies the supplier.

    c. *Range_to_sum:* The Current Investment column in the InventoryTable.

    What is the formula entered into cell C4?

Step 6. Add a total row to the table. Format the grand total for column C as currency with two decimal places. What is the grand total for current investments? Is this value the same total that is calculated on the Inventory worksheet when no filtering is applied?

Step 7. Adjust column width as necessary and don't forget to save your work.

Answer the following questions about which type chart to use on the worksheet:

    1. What type chart would you use to visualize the data in column C as the parts of a whole?

    2. Would a line chart be useful to represent the data in column C? Explain your answer.

    3. What type chart is best to use on this worksheet to identify high and low values in column C?

Do the following to insert a chart in the Inventory Summary worksheet:

Step 1. Select the data in column A and column C. Using that data, insert a bar chart in the worksheet. Select an upright **Clustered Cylinder** bar chart as shown earlier in Figure 11-32.

> **Hint** To locate the upright Clustered Cylinder bar chart, click **Bar** on the Insert ribbon and then click **All Chart Types** on the drop-down menu.

Step 2. Add the title **Investment by Supplier** to the chart.

Step 3. Add Data Labels to the chart. Delete the legend from the chart.

Step 4. Save your work.

Mastery Project Part 4: Introducing Excel Macros and Microsoft Access

If you need help completing this part of the mastery project, review the "Introducing Excel Macros and Microsoft Access" section in the chapter.

Answer the following questions about Excel macros and Microsoft Access:

1. What is the purpose of an Excel macro and why would you use one?

2. Looking at the HardwareStore workbook you built in this project, suppose you want to move this data from Excel to Access. Which two of the four worksheets do you think should be used to create two database tables? Why?

3. How does Access relate one table to another table in the same database?

4. Suppose the InventoryTable is converted to an Access database table. Which three columns would not be stored in the database? Why?

5. Which two worksheets might be used to build two Access reports?

6. What Access tool would you use to create a list of printed letters to mail to suppliers?

Becoming an Independent Learner

The most important skill learned in this chapter is how to teach yourself a computer skill. Rate yourself at Level A through E on how well you are doing with this skill. What is your level?

○ Level A: I was able to successfully complete the Chapter Mastery Project without the help of doing the On Your Own activities in the chapter.

○ Level B: I completed all the On Your Own activities and the Chapter Mastery Project without referring to any of the solutions in the *Solutions Appendix*.

○ Level C: I completed all the On Your Own activities and the Chapter Mastery Project by using just a few of the solutions in the *Solutions Appendix*.

○ Level D: I completed all the On Your Own activities and the Chapter Mastery Project by using many of the solutions in the *Solutions Appendix*.

○ Level E: I completed all the On Your Own activities and the Chapter Mastery Project and had to use all the solutions in the *Solutions Appendix*.

To continue toward the goal of teaching yourself computer skills, if you are not at Level A, try to move up one level on how you learn in Chapter 12, "Connecting to the Internet and Securing a Computer."

Projects to Help You

Now that you have mastered the material in this chapter, you are ready to tackle the three projects introduced at the beginning of the chapter in the section "How Will This Chapter Help Me?"

Project 1: Using Excel in Your Personal Life

Teaching yourself a computer skill requires exploring on your own and trying new things. Building on the skills you learned in the chapter and exploring on your own, do the following to enhance the HardwareStore workbook created in the Chapter Mastery Project:

Step 1. When the Quantity in Stock is less than the Minimum Quantity, it's time to order more stock. Use the Conditional Formatting command to highlight a cell in the Quantity in Stock column if the value in the cell is less than the Minimum Quantity. Highlight the cell using a green color.

Quantity in Stock	Minimum Quantity	Quantity to Order	Ci In
0.64	3	2	
4.54	0	4	12
2.97	2	2	
5.77	2	3	7
5.04	6	2	
2.68	2	3	7
3.39	1	1	
9.92	5	6	13
8.60	3	2	
2.78	5	4	
4.79	2	2	

PERSONAL PROJECT: I need to build an Excel worksheet that uses conditional formatting. I also want to dress up my worksheets with clip art. And I need to adjust print settings to make large worksheets easier to read when they are printed.

Hint To learn how to enter a conditional formatting formula, search Excel Help on **conditional formatting**.

Step 2. To dress up the Order Form worksheet, insert clip art on the worksheet appropriate for a hardware store.

Step 3. Adjust the Order Form worksheet so the sheet prints on one page using No Scaling.

Step 4. On the Order Form worksheet, insert a Page Break after row 19. Below row 19, build a new order form for another supplier, Cali Supply Company.

Step 5. Verify the two order forms print on two pages, one to a page.

Step 6. Adjust the Inventory worksheet so all columns print on one page. The worksheet rows spill over to a new page. To make printed pages easier to read, set the first six rows on the worksheet to print at the top of each page.

Step 7. Include a footer with a page number at the bottom of each printed page.

Project 2: Using Excel in Your Academic Career

Your instructor has asked for your help in checking some worksheets created by other students. In the Sample Files folder on the DVD in the back of the book, open the **Student01_ConsignmentShop** workbook file. Compare this student's work to the ConsignmentShop workbook you created in the chapter. Find and list the two errors on each worksheet for a total of eight errors.

Use these hints to help you find the errors:

1. Students often have problems with the Merge & Center command. Search for titles in the wrong columns or columns that are not merged.

ACADEMIC PROJECT: My instructor has asked me to help her grade some worksheets.
She specifically wants me to check for errors using tables and formulas in these tables. What types of errors do students typically make in these cases?

2. A common mistake when using the IF function is to put the last two arguments for the function in the wrong order. To view the formulas on a worksheet so you can check for errors, click **Show Formulas** on the Formulas ribbon.

3. To verify that data is formatted as a table, look for the drop-down arrows in the column heading row of the table.

4. Search for missing columns in tables.

5. When building a summary of information by category, make sure each category is represented.

6. Check for misspelled words used in titles, labels, and column headings.

7. Verify text wrap is used as directed.

8. Verify the Seller Statement prints on a single page and identify any problems you see.

Project 3: Using Excel in Your Technical Career

A great way to get an introduction to programming and to Visual Basic for Applications (VBA) is to record and use Excel macros. Do the following to find out about and create Excel macros:

TECHNICAL CAREER PROJECT: I want to take my knowledge of Excel a step further and learn to record and use a macro. Can I create a macro without using a programming language? Will Excel write the program for me?

Step 1. Open your browser and go to **office.com/training**. Click the link to **Excel 2010**, which is under Office 2010 online training. A list of videos about Excel appears.

Step 2. Scroll down the list and click the link **Save time by creating and running macros in Excel 2010**.

Step 3. Watch the four short videos about macros and answer the following questions:

    a. List the steps to display the Developer ribbon on the Excel window.

    b. Which button on the Developer ribbon do you click to record steps in a macro?

    c. What programming language does Excel use to record the steps in a macro?

Step 4. Using Excel, open a blank worksheet. Create a macro to type **Gently Used Consignment Shop** in any cell on the worksheet and format the cell using the **Title** cell style. What is the name you assigned the macro? Run the macro to test it.

Step 5. Create a second macro to type and format the consignment shop name and address on three rows as shown earlier in Figure 11-18. Name the macro **ShopAddress**. Run the macro to test it.

Step 6. View the list of macros. Select the **ShopAddress** macro and click **Edit** to see the code that Excel created for the macro. The code appears in a programming window where it can be edited. What is the name of the programming window?

Project to Help Others

One of the best ways to learn is to teach someone else. And, in teaching someone else, you are making a contribution into that person's life. As part of each chapter's work, you are encouraged to teach someone a skill you have learned. In this chapter, help someone learn to use Excel.

Who is your apprentice? _____

When helping others learn, don't do the work for them. Coach and instruct. Show them how to find information for themselves. Help them be as independent a learner as possible.

Do the following:

Step 1. Show your apprentice the worksheets you created in this chapter. Explain how a table is created and used to track data. Also show him the formulas you used in the worksheet and how you inserted a chart in the worksheet.

Step 2. If your apprentice is interested in building his own worksheet, help him design and create a worksheet of his choosing.

CHAPTER 12

Connecting to the Internet and Securing a Computer

IN THIS CHAPTER, YOU WILL

Connect a computer to the Internet

Secure a computer and its data

Secure a small home network

In previous chapters, you relied on a working computer that is already connected to the Internet. In these last three chapters of the book, you learn to take care of a computer and its Internet connection, fix a computer problem, and buy your own computer. In this chapter, you learn how to connect to the Internet and fix the connection when it stops working. You also learn how to secure your computer so your computer and its data stay safe.

As always, remember the most important computer skill is how to teach yourself a computer skill. Therefore, this chapter is designed to help you teach yourself how to make an Internet connection and secure your computer. Try to do each On Your Own activity without any help. But remember, if you need help, you can always refer to the solutions in the *Solutions Appendix*.

JUMP RIGHT IN

If you want even more of a challenge, try proceeding directly to the Chapter Mastery Project at the end of this chapter. If you need help on the project, refer to the On Your Own activities in the chapter or do your own independent investigating using Windows Help or searching the web for answers. When you complete the project, you will have mastered the skills in this chapter. Then go to the projects where you apply your skills to new situations.

How Will This Chapter Help Me?

These three projects focus on personal, academic, or technical career goals. Depending on your own interests, you might choose to complete any or all of them to help you achieve your goals.

PERSONAL PROJECT: I just bought a laptop, and my roommate already has a desktop computer. We want a small home network where we can share files between the two computers and both computers can connect to the Internet. What equipment do I need to set up a home network to the Internet?

ACADEMIC PROJECT: My study group meets every week in the student center. We all bring our laptops. When we want to share files, we email them to each other. Is there an easier way to share these files? Is there a way each team member can see the files on the other computers?

TECHNICAL CAREER PROJECT: I just moved to a new neighborhood, and I need Internet service. How do I get it? What equipment do I need to buy? Which is better, DSL or cable Internet?

Connecting a Computer to the Internet

When a single computer connects to the Internet, it can connect by way of a **local area network (LAN)**, or it can connect directly to a **wide area network (WAN)**. Let's first look at the different LAN and WAN technologies used, which are summarized in Table 12-1. Then you learn how to make an Internet connection.

> **local area network (LAN)**—A small network of computers and other connected devices covering a small area such as a home, business, school, or airport.
>
> **wide area network (WAN)**—A network that covers a large area. WANs are used to connect networks together such as when several businesses or homes connect to the Internet.

TABLE 12-1 Communication Technologies Used for Internet Connections

Technology	Used on a LAN	Used on a WAN	Wired	Wireless	Broadband Shared With
Ethernet	✔	—	✔	—	—
Wi-Fi	✔	—	—	✔	—
Dial-up	—	✔	✔	—	—
DSL	—	✔	✔	—	Telephone voice
Cable Internet	—	✔	✔	—	TV cable
Mobile broadband	—	✔	—	✔	Cellular voice
Satellite	—	✔	—	✔	—

Wired and Wireless Used on a LAN

When you connect a computer to the Internet at a school or business, you connect by way of a LAN. The connection to the LAN can be wireless or wired (see Figure 12-1). Some homes have a small network with wired and wireless connections. Computers on the local network can share resources such as a printer, a scanner, or data.

Looking at Figure 12-1, you can see a **router** is used to connect the LAN to another network (the Internet). The router is also used to tie together the computers in the network.

> **router**—A device used to connect one network to another.

router

A wired connection on a LAN uses a network cable, also called an **Ethernet** cable. A wireless connection on a LAN uses **Wi-Fi** technology.

Ethernet—A wired networking technology used for local networks. Currently, Ethernet transmits at 100 Mbps (megabits per second or million bits per second) or 1000 Mbps.

Wi-Fi—Wireless standards used for local networks. The latest Wi-Fi standard is called long-range Wi-Fi or 802.11n and has a range up to 1400 feet and transmits at 300 Mbps. The previous standard is called 802.11g and has a range up to 300 feet and transmits at 54 Mbps.

Local Area Network

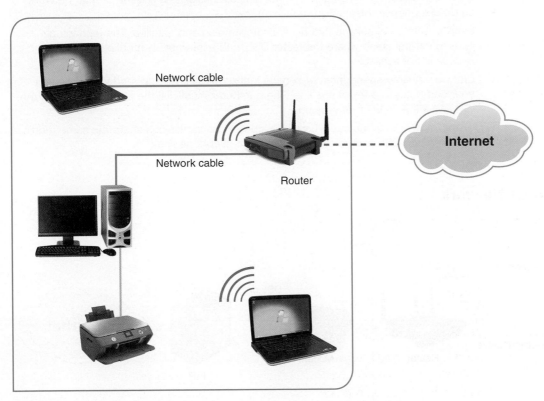

FIGURE 12-1
A wired or wireless connection to a local network connects to the Internet.

Wired and Wireless Used on a WAN

A single computer or network connects to the Internet by way of an **Internet service provider (ISP)**.

Internet service provider (ISP)—An organization that offers access to the Internet for a fee. Most often, an ISP offers email as part of the subscription service.

The ISP uses a WAN communication technology to make the connection. The technology used for the connection to the ISP might be **DSL**, **cable Internet**, **mobile broadband**, **satellite**, or **dial-up**. The most common are DSL and cable Internet (see Figure 12-2). DSL, cable Internet, and mobile broadband are examples of **broadband** technologies.

> **DSL (digital subscriber line)**—Internet service that uses regular telephone lines and shares these lines with voice.
>
> **cable Internet**—Internet service that uses TV cable lines and shares these lines with TV.
>
> **mobile broadband**—A type of Internet access that uses the same cellular network as do cell phones. Also called mobile Internet.
>
> **satellite**—Internet service that uses a satellite dish and satellite. The technology is used in rural areas where the faster DSL, cable Internet, or mobile broadband service is not available.
>
> **dial-up**—A slow-speed Internet service that requires a dial-up modem to connect your computer to a telephone line. The computer must dial the phone number of the ISP to initiate an Internet session.
>
> **broadband**—A technology where two types of transmissions share the same media. For example, DSL and voice share the same telephone lines.

Local Area Network

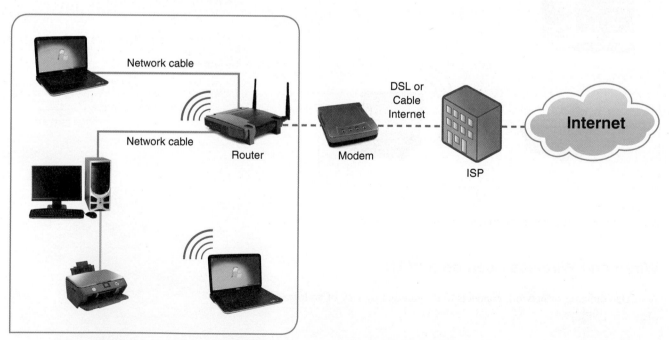

FIGURE 12-2
An ISP stands between a local network and the Internet.

Notice in Figure 12-2 a modem stands between the LAN and the DSL or cable lines. A **modem** is used to make the transition between two communication technologies. In this case, the modem translates between LAN communication and DSL or cable Internet communication.

> modem—A device that converts one type of communication signal to another.

modem

DSL, cable Internet, and dial-up create wired connections to an ISP. Wireless connections to an ISP can be by way of mobile broadband or satellite.

Now that you know a little about the technologies used, let's learn how to make the different type connections.

Manage Network Connections

Regardless of the communication technology used, all network connections are managed using the Windows Network and Sharing Center. An easy way to open this window is to click the network icon in the taskbar (see Figure 12-3).

This taskbar icon might indicate a wired ▤ or wireless ▥ connection. A red X over the icon indicates a problem with the connection. ▤

> **Not Working?** If you don't see the network icon in the taskbar, you can add it. To add an icon to the taskbar, click the white up arrow ▲ in the taskbar and click **Customize**. The Notifications Area Icons window appears. Change the behavior of the Network icon to **Show icon and notifications**.

When you click the icon, a box appears above it, as shown in Figure 12-3. In the box, click **Open Network and Sharing Center**. The Network and Sharing Center window opens (see Figure 12-4).

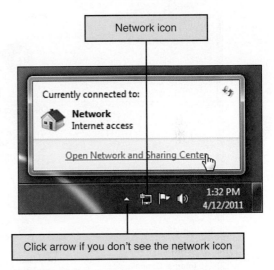

Network icon

Currently connected to:

Network
Internet access

Open Network and Sharing Center

1:32 PM
4/12/2011

Click arrow if you don't see the network icon

FIGURE 12-3
You can use the network icon in the taskbar to access the Network and Sharing Center.

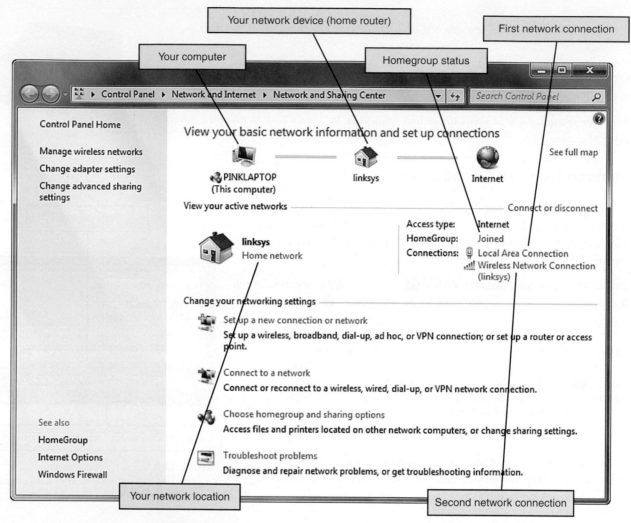

FIGURE 12-4
You can manage network connections using the Network and Sharing Center.

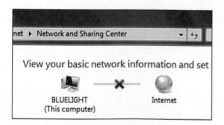

A problem with a network connection is indicated by a red X in this window. To fix the problem, click the red **X**, and Windows repairs the connection or offers suggestions to help you fix the problem.

When you first connect to a network, Windows wants to know the network location so it can set the security level for the network. In Figure 12-4, this option has been set to Home network. Click the setting to see the three choices (see Figure 12-5). These choices are

▶ **Home network.** Other computers on the network can see you, and you can join a **homegroup**. Use this setting when you want to share files or a printer with other computers in a small local network.

▶ **Work network.** Other computers on the network can see you, and you can join a **Windows domain**. You cannot join a homegroup using this setting. Use this setting when connected to a corporate or business network managed by a network administrator.

> **homegroup**—A Windows feature that allows you to share data and other resources with other computers on a local network.
>
> **Windows domain**—A Windows feature used by large corporations to manage the computers, data, and other resources on the corporate network.

▸ **Public network.** Other computers on the network cannot see you. You cannot join a homegroup or Windows domain. Use this setting when connected to any public network—for example, at a hotel or coffee shop.

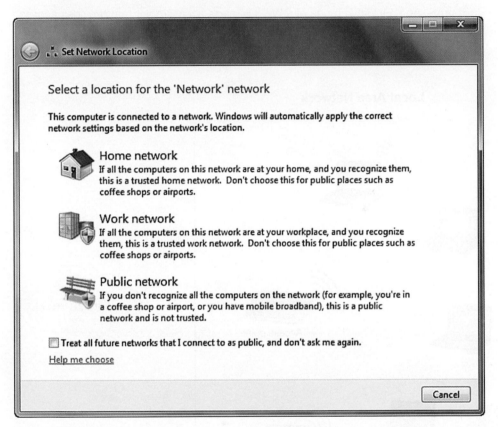

FIGURE 12-5
Tell Windows the network location so it can set the security level for the network.

Examine your computer's network connections and settings and answer these questions:

1. Is the network icon showing in the taskbar? If not, add the icon to the taskbar.
2. Does the network icon in the taskbar indicate a wireless or wired connection?
3. How many network connections do you have?
4. What is the current setting for your network location?
5. Does the Network and Sharing Center report a problem with connectivity? If so, click the red **X** to fix the problem.
6. What happens when you click the Internet icon?
7. What happens when you click the icon for your computer?

On Your Own 12-1
Examine Network Connections and Settings

? Solutions Appendix

For help, see Solution 12-1: How to Examine Network Connections and Settings.

wireless access point

Make a New Wireless Connection

Suppose you want to use the free Wi-Fi service at your local coffee shop to connect your laptop to the Internet. The coffee shop uses a **wireless access point** to provide this **hotspot**. The access point connects to the coffee shop's local network and on to the Internet (see Figure 12-6).

> **wireless access point**—A device that allows a wireless computer, printer, or other device to connect to a network.
>
> **hotspot**—An area within range of a Wi-Fi wireless access point that provides access to a local network. Hotspots can be used at home, in a park, in an office building, or in a restaurant.

Local Area Network

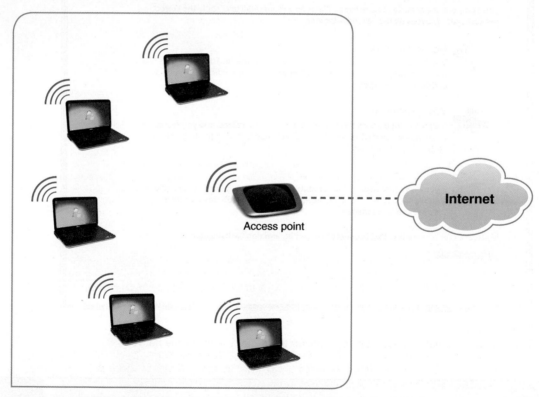

Access point

Internet

FIGURE 12-6
A coffee shop offers a public wireless hotspot.

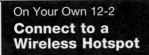

On Your Own 12-2

**Connect to a
Wireless Hotspot**

You can do this activity if you have a wireless computer inside a wireless hotspot. Do the following to connect the wireless computer to a wireless network and on to the Internet:

 Video **12-2**

Step 1. If the computer has a wireless switch, turn on the wireless switch.

Step 2. Click the network icon in the taskbar. A list of wireless networks in the area appears. Connect to one of these networks.

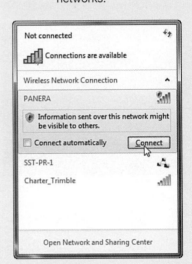

Step 3. If the wireless network is secured, you must enter a password, called the Network Security Key, to use the network. If the network is not secured, no password is required.

Step 4. If the network is not secure, you have no idea who might be using it. To protect your computer and its data, set the network location to **Public network**. If the network is secured and you know and trust other users of the network, set the location to **Home network**.

Tip Never set the network location to Home network unless the hotspot is secured with a password. Even if the hotspot is in your own home, people outside the walls of your house might be using it. Later in the chapter, you learn how to secure your own wireless network so a password is required.

Step 5. After you complete the connection, open **Internet Explorer** and try to surf the web. Some public hotspots require you to agree to the terms of use. If so, a web page appears when you first open Internet Explorer. You must agree to the terms before you can use the network (see Figure 12-7).

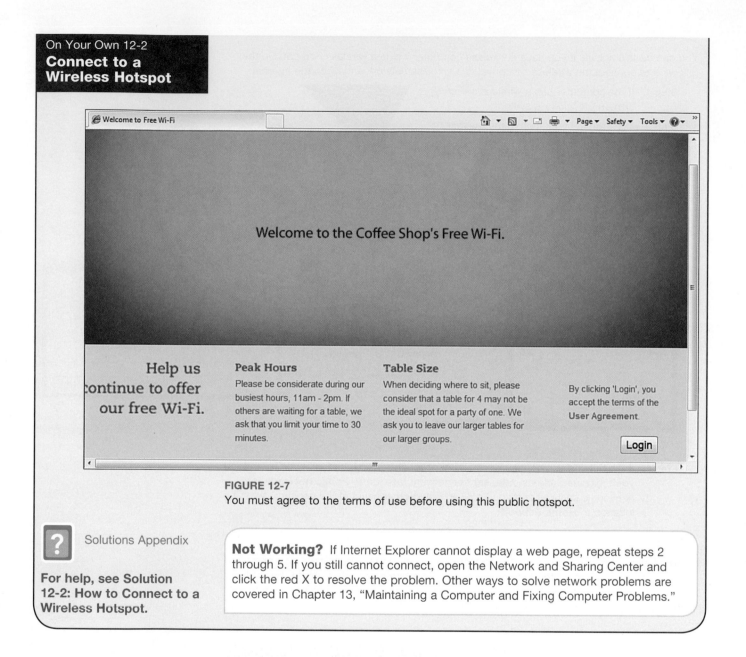

On Your Own 12-2
Connect to a Wireless Hotspot

Welcome to Free Wi-Fi

Page ▾ Safety ▾ Tools ▾

Welcome to the Coffee Shop's Free Wi-Fi.

Help us continue to offer our free Wi-Fi.

Peak Hours

Please be considerate during our busiest hours, 11am - 2pm. If others are waiting for a table, we ask that you limit your time to 30 minutes.

Table Size

When deciding where to sit, please consider that a table for 4 may not be the ideal spot for a party of one. We ask you to leave our larger tables for our larger groups.

By clicking 'Login', you accept the terms of the User Agreement.

Login

FIGURE 12-7
You must agree to the terms of use before using this public hotspot.

? Solutions Appendix

For help, see Solution 12-2: How to Connect to a Wireless Hotspot.

Not Working? If Internet Explorer cannot display a web page, repeat steps 2 through 5. If you still cannot connect, open the Network and Sharing Center and click the red X to resolve the problem. Other ways to solve network problems are covered in Chapter 13, "Maintaining a Computer and Fixing Computer Problems."

Make a Wired Connection

When connecting to a wired network, connect the network cable to the network port on the computer and to the network device. Some computers have one or two lights near the network port to indicate network activity (see Figure 12-8). If the lights are not on, check the cable connections at both ends. When Windows detects connectivity, it automatically sets up the wired connection.

FIGURE 12-8
The lights near the network port indicate network activity.

You can do this activity if your computer is connected to a wired network. Do the following:

Step 1. Does your computer have lights near the network port? If so, what is the status of these lights?

Step 2. Open the **Network and Sharing Center** window. Does Windows report a problem with network connectivity? If so, click the red **X** to solve the problem.

Step 3. Unplug the network cable. If you have wireless connectivity, turn off the wireless switch or disconnect from the wireless network.

Step 4. Windows reports a problem with network connectivity. What is the status of the network indicator lights? Click the red **X**. What useful information does Windows offer to fix the problem?

Step 5. Fix the problem and verify that Internet access has been restored.

For help, see Solution 12-3: How to Verify Your Wired Network Connection.

 Solutions Appendix

Make a Mobile Broadband Connection

Mobile broadband connections use **cellular networks** that are also used by cell phones. To use mobile broadband, you must subscribe to a data service with a wireless provider such as AT&T, Verizon, or Sprint. The data service might use the 3G standards or the faster **4G** standards for data transfers.

> **cellular network**—A wireless network made available by towers and first used by cell phones. Each tower covers the area around it, which is called a cell.
>
> **4G**—The latest standard used for data transfers over a cellular network. 4G networks have a range large enough to cover an entire city. 4G is expected to replace cable Internet and DSL as a way to wirelessly connect a computer or small network to the Internet. Two competing technologies that meet 4G standards are WiMAX and LTE.

Some laptop computers come with the ability to access mobile broadband built in. The technology used is **WiMAX** or **LTE**. To use the feature, you must sign up for a data plan with a wireless provider that supports WiMAX or LTE.

> **WiMAX**—A wireless technology used by Sprint and other carriers to support a 4G network.
>
> **LTE**—A wireless technology used by Verizon, AT&T, and other carriers to support a 4G network.

Some laptop computers have support for WiMAX and/or LTE built in. If the technology is not built in, you can use an external mobile broadband device. Four external devices that a computer can use for mobile broadband connections are shown in Figure 12-9.

The four devices and their setups are described next. To use any of these devices, you must sign up for a data plan with a wireless provider.

▶ **Cell phone tethering.** If your cell phone can handle data and has a data port, you can connect it to your laptop. The phone is said to be tethered to the laptop and serves as the middle-man between the cellular network and laptop. The connection uses a USB cable. If your cell phone and computer both use **Bluetooth**, the cable is not needed. Your cell phone company might require a separate data plan for Internet tethering, and you might need to install an app on your cell phone and/or software on your computer.

a. Cell phone tethered to the computer

b. Portable mobile broadband modem

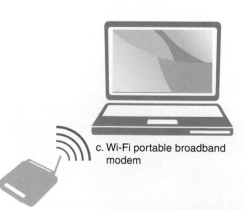

c. Wi-Fi portable broadband modem

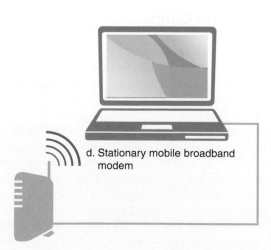

d. Stationary mobile broadband modem

FIGURE 12-9
These four external devices allow a computer to use mobile broadband.

> **Bluetooth**—A wireless technology with a short range that is used to connect personal wireless devices to a computer—for example, to connect a cell phone, wireless keyboard, or wireless printer.

▶ **Portable mobile broadband modem.** Plug the **mobile broadband modem** into your computer to connect it to the cellular network. To use the device, you must subscribe to a data service with a carrier that supports the device.

> **mobile broadband modem**—A device that connects a computer or network to a cellular network. The modem might be portable or stationary. It might connect to a computer using USB, Bluetooth, or another type connection. It goes by many names, including wireless Internet card, laptop connect card, USB broadband modem, and AirCard.

▶ **Wi-Fi portable broadband modem.** The modem uses a battery and is small enough to hold in your hand. It connects to the cellular network and creates a Wi-Fi hotspot that can be used by several Wi-Fi computers. Use it to create your own mobile Wi-Fi hotspot.

▶ **Stationary mobile broadband modem.** This type of modem plugs into an electrical outlet and is used to connect a local network to a cellular network. The computers on the LAN can connect using Wi-Fi or network cables. Use this type of modem as a substitution for DSL or cable Internet.

Now that you know how a computer connects to the Internet, let's focus on securing that connection.

Securing a Computer and Its Data

As you learned in Chapter 2, "Finding and Using Information on the Web," the Internet is a dangerous place where viruses and thieves abound. The three most important ways to keep your computer and its data safe are to

▶ **Use antivirus software.** You learned how to install, update, and run antivirus and antispyware software in Chapter 2.

▶ **Secure your network connection.** Recall from earlier in this chapter that you can set your network location to a public network when connected to a network that strangers might be using.

▶ **Keep Windows updated.** These updates can plug security leaks.

Recall from Chapter 2 that other ways to stay safe when using the web are to use strong passwords for all your online accounts and be careful to buy or download only from websites you trust. In Chapter 6, "Communicating with Others Using the Internet," you learned to use caution when opening an email attachment or clicking a link in an email message.

In this part of the chapter, you learn how to keep Windows updated and how to back up your data in the event the data on your computer gets lost or corrupted. You also learn how to set up a standard user account that offers more protection for your computer than does an administrator account.

Keep Windows Updated

Microsoft releases updates to Windows on its website. These updates improve Windows features and solve known problems with the OS. If a security hole is discovered in Windows, Microsoft fixes the problem and releases a **patch** to plug the hole.

> **patch**—An update to software to fix a known problem (or bug) in the software. These problems might allow hackers or viruses to attack the computer.

Windows can be set to automatically download and install updates when your computer is connected to the Internet. Sometimes you must restart your computer for these updates to be installed. If so, expect to see a message on your screen similar to that in Figure 12-10.

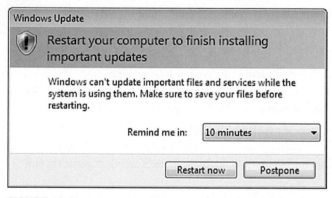

FIGURE 12-10
You must restart the computer so Windows can install its updates.

Occasionally, Microsoft releases a collection of major updates called a **service pack**. At the time of this writing, Microsoft has released one service pack for Windows 7 called Service Pack 1. Windows does not install a service pack or an optional update unless you agree to the installation.

> **service pack**—In Windows or Office, a collection of updates delivered as a single installation package. These updates might include improvements to the software and solutions to known problems.

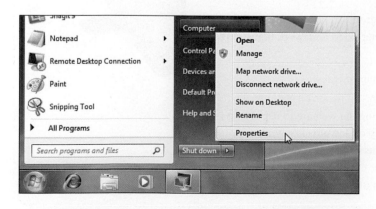

Updates might not be current on your computer. To find out whether service packs are already installed, use the System window. To access the window, click **Start**, right-click **Computer,** and select **Properties** from the shortcut menu. The System window appears which displays information about the system (see Figure 12-11). If a service pack is installed, it is listed on this window.

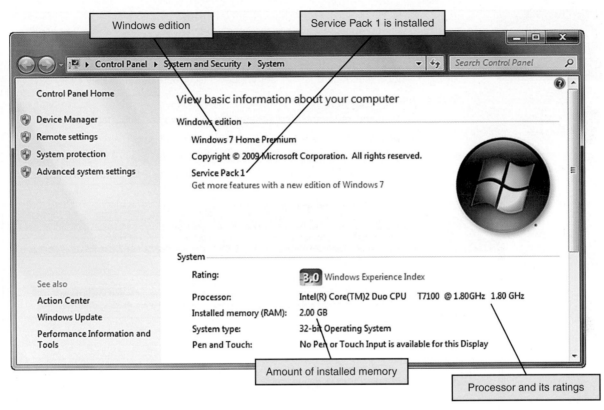

FIGURE 12-11
The System window shows information about the system and reports Service Pack 1 is installed.

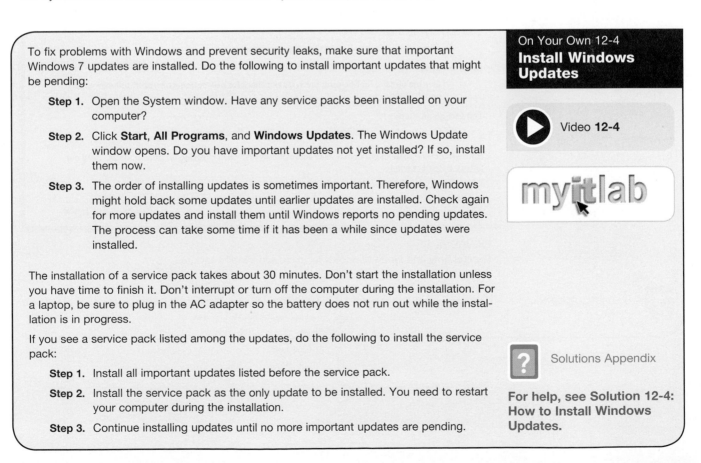

To fix problems with Windows and prevent security leaks, make sure that important Windows 7 updates are installed. Do the following to install important updates that might be pending:

Step 1. Open the System window. Have any service packs been installed on your computer?

Step 2. Click **Start**, **All Programs**, and **Windows Updates**. The Windows Update window opens. Do you have important updates not yet installed? If so, install them now.

Step 3. The order of installing updates is sometimes important. Therefore, Windows might hold back some updates until earlier updates are installed. Check again for more updates and install them until Windows reports no pending updates. The process can take some time if it has been a while since updates were installed.

The installation of a service pack takes about 30 minutes. Don't start the installation unless you have time to finish it. Don't interrupt or turn off the computer during the installation. For a laptop, be sure to plug in the AC adapter so the battery does not run out while the installation is in progress.

If you see a service pack listed among the updates, do the following to install the service pack:

Step 1. Install all important updates listed before the service pack.

Step 2. Install the service pack as the only update to be installed. You need to restart your computer during the installation.

Step 3. Continue installing updates until no more important updates are pending.

On Your Own 12-4
Install Windows Updates

▶ Video **12-4**

myitlab

? Solutions Appendix

For help, see Solution 12-4: How to Install Windows Updates.

On Your Own 12-5
**Verify or Change
Windows Update
Settings**

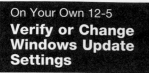

To make sure your computer always has the latest updates, set Windows to automatically install updates daily. Do the following:

Step 1. Click **Change settings** on the Windows Update window. In the Change settings window (see Figure 12-12), set Windows to update automatically every day.

Step 2. Apply these additional settings:

▶ Install recommended updates the same way as important updates.

▶ Allow all users to install updates on this computer.

▶ If you have other Microsoft software installed such as Microsoft Office 2010, set Windows to update this software when it updates Windows.

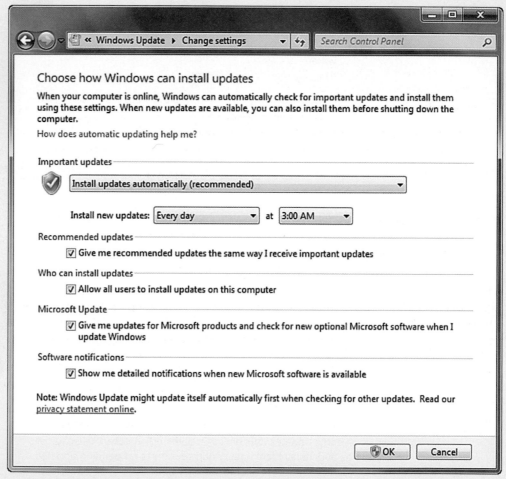

FIGURE 12-12
Control how and when Windows receives and installs updates.

? Solutions Appendix   **For help, see Solution 12-5: How to Verify or Change Windows Update Settings.**

Back Up Important Data

If you keep important data on your computer, be prepared in case the data is accidentally deleted, the computer is lost or stolen, or the data gets corrupted. Keep at least two copies of important data. Store this **backup** of your data on a different media than the original data.

> **backup**—An extra copy of a data file stored on a different storage media. To be extra safe, keep the second storage media at a different location—for example, at a relative's house.

Four general ways to maintain a backup of your data are to

- ▶ **Use an online backup service.** Whenever you connect your computer to the Internet, the service automatically syncs your data files with copies it keeps in the cloud. You pay for the monthly or yearly subscription. Examples of websites that provide reliable online backup services are mozy.com, carbonite.com, and idrive.com. An online backup service is the most reliable and most expensive backup method.

- ▶ **Use Windows Backup and Restore or other backup software.** You can set the software to automatically copy folders on your hard drive to a different storage media.

- ▶ **Manually make copies of the data files on your computer.** This method requires you remember to copy the data to a second media on a regular basis.

- ▶ **Keep your data in the cloud.** Cloud-computing sites keep backups of your data. For example, Windows Live automatically backs up the data kept on a SkyDrive in the event something happens to the server holding your SkyDrive. This method assumes you trust Windows Live to protect your important data.

> **Tip** When deciding what data you want to back up, think about what it would be like to lose those photos, videos, Internet Explorer favorites, email addresses, tax records, or other important documents stored on your computer. If you can't get along without it, back it up.

Use Windows Backup and Restore to back up your Documents library and other important data to a USB flash drive, external hard drive, CD, or other location. To set up a backup using the Windows Backup and Restore utility, you must log on with an administrator account or provide the password to an administrator account. You learned about administrator accounts in Chapter 2.

Do the following:

Step 1. Open the Windows Backup and Restore window. If no backup schedule has been set up on this computer, the window looks like that in Figure 12-13.

Step 2. Set up a backup schedule to run each day to back up the following:

- ▶ Your Documents library
- ▶ The items on your Windows desktop
- ▶ Your Internet Explorer favorites
- ▶ All the email messages and addresses kept by Outlook installed on your computer

Step 3. The backup happens daily unless you turn off the schedule. You can also back up at any time. To do that, on the Backup and Restore window, click **Back up now**.

On Your Own 12-6
Use Windows Backup and Restore

On Your Own 12-6
Use Windows Backup and Restore

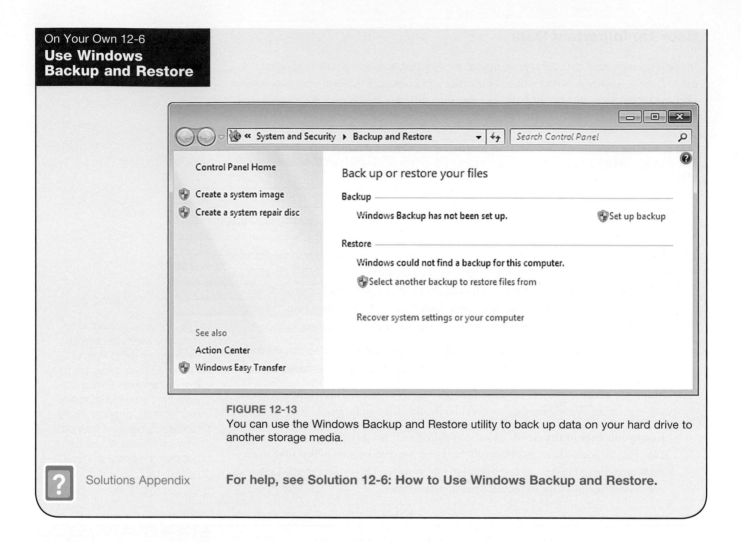

FIGURE 12-13
You can use the Windows Backup and Restore utility to back up data on your hard drive to another storage media.

? Solutions Appendix   **For help, see Solution 12-6: How to Use Windows Backup and Restore.**

If you lose your data or it gets corrupted, you can restore it from backup. First, make sure you really want to restore the data because the process overwrites the original file or folder with the backup version. To be safe, first copy the original file or folder to a different location so you can backtrack if necessary.

Two ways you can recover your data are to

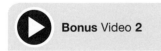

▶ **Use the Backup and Restore window.** In the window, click **Restore my files**. Follow directions onscreen to select folders or files to restore, or restore all the folders and files in the backup.

▶ **Use Windows Explorer.** This method works when the original file or folder still exists but might be corrupted. Right-click this original file or folder and select **Properties** from the shortcut menu. In the Properties box, click the **Previous Version** tab. A list of backup files or folders appears. Select the one you want and click **Restore** (see Figure 12-14). The backup overwrites the original.

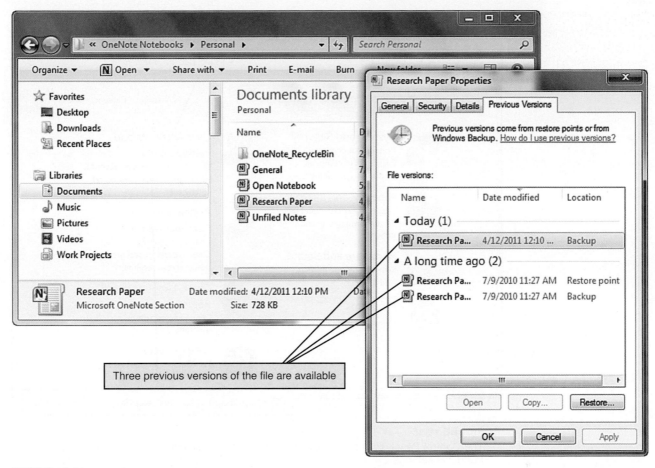

FIGURE 12-14
Use the Previous Versions tab on the Properties box to recover a corrupted file.

When you restore a file or folder using either method, remember the backup overwrites the original. To keep from losing the original, make a copy of it first before you restore it from backup. If the backup is not what you expected, you can return to the original.

Set Up a Standard User Account and Manage Passwords

Recall from Chapter 2 that an administrator user account in Windows has more rights than does a standard user account. When you are responsible for a computer, you need an administrator account to install or uninstall software, change Windows settings, and perform other administrative tasks.

If other people use your computer, set up a standard account for each user. Each user then has his own libraries to hold his data and can set all his user preferences the way he likes. And the limited rights on the standard account prevent other users from making changes to the computer that you don't know about or approve.

Use the Windows **Control Panel** (see Figure 12-15) to change Windows settings, including adding or removing a user account or resetting a user password.

> **Control Panel**—A window used to adjust computer settings. To open the window, click **Start** and click **Control Panel**.

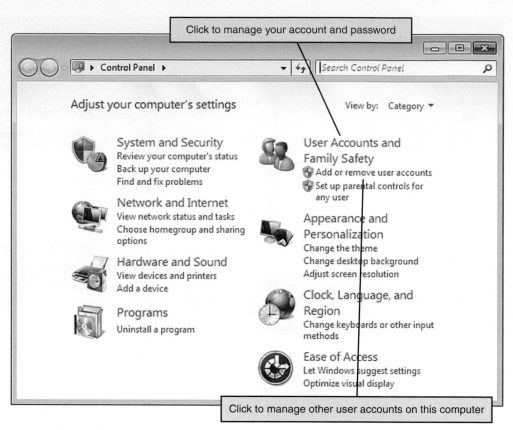

FIGURE 12-15
The Control Panel gives access to many Windows utilities and allows you to change
Windows settings.

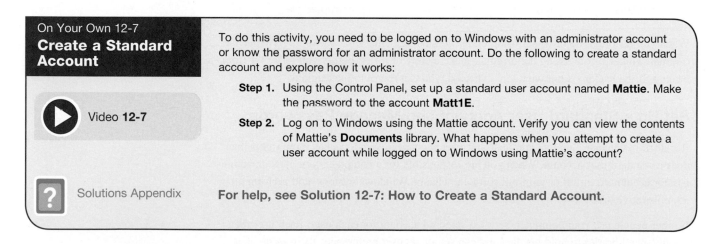

On Your Own 12-7
Create a Standard Account

Video **12-7**

? Solutions Appendix

To do this activity, you need to be logged on to Windows with an administrator account
or know the password for an administrator account. Do the following to create a standard
account and explore how it works:

Step 1. Using the Control Panel, set up a standard user account named **Mattie**. Make
the password to the account **Matt1E**.

Step 2. Log on to Windows using the Mattie account. Verify you can view the contents
of Mattie's **Documents** library. What happens when you attempt to create a
user account while logged on to Windows using Mattie's account?

For help, see **Solution 12-7: How to Create a Standard Account.**

To keep other users from logging on using your account, be sure to assign a strong password to your administrator account. To be safe, you need to occasionally change this password. In addition, a user might forget her password. If this happens and you are responsible for the computer, you can reset her password. Do the following:

On Your Own 12-8
Manage Windows Passwords

Step 1. Log on to your Windows account and change your password. Recall that a strong password contains upper- and lowercase letters and numbers.

Step 2. Suppose Mattie changed her password and you do not know it. She calls you to say she has forgotten her password. Reset the password to **changeme**. When you tell Mattie the new password, remind her to change it to a stronger password when she first logs in.

 Video **12-8**

For help, see Solution 12-8: How to Manage Windows Passwords.

? Solutions Appendix

Securing a Small Home Network

If you have Internet access in your home, most likely you are using DSL or cable Internet to connect to the Internet. More than one computer in your home might share this Internet connection. In this part of the chapter, you learn to secure a wireless home network and share data and a printer with other computers in your home.

> **Hint** How to buy the equipment and set up a home network are not covered in this chapter because there are so many situations and options to cover. Begin by subscribing to an Internet service (for example, DSL, cable Internet, or mobile broadband). When you subscribe to the service, the ISP sells you the right equipment and helps you set it up.
>
> After you have one computer connected to the Internet, it's time to set up your home network. Begin the process by buying a wireless home router. Projects at the end of this chapter can help you get started with setting up your home network.

Secure a Wireless Network

A small home network might use one or more network devices to control the network; they include

- ▶ A DSL modem or cable modem used to connect your home network to your ISP. Recall that a DSL modem uses a phone line to connect to a telephone jack. A cable modem uses a TV cable to connect to a TV wall jack.

- ▶ A router that allows multiple computers to connect in a network and connects that network to the DSL modem or cable modem. A **wireless router** allows for both wired and wireless connections. See Figure 12-16.

> **wireless router**—A network device that allows several wired or wireless computers to connect in a local network. It also connects this network to another network such as the Internet.

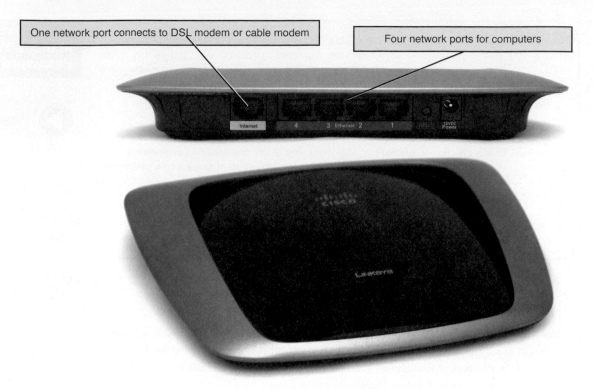

One network port connects to DSL modem or cable modem

Four network ports for computers

FIGURE 12-16

This wireless router designed for a home network connects wireless computers and up to four wired computers in a network.

One setup for a small network is shown in Figure 12-17. A laptop and desktop computer are connected to a wireless router. The router serves as the wireless access point for wireless computers to connect to the network. The router connects to a DSL modem or cable modem, which connects to the Internet.

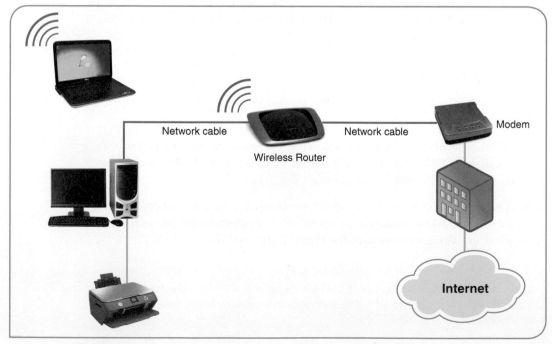

Network cable

Network cable

Modem

Wireless Router

Internet

FIGURE 12-17

This small home network has a wireless router and connects to the Internet.

A wireless network needs to be secured because the wireless range extends past the walls of your home. The wireless range can be up to 1400 feet depending on the Wi-Fi standard used, the strength of the wireless device, and the interference around it. Computers in your neighborhood might be able to connect to your wireless network, use your Internet connection, and copy the data stored on your computers.

Tip Thieves might steal your data and use your unsecured network for illegal activities on the web. These activities can be traced back to you as the owner of the ISP account.

You can do this activity if you have access to a wireless router in a small home network. Do the following to secure the wireless network:

Step 1. Look in the router's user guide and find this information needed to access the router setup program:

  a. The **IP address** of the router—for example, 192.168.1.1.

  b. The router password. You must have this password to view the router setup screens and make any changes.

Step 2. Use a computer that has a wired connection to the router. Open **Internet Explorer**. Enter the IP address of the router in the IE address box. In the Windows Security box that appears, enter the password to the router. For most routers, you do not need to enter the User Name. Click **OK**.

Step 3. The router setup main menu appears. If the router's password is that assigned by the router manufacturer and has not yet been changed, change the password. This standard password is easy for others to guess. You do not want a hacker to hijack your router.

Step 4. Find the window that sets up the wireless security for the router, such as that shown in Figure 12-18. Yours might look different. Assign a password to the wireless network. If you have a choice for the security mode used, know that **WPA2** provides better security than WPA, which is better than the older WEP mode. Save your changes and exit the router setup program.

Step 5. Test your security by using a wireless computer to connect to the network. When you first attempt the connection, you must enter the password to the wireless network. Recall that Windows calls that password the Security Key or the Network Security Key.

On Your Own 12-9
Secure a Wireless Network

▶ Video **12-9**

IP address—Four numbers separated by periods, such as 192.168.1.103. The address can be used to identify a computer or other device on a network.

Tip Write down the password to your wireless network and keep it in a safe place. A good place to record it is on the router documentation.

WPA2—A method of encrypting data on a wireless network so that hackers cannot intercept and read data in transmission. WPA2 stands for Wi-Fi Protected Access, Version 2.

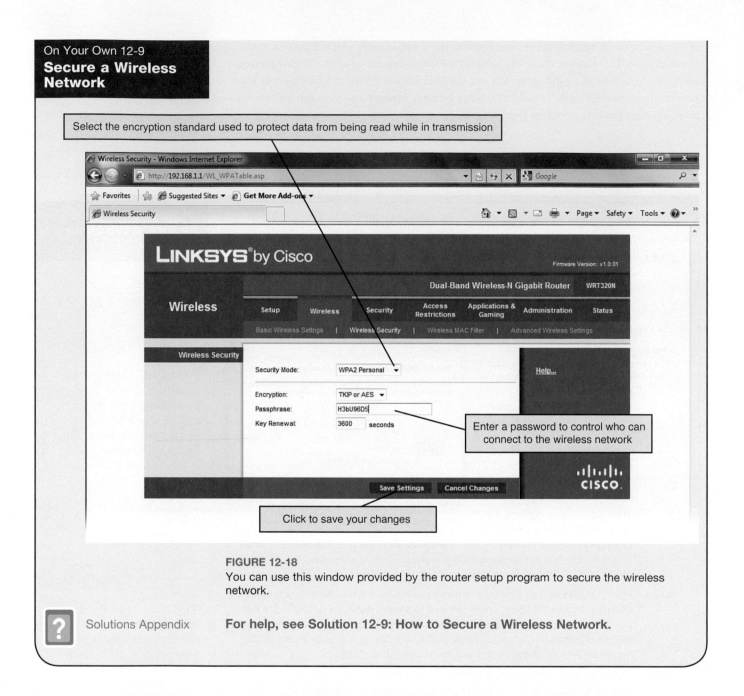

On Your Own 12-9
Secure a Wireless Network

Select the encryption standard used to protect data from being read while in transmission

Enter a password to control who can connect to the wireless network

Click to save your changes

FIGURE 12-18
You can use this window provided by the router setup program to secure the wireless network.

Solutions Appendix   **For help, see Solution 12-9: How to Secure a Wireless Network.**

Use a Homegroup to Share Your Data and Printer

Tip Windows Vista and Windows XP do not support homegroups. If you have Vista or XP computers on your network, you must use more complex methods of sharing that are not covered in this book.

Now that your home network is secure, you might want to share your data and perhaps a printer with other computers connected to your network. Windows offers several methods to share resources. A Windows homegroup is the easiest method to set up and to use.

The first computer that attempts to join a homegroup assigns the password to the homegroup. Windows 7 computers on the network use this password to join the homegroup and then share specific libraries, folders, or files with the homegroup.

Windows 7 comes in several editions, including Windows 7 Starter, Windows 7 Home Basic, Windows 7 Home Premium, and Windows 7 Professional. Windows 7 Starter and Home Basic cannot create a homegroup, but they can join one after it is created. Windows 7 Home Premium and Professional can create and join a homegroup.

Use Windows Explorer to access the shared resources. Look in the Homegroup area of Windows Explorer to see these resources (see Figure 12-19).

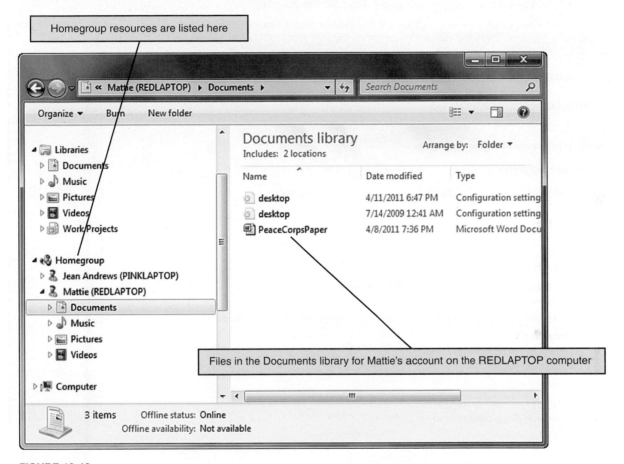

FIGURE 12-19
The Homegroup area of Windows Explorer shows resources shared by other computers on the network.

You can do this activity working with a partner using two Windows 7 computers connected to a network. One of the two computers must be running Windows 7 Home Premium or Windows 7 Professional.

Do the following to set up and use a homegroup:

Step 1. On each computer, use the Network and Sharing Center to verify the network location is set to **Home network** and to join the homegroup. Share the Pictures, Documents, Music, and Videos libraries with the homegroup. If your computer has a printer connected, share the printer with the homegroup.

Video **12-10**

On Your Own 12-10
Use a Homegroup to Share Data

Step 2. To manage a homegroup, click **Homegroup** in the left pane of the Network and Sharing Center. The HomeGroup window appears (see Figure 12-20). Using this window, you can view the homegroup password, leave the homegroup, and change what you share with the homegroup. What is the password to your homegroup?

Step 3. Test the homegroup by using Windows Explorer to copy a file from the **Documents** library on one computer to the **Documents** library on the other computer. What file did you copy?

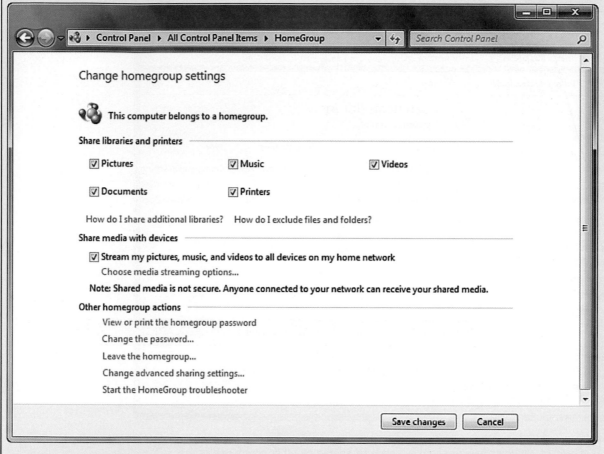

FIGURE 12-20
Use the HomeGroup window to view the homegroup password and to manage the homegroup.

For help, see Solution 12-10: How to Use a Homegroup to Share Data.

Solutions Appendix

If you want to share other folders with the homegroup, use Windows Explorer to locate the folder. Right-click the folder and click **Share with** in the shortcut menu. Then click **Homegroup (Read)** or click **Homegroup (Read/Write)**, as shown in Figure 12-21.

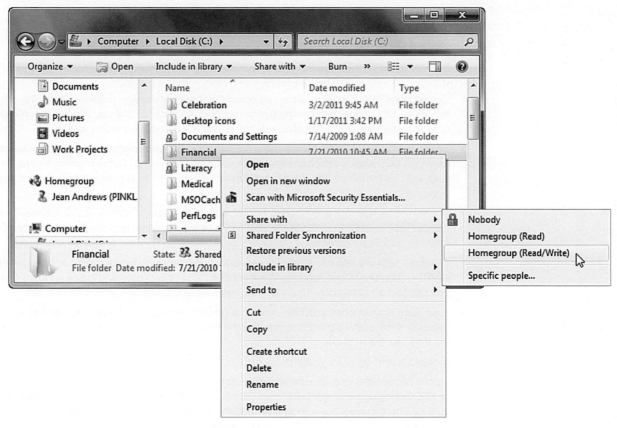

FIGURE 12-21
Use Windows Explorer to share a folder with the homegroup.

To know whether a folder is shared, select the folder. Its shared status appears at the bottom of the Windows Explorer window.

Summary

Connecting a Computer to the Internet

▶ A computer connects to the Internet by way of a local area network (LAN) or wide area network (WAN). The connection can be wired or wireless.

▶ Connections to the Internet are made through an Internet service provider (ISP). The connection might use DSL, cable Internet, mobile broadband, satellite, or dial-up. The most common technologies used are DSL and cable Internet, which are broadband technologies.

▶ Broadband Internet connections share the same media with another type of transmission. For example, DSL shares telephone lines with voice transmissions. Cable Internet shares TV cable lines with TV transmissions. Mobile broadband shares a cellular network with voice transmissions.

▶ The Windows Network and Sharing Center is used to manage network connections. The network taskbar icon is used to indicate the status of a network connection. You can use it to access the Network and Sharing Center.

▶ Windows sets the security level of a network according to its location. The options for the network location are Home network, Work network, and Public network. Using a Home network, you can join a homegroup. Using a Work network, you can join a Windows domain.

▶ A wireless access point provides a hotspot where a wireless computer can connect to the local network. If the access point has secured the network, you must enter a Security Key or password to use the network.

▶ A network port on a computer might have lights near it to indicate network activity.

▶ Mobile broadband uses the same cellular network as does cell phones. 4G networks use WiMAX or LTE technology and are faster than 3G networks. Some laptops come with WiMAX and/or LTE built in. You can also buy a mobile broadband modem to connect a computer or small network wirelessly to the Internet using mobile broadband.

▶ Bluetooth is a technology used to wirelessly connect personal devices to a computer.

Securing a Computer and Its Data

▶ The three most important ways to protect a computer and its data are to use antivirus software, secure your network connections, and keep Windows updates current.

▶ Microsoft releases updates to Windows to fix known problems, which might include a security leak. A collection of updates downloaded and installed as a group is called a service pack.

▶ Use the Windows Update window to install Windows updates and to manage when and how the updates are installed.

▶ To protect important data, always keep two copies of the data. Store the backup on a second storage media. To be extra safe, keep the second storage media at a different location.

▶ Four ways to maintain backups are to use an online backup service, use Windows Backup and Restore or other backup software, manually make copies of all your important data files, and keep your data on a website that maintains its own backups. The safest and most reliable method is to use an online backup service.

▶ If you have made backups using Windows Backup and Restore, you can restore a file or folder using the Backup and Restore window or using the Previous Version tab on the Properties box of the file or folder.

▶ Set up a standard user account for each user of a computer. Protect the administrator account with a strong password.

▶ Use the Windows Control Panel to change computer settings, including managing user accounts and user passwords.

Securing a Small Home Network

▶ A small home network that has Internet access is most likely to use DSL or cable Internet to connect to the Internet. A wireless router designed for home use connects wired and wireless computers to the network.

▶ Always secure a wireless network so that strangers cannot hack into your network, use your Internet connection, and steal your data. Secure the network by using the setup program on the wireless access point device to assign a password that must be used to access the network.

▶ Use your browser to access the setup program on a home router to configure the router. Enter the IP address of the router in the browser's address box.

▶ Data sent wirelessly should be encrypted while in transmission so it cannot be stolen. The best wireless encryption technique is WPA2, which is better than WPA or WEP encryption.

▶ Windows 7 supports homegroups, but Windows Vista and XP do not. The first computer to attempt to join a homegroup assigns the homegroup password. Other computers must use this password to join the homegroup.

▶ Use the Homegroup area of Windows Explorer to access resources shared by other computers in the homegroup. You can also use Windows Explorer to share folders with the homegroup or to remove the share status.

Review Questions

Answer these questions to find out whether you have learned the skills and knowledge in the chapter. Your instructor can provide you with the correct answers when you are ready to check your work. If you answered most of the questions correctly, you are ready for the Chapter Mastery Project. If not, go back and review the chapter before you tackle the project.

1. What group of wireless standards does a wireless LAN use? What is the name of the latest standard in this group, and what is its maximum range?

2. List five technologies a local network might use to connect to the Internet. Which three of these services are broadband?

3. If you don't see the network icon in the taskbar, what do you do to put it there?

4. What three choices does Windows offer for a network location? Which location is represented by a park bench icon?

5. Which network location must you use if you need to join a Windows domain?

6. When a wired network connection is not working, how can you tell if there is activity on the network cable?

7. What two types of technologies are built into a laptop so the laptop can connect to the Internet using mobile broadband?

8. When you are securing a computer, what type network location offers the best protection?

9. What is a collection of Windows updates called that are installed as a single package?

10. How are updates to Microsoft Office installed on a computer?

11. What is the safest and most reliable method to keep backups of important personal data?

12. What device can be used to network several computers together and connect that network to a DSL modem or cable modem?

13. How many numbers are there in an IP address, and what symbol is used to separate these numbers?

14. Which wireless encryption method offers the best security, WPA or WEP?

15. List the steps to find out the homegroup password.

Chapter Mastery Project

Find out how well you have mastered the content in this chapter by completing this project. If you can answer all the questions and do all the steps without looking back at the chapter details, you have mastered this chapter. If you can complete the project by finding answers using Windows Help or the web, you have proven that you can teach yourself about computers.

Hint All the key terms in the chapter are used in this mastery project. If you encounter a key word you don't know, such as *homegroup,* enter **define:homegroup** in the Internet Explorer search box.

If you find you need a lot of help doing the project and you have not yet read the chapter or done the activities, drop back and start at the beginning of the chapter and then return to this project.

Mastery Project Part 1: Connecting a Computer to the Internet

If you need help completing this part of the mastery project, please review the "Connecting a Computer to the Internet" section in the chapter.

Answer the following questions:

1. Which is faster, wireless Wi-Fi using the 802.11n standard or wired Ethernet transmitting at 1000 Mbps? When you need the fastest Internet speeds, is it generally best to use a wired connection or a wireless connection?

2. Suppose you have DSL, satellite, and dial-up services in your area. Which one is the best choice? Why?

3. Why is mobile broadband considered to be a broadband technology?

4. When should you set a network connection to Public network? To Home network?

5. When connecting to a wireless network, how can you tell that the wireless network is secured?

6. Suppose your wired network connection is not working, and you see a blinking light near the network port. What does the blinking light indicate? What do you do next to fix the network problem?

Do the following to manage the network connections on your computer:

Step 1. Remove the network icon from the taskbar. Now restore the network icon to the taskbar. What window did you use to make these changes?

Step 2. If your computer is not already connected, connect it to a wired or wireless network.

Step 3. Find out the current setting for the network location of your computer. Using this setting, can you join a Windows domain? A homegroup?

Step 4. Click the Internet icon in the Network and Sharing Center window. What happens? Why might this icon be helpful when troubleshooting a network connection problem?

Step 5. Unplug your network cable and/or turn off the wireless switch on your laptop so you no longer have network connectivity. How does the Network and Sharing Center report the problem?

Step 6. Fix the problem and make sure connectivity is restored. How do you verify that you have Internet access?

Do the following to find out about Internet connections:

Step 1. Use Google.com to shop for a wireless access point that uses the 802.11n standard. (Search on **wi-fi access point**.) What is the brand and model of the device you found? What other wireless standards does the device support? Does it support 802.11g?

Step 2. Go to the Comcast website at Comcast.com. Find out the two types of broadband services that Comcast offers.

Step 3. Another popular ISP is Verizon (Verizon.com). Check out the Verizon website. What two types of broadband services are offered by Verizon?

Step 4. Suppose you want to connect computers in your home to a router using a network cable. Search the web for a 50-foot Ethernet cable. What website offered the cable? Save or print the web page showing the price of the cable.

Step 5. Suppose you want to use mobile broadband while traveling with your laptop and you decide to use CLEAR 4G WiMAX (www.clear.com). Go to the CLEAR website and find a USB mobile broadband modem. How much does the modem cost, and how much does the least-expensive monthly subscription cost? What is the data limit for one month?

Mastery Project Part 2: Securing a Computer and Its Data

If you need help completing this part of the mastery project, please review the "Securing a Computer and Its Data" section in the chapter.

Answer the following questions:

1. Which is more important to keep a computer safe:

   a. Run antivirus software or use a strong password to your online banking service?

   b. Keep a backup of important data or keep Windows updates current?

   c. Set your network location to Work network or set it to Public network?

2. Why are Windows updates important when securing a computer?

Do the following to install updates for Windows:

Step 1. Use the System window to find out whether Windows 7 Service Pack 1 is installed. If it is not yet installed, how long can you expect the installation to take? What special precaution should you take when installing a service pack on a laptop computer? Why?

Step 2. Find out if there are any important Windows updates not yet installed on your computer. Install any pending and important updates. Verify there are not more important updates pending. Why might new updates appear after you have installed an update?

Step 3. Set Windows Update so that updates are automatically installed every day. Allow all users to install updates. Allow other Microsoft software to receive updates.

You need to be able to write files to the hard drive to do this activity. Do the following to set up a backup schedule and restore a file from backup:

Step 1. Copy two photos from another location into the Pictures library. If you don't have two photo files, use two files in the Sample Files folder on the DVD in the back of this book.

Step 2. Use the Backup and Restore window to back up the Documents and Pictures libraries every day. Make sure the backup occurred.

Step 3. Delete one of the photos from the Pictures library.

Step 4. Use the Backup and Restore window to restore the deleted photo to the Pictures library.

Step 5. After you have restored the file, open its **Properties** box. Does the **Previous Version** tab report any previous versions of the file?

Do the following to check out an online backup service:

Step 1. Using one of the backup services mentioned in the chapter, find out the minimum cost of subscribing to the service.

Step 2. Find out if you are limited to the amount of backup space you can use. If so, what is that limitation?

Step 3. Find one online review of the service. Is the review positive or negative?

Do the following to set up a standard account and manage passwords:

Step 1. Use the Control Panel to create a standard account named **James**. Make the password for the account **JaMes5**.

Step 2. Log on to Windows using the James account. Change the password to the account. View the **Documents** library for the account.

Step 3. Log off Windows. Log back on using an administrator account. Reset the password to the James account making the new password **changeme**. Log onto the James account using the new password.

Step 4. Switch back to the administrator account. Delete the **James** account. What warnings do you get when you delete the account? Even with the warnings, are you still able to delete the account?

Mastery Project Part 3: Securing a Small Home Network

If you need help completing this part of the mastery project, please review the "Securing a Small Home Network" section in the chapter.

Answer the following questions:

1. Why is it important to secure a wireless network in your home? How do you secure the network?

2. Why is it important to change the password to your home router as soon as you install it?

This activity requires access to a wireless router. Do the following:

Step 1. Using the IP address and password to the router, access the router setup program. What are the steps to change the router password?

Step 2. What is the IP address of the router? Can you change the IP address? If so, list the steps to do that.

Step 3. List the wireless encryption standards the router supports to secure the wireless network. Is WPA2 among those it supports?

Work with a partner and two computers to set up and use a homegroup. Do the following:

Step 1. If the two computers are not already joined in a homegroup, join them.

Step 2. Share the **Pictures** library on both computers to the homegroup. Copy a photo from the Pictures library from one computer to the other.

Step 3. If the Documents library is shared with the homegroup, remove it from the homegroup. Verify one computer cannot see the Documents library of the other computer.

Becoming an Independent Learner

Answer the following questions about becoming an independent learner:

1. To teach yourself to manage network connections and secure a computer, do you think it is best to rely on the chapter or on Window Help or the web when you need answers?

2. The most important skill learned in this chapter is how to teach yourself a computer skill. Rate yourself at Level A through E on how well you are doing with this skill. What is your level?

   ○ Level A: I was able to successfully complete the Chapter Mastery Project without the help of doing the On Your Own activities in the chapter.

   ○ Level B: I completed all the On Your Own activities and the Chapter Mastery Project without referring to any of the solutions in the *Solutions Appendix*.

   ○ Level C: I completed all the On Your Own activities and the Chapter Mastery Project by using just a few of the solutions in the *Solutions Appendix*.

   ○ Level D: I completed all the On Your Own activities and the Chapter Mastery Project by using many of the solutions in the *Solutions Appendix*.

   ○ Level E: I completed all the On Your Own activities and the Chapter Mastery Project and had to use all of the solutions in the *Solutions Appendix*.

To continue toward the goal of teaching yourself computer skills, if you are not at Level A, try to move up one level on how you learn in Chapter 13.

Projects to Help You

Now that you have mastered the material in this chapter, you are ready to tackle the three projects introduced at the beginning of the chapter in the section "How Will This Chapter Help Me?"

Project 1: Selecting a Router for a Home Network

Suppose you have DSL or cable Internet coming to your home and you want to set up a home network. You need a home router that connects wired and wireless computers to create the network. The router will also connect to your DSL modem or cable modem. Shop online for a home router and bookmark the URL of the web page showing the router you select. Also bookmark one online review of this router. Email the two links to your instructor. Find a router that meets these requirements:

► The router provides wireless access using the latest 802.11n standard. The router must allow you to secure the wireless network with a password and must support the WPA2 encryption standard.

► The router has a minimum of three network ports to connect three wired computers and another network port to connect to your DSL modem or cable modem.

► The router gets good online reviews that report it is easy to use and technical support from the manufacturer is available.

As you shop for a router, you might encounter unfamiliar technical terms. Don't worry if you don't understand all the terms. Just make sure the router you select gets good online reviews and meets your requirements.

Answer these questions:

1. What is the brand and model of the router?

2. How much does the router cost?

PERSONAL PROJECT: I just bought a laptop, and my roommate already has a desktop computer. We want a small home network where we can share files between the two computers and both computers can connect to the Internet. What equipment do I need to set up a home network to the Internet?

Project 2: Sharing Files in a Homegroup

Working with a partner, do the following to learn how to manage the shared data in a homegroup:

1. Work with a partner and set up a homegroup. Create two folders named Personal and Classwork in your Documents library. Put one document file in each folder.

2. Share the Classwork folder with the homegroup, but do not share the Personal folder.

3. Verify that you can access the file in the Classwork folder on your partner's computer, but you cannot see the contents of your partner's Personal folder.

> **Not Working?** You might not be able to do this project using computers in your school lab if lab computers are locked down so you cannot change the network location to a Home network.

ACADEMIC PROJECT: My study group meets every week in the student center. We all bring our laptops. When we want to share files, we email them to each other. Is there an easier way to share these files? Is there a way each team member can see the files on the other computers?

TECHNICAL CAREER PROJECT: I just moved to a new neighborhood, and I need Internet service. How do I get it? What equipment do I need to buy? Which is better, DSL or cable Internet?

Project 3: Investigating Broadband Internet Services

Do the following to find out about broadband Internet services you might use yourself or recommend to others:

1. Search the Internet and find out if DSL or cable Internet is offered in your neighborhood. If you already have DSL, research cable Internet. If you already have cable Internet, research DSL. If you don't yet have Internet broadband in your home, research both services to decide which is best for you.

2. What company offers DSL or cable Internet in your neighborhood? How much does the service cost? Is there a setup fee? Does a technician come to your home to set up the service, or are you expected to set it up yourself? Is the DSL modem or cable modem included in the subscription, or must you purchase it?

3. Some neighborhoods have access to both DSL and cable Internet. To choose between the two, consider the quality of service and cost. To find out how well the service performs in your neighborhood, ask your neighbors these questions:

   Are they satisfied with the service? Does it go down often or is it reliable? If a problem occurs, does the company provide good technical support?

4. Based on your research, which service would you recommend to a neighbor or might you choose for yourself? Why?

Project to Help Others

One of the best ways to learn is to teach someone else. And, in teaching someone else, you are making a contribution into that person's life. In this chapter, help someone learn to connect to the Internet and secure his computer.

Who is your apprentice? _____

Does your apprentice use a computer that is connected to the Internet? If so, do the following:

Step 1. Show him how to use the Network and Sharing Center to solve a connectivity problem. Make sure the network location is set correctly to protect the computer from attack.

Step 2. Help your apprentice make sure antivirus software is running on his computer.

Step 3. Help your apprentice update Windows and make sure Windows is set to automatically download and install important updates.

If your apprentice does not have an Internet connection in his home, step him through Project 3 to help him understand the different technologies in his area and what they cost.

CHAPTER 13

Maintaining a Computer and Fixing Computer Problems

IN THIS CHAPTER, YOU WILL

Keep a computer running well

Take care of hardware

Solve the most common computer problems

If you are responsible for a computer, you need to know how to take care of it. A computer will run well for many years without giving problems if you take good care of it. In this chapter, you learn how to do just that.

As always, remember the most important computer skill is how to teach yourself a computer skill. Therefore, this chapter is designed to help you teach yourself how to maintain a computer and solve computer problems. Try to do each On Your Own activity without any help. But remember, if you need help, you can always refer to the solutions in the *Solutions Appendix*.

JUMP RIGHT IN

If you want even more of a challenge, try proceeding directly to the Chapter Mastery Project at the end of this chapter. If you need help on the project, refer to the On Your Own activities in the chapter or do your own independent investigating searching Windows Help and Support or the web for answers. When you complete the project, you will have mastered the skills in this chapter. Then go to the projects that require you apply your skills to new situations.

How Will This Chapter Help Me?

This chapter provides three projects focusing on personal, academic, or technical career goals. Depending on your own interests, you might choose to complete any or all of these projects to help you achieve your goals.

PERSONAL PROJECT: My computer is only three years old and has started to run slowly. Is it getting old? Should I replace it, or can I do something to speed it up?

ACADEMIC PROJECT: I've been assigned a computer to use while in school, and I need to take good care of it. I want to make sure it stays protected and runs well. I also want to change some settings on the Windows desktop.

TECHNICAL CAREER PROJECT: I work on a help desk, and we get lots of questions about how to use Windows and how to solve Windows problems. My team leader has asked me to write some tutorials we can send to users when they call. I also need to write a script the help desk can use when we need to find out about the user's computer.

Keeping a Computer Running Well

Most computer problems can be prevented through good **computer maintenance**. If you are responsible for a computer, you need to take the time to set it up so that it is securely protected. Then about every month, you need to do the routine maintenance needed to keep a computer running well.

> **computer maintenance**—Tasks that are done routinely or as needed to keep a computer protected and running well.

In Chapter 12, "Connecting to the Internet and Securing a Computer," you learned to secure a computer. Recall the three most important tasks are to

- ▶ Set Windows Updates to automatically download and install updates

- ▶ Install and run antivirus software

- ▶ Set the Windows network location so the computer is protected from attacks coming from the local network or the Internet

Over time, a computer tends to run slower than it did when first purchased. Ongoing routine maintenance can prevent this from happening. In this part of the chapter, you learn how to clean up the hard drive so your computer has the free space it needs to work, uninstall software you no longer want, and disable a program from launching when you first start Windows.

> **Hint** Many of the activities in this chapter require you to know the password to an administrator account or to log on to Windows using an administrator account. If you are responsible for a computer, you need access to this account.
>
> Recall that if you are logged on to Windows using a standard account and attempt to perform a task that only an administrator can do, the UAC box appears. Enter the administrator password to continue.

Clean Up the Hard Drive

Windows requires at least 15% of free space on the hard drive that it uses to do its work. Even more space is better. When a hard drive gets full, Windows runs slower and might report errors. Use the **Disk Cleanup** utility to free up some hard drive space.

> **Disk Cleanup**—A Windows utility used to delete temporary and optional files on the hard drive to free up hard drive space.

To clean up the hard drive, open Windows Explorer. Right click **Local Disk (C:)** and select **Properties** from the shortcut menu. The Local Disk (C:) Properties box opens (see Figure 13-1). Click **Disk Cleanup** to start the cleanup process.

Not Working? Drive C: is the drive where Windows is installed. It might be shown as Local Disk (C:), OS (C:), or some other name that contains C: in the name.

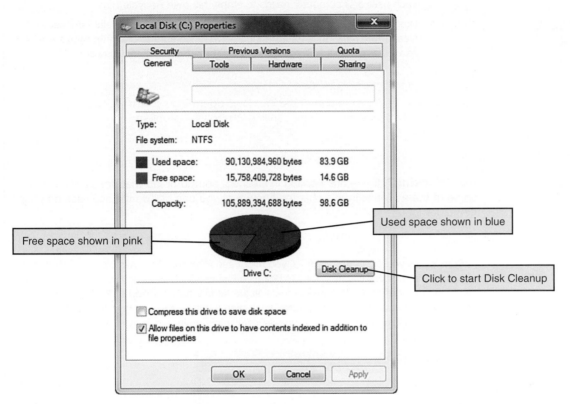

FIGURE 13-1
The Properties box of Local Disk (C:) shows free space on the drive that holds the Windows operating system.

Tip Another way to access Disk Cleanup as well as other useful system tools is to click **Start**, **All Programs**, **Accessories**, and **System Tools**.

Notice on the Local Disk (C:) Properties box you can compress the drive to save disk space. Compression is not considered a best practice and should be done only if you have no other way of freeing up hard drive space. A compressed drive runs slower than one that is not compressed.

Do the following to clean up the hard drive:

Step 1. Recall the Recycle Bin is the place where Windows puts files and folders deleted from the hard drive. Empty the Recycle Bin to free up that space. Note that each user of a computer needs to empty his own Recycle Bin.

Step 2. Use Disk Cleanup on the Local Disk (C:) Properties box to delete unneeded files on the hard drive (refer to Figure 13-1). Be sure to clean up **system files** as well as data files. To do so requires the administrator password.

> **system file**—A file that is part of the Windows operating system. Temporary system files can safely be deleted without causing Windows a problem.

> **Not Working?** If you are working in a school computer lab that does not allow some of the activities in this chapter, know that you can still do the activities on your home computer.

Step 3. As you clean up the drive, you might see *Previous Windows installation(s)* listed in the Disk Cleanup for (C:) box (see Figure 13-2). Deleting this item can free up a lot of space because it holds all the folders for a version of Windows previously installed on this computer. If you see the item and know you no longer need anything from the old Windows installation, include it in the items to delete.

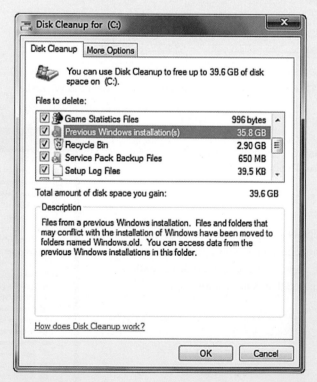

FIGURE 13-2
This computer was upgraded from Windows Vista to Windows 7. The old Windows Vista data is no longer needed and can be deleted to free up 35GB of disk space.

Hint Be sure to delete Temporary Internet Files listed in the Disk Cleanup box. These files can take up a lot of space and are not needed.

Step 4. Use the information on the Local Disk (C:) Properties box to calculate the percentage of free space on the hard drive. If 15% is not free, consider moving some data folders to other devices such as an external hard drive or burn some data files or folders to CDs or DVDs.

Step 5. Windows automatically defragments a hard drive once a week. To verify this is being done, click the **Tools** tab on the disk's Properties box. Then click **Defragment now**. Verify the drive is being defragmented weekly (see Figure 13-3). If the drive has recently been defragmented, you don't need to defrag the drive at this time.

defragment—Rearrange fragments or parts of files on the hard drive so files can be read more quickly.

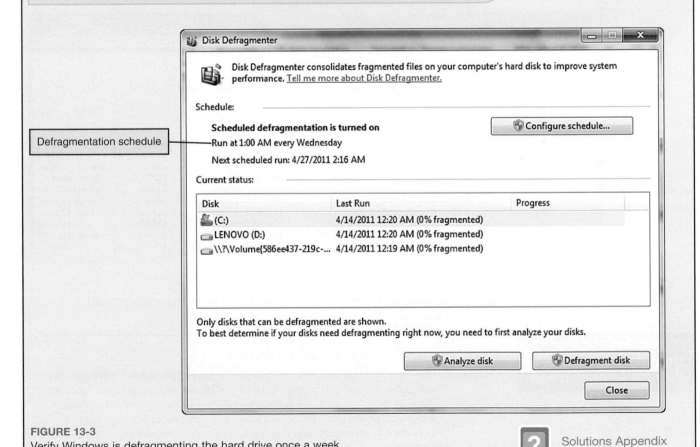

Defragmentation schedule

FIGURE 13-3
Verify Windows is defragmenting the hard drive once a week.

Solutions Appendix

For help, see Solution 13-1: How to Clean Up the Hard Drive.

Uninstall Software You No Longer Need

Most of us install software as we encounter a need for it. This software might be an application, a device driver, or an Internet Explorer **plug-in**. Over time, this installed software can fill up a hard drive and slow down a computer. To free hard drive space and keep Windows running well, uninstall software you no longer want or need.

> **plug-in**—A helper program to another program. The plug-in launches whenever the main program launches to be available when the main program needs it. For example, Internet Explorer might use a plug-in to help build a web page with interactive animation. A plug-in is sometimes called an add-on.

To uninstall software, first open Control Panel and click **Uninstall a program**. The Programs and Features window appears listing all the software installed on this computer (see Figure 13-4). Select a program and then click **Uninstall** to uninstall it.

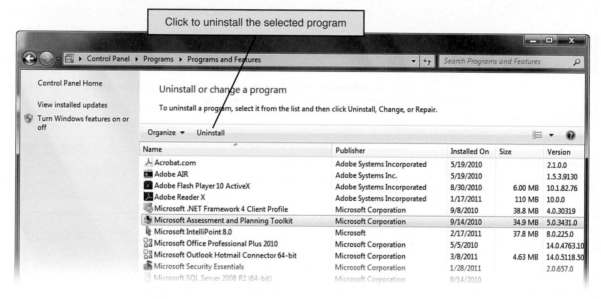

FIGURE 13-4
Use the Programs and Features window to uninstall software you no longer need.

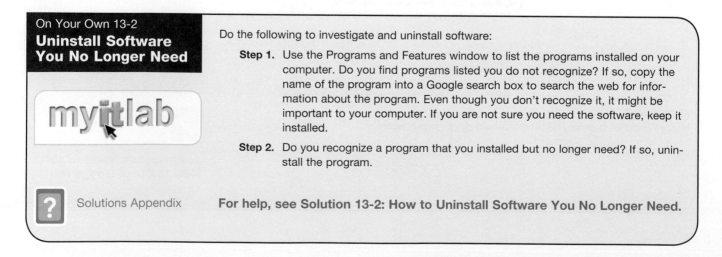

On Your Own 13-2
Uninstall Software You No Longer Need

Do the following to investigate and uninstall software:

Step 1. Use the Programs and Features window to list the programs installed on your computer. Do you find programs listed you do not recognize? If so, copy the name of the program into a Google search box to search the web for information about the program. Even though you don't recognize it, it might be important to your computer. If you are not sure you need the software, keep it installed.

Step 2. Do you recognize a program that you installed but no longer need? If so, uninstall the program.

Solutions Appendix   **For help, see Solution 13-2: How to Uninstall Software You No Longer Need.**

Disable a Program from Launching at Startup

When software is first installed, it sometimes registers itself with Windows so it is launched each time Windows starts. When many programs launch at startup, Windows is slow to start and runs slowly because these programs running in the background are using up system resources. If you seldom use a program, you might want to disable it from launching at startup. You can still launch it manually at any time.

Use the **System Configuration** utility to control the programs that launch at startup. Click **Start**, enter **msconfig** in the *Search programs and files* box, and press **Enter**. If necessary, enter the administrator password in the UAC box. The System Configuration dialog box opens (see Figure 13-5).

System Configuration—A Windows utility used to control what programs launch at startup. To launch the utility, use the **msconfig** command.

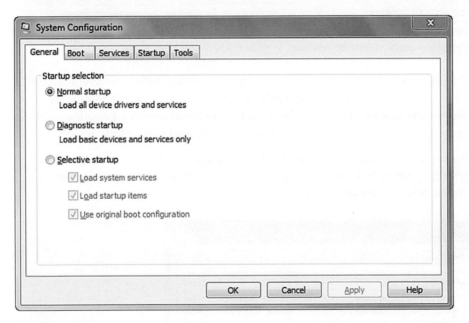

FIGURE 13-5
Using System Configuration, you can disable startup programs and solve problems when Windows starts.

Click the **Startup** tab to view a list of programs that launch at startup (see Figure 13-6). To disable one from launching, uncheck it and click **Apply**. Close System Configuration and restart your computer. Later, if you decide you need the program to launch every time Windows starts, return to the System Configuration box and check the program.

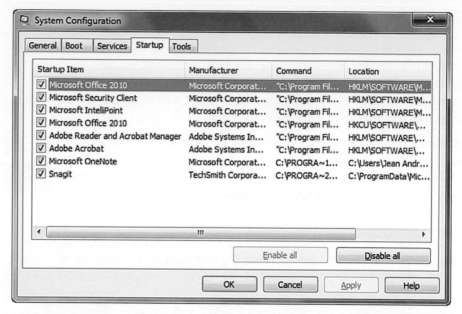

FIGURE 13-6
Uncheck any program you do not want to launch when Windows starts.

You might need to investigate the startup programs to decide whether you want to disable one. For example, in Figure 13-6, the Adobe Acrobat program is listed. A Google search on Adobe Acrobat tells you about the software. If you don't find enough information about the startup program to know whether you can disable it, you need to dig a little deeper.

To dig deeper, resize the columns in the System Configuration box so you can see the program filename in the Command column. Figure 13-7 shows the program filename for the Adobe Acrobat software is Reader_sl.exe.

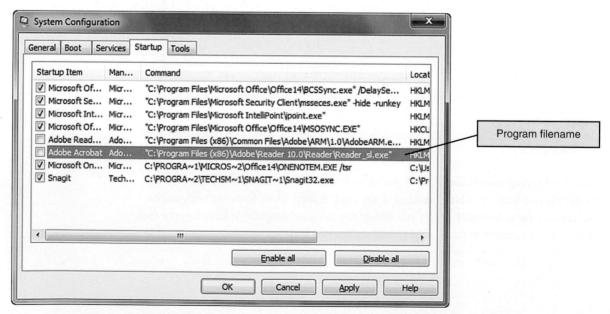

FIGURE 13-7
The Command column shows the program filename launched at startup.

When you do a Google search on Reader_sl.exe, you discover this is a speed launcher program that continually runs in the background. It helps the Adobe Acrobat software to start faster whenever a user starts the application. If you don't use Adobe Acrobat often, you don't need to start Reader_sl.exe each time Windows starts. You can safely disable this startup program.

Tip The two major causes of a computer slowing down over time are lack of free space on the hard drive and too many startup programs. Investigating each startup program might take time, but this time can pay off when Windows starts faster and performs better.

On Your Own 13-3
Limit Startup Programs Using System Configuration

Do the following to use System Configuration:

Step 1. Start System Configuration and investigate the list of programs that launch at startup. Are there any you do not recognize? If so, investigate the purpose of the program. You can do a Google search on the name of the software listed in the Startup Item column or the program filename listed in the Command column.

Step 2. Is there a program you decide you don't need launched each time Windows starts? If so, disable that program.

Step 3. Restart your computer and verify that all is working as you expect. If you see a problem, return to System Configuration and enable the program that you disabled.

 Video **13-3**

For help, see Solution 13-3: How to Limit Startup Programs Using System Configuration.

 Solutions Appendix

Taking Care of Hardware

If a computer is cared for, it should last for many years. When you are responsible for a computer, you need to know how to protect it against power surges, heat, humidity, and other external factors that can damage hardware.

Here are a few tips for protecting computer hardware:

▶ **Use a surge protector.** To protect a computer against lightning or other power surges, use a **surge protector**. Plug the power cord from your computer into the surge protector and plug the surge protector into an electrical wall outlet. The surge protector does not allow electrical surges to pass through to your computer. A small, portable surge protector can be convenient when traveling with a laptop.

> **surge protector**—A device that allows you to plug in several electrical devices and protects these devices from power surges.

surge protector

▶ **Keep computer vents clear and dust free.**
If vents are obstructed, a computer can over-
heat. Never work with a laptop computer
sitting on a fluffy pillow or blanket because
there is not enough airflow for the vents on
the bottom of the laptop. Make sure the vents
of your desktop computer are not obstructed.
If vents get filled with dust, you can use a
can of compressed air to blow them clean.

▶ **Protect a desktop computer sitting under
a desk.** Place the computer so you are not
likely to accidentally kick it. Don't set it on
thick carpet that doesn't allow good airflow.
Don't move a desktop computer while it is
working because doing so can damage the
hard drive.

▶ **Protect a computer from high humidity and heat.** Heat and humidity are not good
for a computer. Never leave your laptop in a hot car during the summer months.
Keeping computers in a damp basement is also not a good idea.

Here are some tips to keep hardware clean and working well:

▶ **Clean your keyboard.** Turn your keyboard upside down and shake it to dislodge
crumbs. Use a can of compressed air to blow out the dust. Use a soft, slightly damp,
lint-free cloth to clean the keyboard. For a really dirty keyboard, you can use cotton
swabs dipped in alcohol to clean around each key.

▶ **Clean your mouse.** Clean the mouse with a damp cloth. For an optical mouse, clean
the feet on the bottom of the mouse so it slides easily. Don't forget to clean the
mouse pad. Built-up dirt on the pad can keep the mouse from sliding easily.

▶ **Clean your monitor screen.** Special electronic cleaning wipes work great to clean a
monitor screen and other computer parts. If you don't have them, use a lint-free, soft
slightly damp cloth to clean the screen. Don't use alcohol or window cleaner on a
monitor screen. And don't use paper towels that can scratch the surface.

▶ **Clean computer vents.** To keep a computer from overheating, you need to keep
computer vents clean of dust and free from obstruction. Clean the vents with a can
of compressed air. If you see a lot of dust built up around the vents, ask a computer
repair technician to show you how to safely open the computer case and clean the
inside.

▶ **Don't unpack or turn on a computer that has just come in from the cold.** Cold
air has a lot of **static electricity**, which is extremely dangerous to a computer. Wait
for a computer to come to room temperature before unpacking it or turning it on.

> **static electricity**—The accumulation of an electrical charge that can cause sparks
> or a crackling sound. Even a small amount of static electricity that you cannot see or
> hear can damage computer components.

▶ **Protect CDs and DVDs.** A scratched or dirty CD or DVD might not work. Heat and sunlight can also damage discs. Protect your optical discs from heat, direct sunlight, scratches, and dirt. If one gets scratched or dirty, use a soft dry cloth or an optical disc cleaning kit to clean it. Wipe from the center of the disc out and not in a circle.

> **Tip** Heat, humidity, power surges, and static electricity can affect hardware over time. Even though you might not see immediate damage, components might not last as long after being exposed.

You can use the power settings on a computer to extend a battery charge on a laptop or to save on electricity. For example, you can control how long a computer is inactive before it turns off the display or puts the computer to sleep. To manage power, open Control Panel, click **Hardware and Sound**, and then click **Power Options**. Figure 13-8 shows the Power Options window for a laptop. The Power Options window for a desktop computer is missing two items, which are labeled in the figure.

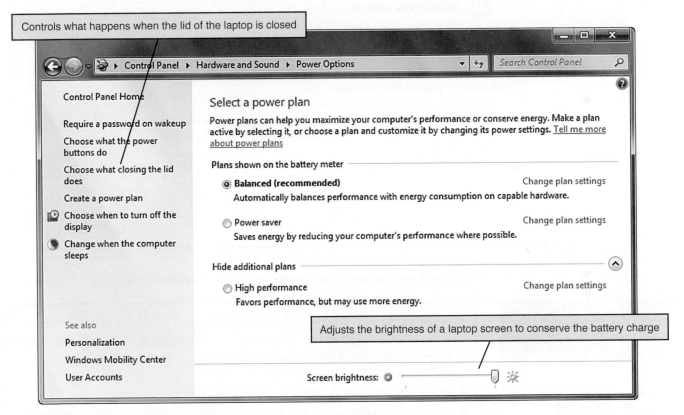

FIGURE 13-8
Windows offers power plans to conserve electricity.

You can extend the battery charge on a laptop or netbook by managing the power settings. Windows uses different powers settings for a laptop or netbook depending on whether the computer is plugged into a power source or is using the battery. To see these settings, click **Choose what closing the lid does**. The System Settings window shown in Figure 13-9 appears.

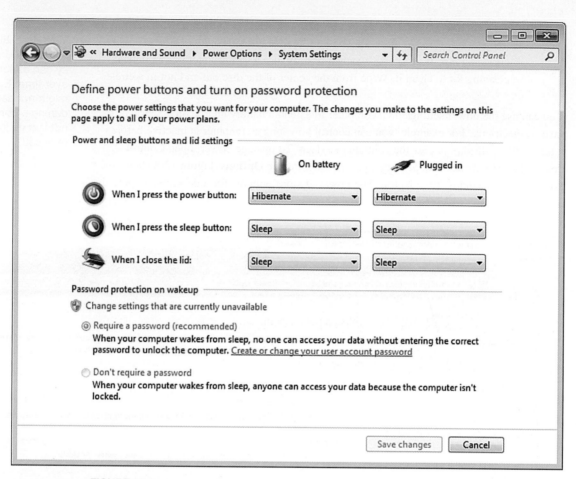

FIGURE 13-9
Power and lid settings are different when a laptop is on battery or plugged in.

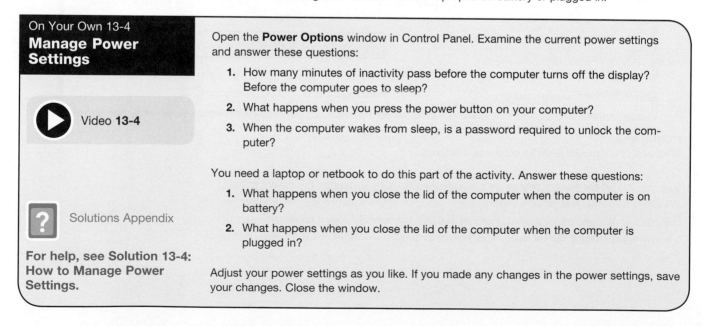

On Your Own 13-4
Manage Power Settings

Video **13-4**

Solutions Appendix

For help, see Solution 13-4: How to Manage Power Settings.

Open the **Power Options** window in Control Panel. Examine the current power settings and answer these questions:

1. How many minutes of inactivity pass before the computer turns off the display? Before the computer goes to sleep?

2. What happens when you press the power button on your computer?

3. When the computer wakes from sleep, is a password required to unlock the computer?

You need a laptop or netbook to do this part of the activity. Answer these questions:

1. What happens when you close the lid of the computer when the computer is on battery?

2. What happens when you close the lid of the computer when the computer is plugged in?

Adjust your power settings as you like. If you made any changes in the power settings, save your changes. Close the window.

Here are some additional tips to make a laptop or netbook battery charge last longer:

▶ Change the power plan settings to reduce the screen brightness. A less bright screen uses less power.

▶ Some USB devices use power even when they are not active. Unplug all USB devices you are not using. Another device that drains a laptop of power is the wireless device. When you're not using wireless, turn off the wireless switch.

▶ Because the optical drive uses a lot of power when in use, don't watch a movie on DVD or listen to a music CD when you need to conserve power.

▶ Keep as many programs closed as you can. Check the taskbar and close any open programs.

▶ Don't allow your battery to completely discharge. Doing so can weaken the battery. When traveling, plug in your AC adapter as often as possible.

▶ Heat can cause components to require more electricity. Keep your laptop cool and vents free.

▶ If you plan to not use your laptop for a time (more than a week), don't store it with the battery fully charged. Doing so can weaken the battery.

▶ A computer uses more power if it does not have enough memory. Installing more memory can make a battery charge last longer. Later in the chapter, you learn about upgrading memory in a computer.

▶ Carry an extra battery to use when the first one is almost discharged.

Solving the Most Common Computer Problems

Most computer problems are easy to solve. In this part of the chapter, you learn how to solve the common ones. You also learn about getting professional help when faced with a problem you cannot solve.

> **Tip** Become an independent investigator. If you are faced with a computer problem and this chapter does not take you far enough to solve it, search the web for more information about the problem and what to do. Be sure to take advice only from reliable websites. If you still cannot solve the problem, get professional help.

A File Is Missing or Was Accidentally Deleted

If you accidentally deleted a file from the hard drive, look in the Recycle Bin to find the file and restore it. To restore a file in the Recycle Bin, right-click it and select **Restore** from the shortcut menu (see Figure 13-10).

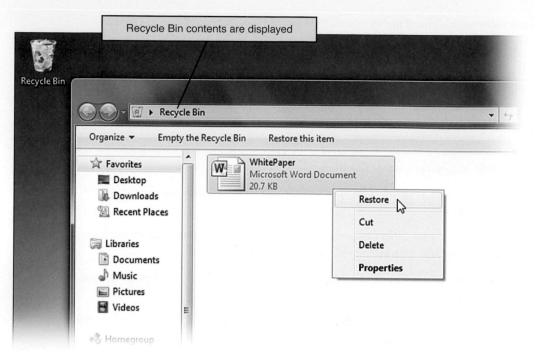

Recycle Bin contents are displayed

FIGURE 13-10
Look in the Recycle Bin for a deleted file.

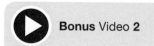

Bonus Video **2**

In Chapter 12, you learned how to recover a previous version of a file. Create a new file in the same folder as the missing file. Use exactly the same name and file extension as the missing file. Then open the file's Properties box and click the **Previous Versions** tab. If a previous version of the original file exists, it is listed here. Click the previous version and then click **Restore**.

The Monitor Screen Is Difficult to Read

To change monitor settings, you use Windows settings or buttons on the front of the monitor. Sometimes you need to make changes in both places. Use the buttons on the front of the monitor to change the brightness and contrast of the screen and the position of the lighted area on the monitor screen. Laptops and netbooks might have buttons near the keyboard to control the display.

The screen resolution is changed using Windows display settings. Right-click somewhere on the desktop and select **Screen resolution** from the shortcut menu. The Screen Resolution window appears.

screen resolution—The number of dots (called pixels) on a monitor screen used to create the screen, for example, 1680×1050. For most monitors, the highest resolution available gives best results and is sometimes called the native resolution.

In the Resolution field, make sure the highest setting is selected (see Figure 13-11). Click **Apply**. In the dialog box that appears, click **Keep changes**. Then close the Screen Resolution window.

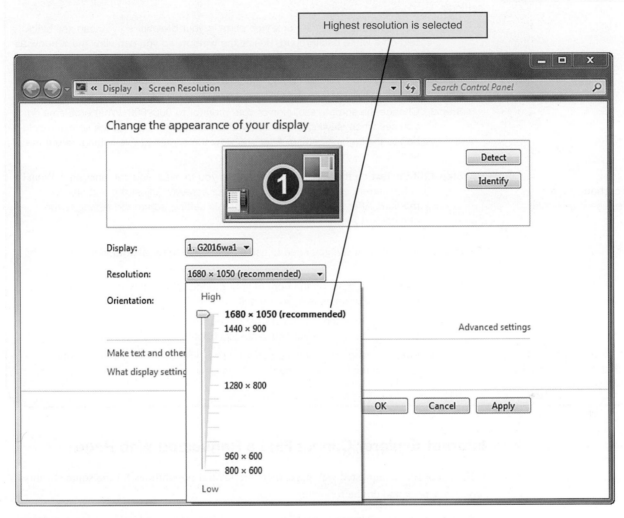

FIGURE 13-11
For best results, select the highest resolution available.

On Your Own 13-5
Practice Changing Monitor Settings

When you're adjusting monitor settings, it is a good idea to first open a Word document so you can see black text against a white background. Adjust the monitor so the text is easy to read and the screen is not too bright. Do the following to practice changing the monitor settings:

Step 1. Open a Word document or a web page in your browser so you can see black text on a white background. Resize the window so you can view the window as well as the Windows desktop.

Step 2. Using Windows, find out your current screen resolution. Note this resolution so you can return to it later.

Step 3. Change the screen resolution of your monitor to 800×600. What problems do you see when viewing the screen at this resolution? Change the screen resolution to the highest setting. After you view the screen at this setting, return the setting to the original screen resolution.

Step 4. If the text on the screen is too small for you to read, you can enlarge it. What is the current setting for text size on your screen? Adjust the text size to medium. After you view the screen at this setting, return the setting to the original text size.

To do this part of the activity, you need to use a desktop monitor and not a laptop. Do the following:

Step 1. Using the buttons on the front of your monitor, find out what is the current setting for the brightness of your monitor.

Step 2. Adjust the brightness and contrast of your monitor so that text on the screen is clear and the monitor lighting is not too bright.

Step 3. Practice using the buttons on your monitor to move the lighted part of the screen to the left and to the right. Then return the lighted screen to a center position.

Hint To change the text size, use the Display window.

? Solutions Appendix

For help, see Solution 13-5: How to Practice Changing Monitor Settings.

Internet Explorer Cannot Find a Requested Web Page

If IE cannot find a requested web page, there are several possibilities for the source of this problem. Check and do the following:

Step 1. If the error message says "Error 404" or "Page not found," the URL might be bad or not typed correctly. Check the spelling. Does another URL work? Try **google.com**.

Step 2. If the error message says "Internet Explorer cannot display the webpage," click **Diagnose Connection Problem**. Windows attempts to solve the problem and offers suggestions (see Figure 13-12). Follow through with the suggestion and click **Check to see if the problem is fixed**.

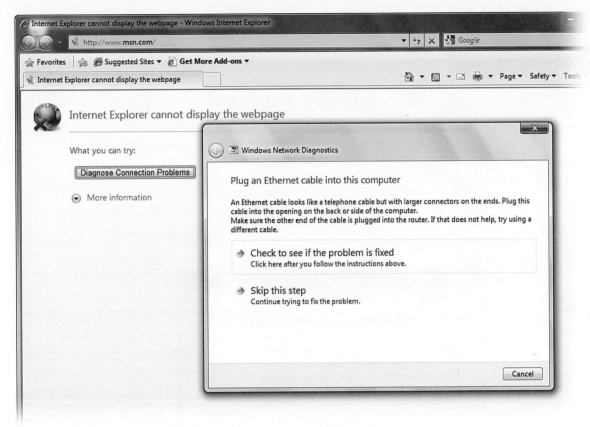

FIGURE 13-12
Windows offers a suggestion to fix a network connectivity problem.

If your problem is still not solved, do the following:

Step 1. The network connection might not be working. Look in the taskbar for the network icon. Does it have a red X over it? If so, open the Network and Sharing Center and repair the connection. Recall from Chapter 12 you can do that by clicking the red **X** in this window.

Step 2. For a wired connection, check cable connections at both ends. Are the status indicator lights near the network port lit?

Step 3. For a wireless connection, check the signal strength. You might need to move the laptop to a stronger area of the wireless network.

Step 4. Are you at home and using a router and cable modem or DSL modem? If so, reset this equipment by following these steps:

   a. Turn off or unplug the cable modem or DSL modem. Turn off or unplug the router. Wait five minutes for the equipment at the ISP to reset.

   b. Plug in or turn on the cable modem or DSL modem and wait for the lights on the front of the device to settle. Then plug in the router.

   c. Watch on your computer taskbar as the network icon shows the connection being restored. If you still have no connection, report the problem to your ISP.

An Application Is Frozen and Will Not Respond

When an application freezes, "Not Responding" usually shows up in the title bar. You can try waiting for the application to respond, or you can force the application to close. If you force the application to close, you might lose any data not saved. To force it to close, do the following:

Step 1. Right-click in the taskbar and select **Start Task Manager** from the shortcut menu. The Windows **Task Manager** window opens (see Figure 13-13).

> **Task Manager**—A Windows utility used to close open applications that are not responding. It can also be used to monitor computer and network performance and programs running in the background (called services).

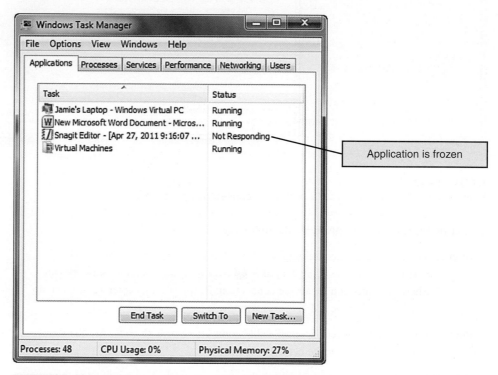

FIGURE 13-13
Use Task Manager to end an application that is not responding.

Step 2. On the Applications tab, select the application that is not responding, click **End Task**, and follow directions onscreen.

Open the Paint application. Open Task Manager. Use Task Manager to close the Paint application. Then close Task Manager.

On Your Own 13-6
Use Task Manager to Close an Application

For help, see Solution 13-6: How to Use Task Manager to Close an Application.

? Solutions Appendix

A Device or Program Will Not Install

Normally, when you plug in a new hardware device such as a USB flash drive or printer, Windows recognizes the device and automatically installs device drivers to support it. You see the progress of the installation reported at the bottom of your screen.

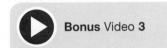
Bonus Video 3

If a problem occurs when you're installing a device or software, the Windows Action Center can help. The **Action Center** is represented by a flag icon in the taskbar. A red X over the flag indicates a problem that requires immediate attention.

Not Working? If you don't see the Action Center flag in the taskbar, click the white arrow ▲ in the taskbar and click **Customize**. In the Notification Area Icons window, show the Action Center flag and click **OK**.

Action Center—A Window utility that is a collection of several utilities and windows. Use it to solve problems with hardware and software installations and other Windows problems.

Click the flag in the taskbar and then click **Open Action Center**. Problems the computer is having are reported in the Action Center window with recommendations for solutions (see Figure 13-14). To resolve a problem, click the button to the right of the problem message. Action Center steps you through the solution.

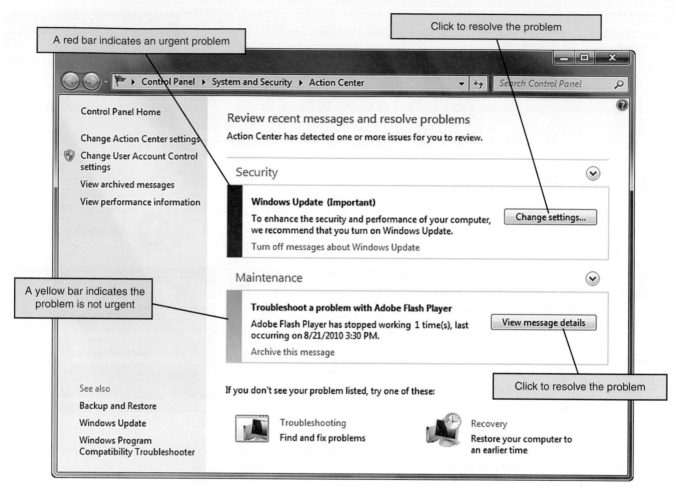

FIGURE 13-14
Use the Windows Action Center to solve problems with hardware and software.

A Document Will Not Print

Printer problems can be caused by the application used to print a document, Windows, connectivity to the printer, or the printer. The reason for a problem at the printer might be that the printer is not turned on or is not online, it is out of paper, the paper is jammed, the ink cartridge or toner cartridge is low, or power is not getting to the printer. When you're solving a printer problem, it helps to have a plan to sort out what works and does not work. Figure 13-15 can help.

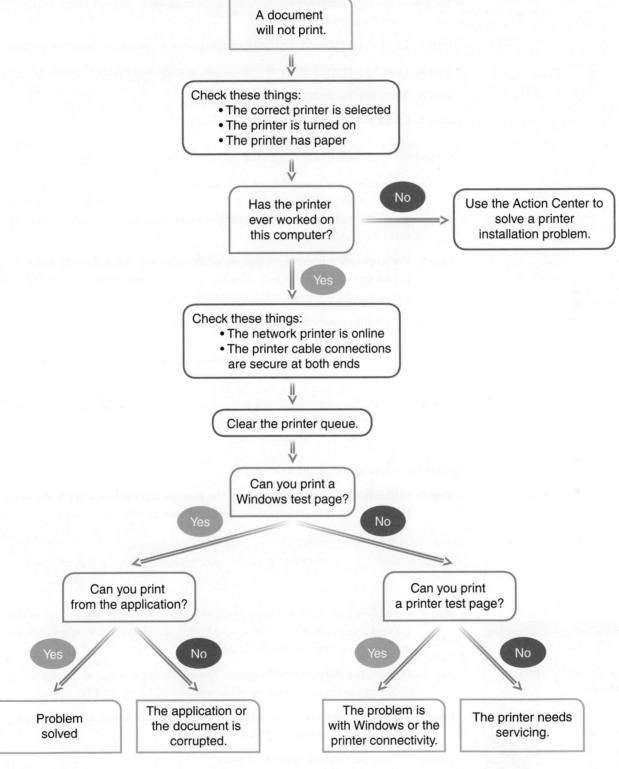

FIGURE 13-15
This plan can help solve a printer problem.

When you're solving a computer problem, check the most likely problems first. Do the following to solve a printer problem:

Step 1. Using the application, verify the correct printer is selected in the Print window.

Step 2. Look for a power light on the front of the printer. Is the printer turned on?

Step 3. Make sure the printer has paper.

Step 4. Check for a paper jam and clear it.

If the problem is still not solved, dig a little deeper and check the following:

Step 1. If the printer has never worked with this computer, perhaps the printer did not install correctly. Check the Action Center to see whether a problem is reported. If you find the printer installation problem listed there, follow directions onscreen to solve the problem.

Step 2. For a network printer, check that the printer is online. A panel on the front of the printer should say *Ready* indicating that it is online and connected to the network. Check that the network cable is connected at both ends.

Step 3. For a USB printer, check the USB cable connections at both ends.

Perhaps the problem is caused by a corrupted document that has blocked the **printer queue**.

> **printer queue**—A list of documents that users have sent to the printer but have not yet printed.

To clear the printer queue, do the following:

Step 1. Click **Start**, **Devices and Printers**. The Devices and Printers window opens (see Figure 13-16). In the window, notice the **default printer** has a green check mark.

> **default printer**—The printer that Windows uses if another printer is not selected.

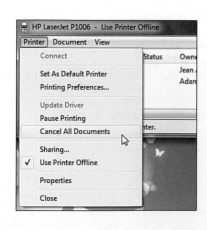

Step 2. Double-click the printer you are trying to reach. The printer window opens (see the background window of Figure 13-17). Any problems that Windows has with the printer are shown at the top of this window.

Step 3. Double-click **document(s) in queue**. The printer queue window appears listing documents in the queue (see the active window of Figure 13-17).

Step 4. To clear the print queue, click **Printer** and then click **Cancel All Documents**. Clearing the queue might take a few moments.

Step 5. Try to print from the application again.

> **Not Working?** You cannot cancel a document in a printer queue that was put there by another user unless you are logged on as an administrator.

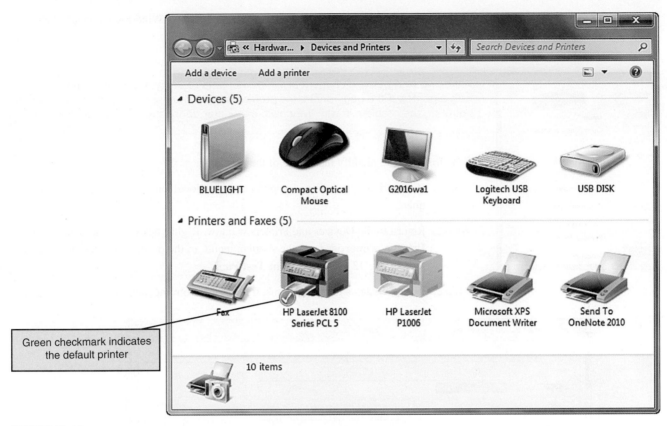

Green checkmark indicates
the default printer

FIGURE 13-16
Use the Devices and Printers window to manage installed printers.

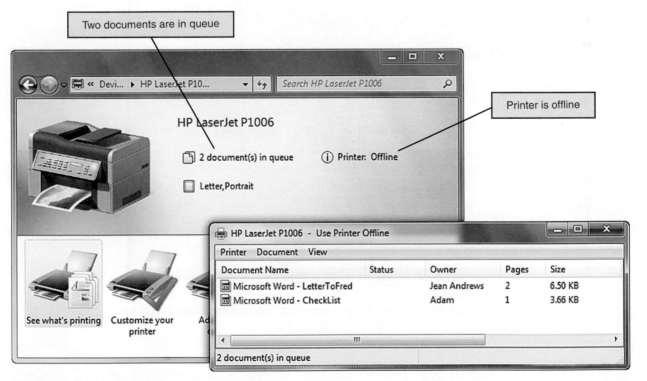

Two documents are in queue

Printer is offline

FIGURE 13-17
The printer window reports a problem with the printer.

If the problem is still not solved, it's time to find out whether Windows can reach the printer. To find out, you can print a **Windows test page**.

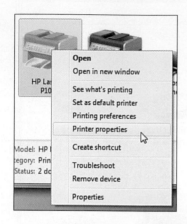

> **Windows test page**—A page that Windows prints to verify that it can communicate with a printer. If the page prints, the problem is with the application. If the page does not print, the problem is with Windows, the printer connectivity, or the printer.

Do the following to identify the source of the problem:

Step 1. If the printer queue is not empty, cancel all documents in the queue to empty the queue.

Step 2. Return to the Devices and Printers window. Right-click the printer and select **Printer properties** from the shortcut menu. In the printer's Properties window (see Figure 13-18), click **Print Test Page**.

Step 3. If the Windows test page prints, try printing from the application again.

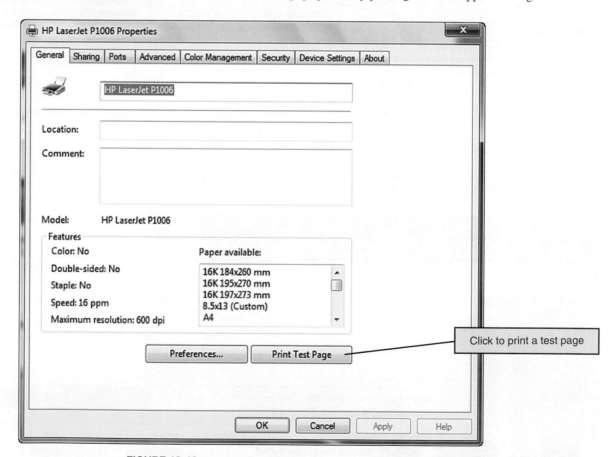

FIGURE 13-18
Print a Windows test page to verify that Windows can reach the printer.

Step 4. If the Windows test page does not print, try to print a **printer test page**. Look in the printer user guide and find out how to print a printer test page. You can do that by pressing certain buttons on the printer. If the printer test page does not print, the printer needs servicing.

> **printer test page**—A page you print by pressing buttons on the printer to verify that the printer is working correctly.

To do this activity, you need access to a printer. Do the following to practice solving printer problems by using the printer queue:

Step 1. To set up the problem, turn off your printer. Open a Word document that you want to print. Command Word to print the document. Command Word to print the document a second time. Neither printout happens because the printer is turned off.

Step 2. Open the printer window, which should show the printer is offline and two documents in queue. Open the queue so you can see the list of documents in the queue.

Step 3. Delete one of these documents in the printer queue.

> **Hint** To delete a single item in the printer queue, right-click it and select **Cancel** from the shortcut menu.

Step 4. Turn on the printer. The one document should now print. Watch the printer queue as the document prints and the queue is empty. Then close all windows.

On Your Own 13-7
Use the Printer Queue

 Video **13-7**

 Solutions Appendix

For help, see Solution 13-7: How to Use the Printer Queue.

Windows Gives Strange Errors

Unknown Windows errors can be caused by a variety of problems. Here are some steps to try:

Step 1. Copy or type the exact error message in a Google search box and search for information about the error. Be careful because some websites cannot be trusted. Microsoft.com is the best source of information about a Windows error.

Step 2. Restart the computer. A good rule of thumb when Windows or an application gives errors is to restart the computer. A fresh restart is sometimes all that is needed to solve a problem.

> **Not Working?** If Windows is frozen so that you cannot restart from the Windows Shutdown menu, press **Ctrl-Alt-Del**. The screen shown in Figure 13-19 appears. Click the up arrow in the red box and select **Restart** as shown in the figure.

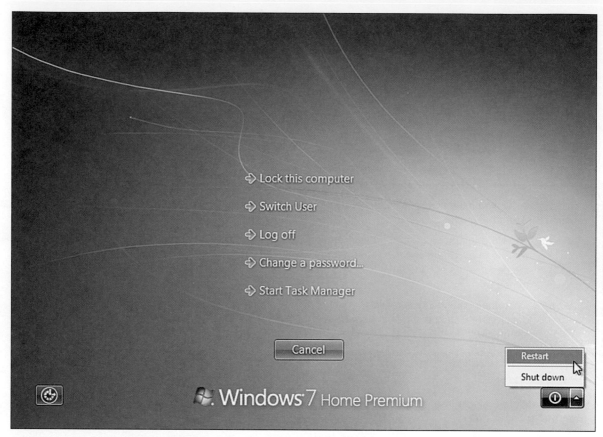

FIGURE 13-19
Use the recovery screen to manage Windows when the Windows desktop is frozen.

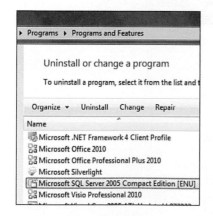

Step 3. If you find the error is caused by an application, consider the problem might be caused by a data file the application is using and not the application itself. Close the application. Open it again and try a different data file with the same application.

Step 4. If you are convinced the problem is a corrupted application, try repairing the application. If that doesn't work, use the Control Panel to uninstall the application and then install it again.

> **Hint** To repair a program, select it in the Programs and Features window and then click **Repair** or **Change** in the menu bar.

Step 5. The problem might be caused by malware. Use antivirus software to scan the computer for malware. You learned to use this type of software in Chapter 2, "Finding and Using Information on the Web."

Step 6. Windows updates can sometimes solve application or Windows problems. Make sure all important or recommended Windows updates are installed. You learned how to do that in Chapter 12.

Step 7. A healthy hard drive is essential to a healthy computer. A corrupted or failing hard drive often presents itself as a Windows or application error. To check the hard drive for corruption, use the **Check Disk** utility.

Check Disk—A Windows utility used to find bad or corrupted areas of a hard drive. The utility must be run before Windows is started.

Do the following:

    a. Use Windows Explorer to open the Local Disk (C:) Properties box. Click the **Tools** tab (see Figure 13-20).

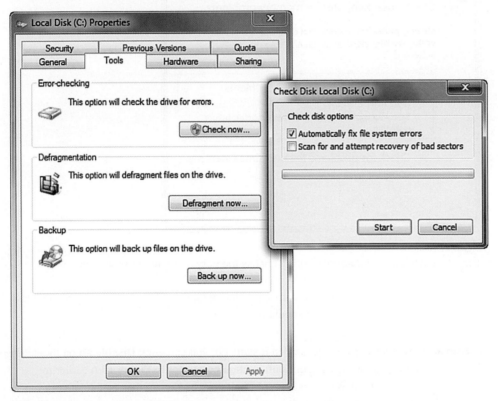

FIGURE 13-20
Check the hard drive for errors or corruption.

    b. Click **Check now**. The Check Disk Local Disk (C:) box appears, which is also shown in the figure. Make sure **Automatically fix file system errors** is checked. Click **Start** and follow directions onscreen. You need to restart your computer for the process to run.

    c. If the program reports the hard drive has errors, don't trust the drive with your important data and plan to replace the drive soon.

Step 8. Another essential hardware device is memory. A memory module might be going bad, which can cause random Windows errors. To check for problems with memory, use the **Memory Diagnostic** utility.

Memory Diagnostic   A Windows utility you use to test for a failing memory module. Use the **mdsched** command to start the utility. The utility then restarts Windows and checks memory before Windows is loaded.

Do the following:

a. Click **Start**, type **mdsched** in the *Search programs and files* box, and press **Enter**. If necessary, provide the administrator password. The Windows Memory Diagnostic box appears (see Figure 13-21). Click **Restart now and check for problems (recommended)**.

FIGURE 13-21
The Windows Memory Diagnostic utility checks memory modules for problems.

b. If the program reports a problem with memory, all the memory modules in the computer should be replaced.

Step 9. If Windows gives errors when it starts up, you can click **Disable all** on the Startup tab of the System Configuration box (refer to Figure 13-6 earlier in the chapter). If Windows starts without errors, you can then enable one startup program after another until you find the one causing the error.

Other problems that might give Windows errors include a failing hardware device, corrupted device driver, or corrupted Windows installation. These types of problems are best handled by an experienced computer repair technician.

On Your Own 13-8
Check Your Hard Drive and Memory for Errors

Application errors and Windows errors are sometimes caused by a failing hard drive or failing memory module. Use the Windows Check Disk utility to test your hard drive for errors. Did the utility report any errors? Use the Memory Diagnostic utility to test the memory modules installed on your computer. Did this utility report any errors?

I Think My Computer Has a Virus

Symptoms of an infected computer include

▸ Pop-up ads appear when you're surfing the web.

▸ The system starts up and runs slowly and programs take longer to launch.

▸ A hardware device such as the optical drive or USB port no longer works.

▸ Filenames and file sizes in Windows Explorer have changed.

▸ Internet Explorer has a toolbar you didn't ask for or your home page has changed.

▸ Your antivirus software reports a problem.

Do the following to remove the malware:

Step 1. If the computer is connected to a local network, immediately disconnect it from the network. You don't want the virus to spread to other computers on the network.

Step 2. Use antivirus software to scan the entire hard drive for malware. If it finds malware, follow its directions to delete the malicious program. Then restart your computer. Reconnect to the Internet and command the antivirus program to download its updates. Then disconnect from the Internet and scan the hard drive again.

Step 3. If new malware is found, keep repeating this process until a scan comes up clean. Then restart the computer one more time checking for errors.

Step 4. Connect to the Internet and make sure that all important Windows updates are installed. Also use the Network and Sharing Center to verify that your network location is set to protect your computer.

> **Not Working?** Sometimes a system is so infected that antivirus software cannot run. If this is the case, start Windows in Safe Mode. In Safe Mode, the virus program might not start and the antivirus software can run. How to start a computer in Safe Mode is covered later in this chapter in the section "My Computer Won't Start."

Do the following to clean up Internet Explorer:

Step 1. Using Control Panel, open the Programs and Features window. Look for plug-in or toolbar programs you don't want. To uninstall a program, select it and then click **Uninstall**.

Step 2. Open Internet Explorer. Click **Tools**, **Internet Options**. The Internet Options box opens. You can change the home page on the **General** tab.

Step 3. To disable any add-ons you have not already uninstalled, click the **Programs** tab and then click **Manage add-ons**. The Manage Add-ons box appears (see Figure 13-22). Select an add-on and click **Disable**.

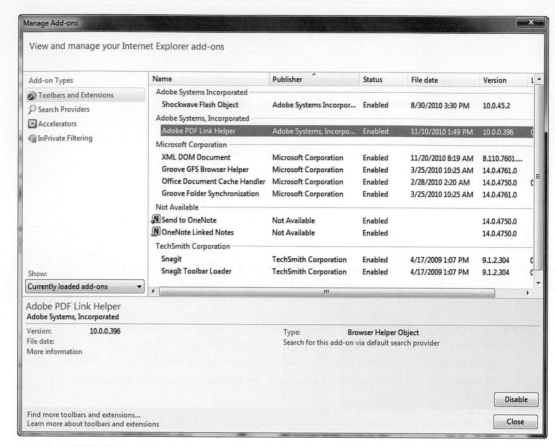

FIGURE 13-22
Disable Internet Explorer add-ons you do not need.

> **Step 4.** Close all windows and then open Internet Explorer. Verify that all is working as it should.

If you are still having problems, know that an experienced technician can dig much deeper to clean up an infected system. It's time to ask for some expert help.

My Computer Is Too Slow

A computer might slow down over time if too many programs are running in the background or the hard drive is full. Other problems that cause a slow computer are not enough memory, a slow **processor**, or a slow Internet connection.

processor

> **processor**—The component where all processing of data and instructions takes place. Processors for personal computers are made by Intel (intel.com) and AMD (amd.com) and vary greatly in speed and other features. The processor is also called the central processing unit or CPU.

Do the following to help solve the problem of a slow computer:

Step 1. Follow directions given earlier in the chapter to clean up the hard drive, uninstall software, and disable programs from launching at startup.

Step 2. Consider you might need more memory. Installing more memory (called upgrading memory) is not as expensive as other upgrades such as upgrading your processor or hard drive. A memory upgrade might significantly improve computer performance.

To find out how much memory is installed on a computer, click **Start**, right-click **Computer**, and click **Properties** in the shortcut menu. The System window opens (see Figure 13-23). Information about the system, including the amount of installed memory (RAM), is reported on this window. In Figure 13-23, that amount is 2GB. Also notice in the figure the system type is a **32-bit operating system**.

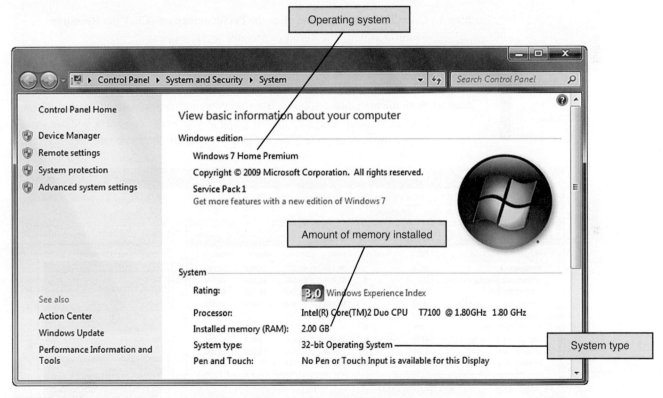

FIGURE 13-23
Use the System window to find out how much memory is installed.

> **32-bit operating system**—An operating system that processes 32 bits at a time.

Microsoft recommends a minimum of 1GB of memory for a 32-bit version of Windows 7 and 2GB of memory for a 64-bit version of Windows 7. If you want to improve performance, a 32-bit operating system can benefit from up to 4GB of memory. A **64-bit operating system** can benefit from up to 8GB of memory.

> **64-bit operating system**—An operating system that processes 64 bits at a time. Each edition of Windows 7 comes in a 32-bit or 64-bit version. The 64-bit versions are generally faster and require more memory than the 32-bit versions.

The amount of memory you need depends on how you use your computer. For example, the more applications you have open at the same time, the more memory you need. The **Resource Monitor** tool can help you monitor memory use.

> **Resource Monitor**—A Windows utility that monitors the performance of the CPU, memory, hard drive, and network.

To use Resource Monitor, follow these steps:

Step 1.   Open **Task Manager** and click the **Performance** tab. Click the **Resource Monitor** button. The Resource Monitor window opens.

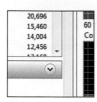

Step 2.   Click the **Memory** tab. Click the down arrow to the right of Physical Memory. A bar graph showing how memory is currently used appears (see Figure 13-24).

Step 3.   With the bar graph displayed, use your computer as you normally would for an hour or so. Keep an eye on the bar graph as you work. You know you can benefit from a memory upgrade if the bar graph frequently shows no free memory.

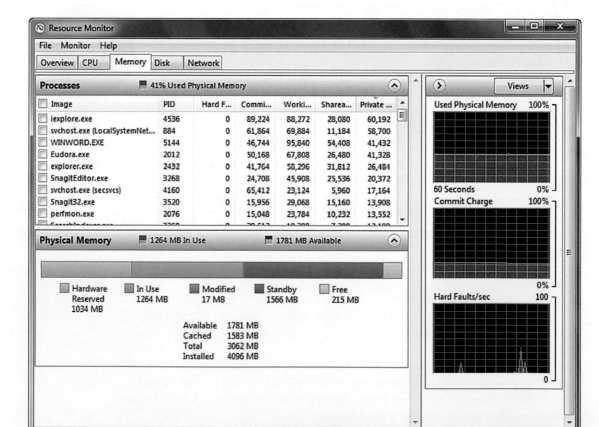

FIGURE 13-24
Use the Resource Monitor to monitor how memory is being used.

If you decide to upgrade memory, be sure to purchase memory modules that are compatible with your computer and have an experienced technician install the modules.

To decide whether your computer needs a memory upgrade, investigate your system and then answer these questions:

Step 1. What edition of Windows is installed on your computer?

Step 2. Is your operating system a 32-bit or 64-bit system?

Step 3. How much memory is installed?

Step 4. Open the memory bar graph in Resource Monitor. With the graph displayed, work at your computer for a few minutes. Did Resource Monitor report that the computer ran out of free memory as you worked?

Step 5. Does your computer need a memory upgrade? If so, what is the total amount of memory you need?

On Your Own 13-9
Decide Whether Your Computer Needs a Memory Upgrade

 Solutions Appendix

For help, see Solution 13-9: How to Decide Whether Your Computer Needs a Memory Upgrade.

My Computer Won't Start

A variety of problems can cause a computer not to start. Here are the general steps to follow to uncover the source of the problem:

Step 1. Look for lights on the front of the computer and listen for the fan spinning. If you don't see lights or hear the fan, the computer might not be getting power. Is it plugged in and turned on? For a desktop computer, check the power switch on the back of the computer case. For a laptop, the battery might be low. Plug in the AC adapter.

Step 2. If the computer has power, but the monitor is blank, check to see whether the monitor is plugged in and turned on. Look for a small light on the front of a monitor to indicate it is getting power.

Step 3. Before Windows starts, the processor goes through the steps of checking hardware and starting up essential hardware devices. Messages on a black screen show up during this stage of starting (also called booting) the system (see Figure 13-25). If the system halts with an error message on a black screen, go to a working computer and use Google to search for the error message.

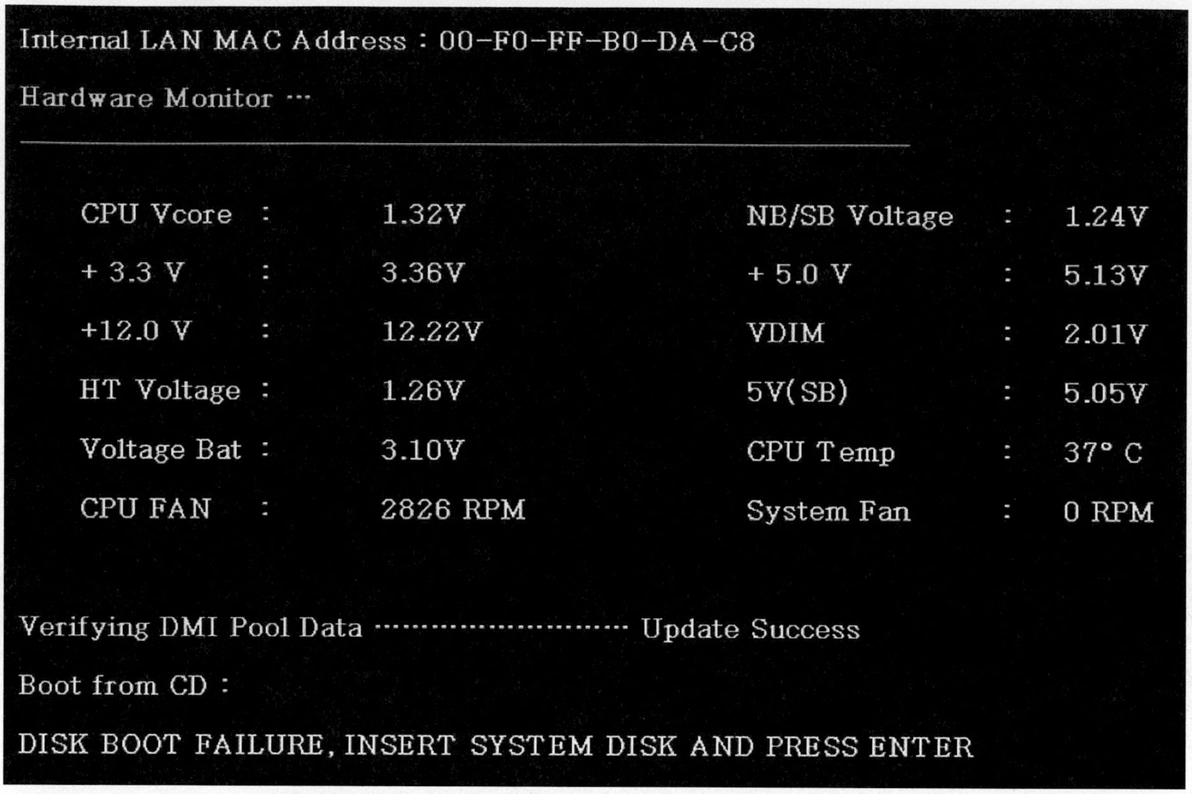

```
Internal LAN MAC Address : 00–F0–FF–B0–DA–C8

Hardware Monitor ···
_____


     CPU Vcore   :      1.32V              NB/SB Voltage   :    1.24V

     + 3.3 V     :      3.36V              + 5.0 V         :    5.13V

     +12.0 V     :      12.22V             VDIM            :    2.01V

     HT Voltage  :      1.26V              5V(SB)          :    5.05V

     Voltage Bat :      3.10V              CPU Temp        :    37° C

     CPU FAN     :      2826 RPM           System Fan      :    0 RPM



Verifying DMI Pool Data ···················· Update Success

Boot from CD :

DISK BOOT FAILURE, INSERT SYSTEM DISK AND PRESS ENTER
```

FIGURE 13-25
A message on a black background indicates a problem with essential hardware devices.

Step 4. When Windows encounters an error it cannot recover from, it displays a STOP error on a blue screen. This screen is called a blue screen of death (BSOD) or STOP error by computer technicians. The number that identifies the STOP error is listed near the middle of this screen (see Figure 13-26). Do a Google search on the characters following STOP. For example, enter this search string in Google:

```
STOP 0x000000F4 error message
```

Rely on the Microsoft.com site for the best advice about the error and what to do about it.

Step 5. If you cannot start Windows normally, try to start in **Safe Mode**. If you can get to the Windows desktop in Safe Mode, you might be able to solve the underlying problem.

> **Safe Mode**—A barebones way to start Windows, which launches only the essential hardware devices and programs. You can sometimes start a computer in Safe Mode when Windows refuses to start in the normal way.

```
A problem has been detected and windows has been shut down to prevent damage
to your computer.

A process or thread crucial to system operation has unexpectedly exited or been
terminated.

If this is the first time you've seen this Stop error screen,
restart your computer. If this screen appears again, follow
these steps:

Check to make sure any new hardware or software is properly installed.
If this is a new installation, ask your hardware or software manufacturer
for any windows updates you might need.

If problems continue, disable or remove any newly installed hardware
or software. Disable BIOS memory options such as caching or shadowing.
If you need to use Safe Mode to remove or disable components, restart
your computer, press F8 to select Advanced Startup Options, and then
select Safe Mode.

Technical information:

*** STOP: 0x000000F4 (0x00000003,0x84AEED40,0x84AEEEAC,0x82850CF0)

Collecting data for crash dump ...
Initializing disk for crash dump ...
Beginning dump of physical memory.
Dumping physical memory to disk:  15
```

Value used to identify the STOP error

FIGURE 13-26
A message on a blue background indicates Windows cannot recover from the error.

Do the following to launch Windows in Safe Mode:

a. Power up the computer and press the **F8** key before Windows starts. The Advanced Boot Options menu appears (see Figure 13-27).

b. Select **Safe Mode with Networking** and press **Enter**. Windows starts up. After you log on to Windows, the Windows desktop loads in Safe Mode (see Figure 13-28). Windows Help and Support automatically opens to offer suggestions as to how to use Safe Mode.

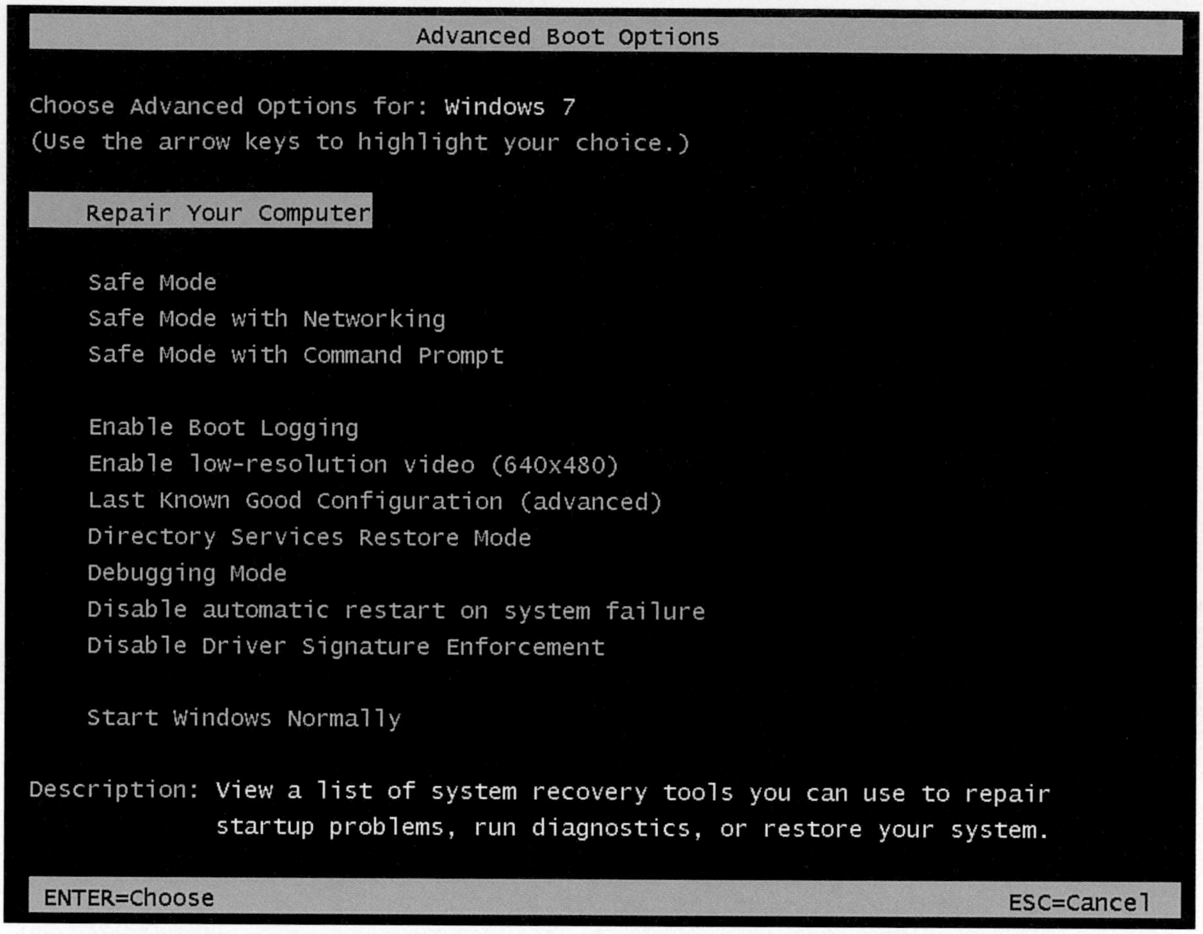

```
┌──────────────────────────────────────────────────────────────┐
│                    Advanced Boot Options                       │
├──────────────────────────────────────────────────────────────┤
│                                                                │
│ Choose Advanced Options for: Windows 7                         │
│ (Use the arrow keys to highlight your choice.)                 │
│                                                                │
│   Repair Your Computer                                         │
│                                                                │
│     Safe Mode                                                  │
│     Safe Mode with Networking                                  │
│     Safe Mode with Command Prompt                              │
│                                                                │
│     Enable Boot Logging                                        │
│     Enable low-resolution video (640x480)                      │
│     Last Known Good Configuration (advanced)                   │
│     Directory Services Restore Mode                            │
│     Debugging Mode                                             │
│     Disable automatic restart on system failure                │
│     Disable Driver Signature Enforcement                       │
│                                                                │
│     Start Windows Normally                                     │
│                                                                │
│ Description: View a list of system recovery tools you can use to repair │
│              startup problems, run diagnostics, or restore your system. │
│                                                                │
├──────────────────────────────────────────────────────────────┤
│ ENTER=Choose                                        ESC=Cancel │
└──────────────────────────────────────────────────────────────┘
```

FIGURE 13-27
When the computer first starts, press F8 to display the Advanced Boot Options menu.

Step 6. Try these steps while in Safe Mode:

    a. A virus might be the problem. Use antivirus software to scan the hard drive.

    b. If you have just installed new software, use the Programs and Features window to uninstall the software.

    c. Open the Action Center and resolve any urgent problems it reports. Urgent problems in the Action Center are indicated by a red bar.

Step 7. Try restarting the system. If you still get errors, it's time to get help from an experienced technician.

FIGURE 13-28
Windows Safe Mode starts up with only the minimum of hardware and software.

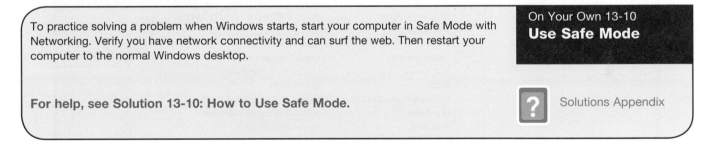

To practice solving a problem when Windows starts, start your computer in Safe Mode with Networking. Verify you have network connectivity and can surf the web. Then restart your computer to the normal Windows desktop.

On Your Own 13-10
Use Safe Mode

For help, see Solution 13-10: How to Use Safe Mode.

? Solutions Appendix

Prepare to Talk with a Computer Repair Technician

You will not always be able to solve every computer problem. If this is the case, you need to turn to professional help. Before you call for help, gather information about the problem and the computer. Do the following:

Step 1. Start at the beginning. Restart your computer and carefully check for error messages or the first time the problem presents itself.

Step 2. Note what works and what does not work. Write down the exact error message.

Step 3. Ask yourself, "When did the problem start? What had just happened when the problem started?" These are important first questions a technician asks when she begins the troubleshooting process.

Step 4. Is the computer under warranty? If so, have the purchase receipt and warranty available. You also need the model and serial number of the computer. For a laptop, look on the bottom of the computer. For a desktop, look on the back of the computer case.

Step 5. A technician needs to know the brand and model of a laptop, netbook, or brand-name computer. Do the following to find this information:

   a. If you can start the computer, click **Start**, enter **msinfo32** in the *Search programs and files* box, and press **Enter**. The System Information window appears (see Figure 13-29). Useful information a technician might ask for is labeled in the figure.

> System Information—A Windows utility that reports technical information about a computer, hardware, and software. To launch the utility, use the msinfo32 command.

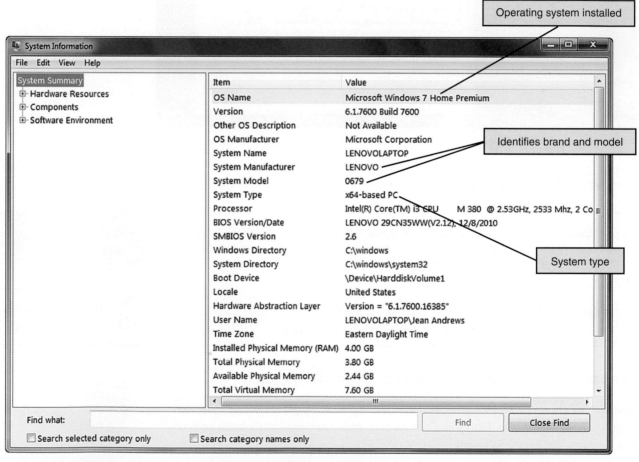

FIGURE 13-29
The System Information window gives useful information a technician can use for trouble-shooting.

   b. If you cannot start the computer, know that you can find the model and serial numbers on the bottom of a laptop or netbook. You also might find them in the documentation that came with your computer.

As you speak with the technician, state the problem as clearly as you can with as much detail as the technician needs.

Summary

Keeping a Computer Running Well

▶ Ongoing routine maintenance can keep a computer from slowing down over time.

▶ Routine maintenance includes keeping the hard drive from filling up; uninstalling software you no longer need; limiting unnecessary startup programs; and protecting hardware from damage caused by power surges, heat, and humidity.

▶ To clean up a hard drive, empty the Recycle Bin, use the Disk Cleanup utility, and make sure Windows is set to defragment the drive weekly.

▶ Use the Programs and Features window in Control Panel to uninstall software.

▶ Use the System Configuration utility (msconfig) to control the programs that are launched when Windows starts. Too many startup programs can slow down Windows.

Taking Care of Hardware

▶ Use a surge protector to protect a computer against surging electricity.

▶ To prevent a computer from overheating, keep vents clear of dust and unobstructed for good airflow. Don't leave a computer in a hot car or humid conditions. Protect a computer from static electricity.

▶ Clean a monitor, mouse, and keyboard using cleaning wipes or a soft cloth. Protect CDs and DVDs from heat, direct sunlight, scratches, and dirt.

▶ Use Windows power settings to conserve electricity and make a battery charge on a laptop last longer.

Solving the Most Common Computer Problems

▶ Look in the Recycle Bin to find a deleted file. Use the Previous Versions tab of the file's Properties box to restore a file.

▶ Adjust screen resolution and text size using Windows display settings to make a screen easier to read.

▶ Use buttons on the front of a desktop monitor to adjust brightness, contrast, and position of the lighted area on the monitor screen.

▶ Use Task Manager to end an application that is not responding.

▶ Use the Action Center to solve problems with Windows, software, and hardware, including problems installing software or hardware devices.

▶ Problems with printing can be caused by the document, the application, Windows, printer connectivity, or the printer. Use the Devices and Printers window to help solve printer problems.

▶ The Check Disk utility can check the hard drive for corruption. The Memory Diagnostic utility can check for a failing memory module. The hard drive and memory modules are essential to a computer working well. If the device gives errors, it needs to be replaced.

▶ If your computer is infected with a virus, run the antivirus software multiple times until the scan returns clean. You might need to make several scans to clean an infected system.

▶ Use the Internet Options box to disable Internet Explorer add-ons. The add-ons can be uninstalled using the Programs and Features window.

▶ To speed up a slow computer, clean up the hard drive, uninstall software, and limit startup processes. Upgrading memory is an inexpensive option that can improve Windows performance.

▶ A 64-bit operating system runs faster than a 32-bit operating system and requires more memory.

- ▶ When a computer first starts, the hardware presents error messages on a black screen before Windows starts. Windows presents error messages on a blue screen called the blue screen of death.

- ▶ Safe Mode is a barebones way to start Windows and might work when starting Windows normally gives errors.

- ▶ Before talking with a computer repair technician, gather information about the problem and the system. The System Information window can help.

Review Questions

Answer these questions to assess your skills and knowledge of the content covered in the chapter. Your instructor can provide you with the correct answers when you are ready to check your work.

1. How often does Windows normally defragment the hard drive?

2. Which window in Control Panel do you use to uninstall software?

3. What utility can you use to control the programs launched at startup? What command do you use to start the utility?

4. What device can you use with your computer to protect the computer against lightning?

5. Why is it not a good idea to use your laptop while it is sitting on a pillow?

6. You accidentally left your laptop in your car on a freezing night and then brought it inside. Why is it important that you not turn it on immediately?

7. List four types of hardware devices on a laptop that consume energy and their use should be limited when you're trying to extend the battery charge.

8. Which screen resolution is likely to give the best results for a monitor?

9. If Microsoft Word attempts to perform an operation it cannot complete, it might lock up. When you try to close the Word window, you see "Not Responding" in the title bar. How can you solve the problem?

10. What Windows utility do you use if you connect a USB scanner to your computer and the scanner does not install properly?

11. Your document will not print, so you decide to clear the printer queue. You notice another document first in the queue that belongs to another user. You are logged on to Windows with a standard user account. What can you do to clear the queue?

12. To demonstrate that the printer is working correctly, do you print a Windows test page or a printer test page?

13. What two essential hardware devices might be the source of random Windows error messages onscreen? What two Windows utilities can you use to check these devices?

14. What two utility windows described in the chapter can you use to display the amount of memory installed in a computer?

15. When first starting a computer, what key do you press to launch the Advanced Boot Options menu?

Chapter Mastery Project

Find out how well you have mastered the content in this chapter by completing this project. If you can answer all the questions and do all the steps without looking back at the chapter details, you have mastered this chapter. If you can complete the project by finding answers using Windows Help and Support or the web, you have proven that you can teach yourself how to care for a computer.

If you find you need a lot of help doing the project and you have not yet read the chapter or done the activities, drop back and start at the beginning of the chapter and then return to this project.

> **Hint** All the key terms in the chapter are used in this mastery project.
> If you encounter a key word you don't know, such as *defragment,* enter **define:defragment** in the Internet Explorer search box.

Mastery Project Part 1: Keeping a Computer Running Well

If you need help completing this part of the mastery project, please review the "Keeping a Computer Running Well" section in the chapter.

You need the Windows administrator password to do many of the activities in this project. Do the following to keep a computer in good running order:

Step 1. Clean up the hard drive by emptying the Recycle Bin and using Disk Cleanup. Using Disk Cleanup, clean up data files and system files. Make sure at least 15% of the hard drive is free space. When cleaning up the drive, did you delete a previous Windows installation? What percentage of the drive is free space?

Step 2. Verify that Windows is automatically defragmenting the drive. What day and time is this happening?

Step 3. Examine the list of software installed on your computer. Are any plug-ins listed? If so, what are the name and purpose of one of these plug-ins?

Step 4. Did you find a program listed that you did not know its purpose? What is that program name? Research on the web and find out the purpose of the program. What is its purpose? Do you need to keep this program installed?

Step 5. Are there any programs listed that you understand the purpose and know that you no longer need? If so, uninstall these programs.

Step 6. Open System Configuration. List the startup item and program filename of four startup programs showing in this dialog box. What is the purpose of each program? If you don't know the purpose, research it on the web.

Step 7. Can you safely disable any of these four programs? If so, disable the program. Restart your computer and verify all is working as you expect. If you have a problem, go back and enable the program.

Mastery Project Part 2: Taking Care of Hardware

If you need help completing this part of the mastery project, please review the "Taking Care of Hardware" section in the chapter.

Do the following to take care of hardware:

Step 1. Research on the web and find one portable surge protector that you can carry with you when traveling with your laptop. What is the brand and model of the device? How much does it cost? What is the guarantee of protection that the manufacturer claims for the device?

Step 2. Research the web and find a can of compressed air to clean your keyboard and your computer vents. How much does one can cost? What is the brand name of the can?

Step 3. Look at your computer and find the air vents. Describe where these vents are located. Are the vents unobstructed and free from dust? What can you do to make sure the vents can get the best airflow to keep your computer cool?

Step 4. If you are using a desktop computer, is it sitting where it might get kicked? If so, move it to a safer place.

Step 5. Feel the bottom and sides of your computer after it has been running for a while. Does it feel too warm? What can you do to keep it cool? List four external factors mentioned in the chapter that can cause hardware devices to not last as long as they should?

Step 6. Suppose you leave a CD on the dashboard of your car in the summer. Why might it not last as long as a CD kept at your desk in your home?

Step 7. Using the Windows power settings, set your power plan to turn off the display after 10 minutes of inactivity and put the computer to sleep after 30 minutes. Require a password when the computer wakes up.

Step 8. Set the power button to shut down the computer. Test the power button function by pressing it. Does the computer perform an orderly shutdown?

Answer the following questions:

1. What two items appear on the Power Options window of a laptop computer that don't appear on the Power Options window of a desktop?

2. You will be away from an electrical outlet all day, but your laptop battery lasts only four hours. What can you do to make sure you can use your laptop all day?

3. To conserve the battery charge, which two activities should you not do:

   a. Use your laptop to watch a movie on DVD.

   b. Dim your monitor screen.

   c. Watch a movie streamed over a public Wi-Fi network.

   d. Watch a movie stored on the hard drive of your laptop.

Mastery Project Part 3: Solving the Most Common Computer Problems

If you need help completing this part of the mastery project, please review the "Solving the Most Common Computer Problems" section in the chapter.

Do the following to practice the skills needed to solve computer problems:

Step 1. Create a file in the Documents library of your hard drive. Delete the file. Use the Recycle Bin to recover the deleted file.

Step 2. Locate a file on the hard drive that has been there for some time. Open the Properties box of this file and look at the Previous Versions tab. Are there any previous versions listed? If so, when were these files created?

Step 3. Verify the screen resolution of your monitor is set to the highest setting. List the steps you took to check this setting. What is another name for the highest screen resolution available for a monitor?

Step 4. Suppose your friend has poor eyesight and needs the text on the screen to be very large. Experiment with customizing the text size on the monitor screen. Set the text size at 200%. After you view the text at this size, return it to the default size.

Step 5. Suggest to your friend that the magnifier tool might be a better solution than having all the text on the screen so large. Experiment using the magnifier tool in Lens view. Pin the magnifier tool to the taskbar so it is handy to access.

Step 6. If you are using a desktop monitor, use the buttons on the front of the monitor to adjust the brightness and contrast to get the most contrast and the most brightness. This setting can help someone with poor eyesight. After you make the adjustments, return them to the settings you are comfortable using.

Answer the following questions about a problem connecting to the Internet:

1. Suppose you are working from home and have a cable modem connection to the Internet and a router for your small home network. List the steps to reset the connection.

2. You notice the lights near the network port on your desktop computer are not on. Is your next step to check the network cable connection or ask Windows to repair the connection?

Do the following to practice using more Windows utilities:

Step 1. Open two instances of the Paint program. Use Task Manager to close both Paint windows.

Step 2. Does the Action Center flag in the taskbar report an urgent problem? If so, use the Action Center to resolve the problem. If you don't see the Action Center flag in the taskbar, use the Notification Area Icons window to place it there.

Step 3. If you have access to a printer, practice solving a printer problem by doing the following:

    a. Check the printer queue and clear any pending print jobs. Why might you not be able to delete print jobs for all users of this computer?

    b. Print a Windows test page.

    c. Print a printer test page.

Answer these questions:

1. What is the name of your Windows default printer?

2. What Windows utility can you use to solve a problem with a USB printer not installing correctly?

3. If you get a Windows error message you do not understand, how can you get help to understand the message?

4. What window in Control Panel can you use to repair an application giving errors?

Do the following:

Step 1. If you have not already done so, use the Windows Check Disk utility to scan your hard drive for errors and corruption.

Step 2. If you have not already done so, use the Windows Memory Diagnostic to scan memory for a failing memory module.

Step 3. Use Control Panel to look at the list of all software installed on your computer. Is there any program you no longer need? If so, uninstall it.

Step 4. Use the Internet Options box of Internet Explorer to look at the list of add-ons installed. Is there any add-on you no longer need? If so, disable it.

Step 5. Examine your system using the System window. Do you have a 32-bit or 64-bit operating system installed?

Step 6. How much memory do you have installed?

Step 7. What is the optimum memory for your system? Would your system benefit from a memory upgrade.

Step 8. Crucial.com sells reliable memory modules and offers a utility that can tell you how much memory you have installed and what memory modules you need to buy for an upgrade. Go to the crucial.com site and run the Crucial System Scanner Tool on your computer. What memory modules did Crucial recommend you buy? Do not make the purchase and attempt to install the memory before first talking with an experienced computer technician.

Step 9. Open the System Information window. What is the reported System Model for your computer? For a laptop, what does the system model information tell you? For a desktop computer, what does the system model information tell you?

A computer startup problem is sometimes caused by a startup program that is giving errors. Suppose you cannot start Windows because it crashes at startup. Do the following to practice solving this type of startup problem:

Step 1. To disable all startup programs so you can eliminate these as the source of the problem, start the computer in Safe Mode. What is the color of the desktop background when the system is in Safe Mode?

Step 2. In Safe Mode, open the System Configuration utility. Write down the items enabled or disabled on the Startup tab so you can return to these settings later. Disable all startup programs. Restart Windows normally.

Step 3. Before continuing with this project, return the startup items in the System Configuration utility box as you found them.

Answer these questions about solving a computer startup problem:

1. Which type of error screen appears first during startup: an error message on a black screen or an error message on a blue screen?

2. What is the best way to find out the source of a problem caused by a STOP error?

Becoming an Independent Learner

Answer the following questions about becoming an independent learner:

1. To teach yourself to solve computer problems, do you think it is best to rely on the chapter or on the web and Windows Help when you need answers?

2. The most important skill learned in this chapter is how to teach yourself a computer skill. Rate yourself at Level A through E on how well you are doing with this skill. What is your level?

   ○ Level A: I was able to successfully complete the Chapter Mastery Project without the help of doing the On Your Own activities in the chapter.

   ○ Level B: I completed all the On Your Own activities and the Chapter Mastery Project without referring to any of the solutions in the *Solutions Appendix*.

   ○ Level C: I completed all the On Your Own activities and the Chapter Mastery Project by using just a few of the solutions in the *Solutions Appendix*.

   ○ Level D: I completed all the On Your Own activities and the Chapter Mastery Project by using many of the solutions in the *Solutions Appendix*.

   ○ Level E: I completed all the On Your Own activities and the Chapter Mastery Project and had to use all of the solutions in the *Solutions Appendix*.

To continue toward the goal of teaching yourself computer skills, if you are not at Level A, try to move up one level on how you learn in Chapter 14, "Buying Your Own Personal Computer."

Projects to Help You

Now that you have mastered the material in this chapter, you are ready to tackle the three projects introduced at the beginning of the chapter in the section "How Will This Chapter Help Me?"

Project 1: Maintaining a Personal Computer

A computer can slow down over time if it is not well maintained. Are you responsible for your own computer, or do you have a friend who needs help maintaining his computer? If so, do the following to make sure this computer is being well maintained:

Step 1. Following directions in the chapter, go through the steps to make sure the computer is secure, the hard drive is clean, and Windows is not bogged down with unnecessary startup processes.

Step 2. Check the hardware to make sure it is being protected from power surges, heat, and humidity. Clean the computer vents, keyboard, mouse, and monitor screen.

Step 3. Adjust the power settings as needed to conserve electricity. For a laptop, adjust the power settings as needed to conserve the battery charge.

PERSONAL PROJECT: My computer is only three years old and has started to run slowly. Is it getting old? Should I replace it, or can I do something to speed it up?

Project 2: Setting Up Windows Maintenance and the Windows Desktop

Suppose you have just received a computer to be used while you are working toward a degree. You need the computer to last for several years, and you want to set it up with your own preferences. To do that, you need the administrator password. If you're not sure how to perform a task, check Windows Help and Support or search the web.

Do the following to make sure the computer is set up for good maintenance:

Step 1. Verify antivirus software is set to run in the background and automatically update itself.

Step 2. Verify Windows Update is set to install updates automatically.

Step 3. Verify the Windows network location is set to protect the computer from attacks.

Step 4. Verify Windows is defragmenting the hard drive weekly.

Step 5. Open the Resource Monitor. Leave the Memory tab displayed while you work at your computer. Does the Resource Monitor show signs you don't have enough memory?

ACADEMIC PROJECT: I've been assigned a computer to use while in school, and I need to take good care of it. I want to make sure it stays protected and runs well. I also want to change some settings on the Windows desktop.

Do the following to customize the Windows desktop:

Step 1. You plan to use the Documents library to hold all your academic papers. Normally, Windows puts only the Recycle Bin on the desktop. Add an icon to the desktop that will open the Documents library in Windows Explorer when you double-click it. This icon on the desktop is called a shortcut icon.

Step 2. Rename the shortcut icon to **My Academic Papers**.

Step 3. Change the desktop wallpaper to the **Nature** theme. After you view this theme when applied, change it to a different theme if you don't like this one.

Step 4. You plan to use Microsoft Word and Excel in your academic career. Normally, Windows puts only the Internet Explorer and Windows Explorer Quick Launch icons in the taskbar. To make Word and Excel easier to access, add these two program icons to the taskbar.

Step 5. Log off and then log back on to Windows to verify all your preferences are applied when you first log on.

After you complete this project, you might want to undo all the changes you made to the Windows desktop.

Project 3: Solving Computer Problems for Others

Part 1: Write and Edit User Tutorials

As a computer help desk techie, you find that users often ask you how to change a Windows setting or solve a computer problem. Work with a partner on this project to develop some help desk tutorials that you can pass on to the users you support. You develop two of the tutorials, and your partner develops two. Write clear and concise directions for a novice user. Include screenshots where appropriate. Recall from Chapter 1, "Using Windows 7 to Manage Applications and Data," that you can use the Windows Snipping Tool to make a screenshot.

Exchange the tutorials and edit the tutorials written by your partner. Be sure to read the tutorials as though you are a novice user who needs the help the tutorial offers. Mark anything that is not a clear direction with the explanations you need.

Return the tutorials to your partner for her to approve your edits or redo the changes. Present the four tutorials to your instructor as a team project. Here are the tutorials to write:

1. How to add a shortcut to the Windows desktop pointing to a folder on the hard drive
2. How to install a photograph as the Windows desktop wallpaper
3. How to use Task Manager to end an application that is hung
4. How to restart the computer in Safe Mode, disable all startup programs, and restart the computer normally

Part 2: Use the System Information Utility

Help desk technicians speaking with a user on the phone often use the System Information utility to find out basic information about the user's computer. Write a script that help desk personnel can use during a phone call to find the answers to these questions:

1. What edition of Windows is installed?
2. What service packs are installed?
3. What is the system model?
4. What is the system type?
5. How much physical memory (RAM) is installed?

The system type tells a technician if the operating system installed is a 32-bit or 64-bit OS. The two possibilities for system type are X86-based PC or x64-based PC. Research on the web and find out how to interpret this information to decide if the OS is 32-bit or 64-bit.

What is the system model of your computer as reported by the System Information window? Research this system model on the web. What information did you find about the model?

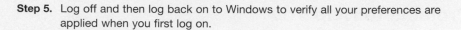

TECHNICAL CAREER PROJECT: I work on a help desk, and we get lots of questions about how to use Windows and how to solve Windows problems. My team leader has asked me to write some tutorials we can send to users when they call. I also need to write a script the help desk can use when we need to find out about the user's computer.

Project to Help Others

One of the best ways to learn is to teach someone else. In teaching someone else, you are making a contribution into that person's life. As part of each chapter's work, you are encouraged to teach someone else a skill you have learned. In this chapter, help someone learn to maintain a computer and fix a computer problem.

Who is your apprentice? _____

People learn best when they want to learn and when they are ready to learn. Consider the computer skills your apprentice already knows. Based on these skills, list five tasks covered in this chapter that you believe your apprentice is ready to learn. Here are some suggestions, but you might have other ideas:

1. How to find a deleted file in the Recycle Bin
2. How to clean up the hard drive
3. How to change monitor settings
4. How to rid a system of a virus

Ask your apprentice which of these skills he would like to learn and then help your apprentice learn these skills. Remember, a coach teaches from the sidelines. Watch as your apprentice explores and help him learn the art of teaching himself a computer skill.

CHAPTER 14

Buying Your Own Personal Computer

IN THIS CHAPTER, YOU WILL

Decide whether you need an upgrade or a new computer

Decide what type of computer you need

Learn about extra features a computer might have

Shop for a computer and peripherals

Learn to set up a new computer and recycle an old computer

The computer market is constantly changing. The facts about the current computer market presented in this chapter are likely to be outdated quickly. Therefore, you must learn how to investigate hardware and software offerings on your own and make decisions based on your findings. Try to do each On Your Own activity without any help. But remember, if you need help, you can always refer to the solutions in the *Solutions Appendix*.

JUMP RIGHT IN

If you want even more of a challenge, try proceeding directly to the Chapter Mastery Project at the end of this chapter. If you need help on the project, refer to the On Your Own activities in the chapter or use the web to do your own independent investigating. When you complete the project, you will have mastered the skills in this chapter. Then proceed to the other projects that require you apply your skills to new situations.

How Will This Chapter Help Me?

Recall that each chapter provides three projects focusing on personal, academic, or technical career goals. Depending on your own interests, you might choose to complete any or all of these projects to help you achieve your goals.

PERSONAL PROJECT: I want to buy a super responsive gaming computer with realistic graphics to annihilate my enemies online. What makes a gaming computer perform better than any machine out there? What can I do to beef it up?

ACADEMIC PROJECT: I've decided to buy a computer to use during my academic career. I want to research and find the best buy for my money with all the features I need. It must last me for four years, so I don't want to make a mistake.

TECHNICAL CAREER PROJECT: One day I want to build a computer. I work with technical people who have bought parts and built their own computer from these parts. What parts do I need and where do I purchase them?

Do I Need an Upgrade or a New Computer?

You might be ready to buy your own computer or help someone else buy one. If you already have a computer, the first question to ask yourself is whether you need to upgrade your computer or buy a new computer. Computers tend to need replacing about every four to seven years. If you already have a computer that is less than five years old, consider upgrading it rather than replacing it.

People replace a computer for two reasons: the computer does not have a device they want, or the computer is too slow. Figure 14-1 can help you decide whether an upgrade can satisfy your needs. The following sections describe each step in more detail.

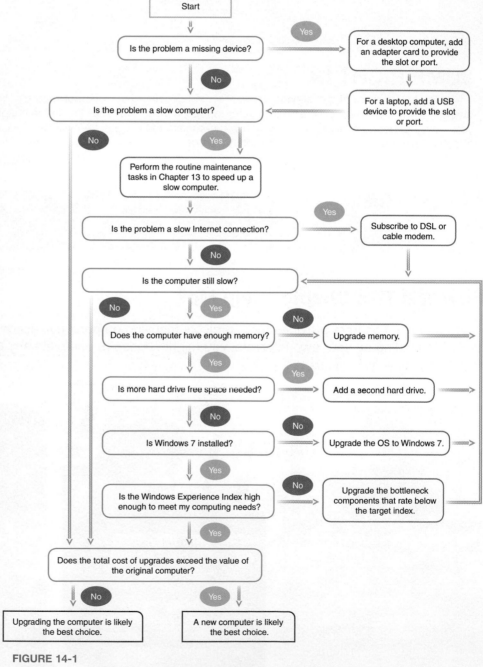

FIGURE 14-1
Can I solve my computer problem by upgrading my current computer?

Generally, the total cost of upgrades should not exceed the current value of your computer. The cost of each upgrade includes the cost of the component and the cost of labor to install it.

Let's work our way through the diagram in Figure 14-1 to see whether an upgrade is your best option.

Is Your Computer Missing a Device?

You might be able to install a port, slot, or other hardware device that is missing. For example, suppose you want a **memory card reader** in your computer for the Secure Digital (SD) card that your digital camera uses. You can install an **adapter card** in a desktop computer to provide several memory card slots. Another option is to purchase a USB memory card reader that plugs into a USB port and provides memory card slots (see Figure 14-2).

> **memory card reader**—A device that includes one or more slots to insert a memory card. The device can read and write to the card.
>
> **adapter card**—A circuit board that attaches to the motherboard inside the desktop computer case and provide ports that stick out the back of the case to connect a peripheral device. For example, the adapter card in Figure 14-3 provides extra USB ports for a computer.

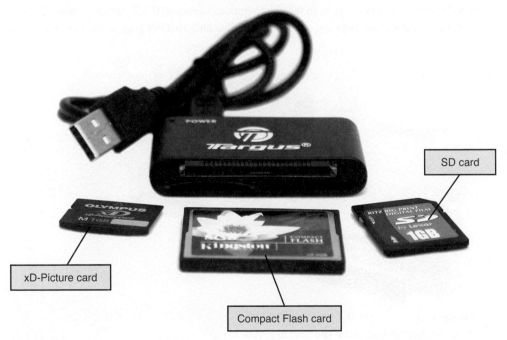

FIGURE 14-2
This USB memory card reader has three slots for three types of memory cards.

FIGURE 14-3
Use this adapter card to add three USB ports to your computer.

In another example, your desktop computer has a VGA video port and your new monitor uses the newer DVI video port. In this case, you can use a small adapter (see Figure 14-4) to make the conversion between a VGA video cable and the DVI port on the monitor.

FIGURE 14-4
Use an adapter to connect a DVI port to a VGA cable.

video card

Another option is to install a new **video card** in your computer that provides a DVI port and a faster graphics experience. Another reason you might want to install a new video card is to provide an extra video port on your computer for a second monitor.

> **video card**—A type of adapter card that provides one or more video ports for one or more monitors.

Not all video cards or adapter cards fit every computer, so check with a computer technician to find out what types of cards your computer can handle.

Is My Computer Slow?

After you determine whether your computer is missing a device, the next question to ask is,
"Is my computer slow?" A slow computer can be caused by a variety of problems discussed
next.

Lack of Routine Maintenance

As you learned in Chapter 13, "Maintaining a Computer and Fixing Computer Problems,"
a computer can slow down over time if too many programs are running in the background or the hard drive does not have enough free space. Both problems can be helped
by routine maintenance. See Chapter 13 if you need a refresher about how to perform this
maintenance.

Slow Internet Connection

Are you using an old dial-up connection to the Internet at home? Dial-up is painfully slow,
and upgrading your computer will not solve the problem. Check into subscribing to DSL,
cable Internet, or mobile broadband. You learned about these types of Internet connections
in Chapter 12, "Connecting to the Internet and Securing a Computer."

Not Enough Memory

Upgrading memory is the easiest and least expensive type of computer
upgrade. Adding more memory can sometimes make a big difference in
computer performance. See Chapter 13 to find out how much memory you
have and how much your system needs.

Not Enough Hard Drive Space

In Chapter 13, you learned that Windows needs about 15% of free hard drive
space to do its work. After you follow the directions in Chapter 13 to clean
up your hard drive, you still might not have enough space. You can purchase
a second hard drive and use it to hold your music, photos, movies, backups, and other data.

Most desktop computers can accommodate a second hard drive installed inside the
computer case. For desktops and laptops, you can also install an external hard drive (see
Figure 14-5).

> **Tip** When upgrading
> memory, be sure to have
> an experienced technician
> select the memory modules
> that are compatible with
> your system and install the
> modules.

FIGURE 14-5
Use an external hard drive to add to the available hard drive space.

Most external drives plug into a USB port. If you are considering this option, make sure the USB port on your computer is a **Hi-Speed USB** port or **SuperSpeed USB** port rather than an original USB port. Also make sure the hard drive uses SuperSpeed or Hi-Speed USB.

> **Hi-Speed USB**—USB standard 2.0 that is about 40 times faster than original USB.
>
> **SuperSpeed USB**—USB standard 3.0 that is about ten times faster than Hi-Speed USB.

To find out what type USB ports your computer has, use the msinfo32 command you learned about in Chapter 13. In the System Information window, click **USB** in the Components group. For example, the computer in Figure 14-6 has one SuperSpeed USB port and two Hi-Speed USB ports. If you don't have enough USB ports or your USB ports are not fast enough, you can install an adapter card on a desktop to provide the USB ports you need.

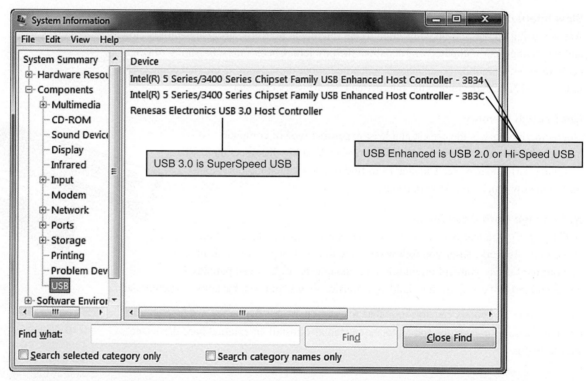

FIGURE 14-6
The System Information window reports the types of USB ports in a system.

A Slow Operating System

Windows 7 is the fastest operating system Microsoft has released so far. If your computer is using Windows XP or Windows Vista, consider upgrading the OS to Windows 7. First, make sure your computer can support Windows 7 and consider the cost of the upgrade.

Before deciding to upgrade the operating system to Windows 7, make sure the computer can support Windows 7. It needs this hardware:

▸ At least 2 GB of memory, but 4 GB or more is better

▸ A processor that runs at 1 GHz or faster

▸ About 30 GB of free hard drive space

Tip To allow Microsoft to examine your computer and tell you whether the hardware and applications qualify for Windows 7, go to windows.microsoft.com/ upgradeadvisor and download and run the Windows 7 Upgrade Advisor.

In Chapter 13, you learned how to find out what memory, processor, and free hard drive space is installed on your computer.

The Processor, Hard Drive, or Video Is Too Slow for My System

Use the Windows Experience Index to identify a key component installed in your computer that is slowing down performance.

> Windows Experience Index—A score of 2 to 7 that Windows assigns to a computer to rate its overall performance. Windows 7 and Windows Vista use this index.

To see the index, click **Start**, right-click **Computer**, and click **Properties** in the shortcut menu. In the System window, click **Performance Information and Tools**. The Performance Information and Tools window appears (see Figure 14-7).

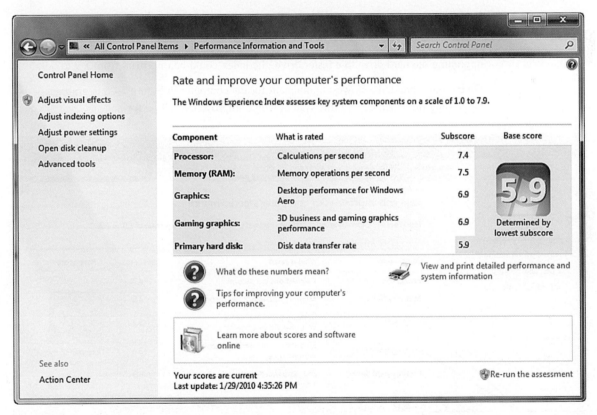

FIGURE 14-7
Use the Windows Experience Index to determine a key component that needs upgrading.

> **Tip** If a change has been made to your computer that will affect the index, the message *Your Windows Experience Index needs to be refreshed* appears on the Performance Information and Tools window. Click the message to refresh the index. A laptop cannot be running on battery when the index is refreshed.

The Windows Experience Index reports performance scores for four key hardware components: The processor, memory, the video subsystem, and the primary hard drive. The index is determined by the lowest score.

Table 14-1 gives you a guide for interpreting the Windows Experience Index.

TABLE 14-1   The Windows Experience Index Measures a Computer's Expected Performance

Index	Minimum Performance
2.0	Fast enough only for surfing the web, but not fast enough for many Windows features or applications.
3.0	Fast enough to surf the web and run most applications if only one application is open at a time. It is not fast enough for graphics or gaming programs.
4.0 or 5.0	Fast enough to run multiple applications and can provide excellent graphics.
6.0 or 7.0	Fast enough for most multimedia applications, several applications open at the same time, and multiplayer gaming.

The component with the lowest score is the component that needs upgrading to improve performance. For example, in Figure 14-7, the slowest component is the hard drive. By upgrading the hard drive to a faster drive, the index could be improved from 5.9 to 6.9.

On the other hand, the slowest component for the computer in Figure 14-8 is graphics. Upgrading the video card in this system would improve overall performance.

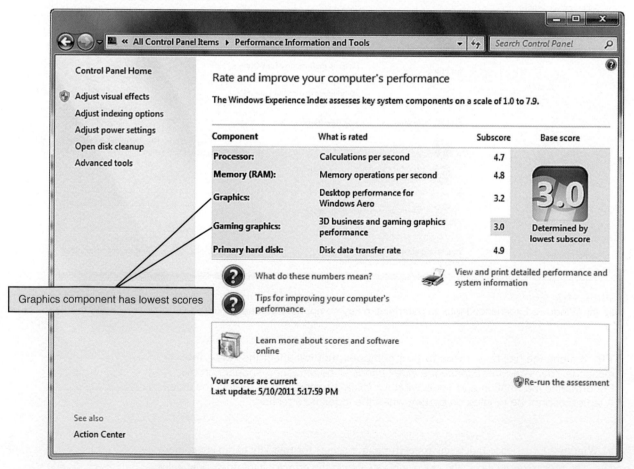

FIGURE 14-8

This computer would benefit from upgrading the video card.

After you decide which component needs upgrading, the next step is to investigate what new component is compatible with your computer. Ask a technician to help you select a compatible component.

What is the Windows Experience Index for your computer? Based on the index value, how would you describe the expected performance of your computer? What component is the slowest component and would benefit from an upgrade?

For help, see Solution 14-1: How to Determine What Upgrade Would Improve Your Computer's Performance.

 Solutions Appendix

How Much Is My Computer Worth?

Generally, the total cost of upgrades should not exceed the value of the current computer. A computer's value is affected by these factors:

► Type of computer (desktop, laptop, netbook, or all-in-one)

► Brand and model unless the computer was assembled from parts

► If the computer was assembled from parts, consider the brand, speed, and features of key components including the processor, **motherboard**, hard drive, and memory

► Operating system installed with original DVD

► Applications installed with original DVD or CD

► Age of the computer and remaining warranty period if any

> **motherboard**—The main circuit board inside a computer case or laptop (see Figure 14-9). The board holds the processor and memory modules and provides ports out the back of a desktop or on the back and sides of a laptop.

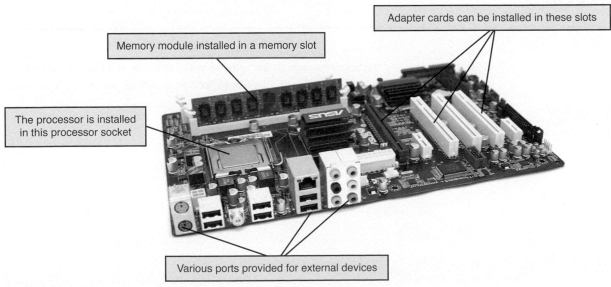

Adapter cards can be installed in these slots

Memory module installed in a memory slot

The processor is installed in this processor socket

Various ports provided for external devices

FIGURE 14-9

A motherboard provides ports for external devices and slots for internal devices.

> **Tip** If you want to move the applications installed on your old computer to your new computer, don't include the applications when determining the value of your old computer. Be sure to uninstall these applications before getting rid of the old computer. Remember, however, that an application designed for an older edition of Windows might not install on Windows 7.

With the information about your computer in hand, search the web for computers for sale that are comparable to yours. You can also talk with a used computer store for advice.

As a rule of thumb, a computer loses about 20% of its value immediately after you purchase it and another 20% each year. That means a computer older than four or five years is not worth much. Its low value probably does not justify expensive upgrades.

On Your Own 14-2
Determine the Value of Your Computer

? Solutions Appendix

For help, see Solution 14-2: How to Determine the Value of Your Computer.

Collect the information about your computer needed to determine its value including the type of computer, hardware, software, age, and warranty.

Collect this specific information about the hardware:

- ▶ For a brand name desktop, laptop, or netbook, find the system manufacturer and system model. This information is often imprinted on the front, back, or bottom of a computer. The System Information window also gives this information.

- ▶ For a desktop built from parts, find the processor model, the amount of installed memory, the size of the hard drive, and the edition of Windows installed.

Search the web for at least three comparable computers for sale. What is the price of each computer? What is the average price of all comparable computers?

Based on your findings, what is the approximate value of your computer? To verify you have the right value, you can ask expert computer technicians you might know.

> **Hint** eBay.com and Craigslist.org offer used computers for sale. Also, try doing a Google.com search on **what is my computer worth**. You might find websites that offer free calculators to determine the value of a computer.

If the total cost of the upgrades exceeds the value of your computer, it's time to consider buying a new computer. Let's turn our attention to the first questions you must ask yourself when deciding what type computer you should buy.

What Type Computer Do I Need?

When you are deciding what type of computer you need, the factors to consider are mobility, performance, compatibility, and budget. Keep in mind two points about budget:

▶ With computers, bigger is not always better. It's best to buy only what satisfies your current needs because computers rapidly decrease in value. You don't want to spend money on what you don't use and won't be worth much in a few short years. Computers are constantly improving. In just a few years, you can buy a much better computer than you can buy today for the same amount of money.

▶ The cost of buying a computer is not just the cost of the computer. You might also want an extended warranty, monitor, printer, applications software, carrying case for a laptop or netbook, or other products.

Now let's consider mobility, performance, and compatibility.

Computers That Offer Mobility

If you need to take a computer with you on the go, a desktop or all-in-one is not your best choice. Your best choices are a laptop, netbook, or tablet. In some situations, a smartphone might do the job. Types of mobile computers are shown in Figure 14-10. Take into account these tips when selecting one:

▶ Mobile computers are built with little room for expansion or upgrades. What you first buy is what you most likely will live with, except for, perhaps, a memory upgrade.

▶ Choose a good manufacturer because almost all the future support for a computer comes from this manufacturer. Be sure to read some reviews about the manufacturer you are considering.

Laptop or notebook is the best-performing mobile computer

Netbook is lightweight and has a small screen

Tablet PC lid can flip around to lie flat on the keyboard

A handheld tablet relies on a touch screen for input

Smartphone contains programs called apps

FIGURE 14-10
Types of mobile computers include a laptop, netbook, tablet PC, handheld tablet, and smartphone.

Here is a brief description of each type of mobile computer:

> ► **Laptop or notebook computer.** Laptops cost more than desktop computers with similar performance. You pay extra for the lighter weight and longer lasting battery, but you can get just as much performance in a laptop as you can a desktop if you are willing to pay for it.

▶ **Netbook.** A netbook is a low-end laptop with a small screen and keyboard and slower performance. It is designed for low-budget general use such as surfing the web and email. Netbooks cannot support applications that require a lot of computing resources. On the other hand, netbooks are much lighter than laptops and the battery can stay charged longer. Most netbooks don't have an optical drive.

▶ **Tablet PC.** The high-end tablet PC can perform just as well as a laptop or desktop. These tablet PCs are more expensive than either because the touch screen has the ability to flip around and lie flat on top of the keyboard. Tablet PCs are designed to receive and interpret handwriting and voice input in addition to touchpad and keyboard input.

▶ **Handheld tablet.** Various handheld tablet devices are currently hitting the market ranging from the more expensive iPad by Apple Computers and PlayBook by BlackBerry to the less expensive **Android**-based tablets with smaller screens and poorer performance. These tablets use a virtual keyboard that appears on the screen when you need it. Some tablet devices are also smartphones.

> Android—An operating system used by small computing devices and smartphones.

▶ **Smartphones.** Smartphones are cell phones that can hold a few applications that don't require much computing resources. A smartphone has Internet applications and personal management functions such as a calendar, an appointment book, an address book, a calculator, and a notepad. You can use a smartphone to keep up on Facebook and Twitter, send and receive email, and access the web. A smartphone might have an embedded camera, MP3 player, or audio recorder. Some smartphones have touch screens; others have mini keyboards.

The key factors to consider when selecting a mobile computer include

▶ **Screen size and size of the keyboard.** If you plan to do a lot of work at your mobile computer, a larger screen and keyboard are more comfortable.

▶ **Weight.** Realize the advertised weight of a mobile computer does not include the weight of the battery.

▶ **Battery charge.** Some netbooks and handheld tablets can keep a battery charge all day. Battery charge on a laptop or tablet PC might not last more than four or five hours.

Batteries for mobile computers are rated by number of cells. Sometimes you can customize the battery for a laptop or netbook. For example, a laptop might come with either a 6-cell Lithium-Ion battery or a 9-cell Lithium-Ion battery. The more cells, the longer the battery charge.

Computers That Offer the Best Performance

The overall performance of a computer is affected by the processor, memory, hard drive, video subsystem, and type of operating system.

The Processor Speed and Number of Cores

The one component that most affects performance in a computer is the processor. Many computer manufacturers allow you a choice of processors. For example, in Figure 14-11, when customizing one HP laptop, you have three choices for a processor. A little explanation about processors might help you choose.

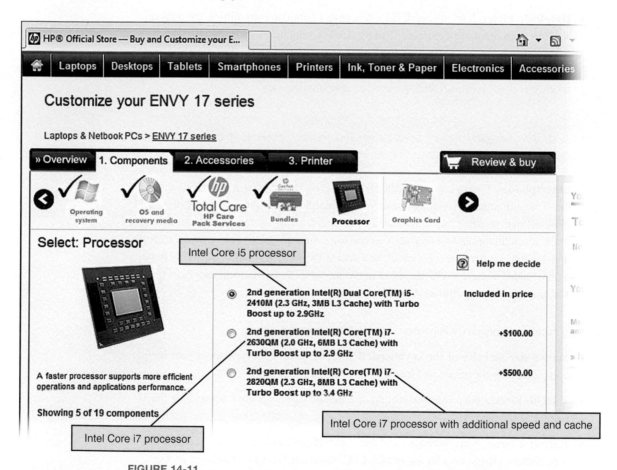

FIGURE 14-11
Three choices of processors are offered for this ENVY 17 series laptop on the hp.com site.

The performance of the processor is primarily determined by its speed (also called its frequency) measured in **MHz** or **GHz**, the number of **cores** the processor has, and the amount of **cache memory** in the processor housing. In today's computers, a processor rated at 512 MHz is considered slow, and a processor rated at 3 GHz is considered fast. Today's processors can have one, two, or more cores. The Intel Core i5 processor mentioned in Figure 14-11 has two cores. The Intel Core i7 processors mentioned in Figure 14-11 have four cores and a 6 or 8 MB cache.

MHz—A megahertz, which is one million hertz. A hertz (Hz) is one activity per second.

GHz—A gigahertz, which is one billion activities per second.

core—A component inside a processor that can process data. A processor with four cores can process data about twice as fast as one with two cores even though the speeds are rated the same.

cache memory—A small amount of memory inside the processor housing used to speed up the overall processor performance. The more cache, the better.

Processors are made by Intel and AMD. Intel processors are more popular than AMD and generally cost slightly more than a comparable AMD processor. AMD processors are popular with hobbyists and gamers and are used in low-end home computers. Table 14-2 lists some top Intel processors for personal computers, and Table 14-3 lists the top AMD processors for personal computers.

TABLE 14-2 Intel Processors for Personal Computers

Intel Processor	Description
Core i7 or Core i5	High-performing processor
Core i3	Moderate to high performance
Core 2, Core Duo, or Core vPro	Moderate performance
Pentium or Celeron	Basic computing
Atom	Low-end performance, used in netbooks

TABLE 14-3 AMD Processors for Personal Computers

AMD Processor	Description
Athlon II and Athlon X2	High to moderate performance
Phenom II and Phenom	High to moderate performance for laptops
Turion II	High to moderate performance for desktops
Athlon	Basic computing
Sempron	Low-end desktops

To learn more about a particular processor you encounter while customizing a computer, copy the details listed about the processor in a Google search box to read reviews about the processor.

Intel is constantly releasing new processors for desktop and laptop computers. By the time this book is in print, Table 14-2 might be out of date. Search the web and find out whether Intel has released a processor for laptops that is newer than the Core i7 or Core i5. If so, what is that processor?

On Your Own 14-3
Investigate the Latest Intel Processor for Laptops

For help, see Solution 14-3: How to Investigate the Latest Intel Processor for Laptops.

 Solutions Appendix

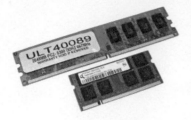

The Amount and Type of Memory

In Chapter 13 you learned the importance of having enough memory for Windows and applications to work. The type of memory can also affect performance. Today's memory modules use a technology called **DDR**. Current versions used today are DDR2 and DDR3. DDR4 is expected to be released by the time this book is in print. Each version of DDR is faster than the previous one.

> **DDR**—A technology used by memory modules. DDR3 is faster than DDR2, which is faster than DDR memory. DDR2 modules can work in pairs to almost double the speed of DDR2 modules (called dual channels). DDR3 modules can work in pairs (dual channels) or three together (triple channels) to almost double or triple the speed of DDR3 modules.

When selecting a computer, pay attention to the amount and type of memory used. For example, Figure 14-12 shows part of a web page comparing two all-in-one computers. The Pentium computer on the left has 2 GB of DDR3 memory, and the Core i3 computer on the right has 3 GB of Dual Channel DDR3 memory. Because the memory in the Core i3 computer is configured as Dual Channel, this memory will run almost twice as fast as the memory in the Pentium computer.

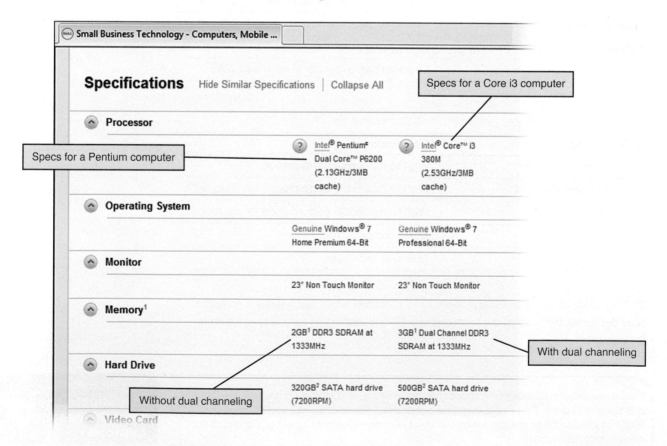

FIGURE 14-12
Dual Channel DDR3 memory runs faster than DDR3 memory that is not configured for dual channeling.

Tip For dual channeling to work, two matching memory modules must be installed side by side. For triple channeling to work, three matching memory modules must be installed side by side. These matching modules can then move data in and out of memory in sync at the same time.

The Size, Speed, and Type of Hard Drive

Recall from Chapter 1, "Using Windows 7 to Manage Applications and Data," that today's hard drives hold up to 2 TB of data. Earlier in this chapter, you learned that the speed of the hard drive can affect overall performance. Two types of hard drives are used in computers: magnetic hard drives and solid state drives.

A **magnetic hard drive** has platters inside that spin at 5400, 7200, or 10,000 **RPM**. A solid state drive, also called an **SSD**, has no moving parts and is faster and more expensive than a magnetic drive. Figure 14-13 shows six options for a hard drive when the buyer is customizing one HP laptop.

magnetic hard drive—The most common hard drive technology where data is written as magnetic spots on spinning platters.

RPM—Revolutions per minute.

SSD—Solid state disk or solid state drive, which is a hard drive with no moving parts. SSDs are faster than magnetic drives and use less battery charge in mobile computers.

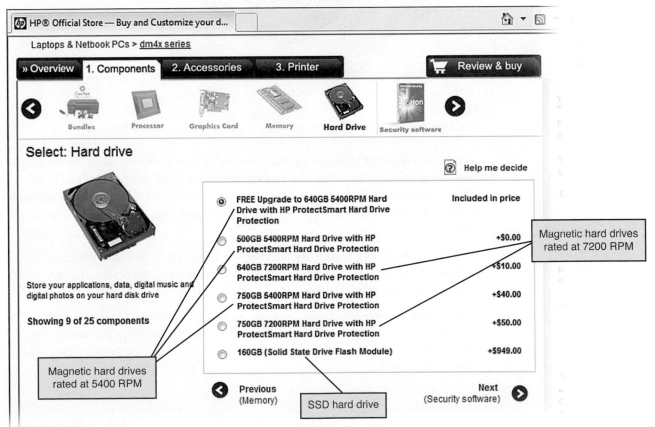

FIGURE 14-13
Choose the type, speed, and size of the hard drive for an HP laptop.

The Quality of the Video Subsystem

The video subsystem can be **integrated video** or a dedicated video card. In most cases, integrated video is sufficient and is less expensive.

> **integrated video**—Video circuitry embedded on the motherboard, and the motherboard provides a video port. The quality of video is not as good as when a dedicated video card is used.

A desktop, laptop, or all-in-one computer can use a video card, which gives better video performance than integrated video. Figure 14-14 shows a video card used in a desktop. Video cards come in a wide variety of quality and price.

FIGURE 14-14
This high-end video card used in a desktop includes a fan to keep it cool.

A high-end video card is used in a gaming computer or other situation when you need high-quality graphics. The best video card for extreme gaming is one that has 1 or 1.5 GB of video memory installed on the video card. A video card with less video memory works well if you want only two or more video ports for extra monitors that you don't intend to use for gaming.

For example, look at the comparison ads shown in Figure 14-15. The third computer includes a better-performing graphics card (another name for a video card). The fifth computer has support for dual monitors.

When you click **Compare** in the ad, you can see the model of the video card and the amount of video memory installed on it. Figure 14-16 shows the details for the first four systems in Figure 14-15 listed in reverse order. Before you decide on the video card, read some reviews about it.

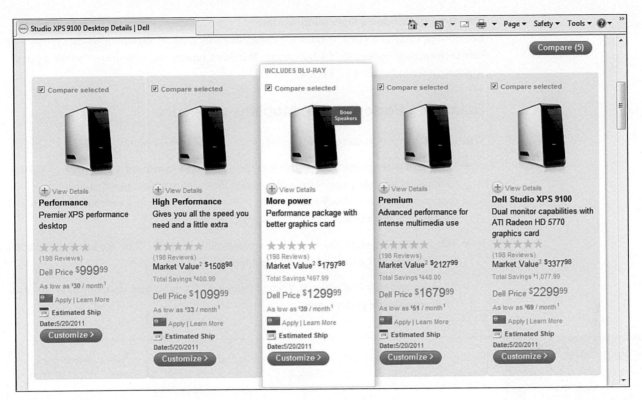

FIGURE 14-15
These desktops offer choices for the video subsystem.

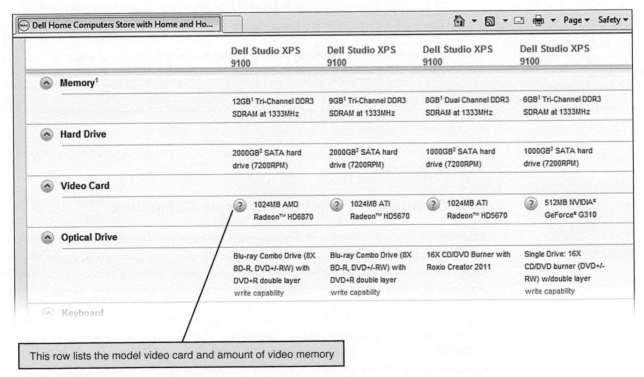

FIGURE 14-16
Dell offers a choice of video cards for one multimedia desktop model.

The Type of Windows Operating System

Recall from Chapter 13 that Windows 7 comes in either a 32-bit system or 64-bit system. For best performance, choose the 64-bit system. Windows reports the system type on the System window (refer to Figure 13-23 in Chapter 13).

Balancing Performance, Mobility, and Price

When balancing performance, mobility, and price, consider these points:

▶ The right desktop computer offers you the most performance for your money. Desktop computers are easily upgraded and cost less than comparable laptops or all-in-one computers. Desktops vary widely from low-end general-purpose computers to high-end powerful gaming computers.

▶ All-in-one computers cost more than a comparable desktop. They are likely to include a touch screen and wireless keyboard and mouse.

▶ Laptops and high-end tablet PCs are mobile and cost more than desktops or all-in-ones with comparable performance.

On Your Own 14-4

Compare Prices for a Desktop and a Comparable Laptop

? Solutions Appendix

For help, see Solution 14-4: How to Compare Prices for a Desktop and a Comparable Laptop.

Desktop computers generally cost less than a laptop with comparable features and performance. To verify that, begin by shopping online for a low-priced Windows 7 desktop computer that does not have many extra features. Answer these questions:

1. What are the brand, model, and price of the desktop you found?

2. What is the processor model? How much memory is installed? What size is the hard drive? Which type optical drive is installed? Which edition of Windows 7 is installed?

3. What extra features does the computer have? (For example, web cam or speakers?)

Now find a laptop computer that matches these specifications as closely as you can. How does the price of the laptop compare to the price of the desktop?

When deciding on the type of computer to buy, you also need to decide whether you want an IBM-compatible computer or an Apple computer.

IBM-Compatible Computers or Apple Computers

IBM-compatible computers and computer parts are made by many different manufacturers including Dell, IBM, HP, Asus, and Sony. All these computers are generally designed to use a Windows operating system by Microsoft or a Linux operating system. Currently, about 80% of personal computers sold are IBM-compatible and use the Windows operating system.

> **IBM-compatible computer**—Any computer that uses the Windows OS or the Linux operating system and is not made by Apple.
>
> **Linux**—A free or low-cost operating system developed by volunteer contributors. Linux is open source software meaning that the code to write the software is openly available for anyone to see and edit. Linux is used on mainframe computers, personal computers, and mobile devices. The Android OS is based on Linux.
>
> **mainframe**—A large computer that supports many other smaller computers.

The other computer design is produced solely by one manufacturer: Apple Inc (www.apple. com). Apple makes desktop, all-in-one, notebook, netbook, and tablet computers. All Apple computers come with the **Mac operating system** preinstalled. The Mac OS is also made by Apple, and an Apple computer is called a Mac.

> **Mac operating system**—The operating system used on all Apple computers.

Users of Macs generally like the intuitive user interface and beautiful graphics of the Mac OS. Here are the important points to consider when you are thinking of purchasing a Mac:

- ▶ A good reason to buy a Mac is you are already familiar with the Mac OS and you like the way it works.

- ▶ Another good reason to buy a Mac is your friends or coworkers use a Mac and you need to share data and work on the same projects as a team. If all team members are using Macs, compatibility is not a problem.

- ▶ All the applications you install on your Mac must be specifically written for the Mac OS. Applications in desktop publishing, graphics design, music, entertainment, and education abound for the Mac. If you are considering a career in one of these fields, knowing how to use a Mac can be a strong asset.

- ▶ Although you can install a Windows operating system on a Mac, a Mac computer comes with the Mac OS already installed. To save money, if you want to use the Windows operating system, it's best to buy an IBM-compatible computer.

- ▶ All internal components you replace or add to your Mac must be Apple components or approved by Apple.

- ▶ Macs generally cost more than a comparable IBM-compatible computer.

Because IBM-compatible computers are so popular, this book focuses on these computers along with the Windows 7 operating system they are most likely to use.

Extra Features a Computer Might Have

When buying a computer, consider the extra features you might need. For example, you might want a web cam for video chat or an HDMI port to use your computer to stream movies to your TV. Extra features cost extra money, so buy only the features you will use.

Web Cam, Card Reader, Sound Ports, and Other Standard Features

All computers have some type of sound port. Look for a speaker port and microphone port. Most mobile computers have a web cam and card reader. Check to make sure the card reader supports the type memory cards you use with your digital camera or other electronic devices. If a computer does not have a built-in device, you can substitute an external one (see Figure 14-17).

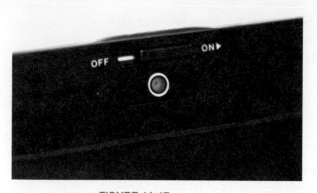

FIGURE 14-17

A web cam can be built into the lid of a notebook or netbook, or you can use an external USB web cam.

The Edition of Windows 7

When you purchase a new computer, the operating system is already installed. Sometimes you have a choice as to which type or edition of Windows 7 comes preinstalled on the computer. For example, Figure 14-18 shows choices for the operating system to be installed on one Dell desktop.

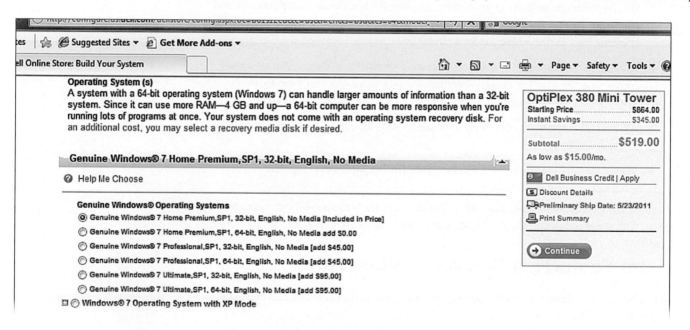

FIGURE 14-18

Dell offers a choice of operating systems for the OptiPlex 380 desktop.

Recall that the system type might be a 32-bit system or 64-bit system. Select the 64-bit system for best performance.

The edition of Windows 7 you select affects the features of the OS and not its performance. Your choices might include

> ▶ **Windows 7 Starter** is the most limited, bare-bones edition. In the United States, this edition is used only on netbooks.

> ▶ **Windows 7 Home Premium** is the most popular edition for personal use. Choose this edition for a laptop, desktop, or all-in-one computer you plan to use at home, at school, when traveling, or in a small office.

▶ **Windows 7 Professional** contains all the features of Windows 7 Home Premium plus features used in a corporate or professional setting. Choose this edition if

- ▶ You expect you might need to connect your computer to a corporate network.

- ▶ You want more security features or professional tools than the Home Premium edition offers.

▶ **Windows 7 Ultimate** contains support for multiple languages. Choose this edition if you need Windows to work in a language other than English.

Find a computer ad that offers a choice of operating systems and answer these questions about the cost of Windows 7:

On Your Own 14-5
Compare Prices for Windows 7 Editions

1. How much extra would you expect to pay if you request that Windows 7 Home Premium 32-bit be changed to Windows 7 Home Premium 64-bit?

2. How much extra would you expect to pay for a computer when you request that Windows 7 Home Premium be changed to Windows 7 Professional? To Windows 7 Ultimate?

For help, see Solution 14-5: How to Compare Prices for Windows 7 Editions.

 Solutions Appendix

Video Ports

Four types of video ports used on today's computers are VGA, DVI, DisplayPort, and HDMI. **DisplayPort** and **HDMI** give better video than DVI, which is better than VGA. Some laptops and netbooks use the **Mini DisplayPort (mDP)**. DisplayPort, HDMI, and Mini DisplayPort can output audio as well as video.

DisplayPort

> **DisplayPort**—A type of video port that gives high-definition video to a computer monitor or can stream video and audio to a TV or home theater system. DisplayPort is expected to replace VGA and DVI video ports on computers.
>
> **HDMI**—A type of video and audio port technology used to transmit video and audio to a high-definition TV (HDTV) or home theater system.
>
> **Mini DisplayPort (mDP)**—A smaller version of the DisplayPort used on laptops and netbooks.

HDMI

Be sure the video port on your computer matches your monitor or TV. Sometimes you can use an adapter or converter cable if the connectors don't match. Figure 14-19 shows a DVI to DisplayPort adapter, and Figure 14-20 shows a VGA to DisplayPort adapter.

Mini DisplayPort

FIGURE 14-19
Use a DVI to DisplayPort adapter to connect a DVI monitor to a DisplayPort on a computer.

FIGURE 14-20
Use a VGA to DisplayPort adapter to connect a VGA monitor to a DisplayPort on a computer.

Wireless Capabilities

Most mobile computers come with Wi-Fi to connect to a hotspot. Many computers also include Bluetooth to connect to personal devices in close range. Other wireless technologies that might be available on high-end laptops are 3G mobile broadband to connect to a 3G cellular network, WiMAX or LTE to connect to a 4G cellular network, and **Wireless Display (WiDi)** to connect to high-definition TVs. Figure 14-21 shows an HP laptop that has Wi-Fi (802.11a/b/g/n), Bluetooth, and Wireless Display (WiDi) included in the price.

> **Wireless Display (WiDi)**—A wireless technology that connects a computer to a high-definition TV (HDTV). You must connect a wireless receiver to the TV to receive the wireless signal. Wireless Display is a wireless alternative to an HDMI cable.

> **Tip** Recall from Chapter 12 that you must subscribe to a data plan with a wireless carrier such as Verizon or Sprint to connect your computer to 3G or 4G cellular networks. The wireless technology your laptop uses must match what the carrier supports.

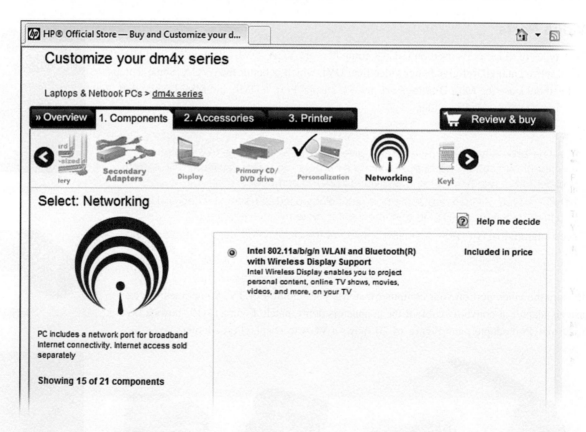

FIGURE 14-21

This HP laptop includes Wi-Fi, Bluetooth, and Wireless Display wireless technologies.

Optical Drive

Netbooks generally don't have an optical drive, but other computers do. Some choices for optical drives are listed in Table 14-4.

TABLE 14-4 Optical Drives Might Support CD, DVD, and Blu-ray Discs

Optical Drive	Description	Type Discs It Can Use
CD-ROM	Reads a CD	Any CD
CD-RW	Write to and rewrite to a CD	Recordable CD (CD-R)
		Rewritable CD (CD-RW)
DVD-R	Write a single or double layer of data to a DVD	Recordable DVD (DVD-R)
		Compatible with CDs
DVD+/-RW	Writes to and rewrites to a DVD	Recordable DVD (DVD+R)
		Recordable DVD (DVD-R)
		Rewritable DVD (DVD+RW)
		Rewritable DVD (DVD-RW)
		Compatible with CDs
BD-ROM	Read Blu-ray Discs (BD)	Compatible with DVDs and CDs and might write to a DVD or CD
BD-R	Write to a BD, single or double layer	Recordable BD (BD-R)
		Compatible with DVDs and CDs and might write to both
BD-RE	Writes to and rewrites to a BD, single or double layer	Rewriteable BD (BD-RE)
		Compatible with DVDs and CDs and might write to both

Combo drives support a variety of optical discs. For example, look back at Figure 14-16 at the choices for the optical drive for a Dell desktop. Unless you plan to use Blu-ray discs, you don't need to pay the extra money for a Blu-ray drive.

As you can see from Table 14-4, lots of standards exist for CDs, DVDs, and BDs. Be sure you buy the discs that your computer supports. Figure 14-22 shows how much each type of optical disc can store.

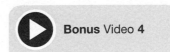
Bonus Video 4

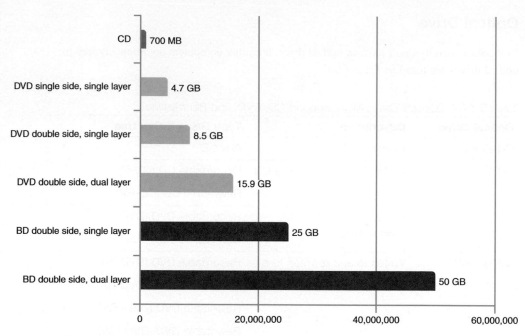

FIGURE 14-22
Optical discs come in a variety of types and storage capacities.

On Your Own 14-6
Compare Prices for a Computer with a Blu-ray Burner

Search the web for the least expensive new computer you can find that includes a Blu-ray burner (a drive that writes to Blu-ray discs). What are the website, brand, model, and price of the computer? Compare your price with other students in your class to see who can find the least expensive computer with a Blu-ray burner.

 Solutions Appendix

For help, see Solution 14-6: How to Compare Prices for a Computer with a Blu-ray Burner.

TV Tuner

A computer might include a **TV tuner** so your computer can also be a television. Plug the TV cable into the computer and use software on the computer to watch TV. The computer is likely to come with a remote control to control the TV from across the room. If your computer does not have an internal TV tuner, you can use a USB TV tuner such as the one shown in Figure 14-23.

> **TV tuner**—An internal or external device that turns a computer into a television. You might be able to use the TV tuner to record TV programs.

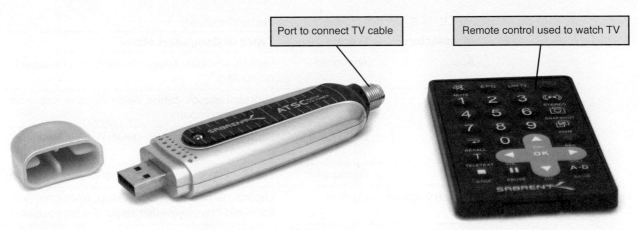

Port to connect TV cable

Remote control used to watch TV

FIGURE 14-23
Connect this USB TV tuner to a computer and plug in a TV cable to watch TV on the computer.

Now that you know what type of computer you want and the extra features it might have, you are ready to start shopping.

Shopping for a Computer and Peripherals

When shopping for a computer, keep these tips in mind:

▶ Be aware of "great deals" that might disappoint you later. Realize you will be tied to the manufacturer's customer support for your computer for many years to come. Select your brand carefully.

▶ Read product reviews. Some websites that offer excellent reviews and ratings you can count on are toptenreviews.com, reviews.cnet.com, pcmag.com, pcworld.com, and computershopper.com.

Tip When reading reviews about a product, search for reviews posted on sites other than the manufacturer's website.

When you shop for a computer, you can

▶ Buy the computer directly from the website of the computer manufacturer such as those listed in Table 14-5.

▶ Search retail sites that sell electronic equipment. Reputable retail sites include amazon.com, microcenter.com, newegg.com, compusa.com, tigerdirect.com, bestbuy.com, and computershopper.com.

▶ Walk into an electronics retail store and talk with an experienced sales technician.

TABLE 14-5   Manufacturers of Brand-Name Computers

Manufacturer	Website	Types of Computers Made
Acer	Acer.com	Laptop, netbook, tablet, desktop, and handheld computers
Apple	Apple.com	Laptop, netbook, tablet, desktop, all-in-one, and handheld computers
Dell	Dell.com	Laptop, netbook, tablet, desktop, all-in-one, and handheld computers
Fujitsu	Fujitsu.com	Laptop, tablet, desktop, and handheld computers
Hewlett Packard (HP)	Hp.com	Laptop, netbook, tablet, desktop, all-in-one, and handheld computers that target the home user
Lenovo	Lenovo.com	Desktop, all-in-one, laptop, netbook, and handheld computers that target the professional and corporate user
Sony	Sonystyle.com	Laptop, netbook, desktop, all-in-one, and handheld computers
Toshiba	Toshiba.com	Laptops and netbooks

Tip As you read a computer ad, you might encounter a term you don't understand. If so, open a new tab in Internet Explorer to do a Google search on the term. Then return to the IE tab displaying the ad.

Don't buy the first computer you find. Take your time, make comparisons, and read reviews. Expect to learn about computers as you shop. After you settle on the computer, search different retailers for the best price and decide how to customize the computer.

On Your Own 14-7

Investigate Computer Manufacturers

Each of the top computer manufacturers has a reputation in the computer industry. For example, Lenovo is known for its high-quality products and has a great reputation for customer service. Working with a team of three other students, do the following to investigate computer manufacturers:

Step 1. Search the web and find one review or comment from a user about each of the eight companies listed in Table 14-5. The review can be about a product the company sells, the customer service experience, or a warranty a company offers. Bookmark the review (add it to your Favorites), save the web page of the review, or print the review.

Hint When searching for a review about a company, find reviews posted on websites other than the company's website.

Step 2. Share your eight reviews with the three other students on your team.

Step 3. Discuss your findings. As a team, rate the eight companies in order from the company you would most prefer to buy from to the least preferred.

Step 4. In a classroom, discuss your findings and compare them to other teams' findings.

Step 5. Which company came out on top of the list? Why? Which company came out on the bottom? Why?

Step 6. What other computer manufacturers came up during the research and discussions? Do you think one of these should have been included in Table 14-5? If so, explain why.

? Solutions Appendix

For help, see Solution 14-7: How to Investigate Computer Manufacturers.

> **Tip** When deciding what computer manufacturer to buy from, ask an experienced computer technician—one who does not work for one of these manufacturers— for advice.

A manufacturer's website might offer you the ability to customize a computer. When you are customizing a computer, the most important items to consider are the operating system, processor, memory, and extra features you might need.

Suppose you are ready to buy a new laptop to use for entertainment and work. For each laptop you find, bookmark, print, or save the web page(s) showing the brand, model, and price of the laptop and a list of features. Do the following:

Step 1. Find a laptop that has at least a 15-inch screen and a 3D display that lets you watch high-definition movies and play 3D games. Find one review on this laptop.

Step 2. Find a laptop that lets you connect wirelessly to your high-definition TV. Find one review on this laptop.

On Your Own 14-8
Find Laptops with Extra Features

 Solutions Appendix

For help, see Solution 14-8: How to Find Laptops with Extra Features.

Consider an Extended Warranty

Most computers come with a complimentary warranty that covers parts and labor for one year. The manufacturer or retailer might offer an extended warranty. Pay attention to how long the warranty lasts (one to five years is common) and how much it costs. Figure 14-24 shows the screen when purchasing an Alienware laptop where you must select the warranty. (Alienware is Dell's line of gaming computers.)

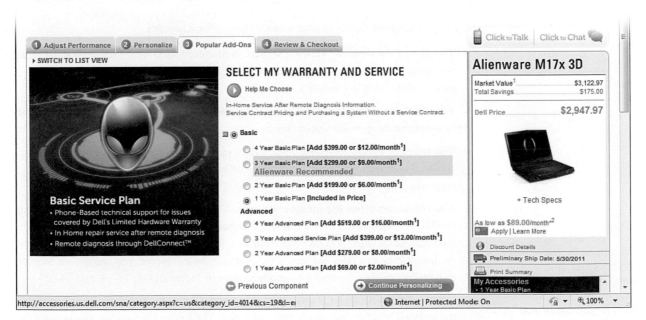

FIGURE 14-24
Dell offers basic and advanced warranties that cover one to four years.

Find out what the warranty covers. Does it cover just manufacturer defects? Does the warranty include failing hardware or accidents such as spilling a soda across a laptop keyboard? You might have to read the fine print to find out.

Consider how the warranty works. Do you have to ship the computer back to the manufacturer? Do you get phone support? Is there a local computer service center where you can take the computer?

Shop for a Monitor

For a desktop computer, you need a keyboard, mouse, and monitor. Figure 14-25 shows an ad listing four LCD flat-screen monitors.

FIGURE 14-25
This ad at compusa.com lists key details for four monitors.

Here are the important details to note when shopping for a monitor:

▶ **The size of the monitor viewing screen.** A monitor size is measured diagonally from one corner to the other. Typical sizes for desktop monitors are 18, 22, 26, and 27 inches, although you can buy larger ones.

▶ **The resolution.** Recall that the resolution is the number of horizontal and vertical dots or pixels on the monitor screen, for example, 1920 × 1200. The higher, the better.

▶ **The monitor speed.** Response time is the time it takes for the monitor to build one screen. The lower, the better. A response time of 1 ms (millisecond) is faster than a response time of 3 ms.

▶ **The connector types the monitor can use.** Choices are VGA, DVI, DisplayPort, and HDMI. HDMI is better than DVI, which is better than VGA. Make sure the connector type matches a video port on your computer. If, however, you buy a monitor with a connector type that does not match the port on your computer, you can use an adapter to convert one type connector to another (refer to Figures 14-4, 14-19, and 14-20).

▶ **Contrast ratio.** Contrast is measured as a contrast ratio, for example, 1000:1, which is the contrast between true black and true white. The higher the number, the better.

▶ **Extra features.** Some monitors have touch screens, built-in speakers, iPod ports, and USB ports.

Tip Don't confuse the contrast ratio with the dynamic contrast ratio that you might see advertised. The dynamic contrast ratio is a much higher value and not a true indication of the contrast.

Shop for a Printer

Another purchase you might need to make is a printer. The least expensive type printer is an **inkjet printer**. Some inkjet printers are photo printers (see Figure 14-26a), meaning they are of high enough quality to print lab-quality photos on photographic paper. A **laser printer** (see Figure 14-26b) is more expensive, but the quality of the printout is much better.

> **inkjet printer**—A color printer that uses ink cartridges with small nozzles that jet the ink out onto the paper.
>
> **laser printer**—A black-and-white or color printer that creates an image on the page using a laser beam inside the printer and powdered ink called toner. The toner cartridge holds the toner.

(a) Inkjet printer   (b) Laser printer

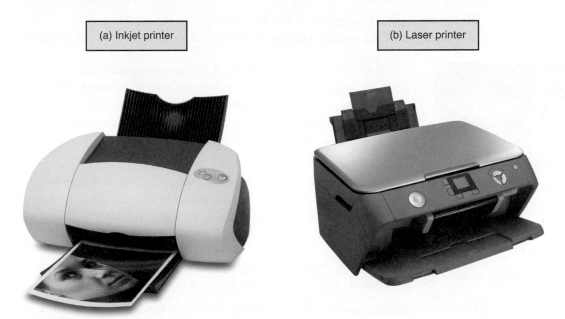

FIGURE 14-26
Two types of printers: (a) an inkjet printer and (b) a laser printer.

When selecting a printer, consider these features:

- ▶ **Type of printer.** Inkjet printers are less expensive and produce lower-quality printouts over laser printers. A color laser printer costs more than a black-and-white laser printer.

- ▶ **Connection types.** Printers connect to a computer by way of a USB cable or wirelessly (Wi-Fi or Bluetooth). A network printer connects directly to the network.

- ▶ **Cost of toner cartridges (for laser printers) and ink cartridges (for inkjet printers).** These cartridges can be quite expensive. Be aware that when you first buy a printer, the cartridges are only partially full so you need to buy new cartridges right away.

- ▶ **All-in-one device.** Some printers are also a scanner, copier, and fax machine rolled into one machine (called an all-in-one device).

- ▶ **The warranty and online support.** Check out the printer manufacturer's website. You should find support information for the printer and the option to download the device drivers and the user manual.

Before making a final buying decision, be sure to read reviews about the printer.

Setting Up a New Computer and Recycling Your Old Computer

After you purchase your computer, it's time to take it out of the box and set it up for the first time. Here are the steps to follow:

Step 1. Don't unpack a computer that has just come in out of the cold. Very cold electronic equipment moved into a warm room can attract static electricity, which can damage internal components. Wait an hour or so for the computer to reach room temperature.

Step 2. Open the box and remove the computer and other equipment, setting it out on your work area. Remove any cellophane from the work area. (Cellophane attracts static electricity.)

Step 3. For a desktop computer, plug in the power cord, network cable, mouse, keyboard, and monitor. Plug the monitor power cord into an electrical outlet.

Step 4. For a laptop, if the battery is not already installed in the laptop, install it. Plug the AC adapter cable into the computer and into the surge protector or an electrical output. Even if the battery is not fully charged, you can still turn on the laptop because it receives power through the AC adapter cable.

Step 5. Turn on the computer. Most likely the opening windows step you through the process of entering your username and password into Windows 7. Follow specific instructions in the Getting Started document that came with your computer. Be sure to write down your password in a safe place so you don't forget it.

Step 6. As soon as you can, register your computer with the manufacturer so that you can get technical support and warranty service when you need it.

Step 7. Use a large envelope or folder to collect all the documentation that came with your computer including the sales receipt, packing and shipping list, warranty information, and software documentation. Also include in the envelope any CDs or DVDs that came with your computer. Label the envelope and keep it in a safe place. If later you have problems with your computer, you will need the sales receipt and warranty documentation to get help from the retail store's service center or the computer manufacturer.

Step 8. If you purchased additional equipment such as a printer, scanner, or game controller, now is the time to unpack the device, connect it to your computer, and turn it on. Windows 7 should recognize the device immediately without any further action on your part.

If you decide to donate, sell, recycle, or trash your old computer, do the following before it goes out the door:

Step 1. Copy any personal data on the hard drive to another storage device or to your new computer. Verify the data is safely stored on the device or new computer.

Step 2. Uninstall any application that you intend to use on your new computer. If you decide to leave the application installed, be sure to include with the computer the original CD or DVD and documentation.

Step 3. To protect your personal data stored on your old computer, delete it from the old hard drive. Don't forget to empty the Recycle Bin.

Step 4. If you are concerned a thief might attempt to recover your personal data from the hard drive, you can take extra measures to thoroughly erase all traces of the data. Ask a computer technician to erase everything on the drive using a **zero-fill utility**. Or you can ask him to remove the hard drive from the computer and then you can destroy the drive.

Step 5. If the computer will be used by someone else, include with the computer any documentation, CDs, or DVDs for the installed software or hardware.

> **zero-fill utility**—A utility program that overwrites everything on the hard drive with zeros. After the zero-fill utility is finished, Windows and applications must be reinstalled.

Summary

Do You Need an Upgrade or a New Computer?

▶ You might want to replace or upgrade a computer if it is missing a device or is too slow.

▶ The total cost of upgrades should not exceed the current value of the computer. This cost includes parts and labor.

▶ Computer performance can be improved by routine maintenance; subscribing to a faster Internet connection; adding memory; adding an external hard drive; or upgrading the operating system, processor, hard drive, or video card.

▶ The Windows Experience Index can help you identify a component that can be upgraded to improve performance.

▶ To find out how much your computer is worth, find comparable computers for sale.

What Type Computer Do You Need?

▶ When you are deciding what type of computer you need, the factors to consider are mobility, performance, compatibility, and budget.

▶ Mobile computers include laptops, netbooks, tablet PCs, handheld tablets, and smartphones.

▶ Components that most affect computer performance are the processor, memory, hard drive, video subsystem, and type of operating system.

▶ Processor performance is rated by the speed of the processor and number of cores.

▶ Current memory technologies that affect performance are DDR2 and DDR3 memory modules, dual channeling, and triple channeling.

▶ Hard drive performance is affected by the RPM rating of a magnetic hard drive. Solid state disks (SSDs) are faster than magnetic drives but cost more.

▶ A video card in a computer is faster than integrated video. Video cards vary widely in price and performance.

▶ A 64-bit Windows operating system is faster than a 32-bit OS.

▶ Computers fall into two categories: IBM-compatible computers that use the Windows operating system and Apple computers that use the Mac OS.

Extra Features a Computer Might Have

▶ Windows 7 Ultimate has more features than does Windows 7 Professional, which has more features than does Windows 7 Home Premium. Windows 7 Starter is used only in netbooks and is a bare-bones OS.

▶ Video ports on today's computers include VGA, DVI, DisplayPort, and HDMI.

▶ Wireless technologies on computers include Wi-Fi, Bluetooth, mobile broadband for 3G networks, WiMAX and LTE for 4G networks, and Wireless Display (WiDi) for high-definition television.

▶ An optical drive might write to or read a variety of optical discs including Blu-ray, DVD, and CD.

▶ A TV tuner makes your computer into a television. Plug in a TV cable to the port on the TV tuner.

Shopping for a Computer and Peripherals

▶ You can buy a new computer directly from the manufacturer or from retail websites or stores. Buy from reputable manufacturers because you might be dependent on them for future service of your computer.

▶ An extended warranty might cover manufacturer defects, failed hardware, accidents, and phone support.

▶ When selecting a monitor, consider size of the screen, resolution, speed, connectors, contrast ratio, and extra features.

▶ Two types of printers are inkjet printers and laser printers. Laser printers are a little more expensive and produce better quality than inkjets.

Setting Up a New Computer and Recycling Your Old Computer

▶ When you first turn on a new computer, Windows steps you through the process of entering your username and password into Windows. Keep all documentation, discs, and receipts in an envelope in a safe place. You will need this information if you have problems with your computer.

▶ Before donating, selling, recycling, or trashing your old computer, copy and delete any personal data on it. Uninstall any applications you want to use on your new computer.

Review Questions

Answer these questions to assess your skills and knowledge of the content covered in the chapter. Your instructor can provide you with the correct answers when you are ready to check your work.

1. If your desktop computer has only one video port but you want to use two monitors, what can you do to upgrade your computer?

2. How much memory must a computer have before it can be upgraded from Windows Vista to Windows 7?

3. What four components in a computer does the Windows Experience Index measure?

4. Which is the main difference between a laptop and tablet PC?

5. What two factors are used to rate processors? What two companies manufacture processors for personal computers?

6. Which is a better-performing processor, the Intel Core i5 or the Intel Pentium?

7. Which is a better-performing processor, the AMD Phenom or the AMD Sempron?

8. DDR2 memory runs faster if two matching modules are installed side by side. What is this technology called?

9. Which is faster, a magnetic hard drive running at 5400 RPM or an SSD?

10. All Apple computers use what operating system?

11. Which edition of Windows 7 should someone use if she wants text on Windows screens to be displayed in Spanish?

12. Which is faster, a VGA port or a DisplayPort?

13. Which port on a computer would you expect to use to connect a cable from the computer to your high-definition television?

14. What device can connect to a computer using Wireless Display (WiDi)?

15. Which monitor is faster, one with a rating of 3 ms or one with a rating of 5 ms?

Chapter Mastery Project

Find out how well you have mastered the content in this chapter by completing this project. If you can answer all the questions and do all the steps without looking back at the chapter details, you have mastered this chapter. If you can complete the project by finding answers using the web, you have proven that you can teach yourself how to make computer upgrade and buying decisions.

If you find you need a lot of help doing the project and you have not yet read the chapter or done the activities, drop back and start at the beginning of the chapter and then return to this project.

> **Hint** All the key terms in the chapter are used in this mastery project. If you encounter a key word you don't know such as *zero-fill utility,* enter **define:zero-fill utility** in the Internet Explorer search box.

Mastery Project Part 1: Do You Need an Upgrade or a New Computer?

If you need help completing this part of the mastery project, please review the "Do You Need an Upgrade or a New Computer?" section in the chapter.

Before deciding to buy a new computer, consider the cost and benefits of upgrading your old computer. Answer these questions:

1. If your old computer is six years old and the total cost of upgrades is about $400, why is it better to buy a new computer than upgrade this one?

2. What is the first thing you should do to speed up a slow computer before you consider an upgrade?

3. Suppose your old computer has a DVD reader rather than a DVD burner, but you want to burn some DVDs. What are two ways you can upgrade your computer?

4. What type of adapter card can be installed in a desktop so the desktop has an extra video port?

5. You decide you need extra hard drive space and plan to buy an external hard drive that uses SuperSpeed USB. Your desktop computer uses regular USB. What are two possible solutions to this problem?

6. Your friend's old Windows XP computer has 512 MB of memory, a 1.88 GHz Pentium processor, and 50 GB of free hard drive space. What hardware upgrades must be made before the OS can be upgraded to Windows 7?

Do the following:

Step 1. Find out the Windows Experience Index of a computer. Which component would improve performance?

Step 2. Your friend's laptop is a Lenovo G560-0679 with Windows 7 Home Premium, 64-bit, installed. It uses an Intel Core i3 2.53 GHz CPU with 4 GB of RAM. The hard drive holds 500 GB. What is the laptop worth? Print or save web pages that support your answer. Based on its current value, calculate about how much this computer will be worth in one year.

Mastery Project Part 2: What Type Computer Do You Need?

If you need help completing this part of the mastery project, please review the "What Type Computer Do You Need?" section in the chapter.

Answer the following:

1. Why is it not always a good idea to buy the best computer you can afford?

2. Which type of computer has the longer battery charge, a tablet PC or a handheld tablet such as an iPad?

3. Which type of computer uses the Android OS, a netbook or a handheld tablet?

4. What is one Intel processor that has six cores? An AMD processor? Print or save web pages supporting your answers.

5. Which memory configuration gives better performance, one DDR3 module installed as a single module or two DDR2 modules installed in dual channeling?

6. An Inspiron all-in-one computer includes the ATI HD4270 Radeon video card. Does this computer support 3D graphics display? Print or save web pages to support your answer.

7. Find a laptop that uses a SSD drive. What is the size of the drive? Print or save the web page describing the laptop.

8. Find one IBM-compatible computer (desktop, laptop, or all-in-one) and a comparable Apple computer. How do the prices compare? Print or save web pages showing the two comparable computers and their prices.

Mastery Project Part 3: Extra Features a Computer Might Have

If you need help completing this part of the mastery project, please review the "Extra Features a Computer Might Have" section in the chapter.

Do the following to investigate extra features a computer might have:

1. Find an all-in-one computer that uses Windows 7 Professional, 64-bit. Print or save the web page describing the computer. Can you buy this computer with a 32-bit OS installed?

2. Which type of computer uses Windows 7 Starter, a netbook or a tablet?

3. Which costs more, Windows 7 Ultimate or Windows 7 Professional?

4. What factor is used to rate the quality of a laptop battery?

5. Find photos of a DisplayPort and an HDMI port on laptops. Print or save the web pages showing the photos. Which of these two ports is expected to replace VGA and DVI on future computers?

6. Which wireless technology might you buy on a laptop to connect to a wireless keyboard? To connect to a 4G cellular network? To connect to an HDTV?

7. What type of DVD do you need so that you can burn data to the DVD multiple times, overwriting the existing data? Print or save a web page that shows a pack of these DVDs for sale.

8. What is the maximum amount of data a dual-layer Blu-ray disc can hold? How many CDs would it take to hold all this data?

9. Find one computer that has a BD reader and a DVD burner combo drive. Print or save web pages describing the computer.

10. Find a USB TV tuner for sale. Print or save a web page describing the device.

Mastery Project Part 4: Shopping for a Computer and Peripherals

If you need help completing this part of the mastery project, please review the "Shopping for a Computer and Peripherals" section in the chapter.

Do the following:

Step 1. Find a web page describing the warranty that Acer offers on one of its computers. Compare this warranty to a warranty offered by Sony. Which company offers the better warranty? Explain your answer.

Step 2. Acer currently offers the Aspire and TravelMate laptops. Research on the web and write one sentence briefly explaining the purpose of each laptop family.

Step 3. Dell offers the Latitude, Vostro, Inspiron, XPS, and Alienware laptops. Which laptop family is designed for gaming? For small business? For low cost?

Step 4. Shop for the next computer you would like to buy. Print or save web pages that give the following information about the computer:

- ▶ Desktop, all-in-one, laptop, or netbook
- ▶ Brand, model, and price
- ▶ Operating system
- ▶ Processor, memory, and hard drive
- ▶ Optical drive
- ▶ Display and graphics including the types of video ports
- ▶ Wireless communication
- ▶ Built-in devices
- ▶ Battery cells and charge time for a mobile computer
- ▶ Warranty

Step 5. Find two reviews about the computer you selected. What are the positive and negative points made in these reviews?

Step 6. Shop for a monitor. Print or save the web pages showing the brand, model, price, and ratings of the monitor including the monitor size, speed, resolution, contrast ratio, and connectors. Find one review about this monitor. Is the review positive or negative?

Step 7. Shop for a printer. Print or save the web pages showing the brand, model, price, and ratings of the printer. Find one review about this printer. Is the review positive or negative?

Step 8. Shop for the ink or toner cartridges for the printer. Print or save the web pages showing the type of cartridge and its price.

Mastery Project Part 5: Setting Up a New Computer and Recycling Your Old Computer

If you need help completing this part of the mastery project, please review the , "Setting Up a New Computer and Recycling Your Old Computer" section in the chapter.

Why is it important to gather up documentations, discs, and receipts and save them in an envelope?

It's better to donate or recycle an old computer rather than throw it in the trash. Do the following:

Step 1. Search the web and find an organization in your area that will receive a computer as a donation. The PC repair instructor at your school might take an old computer so that her class can fix it up and donate it.

Step 2. Find an organization in your area that will recycle a computer. For example, try doing a Google search on **where to recycle computers in Cleveland**. What organization or business in your area will receive a computer for recycling?

Becoming an Independent Learner

Answer the following question about becoming an independent learner:

The most important skill learned in this book is how to teach yourself a computer skill. In the Chapter Mastery Project for each chapter you have been rating yourself on how well you are doing with this skill. What is your overall rating for the entire book?

○ Level A: I was able to successfully complete the Chapter Mastery Projects without the help of doing the On Your Own activities in the chapter. **I have proven that I can teach myself a computer skill without directions given by others.**

○ Level B: I completed all the On Your Own activities and the Chapter Mastery Projects without referring to any of the solutions in the *Solutions Appendix*. **I have proven that I am able to teach myself a computer skill without directions given by others.**

○ Level C: I completed all the On Your Own activities and the Chapter Mastery Projects by using just a few of the solutions in the *Solutions Appendix*. **I need some help, but for the most part I can teach myself computer skills.**

○ Level D: I completed all the On Your Own activities and the Chapter Mastery Projects by using many of the solutions in the *Solutions Appendix*. **I still need some help when learning a new computer skill.**

○ Level E: I completed all the On Your Own activities and the Chapter Mastery Project and had to use all the solutions in the *Solutions Appendix*. **I learn new computer skills by following directions given by others.**

Projects to Help You

Now that you have mastered the material in this chapter, you are ready to tackle the three projects introduced at the beginning of the chapter in the section "How Will This Chapter Help Me?"

Project 1: Customizing a Gaming Computer

Go to Dell.com and pretend money is no object when buying a gaming computer. Dell offers some extreme (and expensive) gaming computers that you can customize. Compete with others in your class to see who can design the most expensive gaming computer. Pump up Dell's best gaming computer with all the extras Dell offers. Print or save the web page showing the details of the system and its price. Compare prices with others in your class to see who designed the most expensive gaming computer. Collect this information about the computer:

▶ Model

▶ Processor speed and number of cores

▶ Memory amount and type

▶ Hard drive size and type

PERSONAL PROJECT: I want to buy a super responsive gaming computer with realistic graphics to annihilate my enemies online. What makes a gaming computer perform better than any machine out there? What can I do to beef it up?

- ▶ Optical drive
- ▶ Operating system edition and version
- ▶ Video card(s)
- ▶ Game controllers
- ▶ Other extra devices or software
- ▶ Warranty
- ▶ Price

ACADEMIC PROJECT:
I've decided to buy a computer to use during my academic career. I want to research and find the best buy for my money with all the features I need. It must last me for four years, so I don't want to make a mistake.

Project 2: Using Comparison Tables to Select a Computer

Suppose you have decided to buy a computer to use during your academic career. Because you are a good researcher, you decided to use a comparison table to help make up your mind. For a laptop computer, Table 14-6 can help you compare features. For a desktop computer, Table 14-7 should help. You can find both tables in the document file named CompareComputersTable in the Sample Files folder on the DVD in the back of this book.

Research either laptop or desktop computers. Find three computers that you like and enter the information in the table. Based on your comparisons, which computer would you consider buying? Why?

TABLE 14-6   Comparison Chart When Buying a Laptop

Feature	Laptop 1	Laptop 2	Laptop 3
Brand and model			
Processor speed and number of cores			
Memory amount and type			
Hard drive size and type			
Weight			
Screen size			
Time battery charge lasts			
Optical drive			
Windows edition and type			
Video (integrated or video card)			
Bluetooth			
Other extra features			
Warranty			
Price			

TABLE 14-7   Comparison Chart When Buying a Desktop

Feature	Desktop 1	Desktop 2	Desktop 3
Brand and model			
Processor speed and number of cores			
Memory amount and type			
Hard drive size and type			
Optical drive			
Windows edition and type			
Video (integrated or video card)			
Wireless technologies			
Other extra features			
Warranty			
Price			

Project 3: Advancing Your Technical Knowledge by Selecting a Motherboard

Most people buy a brand-name computer sold directly from the computer manufacturer or retail store. A technical person might prefer to build a desktop computer from parts. (A techie calls a computer built from parts a *white box*.) The advantages of a desktop built from parts are

TECHNICAL CAREER PROJECT: One day I want to build a computer. I work with technical people who have bought parts and built their own computer from these parts. What parts do I need and where do I purchase them?

▶ You have complete control over what parts go into your computer.

▶ You learn a great deal about computers as you research and select the parts for your custom-built computer.

▶ You can sometimes save money over a brand-name desktop.

Don't attempt to build the computer yourself unless you have technical experience working inside a computer. A reputable computer parts store might build a computer for a small fee or for free. The store might also offer a warranty on the computer and provide technical support and service.

When you are buying a brand-name computer, selecting the motherboard is not likely to be an option. For a computer built from parts, the motherboard is your most important and first choice because it determines the type of processor and memory the computer can have. Select parts in this order:

1. Select the motherboard, which determines what type computer case, power supply, processor, and memory modules you can select.

2. Select the video card (or use integrated video), optical drive, and hard drive.

Suppose you are considering a desktop computer built from parts. Start your research by finding a motherboard. Fill in the information in Table 14-8 to compare three motherboards. (A techie sometimes calls a motherboard a *mobo*.) You can find the table in the file CompareMotherboardsTable in the Sample Files folder on the DVD.

TABLE 14-8   Comparison Chart When Selecting a Motherboard

Feature	Mobo 1	Mobo 2	Mobo 3
Brand and model			
Type processors the board accepts			
Type memory the board accepts			
Type USB ports (Hi-Speed or SuperSpeed)			
Network port onboard (might be labeled gigabit LAN)			
If the board has integrated video, type video ports onboard			
Wi-Fi onboard			
Bluetooth onboard			
Price			

Three reputable manufacturers of motherboards that you might consider are

- Intel at intel.com
- Asus at asus.com
- GIGABYTE at gigabyte.com

Reputable retail sites where you can find motherboards for sale are tigerdirect.com, compusa.com, and computershopper.com.

Project to Help Others

One of the best ways to learn is to teach someone else. And, in teaching someone else, you are making a contribution in that person's life. As part of each chapter's work, you are encouraged to teach someone else a skill you have learned. In this chapter, help someone learn about upgrading or buying a computer.

Who is your apprentice? _____

Do the following:

Step 1. Ask your apprentice to assume he is in the market for a new computer or to upgrade his old computer.

Step 2. If he has a computer, help him determine what upgrades he might want and how much the upgrades will cost. Try to determine the value of his computer to decide if an upgrade is appropriate.

Step 3. Help your apprentice go shopping online for a new computer. Help him choose the type computer, key components, and extra features that will best meet his needs.

Step 4. Ask your apprentice to tell you how much he has learned from your helping him in this course and how he thinks the learning and teaching sessions went.

Solutions Appendix

CHAPTER 1 SOLUTIONS

Using Windows 7 to Manage Applications and Data

The solutions in this appendix are for you to use if you get stuck when doing an On Your Own activity in the chapter. To learn how to teach yourself a computer skill, always try the On Your Own activity first before turning to these solutions.

On Your Own Solution 1-1 How to Turn on Your Computer

Follow these steps to turn on your computer and start Windows:

Step 1. If your computer is not already turned on, press the power button on your computer to turn it on.

Step 2. Windows might provide a logon screen like the one shown in Chapter 1 in Figure 1-1. If the username is not correct, use your mouse or touch pad to click **Switch User**. A list of other user accounts set up on this computer appears. Click your user account.

> **Not Working?** If you don't see your user account, use both hands to press three keys at the same time: **Ctrl**, **Alt**, and **Delete** (commonly written as **Ctrl-Alt-Delete**). You might need to enter your user account in the box that appears. When you're using a lab computer, ask your instructor for specific directions for logging on.

Step 3. Enter the password and press the **Enter** key. The Windows desktop appears.

On Your Own Solution 1-2 How to Start a Program

Follow these steps at your computer to start the Paint program:

Step 1. Click the **Start** button. [image] The Start menu appears, listing some programs installed on your computer. Your list might be different than the one in Figure S1-1, depending on the programs installed on your computer.

> **Not Working?** This book uses Windows 7. If you have another operating system installed, your screen might not look the same as the one shown and the steps to use the operating system might be different. To find out what Windows operating system is installed, click **Start**, right-click **Computer**, and click **Properties** in the drop-down menu. The edition of Windows appears on the System window.

Step 2. Click **All Programs**. A more extensive list of installed programs appears.

Step 3. Click **Accessories** to see a list of these programs.

Step 4. Click **Paint** to open the Paint program. The Paint window opens.

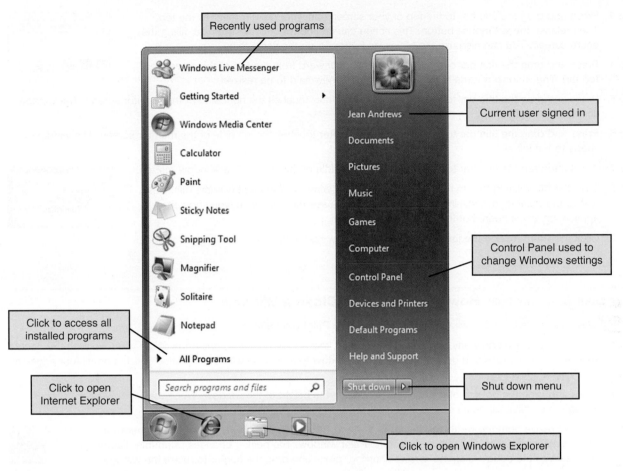

FIGURE S1-1
The Start menu lists programs installed on a computer.

On Your Own Solution 1-3   **How to Manage a Window**

Follow these steps to learn how to manage a window:

Step 1. Open the Paint program if it is not already open.

Step 2. Position your pointer in the blue title bar at the top of the Paint window. Press and drag the title bar over the screen to move the window.

Step 3. Press and drag the title bar to the top of your screen until your pointer reaches the top. Then release the left mouse button. This action causes the window to maximize, filling the entire screen. You can also use the Maximize button to do the same thing.

Step 4. Press and drag the title bar of the Paint window downward from the top of the screen (not too far). The window returns to its original size. It is now said to be resized.

Step 5. Press and drag the title bar to the right until your pointer touches the right side of the monitor screen. The window snaps to the right side.

Step 6. Press and drag the title bar to the left until your pointer touches the left side of the monitor screen. The window snaps to the left side.

Step 7. Press and drag the title bar to somewhere in the middle of the screen. The window resizes.

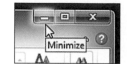

Step 8. Click the Minimize button in the title bar of the Paint window. The Paint window minimizes. Notice the Paint icon is still in the taskbar. When you see the Paint icon, you know the application is still open, but the window is not visible.

Step 9. Click the **Paint icon** in the taskbar. The Paint window restores.

On Your Own Solution 1-4   How to Resize and Close a Window

Follow these steps to resize the Paint window and then close the Paint program:

Step 1. You can make a window any size you like. To do so, move your pointer to one edge of the window. With the double arrows showing, press and drag the edge of the window to resize the window. Practice resizing on all four edges of the Paint window.

Step 2. Press and drag the bottom of the window to shorten the height of the window. When the window height is short enough, a scrollbar appears on the right side of the window.

Step 3. You can resize both the width and height of a window at the same time by grabbing a corner of a window. Move your pointer to a corner of the Paint window. The pointer changes to double diagonal arrows. With the double diagonal arrows showing, press and drag the corner to resize the window.

Step 4. To close the Paint window, click the red **X** ![X button] in the upper-right corner of the window. If you have drawn on the window, Paint asks whether you want to save your work. Click **Don't Save**. The Paint window closes.

On Your Own Solution 1-5   How to Manage Multiple Windows

Follow these steps to manage two windows:

Step 1. Click **Start**, **All Programs**, **Accessories**, and **Paint**. The Paint window opens.

Step 2. In the Windows taskbar, click the **Windows Explorer Quick Launch** icon. ![icon] Windows Explorer opens; this program allows you to manage files and folders on your computer. You now have two windows open.

> **Not Working?** If the Windows Explorer icon is not showing in the taskbar, to open Explorer, click **Start**, **All Programs**, **Accessories**, **Windows Explorer**.

Step 3. Press and drag the title bar of the Windows Explorer window so that the two windows overlap on the monitor screen. Your screen should look similar to that in Figure S1-2.

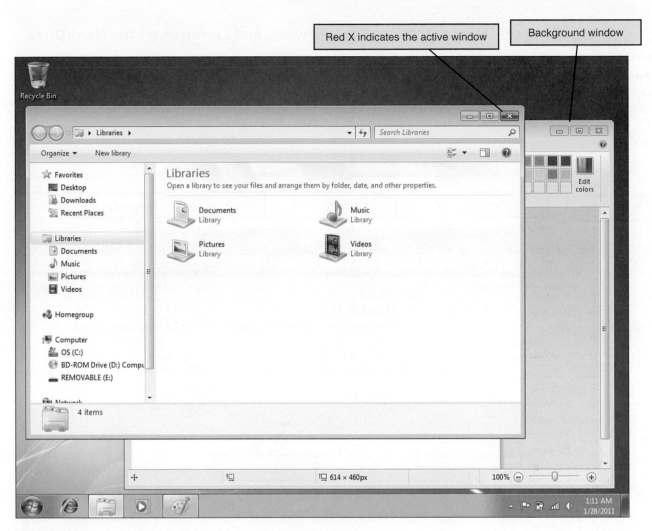

FIGURE S1-2

Two application windows overlap. The Windows Explorer window is the active window. The active window always has a red close button.

Step 4. Click anywhere in the **Paint** window. Notice the Paint window comes to the foreground. The window in the foreground is called the active window, the window you are currently using. To use another window, you can click on it to make it the active window. You can easily tell which window is the active window because the close button is red.

Not Working? If Windows is not using default display settings, the active window might not have the red X.

Step 5. Another way to make a window the active window is to use the program icon in the taskbar. Click the **Windows Explorer icon** in the taskbar to make it the active window.

Step 6. Close both windows by clicking the close button on each window.

On Your Own Solution 1-6   How to Explore Files, Folders, and Libraries on the Hard Drive

Follow these directions to explore the folders and files on the hard drive:

Step 1.   Click the **Windows Explorer icon** in the taskbar. Windows Explorer opens (see Figure S1-3). The window is divided into two parts called panes. You use the left pane, called the navigation pane, to navigate through devices and folders. You use the right pane to view the contents of a device, folder, or library. A scrollbar might be provided to scroll through the contents in a pane if the window is too small to show all the contents.

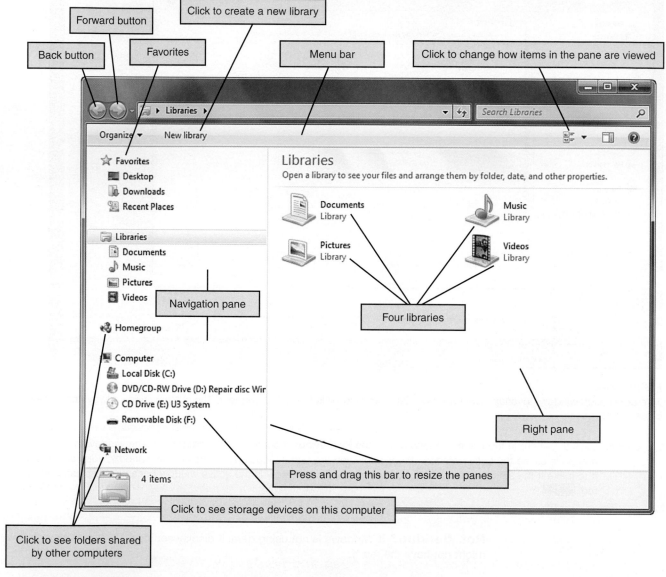

FIGURE S1-3

Windows Explorer allows you to manage folders and files on your computer.

Step 2.   In the navigation pane, click **Libraries**. The right pane displays four libraries.

Step 3.   In the right pane, double-click **Documents**. The contents of the Documents library appear in the right pane. It is said that you have drilled down to the Documents library. As you drill down into libraries, folders, and subfolders, you might find you are denied access. Some folders are secured to protect their contents.

Step 4.   Click the **back arrow button** in the Windows Explorer title bar to move back up one level in the folder tree.

Step 5. In the navigation pane, click **Computer**. All the drives on the computer are listed in the right pane (see Figure S1-4). Each drive is identified by a drive letter, and the drive letter is always followed by a colon. Notice in Figure S1-4 the hard drive is called Local Disk (C:). Your drive C: might be written another way, such as OS (C:). Also notice in the right pane the size of the hard drive (421GB) and the fact that 388GB of space on the drive is free. What is the size of the drive C: on your computer?

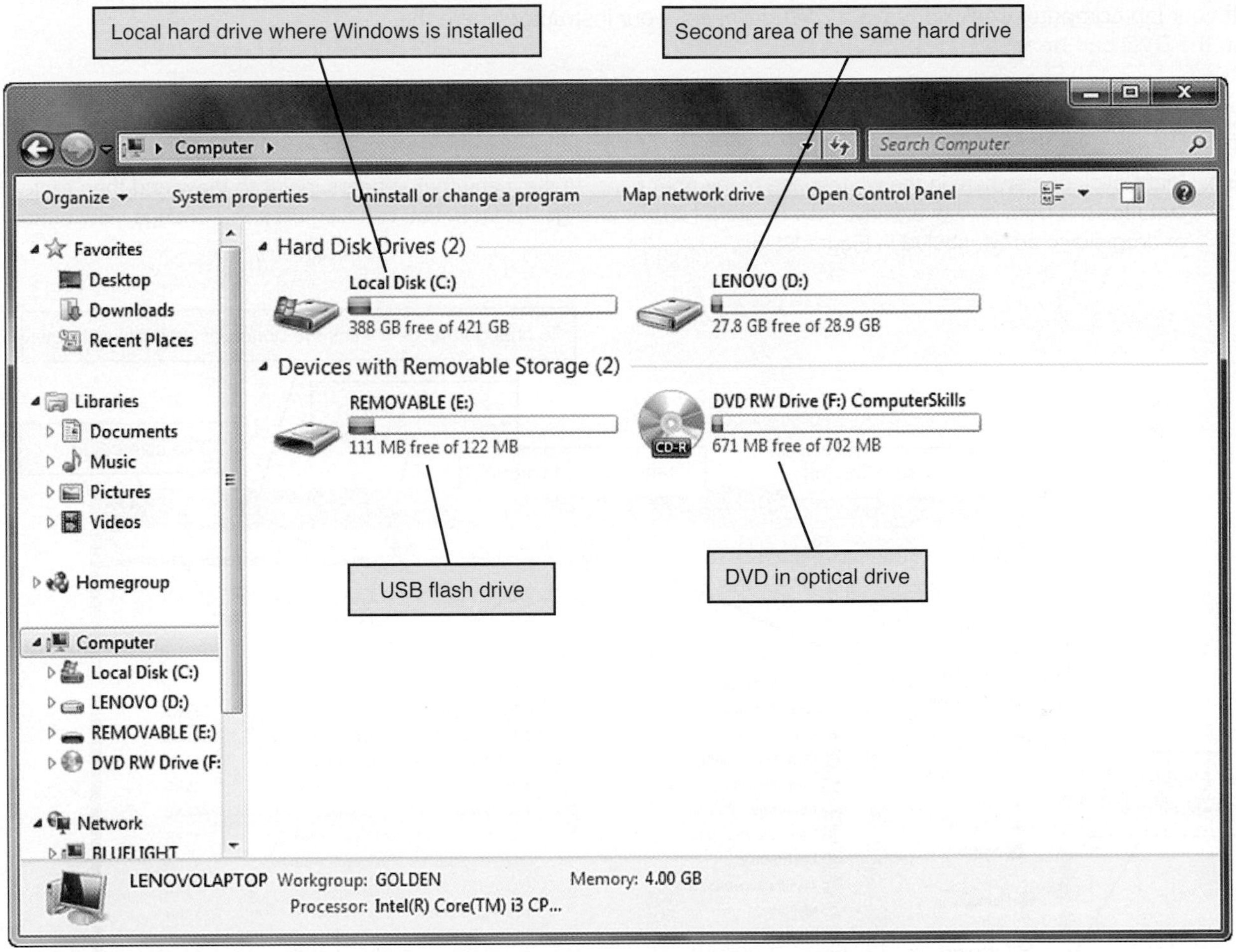

FIGURE S1-4

The Computer view of Windows Explorer shows all drives connected to the computer.

Step 6. In the navigation pane, click drive C:. For example, in Figure S1-4, you would click **Local Disk (C:)**. The many files and folders on the hard drive display in the right pane. These files and folders are said to be stored in the root, or top level, of drive C:.

On Your Own Solution 1-7 **How to Explore Files and Folders on the DVD**

Follow these steps to explore the contents of the DVD in the back of this book:

Step 1. Insert the DVD into the optical drive. If the AutoPlay dialog box opens, close it by clicking the red **X** in the upper-right corner of the box.

Step 2. In the navigation pane of Windows Explorer, click **Computer**. The devices appear in the right pane. Double-click DVD Drive. The folders and files at the root of the DVD appear in the right pane.

> **Not Working?** If your computer has a CD drive rather than a DVD drive, it cannot read the DVD.

> **Tip** If your lab computer does not have a DVD drive, ask your instructor where the files on the DVD can be found.

Step 3. Double-click the **Sample Files** folder. The contents of the Sample Files folder appear in the right pane.

Step 4. Right-click somewhere in the whitespace of the right pane. In the menu that appears, point to **View** and then click **Details**. The Details view displays (see Figure S1-5). To change the view, you can also click the Change view button or drop-down arrow labeled in Figure S1-5.

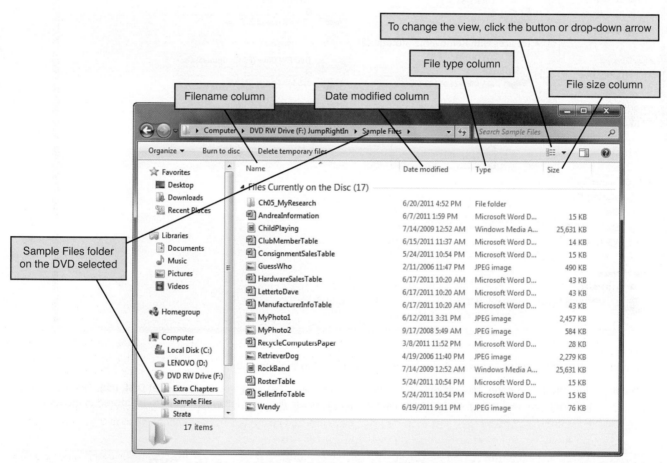

FIGURE S1-5
Files in the Sample Files folder are displayed using the Details view.

Step 5. Right-click the **Name** column heading. A menu of columns appears. In the list of columns, make sure that **Name**, **Date modified**, **Type**, and **Size** are checked and other columns are not checked.

Step 6. To sort the list by Name, click the **Name** column heading. To sort the list in reverse order by Name, click the **Name** column heading again.

Step 7. To sort the list by Type, click the **Type** column heading. To sort the list in reverse order by Type, click the **Type** column heading again.

Step 8. To view the properties of the **Wendy** file, right-click the file. In the shortcut menu, click **Properties**. The Properties box displays. The file extension shows as jpg.

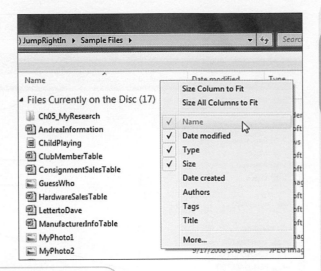

Hint When you are finished with a drop-down menu, click off it to make the menu disappear.

On Your Own Solution 1-8   How to Manage Folders on a USB Flash Drive

This solution has four parts:

▶ How to create a folder on a USB flash drive

▶ How to delete a folder

▶ How to use a shortcut menu in Windows Explorer

▶ How to copy a folder from one storage device to another

How to Create a Folder on a USB Flash Drive

Follow these steps to create a folder named Computer Class on your USB flash drive:

Step 1. If necessary, open Windows Explorer.

Step 2. Plug your USB flash drive into a USB port. If Windows displays the AutoPlay dialog box, close the dialog box.

Step 3. If necessary, click the white arrow to the left of Computer in the left pane to open the Computer group. The USB flash drive is listed as Removable. Your USB flash drive might be listed under a different name, such as Removable Disk or Lexar Media, which is the brand of the USB drive. Click the drive; in the example, click Removable. The right pane now shows the contents of your USB flash drive.

Step 4. Click New folder in the menu bar under the title bar of Windows Explorer. A new folder appears on your flash drive. The name of the folder is New folder, and that name is highlighted so that you can change the name. Type **Computer Class** as the name of the new folder and press **Enter**.

Step 5. Double-click **Computer Class**. The right pane shows the folder is empty. Notice the Computer Class folder is listed in the address bar at the top of Windows Explorer (see Figure S1-6).

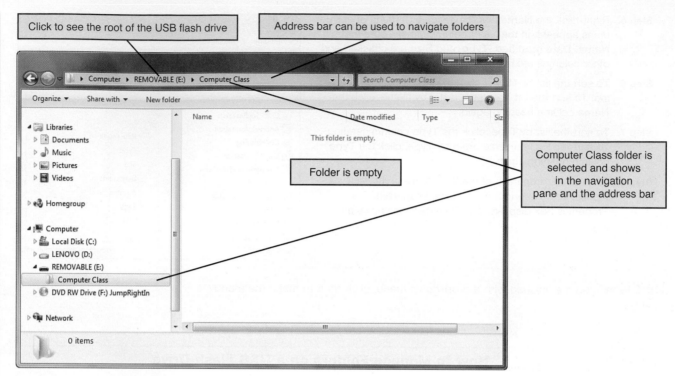

FIGURE S1-6
The Computer Class folder is empty.

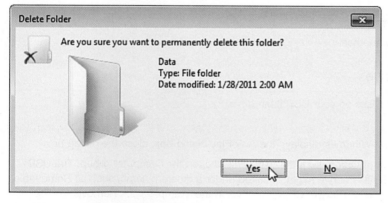

FIGURE S1-7
Click Yes to delete the Data folder.

How to Delete a Folder

Now let's practice creating and deleting a folder. Follow these steps:

Step 1. Click **New folder** and enter **Data** for the name of the new folder. The Data folder is now a subfolder of the Computer Class folder.

Step 2. Click the **Data** folder to select it.

Step 3. To delete the folder, press the **Delete** key. The Delete Folder dialog box appears (see Figure S1-7). Click **Yes**. The Data folder is deleted.

How to Use a Shortcut Menu in Windows Explorer

Follow these steps to learn how to use a shortcut menu in Windows Explorer:

Step 1. In the navigation pane of Windows Explorer, click your USB drive. (In the example, click **Removable**.) The Computer Class folder appears in the right pane of Explorer.

Step 2. Right-click anywhere in the whitespace of the right pane. A shortcut menu appears similar to the left menu in Figure S1-8.

Not Working? When you right-click an item and the wrong menu appears, try right-clicking again. Most likely, your pointer was not in the correct position.

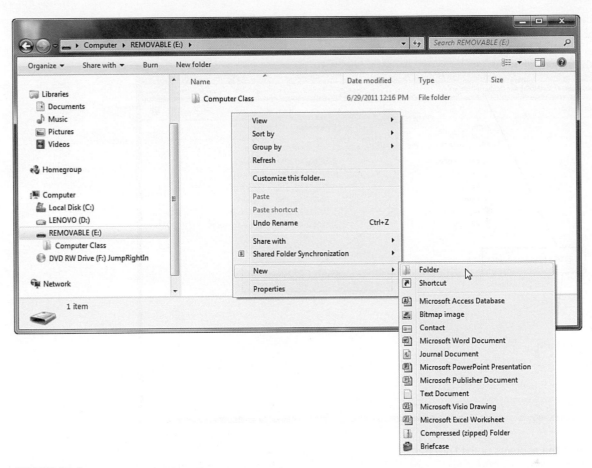

FIGURE S1-8
Create a new folder using the shortcut menu in the right pane.

Step 3. Using your pointer, point to **New**, as shown in the figure. A second menu appears showing all the items that you can create. Click **Folder**. A new folder is created. Name the folder **History Class**.

Step 4. Click anywhere in the whitespace in the right pane so that the History Class folder is not selected. You now have two folders at the top level of your USB flash drive: Computer Class and History Class.

Step 5. To rename the History Class folder, right-click it and select **Rename** from the shortcut menu. Name the folder **English Class**.

How to Copy a Folder from One Storage Device to Another

Follow these steps to copy the Sample Files folder from the DVD to your USB drive using two windows and the drag and drop operation:

Step 1. Insert the DVD taken from the back of this book into the optical drive. If the AutoPlay dialog box appears, close the box by clicking the red **X** in the upper-right corner.

Step 2. In the navigation pane of Windows Explorer in the Computer group, double-click the DVD drive. The contents of the root of the DVD appear in the right pane as shown in Figure S1-9.

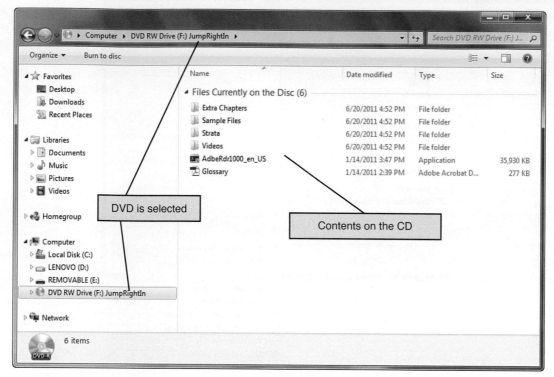

FIGURE S1-9
The right pane shows the contents of the DVD root.

Step 3. Drag the Windows Explorer window to the left side of your screen so that it snaps to the left.

Step 4. To open a second Windows Explorer window, right-click the **Windows Explorer** icon [image] in the taskbar. In the shortcut menu that appears, click **Windows Explorer**. A second window opens. Drag this window to the right side of your screen so that it snaps to the right side.

Step 5. In the Windows Explorer window on the right, in the navigation pane, click **Computer**. Then in the right pane of this window, double-click the removable USB flash drive. The contents of the root of the USB drive appear in the right pane.

Step 6. Click the title bar of the left window to make it the active window. Then press and drag the **Sample Files** folder from the left window to the right window, placing the folder in the root of the USB flash drive.

Step 7. To verify the folder copied without errors, in the right window, double-click **Sample Files**. A list of files in the folder appears (see Figure S1-10).

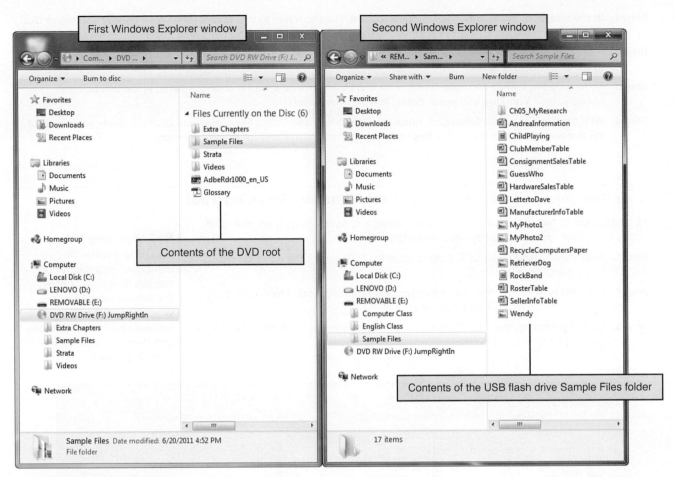

FIGURE S1-10
Verify the contents of the Sample Files folder on the USB flash drive.

On Your Own Solution 1-9   How to Open, Copy, Move, and Delete a File

Follow these steps to view the contents of the Wendy file. Then copy it to the Computer Class folder:

Step 1. If necessary, insert your USB flash drive in the USB port. If the AutoPlay dialog box opens, close it.

Step 2. If necessary, open **Windows Explorer**.

Step 3. Drill down to **Computer** and then to the removable USB flash drive. The list of folders on the USB flash drive appears in the right pane. Double-click the **Sample Files** folder to view its contents.

Step 4. To open the **Wendy** file, double-click it. The photo displays. Close the photo window.

Step 5. In Windows Explorer, right-click the **Wendy** file and select **Copy** from the shortcut menu. The file is copied into the Windows Clipboard.

Step 6. In the navigation pane, double-click **Computer Class**. This folder's contents appear in the right pane, and the folder name appears in the title bar of the Windows Explorer window.

Step 7. Right-click in the white area of the right pane and select **Paste** from the shortcut menu. The Wendy file is copied into the Computer Class folder.

Step 8. Double-click the **Sample Files** folder and verify the Wendy file is still there.

Follow these steps to move the Wendy file from the Computer Class folder to the English Class folder. Then rename the file and finally delete it:

Step 1. In the navigation pane, click the **Computer Class** folder to return to that folder. Right-click **Wendy** and select **Cut** from the shortcut menu. The file is moved to the Clipboard. Click the **English Class** folder.

Step 2. Right-click in the whitespace of the right pane and select **Paste** from the shortcut menu. The Wendy file is moved to the English Class folder.

Step 3. To rename the Wendy file, right-click the file and click **Rename** from the shortcut menu. In the text box that appears, type **YourDog** and press **Enter**. The file is renamed.

Step 4. With the YourDog file still selected, press the **Delete** key. The Delete File dialog box appears. Verify you are deleting the correct file and then click **Yes** to delete it. The English Class folder is now empty.

On Your Own Solution 1-10   **How to Use the Windows Snipping Tool**

Follow these steps to take a snip of your Windows screen and save it to a file on your USB flash drive or another location given by your instructor:

Step 1. If necessary, insert your USB flash drive in the USB port. If the AutoPlay dialog box opens, close it.

Step 2. Click **Start**, **All Programs**, **Accessories**, and **Snipping Tool**. The screen goes dim and the Snipping Tool box opens.

Step 3. Click the arrow to the right of New to see a list of types of snips you can capture (see Figure S1-11). Click one.

> **Not Working?** If you are using a netbook computer, you might not see the Snipping Tool in the Accessories group. Windows 7 Starter is installed on many netbooks and does not include the Snipping Tool.

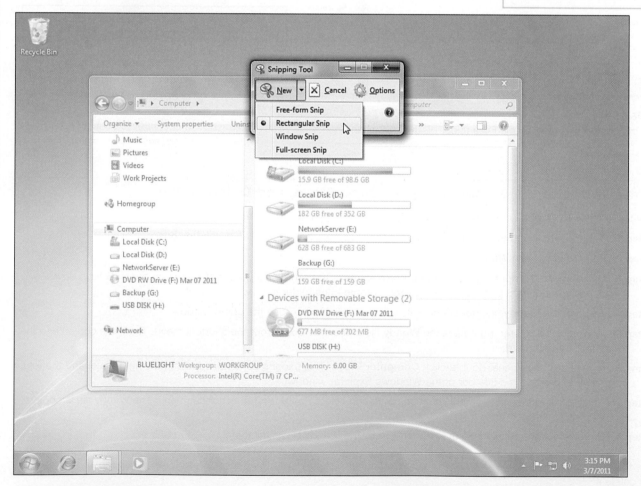

FIGURE S1-11
Select the type of snip.

Step 4. If you selected a free-form snip or rectangular snip, your pointer changes to a crosshair $+$. Press and drag to select the area of your screen you want to capture.

Step 5. If you selected a window snip, click the window on your desktop you want to snip.

Step 6. The Snipping Tool window opens showing your snip. Click **File**, **Save As**. The Save As box opens (see Figure S1-12).

Step 7. In the left pane, click your USB flash drive.

Step 8. Under *File name*, replace the text with **MySnip1**. Notice the *Save as type* is PNG. The file will be saved as a PNG file.

Step 9. Click **Save**. The file is saved to your USB flash drive.

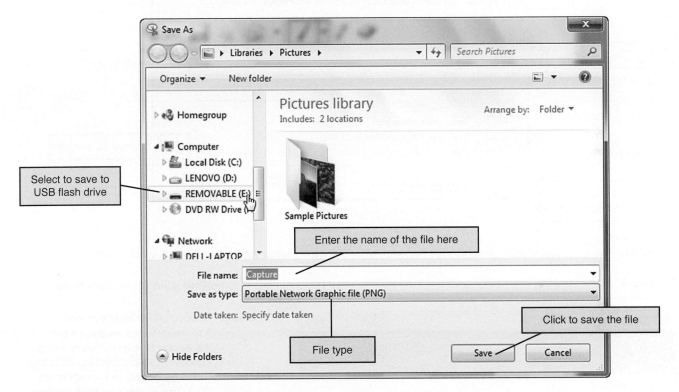

FIGURE S1-12
Tell Windows where to save the file and what to name it.

On Your Own Solution 1-11   **How to Install Software from DVD**

The program file AdbeRdr1000_en_US.exe in the root of the DVD is the setup program used to install the Adobe Reader software. Follow these steps to install the software using the DVD in the back of this book:

Step 1. If the DVD is not already in the optical drive, insert it.

Step 2. If the Autoplay dialog box appears, click **Run AdbeRdr1000_en_US.exe**. A UAC (User Access Control) box appears. Refer to Figure 1-20 in the book to see what the UAC box looks like.

Step 3. If the dialog box does not display, open Windows Explorer and display the contents of the DVD. Double-click the **AdbeRdr1000_en_US.exe** program file. A UAC box appears asking if you want to allow the program to change your computer.

Step 4. Respond to the UAC box: If you are logged on with an administrator user account, click **Yes** to continue with the installation. If you are logged on with a standard user account, enter the password of the administrator and click **Continue**. Either way, the installation is allowed to proceed.

Step 5. The setup program launches and the *Adobe Reader X – Setup* window appears. After the program prepares the installation files, the window shown in Figure S1-13 displays. In the window, notice you can change the location of the installed software, which is currently set to C:\Program Files\Adobe\Reader 10.0\. You don't need to change this location. Click **Install** to install the software.

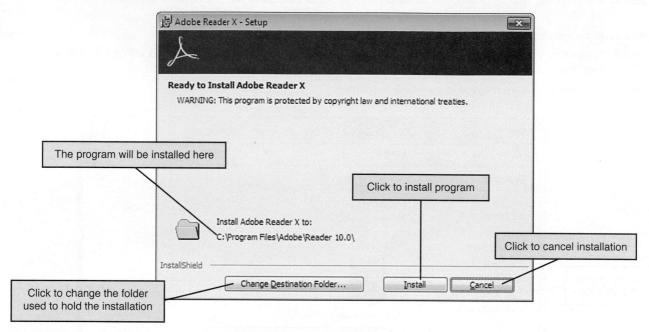

FIGURE S1-13
The Adobe Reader setup program gives you the opportunity to change the folder where the installed software will be stored.

Step 6. The installation proceeds. When it is finished, the setup program window looks like Figure S1-14. Click **Finish**.

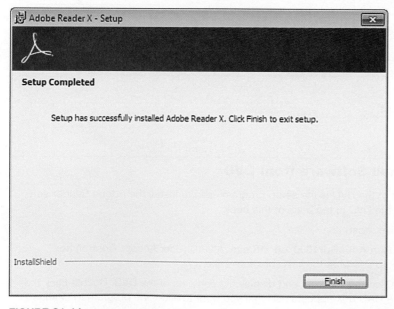

FIGURE S1-14
The software installed successfully.

Step 7. After you first install software, test it to make sure it works. To test the Adobe Reader software, using Windows Explorer, double-click the **Glossary.pdf** file in the root of the DVD. This action causes the Adobe Reader software to launch, which can display the contents of a .pdf file.

Step 8. The first time you use the software, a licensing agreement displays, asking you to accept the terms of the license (see Figure S1-15). After you view the agreement, click **Accept**. Adobe Reader then displays the contents of the Glossary.pdf file.

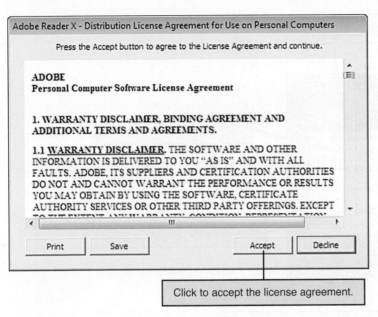

FIGURE S1-15
The Adobe Reader application asks you to accept the terms of the Software License Agreement.

Step 9. Close the **Glossary.pdf** file and close **Windows Explorer**. Remove the DVD from the optical drive and store it in a safe place.

On Your Own Solution 1-12   **How to End a Windows Session**

This solution has four parts:

- ▶ How to log off a computer
- ▶ How to put your computer in sleep mode
- ▶ How to shut down a computer
- ▶ How to put a laptop or netbook in hibernation

How to Log Off a Computer

Follow these steps to log off:

Step 1. Click the **Start** button and then click the **arrow** to the right of Shut down. See Figure S1-16.

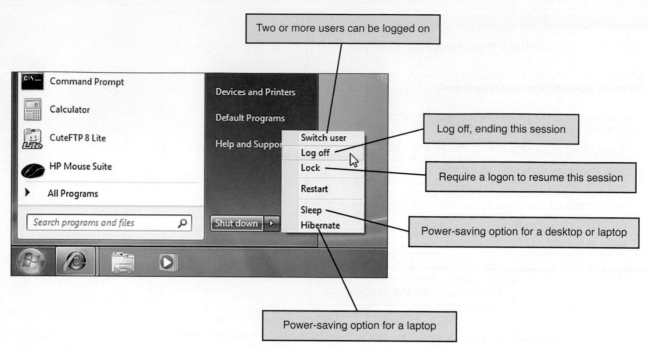

FIGURE S1-16
Shutdown menu on a laptop shows hibernation as an option.

Step 2. Click **Log off**. Windows logs you off your account.

Step 3. To log back on, press any key or move the mouse or touchpad. The logon screen appears and you can log back on.

How to Put Your Computer in Sleep Mode

To put a computer in sleep mode, follow these steps:

Step 1. Click the **Start** button and then click the **arrow** to the right of Shut down.

Step 2. Click **Sleep**. Windows puts the computer to sleep.

Step 3. To wake up the computer, press any key or move the mouse or touch pad.

How to Shut Down a Computer

To shut down Windows, follow these steps:

Step 1. Close any open windows.

Step 2. Click the **Start** button and click **Shut down**. Windows closes, and the computer is powered down.

Step 3. To power the computer back up, **press** the power button.

How to Put a Laptop or Netbook in Hibernation

To put Windows in hibernation on a laptop or netbook, follow these steps:

Step 1. Click the **Start** button and then click the **arrow** to the right of Shut down.

Step 2. Click **Hibernate**. All the work in open applications is saved to the hard drive, and the computer powers down.

Step 3. To resume work, press the power button. The system powers up, and Windows reloads any open applications and documents so that you can resume your work where you left off.

CHAPTER 2 SOLUTIONS
Finding and Using Information on the Web

The solutions in this appendix are for you to use if you get stuck when doing an On Your Own activity in the chapter. To learn how to teach yourself a computer skill, always try the On Your Own activity first before turning to these solutions.

> **Not Working?** Websites change from time to time. The step-by-step instructions were accurate when we wrote them, but be aware that you might have to adjust them to account for later website changes.

On Your Own Solution 2-1 **How to Use Internet Explorer**

This solution has two parts:

▶ How to navigate to new web pages

▶ How to use the address box and back and forward buttons

How to Navigate to New Web Pages

Follow these steps to open and use Internet Explorer:

Step 1. Click the **Internet Explorer** icon ⬚ in the taskbar. Internet Explorer opens, and a web page displays inside the IE window (see Figure S2-1). Look in the address box of your browser for the text beginning with http://. This text is the address of your home page. Windows 7 automatically makes the home page http://www.msn.com, but your home page might have been changed to some other page.

FIGURE S2-1
The home page is the first page that displays when you open your browser.

Step 2. Move your pointer over the web page. When the shape of your pointer changes from an arrow ↳ to a hand ☝ , you have located a link.

Step 3. Click a link, and another web page displays. Moving from web page to web page is called surfing the web. When you click a link and a new web page displays, notice the address in the address box changes. The address showing is the address of the new web page. Also notice the name of the web page appears in the tab above the page.

Step 4. You can return to your home page at any time. To return, click the **Home** button 🖼, which is labeled in Figure S2-1.

How to Use the Address Box and Back and Forward Buttons

Besides clicking links to find new web pages, you can also enter the address in the address box. Follow these steps:

Step 1. Press and drag your pointer over all the text in the address bar so that all the text is selected. Selected text is highlighted in blue.

Step 2. Let's get some CNN news. Type **www.cnn.com**, which replaces the highlighted text. Press **Enter**. The CNN web page appears. Notice that when you enter www.cnn.com in the address box, Internet Explorer automatically adds http:// to the beginning of the address.

> **Not Working?** Make sure all the old address is deleted. Only one address at a time can be in the address box. You can use your Backspace key to delete an old address.

Step 3. Click a link on the www.cnn.com page to display another page.

Step 4. Click the back button 🔵 in the title bar. Your browser goes to the last previously visited page, returning you to the www.cnn.com page.

Step 5. Click the forward button 🔵 in the title bar. The browser goes forward to the web page you just left. By using the back and forward buttons, you can revisit web pages you have seen since the browser was opened.

On Your Own Solution 2-2   **How to Manage Multiple Web Pages**

Follow these steps to visit four websites:

Step 1. If **Internet Explorer** is not already open, open it.

Step 2. Type **www.nytimes.com** in the address box and press **Enter**. The New York Times page appears.

> **Not Working?** If a web page does not immediately appear after you press Enter, try pressing the Refresh button ⟳ to the right of the address box. If it still does not appear, the website might be having problems. To cancel the request for a page, press the Cancel button ☒.

Step 3. You can open more than one web page at a time. Click the **New Tab** button (refer to Figure S2-1) to open a new tab. The New Tab appears (see Figure S2-2).

Step 4. In the address box, the text is already highlighted. Type **news.yahoo.com** to replace the highlighted text and press **Enter**. The Yahoo! News web page appears.

Step 5. Open a third tab. Type **news.google.com** in the address box and press **Enter**. The Google News web page appears.

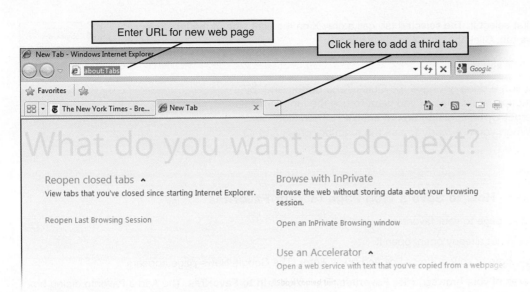

FIGURE S2-2

A new tab allows you to view a new page without losing the previous page.

> **Not Working?** If you get an error, make sure you have deleted all the text in the address box before you enter a new address.
>
> If a web page does not immediately appear after you press **Enter**, try pressing the **Refresh** button ⟳ to the right of the address box.

Step 6. Open a fourth tab and visit the web page **cnn.com**.

Step 7. You now have four tabs open. You can view any one of the four pages by clicking its tab button. Click **The New York Times** tab to return to that page.

Step 8. Click the **Quick Tabs** button to the left of the open tabs. All the web pages appear (see Figure S2-3). Click the **Google News** page to view it.

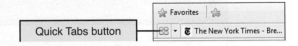

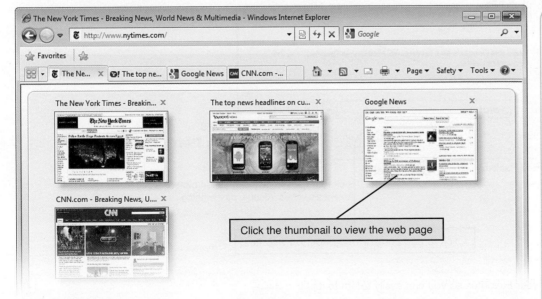

> **Not Working?**
> If you don't see the Quick Tabs button, it might be disabled. To fix the problem, click **Tools**, **Internet Options**. The Internet Options dialog box appears. In the Tabs group, click **Settings**, and then click **Enable Quick Tabs**. Click **OK**. Click **OK** again to close the dialog box. Close Internet Explorer and open it. The Quick Tabs button appears after you open a second IE tab.

FIGURE S2-3

The Quick Tabs view allows you to see all open pages and select one.

Step 9. To close a tab, first select it. The selected tab has a gray X on the right side of the tab. Select the **Google News** tab. Click the gray **X** to close this tab.

> **Hint** Internet Explorer version 9 does not have the Quick Tabs button and, by default, the Quick Tabs function is disabled. If you want to use the function in IE version 9, first use the Internet Options dialog box to enable it. Then close and reopen Internet Explorer. When you are ready to use the function, press Ctrl+Q.

On Your Own Solution 2-3   How to Save a Web Page to Your Favorites

Follow these steps to save a web page to your favorites:

Step 1. If Internet Explorer is not already open, open it.

Step 2. Type **news.google.com** in your address box and press **Enter**. The Google News page appears.

Step 3. In the upper-left area of your browser, click **Favorites**. Then click **Add to Favorites**. The Add a Favorite dialog box appears (see Figure S2-4). Click **Add**. The Google News site is added to your Favorites list. (You can also click the gold star to the right of Favorites to add a web page to Favorites.)

Step 4. Later when you want to revisit the site, click **Favorites** and then click the site in the list of Favorites that appears.

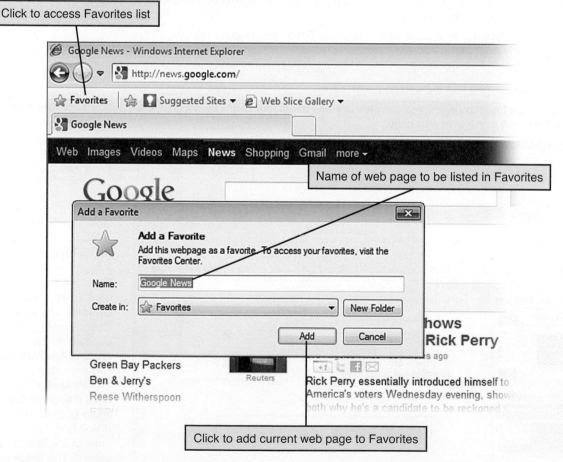

FIGURE S2-4
Add a website address to your Favorites so you can easily return to it.

On Your Own Solution 2-4   **How to Use a Search Engine**

The Google.com website changes often. The instructions here were correct when we wrote them, but they might need adjusting. Follow these steps to learn to use Google to find information on the web:

Step 1. If Internet Explorer is not already open, open it.

Step 2. To go to the Google site, type **google.com** in the address box and press **Enter**. The Google web page appears.

Step 3. Enter **seattle weather** in the search box. As you type, notice the autosuggest feature of Google is offering suggestions for the completion of your search string (see Figure S2-5).

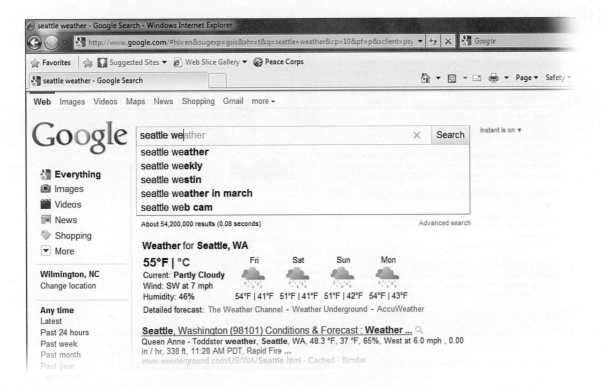

FIGURE S2-5
Google autosuggest offers suggestions to complete your search string.

Step 4. Also notice the instant search feature of Google gives search results as you type. Before you finish typing seattle weather, the weather forecast for Seattle, Washington, displays. To use a suggestion, click it. Click **seattle weather** in the drop-down list of suggestions. (On the other hand, if you don't want to use a suggestion, finish typing your search string and press **Enter** or click **Search**.)

Step 5. The list of hits Google found about your search appears. Mouse over the area to the right of a hit. A double arrow appears. When you mouse over the double arrow, a preview of the page appears on the right, as shown in Figure S2-6. As you move your mouse pointer over other hits, other previews appear.

Not Working? The step-by-step instructions given here were accurate when we wrote them, but be aware that you might have to adjust them to account for later website changes.

Hit count (number of web pages found)

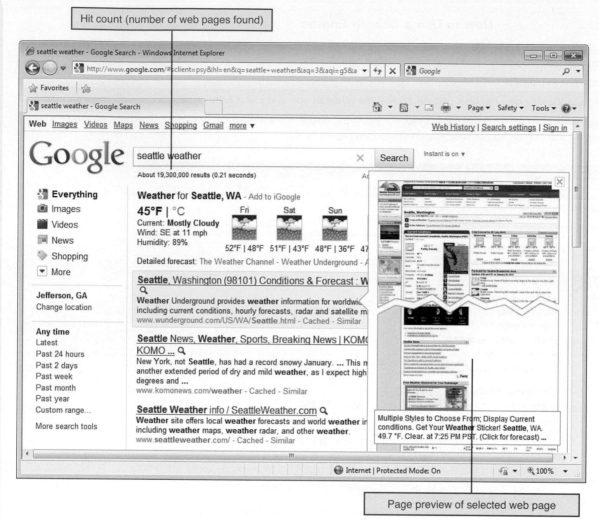

Page preview of selected web page

FIGURE S2-6

Page previews allow you to view a page without leaving the Google hit list.

Step 6. Mouse over the first line in a hit (the line that is blue and underlined). Your pointer changes to a hand. ✋ Click this first line to drill down to the link.

Follow this step to practice using the Internet Explorer search box:

Step 1. In the search box, type **how to change the oil in my car** and press **Enter**. The page showing the results includes the name of the search engine used. Bing.com is used unless the default setting for the search box has been changed.

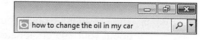

On Your Own Solution 2-5 **How to Perform Google Advanced Searches**

Follow these steps to get information on how a search engine works searching only the wikipedia.org website:

Step 1. If Internet Explorer is not already open, open it. In the address box, type **google.com** and press **Enter**. The Google search page opens.

Step 2. Type **site:wikipedia.org how a search engine works** and press **Enter**. The list of hits appears. Notice all the hits come from the wikipedia.org site.

Follow these steps to limit the preceding search to content updated in the past 24 hours and then remove the limitation:

Step 1. In the left column of the Google page, click **More search tools**. A list of advanced tools appears.

Step 2. In the list of tools, click **Past 24 hours**. Notice the hit count is greatly reduced.

Step 3. To undo the time limitation placed on the search, at the top of the hit list, click the blue **X** to the right of Past 24 hours (see Figure S2-7).

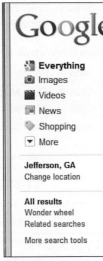

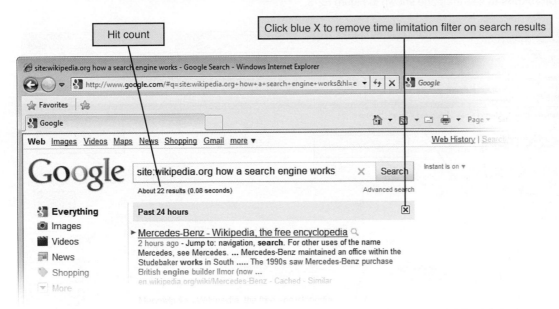

FIGURE S2-7
Click the blue X to remove the time limitation on the search.

Follow these steps to limit the search to exact words and to exclude a word from the search:

Step 1. To search for exact wording, put quotation marks around the phrase. In the Google search box, type **"who invented google earth"** and press **Enter**. Be sure to include the quotation marks as you type. Only sites that use this exact phrase are listed.

Step 2. Use a hyphen before a word to exclude it from search results. To search for an apartment near Emory University but eliminate luxury apartments from your search, type **rent apartment near emory university –luxury** in the Google search box and press **Enter**.

> **Not Working?** Don't type a space following the hyphen.

On Your Own Solution 2-6   **How to Find Images, Videos, Driving Directions, and Translations**

Follow these steps to find images and videos:

Step 1. If Internet Explorer is not already open, open it. Go to the **google.com** search page.

Step 2. Enter **2010 gulf oil spill** in the Google search box.

Step 3. Click **Images** in the menu at the top of the Google page. Images of the spill appear.

Step 4. Enter **how to make a homemade pizza** in the Google search box. Click **Videos** in the menu at the top of the Google page. Links to videos appear.

Follow these steps to find driving directions from Baltimore, Maryland, to Newark, New Jersey:

Step 1. Return to the Google search page by entering **google.com** in the Internet Explorer address box and pressing **Enter**.

Step 2. Click **Maps**. The Google maps page appears. (You can also get to this page by entering **maps.google.com** in the Internet Explorer address box.)

Step 3. Click **Get Directions** to see the page shown in Figure S2-8.

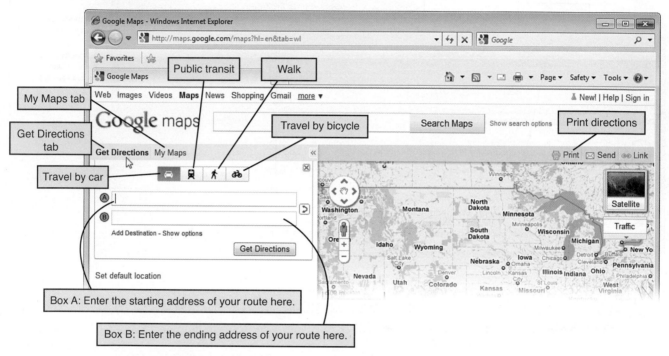

FIGURE S2-8

Use Google Maps to find driving, transit, walking, and bicycling directions.

Step 4. In box A, enter **baltimore, md**.

Step 5. In box B, enter **newark, nj**.

Step 6. Select the car icon above the boxes, indicating that your search will give you driving directions. Click the **Get Directions** button below the destination boxes. Driving directions appear. You can also enter full addresses including street address, city, and state in boxes A and B to get driving directions to a specific address.

Step 7. You might need printed directions that you can take with you as you drive. To print the directions, click **Print** near the top of the window above the map. A new window opens showing directions designed for printing.

Step 8. Click **Print** in the upper-right corner of the window. The Print dialog box appears (see Figure S2-9). Select your printer and click **Print**. The document prints.

Follow these steps to translate text:

Step 1. Return to the Google search page by entering **google.com** in the Internet Explorer address box and pressing **Enter**.

Step 2. In the menu at the top of the Google page, click **more**. In the drop-down list that appears, click **Translate**. The Google translate page appears.

Step 3. In the text box, type **Good morning. Welcome to my home.** As you type, notice the translator detects you are typing English.

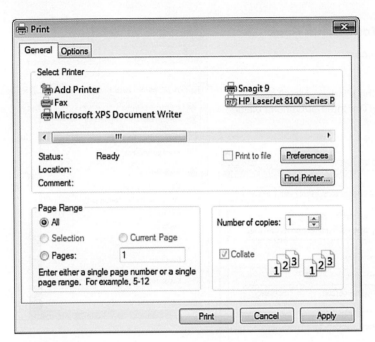

FIGURE S2-9
The Print dialog box allows you to select a printer and then print.

Not Working? If the document does not print, verify the printer is connected to your computer. Does the printer have paper? Is the printer turned on? Chapter 13 gives more tips when solving a printer problem.

Step 4. To the right of To, select **Spanish** from the list of languages. The translation happens instantly (see Figure S2-10).

Step 5. To hear the translation, click **Listen**.

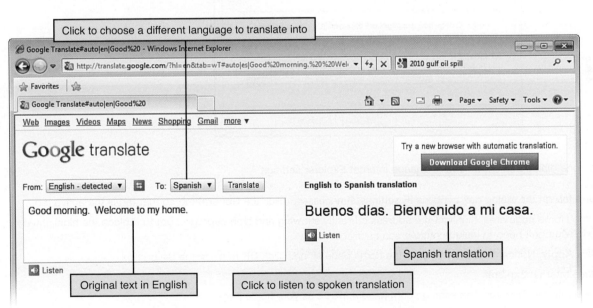

FIGURE S2-10
Translate text from English to Spanish and listen to the translation.

Not Working? To hear the translation, the volume on your computer must be turned up high enough. To turn up the volume, use the volume icon in the taskbar.

On Your Own Solution 2-7 **How to Change Your Home Page**

Follow these steps to change your home page to **espn.go.com**:

Step 1. If Internet Explorer is not open, open it.

Step 2. In the menu bar on the upper-right corner of the window, click **Tools**. In the drop-down menu, click **Internet Options**. The Internet Options dialog box appears (see Figure S2-11).

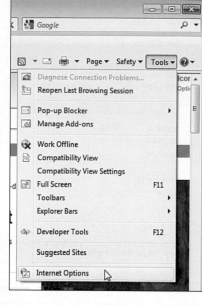

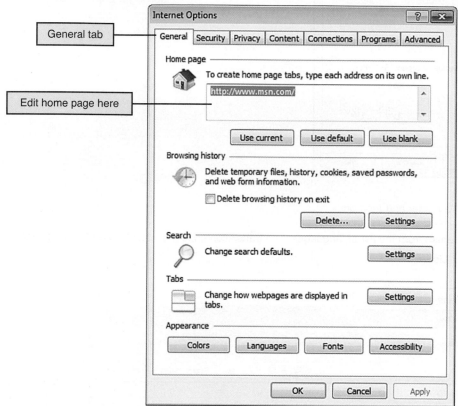

FIGURE S2-11

The Internet Options dialog box allows you to change Internet Explorer settings.

Step 3. Each tab on the dialog box contains IE settings. If necessary, click the **General** tab so that tab is the active tab.

Step 4. In the Home page area, highlight the address currently showing and type **espn.go.com** to replace the highlighted text. You don't need to include http://.

Step 5. Click **Apply**. Notice IE added http:// to the home page string. Click **OK** to close the dialog box.

Step 6. Close Internet Explorer.

Step 7. Open Internet Explorer. The espn.go.com page appears as your home page.

Not Working? If espn.go.com does not appear as your home page, open the Internet Options dialog box again and check your spelling. Perhaps you misspelled the address.

On Your Own Solution 2-8   **How to Set Up and Use a SkyDrive**

This solution has two parts:

▶ How to set up a SkyDrive

▶ How to upload a file to a SkyDrive and share a SkyDrive folder

How to Set Up a SkyDrive

When you sign up for a Windows Live account, your SkyDrive is automatically created.

The live.com website changes often, so the instructions given below might need adjusting. If you do not yet have a Windows Live account, follow these steps to sign up for the account:

Step 1. If Internet Explorer is not open, open it. Go to the **live.com** site. See Figure S2-12.

FIGURE S2-12
Sign up for a Live account or log in to an existing account.

Step 2. Click **Sign up**. The Create your Windows Live ID page appears (see Figure S2-13).

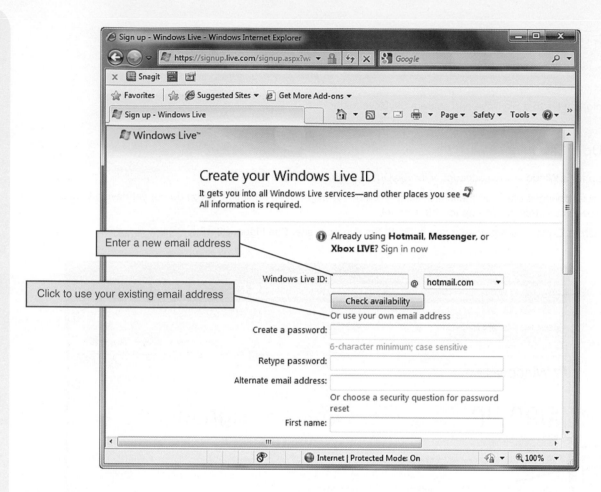

FIGURE S2-13
Create your Windows Live ID and Hotmail email account.

Step 3. If you already have an email address, click **Or use your own email address** and enter the address. Email addresses have the form someone@example.com.

Step 4. If you don't already have an email address, enter your name or some other group of characters in the Windows Live ID box.

Step 5. Notice that @hotmail.com will be added to the characters to complete your email address. You can use the down arrow to the right of hotmail.com to change the ending to live.com. Then click **Check availability**.

Step 6. If the email address is taken, a drop-down box appears with suggestions. Select one or try a new address. For example, I discovered jeanandrews@live.com was available and took it.

Step 7. Fill in the other information in the boxes and click **I accept** at the bottom of the page. Be sure to write down your new email address and your password to Windows Live. After the account is created, you are automatically signed in.

If you already have a Windows Live account, follow these steps to sign in:

Step 1. If Internet Explorer is not open, open it. Go to the **live.com** site. (Refer to Figure S2-12 shown earlier.)

Step 2. Click **Sign in** and enter your password. Then click **Sign in** again.

How to Upload a File to a SkyDrive and Share a SkyDrive Folder

The live.com website changes often, so the instructions given below might need adjusting. Follow these steps to upload a photo file to your SkyDrive:

Step 1. Now that you are signed in to Windows Live, you should see your name in the upper-right corner of the web page (see Figure S2-14). In the menu at the top of the page, click **SkyDrive**.

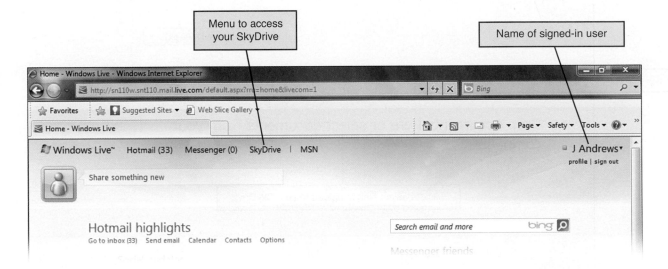

FIGURE S2-14
Access your SkyDrive after you are signed into Windows Live.

Step 2. Your SkyDrive folders appear. Initially, you have the My Documents and Public folders, but you can create others. Double-click the **Public** folder to open it.

> **Not Working?** At the time we wrote this book, Windows Live assigned a new SkyDrive a Public folder and a My Documents folder. Your SkyDrive might contain different folders. Add your files to whatever folder the SkyDrive offers.

Step 3. Click **Add files**. The Add documents to Public page appears (see Figure S2-15). Click **select documents from your computer**. The Open dialog box appears.

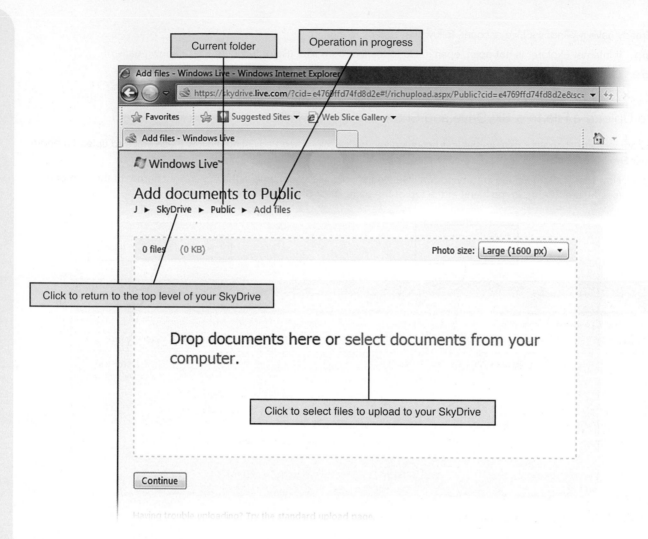

FIGURE S2-15
Add files to a folder on your SkyDrive.

Step 4. Locate your photo file. If you don't have a photo of yourself, you can use the **MyPhoto1.jpg** file in the Sample Files folder on the DVD in the back of the book. Click **Open**. The file appears in the box of files ready to upload.

Step 5. Click **Continue**. The file is uploaded and stored on your SkyDrive in the Public folder. To return to the top level of your SkyDrive, click **SkyDrive**. The **SkyDrive** page appears showing two folders. Double-click a folder to see its contents.

Everyone has access to the Public folder. If your instructor wants you to store your homework files in the My Documents folder and give him access to this folder, follow these steps to give access:

Step 1. On the far right of the SkyDrive window, look for links that you can use to delete the folder, edit permissions, and get and send a link to a folder. If you don't see these links, mouse over the last column in the My Documents row until the Show information icon appears (see Figure S2-16). Click the icon.

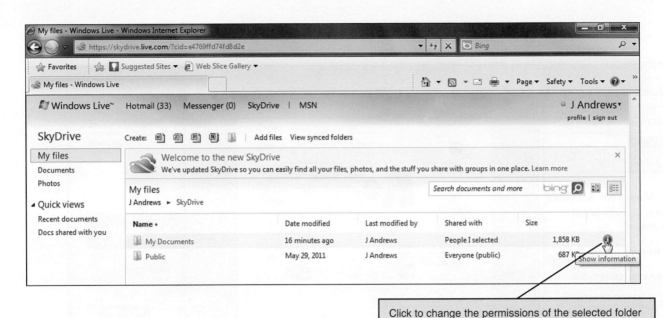

Click to change the permissions of the selected folder

FIGURE S2-16
Click the Show information icon to view and change the folder settings.

Step 2. Links appear where you can delete the folder, edit permissions, and get and send a link to the folder. Click **Edit permissions** and enter the email address of your instructor. Click **Save**. The Send a notification window appears.

Step 3. Enter a message to your instructor and click **Send**. Your instructor is sent an email message with the link to your SkyDrive. If your instructor has a Windows Live account, he can click this link to find files you place in the My Documents folder of your SkyDrive. In later chapters, you learn how to save documents to this folder using Office applications.

Not Working? Remember, the live.com website changes often. If you are having problems with these instructions, look for help on the SkyDrive page. For example, in Figure S2-16, click Learn more. You can also search Google on **how to use a skydrive**.

On Your Own Solution 2-9   **How to Print and Save a Web Page**

This solution has two parts:

▶ How to print a web page
▶ How to save a web page to a data file

How to Print a Web Page

Follow these steps to print a web page:

Step 1. If Internet Explorer is not already open, open it. Go to the web page **wellsfargo.com**.

Step 2. To print the page, click the down arrow [icon] next to the printer icon. Click **Print Preview** in the drop-down menu that appears. A new window opens containing a preview of how the printout will appear (see Figure S2-17). It might be a messy view of the page, but important text on the page is present.

Click to print

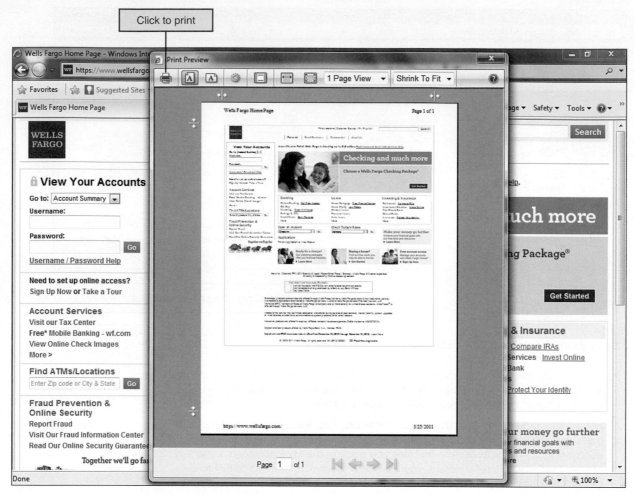

FIGURE S2-17
A printed web page might be disorderly but does contain important text.

Step 3. To print the page, click the printer icon in the menu bar of the Print Preview window. The Print dialog box appears.

Step 4. Click your printer to select it and click **Print**. The page prints.

How to Save a Web Page to a Data File

Follow these steps to save a web page and verify it is saved correctly:

Step 1. With the Wells Fargo web page displayed in your browser window, click **Page** in the menu bar of the browser. Click **Save As** from the drop-down menu that appears.

Step 2. The Save Webpage dialog box appears (see Figure S2-18). Notice the file has been assigned a filename and an .mht file extension. (The file is named Wells Fargo Home Page.mht.) Navigate to the device and folder where you want to save the file. For example, in Figure S2-18 to save to the USB flash drive, click **REMOVABLE** in the left pane. (Your USB flash drive might have a different name and different drive letter.) Click **Save**. The file saves.

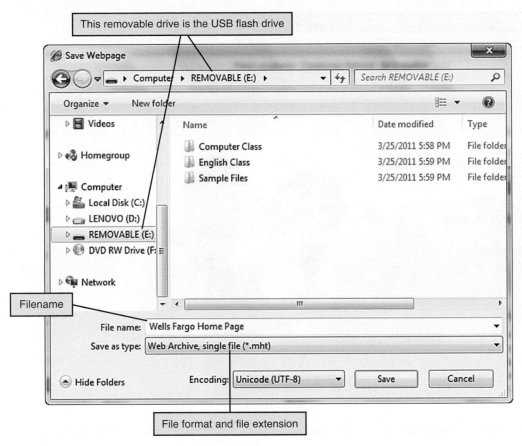

FIGURE S2-18
Save the web page in the .mht file format to the USB flash drive.

Step 3. To verify the file saved correctly, first close the Internet Explorer window.

Step 4. Open Windows Explorer and locate the **Wells Fargo Home Page.mht** file on the storage device where you saved it.

Step 5. Double-click the file **Wells Fargo Home Page.mht** to open it. Internet Explorer opens and the file displays. Notice the location and name of the file displays in the address box of Internet Explorer.

On Your Own Solution 2-10   **How to Download, Install, and Run Microsoft Security Essentials**

Follow these steps to download Security Essentials, saving the downloaded file to your Windows desktop:

Step 1. If it is not already open, open Internet Explorer. Go to the web page www.microsoft.com/security_essentials, which is shown in Figure S2-19.

> **Not Working?** Websites change often. If the URL does not work, go to the www.microsoft.com website and search for Microsoft Security Essentials.

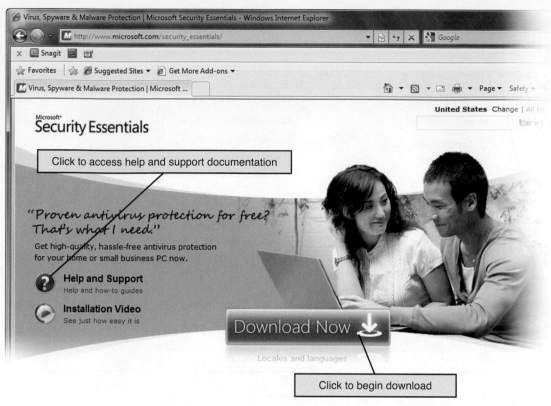

FIGURE S2-19
The home page for Microsoft Security Essentials provides links to view documentation and videos and to download the software.

Step 2. Click **Download Now**. The File Download–Security Warning dialog box appears (see Figure S2-20). In the box, notice the name and size of the file to be downloaded.

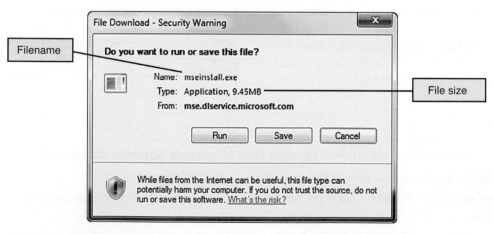

FIGURE S2-20
Download the file and save it on your computer.

Step 3. To save the file to your computer, click **Save**. The Save As dialog box appears, asking you to decide where to save the file. In the navigation pane, click **Desktop**. See Figure S2-21.

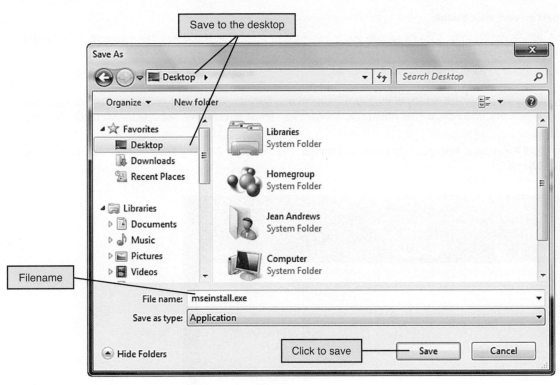

FIGURE S2-21
Save the file to your Windows desktop.

> **Not Working?** In the left pane, you might need to use the scrollbar to see Desktop listed in the Favorites group.

Step 4. Do not change the filename. Click **Save**. The file downloads and is saved to your Windows desktop.

Step 5. Close Internet Explorer.

> **Not Working?** Installation procedures for a software product might change over time or from one computer to another. For example, one installation might require you to restart the computer and another installation might skip this step. Always follow the directions onscreen as you install software.

Follow these steps to install Security Essentials:

Step 1. On your desktop, double-click the **mseinstall.exe** file you just downloaded.

Step 2. Respond to the UAC (User Access Control) box.

Step 3. The Microsoft Security Essentials window appears. Click **Next**.

Step 4. On the next screen, click **I accept** to agree to the license agreement.

Step 5. On the next screen, you are asked whether you want to join the Customer Experience Improvement Program. Make your selection and click **Next**.

Step 6. On the next screen, you are asked whether you want to turn on Windows Firewall. A firewall is software that prevents uninvited intrusion. Leave the check box checked to turn on Windows Firewall unless you know that another firewall program is running on your computer. Click **Next**.

Step 7. On the next screen, click **Install**.

Step 8. When the installation finishes, it might require you to restart your computer. If you see this message, click **Restart now** to restart your computer.

Step 9. After the computer restarts, log back on to Windows.

Antivirus software should be set to run continually in the background to monitor computer activity and scan downloaded files for viruses. The software calls this feature *real-time protection*. Follow these steps to verify the settings for Microsoft Security Essentials:

Step 1. Click **Start**, **All Programs**, **Microsoft Security Essentials**. The Microsoft Security Essentials window opens (see Figure S2-22).

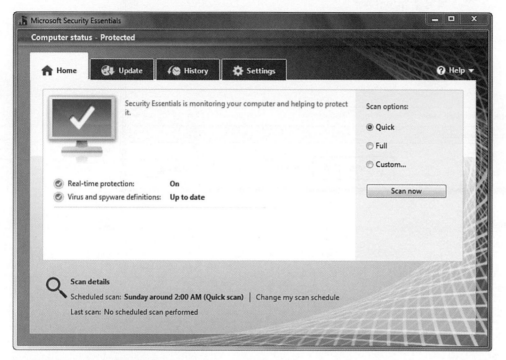

FIGURE S2-22
The Microsoft Security Essentials window is used to perform an immediate scan for malware and to control software settings.

Step 2. On the Home tab shown in the figure, verify that Real-time protection is On.

Step 3. Click the **Settings** tab. On the Settings tab, verify that **Run a scheduled scan on my computer (recommended)** is checked (see Figure S2-23).

Step 4. Click **Real-time protection** in the left pane. Notice that you can now use the right pane to turn real-time protection on or off and control its options.

Step 5. If you made changes to the settings, click **Save changes**.

Step 6. Close the Microsoft Security Essentials window.

Step 7. After you have installed software you download from the web, it is not necessary to keep the downloaded installation file. To clean up your desktop, right-click the downloaded file on the desktop and select **Delete** from the shortcut menu (see Figure S2-24).

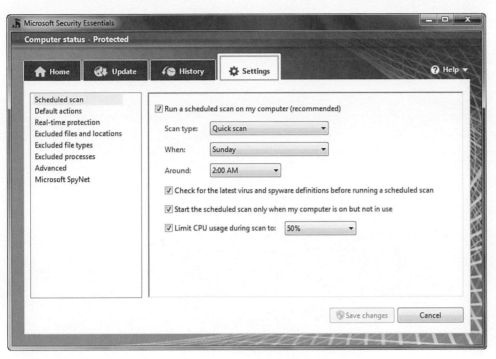

FIGURE S2-23
Use the Settings tab to configure the software.

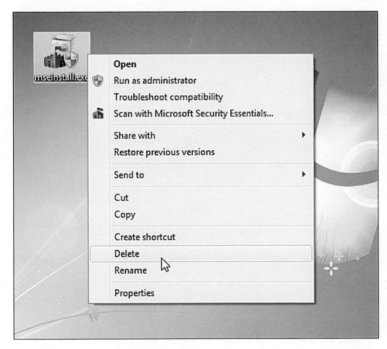

FIGURE S2-24
Delete the downloaded file on the Windows desktop.

CHAPTER 3 SOLUTIONS
Creating Documents with Microsoft Word

The solutions in this appendix are for you to use if you get stuck when doing an On Your Own activity in the chapter. To learn how to teach yourself a computer skill, always try the On Your Own activity first before turning to these solutions.

On Your Own Solution 3-1 **How to Use the Word Window**

Follow these steps to open Word and examine the Word window:

Step 1. Click **Start**, click **All Programs**, click **Microsoft Office**, and click **Microsoft Word 2010**. The Microsoft Word window opens with a new document. If the window is not maximized, maximize it.

Step 2. Study Figure 3-1 shown earlier in the chapter and compare it to your open window.

Step 3. If you don't see the horizontal or vertical rulers, click the **View Ruler** button on the right side of the Word window under the ribbon.

Step 4. If the **Print Layout** button 📄 is not yellow, click it to make it the selected layout.

Step 5. Find your insertion point ▯, which is in the upper-left area of the document inside the document margins.

Step 6. To open the Word Help window, click the **Help** button 🔳 in the upper-right area of the Word window. The button is shaped like a question mark.

Step 7. In the Search box of the Word Help window, type **backstage view** and click **Search**.

Step 8. Click **What and where is Backstage view** to find out what Backstage view is.

Step 9. Close the **Word Help** window.

> **Not Working?** As you work, if you accidently attempt to close the Word window, Word displays a dialog box asking whether you want to save your work. Click **Cancel**. The Word window stays open.

On Your Own Solution 3-2 **How to Enter and Edit Text**

Follow these steps at your computer to enter text in Word 2010:

Using the new document that was created when you opened Word 2010, move the Zoom gauge so that the size of the document is set to 100%. This size makes it easier to see what you're typing.

Step 1. Type the following text. Press **Enter** after each line.

> Overnight Trip to Piedmont Falls State Park
>
> Dear Parent or Guardian:

Step 2. Check your work for errors. Here are a few tips on editing text:

- ▸ To delete what you just typed, press the **Backspace** key.
- ▸ To move the insertion point to a new location, click somewhere in the text. You can also use your arrow keys to move the insertion point. Then press the **Backspace** key to delete text to the left of the insertion point.
- ▸ To insert new text, click where you want the text. Then type the new text.

▶ You can also select large amounts of text and delete or replace the selected text. Use the press and drag operation to select text. The selected text is highlighted in blue. To delete highlighted text, press **Delete**. To replace selected text, just start typing. Whatever you type replaces the text that was highlighted in blue.

▶ To select and highlight one word, double-click the word. What you type next replaces that word. Or you can press **Delete** to remove the word.

▶ To undo what you have just done, click the **Undo** button 🔄 found on the Quick Access Toolbar.

Step 3. To move your insertion point to the end of the document, press **Ctrl-End**. The insertion point is now on a blank line. Type the following paragraph. Do not press Enter until you finish typing all the text. Then press **Enter**.

The team will take an overnight trip to Piedmont Falls State Park on June 3, and return on June 4. Please have your child at the ballpark at 4:00PM on Friday, June 3, ready to go. Plan to pick up your child at the ballpark between 3:30 and 4:00PM on Saturday, June 4. Please do not be late when picking up your child.

Not Working? If your insertion point is at the end of the last line after you press Ctrl-End, press **Enter** to advance to a new line.

Step 4. Your document should now look like that in Figure S3-1. Check your document and correct any mistakes you find.

Overnight Trip to Piedmont Falls State Park

Dear Parent or Guardian:

The team will take an overnight trip to Piedmont Falls State Park on June 3, and return on June 4. Please have your child at the ballpark at 4:00PM on Friday, June 3, ready to go. Plan to pick up your child at the ballpark between 3:30 and 4:00PM on Saturday, June 4. Please do not be late when picking up your child.

|

FIGURE S3-1
The first lines of text have been added to the document.

On Your Own Solution 3-3   How to Save, Close, and Open a Document

This solution has four parts:

▶ How to save the document to your hard drive

▶ How to save the document to your USB flash drive

▶ How to save the document to your SkyDrive

▶ How to resave, close, and reopen your document

How to Save a Document to Your Hard Drive

Follow these steps to save a document to your hard drive:

Step 1. Click the **File** tab ▭ File ▭ to access the Backstage view.

Step 2. Click **Save As**. The Save As box appears (see Figure S3-2). Using this box, follow these four steps labeled in the figure:

1. By default, the location to save the document is the Documents library of your hard drive. This location is a good choice when saving to the hard drive. However, if you want to change the location, use the left pane of the Save As box to find and select a new location.

2. In the *File name* box, type **CheckList** as the filename.

3. Verify the document type. Word Document is correct.

4. Click **Save**. The file is saved in the Documents library of your hard drive or another location you have selected.

> **Not Working?** If you try to save a document to the hard drive and get an error such as "Path Not Found," most likely you do not have permission to save to the hard drive. Try saving to a USB flash drive instead.

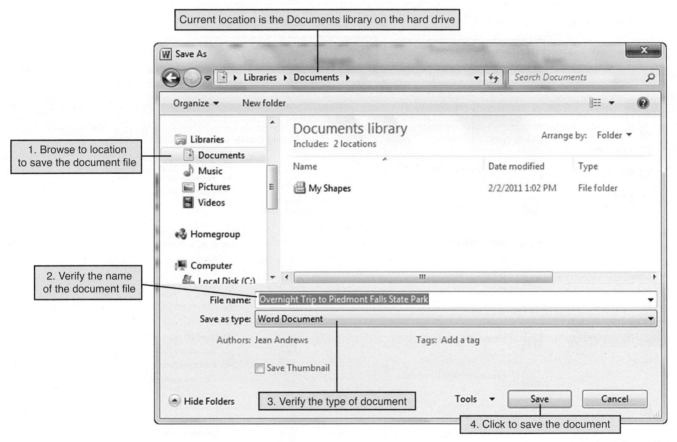

FIGURE S3-2
The Save As box allows you to enter the name, location, and file type for the document you are saving.

How to Save a Document to a USB Flash Drive

Follow these steps to save a document to a USB flash drive:

Step 1. Insert the USB flash drive into a USB slot on your computer.

Step 2. Click the **File** tab File . The Backstage view appears.

Step 3. Click **Save**. The Save As box appears (refer to Figure S3-2).

Step 4. On the left pane, make sure the Computer group is open and items are listed under it. Scroll down until you find your USB flash drive. It might be named Removable Disk, Removable, or some other name. Click the drive. The folders and files on the USB flash drive appear.

Step 5. If you are using the same USB flash drive that you used in Chapter 1, you see the folder Computer Class. If so, double-click **Computer Class** to save the file to that folder. If the folder is not there, save the file to the root of the USB drive.

Step 6. In the *File name* box, type **CheckList** as the filename.

Step 7. Click **Save**. The file is now saved on your flash drive.

How to Save a Document to Your SkyDrive

Follow these steps to save a document to your SkyDrive:

Step 1. Make sure you are connected to the Internet. You must have an Internet connection to access your SkyDrive.

Step 2. Click the **File** tab to access the Backstage view.

Step 3. Click **Save & Send** to access the Save & Send menu (see Figure S3-3).

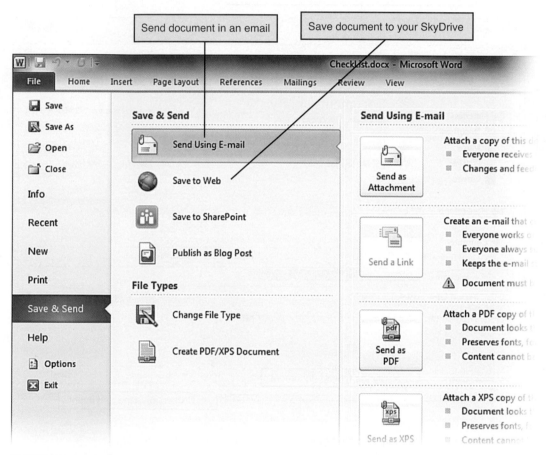

FIGURE S3-3

The Save & Send menu allows you to quickly save your document to a SkyDrive or email the document.

Step 4. Click **Save to Web**. In the right pane, the Save to Windows Live SkyDrive section appears. The first time you save to a SkyDrive, the window looks like that in Figure S3-4.

Step 5. Click **Sign In**. In the dialog box that appears, enter your email address and password to your SkyDrive account that you created in Chapter 2, "Finding and Using Information on the Web." Check **Sign me in automatically**. Click **OK**.

Step 6. The SkyDrive folders appear. Click **My Documents**. Then click **Save As**. The Save As dialog box appears.

Step 7. Change the filename to **CheckList** and click **Save**. The file CheckList.docx is saved to the My Documents folder on your SkyDrive.

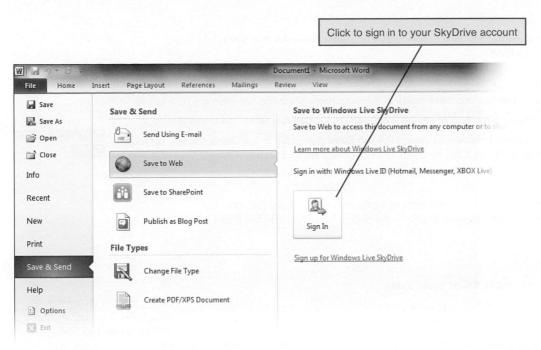

FIGURE S3-4
Sign in to your SkyDrive account.

How to Save, Close, and Reopen Your Document

To practice saving your document after it has been saved the first time, follow these steps:

Step 1. Click the **File** tab. Notice the location and name of the document displays at the top of the Info page (see Figure S3-5). This document is saved to a USB flash drive.

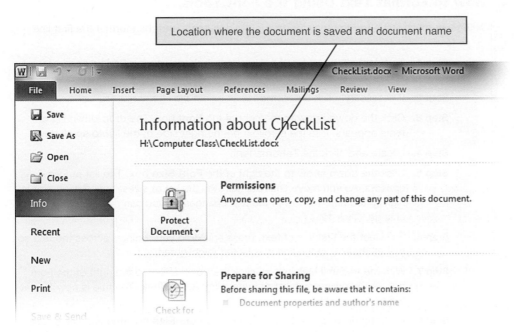

FIGURE S3-5
The document location is the Computer Class folder on the USB flash drive.

> **Hint** If the location displayed is not the correct location, click **Save As** and save the document to a new location.

Step 2. Click **Save**. Any changes you have made to the document since the last save are now saved to the drive.

Step 3. To practice a shortcut method of saving, hold down your **Ctrl** key while you press **S**.

Step 4. To demonstrate a third method to save, click the **Save** button 🔲 in the Quick Access Toolbar. (The button is shaped like a floppy disk.) The document saves again.

> **Tip** When you use any of these three methods to save, if the document has not been saved the first time, Word displays the Save As dialog box. You can tell it the save location.

To close and reopen your document, follow these steps:

Step 1. Close the **Word** window.

Step 2. Open Microsoft Word.

Step 3. Click the **File** tab. If **Recent** is not already selected in the left pane, select it.

Step 4. In the list of Recent Documents, click the **CheckList.docx** document. If the document is saved to your SkyDrive account, you might be asked to sign in by entering your email address and password.

> **Hint** Before removing your USB flash drive, don't forget to use the Safely Remove Hardware and Eject Media icon in the taskbar.

Another method of opening a document is to use **Windows Explorer**. Locate the document and double-click the document file-name. The document opens.

On Your Own Solution 3-4   **How to Format Text Using the Font Tools**

Follow these steps to format all the text in the document and then format the first line of text:

Step 1. To select all the text in the document, hold down your **Ctrl** key and press **A**. All the text is highlighted.

Step 2. If necessary, click the **Home** tab to select the Home ribbon.

Step 3. Click the down arrow to the right of the **Font** box. The drop-down list of fonts appears. Use the scrollbar on the right side of the list to scroll down.

Step 4. Locate and click the **Tahoma** font.

Step 5. Click the down arrow to the right of the **Font Size** box. The list of font sizes appears. As you move your pointer over the list of sizes, notice each size is highlighted and the size of the text changes so you can see the effect of the change. Click **12**.

Step 6. To select the first line of text, press and drag your pointer across the text so that all the text in the line is selected (highlighted).

Step 7. With the text still highlighted, click the down arrow to the right of the Font box. In the drop-down list of fonts, click **Arial Black**. The title is now formatted as Arial Black.

Step 8. Click the down arrow to the right of the **Font Size** box (the first line of text should still be highlighted). Click **14**. If you decide a larger or smaller size is better, you can change it later.

Step 9. With the first line still highlighted, click the down arrow to the right of the **Change Case** button and select **UPPERCASE** from the drop-down menu. The first line is now in all uppercase.

Follow these steps to format text using underline and bold:

Step 1. Press and drag your pointer over the text **4:00PM on Friday, June 3**. Be sure not to include the comma following the text.

Step 2. Click the **Underline** button in the Font group.

Step 3. Press and drag your pointer over the text **3:30 and 4:00PM on Saturday, June 4**. Be sure not to include the period following the text.

Step 4. Click the **Underline** button in the Font group.

Step 5. Press and drag your pointer over the text **Please do not be late when picking up your child.** Be sure to include the period as part of the selected text.

Step 6. Click the **Italic** button in the Font group.

Step 7. Check the document for errors and save it.

On Your Own Solution 3-5   How to Format Text and Create a Bulleted List

Follow these steps to center text:

Step 1. Using the **CheckList** document, click anywhere in the title line. The line does not need to be highlighted, but your insertion point should be inside the line. Word considers the line a paragraph and the paragraph is currently selected.

Step 2. In the Paragraph group, click **Center**.

Step 3. Press **Ctrl-End** to move your insertion point to the bottom of the document.

Step 4. Type the following text, pressing **Enter** after each line:

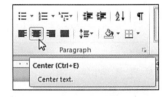

> Items your child should bring:
>
> Rain gear
>
> Sleeping bag
>
> Flashlight
>
> Change of clothes
>
> Extra pair of shoes

Hint Don't forget to press **Enter** after the last line.

Follow these steps to use the Format Painter to format text:

Step 1. Click anywhere on the second line of the document, *Dear Parent or Guardian:*. Click the **Format Painter**. Your pointer changes to a paint brush.

Step 2. Press and drag the paint brush over the six lines of text at the bottom of the document. The text is formatted the same as the second line, which is Tahoma, 12 point.

Step 3. Select the last five lines of text. Click the **Bullet** button in the Paragraph group. The five lines become a bulleted list.

Step 4. To complete the text in the document, move your insertion point to the bottom of the document and press **Enter** twice. Type the following line and press **Enter**:

> Signature of parent or guardian: _____

Step 5. The text in the document is now finished. Save the document.

> **Not Working?** If you don't like a format that you just applied, click the **Undo** button 🔄 to undo the formatting.

On Your Own Solution 3-6   How to Insert Clip Art into a Document

Do the following to insert clip art of campers into the document:

Step 1. Position your insertion point at the beginning of the line **Items your child should bring**. Or you can press **Ctrl-Home** to move your insertion point to the top of the document.

Step 2. Click the **Insert** tab. On the Insert ribbon, click **Clip Art**. The Clip Art pane opens on the right side of the Word window. In the *Search for* box, type **campers** and click **Go**.

> alls State Park on June 3, and
> t 4:00PM on Friday, June 3, re
> een 3:30 and 4:00PM on Satur

Step 3. In the list of clip art that appears, click the clip art of three campers. The clip art is inserted in the document.

Step 4. The clip art is inserted as an inline graphic. With the clip art still selected, click the **Format** tab.

> **Hint** To know if an object is selected, look for sizing handles around the object.

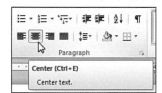

Step 5. Click the **Wrap Text** button on the Format ribbon. In the drop-down box of positions, select **Square**. The graphic can now be moved into position.

Step 6. To clear your Word window, close the Clip Art pane by clicking the **close** button ❌ in the upper-right corner of the pane.

Step 7. With the graphic still selected, position your pointer inside the graphic. Your pointer changes to a four-directional arrow. ✥ Press and drag the graphic. Position the graphic to the left of the bulleted list.

Step 8. You might want to resize the graphic. To do so, grab a resizing handle on a corner of the graphic and drag the handle. The exact size of the graphic is not important.

Step 9. The CheckList document is now finished. Save the document.

> **Tip** To delete a picture or other object, first select it by clicking the object and then press **Delete**.

On Your Own Solution 3-7   How to Change Document Properties

Follow these steps to view and change the document properties:

Step 1. Click the **File** tab to show the Info group in the Backstage view. The document properties are shown in the right pane. Who is the document author?

Step 2. If you need to change the author, right-click the author and select **Edit Property** from the shortcut menu that appears. The Edit person dialog box appears.

Step 3. Replace the name with your name and click **OK**.

Step 4. Save the document.

On Your Own Solution 3-8   **How to Print a Document**

Before printing a document, verify that the number of pages makes sense and save the document. Do the following:

Step 1. If the **Home** ribbon is not selected, select it.

Step 2. Look in the bottom-left corner of the window for the page count. It should be displayed as Page 1 of 1.

Step 3. If the document has more than one page, look for extra lines at the bottom of the document. To do that, click the **Show/Hide** button ¶ in the Paragraph group. Paragraph marks (also called hard returns) appear. Delete any unnecessary paragraph marks, which delete the unnecessary lines.

Step 4. Save the document.

Step 5. Click the **File** tab. Click **Print**. The Print window appears. See Figure 3-11 shown earlier in the chapter.

Step 6. Verify the printer listed is the one that you want to use. To change printers, click the down arrow to the right of the printer name and select a printer from those listed.

Step 7. Click **Print**. The document prints.

Step 8. Close the document.

On Your Own Solution 3-9   **How to Add Page Color and Text Boxes**

In this and following solutions, you are creating the Jazz in the Park document shown in Figure S3-6.

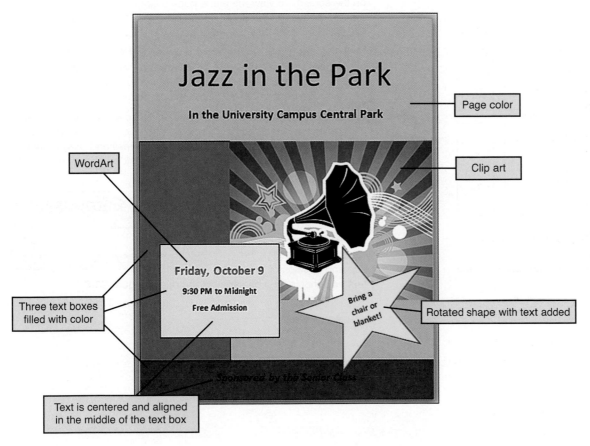

FIGURE S3-6

This Jazz in the Park document uses three text boxes, page color, WordArt, clip art, and a shape.

Follow these steps to create the document and add page color and the first two lines of text:

Step 1. To open a new document, if Word is not already open, open **Word**. A new document is automatically opened. If Word is already open, click the **File** tab and click **New**. Then click **Create**. A new blank document is created.

Step 2. Click the **Page Layout** tab. Then click **Page Color**. A group of Theme Colors appears. As you mouse over a color, the document color changes. Select a medium orange. **Orange, Accent 6, Lighter 40%** works well.

Step 3. Type the following two lines of text and press **Enter** after each line:

Jazz in the Park

In the University Campus Central Park

Step 4. Select the first line of text. Format it to **Calibri (Body) font, 72 point**.

Step 5. Select the second line of text. Format the text to **Calibri (Body)**, **26 point**, and **bold**.

Step 6. Select both lines of text and **Center** the text on the page.

Step 7. Save the document to your USB flash drive, hard drive, SkyDrive, or other location given by your instructor. Name the document **JazzConcert**. If you need help, see directions given earlier in Solution 3-3 for saving a document.

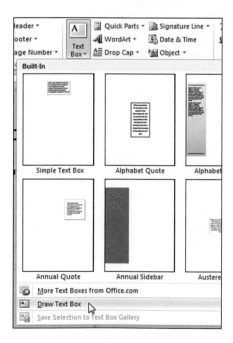

Do the following to create the text box on the left side of the page:

Step 1. If you want to position large text boxes, it helps to see the entire page on the screen. To view the entire page, click the percent to the left of the Zoom slider. In the Zoom dialog box, click **Whole page** and click **OK**. You can now view the entire page.

Step 2. Click the **Insert** tab. On the Insert ribbon, click **Text Box**. A drop-down list appears. Click **Draw Text Box**. Your pointer changes to a crosshair. ➕ Press and drag to draw the text box. Don't worry about its exact size or position. You can change that in Step 4.

Step 3. The next step is to move the text box. To move a text box, position your pointer on the edge of the selected text box until your pointer is shaped like four directional arrows. Then press and drag to move the box. Move the box to the edge of the left side of the page and just below the second line of text.

Step 4. Use the bottom-right corner sizing handle to resize the text box so that it is tall and goes down the left side of the page. The size and position of the text box should now be same as the one in Figure S3-6.

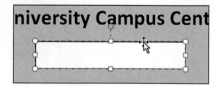

Step 5. With the text box still selected, click the **Format** tab. On the Format ribbon, click **Shape Fill**. A list of colors appears. Select a dark orange. **Orange, Accent 6, Dark 25%** works well.

Step 6. Save the document. Click somewhere off the text box so it is no longer selected.

Step 7. Insert a second text box that will fit at the bottom of the page. Move and resize the text box so that it fits along both sides and across the bottom of the page, as shown in Figure S3-6. Fill the text box with the color **Red**.

Follow these steps to add text to the second text box:

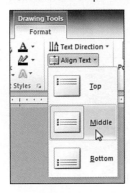

Step 1. Zoom in from the whole page view so you can view the page at 100%.

Step 2. Click in the red text box. An insertion point appears inside the box. Type **Sponsored by the Senior Class.**

Step 3. Select the text you just typed. Make the text **Italic**. Change its size to **24 point**. **Center** the text.

Step 4. Click the **Format** tab. Click **Align Text**. Then click **Middle**. The text is now positioned in the middle of the text box.

Step 5. Save the document.

On Your Own Solution 3-10   **How to Add Clip Art to a Document**

Do the following to add the gramophone clip art to the document:

Step 1. Change the page view so that you can see the entire page in your Word window.

Step 2. Position your insertion point outside the text boxes and after the two lines of text at the top of the document.

Step 3. Click the **Insert** tab. Click **Clip Art**. In the *Search for* box, enter **gramophone**. Scroll down in the list of clip art to locate the gramophone clip art and click it. The clip art appears in the document and is selected.

> **Not Working?** The gramophone clip art is downloaded from the Office.com site. To see it listed in the Clip Art pane, check **Include Office.com content**. You need to be connected to the Internet.

Step 4. Click the **Format** tab. Click **Position** and choose any position under the With Text Wrapping group. The graphic is now a floating graphic.

Step 5. Move the graphic into position, aligning the top of the graphic with the top of the tall text box. Don't worry if the graphic spills off the page on the right side. See Figure S3-7.

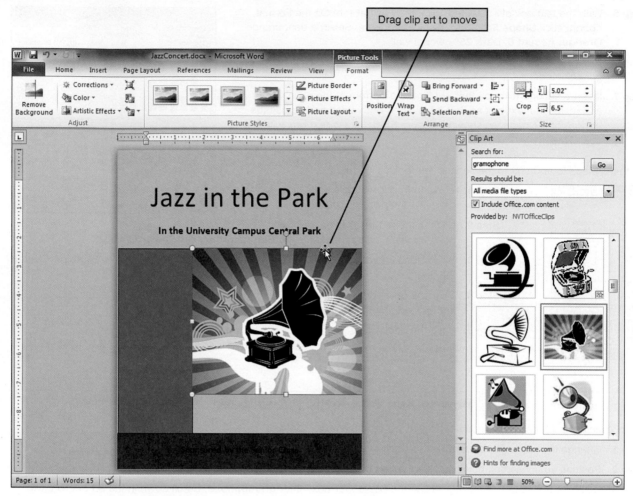

FIGURE S3-7
Position the clip art graphic along the top and left side of the tall text box.

> **Step 6.** To clean up your Word window, close the **Clip Art** pane.
>
> **Step 7.** Save your document.

On Your Own Solution 3-11   How to Add a Shape to a Document

Follow these directions to insert a star and format it, adding text inside the star:

> **Step 1.** Using the JazzConcert document, click the **Insert** tab. Click **Shapes** and then click the star.
>
> **Step 2.** A cross insertion point + appears. Press and drag to create the star. Make it large enough to hold text. The exact size and position can be changed later. The star is created with a blue fill color.
>
> **Step 3.** With the star still selected, press and drag the green rotation handle ⚲ to the left to rotate the star. Point the star toward the upper-left corner of the document.
>
> **Step 4.** Right-click the star and click **Add Text** from the shortcut menu that appears. An insertion point blinks inside the star.

Step 5. Type the following text inside the star. You might need to use the Zoom slider to enlarge the page so you can better see what you are typing:

Bring a chair or blanket!

Step 6. Select the text and change the text color to **Black**. Change the size of the text to **18 point**. Click somewhere off the star so the text inside the star is no longer selected.

Step 7. Select the star. If you need to resize it so that all the text appears, do so now. On the **Format** ribbon, click **Shape Fill**. Select **yellow** for the star.

Step 8. Save the document.

On Your Own Solution 3-12   How to Add WordArt to a Document

Follow these directions to add a text box with WordArt to the document:

Step 1. Using the JazzConcert document, insert a text box into the document. Position the box as shown earlier in Figure S3-6.

Step 2. Use the Shape Fill tool on the Format ribbon to fill the text box with a light orange. **Orange Accent 6, Lighter 80%** works well.

Step 3. Enter the following text in the text box:

Friday, October 9

9:30 PM to Midnight

Free Admission

Step 4. Select the first line of text. On the Format ribbon, click the drop-down arrow beside WordArt selections. Click **Gradient Fill – Orange, Accent 6, Inner Shadow.** Format the text size to **26 point**.

Step 5. Format the last two lines of text in **Calibri (Body), 18 point, bold**.

Step 6. Center all the text in the text box. Align the text in the middle of the text box.

Step 7. The document is finished! Take a moment to look back at Figure S3-6. Correct any problems you see with your work and save the document.

On Your Own Solution 3-13   How to Save a Document as a PDF File

Follow these steps to save a document as a PDF file to your hard drive, USB flash drive, or another local storage device:

Step 1. Save the document as usual.

Tip You should save the file as a Word document before saving it as a PDF file to make sure you have your changes saved in each file type.

Step 2. Click the **File** tab. Click **Save As**. The Save As box appears.

Step 3. In the field labeled *Save as type*, select **PDF** (see Figure S3-8). Save the file in the same location where you saved the Word document file.

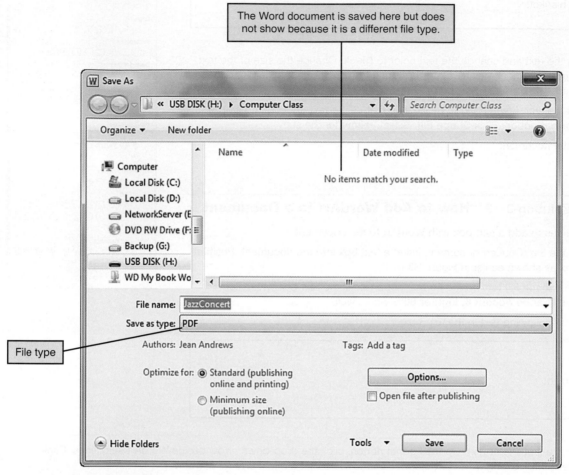

The Word document is saved here but does not show because it is a different file type.

FIGURE S3-8
The PDF file is saved to the USB flash drive where the Word document file was previously saved.

Step 4. Click **Save**. A PDF file is created. Close the Word window.

Step 5. Open **Windows Explorer** and verify you have saved two files: the JazzConsert.docx file and the JazzConcert.pdf file. Double-click the PDF file. The PDF file opens and can be viewed, but you cannot edit the file.

Follow these steps to save a document as a PDF file to your SkyDrive:

Step 1. Save the document as usual.

Step 2. Click the **File** tab. Click **Save & Send**. Click **Save to Web**. Click the folder on your SkyDrive. Click **Save As**. The Save As dialog box appears.

Step 3. In the field labeled *Save as type*, select **PDF**. Click **Save**. The PDF file is saved to your SkyDrive.

Step 4. Open **Internet Explorer**, go to the **live.com** site, and verify the files are saved to your SkyDrive folder.

On Your Own Solution 3-14   **How to Use a Party Invitation Template**

To use a template, you start by selecting it. Follow these steps:

Step 1. Open Microsoft Word.

Step 2. Click the **File** tab. Click **New**. A list of templates appears (see Figure S3-9).

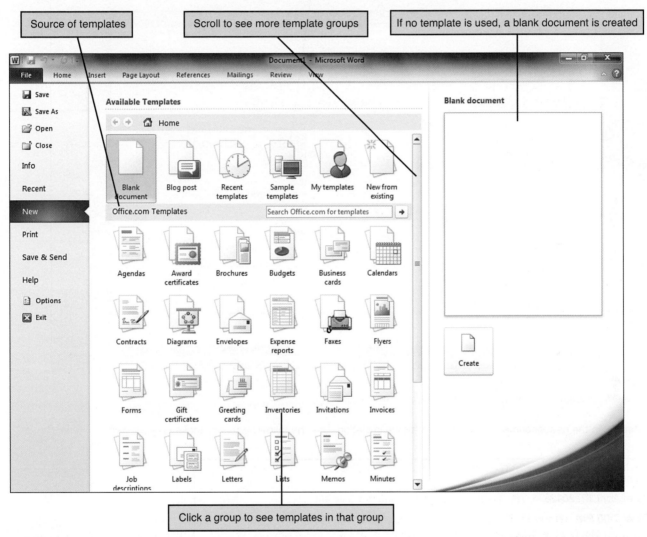

FIGURE S3-9
Templates are made available from the Office.com website.

Step 3. Click **Invitations**. Click **Party invitations**. Scroll down through the list of templates and click **Birthday party invitation**. The design displays in the right pane.

Step 4. Click **Download**. A new document is created.

Step 5. If necessary, zoom in on the document so you can read and edit the text.

Step 6. To edit the text, select it. For example, to change the name of the person having a birthday, select **Stephanie** (see Figure S3-10). Then type the new name.

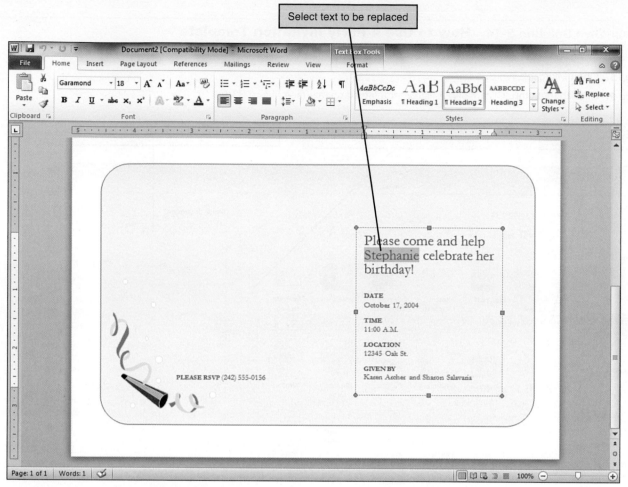

FIGURE S3-10
Select and replace text in the document to suit your own needs.

> **Step 7.** In the new document, type the text for the invitation. Use the following text or make up your own:

Name of person: Mary Ann

Date: April 12, 2012

Time: 7:00 PM

Location: 1234 James Street

Given by: Tom Anderson and Jerry Baskin

RSVP to: tom@sample.edu

> **Step 8.** Check the document properties and verify the author of the document is your name. Save the document to your USB flash drive, hard drive, SkyDrive, or other location given by your instructor. Name the document **Party**. When you click Save, Word asks if you want to save the document using one of the new file formats. Click **OK** to complete the save operation.

> **Step 9.** Print the document. Fold the printed page so the document looks like a party invitation card.

CHAPTER 4 SOLUTIONS
Using the Web for Research

The solutions in this appendix are for you to use if you get stuck when doing an On Your Own activity in the chapter. To learn how to teach yourself a computer skill, always try the On Your Own activity first before turning to these solutions.

> **Not Working?** Websites change from time to time. The step-by-step instructions were accurate when we wrote them, but be aware that you might have to adjust them to account for later website changes.

On Your Own Solution 4-1 **How to Create and Set Up a New Notebook in OneNote**

This solution has two parts:

▶ How to create a new notebook

▶ How to set up the notebook for research

How to Create a New Notebook

Follow these steps to open OneNote:

Step 1. Click **Start**, **All Programs**, **Microsoft Office**, and **Microsoft OneNote 2010**. When OneNote is started, it opens any notebooks already identified on your computer. Compare your OneNote window to Figure S4-1. Open notebooks are listed along the left side of the OneNote window.

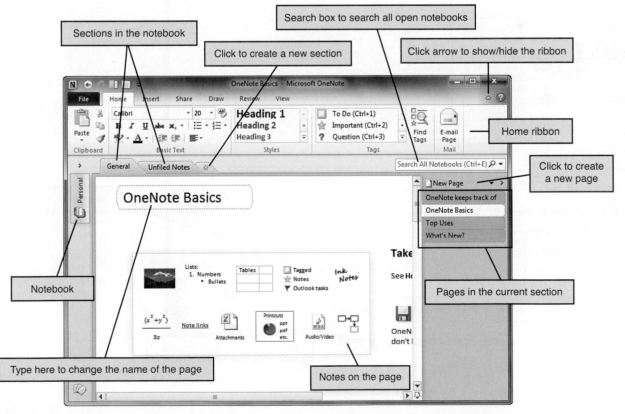

FIGURE S4-1
The OneNote window is used to manage notebooks, sections, pages, and notes.

Step 2. The ribbon at the top of the OneNote window should be displayed as shown in the figure. If you cannot see the ribbon, click the down arrow in the upper-right corner of the window to expand the ribbon.

Create a new notebook and save it to your USB flash drive, hard drive, SkyDrive, or another location given by your instructor. Follow these steps to create a new notebook on your USB flash drive or hard drive:

Step 1. If you are saving your notebook to your USB flash drive, insert the drive.

Step 2. Click the **File** tab and click **New**. The New Notebook window appears.

Step 3. Click **My Computer**.

Step 4. Enter **MyResearch** as the Name for the new notebook.

Step 5. Click **Browse**. The Select Folder dialog box appears.

Step 6. To save the notebook to your USB flash drive, point to it in the left pane. If you want to save the notebook in a folder on the USB flash drive, click the folder in the right pane. Click **Select** to close the dialog box.

Step 7. To save the notebook to your hard drive, know that Windows has already created the OneNote Notebooks folder in the Documents library. This folder is the default location for saving notebooks. Point to **Documents** in the Libraries group. Click the **OneNote Notebooks** folder. Click **Select** to close the dialog box.

Step 8. Verify the notebook name and location is correct. Figure S4-2 shows the MyResearch notebook about to be saved to the Computer Class folder on the USB flash drive. Click **Create Notebook**. A new blank notebook is created.

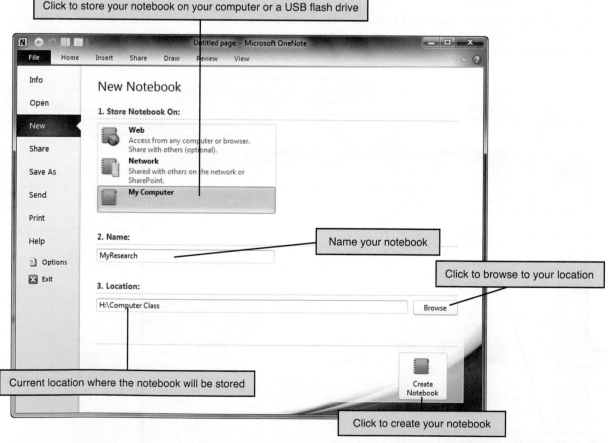

FIGURE S4-2
The new notebook will be created in the Computer Class folder on the USB flash drive.

To save the notebook to the SkyDrive you created in Chapter 2, "Finding and Using Information on the Web," follow these steps:

Step 1. Click the **File** tab and click **New**. The New Notebook window appears.

Step 2. Click **Web**. Enter **MyResearch** as the name of the notebook.

Step 3. To sign in to your SkyDrive account, click **Sign In**. Enter your email address and password to your SkyDrive account and click **Sign in**.

Step 4. The folders on your SkyDrive appear. Click **My Documents** (see Figure S4-3). Click **Create Notebook**. The new blank notebook is created.

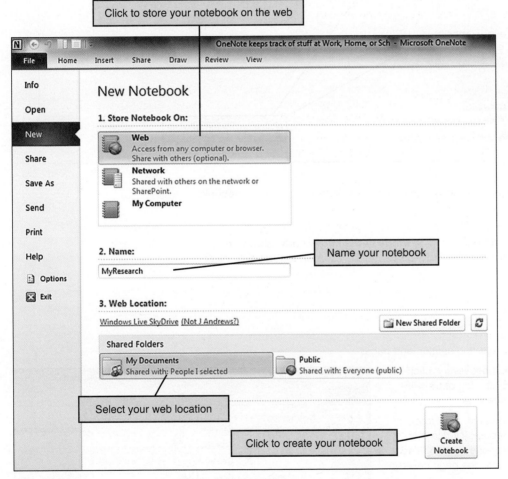

FIGURE S4-3
The new notebook will be created in the My Documents folder on your SkyDrive.

Do the following to verify where your OneNote notebooks are stored:

Step 1. Click the **File** tab.

Step 2. Click **Info**. All open notebooks are listed along with their locations. In Figure S4-4, notice the first two notebooks are located on the hard drive. The MyResearch notebook is stored in the Computer Class folder on the USB flash drive. Your locations might be different.

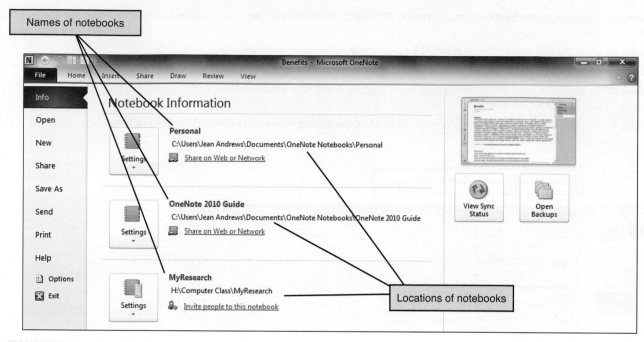

FIGURE S4-4
The Info window in the Backstage view displays the names and locations of open notebooks.

> **Tip** If you want to close a notebook, click **Settings** in the Info window shown in Figure S4-4 and then click **Close** in the drop-down menu. To open a notebook, click the **File** tab and click **Open**.

How to Set Up OneNote for Research

Follow these steps to rename the existing section and page:

Step 1. Click the **Home** tab. If necessary, click **MyResearch** on the left side of the window to select that notebook.

Step 2. After a notebook is created, OneNote shows the blank notebook. Notice that the notebook has only one section titled *New Section 1* and only one page called *Untitled page*.

Step 3. Right-click the **New Section 1** tab. In the shortcut menu that appears (see Figure S4-5), click **Rename**. Type **Peace Corps** and press **Enter**. The section is now named Peace Corps.

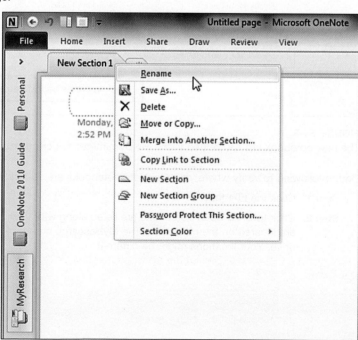

FIGURE S4-5
Rename the section.

Step 4. The text bubble in the upper-left corner of a page is the page name. Click in the text bubble and type **Outline**. As you type, the page tab on the right side of the screen changes names.

Follow these steps to add three new pages to the Peace Corps section:

Step 1. If the page tabs need expanding, click the left arrow in the upper-right corner of the OneNote window to expand the page tabs.

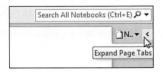

Step 2. Click **New Page** on the right side of the screen to create a new page. Then type **Requirements** in the text bubble at the top of the notebook page to name the page.

Step 3. Create a page titled **Service** and a page titled **Benefits** using the same process as in step 2. You now have four pages to hold your research named Outline, Requirements, Service, and Benefits.

Follow these steps to add the outline to the Outline page:

Step 1. Because you already know some subtopics, you can type those subtopics on the Outline page. Click the **Outline** page tab to return to that page.

Step 2. Click anywhere on the page and a container appears. Type the following:

Outline:

Requirements

Service

Benefits

Step 3. To make the three subtopics a bulleted list, highlight them. On the Home ribbon, click **Bullets** (see Figure S4-6).

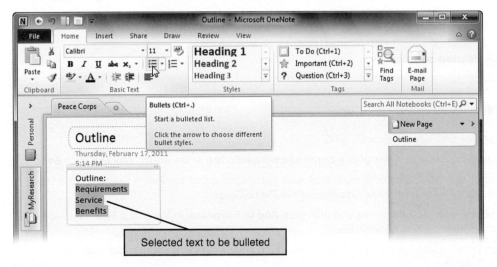

FIGURE S4-6
Create and format the outline on the Outline page to help you plan and organize your research.

Tip As you work with OneNote, notice how the commands are similar to the Word ribbons and commands. All Office applications have many common commands and elements.

On Your Own Solution 4-2   How to Use Google.com and Wikipedia.org for Preliminary Research

This solution has two parts:

▶ How to use Google.com for preliminary research

▶ How to use Wikipedia.org for preliminary research

How to Use Google.com for Preliminary Research

Do the following to use Google.com for preliminary research:

Step 1. Using Internet Explorer, go to **google.com** and enter **peace corps** in the search box. As you type, Google autosuggest completes the search string. These suggestions might give you ideas for subtopics.

Step 2. In the Google results window, look for a list titled *Something Different*, *Searches Related*, or a similar title. In the list, Google gives suggestions for other topics that are similar. Look through these topics to see whether anything interests you. These topics may be useful if you need to broaden your topic. For example, a broader topic than the Peace Corps might be *volunteer service organizations*.

> **Not Working?** If you don't see the Something Different list, click **More search tools** in the left pane. Then click **Related searches**.

How to Use Wikipedia.org for Preliminary Research

Do the following to use Wikipedia.org for preliminary research:

Step 1. Return to the **Google.com** home page. Enter **peace corps site:wikipedia.org** in the search box and click **Search**.

Step 2. Google returns web pages only from Wikipedia.org and all have information about the Peace Corps. Click a few links and find an article that gives general information about the Peace Corps.

Step 3. To bookmark the article you find, click **Favorites** and then click **Add to Favorites**. In the Add a Favorite dialog box, click **Add**. The URL of the article is now bookmarked.

Step 4. Highlight the paragraph in the Wikipedia article and right-click the highlighted text. In the shortcut menu that appears, click **Send to OneNote**.

Step 5. The Select Location in OneNote window appears so that you can select the notebook, section, and page in OneNote that will receive the text. See Figure S4-7. If you don't see the Outline page, click the **+** sign to the left of MyResearch. Drill down to the **Peace Corps** section and click the **Outline** page. Click **OK**. The selected text is copied into OneNote.

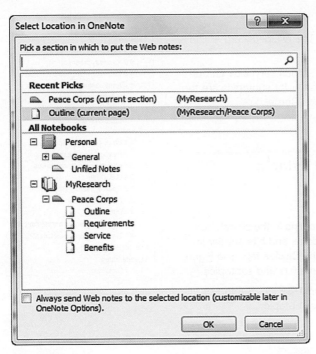

FIGURE S4-7
Select the notebook, section, and page to receive the text.

Step 6. Go to the OneNote window and the Outline page to find the paragraph. The URL is listed below the paragraph as a link to the page where the paragraph was taken. If needed, you can return to the page in your browser by clicking this link.

Step 7. Press and drag to select one sentence in the paragraph that you find important. With the text selected, click the **Home** tab. On the Home ribbon, select a color from the highlighting tool (see Figure S4-8). The sentence is now highlighted.

Not Working? If you don't see the ribbons in the OneNote window, click the down arrow in the upper-right corner of the Notebook window to expand the ribbon.

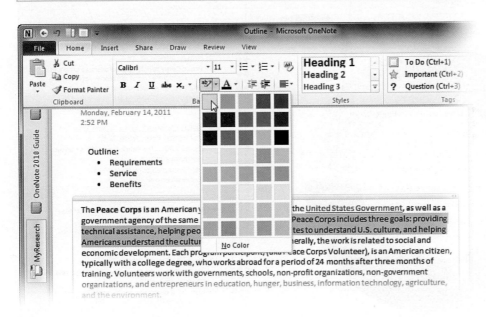

FIGURE S4-8
Highlight selected text in OneNote to mark important information for your research.

Do the following to explore subtopics of the Peace Corps topic:

Step 1. Make the **Internet Explorer** window the active window. The Wikipedia.org article is still showing.

Step 2. Scroll down the page until you find the Contents section, which serves as an outline to a Wikipedia.org article. Two topics you might consider for subtopics are the history of the Peace Corps and laws concerning the Peace Corps.

Contents [hide]

1 History
  1.1 Humphrey proposal
  1.2 Kennedy proposal
  1.3 Establishment and authorization
  1.4 Early controversy
  1.5 Independent status
  1.6 Murder Controversies
  1.7 Programs diversified
2 Evolution
  2.1 Work with the Environment
  2.2 Peace Corps Response
3 Laws governing the Peace Corps
  3.1 U.S. Code
  3.2 Code of Federal Regulations
  3.3 Executive orders
  3.4 Public laws
  3.5 Limitations on former volunteers
  3.6 Time limits on employment
4 Union Representation
5 Leadership
  5.1 Directors

On Your Own Solution 4-3   How to Find Subtopics Using a Clustering Search Engine

Do the following to use the carrot2.org search engine:

Step 1. Using Internet Explorer, go to **carrot2.org**. Enter **peace corps** in the search box and click **Search**. A list of subtopics appears in the left pane, and hits appear in the right pane. To see a circle visual of subtopics, click the **Circles** tab. See Figure S4-9. Click or double-click an item in the circle to see more hits and subtopics.

Step 2. To see a more detailed visual of subtopics, click the **FoamTree** tab. Subtopics appear in a foam tree. Click an item to see hits about this subtopic.

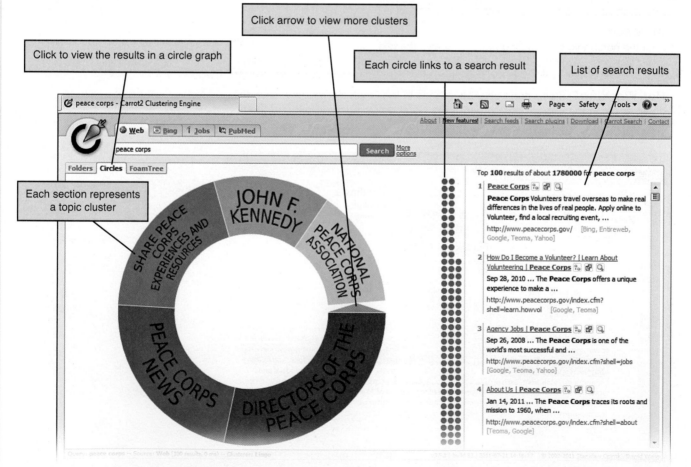

FIGURE S4-9
Carrot2.org gives a visualization of subtopics.

On Your Own Solution 4-4   How to Use a Google Timeline

Do the following to view a Google Timeline, copy it into OneNote, and use the Timeline in Google:

Step 1. Using Internet Explorer, go to **www.google.com**. Type **peace corps** in the search field and press **Enter**. Click **More search tools**. Click **Timeline** and a Google Timeline appears similar to the one shown in Figure 4-7 in the chapter.

Step 2. Make the **OneNote** window the active window. Select the **Outline** page. Click the **Insert** tab in OneNote and then click **Screen Clipping**. See Figure S4-10.

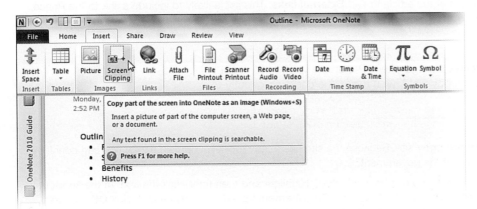

FIGURE S4-10
The Insert ribbon allows you to easily insert graphics into OneNote.

Step 3. The OneNote window disappears, and a crosshair + appears for your pointer. Press and drag the pointer to select the timeline in the Google window. The timeline is copied onto the Outline page of OneNote.

Step 4. If you don't like the location of the containers on the page, press and drag them to move them on the page.

Step 5. Return to Internet Explorer. Drill down on the timeline to view hits found at the peak on the timeline, which turns out to be March 1961. What event happened this month? Figure S4-11 gives the answer.

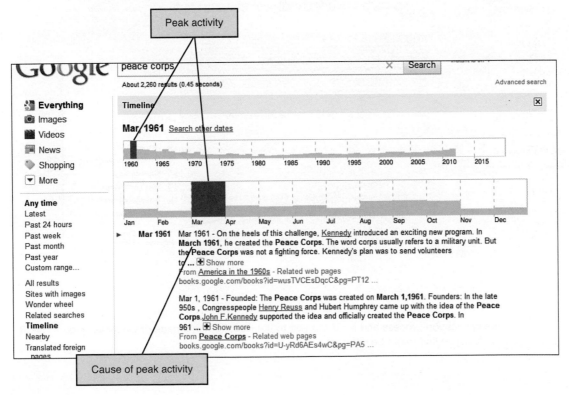

FIGURE S4-11
The peak month for activity in the timeline is March 1961.

On Your Own Solution 4-5   **How to Use Wikipedia.org to Locate Authoritative Content**

Wikipedia.org is not an authoritative source, but it can lead you to these sources. Do the following to use Wikipedia.org to locate authoritative content:

Step 1. Using Internet Explorer, click **Favorites**. In the list of Favorites, click the Peace Corps Wikipedia article you book-marked earlier. The article appears in your browser window.

Step 2. Scroll down the article to find a section labeled **Books** and another section labeled **References**. Links in these sections can lead you to authoritative content.

Step 3. Scroll down toward the bottom of the article to find **External links**. This list is likely to include a link to the Peace Corps website at www.peacecorps.gov. Click that link.

> **Not Working?** Wikipedia.org articles change often. The article you found might not have a link to the www.peacecorps.gov website. If this is the case, go directly to the **www.peacecorps.gov** site.

Step 4. Bookmark the **www.peacecorps.gov** site. Because the site has a .gov top-level domain name, you can conclude the Peace Corps is an agency of the government.

Step 5. Find information on the site about who can be a volunteer. Highlight and then right-click the text. In the shortcut menu that appears, click **Send to OneNote**. Select the **Requirements** page of OneNote and click **OK**. The text goes to OneNote. Figure S4-12 shows text on the Peace Corps site that answers this question along with several others in this activity. However, remember websites might change, so the text you find on the site might be different.

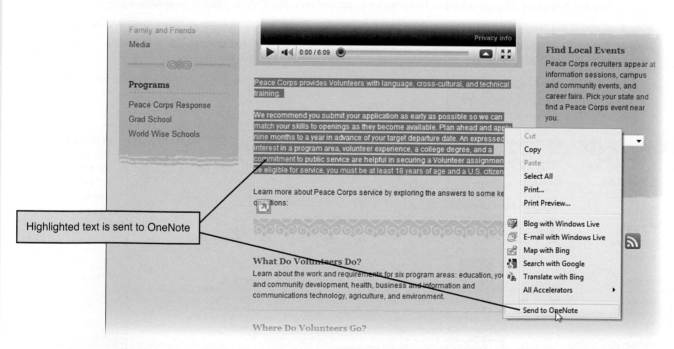

FIGURE S4-12
Text on the www.peacecorps.gov site answers several research questions.

Step 6. Find text describing the application process and send the text to the Requirements page of OneNote. Figure S4-13 shows this text, but the text you find might be different.

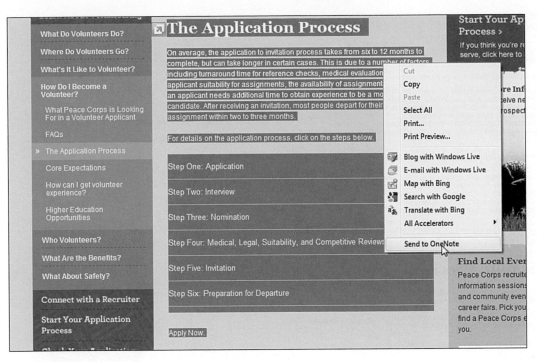

FIGURE S4-13
Text on the application process to be copied into OneNote.

Step 7. Find text on how long is the commitment a volunteer makes to the Peace Corps. If you have not already sent the text to OneNote, do so now.

Step 8. Find text describing the training. If you have not already sent the text to OneNote, do so now.

Step 9. Find text on the types of jobs a volunteer might do. If you have not already sent the text to OneNote, do so now.

Step 10. Click the **OneNote** icon in the taskbar to view the OneNote window. Verify all your research text got copied into OneNote.

Step 11. Use the highlighting tool you learned to use earlier in the chapter to highlight important text.

In our example, we found all the answers to our research questions in two segments of text copied from the www.peacecorps.gov site. These two segments are stored on the Requirements page of OneNote.

Follow these steps to include citation information in OneNote:

Step 1. Citation information for a website includes the title of the website. The title of this site showing on its home page is Peace Corps. Copy the text **Peace Corps** from the web page to OneNote or type the text in OneNote.

> **Not Working?** If the title of a web page is a link or a graphic, you might have trouble copying the text. In this case, type the web page title into OneNote, or use the Screen Clipping tool to copy the title into OneNote.

Step 2. To insert the date you accessed the site, right-click on the OneNote page where you want the date to appear. A shortcut menu appears. Click the date as shown in Figure S4-14. The date is inserted on the page.

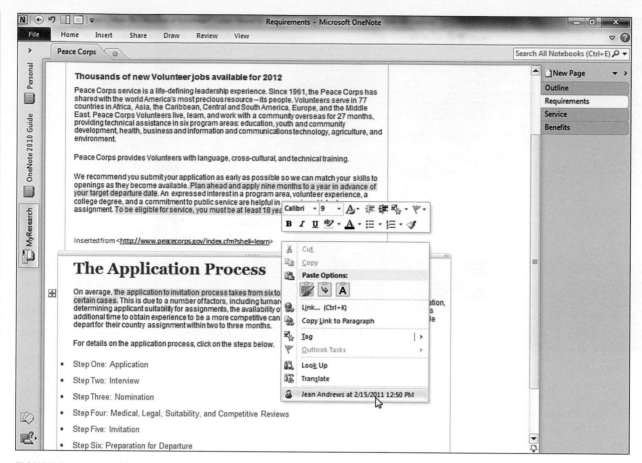

FIGURE S4-14
Insert the date a website was accessed.

On Your Own Solution 4-6   **How to Find Newspaper Articles and Blogs**

Follow these steps to find a newspaper article about the Peace Corps and save the information to OneNote:

Step 1. Using Internet Explorer, go to the New York Times site at **www.nytimes.com**. Look for a search box on the page to search the site.

Step 2. Enter this search string: peace corps volunteers make a difference.

Step 3. Find one article describing the difference a Peace Corps volunteer has made in a foreign country. Select text from the article and copy it into the OneNote Service page.

Step 4. Include on the page in OneNote all the information you will need to cite the newspaper article later in your Works Cited list. This information includes

▶ Author of the article (might not be available)

▶ Article title

▶ Newspaper title (*New York Times*)

▶ Date published (month, day, year)

▶ URL (www.nytimes.com)

▶ Date you accessed the web page

Figure S4-15 shows the content and citation information for one article. Yours might be different.

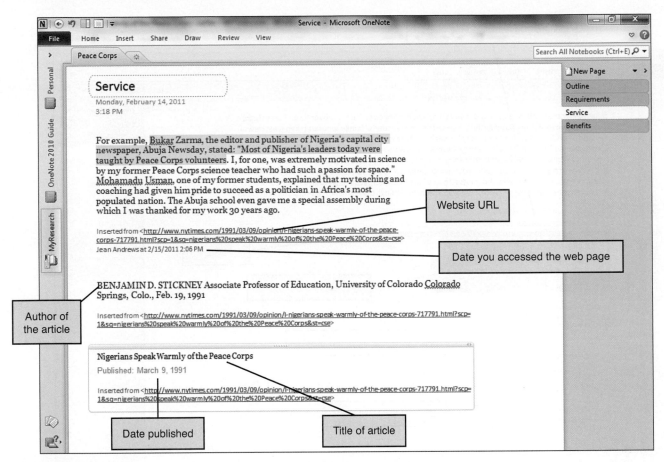

FIGURE S4-15
An online newspaper article requires you cite the author, title of the article, newspaper, date published, and the date you accessed the article online.

Follow these steps to find a recent blog written by a Peace Corps volunteer:

Step 1. Using Internet Explorer, go to **google.com**.

Step 2. The two most popular blogging sites are wordpress.com and blogspot.com. Use one of these search strings in the Google search box:

peace corps blog site:blogspot.com

peace corps blog site:wordpress.com

Step 3. In the left pane of the Google window, click **More search tools**. Click **Past year**.

Step 4. Click links and find a blog entry that describes what it's like to serve in the Peace Corps. Copy the text into OneNote on the Service page or the Benefits page.

Step 5. Use either the text selection method or the Screen Clipping method to copy the citation information into OneNote. Include this information:

- ▶ Author of the blog
- ▶ Title of the blog
- ▶ Date of the blog entry
- ▶ URL
- ▶ Date you accessed the site

Figure S4-16 shows one blog entry and citation information in OneNote, but yours might look different.

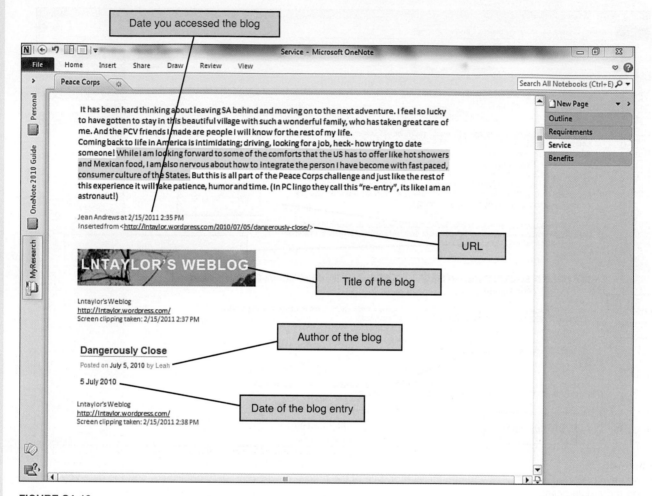

FIGURE S4-16
A blog written by someone directly involved in an activity is a great primary source.

On Your Own Solution 4-7   **How to Find Books Using Wikipedia.org, Google Books, and Worldcat.org**

Do the following to use Wikipedia.org and Google Books to find a book online:

Step 1. Using Internet Explorer Favorites, return to the Wikipedia.org article about the Peace Corps that you bookmarked earlier.

Step 2. Look in the **Books** section and find a book written by someone who served in the Peace Corps. One book is *Living Poor*, by Moritz Thomsen.

Step 3. Go to **google.com** and enter **living poor by moritz thomsen** in the search box. Click **more** and click **Books**. A list of books appears (see Figure S4-17).

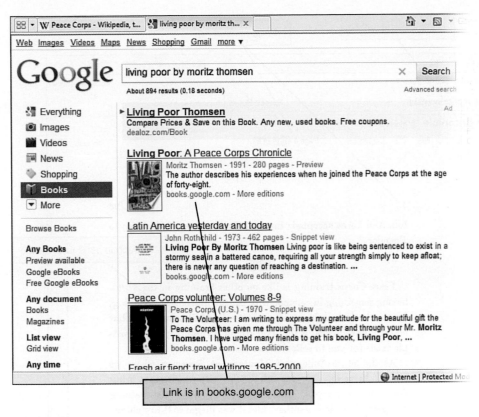

Link is in books.google.com

FIGURE S4-17

Google Books provides books online.

Step 4. Click the book in the hit list. Be sure to select a link provided by the books.google.com site.

Step 5. Scroll down through the pages of the book to find a paragraph that describes training in the Peace Corps. One good paragraph in *Living Poor, A Peace Corps Chronicle,* can be found on page 4 (see Figure S4-18). In the figure, notice the search box in the left pane that you can use to search for text in the book.

Step 6. You cannot select text on the book pages for copying into OneNote, but you can do a Screen Clipping of the paragraph. Go to the OneNote window.

Step 7. In the Peace Corps section of OneNote, select the **Requirements** page. Click somewhere on the page where you want the clipping to go. Click the **Insert** tab and click **Screen Clipping**. Select the paragraph on the Google Books page. The selection is copied into OneNote.

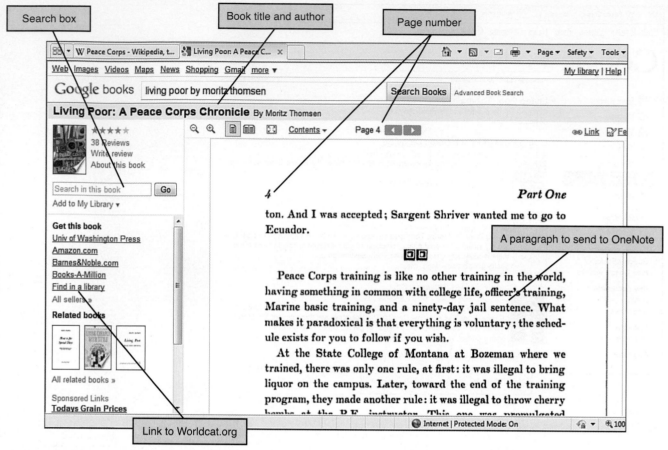

FIGURE S4-18
Google Books presents some of the pages in a book.

Do the following to put the citation information into OneNote:

Step 1. Click **Screen Clipping** on the Insert ribbon. Return to the Google Books page and select the title and author of the book. The information can be found under the search box on the Google Books window. The selection is copied into OneNote.

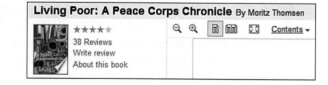

Step 2. Type on the OneNote page the page number in the book where you found the paragraph.

Step 3. Locate the publisher, city of publication, and year of copyright on the page following the front cover. Use the Screen Clipping tool to copy this area into OneNote (see Figure S4-19).

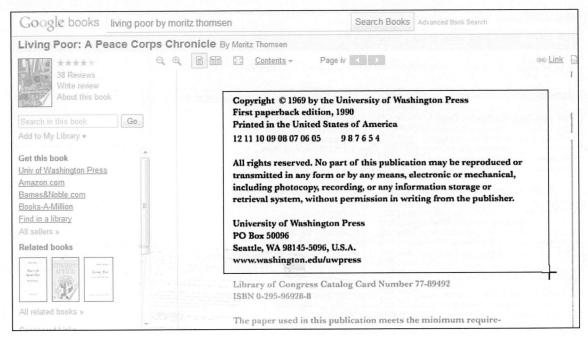

FIGURE S4-19
Look for publication information about a book on the first page of the book.

If you cannot find a book online or the pages in the book are not available online, use Worldcat.org to find a library that holds the book. Follow these steps:

Step 1. With the book displayed in Google Books, under **Get this book** in the left pane, click **Find in a library**. The link takes you to the Worldcat.org site, which shows libraries near you that hold the book.

Step 2. To get more accurate results, enter your ZIP Code in the *Enter your location* box on the Worldcat.org page. Then click **Find libraries**. Which is the closest library to you that holds the book?

On Your Own Solution 4-8   How to Use Google Scholar to Find a Journal Article

Do the following to use Google Scholar to find a journal article:

Step 1. Using Internet Explorer, go to **google.com**. Enter **peace corps volunteer benefits** in the search box. In the menu at the top of the page, click **more** and then click **Scholar** in the drop-down list. A list of scholarly articles and books appears.

Step 2. Notice near the top of the page you can limit the search to recent years to find current sources (see Figure S4-20). Limit your search to articles written since 2008.

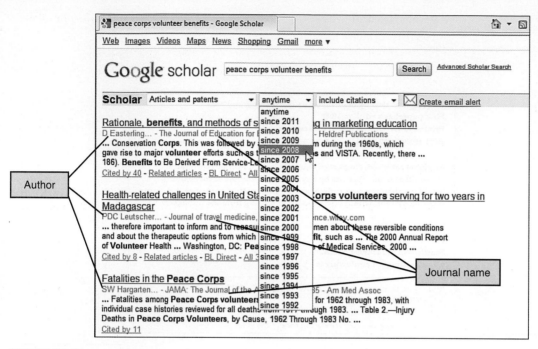

FIGURE S4-20
Google Scholar returns journals and books.

Step 3. Notice that the journal names are listed under the link for each search result. Click some links and find an article that you think is useful. For example, one article is shown in Figure S4-21, but you might find a different article.

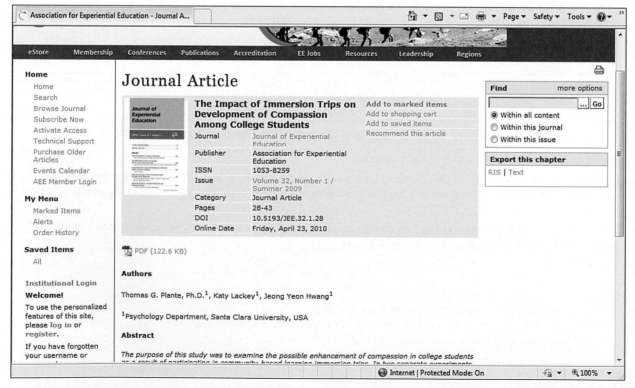

FIGURE S4-21
This web page shows an article abstract taken from the Journal of Experiential Education.

Step 4. Select and copy the abstract of the article onto the Benefits page of OneNote. In OneNote, highlight any text that you think is important.

Step 5. Copy into OneNote all the information you need to cite the article. For a journal article, you need

- ▶ Author name
- ▶ Title of the article
- ▶ Journal title
- ▶ Volume and issue number
- ▶ Date published
- ▶ Pages the article spans or first page if the article jumps pages

Select the text or use the Screen Clipping tool to copy the citation information for your article into OneNote. Figure S4-22 shows the information to be copied into OneNote for the article shown earlier in Figure S4-21, but your citation information might be different.

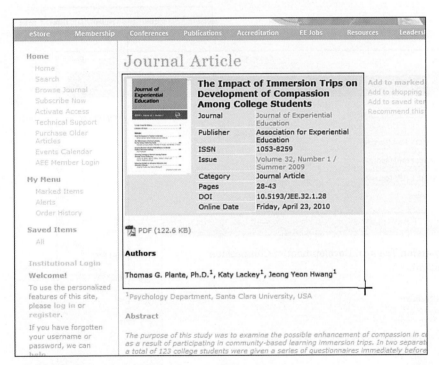

FIGURE S4-22
The selection includes the citation information for this journal article.

Not Working? In OneNote, if you need to move containers down on a page to make more room, click the **Insert** tab and then click **Insert Space**. Then press and drag to make more room.

Step 6. Many websites display the abstract, but not the full article. To view the full text of the article, click a link on the page. For example, in Figure S4-21, you would click **PDF (122.6 KB)** to view the full PDF of the article. However, when this link is clicked, a message appears saying the PDF of the article costs $10.

Your school pays for subscriptions to many journals. Rather than pay for the article yourself, use your school library website to locate and view the article.

On Your Own Solution 4-9   How to Explore Your School Library's Website

Do the following to use your school library website:

Step 1. Determine the URL of your school's website. If you are not sure, ask your instructor.

Step 2. Using Internet Explorer, access that website. Look on the home page to find a link to sign on to the site.

Step 3. Log on to the site using your user ID and password assigned by your school. If you don't know your user ID and password, ask your instructor to whom you should go to find out. You might have to retrieve the information through your school's website.

Step 4. Go to the online library and explore the online databases that your library provides.

Step 5. Try to find the journal article you found using Google Scholar earlier in the chapter. For example, for one school library website, the article shown earlier in Figure S4-21 can be found on the library site and is shown in Figure S4-23. Can you find your article?

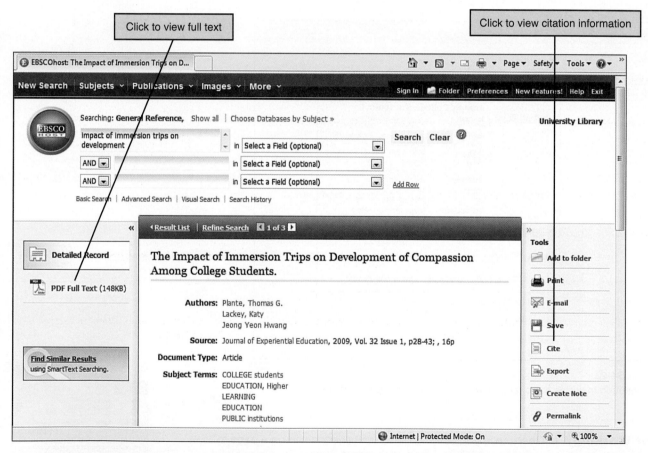

FIGURE S4-23

The full text of a journal article is available by way of a school library's website.

Step 6. Try to view the full article. For example, in Figure S4-23, to view the full article, you would click **PDF Full Text**. Can you view the full text of your article?

Step 7. Is there a link on your web page to view the citation information? For example, in Figure S4-23, to view the citation information for this article, click **Cite**. The citation information is shown in Figure S4-24. Copy the text under **Works Cited** into OneNote. This text is formatted exactly as it should appear in a Works Cited list. Can you find citation information already prepared for a Works Cited list?

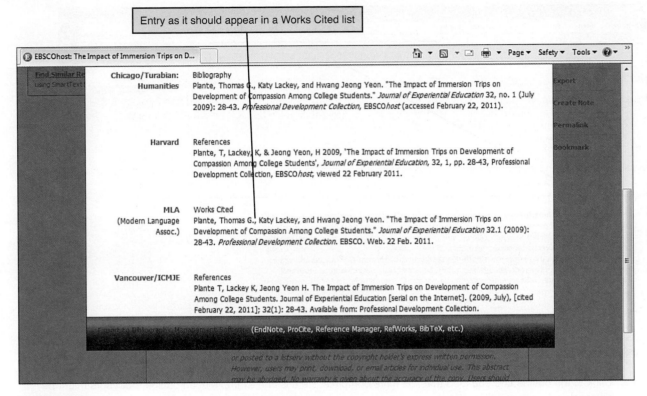

Entry as it should appear in a Works Cited list

FIGURE S4-24
The web page provides citation information already arranged and formatted for a Works Cited list.

On Your Own Solution 4-10   **How to Organize, Print, and Export Your Research in OneNote**

Your outline in OneNote will guide you when you are writing your research paper. Follow these steps to refine your outline:

Step 1. Go to the Outline page of OneNote.

Step 2. To open some space under the outline, click the **Insert** tab. Click **Insert Space**. Position your pointer under the outline and press and drag it down to open space under your outline. See Figure S4-25.

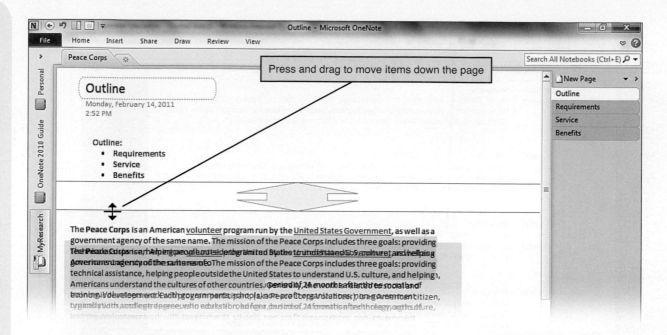

FIGURE S4-25
Insert space under the outline to make room for more text.

Step 3. Click in the outline and edit it so that it is more complete. Here is one example of an outline, but yours might be different:

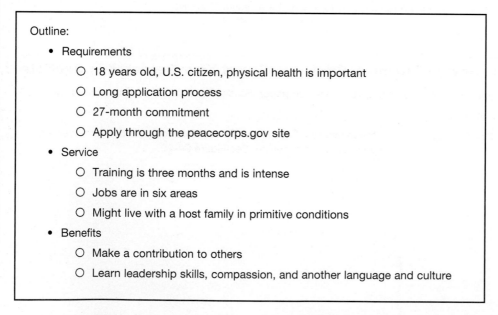

Outline:
- Requirements
    - ○ 18 years old, U.S. citizen, physical health is important
    - ○ Long application process
    - ○ 27-month commitment
    - ○ Apply through the peacecorps.gov site
- Service
    - ○ Training is three months and is intense
    - ○ Jobs are in six areas
    - ○ Might live with a host family in primitive conditions
- Benefits
    - ○ Make a contribution to others
    - ○ Learn leadership skills, compassion, and another language and culture

Step 4. To indent a line, use the **Increase Indent Position** command on the Home ribbon in the Basic Text group. As you type, if you need more space, use the **Insert Space** command on the **Insert** ribbon.

To practice copying a note container from one page to another page in OneNote, follow these steps:

Step 1. Go to the Requirements page. Right-click the title bar of any container on the page. The container is selected and a shortcut menu appears. Click **Copy** on the shortcut menu.

Step 2. Click the **Service** tab to go to that page. Scroll down to the bottom of the page and right-click whitespace below the last entry on the page. In the shortcut menu, click the leftmost **Paste** icon. The container is copied to the page.

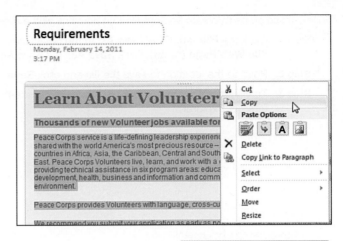

> **Hint** If you want to move a container from one page to another rather than copy the container, use **Cut** and **Paste** rather than Copy and Paste on the shortcut menus.

Step 3. To delete the new entry on the Service page, right-click in the title bar of the container and click **Delete** from the shortcut menu.

If you have access to a printer, follow these steps to print the entire Peace Corps section of your OneNote notebook:

Step 1. Click the **File** tab. Click **Print**. Click **Print Preview**. The Print Preview and Settings dialog box appears. In the drop-down list under **Print range**, select **Current Section**, as shown in Figure S4-26.

Step 2. Click **Print**. The Print dialog box appears. Select your printer and click **Print**. All the pages in the section print.

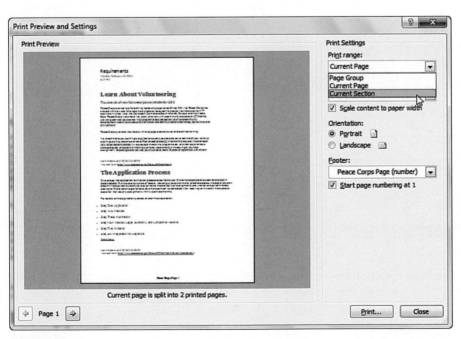

FIGURE S4-26
Print all the pages in the current section of your OneNote notebook.

Follow these steps to create an .mht file that contains all the research notes in the Peace Corps section of your notebook:

Step 1. Click the **File** tab. Click **Save As**. In the Save Current area, click **Section**. In the Select Format area, click **Single File Web Page (*.mht)**. Click **Save As**. The Save As dialog box appears.

Step 2. Point to the location to save the file and click **Save**. The Peace Corps file is created.

Step 3. To view the file, open **Windows Explorer**. Locate the **Peace Corps** file and double-click it. The file displays in Internet Explorer.

CHAPTER 5 SOLUTIONS
Writing Papers Using Microsoft Word Templates and Tools

The solutions in this appendix are for you to use if you get stuck when doing an On Your Own activity in the chapter. To learn how to teach yourself a computer skill, always try the On Your Own activity first before turning to these solutions.

On Your Own Solution 5-1 How to Open the OneNote Notebook to View Research Notes

Follow these steps to open the notebook:

Step 1. Insert the DVD from the back of the book into the optical drive. If the **AutoPlay** dialog box opens, close it.

Step 2. Open **Windows Explorer**. In the Computer group, locate the DVD. Drill down into the **Sample Files** folder. In that folder, drill down into the **Ch05_MyResearch** subfolder (see Figure S5-1). There you find the Peace Corps file. Double-click the **Peace Corps** file. If Windows asks whether you want to open the notebook or just the Peace Corps section, choose to open the entire notebook.

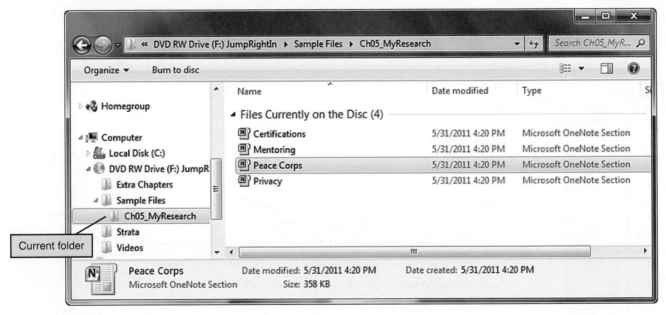

FIGURE S5-1
Find the Peace Corps file on the DVD.

Step 3. The Ch05_MyResearch notebook opens in a OneNote window. Click each page in the Peace Corps section to view the research.

Step 4. To save you typing time, we created the text for the research paper for you. To view the text, click the **Text for Research Paper** page tab.

Leave the OneNote window open so you can copy research and text from the OneNote window into the Word window as you build the paper.

On Your Own Solution 5-2 How to Create a Document Using an MLA Template

Do the following to download an MLA template and create a document using this template:

Step 1. Open **Microsoft Word**. Click the **File** tab and click **New**. In the list of templates, drill down into **Reports** and then **Academic papers and reports**.

Step 2. Select **Research paper in MLA style** and click **Download**. The new document is created.

Office.com occasionally changes the templates it makes available. If you cannot find the Research paper in MLA style template, know that we have provided on the DVD the MLA_Research_Paper document that was created using the template. Do the following to use the document:

Step 1. Insert the DVD into the optical drive. If the Auto Play box opens, close it.

Step 2. Open Windows Explorer and drill down to the **Sample Files** folder on the DVD.

Step 3. Double-click the **MLA_Research_Paper** document. The document opens in Read-Only mode.

Do the following to examine the document that was created using the MLA template:

Step 1. To display paragraph marks, click the **Show/Hide** button on the **Home** ribbon. Identify on your screen the items labeled in Figure S5-2.

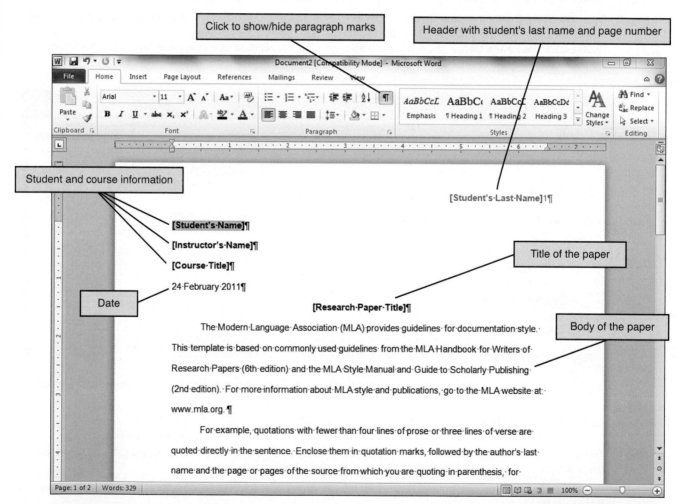

FIGURE S5-2
A document is created using an MLA template for a research paper.

Step 2. In the Styles section, click the down arrow ▣ under Change Styles. The Styles box opens. Drag the title bar of the Styles box to the far right side of the Word window until it snaps to the window as shown in Figure S5-3.

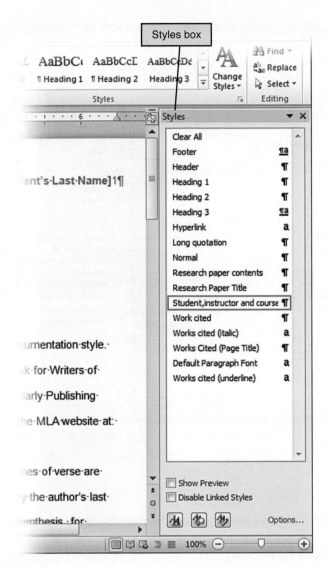

FIGURE S5-3
The Styles box is snapped to the right side of the Word window.

Step 3. To determine what style is applied to the first paragraph, click somewhere in the paragraph. The style that is applied to the text is selected in the Styles box. The selected style is the **Research paper contents** style.

Step 4. In the Styles box, right-click the style and select **Modify** from the shortcut menu. The Modify Style box appears.

Step 5. In the lower-left corner of the box, click **Format** and select **Paragraph** from the menu. The Paragraph box appears. You can view all the paragraph formatting required by MLA for the style. See Figure S5-4. If necessary, you can make changes to the style using this box.

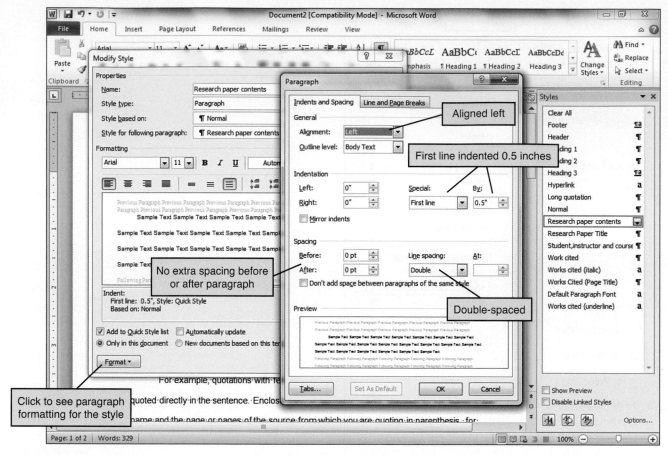

FIGURE S5-4
The formatting for a style can be viewed and modified.

Step 6. Click **Cancel** twice to close both boxes (If you had made changes to the style, you would click OK to save these changes.)

Step 7. To save the document, click the **File** tab and click **Save As**. Following instructions given in Chapter 3, "Creating Documents with Microsoft Word," save the document to your USB flash drive, hard drive, SkyDrive, or other location given by your instructor. Name the document **PeaceCorpsPaper**. When Word asks whether you want to save the document using a new document format, click **OK**.

On Your Own Solution 5-3 How to Enter Header, Student and Course Information, and Paper Title

Do the following to enter the header, student and course information, and paper title:

Step 1. Double-click somewhere in the header of the document to select it. When the header is selected, the body of the document is grayed. Click **[Student's Last Name]** to select it and type **Witt**. Put one space between the last name and the page number. Double-click somewhere in the body of the document to return to this area.

Step 2. Click **[Student's Name]** and type **Jos**. Then click the **Insert** tab. Click **Symbol** and click **More Symbols**. The Symbol dialog box appears.

Step 3. Under Subset, click **Latin-1 Supplement**. Scroll down through the symbols and click **é** (see Figure S5-5).

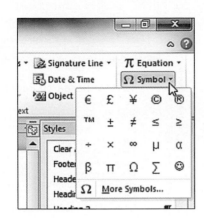

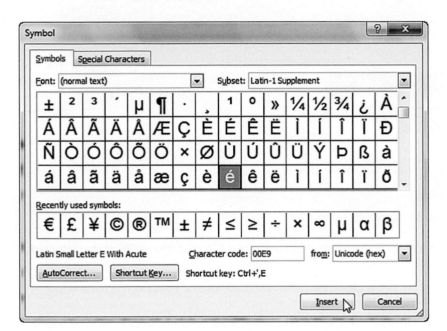

FIGURE S5-5
Symbols can be inserted into a Word document.

Step 4. Click **Insert**. Close the Symbol box. Type a space followed by **Witt**.

Step 5. Click **[Instructor's Name]** and change it to **Professor Chen**.

Step 6. Click **[Course Title]** and change it to **English Composition 101.**

Step 7. The date field should be today's date. If the date is wrong, click it and then click **Update**. Click off the date to unselect it.

Step 8. Click **[Research Paper Title]** and change it to **So You Want to Know About the Peace Corps**.

Step 9. Press and drag to select all the text in the paper following the title down through the end of the paper including the Works Cited page and press **Delete** to delete it.

Step 10. Save the document.

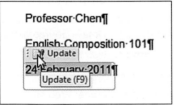

On Your Own Solution 5-4 **How to Enter the First Paragraph and Create a Citation**

Follow these steps to copy the text for the introductory paragraph from OneNote into your document and format the paragraph:

Step 1. In OneNote, select the **Text for Research Paper** page. Press and drag your pointer to select the first paragraph on that page (see Figure S5-6). Do not include in your selection the title above the paragraph.

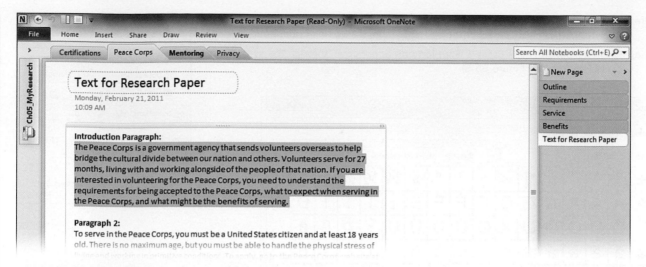

FIGURE S5-6

Select the first paragraph on the **_Text for Research Paper_** page of OneNote.

Step 2. Right-click the selected text and click **Copy** on the shortcut menu. The text is copied into the Windows Clipboard.

Step 3. Return to the Word window.

Step 4. Position the insertion point below the title of the paper. Right-click and click the first **Paste** icon in the shortcut menu. The paragraph is inserted in the Word document.

Step 5. Click somewhere in the paragraph. In the Style box, click the **Research paper contents** style. The style is applied to the paragraph.

Follow these steps to insert a citation:

Step 1. Position the insertion point before the period at the end of the second sentence in the paragraph.

Step 2. Click the **References** tab. In the Citations & Bibliography section, click **MLA Sixth Edition** if it is not already selected under Style.

Step 3. Click **Insert Citation**. In the drop-down menu, click **Add New Source**. The Create Source box opens.

Step 4. Use this information in the Create Source box (see Figure S5-7):

Type of Source: Web site

Name of Web Page: Peace Corps

Year Accessed: 2011

Month Accessed: February

Day Accessed: 15

URL: http://www.peacecorps.gov

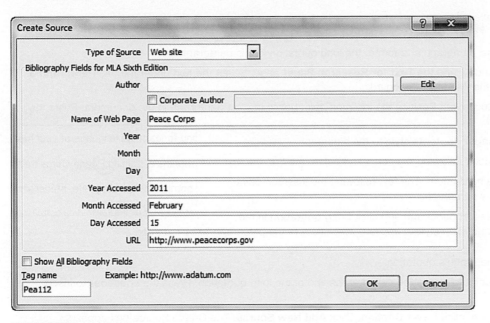

FIGURE S5-7
Citation information is entered in the Create Source dialog box.

Step 5. Click **OK**. The citation (Peace Corps) is added to the paragraph.

Step 6. Save the document.

others. Volunteers serve for 27 m

at nation (Peace Corps). If you are

ed to understand the requirements

On Your Own Solution 5-5 **How to Enter the Second Paragraph and a Citation**

Do the following to add the second paragraph to the paper:

Step 1. Go to the OneNote window and the **Text for Research Paper** page. Select the text under the title **Paragraph 2**. Do not include the title. Right-click and select **Copy** to copy the text into the Windows Clipboard.

Step 2. Return to your Word document. Position the insertion point below the first paragraph.

Step 3. Right-click and select **Paste** to place the text at the end of the document.

Step 4. Apply the **Research paper contents** style to the paragraph.

Step 5. The URL, www.peacecorps.gov, is not formatted correctly. Right-click the link, **www.peacecorps.gov**, and select **Remove Hyperlink** from the shortcut menu.

Step 6. Press and drag your pointer over **www.peacecorps.gov** to highlight this text. Click the **Research paper contents** style in the Styles box. The text is now formatted correctly.

Follow these steps to add a citation at the end of the second paragraph:

Step 1. Position the insertion point before the period at the end of the last sentence of the paragraph.

Step 2. On the References ribbon, click **Insert Citation**. Because the Peace Corps source has already been used, it is listed in the drop-down menu. Click **Peace Corps**. The citation is inserted in the text.

Step 3. Save the document.

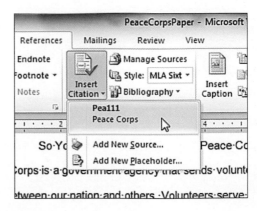

On Your Own Solution 5-6 How to Enter More Text, a Long Quotation, and a Book Citation

Follow these steps to insert the third paragraph and format the long quotation in this paragraph:

Step 1. Go to the **OneNote** window and the **Text for Research Paper** page. Select the text under the title **Paragraph 3**. Copy the selection to the Windows Clipboard.

Step 2. Return to your Word document. Position the insertion point below the last paragraph in the document. Paste the text into the document.

Step 3. Apply the **Research paper contents** style to the paragraph.

Step 4. Position the insertion point following the colon and before the *P* in the text.

Step 5. Press **Enter** to insert a hard return. The text following the insertion point moves down into a new paragraph.

Step 6. Click somewhere in this last paragraph and click **Long quotation** in the Styles box. The Long quotation style is applied, which causes the paragraph to be indented.

Follow these steps to add the citation to this quotation:

Step 1. Position the insertion point following the period at the end of the long quotation. Press the **spacebar** to insert a space.

Step 2. On the References ribbon, click **Insert Citation**. Click **Add New Source**. The Create Source box appears.

Step 3. For Type of Source, select **Book**.

Step 4. For Author, type **Thomsen, Moritz**.

Step 5. To copy the book title from the citation information in OneNote, go to the **OneNote** window. Select the **Requirements** page. Scroll down and select the book title, which is **Living Poor: A Peace Corps Chronicle**, as shown in Figure S5-8. Right-click and copy the selected text.

Step 6. Return to the Word window. Click in the field labeled **Title**. Right-click and paste the text. The title appears in the Title box.

Step 7. The citation information recorded in OneNote shows the year published is 1969 (refer to Figure S5-8). In the Create Source box, enter **1969** in the Year field.

Step 8. For City, enter **Seattle**.

Step 9. For Publisher, enter **University of Washington Press**. Your Create Source box should now look like that in Figure S5-9. Click **OK**. The citation is inserted.

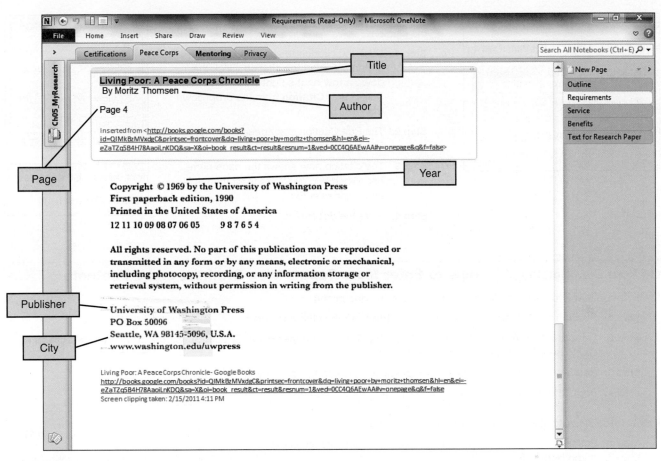

FIGURE S5-8
Select the title of the book in the OneNote research notes.

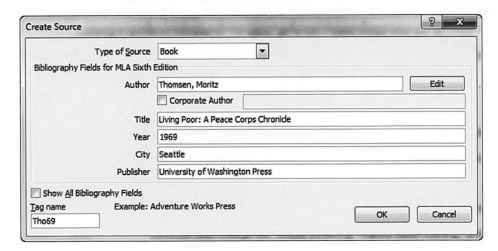

FIGURE S5-9
The book citation information is entered in the Create Source box.

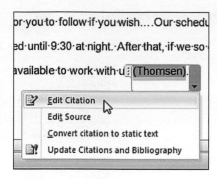

Follow these steps to insert the page number in the citation:

Step 1. Click the citation to select it. A box appears around the citation. Click the down arrow on the right side of the box. Select **Edit Citation** from the drop-down menu.

Step 2. The Edit Citation box appears. Under Pages, enter **4**. Click **OK**.

Step 3. The citation now shows the page number. When you click off the citation, it is no longer selected.

Step 4. Save the document.

On Your Own Solution 5-7   How to Enter More Text, a Blog Citation, and a Footnote

Follow these steps to insert the fourth paragraph into the document:

Step 1. Position the insertion point below the last paragraph in the document.

Step 2. Go to the **OneNote** window and the **Text for Research Paper** page. Select the text under the title **Paragraph 4**. Copy the selection to the Windows Clipboard.

Step 3. Return to your Word document and paste the text into the document.

Step 4. Apply the **Research paper contents** style to the paragraph.

Follow these steps to insert a citation for a blog:

Step 1. Position the insertion point at the end of the first sentence in the paragraph before the period.

Step 2. On the References ribbon, click **Insert Citation**. Click **Add New Source**. The Create Source box appears. The citation information can be found on the Service page of OneNote and is shown in Figure S5-10.

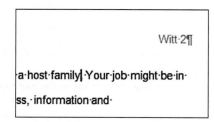

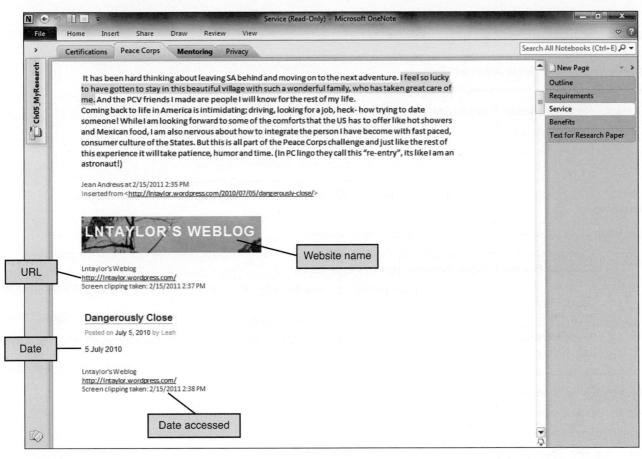

FIGURE S5-10
Blog entry and citation information are shown for Lntaylor's Weblog.

> **Step 3.** Use the following information to create the source:

Type of Source: Web site

Author: Taylor, Leah

Name of Web Page: Lntaylor's Weblog

Date: July 5, 2010

Date accessed: February 15, 2011

URL: http://lntaylor.wordpress.com

Follow these steps to add a footnote:

> **Step 1.** Position the insertion point at the end of the paragraph, following the last period.
>
> **Step 2.** On the References ribbon, click **Insert Footnote**. The footnote area appears at the bottom of the page.

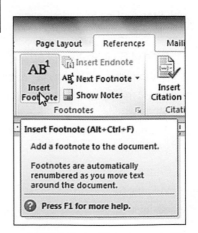

Step 3. Type this text in the footnote area:

> To find blogs written by Peace Corps volunteers, use Google.com and the following search string: Peace Corps volunteer blogs.

Step 4. Apply the **Research paper contents** style to the footnote.

Step 5. Save the document.

On Your Own Solution 5-8 **How to Enter the Conclusion Paragraph and Two More Citations**

Follow these steps to insert the conclusion paragraph and a citation:

Step 1. Copy the **Conclusion Paragraph** from the **Text for Research Paper** page in OneNote into the Word document. Apply the **Research paper contents** style to the paragraph.

Step 2. In the fourth sentence of the paragraph, position the insertion point after the last quotation mark and before the period.

help·others·change·for·the·better.·E

newspaper·publisher,·Bukar·Zarma

Corps·volunteers"|·In·helping·others

in·compassion,·courage,·and·leade

Step 3. Insert a citation. The citation information is taken from *The New York Times* article recorded on the Service page of OneNote. Use this citation information:

> Type of Source: Article in a Periodical
>
> Author: Strickney, Benjamin D.
>
> Title: Nigerians Speak Warmly of the Peace Corps
>
> Periodical Title: The New York Times
>
> Date: March 9, 1991

Step 4. Click **OK** to close the Create Source box. The citation is inserted in the document.

Follow these steps to insert a citation for a journal article:

Step 1. Position the insertion point at the end of the sixth sentence in the paragraph and before the period.

s·to·change,·expect·that·you·wi

leadership·skills|·You·can·also·l

ne·home,·you·are·likely·to·find·t

Step 2. On the **References** ribbon, click **Insert Citation**. Click **Add New Source**. The Create Source box appears. All the information to cite a journal article is not displayed in the box. To display all fields, check **Show All Bibliography Fields**.

Step 3. Use this information:

> Type of Source: Journal Article
>
> Author: Plante, Thomas G., Katy Lackey, and Hwang Jeong Yeon
>
> Title: The Impact of Immersion Trips on Development of Compassion Among College Students
>
> Journal Name: Journal of Experiential Education
>
> Year: 2009
>
> Pages: 28-43
>
> Volume: 32
>
> Issue: 1

Step 4. Click **OK** to close the Create Source box. The citation is inserted in the document.

Step 5. Edit the citation, adding the page numbers **28-43**.

On Your Own Solution 5-9 **How to Create a Works Cited Page**

Do the following to create a Works Cited page:

Step 1. Position the insertion point at the end of the last paragraph in the document. Display paragraph marks and make sure only one hard return is at the end of this paragraph. On the Insert ribbon, click **Page Break**. A new page is created.

Step 2. On the References ribbon, click **Bibliography**. Click **Works Cited** in the drop-down list. The list is inserted in the document.

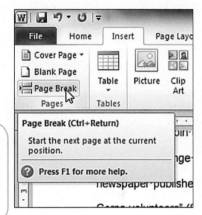

Hint If you find a mistake in the source information used to generate the Works Cited list, go back and find the citation in the body of the paper. Select the citation and click **Edit Source** from the drop-down menu. Correct the source information and then generate a new Works Cited page. Any edits you made to the Works Cited page are lost and must be done again.

Step 3. To center the page title, select it and apply the **Works Cited (Page Title)** style.

Step 4. Select each title in the list that is underlined and apply the **Works Cited (italic)** style. Make sure all underlining is removed.

Step 5. In the Peace Corps entry, change **February** to **Feb.**, including the period.

Step 6. In the Strickney entry, change **March** to **Mar.**, including the period.

Step 7. In the Taylor entry, change **February** to **Feb.**, including the period.

Step 8. Position the insertion point at the end of the Plante, Thomas G. entry and add the following, beginning with a space:

> *EBSCO*. Web. 14 Feb. 2011.

Step 9. Select the *EBSCO* database name and apply the **Works cited (italic)** style. Position the insertion point at the end of the Strickney, Benjamin D. entry and add the following, beginning with a space:

> Web. 15 Feb. 2011.

Step 10. Position the insertion point at the end of the Thomsen, Moritz entry and add the following, beginning with a space:

> *Google Book Search*. Web. 15 Feb. 2011.

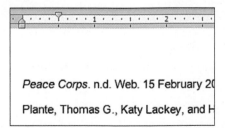

Step 11. Select the *Google Book Search* database name and apply the **Works cited (italic)** style. In the Peace Corps entry, insert the word **Web** and a period before the date accessed.

Step 12. In the Taylor entry, insert the word **Web** and a period before the date accessed.

Step 13. Save the document.

The solutions in this appendix are for you to use if you get stuck when doing an On Your Own activity in the chapter. To learn how to teach yourself a computer skill, always try the On Your Own activity first before turning to these solutions.

> **Not Working?** Websites change from time to time. The step-by-step instructions here were accurate when we wrote them, but be aware that you might have to adjust them to account for later website changes.

On Your Own Solution 6-1   How to Manage Email Using a Website

Follow these steps to use a website to view and print email messages:

Step 1. Open Internet Explorer and go to the website of your email provider. For example, if your email address is andrewsjean7@gmail.com, enter **gmail.com** in your browser address box. Sign in to your email account using your email address and password. In this solution, we are using the gmail.com website. Your website might work differently, but the functions should be the same.

Most websites show your inbox when you first log on. How many messages are in your **inbox**? For gmail.com, the number of messages in the inbox shows up in the lower-right corner of the inbox.

Step 2. To read a message, you might need to click it or double-click it. For gmail.com, when you click a message, it opens so you can read it. For example, in Figure 6-3 shown in the chapter, when I click the first message in the inbox, the message from Joy Dark appears. If you have a message in your inbox, open it now.

Step 3. To print a message you are viewing, look for a Print button on the screen. For gmail.com, click **Print all** on the right side of the window. The print preview of all open messages appears. The Print dialog box also appears (see Figure S6-1). Select your printer and click **Print**.

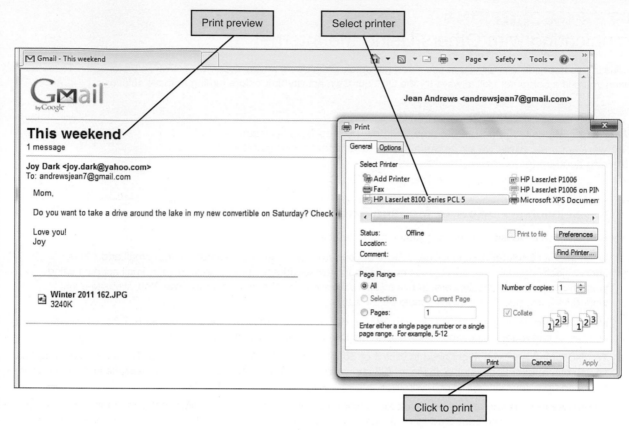

FIGURE S6-1

To print a message, select the printer and click **Print**.

Follow these steps to compose and send a new message:

Step 4. To start the process, look for a button on the screen such as New or Compose. For gmail.com, click **Compose mail** in the left pane. A blank message area appears where you can type your message.

Step 5. Enter the email address of the receiver, subject line, and body of the message. Figure S6-2 shows the message after these items have been entered. Notice the formatting buttons above the body of the message where you can format the text.

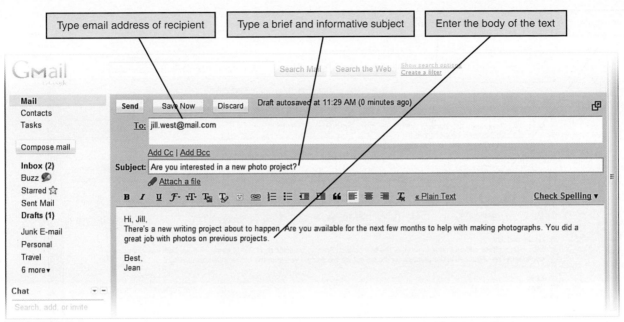

FIGURE S6-2

A new email message needs the receiver's email address, subject line, and body of the message.

> **Step 6.** Reread the message and check it for errors. Then click **Send**. The message is sent. The window returns to your inbox.
>
> **Step 7.** Open your Sent folder to verify the message is there. For gmail.com, click **Sent Mail** in the left pane.

Follow these steps to delete messages:

> **Step 1.** Return to your inbox. For gmail.com, click **Inbox** in the left pane. The inbox appears.
>
> **Step 2.** To delete messages you no longer need, first select a message and then delete it. For gmail.com, you click the check box beside the message to select it. Selected messages are highlighted in yellow (refer to Figure 6-2 in the chapter). Click **Delete** to delete selected messages.
>
> **Step 3.** To see deleted messages so that you can recover them if necessary, look for a folder labeled Trash, Deleted Items, or a similar name. For gmail.com, in the left pane, click **6 more** and then click **Trash**. The Trash folder appears. If you want to recover a deleted message, move it to another folder. To move a message using gmail.com, select the message and then click **Move to**.

Follow these steps to send a message with an attachment:

> **Step 1.** Write a second message to one or more friends. First, enter the email address, subject line, and body of the message. One example of a message is shown in Figure S6-3, which is addressed to two recipients. In the To box, separate each email address with a comma or semicolon.

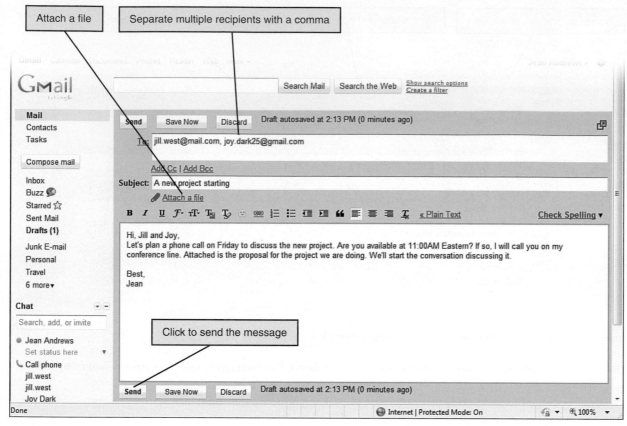

FIGURE S6-3

A new message has two recipients.

Step 2. Look on your screen for a way to attach a file. For example, in Figure S6-3, click **Attach a file**. The Select file(s) to upload by mail.google.com box appears. Drill down on your computer storage device to find the file and then click **Open**. Figure S6-4 shows the box when the **MyPhoto1** file in the Sample Files folder on the DVD is selected.

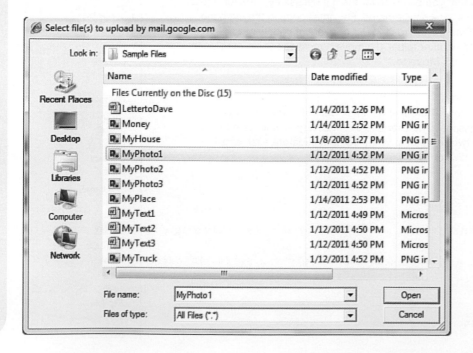

FIGURE S6-4

Find and select the file to attach to the email message.

Step 3. The file is attached. You should see the filename somewhere in the new message area. Click **Send** to send the message.

When you open an email message with an attached file, the file does not immediately open. Follow these steps to open and save the attachment:

Step 1. Messages with attachments have a paper clip icon or some other way to identify the attachment. For example, the message from Joy Dark shown in the chapter in Figure 6-2 has an attached file. In Figure 6-3 in the chapter, you can see the filename at the bottom of the open email message. Click **View** to open the file in a new window. Your screen might work differently.

Step 2. To download the file to your computer so you can save it, click **Download**. The File Download box appears. Click **Save**. The Save As box appears. Navigate to your USB flash drive or other location and click **Save**.

Look back at Figure 6-3 in the chapter and note that you can click Reply to reply to the sender or click Forward to send the message to a third person. Follow these steps to reply to the sender:

Step 1. To reply to the message, look for a Reply button. For gmail.com, click **Reply** at the bottom of the message. A new message is created so that you can reply to the sender (see Figure S6-5). The insertion point is positioned at the top of the original message.

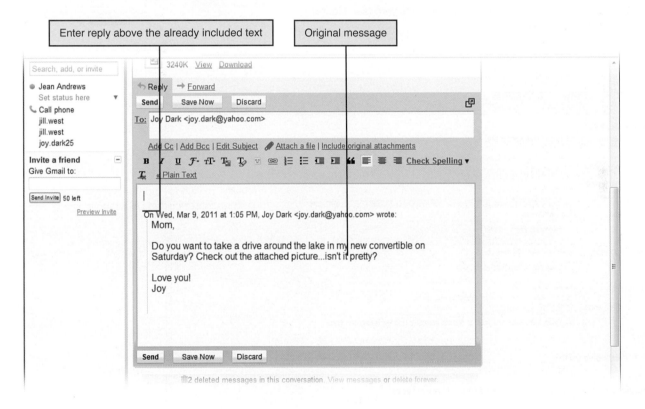

FIGURE S6-5
Reply by typing your message above the original message. The latest reply is always put at the top of the thread of replies.

Step 2. Notice in Figure S6-5 if you need to save the message to finish it later, you can click Save Now. All websites offer a similar way to save drafts of messages not yet finished. Type your reply and send the message. For gmail.com, click **Send** at the bottom of the message (refer to Figure S6-5). Your Send button might be some other place on the window.

On Your Own Solution 6-2   How to Set Up Outlook to Manage an Email Account

This solution has two parts:

▶ How to set up an email account in Outlook that is not a hotmail.com or live.com account

▶ How to set up a hotmail.com or live.com email account in Outlook

How to Set Up an Email Account in Outlook That Is Not a Hotmail.com or Live.com Account

Follow these steps to open Outlook for the first time and use the Startup Wizard to set up an email account:

Step 1.   Open **Microsoft Outlook 2010**. If this is the first time to open the program, the Microsoft Outlook 2010 Startup window appears. Click **Next**.

Step 2.   Follow directions on screen to enter your name, email address, and password. A connection is made to the server, and your email is downloaded to Outlook. Click **Finish**. The Microsoft Outlook window opens.

Follow these steps to set up an email account without using the Startup Wizard:

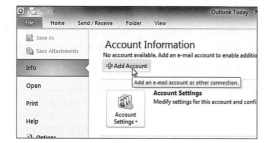

Step 1.   Open **Microsoft Outlook 2010**. Click the **File** tab and click **Add Account**. The Add New Account dialog box opens.

Step 2.   Enter your name, email account, and password (see Figure S6-6). Click **Next**.

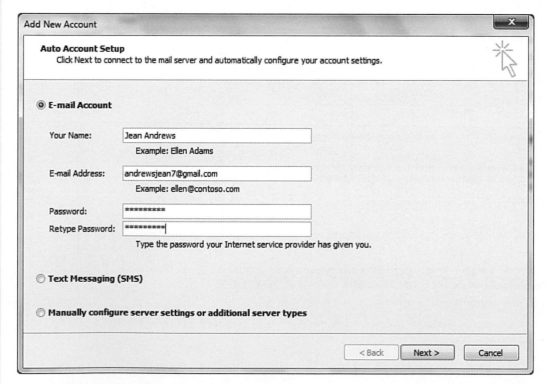

FIGURE S6-6

Enter email account information.

Step 3. The connection is made to your email server. A test email message is sent, and email messages on the server are downloaded to Outlook. Click **Finish**. The Outlook window appears.

Step 4. Look for your email address listed in the left pane. Click **Inbox** under the email address to view messages in the inbox. Your screen should look similar to Figure 6-4 shown in the chapter.

How to Set Up a Hotmail.com or Live.com Email Account in Outlook

Before you can set up a hotmail.com or live.com email account in Outlook, you must download and install the Microsoft Outlook Hotmail Connector. Recall that to install software, you must be logged in to Windows using an administrator account, or you must have an administrator password. Follow these steps:

Step 1. Open **Microsoft Outlook 2010**. If this is the first time to open the program, the Microsoft Outlook 2010 Startup window appears. Click **Next**. Select **Yes** to set up a new email account and click **Next**.

Step 2. Follow directions onscreen to enter your name, email account, and password (refer to Figure S6-6). Click **Next**.

Step 3. The Microsoft Outlook dialog box appears. Click **Install Now**.

Step 4. Internet Explorer opens and the File Download – Security Warning box appears (see Figure S6-7). In the box, click **Run**.

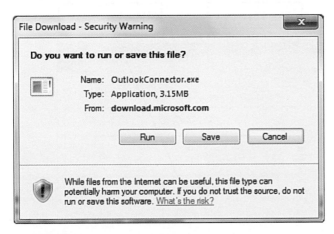

FIGURE S6-7
Click Run to install the Outlook Connector software.

Step 5. The User Account Control dialog box appears. Respond to the box by clicking **Yes** or entering an administrator password and clicking **Yes**.

Step 6. The Microsoft Outlook Hotmail Connector Setup box appears. Accept the license agreement and click **Install**. The software installs. Click **Finish** to close the Setup box.

Step 7. Close **Internet Explorer**. Close **Outlook**.

Step 8. Open **Outlook**. It finds the new software installed. Click the **File** tab. Click **Add Account** and follow directions onscreen to set up the account.

On Your Own Solution 6-3   **How to Use Outlook to Manage Email**

Follow these steps to use Outlook to view and print your email messages:

Step 1. If Outlook is not already open, open it. In this book, we are not using the Outlook Data Files feature of Outlook. If Outlook Data File details are showing, click the black triangle to hide the details.

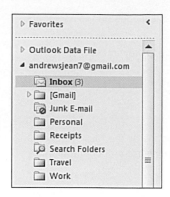

Step 2. To view a list of folders under your email account, if necessary, click the white triangle in the left pane beside your account. The triangle is now black.

Step 3. Under your email account in the left pane, click **Inbox**. The items in your inbox appear in the middle pane.

Step 4. To reorder the items by sender, right-click the title **Arrange By:**. A drop-down menu appears. Click **From**.

Step 5. To read a message, click it to select it. A selected message appears in blue. The contents of the message appear in the right pane.

Step 6. To print a message or messages, first select the messages. To select multiple messages, hold down the **Ctrl** key as you click messages. Click the **File** tab and then click **Print**. Print previews appear (see Figure S6-8). Select your printer and click **Print**.

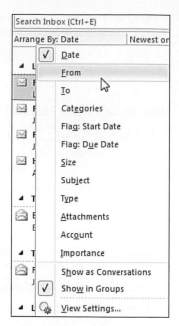

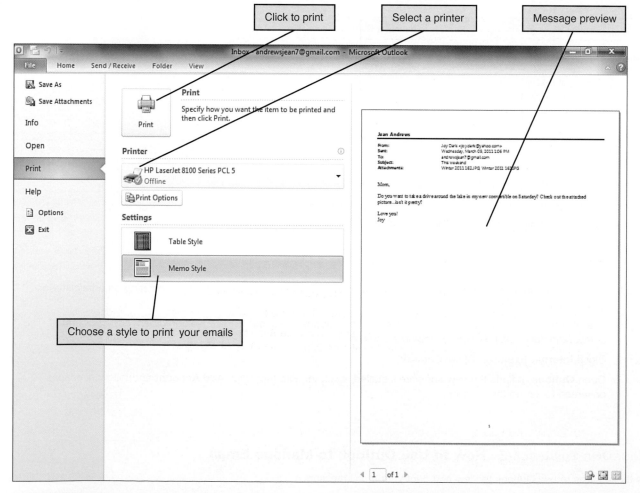

FIGURE S6-8
Selected messages are ready to print.

Follow these steps to compose and send a new message:

Step 1. On the **Home** tab, click **New Email**. A new Message window opens.

Step 2. Enter the email address of the receiver, subject line, and body of the message. Figure S6-9 shows the message after these items have been entered. Notice that when the body of the message is selected, all the formatting tools on the Message tab are available for you to format the text.

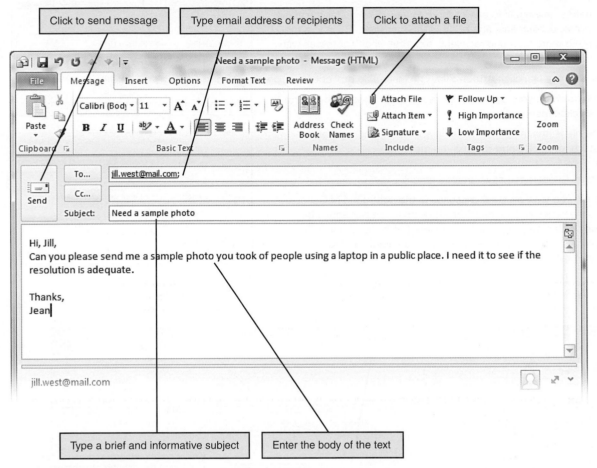

FIGURE S6-9
A new email message needs the receiver's email address, subject line, and body of the message.

Step 3. Reread the message and check it for errors. Then click **Send**. The message is sent.

Step 4. To view sent messages, click the folder in the left pane. Here are two possible folders:

- If the account is set up to keep mail on the server, click the **Sent Mail** folder under the server folder name. In our example, the server folder is **Gmail**. Sent Mail is in the Gmail group.

- If the account is set up to keep mail on the local computer, click **Sent Items**.

Not Working? If you want to change where mail is kept, on the **File** tab, click **Account Settings**. In the Account Settings box, select the email account and click **Change**. Then click **More Settings**. Settings for the account can be changed using the dialog box that appears.

Follow these steps to delete messages:

Step 1. Click the **Inbox** or other folder where you want to delete files.

Step 2. Select messages to delete. On the **Home** tab, click **Delete**. The messages are moved to the Trash folder. Messages remain in the Trash folder until you delete them. Click the **Trash** folder to view your trash.

Follow these steps to send a message with an attachment:

Step 1. Create a new email to one or more friends. First, enter the email address, subject line, and body of the message. To send a message to more than one recipient, separate email addresses with a comma.

Step 2. To attach a file, click **Attach File**. The Insert File box opens.

Step 3. Drill down on your computer storage device to find the file and then click **Insert**.

Step 4. The file is attached. The filename appears to the right of Attached. Click **Send** to send the message.

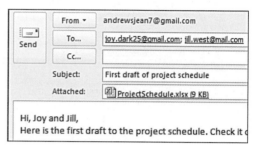

Follow these steps to open and save an attachment:

Step 1. When you view an email message in the right pane of Outlook, the filenames of attached files show up in the bar above the body of the message. Refer to Figure 6-4 in the chapter. To view the file, click the filename. The file appears in the right pane (see Figure S6-10).

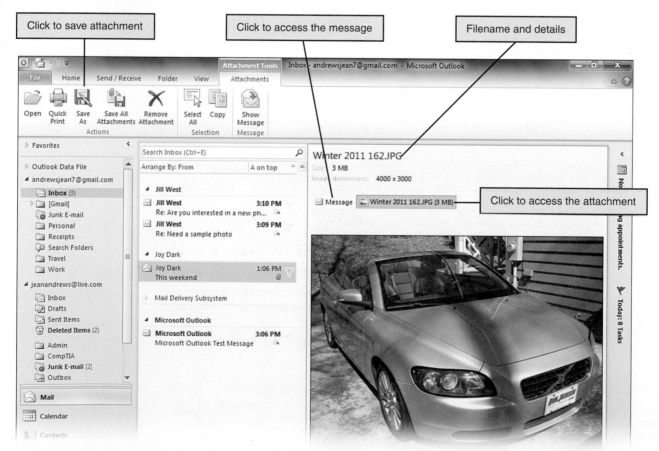

FIGURE S6-10

Outlook displays a photo file that was attached to an incoming email message.

Step 2. To save the file to a new location, on the **Attachment** tab, click **Save As**. The Save Attachment box opens. Navigate to the location to save the file and click **Save**.

Step 3. To return to the message, click **Message**. The message appears in the right pane.

To respond to the selected message, use the Reply, Reply All, or Forward buttons on the Home tab. Follow these steps to reply to the message:

Step 1. With the message selected, click the **Home** tab and click **Reply**. The Message window opens.

Step 2. Type your reply and click **Send**.

On Your Own Solution 6-4   How to Sign Up for Facebook and Build Your Profile

Because the Facebook website changes often, the step-by-step instructions that are accurate at this time would not be accurate by the time the book is in print. For this reason, detailed instructions are not provided.

On Your Own Solution 6-5   How to Find Friends on Facebook

Because the Facebook website changes often, the step-by-step instructions that are accurate at this time would not be accurate by the time the book is in print. For this reason, detailed instructions are not provided.

On Your Own Solution 6-6   How to Build Online Relationships with Facebook Friends

Because the Facebook website changes often, the step-by-step instructions that are accurate at this time would not be accurate by the time the book is in print. For this reason, detailed instructions are not provided.

On Your Own Solution 6-7   How to Find and Like Facebook Pages

Because the Facebook website changes often, the step-by-step instructions that are accurate at this time would not be accurate by the time the book is in print. For this reason, detailed instructions are not provided.

On Your Own Solution 6-8   How to Set Up and Use a Twitter Account

Because websites change often, the steps listed here might need changing. Follow these steps to set up a Twitter account:

Step 1. Use Internet Explorer and go to **twitter.com**. On the home page, click **Sign Up** and follow directions to create an account. You must enter your name, the name for your Twitter account, a password for Twitter, and a valid email address.

Step 2. After you create an account, you are taken to the Interests page to find Twitter accounts to follow. Figure S6-11 shows the page after several accounts are selected.

FIGURE S6-11
Search or drill for Twitter accounts to follow.

Step 3. Drill down in the topics to find accounts or type a name in the search box. For example, if you want to follow the White House, enter **White House** and click **Search**. Results appear. To follow an account, click **Follow**. As you select accounts, the accounts you are following show up on the right side of the window.

Step 4. To get the full benefits of Twitter, you must confirm your email account. Look in your email inbox for a message from Twitter and click the link in the message (see Figure S6-12).

Step 5. Whenever you go to twitter.com and sign in, the Tweets of those you follow appear (see Figure S6-13). Using this window, you can write a Tweet to those following you and set up your profile to make it easier for others to find you on Twitter. Also notice in Figure S6-13 that you can set up Twitter to get Tweets on your phone.

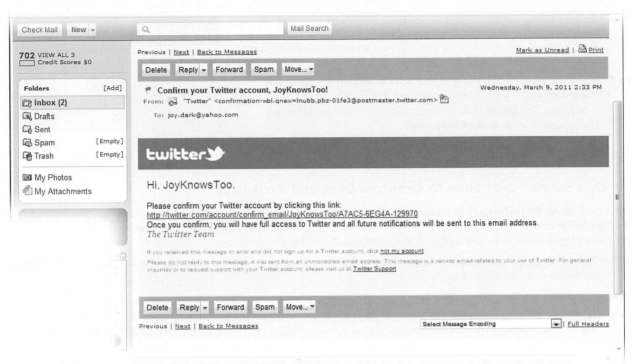

FIGURE S6-12
Click the link in the email message to confirm your email address to Twitter.

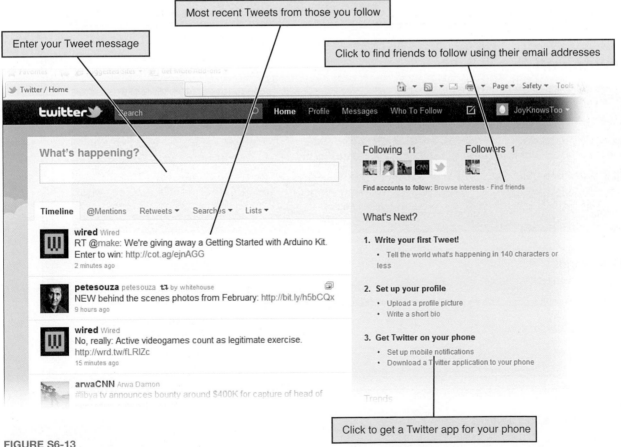

FIGURE S6-13
Read Tweets from those you follow and write your own Tweets to your followers.

Step 6. If you're searching for a friend to follow on Twitter, try clicking **Find friends** shown in Figure S6-13. In the window that appears, enter the email address of a friend. Your friend is sent an email invitation asking whether you can follow him on Twitter.

Step 7. If you want others to be able to find you by email in the same way, make sure your Twitter settings allow your email address to be used in this way. To change your settings, click the down arrow beside your account name and click **Settings**.

On Your Own Solution 6-9 **How to Create a Blog and Post to It**

To create a blog, go to the home page of a blogging site such as blogspot.com or wordpress.com and sign up for a blog account. Then follow directions onscreen to create your blog. Because websites change often, the steps here might need changing. Follow these steps to create a blog on the wordpress.com site:

Step 1. Go to **wordpress.com** and click **Sign up now**. On the signup window, enter a name for your blog, username, password, and your email address.

Step 2. WordPress sends an email message to you. You must click the link in the email message to activate your account.

Step 3. Using your browser, enter the URL to your blog to see what the world sees. My blog is named lifewithjean, so the URL is lifewithjean.wordpress.com. Yours will be different. Figure S6-14 shows my blog before I added anything.

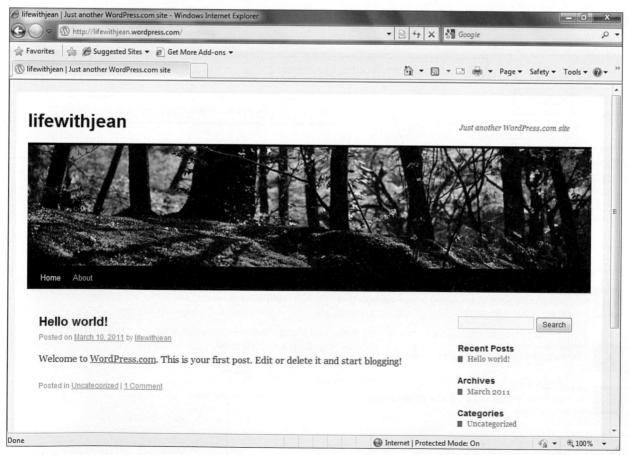

FIGURE S6-14
Here's my blog before I did anything to it.

Step 4. Open a new tab in Internet Explorer and go to **wordpress.com** and log on using your blog name and password. Then click **My Blog** and click **Dashboard**. The Dashboard window is the place where you manage your blog. See Figure S6-15. As you make changes to your blog from the Dashboard, you can switch back to the first tab in Internet Explorer to see the results. Don't forget to refresh the page when you return to the first tab.

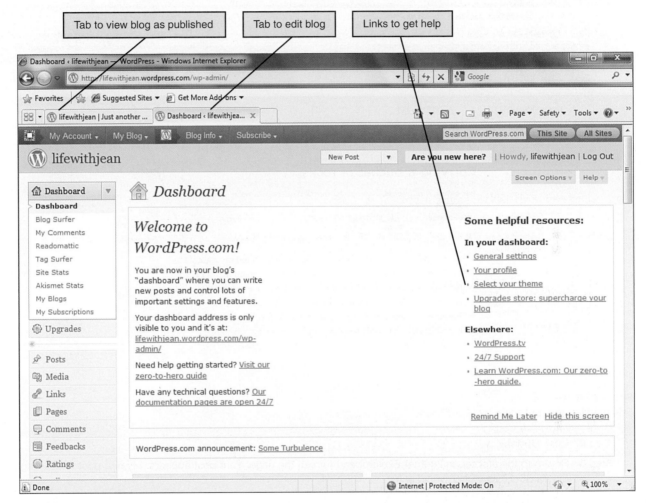

FIGURE S6-15
Use the Dashboard to manage your blog.

Step 5. When you are first learning new software, what should you always do first? Find out how to get help. You can find links on the Dashboard for getting started and to other documentation pages. Take a few minutes to check them out so you know where to go when you have questions.

Step 6. Click **Select your theme**. You can choose from the WordPress themes that appear for your blog design. Let's go with the default theme. After you learn the basics of blogging, you might want to go back and pick a different theme.

Step 7. To return to the Dashboard, click **Dashboard** in the left pane.

Follow these steps to make your first post:

Step 1. WordPress already made the first post called *Hello world!* Let's change it. Using the Dashboard page, scroll down the page to the Your Stuff box. Click **Edit** beside Hello world! The Edit Post window appears. Change the title of the post. In place of the current post contents, write your own post. See Figure S6-16.

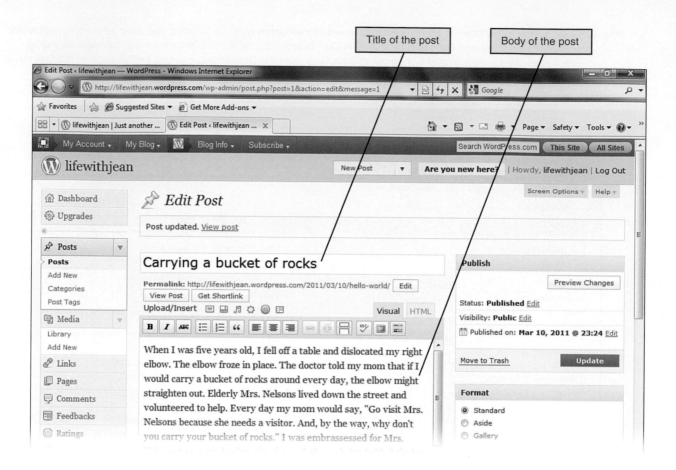

FIGURE S6-16
Edit the first post put there by WordPress.

> **Step 2.** Click **Update**.

> **Step 3.** Return to the first tab in Internet Explorer and refresh the page. Your post appears. My first post is showing in Figure S6-17 as a user would see it.

To email a link to your blog to your instructor, follow these steps:

> **Step 1.** With your blog showing in the first tab, highlight the address box. Right-click and select **Copy** from the shortcut menu. The URL is copied to the Windows Clipboard.

> **Step 2.** Access your email account. Compose a new email message to your instructor. When you are ready for the URL, right-click somewhere in the body of the message and select **Paste** from the shortcut menu. The URL is copied into the email message.

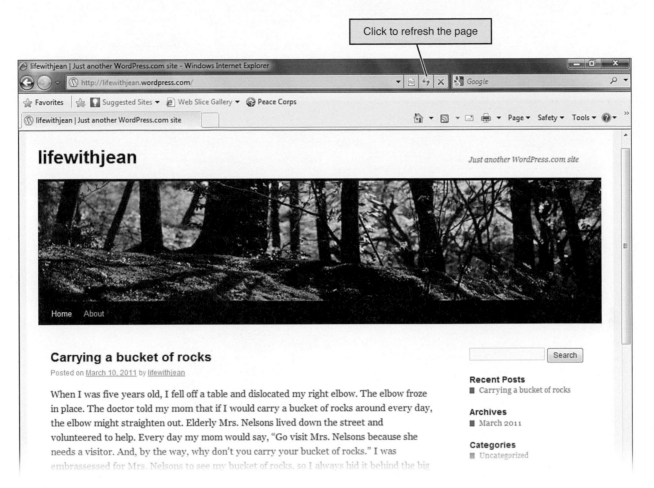

FIGURE S6-17
My blog as the world sees it.

Finding a Job Using the Web, a Résumé, and a Business Letter

The solutions in this appendix are for you to use if you get stuck when doing an On Your Own activity in the chapter. To learn how to teach yourself a computer skill, always try the On Your Own activity first before turning to these solutions.

On Your Own Solution 7-1 **How to Create a Contacts Document Including Tables**

Follow these steps to create one table ready for contact information:

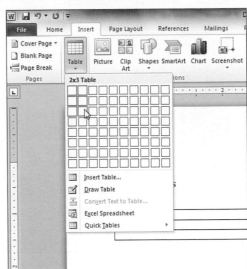

Step 1. Create a new blank document in Word.

Step 2. Type **My Contacts** and apply the **Heading 1** style to the title. Press **Enter** twice.

Step 3. On the Insert ribbon, click **Table**. In the drop-down box that appears, click the third row, second column. A table with two columns and three rows appears in the document.

Step 4. Click the insertion point in the first cell of the table. Enter the following text in the table. Press **Tab** to move from column to column or to create a new row. If you need to go back to a column or row, click a new insertion point.

Company	
Name	
Title	
Phone	
Email	
Address	
Actions	

Step 5. Save the document to your USB flash drive, hard drive, SkyDrive, or another location given by your instructor. Name the document **MyContacts**.

> **Not Working?** If you try to save a document to the hard drive and get an error such as "Path Not Found," most likely you do not have permission to save to the hard drive. Try saving to a USB flash drive instead.

You can change a column width in a table by dragging a column pointer on the horizontal ruler above the document. First, you must select the table. One way to select a table is to use a grabber handle that appears when you mouse over a table. Follow these steps:

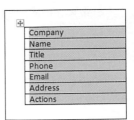

Step 1. Mouse over the table, which causes a box, called a grabber handle, to appear above the upper-left corner of the table. Click the grabber handle to select the entire table. The entire table is highlighted.

> **Hint** When a table is first created or selected, the Table Tools Design tab and Layout tab show up. Use the Layout ribbon to insert or delete rows and columns in the table.

Step 2. With the table highlighted, press and drag the second column pointer in the ruler. Drag the pointer to the left to narrow the column width so that it is about one inch wide. See Figure S7-1.

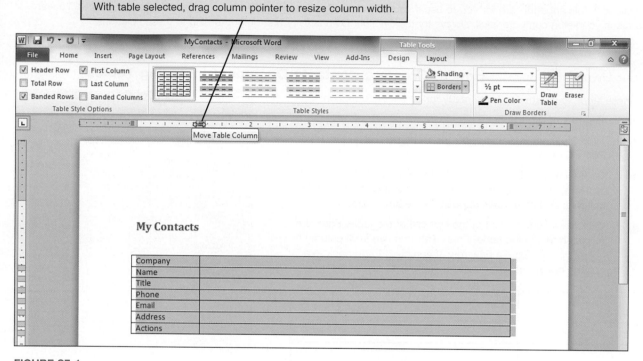

With table selected, drag column pointer to resize column width.

FIGURE S7-1
With the table selected, drag a column pointer on the ruler to resize a column width.

> **Not Working?** If you don't see the rulers, click the View Ruler button on the right side of the Word window.

Step 3. Widen the second column width so that it is about five inches wide.

Follow these steps to make two copies of the table and add data:

Step 1. Press **Ctrl-End** to move the insertion point to the end of the document. Press **Enter** to create a blank line under the table.

Step 2. Select the table again. Right-click on the table and select **Copy** from the shortcut menu.

Step 3. Press **Ctrl-End**. The insertion point is placed at the end of the document. Right-click and select the first **Paste** icon from the shortcut menu. A copy of the table is inserted in the document.

Step 4. Place one more copy of the table in the document.

> **Hint** If two tables in the document join together as one and you want to split them, click in the row where you want to split the table and click **Split Table** on the Layout ribbon.

Step 5. Go back to the first table and enter the contact information for Andy Knight. The contact information can be found in the On Your Own 7-1 activity in the chapter.

Step 6. The text in the second column to the right of Actions needs to be formatted as a bulleted list. Select this text in the second column and click the Bullets icon 🔲 on the Home ribbon. The text becomes a bulleted list, as shown in Figure S7-2.

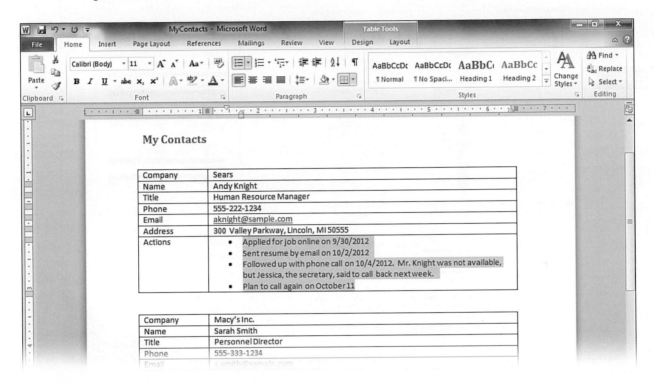

FIGURE S7-2
Format the list of actions as a bulleted list.

Step 7. Enter and format the contact information for **Sarah Smith** in the second table. The contact information can be found in On Your Own 7-1 activity in the chapter.

Step 8. Make sure the document properties show you as the author of the document. Save and close the document.

On Your Own Solution 7-2   **How to Create a Résumé Using a Résumé Template**

The finished résumé for Andrea Champion is shown in Figure 7-4 in the chapter. Follow these steps to create the résumé:

Step 1. In Word, click the **File** tab, select **New**, select **New resume samples**, and then select **Seasonal retail resume sample** (see Figure S7-3). Click **Download**.

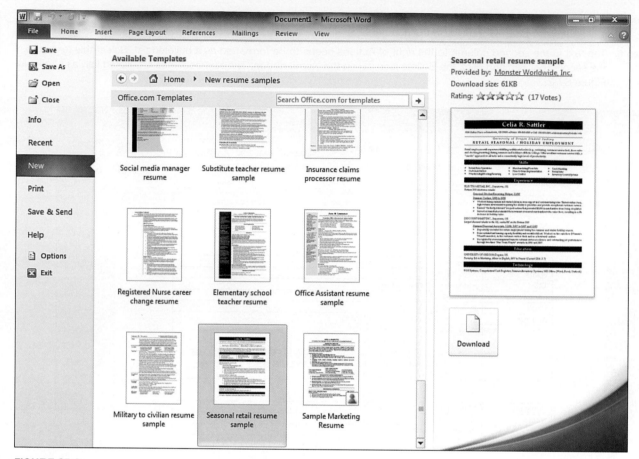

FIGURE S7-3
Download the Seasonal retail resume sample template.

> **Step 2.** When you open the résumé template, you find a text box with instructions for uploading your résumé to Monster.com. Click the border of the text box and then press **Delete**.
>
> **Step 3.** Save the document using the filename **AndreaChampionResume**.
>
> **Step 4.** Referring to the following table, highlight the information on the résumé template (listed on the left side of the table) and type over it with the information on the right side of the table. After the information is highlighted, it is replaced as you type.

Template	Replace With
Celia R. Sattler	Andrea Champion
9358 Sutton Place	138 Walnut Avenue
Sometown, OR 89000	Grand Rapids, MI 49503
555-555-5555	616-555-3825
555-555-5500	616-555-7760
fakename@anydomain.com	andreachampion@sample.com
University of Oregon	University of Michigan

> **Step 5.** Andrea does not have experience in stocking and receiving. To make that change in the Retail Seasonal/Holiday Employment section, change **floor sales and stocking/receiving** to **and floor sales**.

Step 6. The Skills section of the résumé template lists nine skills. Change these nine skills to the six skills that Andrea has:

- Customer Service
- Cash Handling
- Retail Sales
- Inventory
- Display Design
- Gift Wrapping

Step 7. In the Experience section of the résumé, highlight specific information on the template and replace it with the following:

Employer #1	Sears, Roebuck and Co.,
Location	Holland, MI
Type of Company	Department retailer
Job/Dates Performed	Summer/Seasonal Associate, 5/11 to 8/11
Duties	Demonstrated fast learning capacity, flexibility, and versatile skill-set. Worked on the sale floor (Major Appliances), in the customer service desk and as a front-end cashier. Responsible for inventory records for department. Recognized by store management team for customer service excellence and outstanding job performance through the "Rising Star" award in July 2011.
Employer #2	JC Penney Company, Inc.
Location	Holland, MI
Type of Company	Department retailer
Job/Dates Performed	Gift Wrapping, 10/10 to 12/10
Duties	N/A (leave blank)
Job/Dates Performed	Seasonal Customer Service Desk, 1/11
Duties	Worked during the Fall and Winter breaks in the Gift Wrapping department. Thrived during the fast-paced holiday seasons providing exceptional and expedient customer service. Worked in the Customer Service department after the holiday season. Assisted with returns and exchanges until the end of Winter break.

Step 8. In the Education section, use the following table to make the necessary changes to the résumé.

Template	Replace With
UNIVERSITY OF OREGON	UNIVERSITY OF MICHIGAN
Eugene, OR	Grand Rapids, MI
BA in Marketing	Pursuing BS in Psychology
Minor in English	Minor in Music
8/07 to Present	8/10 to Present
Current GPA: 3.7	Current GPA: 3.2

Step 9. In the Technology section of the résumé, change the technologies listed to:

POS Systems

Computerized Cash Registers

Inventory Control Systems

MS Office (Word, OneNote, Outlook)

Step 10. Save the document.

Step 11. Save the document again, this time as a PDF file. Name the PDF file **AndreaChampionResume**. If you need help saving the document as a PDF, see On Your Own Solution 3-13 in Chapter 3 Solutions, "Creating Documents with Microsoft Word."

On Your Own Solution 7-3   How to Email a Résumé PDF

Follow these steps to send an email message with the résumé PDF attached and request a read receipt:

Step 1. Open Outlook. Create a new email message. Type **Interested in Holiday Employment** in the subject line.

Step 2. Type the body of the email message. You can find the message in the On Your Own 7-3 activity in the chapter.

Step 3. Double-check the message for errors.

Step 4. On the Message ribbon, click **Attach File**. The Insert File box opens. Locate the **AndreaChampionResume.pdf** file. See Figure S7-4.

Step 5. Click **Insert**. The file is listed in the Attached field.

Step 6. Click the **Options** tab and select **Request a Read Receipt**. The receipt is emailed to you when the receiver opens the message and agrees to send the read receipt.

Step 7. Type your teacher's email address in the To field. Click **Send** to send the message.

Tip Leave the To field blank until you have double-checked your message for errors. Even if you accidently click **Send** before it is perfect, the email won't go to the potential employer.

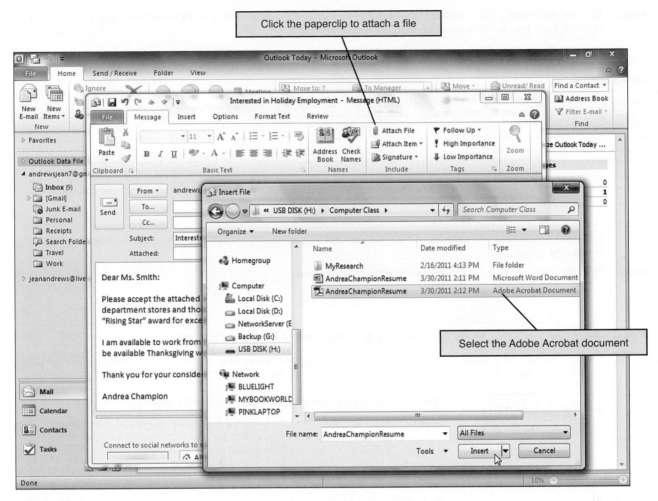

FIGURE S7-4
Be sure to attach the PDF file and not the Word document file to the email message.

On Your Own Solution 7-4   **How to Create a Personal Letterhead for Business Letters**

Follow these steps to create a personal letterhead document:

Step 1.   In Word, click the File tab and click **New**. Under Office.com Templates, click **Letterhead**. Click **Business letter-head (Level design)**. Click **Download**. A new document opens.

Step 2.   To open the header, click the **Insert** tab, click **Header**, and click **Edit Header**. Select the **YOUR LOGO HERE** box and delete it. Replace **Company Name** with **Andrea Champion**. To close the header, click **Close Header and Footer** on the Design ribbon or double-click somewhere outside the header area.

Tip For your own personal letterhead, you can insert a photo of yourself in place of the YOUR LOGO HERE box.

Step 3. To open the footer, click the **Insert** tab, click **Footer**, and click **Edit Footer**. The footer is divided into four parts. Replace each part with the information in the following table:

Template	Replace With
Street Address	138 Walnut Avenue
Address 2	Grand Rapids, MI 49503
Phone: 555.555.0125	Home: 616.555.3825 Cell: 616.555.7760
Email address	andreachampion@sample.com

Step 4. Word might format the email address as a hyperlink. If it does that, remove the hyperlink. Right-click the address and click **Remove Hyperlink** in the shortcut menu.

Step 5. The font size of the footer is 8 point, which is a little small. Select all the text in the footer and change the font size to **9** point. To close the footer, click **Close Header and Footer** on the Design ribbon or double-click somewhere outside the footer area.

Step 6. Save the document, naming it **AndreaChampionLetterhead**.

On Your Own Solution 7-5   How to Create an Interview Follow-up Letter

Not all letterhead templates work the same way. The template we're using provides a structure for you to enter the details of a business letter, and useful styles are also provided. Do the following to use the letterhead to create an interview follow-up letter:

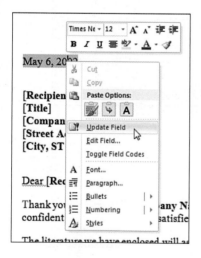

Step 1. If necessary, open the **AndreaChampionLetterhead** document.

Step 2. Click the File tab and click **Save As**. Name the new document file **SarahSmith**. Save the document to your USB flash drive, hard drive, SkyDrive, or other location given by your instructor.

Step 3. Right-click the date and select **Update Field** from the shortcut menu. Today's date appears.

Step 4. Replace the inside address fields as shown in the following table:

Template	Replace With
[Recipient Name]	Ms. Sarah Smith
[Title]	Personnel Director
[Company Name]	Macy's Inc.
[Street Address]	1603 Commerce Way, Suite 200
[City, ST ZIP Code]	Grand Rapids, MI 49500

Step 5. In the salutation, replace [Recipient Name] with **Ms. Smith**.

Step 6. Select the three paragraphs in the body of the letter (see Figure S7-5) and delete the selected text. Save the document.

Step 7. Without closing the SarahSmith document, click the **File** tab and click **New**. In the templates, click **Letters**. Click **Employment and resignation letters**. Click **Interview letters**. Click **Thank you for interview**. Click **Download**. The document appears (see Figure S7-6). After you see the body of the text that was used as a guide to create the body of the letter to Ms. Smith, close the document without saving it.

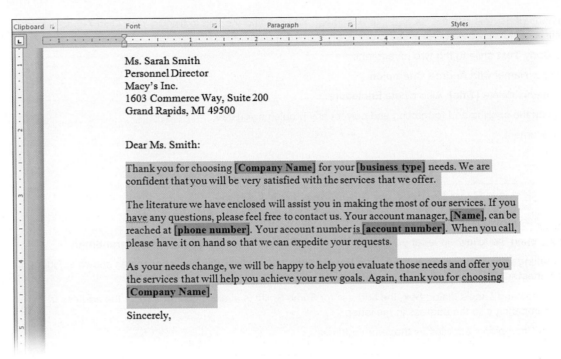

Ms. Sarah Smith
Personnel Director
Macy's Inc.
1603 Commerce Way, Suite 200
Grand Rapids, MI 49500

Dear Ms. Smith:

Thank you for choosing [Company Name] for your [business type] needs. We are confident that you will be very satisfied with the services that we offer.

The literature we have enclosed will assist you in making the most of our services. If you have any questions, please feel free to contact us. Your account manager, [Name], can be reached at [phone number]. Your account number is [account number]. When you call, please have it on hand so that we can expedite your requests.

As your needs change, we will be happy to help you evaluate those needs and offer you the services that will help you achieve your new goals. Again, thank you for choosing [Company Name].

Sincerely,

FIGURE S7-5
Select and delete the body of the letter.

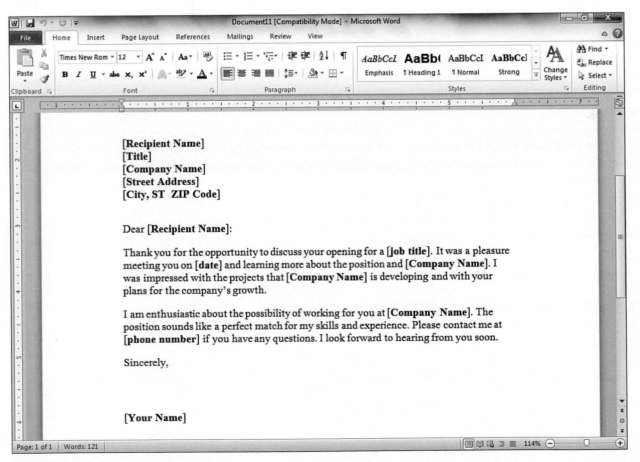

[Recipient Name]
[Title]
[Company Name]
[Street Address]
[City, ST ZIP Code]

Dear [Recipient Name]:

Thank you for the opportunity to discuss your opening for a [job title]. It was a pleasure meeting you on [date] and learning more about the position and [Company Name]. I was impressed with the projects that [Company Name] is developing and with your plans for the company's growth.

I am enthusiastic about the possibility of working for you at [Company Name]. The position sounds like a perfect match for my skills and experience. Please contact me at [phone number] if you have any questions. I look forward to hearing from you soon.

Sincerely,

[Your Name]

FIGURE S7-6
A letter template can help you write the body of a business letter.

Step 8. Type the body of the text into the SarahSmith document. You can find the text in the On Your Own 7-5 activity in the chapter. It is not repeated here. Press **Enter** once after each paragraph.

Step 9. Apply the **Body Text** style to the two paragraphs.

Step 10. Replace [Your Name] with **Andrea Champion**.

Step 11. Below the name, delete **[Title]**. Also delete **Enclosure:**.

Step 12. Double-check the spelling and formatting and correct any problems you see.

Step 13. Save the document.

On Your Own Solution 7-6   How to Add an Envelope to a Letter

Follow these steps to add an envelope to a letter:

Step 1. If necessary, open the follow-up letter you wrote for Andrea Champion to Ms. Smith named **SarahSmith**.

Step 2. Click the **Mailings** tab and click **Envelopes**. The **Envelopes and Labels** dialog box appears, as shown in Figure 7-10 in the chapter.

Step 3. In the Envelopes and Labels dialog box, the address for Sarah Smith is already entered. Verify the address is correct by comparing it to the address in the letter.

Step 4. Enter Andrea Champion's address as the return address:

> Andrea Champion
>
> 138 Walnut Avenue
>
> Grand Rapids, MI 49503

Step 5. Click **Add to Document**. A dialog box appears asking whether you want to save the new return address as the default return address. Click **No**.

Step 6. The envelope appears as the first page of the document (see Figure S7-7). Save the document.

Step 7. If you have access to a printer and an envelope, insert the envelope in the printer. Orient the envelope according to the instructions in your printer manual. Print the document. The envelope prints first, followed by the letter.

Step 8. To see the print preview of the envelope and document, click the **File** tab and click **Print**. The print preview appears.

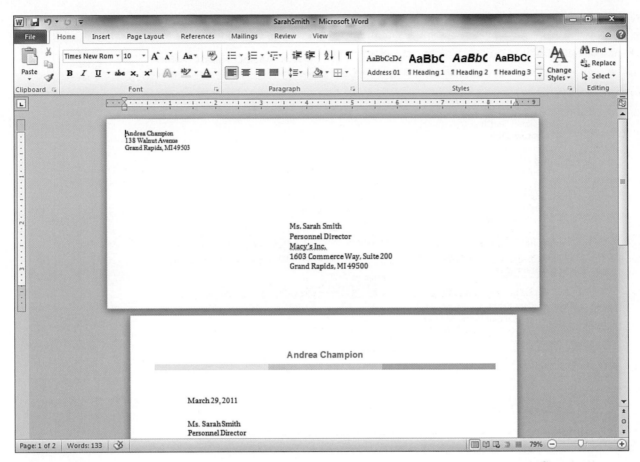

FIGURE S7-7
An envelope has been added as the first page of the document.

On Your Own Solution 7-7   How to Email the Follow-up Letter

Follow these steps to email the follow-up letter:

Step 1. In Word, open the follow-up letter you wrote for Andrea Champion named **SarahSmith**.

Step 2. Press and drag to select the text beginning with *Dear Ms. Smith* through the name *Andrea Champion.* Right-click the selected text and click **Copy** from the shortcut menu (see Figure S7-8). The text copies to the Windows Clipboard.

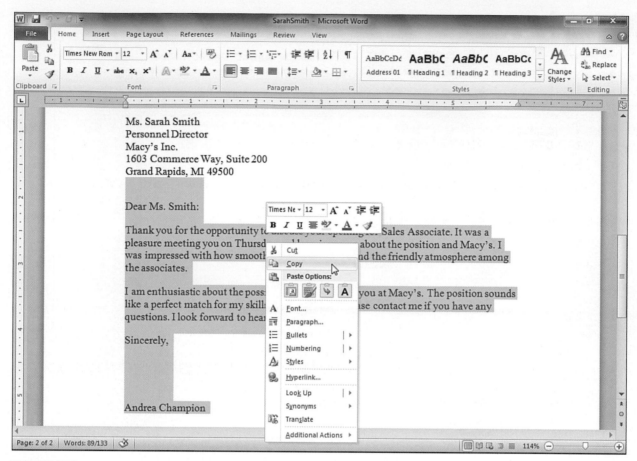

FIGURE S7-8
Select the portion of the follow-up letter to be inserted in an email message.

Hint Besides using a shortcut menu, you can press **Ctrl-C** to copy selected text.

Step 3. In Outlook, create a new email message. In the body of the message, right-click and select **Paste** from the shortcut menu. The text is copied into the message.

Step 4. To remove the text formatting, press **Ctrl-A** to select all the text in the message. Then click the **Clear Formatting** button on the Message ribbon.

Step 5. Insert a double-space following the salutation and each of the two paragraphs.

Step 6. Insert Andrea's cell phone number below her name at the bottom of the message: **Cell: 616-555-7760**.

Step 7. Type **Sales Associate Position** in the subject line of the email.

Step 8. Double-check the spelling and formatting and correct any problems you see.

Step 9. Type your instructor's email address in the **To:** field and send the email to your instructor.

CHAPTER 8 SOLUTIONS
Using PowerPoint to Give a Presentation

The solutions in this appendix are for you to use if you get stuck when doing an On Your Own activity in the chapter. To learn how to teach yourself a computer skill, always try the On Your Own activity first before turning to these solutions.

On Your Own Solution 8-1   How to Explore the PowerPoint Window

Follow these steps to learn about the PowerPoint window:

Step 1. To open PowerPoint, click **Start**, **All Programs**, **Microsoft Office**, and **Microsoft PowerPoint 2010**. Maximize the window.

Step 2. To change views in the Slide/Outline pane on the left, click **Slides** or **Outline** at the top of the pane.

> **Not Working?** If you don't see the Slide/Outline pane on your window, click **Normal** on the View ribbon.

Step 3. To see a ribbon, click the ribbon tab.

Step 4. To add a new slide, click the **Home** tab and click **New Slide**.

Step 5. To add a third slide that uses the Comparison layout, click the down arrow next to New Slide. In the list that appears, click **Comparison**. The Comparison slide layout has five text boxes.

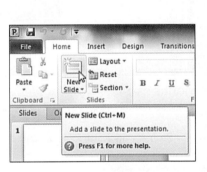

Step 6. To open PowerPoint Help, click the Help icon in the upper-right corner of the window.

Step 7. To find out how to apply a theme, type **apply a theme** in the Help search box and press **Enter**. In the list that appears, click **Apply a theme to add color and style to your presentation**.

Step 8. To find out how to add slide numbers to a presentation, type **slide numbers** in the Help search box and press **Enter**.

Step 9. To close the presentation without saving your changes, click the **File** tab. Click **Close**. In the dialog box that appears, click **Don't Save**.

On Your Own Solution 8-2   How to Choose a Theme

Follow these steps to open a blank presentation:

Step 1. If PowerPoint is not open, open it. A blank presentation is automatically created.

Step 2. If PowerPoint is already open and you need to create a blank presentation, click the **File** tab. Click **New**, click **Blank presentation**, and click **Create**. A blank presentation is created.

Step 3. Maximize the window.

Follow these steps to apply a theme to the presentation:

Step 1. Click the **Design** tab. Click the More arrow to the right of the themes to see more themes. In the gallery of themes, click the **Flow** theme to apply it to all slides.

Hint The name of a theme appears when you move your mouse pointer over a theme.

Step 2. To view the color schemes of the Flow theme, click **Colors** on the Design ribbon. Mouse over the colors and watch how the colors change on the title slide. Click off the color gallery so it disappears.

Step 3. Click **Background Styles**. Click **Style 3** (see Figure S8-1).

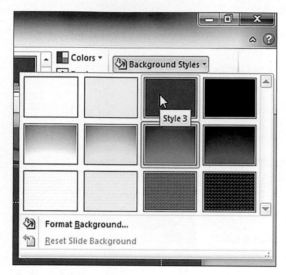

FIGURE S8-1
Choose a background style that will apply to all slides.

Step 4. Click the **File** tab and change the author to your name.

Hint If you need help changing the author to your name, refer to On Your Own Solution 3-7 in Chapter 3 of this *Solutions Appendix*.

Step 5. Save the PowerPoint file to the hard drive, USB flash drive, SkyDrive, or other location.

Hint Saving a file in PowerPoint works the same as it does in Word. If you need help, see the instructions in On Your Own Solution 3-3 in Chapter 3 of this *Solutions Appendix*.

On Your Own Solution 8-3   How to Create a Title Slide

Follow these steps to create the title slide, which is shown in the chapter in Figure 8-7:

Step 1. Click in the first text box and type **What Motivates Us**.

Step 2. Press and drag to select the text. With the text selected, click the **Home** tab. Click the **Increase Font Size** button A˄ to increase the font size. Keep clicking until the title fills the text box without spilling over to a new line.

Hint If the font size is too big, click the **Decrease Font Size** button. A˅

Step 3. Click in the second text box and type **By Jawana Washington**.

Step 4. Select the text. In the font size box on the Home ribbon, select **40** points. Click the **Bold** button to bold the text.

Follow these steps to add a text box and the Einstein quote:

Step 1. Click the **Insert** tab and click **Text Box**. Press and drag to create a text box near the bottom of the slide. In the text box, type the following text:

"Try not to become a person of success, but rather a person of value."

Albert Einstein

Step 2. Select all the text in the text box. Set the font size to **32** points. If necessary, resize and move the text box so all the text fits on the slide.

Step 3. Click somewhere in the name **Albert Einstein**. Click the **Align Text Right** button ≡ on the Home ribbon.

Step 4. Select the text **Albert Einstein**. Click the **Italic** button I on the Home ribbon.

Step 5. Compare the slide to that shown in Figure 8-7 in the chapter and correct any problems you see. You might need to move the third text box so the quote is in the right position.

Hint To move a text box, click on the box to select it. Mouse over the edge of the box until your pointer changes to a cross and arrow. ✛ Press and drag to move the box.

Follow these steps to finish the slide:

Step 1. Speaker notes are typed in the notes pane at the bottom of the slide labeled *Click to add notes*. To increase the height of this pane, press and drag the top of the pane upward. Type the following in the pane:

Motivated people tend to be happier and produce more than others.

We all need to know our strongest motivators.

Step 2. To view the slide as it appears in a slide show, click the **Slide Show** tab. Click **From Current Slide**. Press **Escape** to return to Normal view.

Step 3. To save your work, click the **Save** button ⊟ in the title bar of the PowerPoint window.

On Your Own Solution 8-4   How to Add a Slide with a Bulleted List and Graphics

Do the following to create the second slide:

Step 1. On the Home ribbon, click the arrow beneath the New Slide button and click the **Title and Content** slide. A new slide is added to the presentation.

Step 2. Click inside the first text box and type **Others Motivate Us**. Select the text and click the **Increase Font Size** button A on the Home ribbon. Keep clicking until the title fills the text box.

Step 3. Click in the second text box and type the following text:

Incentives

Reward

Punishment

Step 4. Select the last two lines of text and click the **Increase List Level** button.

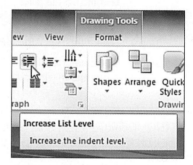

Step 5. Click an insertion point before **Incentives** and press the **Backspace** key to delete the bullet.

Step 6. Select all three lines of text and set the font size to **32** points.

Step 7. The two bullets are blue against a blue background. To correct the problem, select the last two lines of text. Click the down arrow next to the Bullets icon. Click **Bullets and Numbering** in the drop-down list. In the Bullets and Numbering box, change the color to **White**.

Follow these steps to insert a clip art photo about rewards:

Step 1. On the Insert ribbon, click **Clip Art**. The Clip Art box appears. Enter **grade A+** in the search box. Click the down arrow under *Results should be*. Uncheck **All media types**. Check **Photographs**. Then click **Go**.

Step 2. Click a photo. It then appears on the slide. Press and drag a corner sizing handle to resize the photo and to keep proportions the same. Make the size about the same as that in Figure S8-2.

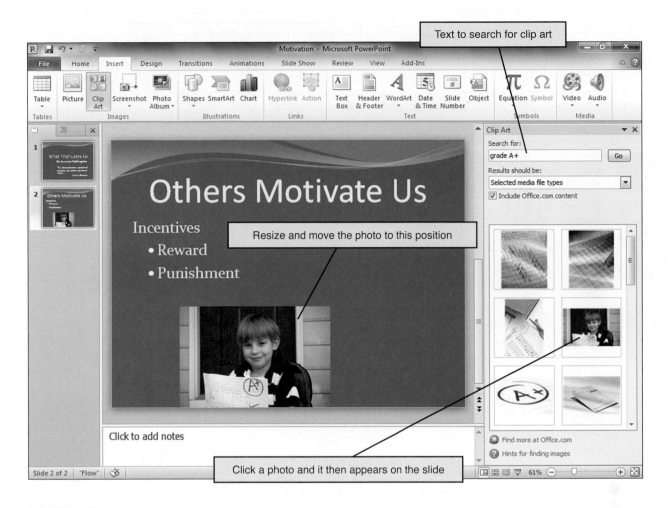

FIGURE S8-2
Resize and position the photo that represents rewards.

> **Step 3.** Press and drag to move the photo to the position shown in the figure. Align the bottom of the photo with the bottom of the slide.

Follow these steps to insert a clip art photo about punishment:

> **Step 1.** Following the directions above, search for a clip art photo on punishment. Enter **punishment** in the Clip Art search box. Resize and position the photo as you see in Figure S8-3. Align the photo along the side of the slide.

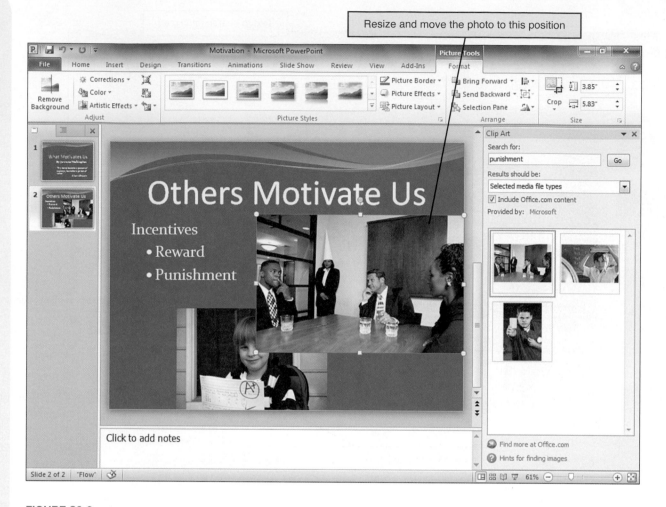

FIGURE S8-3
Resize and position the photo that represents punishment.

> **Step 2.** To send the photo behind the photo about rewards, right click the punishment photo. On the shortcut menu, click **Send to Back**.

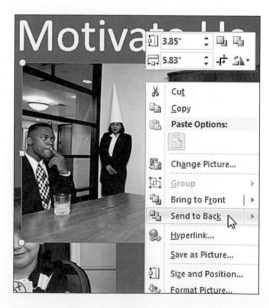

To insert and format the star shape, follow these steps:

Step 1. On the Insert ribbon, click **Shapes**. In the drop-down list, click **24-Point Star**. Your pointer changes to a cross $+$. Press and drag to draw the star on the slide. The star overlaps the photo about rewards.

Step 2. Right-click the star. In the formatting box that appears, click the down arrow next to the Shape Fill button. Under Standard Colors, click **Orange** (see Figure S8-4). You can also use the Shape Fill command on the Format ribbon to change the fill color.

FIGURE S8-4
Set the fill color to orange.

Step 3. Right-click the shape and click **Edit Text** in the shortcut menu. An insertion point appears in the star. Type **Star Student**.

Step 4. Select the text. Use tools on the Home ribbon to set the text color to **Black** and the font size to **28** points.

Step 5. Press and drag a corner sizing handle to resize the star so the text fits.

Step 6. Press and drag the green rotating handle to rotate the star.

Step 7. Compare your slide to that in Figure 8-8 in the chapter and correct any problems you see.

Step 8. To view the slide as it will appear in a slide show, click the **Slide Show** tab and click **From Current Slide**. Press **Escape** to return to Normal view.

Follow these steps to finish the slide:

Step 1. In the notes pane below the slide, enter the following speaker notes:

Carrot in front of us. Stick behind us.

Step 2. Select the word **Carrot** and bold it. Select the word **Stick** and bold it.

Step 3. Save your work.

On Your Own Solution 8-5 How to Add a Slide with SmartArt

Follow these steps to add a slide with SmartArt:

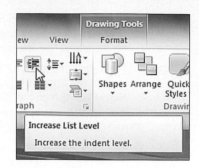

Step 1. Click the **New Slide** button 🗔 on the Home ribbon. A new slide is added.

Step 2. Type **We Motivate Ourselves** in the first text box. Select the text and increase the font size to fill the space.

Step 3. Click in the second text box. Click the **Insert** tab and click **SmartArt**. The Choose a SmartArt Graphic box appears.

Step 4. Scroll down a bit and click **Vertical Curved List** (see Figure S8-5). Click **OK** to insert the SmartArt.

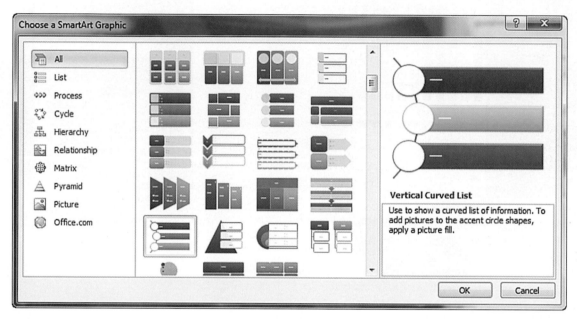

FIGURE S8-5
Choose the SmartArt graphic.

Step 5. When the SmartArt is selected, you can see the SmartArt container box, as shown in Figure S8-6. In the figure, you can also see the SmartArt text pane where you can type, view, and format the text in the SmartArt graphic. Type **Mastery** for the first bullet in the text pane.

> **Tip** You can also type directly in the text boxes inside the SmartArt container box.

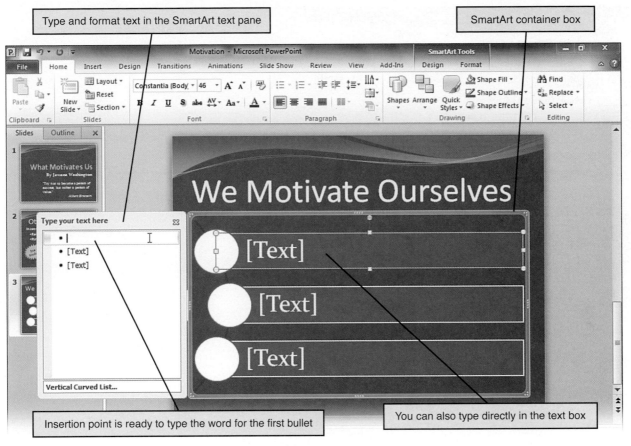

FIGURE S8-6
SmartArt provides a text pane you use to type, view, and format the text in the SmartArt graphic.

Step 6. Click in the next text area and type **Independence**.

Step 7. Click in the third text area and type **Contribution**.

Step 8. Using the SmartArt text pane, press and drag to select the three lines of text. Then use the Home ribbon to set the font size to **54** points and to center and bold the text.

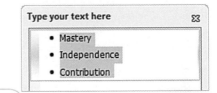

Not Working? If you accidentally close the SmartArt text pane, first select the SmartArt so the SmartArt container box appears. Then click the bar on the left side of the SmartArt container box. The text pane appears. You can also click **Text Pane** on the Design ribbon.

Step 9. With the SmartArt still selected, click the **Design** tab. Click **Change Colors**. Click **Colorful - Accent Colors**, as shown in Figure S8-7.

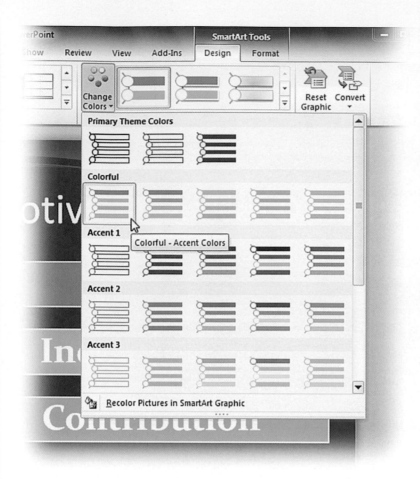

FIGURE S8-7
Change the colors of the SmartArt elements.

> **Step 10.** Compare the slide to that shown in Figure 8-9 in the chapter and correct any problems you see. View the slide as it will appear in a slide show and correct any problems.

Follow these steps to enter speaker notes for this slide:

> **Step 1.** Increase the height of the notes pane below the slide.

> **Step 2.** Type the following text into the notes pane:

Mastery

Opportunity to do something very well

Independence

Right to make our own decisions

Decide what, when, how, and with whom we work

Contribution

Make a difference for others

This is the most powerful motivator

Step 3. Select **Mastery** and use the Home ribbon to bold it. Also bold **Independence** and **Contribution**.

Step 4. Click on the second line and then click the **Increase List Level** button 🔲 on the Home ribbon to indent the line. Do the same for other lines in the notes that need indenting.

Step 5. Save your work.

On Your Own Solution 8-6   **How to Add the Final Slide with Artistic Effects**

Follow these steps to insert the slide and add the title:

Step 1. On the Home ribbon, click the arrow beside **New Slide**. In the drop-down list of slide layouts, select **Title Only**. A new slide is added.

Step 2. In the text box, type the title **How Do You Find Flow?**

Step 3. Using the Home ribbon, apply this formatting to the title:

    a. Select the word **Flow** and set it to italic.

    b. Select all the text in the title. Change the text color to black.

    c. Right-justify the text. Set the font size to **66** points.

    d. Notice the text sits on the bottom of the text box. To align the text with the top of the text box, click the **Align text** button in the Paragraph group (see Figure S8-8). Then click **Top**.

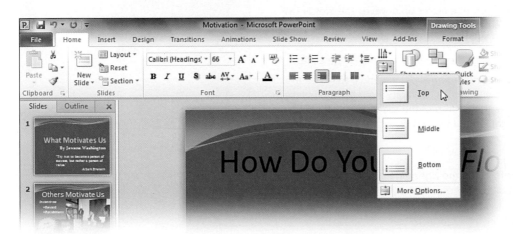

FIGURE S8-8
Align the text with the top of the text box.

Step 4. Press and drag the lower-left corner sizing handle to resize the text box so text wrap causes the text to flow to three lines (see Figure S8-9).

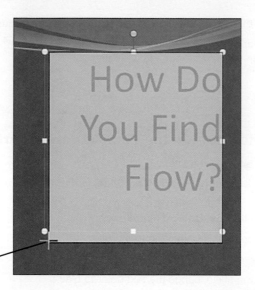

Grab the lower-left corner sizing handle.

FIGURE S8-9
Resize the text box to make the title wrap to three lines.

Follow these steps to insert a clip art photo and format the photo:

Step 1. Insert a clip art photograph of a surfer on a wave. The words **riding a wave** can be used in the clip art search box. The photo is inserted in the center of the slide.

Step 2. Press and drag the photo to the upper-left corner of the slide.

Step 3. Press and drag the lower-right corner sizing handle to resize the photo so that it fills the entire slide, covering even the title. Make sure the photo reaches the bottom of the slide. As you do so, the photo spills off the right side of the slide.

Hint You don't need to cut off (crop) the right side of the photo that spills off the slide. However, if you want to crop a photo, first select the photo. Then click **Crop** on the Format ribbon.

Step 4. Right-click the photo. In the shortcut menu, click **Send to Back**. The title appears on top of the photo.

Step 5. With the photo still selected, click the **Format** tab. Click **Artistic Effects**. In the drop-down gallery of effects, click **Glow Diffused** (see Figure S8-10).

FIGURE S8-10
Artistic effects can make a photo more interesting and appealing.

> **Step 6.** With the photo still selected, click the **Format** tab and click **Color**. Then click **Turquoise Accent color 3 Dark** (see Figure S8-11).

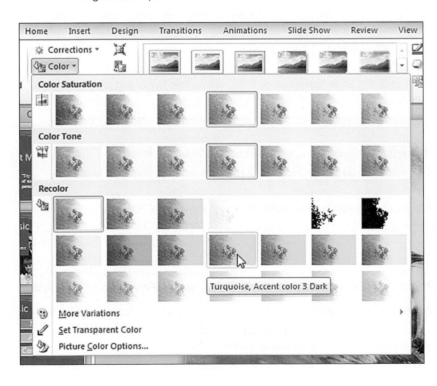

FIGURE S8-11
Apply color to a photo.

Step 7. Compare the slide to that shown in Figure 8-11 in the chapter and correct any problems you see. View the slide as it will appear in a slide show and correct any problems.

Follow these steps to complete the slide and speaker notes:

Step 1. The last slide invites the audience to apply the presentation to their own lives. You can ask questions to encourage thought and discussion. Enter the following notes in the notes pane for this slide:

> To know what motivates you, look for flow in your life.
>
> Flow is when you "lose yourself" in what you're doing.
>
> When do you lose track of time and are not aware of distractions?
>
> What are you doing? Where are you? Who are you with? When does this flow stop?

Step 2. To format the notes, bold the word **flow** and indent all but the first line of text.

Step 3. Save your work.

On Your Own Solution 8-7   How to Review and Revise the Presentation

Follow these directions to practice revising a presentation:

Step 1. Click a slide in the Slide/Outline pane to move to it.

Step 2. To use the spell checker, click **Spelling** on the Review ribbon. Then use the Spelling dialog box to step through any words that PowerPoint thinks are misspelled.

Step 3. Use the Slide/Outline pane to move a slide. Press and drag the slide up or down to a new position. Then return it to its original location.

Step 4. On the View ribbon, click **Slide Sorter** or click the Slide Sorter button in the status bar. Press and drag to move a slide. Then return it to its original location.

Step 5. To insert a new slide following the first slide, right-click the first slide in the Slide/Outline pane. Then click **New Slide** in the shortcut menu.

Step 6. To delete a slide, right-click it in the Slide/Outline pane. Then click **Delete Slide** in the shortcut menu.

Step 7. To view slides in the Notes Page view, click the **View** tab and then click **Notes Page**. Click **Normal** to return to Normal view.

Step 8. To view your presentation as a slide show, click the Slide Show button 🖳 in the status bar. Use the up- and down-arrow keys to step though all the slides.

On Your Own Solution 8-8   How to Print the Presentation and Save as a PowerPoint Show

Follow these steps to find out about printing a presentation and to print:

Step 1. Click the **File** tab. Click **Print**. Slides appear on the screen and print in shades of black and white (called grayscale). If you want to print in color, click the down arrow next to Grayscale and click **Color**.

Step 2. To see how you can print handouts, click the down arrow next to **Full Page Slides**. Print Layout options appear (see Figure S8-12).

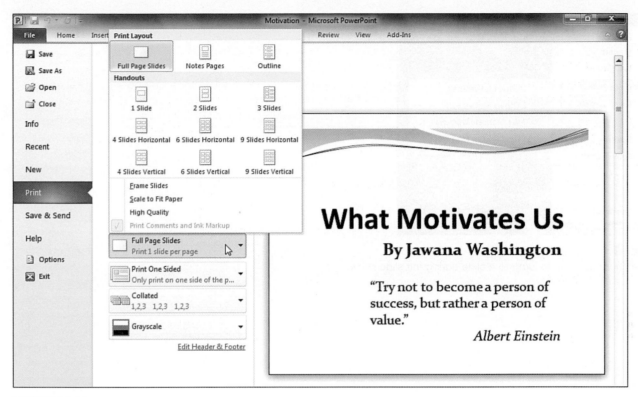

FIGURE S8-12
Select a method to use for printing the slides.

Step 3. Under Handouts, click **3 Slides**. The write-on lines next to the slide are for your audience to take notes during the presentation. To print the handouts, make sure your printer is selected and click **Print**.

Step 4. Click **3 Slides**. In the list of Print Layout options, click **Notes Pages**. The preview shows that one slide prints to a page with speaker notes printed under the slide. To print the notes, click **Print**.

Follow these steps to create and use a PowerPoint show:

Step 1. If necessary, click the **File** tab. Click **Save As**. The Save As dialog box appears. Click the down arrow next to *Save as type* and click **PowerPoint Show**.

Step 2. In the *File name* box, type **MotivationShow**. Click **Save**. The presentation is saved as a slide show, and the file extension is .ppsx.

Step 3. Close the PowerPoint window.

Step 4. Open Windows Explorer. Locate and double-click the file **MotivationShow**. The show starts and the title slide appears. Use the down-arrow key to step to the next slide.

Step 5. To jump to a slide, right-click a slide in the show. Click **Go to Slide** in the shortcut menu. In the list of slides that appears, click the slide you want to see (see Figure S8-13).

Step 6. To end the show, press the **Escape** key.

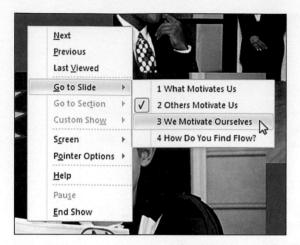

FIGURE S8-13
Use the shortcut menu to jump to a slide during the slide show.

CHAPTER 9 SOLUTIONS
Adding Action and Sound to a PowerPoint Presentation

The solutions in this appendix are for you to use if you get stuck when doing an On Your Own activity in the chapter. To learn how to teach yourself a computer skill, always try the On Your Own activity first before turning to these solutions.

On Your Own Solution 9-1   **How to Edit the Slide Master**

Follow these steps to add shapes to the slide master:

Step 1. Open a new blank presentation in PowerPoint.

Step 2. Click the **View** tab and click **Slide Master**. The Slide Master view opens. Click the first thumbnail in the left pane, which is the slide master.

Step 3. On the Insert ribbon, click **Shapes** and click the **Freeform** shape. Your pointer changes to a crosshair. +

Step 4. Press and drag to draw a jagged long shape on the left side of the master slide. First draw down and then draw up. When the end of the line overlaps the beginning of the line, double-click to stop the drawing. The shape is created and is selected.

Step 5. Right-click the shape and click **Format Shape** in the shortcut menu (see Figure S9-1).

Not Working? If you right-click and a different shortcut menu appears other than the one in Figure S9-1, click off the menu and try again. Most likely, you did not right-click exactly on the shape.

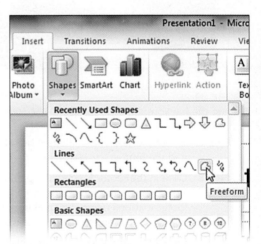

FIGURE S9-1
Right-click a shape to see the shortcut menu for the shape.

Step 6. In the Format Shape box, click **Fill** and click **Solid Fill**. Change the fill color to **Dark Red**.

Step 7. Click **Line Color** and click **No line**. To close the box, click **Close**.

Step 8. To add the second shape on the right side of the slide master, you can copy the first shape and paste it on the right, or you can draw a new shape.

> **Hint** To copy an object, right-click it and select **Copy** from the shortcut menu. To paste it, right-click the slide and select **Paste** from the shortcut menu. Then drag the new object to its correct position.

Follow these steps to format the background and text on the slide master:

Step 1. On the Slide Master ribbon, click **Background Styles** and click **Style 4** (see Figure S9-2). The background is now black.

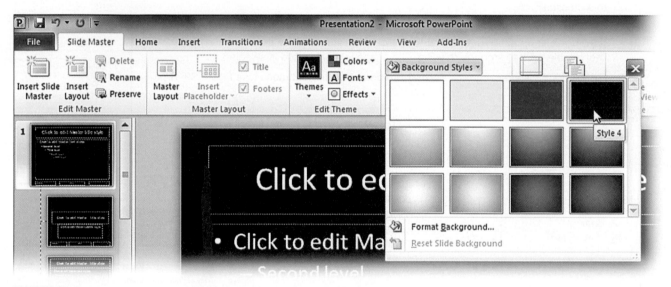

FIGURE S9-2
Change the background style to black.

Step 2. Select the text in the title text box. Click the **Home** tab. Change the font to **Trebuchet MS**, the font color to **White**, and the font size to **44** points.

Step 3. Click in the footer text box. The text disappears, but don't worry, you are still changing the formatting in this box. On the Home ribbon, format the footer text box using the **Chiller** font, **Dark Red**, and **32** points. When you click outside the box, you can see the footer text is formatted.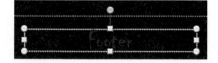

Step 4. Click the **Slide Master** tab and click **Close Master View**.

Step 5. Click the **Home** tab. Click the down arrow next to the New Slide button. Slide layouts appear. Each layout should have the red shapes and black background.

> **Not Working?** If the design is not applied to all layouts, most likely you made changes to a slide master layout and not to the slide master. Return to Slide Master view and click the first thumbnail in the left pane. All your work should be done on this slide.

Step 6. Save the presentation to your hard drive, USB flash drive, SkyDrive, or another location, naming the file **GarageBand**. A PowerPoint presentation file is saved the same way as a Word document file. If you need help saving the file, see On Your Own Solution 3-3 in Chapter 3 of this appendix.

On Your Own Solution 9-2   **How to Add Video to the Title Slide**

Follow these steps to add text to the title slide:

Step 1. On the title slide, enter the title **Out of the Garage Onto the Road**.

Step 2. Select the text and format it using the **Chiller** font, **80** point, **Dark Red**.

Step 3. Press and drag the rotating handle to rotate the text box to the left so the box tilts downward to the left.

Step 4. If necessary, press and drag the lower-right corner sizing handle to shorten the width of the text box. When you do that, the text wraps to two lines, as shown in Figure S9-3.

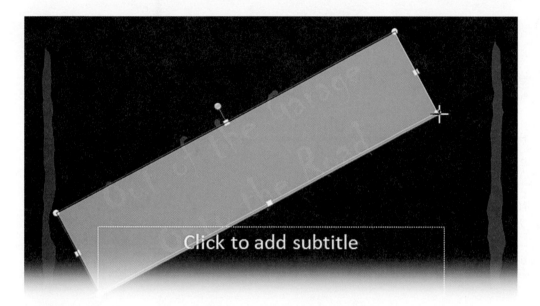

FIGURE S9-3
Resize the text box using the bottom-right corner sizing handle.

Step 5. Move the text box to the top-left area of the slide.

Step 6. Enter the subtitle **By Aimee Peters**. With the text box selected, click the **Align Text Right** button ≡ on the Home ribbon. Move the text box up to make room for the video box below the text box.

Follow these steps to add a video clip to the slide:

Step 1. Insert the DVD from the back of the book into your optical drive. If the AutoPlay box opens, close the box.

Step 2. On the Insert ribbon, click **Video**. The Insert Video box appears. Locate the file **RockBand** in the Sample Files folder on the DVD (see Figure S9-4). Click **Insert**. The video box appears on the slide.

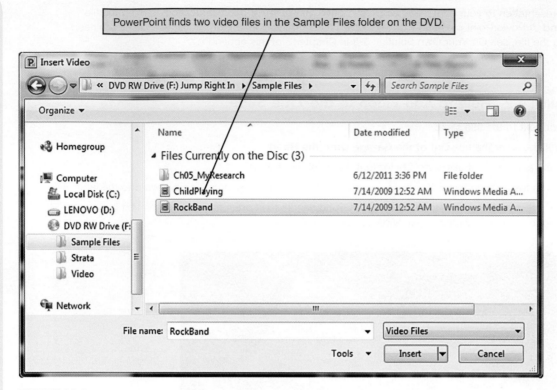

PowerPoint finds two video files in the Sample Files folder on the DVD.

FIGURE S9-4
Find the RockBand video file in the Sample Files folder on the DVD.

> **Step 3.** Resize and position the video box as shown in the chapter in Figure 9-6.
>
> **Step 4.** To test the video, click the video box. The controls at the bottom of the box appear. Click the **Play** button. ▶ The video plays.
>
> **Step 5.** To test the slide, click the **Slide Show** button 🖵 at the bottom of the PowerPoint window. Click the video box and play the video. Press **Escape** to close the slide show.
>
> **Step 6.** Save your work.

On Your Own Solution 9-3   How to Create the Second Slide with Audio and Animation

Follow these steps to add the second slide with a title, footer, and bulleted list:

> **Step 1.** On the Home ribbon, click the down arrow next to New Slide and select the **Two Content** slide layout.
>
> **Step 2.** Enter the slide title: **Start with the Press Kit**.
>
> **Step 3.** To add the footer, on the Insert ribbon, click **Header & Footer**. The Header and Footer box opens.
>
> **Step 4.** Check **Footer** and add the text **Out of the Garage onto the Road**. Check **Don't show on title slide**, as shown in Figure S9-5.

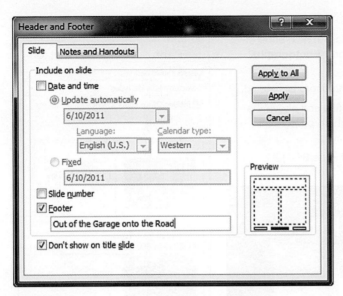

FIGURE S9-5
Type the footer to go on every slide except the title slide.

> **Step 5.** To apply the footer to all slides except the title slide, click **Apply to All**.

> **Step 6.** Notice the footer is using text wrap and fills two lines. To fix this problem, press and drag each side of the text box so that it is wide enough for the footer to fit on one line (see Figure S9-6).

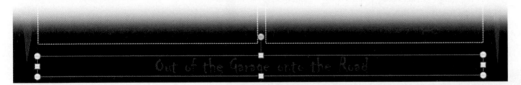

FIGURE S9-6
Widen the footer text box and center it on the slide.

> **Hint** If the text box is centered on the slide as shown in the figure, the footer text is centered on the slide.

> **Step 7.** Click in the text box on the right side of the slide and enter the following text:

Band bio and photo

Past and future gigs

Song & equipment list

Website & Facebook

Business cards

Who to contact

> **Step 8.** Select the text and change the font size to **32** points. **Bold** the text. To widen the text box, press and drag the sizing handle on the left side of the box.

Follow these steps to add clip art:

Step 1. On the Insert ribbon, click **Clip Art**. In the Clip Art search box, enter **garage door**. In the *Results should be* box, check only **Photographs**. Click **Go**.

Step 2. In the list of photos, click the garage door photo. The photo is inserted.

Step 3. Resize and move the photo so that it fits under the title and above the footer. Use a corner sizing handle to resize so the photo proportions don't change.

Step 4. Right-click the photo and click **Send to Back** (see Figure S9-7).

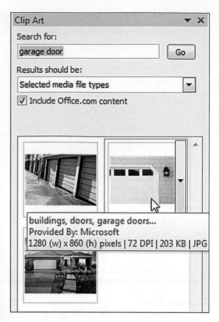

FIGURE S9-7
The photo is in position and is about to be sent behind the text.

Step 5. With the photo selected, click the **Format** tab. Click **Artistic Effects** and click **Paint Strokes**.

Step 6. Click **Color** and in the Color Saturation group, click **Saturation 0%**.

Step 7. Save your work.

Follow these steps to add an audio clip to the slide:

Step 1. On the Insert ribbon, click **Clip Art**. In the Clip Art search box, enter **revving car engine**. In the *Results should be* box, check only **Audio**. Click **Go**.

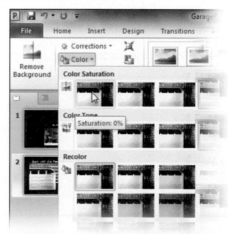

Step 2. In the list of audio clips, click **Revving car engine**. The audio clip icon is added to the slide. Move the audio clip icon to the lower-right corner of the slide (see Figure S9-8). To hear the audio, click the **Play** button.

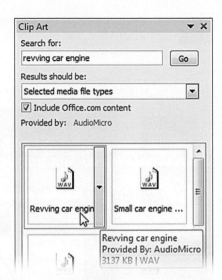

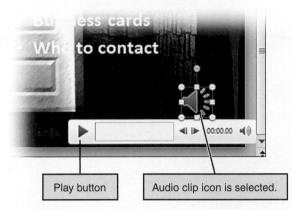

Play button — Audio clip icon is selected.

FIGURE S9-8
Position the audio text box in the lower-right area of the slide.

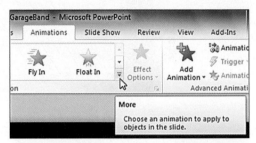

Step 3. Click the **Slide Show** button 🖳 to view the slide as a slide show and play the audio. Press **Escape** to return to Normal view. Correct any errors you see.

Step 4. Save your work.

Follow these steps to add animation to the objects on the slide:

Step 1. Select the audio icon. Click the **Animation** tab and click **Play**.

Step 2. Run the slide show again. When you click anywhere on the slide, the sound plays.

Step 3. Select the photo. On the Animation ribbon, click the down arrow to the right of the animations.

Step 4. Click **Transparency** in the Emphasis group.

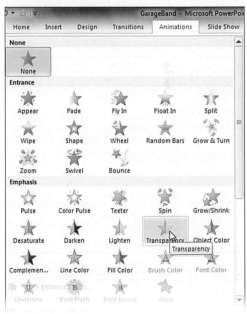

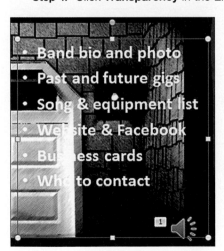

Step 5. Select the text box that contains the bulleted list. Be careful to select the box and not the text inside the box. The text box is selected when the line around the box is solid and not dashed.

Step 6. On the Animation ribbon, click **Grow & Turn** in the Entrance group. Watch as each bulleted item grows and turns onto the slide.

Step 7. View the slide as a slide show. As you click, the sound, photo, and text animations happen. Keep clicking the slide until all the bulleted items display. Then return to normal view.

Step 8. PowerPoint displays on the slide the order that animation happens. The correct order is shown in Figure S9-9. If the order on your slide is not correct, click the **Animations** tab and click **Animation Pane**. The Animation Pane appears as shown in Figure S9-9. You can press and drag an item in this pane to change the animation order.

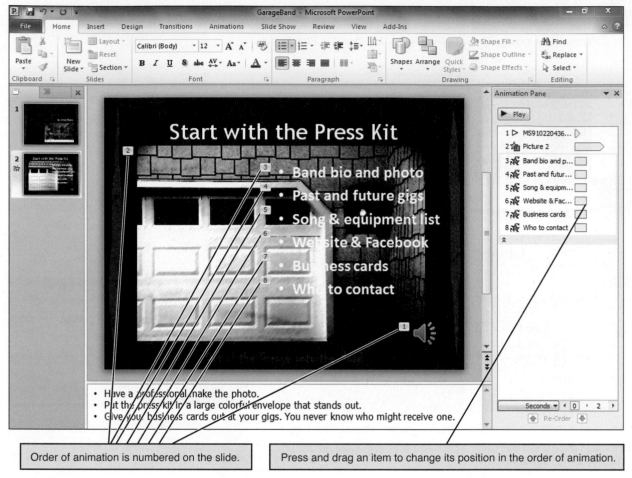

| Order of animation is numbered on the slide. | Press and drag an item to change its position in the order of animation. |

FIGURE S9-9
Animations 1 through 8 are identified on the slide.

> **Hint** If all the animated items are not listed in the Animation Pane, click the down arrow in the pane to see hidden items.

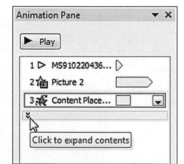

Follow these steps to add speaker notes for this slide:

Step 1. Enter this text for the speaker notes in the notes pane (see Figure S9-9):

Have a professional make the photo.

Put the press kit in a large colorful envelope that stands out.

Give your business cards out at your gigs. You never know who might receive one.

Step 2. Format the notes as a bulleted list.

Step 3. Save your work.

On Your Own Solution 9-4   **How to Create the Third Slide with WordArt**

When this activity is completed, the third slide should look like that in Figure S9-10.

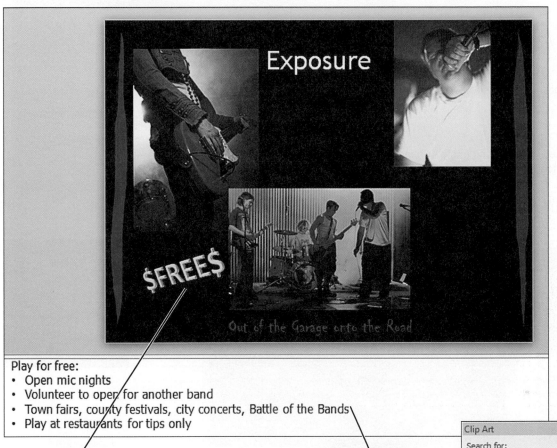

FIGURE S9-10
The third slide has three photos and WordArt.

Follow these steps to create the third slide with photos:

   Step 1. Add a new slide using the **Title Only** layout. Enter the slide title **Exposure**.

   Step 2. Widen the footer text box so the footer fits on one line. Be sure to keep the text box centered on the slide.

   Step 3. On the Insert ribbon, click **Clip Art**. Enter **electric guitar** in the search box. In the *Results should be* box, check only **Photographs**. Click **Go**. Click the electric guitar photo. The photo appears on the slide.

Step 4. With the photo selected, click the **Format** tab and click **Crop**. Cropping bars appear on the corners and sides of the photo. Hover over the crop bar on the right side of the photo until your pointer changes to a crop shape. ⊩

Step 5. Press and drag to crop the right side of the photo. When you are cropping a photo, your pointer changes to a crosshair.

> **Not Working?** If your pointer is not a crosshair as you press and drag, you are resizing or moving the object and not cropping it. Click **Undo** and try again.

Step 6. Crop the left side of the photo. When cropping is done, the photo should look like that in Figure S9-11.

Sides of original photo

Sides of photo after cropping

FIGURE S9-11
The photo has been cropped on both sides.

Step 7. Click **Crop** on the Format ribbon to remove the cropping handles from the photo.

Step 8. Resize and position the photo as shown in Figure S9-10. The top of the photo is aligned with the top of the title.

Step 9. Search for a clip art photo of a **singer**. After you insert the photo, align the photo with the top of the slide.

Step 10. Search for a clip art photo of a **band**. After you insert the clip art, move the photo above the footer.

Follow these steps to insert WordArt and speaker notes:

Step 1. Click the **Insert** tab and click **WordArt**. In the list of WordArt fill styles, click **Olive Green, Accent 3, Powder Bevel**. The WordArt text box appears on the slide.

Step 2. Select the text in the WordArt text box and replace it with **$Free$**.

Step 3. Select the WordArt text. On the Format ribbon, click **Shape Effects**. Point to **3-D Rotation**. Click **Perspective Heroic Extreme Left**.

Step 4. Press and drag the WordArt text box to position it in the lower-left area of the slide (see Figure S9-10). Rotate the text box upward.

Step 5. View the slide as a slide show and check your work.

Step 6. Enter these speaker notes:

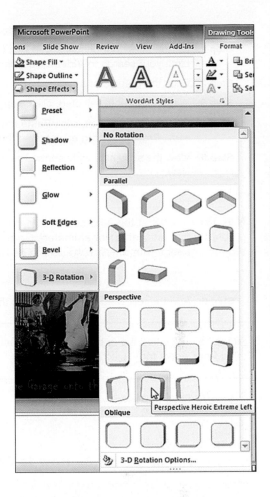

Play for free:

Open mic nights

Volunteer to open for another band

Town fairs, county festivals, city concerts, Battle of the Bands

Play at restaurants for tips only

Step 7. Make the last four lines in the speaker notes a bulleted list.

Step 8. Save your work.

On Your Own Solution 9-5   **How to Add Animated Graphics and a Screen Clipping to a Slide**

Follow these steps to add a screen clipping to a slide:

Step 1. Add a new slide, using the **Title Only** layout. Enter the slide title: **Not Enough Fans?**

Step 2. Widen the footer text box so the footer fits on one line. Be sure to keep the text box centered on the slide.

Step 3. To find the photo, open Internet Explorer and go to **lifewithjean.wordpress.com**. Scroll down the page to find the photo of fans. Make sure the full photo is displayed in your browser window.

Step 4. Click **Start**, **All Programs**, **Accessories**, and **Snipping Tool**. The screen dims, the Snipping Tool box appears, and your pointer changes to a crosshair.

> **Not Working?** Windows 7 Starter installed on a netbook does not include the Snipping Tool. In this case, you cannot complete this part of the activity.

Step 5. Click the down arrow next to New and make sure **Rectangular Snip** is selected.

Step 6. Press and drag to select the photo. Your snip appears in the Snipping Tool box and is copied to the Windows Clipboard.

Step 7. Return to PowerPoint. On the Home ribbon, click **Paste** and click the first Paste icon. The screen clipping appears on the slide.

Step 8. Resize the photo to fill most of the slide as shown in Figure 9-10 in the chapter.

Follow these steps to add animated clip art to the slide:

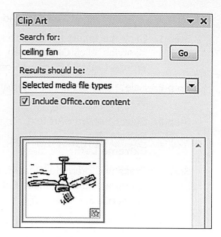

Step 1. On the Insert ribbon, click **Clip Art**. Enter **ceiling fan** in the search box. Limit your search to **Videos** file types. Click **Go**.

Step 2. Click the graphic of a ceiling fan. It appears on the slide.

Step 3. With the graphic selected, click **Copy** on the Home ribbon.

Step 4. On the Home ribbon, click **Paste** multiple times to add many fans to the slide. Press and drag each fan so the fans are scattered over the slide.

Step 5. View the slide as a slide show. The fans turn. Then return to normal view.

> **Not Working?** If the fans do not turn, most likely you selected a graphic in clip art that is not animated. Go back and make sure only **Videos** is selected in the *Results should be* box.

Step 6. Add the following speaker notes to the slide:

> If you're not getting the opportunities you want, change what you're doing until you find what works for you.

Step 7. Save your work.

On Your Own Solution 9-6   How to Embed a Link in a Slide

Follow these steps to embed a link in a slide:

Step 1. Select the third slide titled Exposure. Select the upper-right photo on the slide.

Step 2. Click the **Insert** tab and click **Hyperlink**. The Insert Hyperlink box appears. Click **Existing File or Web Page**. In the Address box, type **http://www.battleofthebands.com**. Click **OK** to close the box.

Step 3. On the Slide Show ribbon, click **From Beginning**. When you get to the third slide, click the photo. Internet Explorer opens and finds the requested link.

Step 4. When you close or minimize the Internet Explorer window, you return to the slide show. Press **Escape** to return to Normal view. Save your work.

On Your Own Solution 9-7   How to Add Transitions to the Presentation

The details of adding transitions to a slide are given in the chapter and are not repeated here.

CHAPTER 10 SOLUTIONS
Managing Numbers and Text Using Excel

The solutions in this appendix are for you to use if you get stuck when doing an On Your Own activity in the chapter. To learn how to teach yourself a computer skill, always try the On Your Own activity first before turning to these solutions.

On Your Own Solution 10-1   How to Examine the Excel Window and Tools

Follow these steps to examine the Excel window and tools:

Step 1. To open Excel, click **Start**, **All Programs**, **Microsoft Office**, and **Microsoft Excel 2010**. A blank workbook opens, as shown in Figure S10-1.

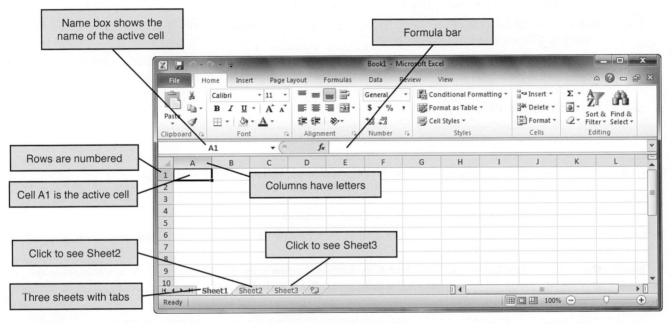

FIGURE S10-1
The Excel spreadsheet program opens a blank workbook with three worksheets.

Step 2. Click each ribbon tab (**File**, **Home**, **Insert**, **Page Layout**, **Formulas**, **Data**, **Review**, and **View**). Take a look at the items on each ribbon. Some of these items work as they do in Microsoft Word and PowerPoint.

Step 3. By default, the active cell is A1. Click a different cell and notice that the name box changes to identify the active cell. Enter text in this cell. The text is left-aligned in the cell.

Step 4. Click another cell and enter a number in the cell. The number is right-aligned in the cell.

Follow these steps to use an Excel template to manage a monthly budget:

Step 1. Click the **File** tab. Click **New**. In the Templates pane, click **Budgets**. Click **Home budgets**, click **PersonalMonthlyBudget**, and click **Download**. A workbook is created using this template.

Step 2. Click on cell **C16**, type **75**, and press the **Tab** key. Notice the dollar sign is added to cell C16, and D16 is now the active cell.

Step 3. Type **80** in cell D16 and press **Enter**. The difference is automatically calculated and appears in cell E16 along with a color-coded symbol.

Step 4. Type a number in cell **C17** and a number in cell **D17**. Be sure to press **Enter** after you type the last number. The difference is calculated.

> **Hint** Data must be entered into the cell before calculations using the cell are updated. To enter the data, you must make another cell the active cell or press Enter.

Step 5. To close this workbook without saving it, click the **File** tab and click **Close**. In the dialog box that appears, click **Don't Save**.

Follow these steps to see a template to track a couple's weight:

Step 1. On the File ribbon, click **New**, click **Charts and diagrams**, click **Business charts**, click **His & Her 12 months Weight Loss chart**, and click **Download**. The new workbook is created.

Step 2. Enter new numbers for Sargon's weight in column E. As you enter a number and then move off the cell, watch how the weight chart and summary calculations for Sargon change.

Step 3. Notice at the bottom of the Excel window there are 12 sheets, one for each month of the year. Click a sheet tab to move to a different sheet.

Step 4. Click the Help button 🔘 in the upper-right corner of the Excel window. In the Excel Help box, enter **rename a worksheet**. To rename a worksheet, right-click the sheet tab and click Rename in the shortcut menu. Type a new name for the worksheet, and then click off the sheet tab.

Step 5. Close the workbook without saving it.

On Your Own Solution 10-2   How to Enter Worksheet Titles and Headings

Follow these steps to enter titles and headings:

Step 1. If Excel is not open, open it. A new blank workbook is created.

Step 2. If Excel is already open and no worksheet is open, click the **File** tab, click **New**, click **Blank workbook**, and click **Create**. A new workbook is created.

Step 3. Verify cell A1 is the active cell. Type **2012 Girls Softball Season** in the cell. As you type, the text appears in the formula bar. It also appears in cell A1 and spills across the row of empty cells.

Step 4. Continue by entering the following text in the indicated cells:

Cell	Text
A3	Coach Chris Stevens
A4	Phone: 251-555-2574
A5	Email: chris.stevens@sample.com
C7	Player
D7	DOB
E7	Parents
F7	Phone
G7	Email
H7	Fees Paid
I7	Fees Due

Step 5. Click the **File** tab and click **Info**. If you are not the author of the file, right-click the author's name and click **Edit Property** in the shortcut menu that appears. In the Edit person dialog box, enter your name and click **OK**.

Step 6. Save the workbook file, naming the file **Roster**. If you need help saving the file to the hard drive, USB flash drive, SkyDrive, or other location, see the instructions in On Your Own Solution 3-3 in Chapter 3 of this *Solutions Appendix*.

On Your Own Solution 10-3   How to Format Using Styles and Themes

Follow these steps to format using styles and themes:

Step 1. Open the **Roster** workbook if you do not have it open already.

Step 2. Press and drag over cells **A1** through **I6**. A selection box appears over these cells. Click the **Home** tab and click **Cell Styles**. A gallery of available styles appears (see Figure S10-2). Click **Accent 5**. The style colors are applied.

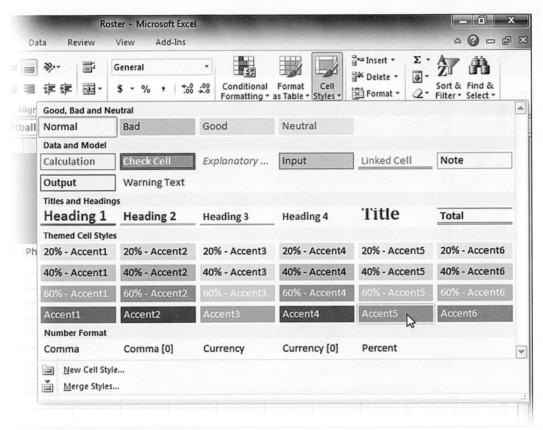

FIGURE S10-2
The Cell Styles offers options for applying styles to cells.

Step 3. Click in cell **A1**. On the Home ribbon in the Font group, click the Font size box. In the drop-down list of font sizes, click **26**.

Step 4. Click in cell **A3**. Change the font size to **14**.

Step 5. Press and drag to select cells **A4** and **A5**. Change the font size to **12**.

Step 6. Press and drag to select cells **C7** through **I7**. On the Home ribbon in the Alignment group, click the Orientation button. In the drop-down menu, click **Angle Counterclockwise**. The text in the cells is now tilted upward.

Step 7. To see the themes, click the **Page Layout** tab and click **Themes**. As you hover over a theme, the worksheet formatting changes (see Figure S10-3). Click **Concourse** to select this theme. The font and color changes appear in the worksheet.

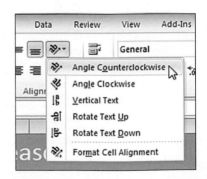

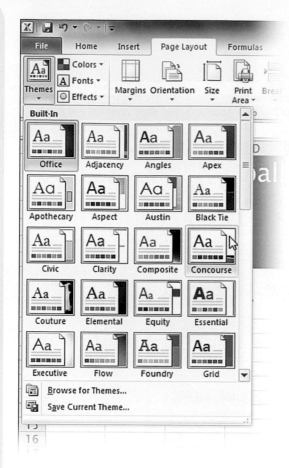

FIGURE S10-3
Themes in Excel apply professional formatting to a worksheet.

> **Step 8.** To save the workbook file, click the Save icon 🔲 in the Excel window title bar.

On Your Own Solution 10-4   How to Format Rows for Team Data and Add One Team Member

Follow these steps to format the cells in row 8 and enter data in the row:

> **Step 1.** Using the Roster workbook, click on cell **D8**. On the Home ribbon, click **Format**. In the drop-down menu, click **Format Cells**. The Format Cells box appears. Under Category, click **Date**. Click the **14-Mar-01** format. Click **OK**.

> **Step 2.** Click on cell **F8**. On the Home ribbon, click **Format**. In the drop-down menu, click **Format Cells**. The Format Cells box appears. Under Category, click **Special**. Click **Phone Number**. Click **OK**.

> **Step 3.** Select cells **H8** and **I8**. On the Home ribbon, click **Format**. In the drop-down menu, click **Format Cells**. The Format Cells box appears. Under Category, click **Currency**. Under Decimal places, verify that **2** is selected. Click **OK**.

> **Step 4.** Enter the following data in the indicated cells:

Cell	Data
C8	West, Jessica
D8	5/14/2000
E8	Mike and Jill West
F8	2515558549
G8	mjwest@sample.com
H8	33

Step 5. Notice that Excel makes the email address in cell G8 a hyperlink. To remove the hyperlink from the email address, right-click it and click **Remove Hyperlink** in the shortcut menu. Select cells **C7** through **I8**. Click **Format** on the Home ribbon and click **AutoFit Column Width** on the drop-down menu.

The details of copying the formatting in row 8 to other rows for team data are given in the chapter in On Your Own 10-4 and are not repeated here. After you complete this activity, don't forget to save your work.

On Your Own Solution 10-5   How to Copy Team Data from a Word Table and Edit the Data

Follow these steps to copy team data from a Word table and edit data:

Step 1. Insert the DVD in the back of the book in the optical drive. Open Windows Explorer and locate the **RosterTable** file in the **Sample Files** folder on the DVD. Double-click the file to open it in Word.

Step 2. Press and drag to select all columns and rows in the table except the column headings.

Step 3. Right-click the selection and click **Copy** in the shortcut menu (see Figure S10-4). The selection is copied into the Windows Clipboard.

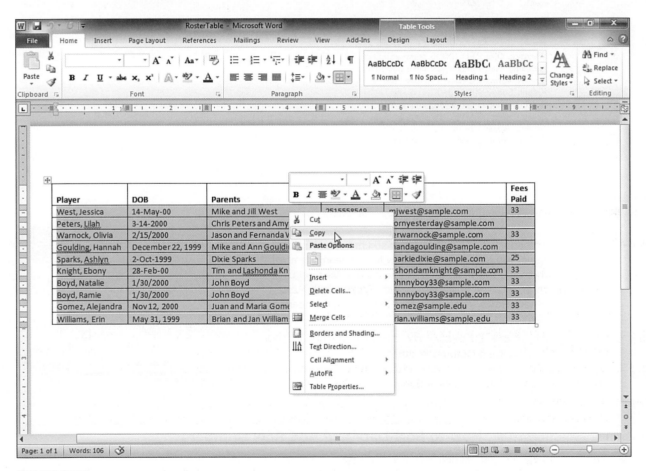

FIGURE S10-4
Copy the roster table in the Word document.

Step 4. If the **Roster** workbook is not already open in Excel, open it.

Step 5. Using the Roster workbook, click in cell **C9**. On the Home ribbon, click the drop-down arrow next to Paste. In the shortcut menu that appears, click the second Paste Options icon, as shown in Figure S10-5. This icon is the Match Destination Formatting icon. The data is pasted in the worksheet, and formatting in the worksheet cells is applied.

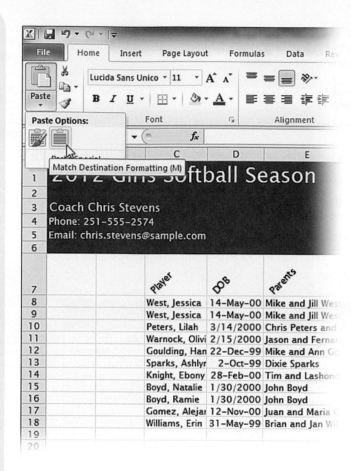

FIGURE S10-5
Paste the data into the worksheet and use the destination formatting.

Step 6. Because you typed a row for Jessica West and her data was also in the Word table, you have a duplicate row for this team member. Click somewhere in a row that contains the Jessica West data. On the Home ribbon, click the down arrow by the **Delete** button and click **Delete Sheet Rows**. Team data for the ten team members is now in rows 8 through 17.

Step 7. Select the block of cells **C7** through **I17** . On the Home ribbon, click **Format** and click **AutoFit Column Width**.

Step 8. Save your work.

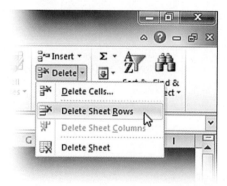

On Your Own Solution 10-6   How to Sort Data and Add Row Numbers

Follow these steps to sort team members and add row numbers:

Step 1. Using the Roster workbook, select the block of cells **C8** through **H17**.

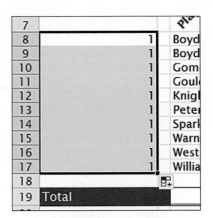

> **Hint** When selecting a block of cells, be careful not to accidentally grab the fill handle.

Step 2. On the Home ribbon, click **Sort & Filter**. Then click **Sort A to Z** in the drop-down menu. The data is sorted by the first column in the range of cells.

Step 3. To enter counting numbers in column A, first type the number **1** in cell **A8** and press **Enter**. Then click on cell A8. The selection box appears.

Step 4. With your pointer shaped like a black cross ✛, press and drag the fill handle down through cell A17.

Step 5. Click the **Auto Fill Options** box that appears. In the drop-down menu, click **Fill Series**. Counting numbers fill the selected area.

Step 6. To change the width of column A, locate the vertical bar to the right of column A above the worksheet area. Press and drag this vertical bar to adjust the column width. Change the width of column B using the same method.

Step 7. Save your work.

On Your Own Solution 10-7   **How to Enter Labels and Values for the Calculations**

Follow these steps to enter and format the labels:

Step 1. Enter the text as follows:

Cell	Text
A19	Total
A21	Operating expenses
C21	Uniform fee
C22	Party fee
A24	Total fee per child
A26	Percentage paid

Step 2. To format the cells, start by clicking cell **A5**.

Step 3. Double-click the Format Painter on the Home ribbon.

Step 4. Click cells **A19**, **B19**, **A21**, **B21**, **A24**, **B24**, **A26**, and **B26**. All these cells are formatted the same as cell A5.

Step 5. Click the Format Painter icon again to stop the Format Painter.

Step 6. Select cells **C19** through **I19**. On the Home ribbon, click **Cell Styles**. In the list of cell styles, click **Total**.

Follow these steps to enter and format the values for fees:

Step 1. In cell **D21**, enter **25**. In cell **D22**, enter **8**.

Step 2. Format cells D21 and D22 as numbers with two decimal places. If you need help, see On Your Own Solution 10-4.

Step 3. Save your work.

On Your Own Solution 10-8   How to Enter Two Sums in the Worksheet

Recall that when you enter a formula or number into a cell and the cell is too narrow to display the number, the cell is filled with the hash symbol (#####). To fix the problem, make the cell wide enough to display the number.

Follow these steps to calculate the total fee per child:

    Step 1. In cell **D24**, enter the formula **=D21+D22** and press **Enter**.

> **Not Working?** If the correct value of 33 does not display in the cell, click the formula bar. You can then edit the formula here by typing over the existing formula. When you are finished, press **Enter**.

    Step 2. Click cell **C19** to select it. Click the Format Painter tool on the Home ribbon. Press and drag to select **C24** and **D24**. The Total cell style is applied.

    Step 3. Format cell **D24** using **Currency**, **2** decimal places. Increase the column width to show the contents of the cell.

The details of using AutoSum to sum the Fees Paid column are given in the chapter and are not repeated here. AutoSum puts this formula in cell H19: **=SUM(H8:H18)**.

On Your Own Solution 10-9   How to Calculate Fees Due

Follow these steps to calculate the fees due:

    Step 1. Go to cell **I8**. Enter the following formula and press **Enter**.

```
=$D$24-H8
```

    Step 2. The value displayed in the cell should be zero. If it is not, click in the formula bar and correct your work. Also make sure the formula and displayed value in cell D24 is correct.

    Step 3. Go to cell **I8**. Click the Copy button 🗗▾ on the Home ribbon. A blinking box appears around the cell.

    Step 4. Select cells **I9** through **I17**. On the Home ribbon, click the Paste button. 🗋 The formula in cell I8 is copied to the new cells.

    Step 5. To verify the formula copied correctly, click cell **I9**. The formula in cell I9 that appears in the formula bar should be =$D$24-H9. If this is not the case, go back to step 1 and carefully do the steps again.

> **Hint** As you work, if a blinking box appears around cells and you want to start over, click the **Escape** key to remove the blinking box. Then start again.

Follow these steps to sum the fees due column:

    Step 1. Go to cell **I19**.

    Step 2. On the Formulas ribbon, click **AutoSum**. A SUM function is entered into the cell. The selection box for the range to sum appears around cells I8 through I18. If this is not the case, press and drag the selection box for AutoSum to include the cells **I8** through **I18**. Press **Enter** to enter the formula into cell I19.

    Step 3. Use the Format Painter to copy formatting in cell **H19** to cell **I19**.

On Your Own Solution 10-10   How to Calculate the Percentage Paid

Follow these steps to calculate the percentage paid:

Step 1. Go to cell **D26**, enter the following formula, and press **Enter**.

=H19/(H19+I19)

> **Tip** Just as in math, when Excel makes a calculation using a formula, it always calculates what is inside parentheses first.

Step 2. The value displayed in the cell is $0.78. The formatting is currency because Excel used the same formatting in cell D26 that it found in cells H19 and I19. If this value does not display, return to cell D26, click in the formula bar, and correct your work. If D26 is not formatted as currency, go back and format cells H19 and I19 as currency with two decimal places.

Step 3. Format cells **C26** and **D26** using the **Total** cell style.

Step 4. Make cell **D26** the active cell. On the Home ribbon, click **Format** and click **Format Cells**. In the Format Cells box, click **Percentage**. Change the decimal places to **0**. Click **OK**. The value in the cell displays as 78%.

Step 5. Save your work.

> **Not Working?** Calculations in a cell depend on values and formulas stored in other cells on the worksheet. If your calculations are not correct, the problem might be with values and formulas in other cells. Carefully go back and check your work for the entire worksheet. Compare each value displayed to those shown in Figure 10-3 in the chapter.

On Your Own Solution 10-11   How to Print the Worksheet

Follow these steps to print the worksheet:

Step 1. Click the **File** tab and click **Print**.

Step 2. Click the down arrow to the right of Portrait Orientation and click **Landscape Orientation**.

Step 3. Click the down arrow to the right of **No Scaling** and click **Fit Sheet on One Page**.

Step 4. Make sure your printer is selected and click **Print**. The worksheet prints on a single page.

CHAPTER 11 SOLUTIONS
Organizing Data Using Excel

The solutions in this appendix are for you to use if you get stuck when doing an On Your Own activity in the chapter. To learn how to teach yourself a computer skill, always try the On Your Own activity first before turning to these solutions.

> **Hint** Several formulas used in the worksheets you build in this chapter depend on other formulas already entered in the worksheets. A mistake in a formula or a missing formula can have a snowball effect through the worksheets. As you work your way through these solutions, work carefully so that a mistake does not affect later calculations.

On Your Own Solution 11-1 **How to Enter Titles, Headings, and Data on the Sales Worksheet**

When this activity is completed, the worksheet should look like that in Figure S11-1.

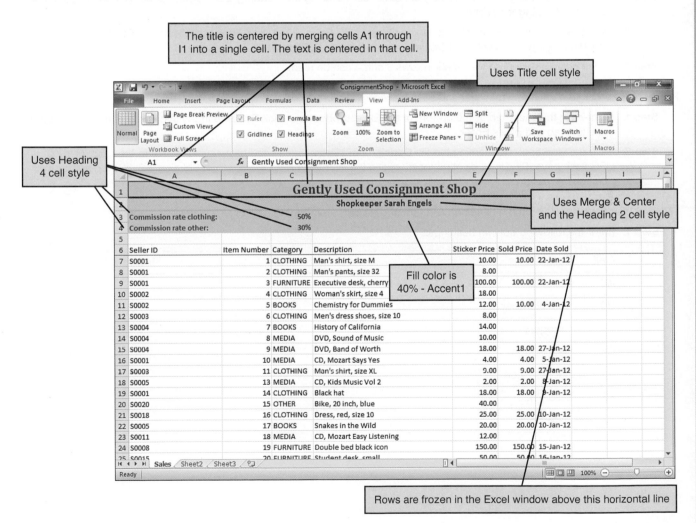

FIGURE S11-1
The Sales worksheet has titles, column headings, and data added.

Follow these steps to enter and format the text in the first four rows:

Step 1. Enter the following text or number in the indicated cells:

Cell	Text or Number
A1	Gently Used Consignment Shop
A2	Shopkeeper Sarah Engels
A3	Commission rate clothing:
C3	0.5
A4	Commission rate other:
C4	0.3

Step 2. Format cells A1 through I4 using the **40% - Accent1** cell style.

Step 3. Select cells A1 through I1. Click **Merge & Center** on the Home ribbon.

Step 4. Select cells A2 through I2. Click **Merge & Center** on the Home ribbon.

Step 5. Format cell A1 using the **Title** cell style. Format cell A2 using the **Heading 2** cell style. Format cells A3 through C4 using the **Heading 4** cell style.

Step 6. Select cells C3 through C4. On the Home ribbon, click **Format** and click **Format Cells**. In the Format Cells box, click **Percentage** and verify that Decimal places is set to **0**. Click **OK**.

Step 7. Widen column A or B so the labels in rows 3 and 4 can be read.

Follow these steps to name the worksheet and save the workbook file:

Step 1. Right-click the sheet tab at the bottom of the Excel window and click **Rename** in the shortcut menu. Type **Sales** on the sheet tab and press **Enter**.

Step 2. Save the workbook file, naming the file **ConsignmentShop**. If you need help saving the file to the hard drive, USB flash drive, SkyDrive, or other location, see the instructions in On Your Own Solution 3-3 in Chapter 3 of this *Solutions Appendix*.

Follow these steps to enter column headings and format data cells:

Step 1. Enter the following column headings:

Cell	Text
A6	Seller ID
B6	Item Number
C6	Category
D6	Description
E6	Sticker Price
F6	Sold Price
G6	Date Sold

Step 2. Select cells **E7**, **F7**, **H7**, and **I7**. Recall that to select nonadjacent cells, you hold down the **Ctrl** key as you click the cells. Use the **Format** command on the Home ribbon to format the cells as numbers with two decimal places.

Step 3. Format cell G7 as a date, using the **14-Mar-01** date format.

Step 4. To use AutoFill to copy formatting, first select cells **A7** through **I7**. Then press and drag the grabber handle in the lower-right corner of the selection box down through row 72 or beyond.

Follow these steps to copy the data from the ConsignmentSalesTable document into the worksheet:

Step 1. Insert the DVD in the optical drive.

Step 2. Open Windows Explorer and use it to locate the **ConsignmentSalesTable** file in the Sample Files folder on the DVD. Double-click the file. The file opens in a Word window.

Step 3. Select all the data in the table except the first row, which contains column headings. The table uses two pages, as shown in Figure S11-2. Be sure to select all the data as shown in the figure.

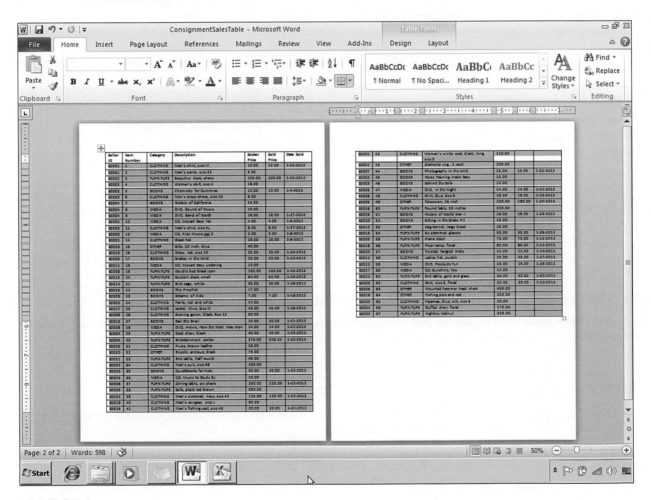

FIGURE S11-2
Select all the data in the table except the column heading row.

Step 4. Click **Copy** on the Home ribbon.

Step 5. Return to the Excel window. Click cell **A7**. On the Home ribbon, click the down arrow under Paste. In the drop-down menu, click the second Paste icon, which is labeled **Match Destination Formatting**. The data is pasted into the worksheet.

Step 6. Select cells A6 through I72. On the Home ribbon, click **Format** and click **AutoFit Column Width**. Column widths are adjusted. If necessary, adjust columns A or B so labels in rows 3 and 4 can be seen.

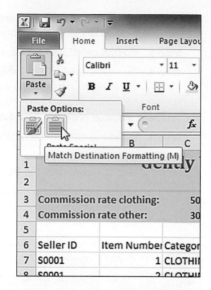

Follow these steps to freeze panes:

Step 1. Click cell **A7** to make it the active cell. On the View ribbon, click **Freeze Panes**. Then click **Freeze Panes** in the drop-down menu. All the rows above row 7 are frozen on the window.

Step 2. To test the frozen rows, use your arrow keys to move down the rows. No matter how far you go down the worksheet, the first six rows stay put.

Step 3. Compare your worksheet to that shown in Figure S11-1 and correct any problems you see.

Step 4. To save your work, click the **Save** icon in the title bar of the Excel window.

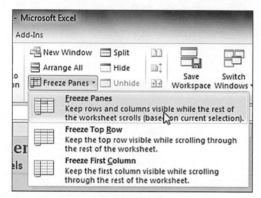

On Your Own Solution 11-2   How to Convert the Data to an Excel Table

The details of converting data to an Excel table and sorting and filtering the data in a table are given in the chapter and are not repeated here.

On Your Own Solution 11-3   How to Add a Total Row to the Table

The details of adding a total row to the table and putting sums in that row are given in the chapter and are not repeated here.

On Your Own Solution 11-4   How to Explore the SUBTOTAL Function in a Table

Follow these steps to explore the SUBTOTAL function:

Step 1. Click the drop-down arrow next to Category in cell C6. In the drop-down menu, uncheck **(Select All)**. Check **BOOKS** and click **OK**. The new sum value displayed in cell E76 is $193.50. Notice the Filter icon appears to the right of the Category heading to indicate the column has a filter applied.

> **Not Working?** If your value in cell E76 is $181.00, most likely you have not yet entered the new data in row 73 in On Your Own 11-2.

Step 2. Click cell E76 in the total row. Click the drop-down arrow that appears to the right of the selected cell. Click **Average**.

Step 3. Click the drop-down arrow next to Category in cell C6. In the drop-down menu, uncheck **BOOKS**. Check **MEDIA** and click **OK**. The average sticker price for Media appears in cell E76, which is $11.10. The SUBTOTAL function in cell E76 uses the function number 101, which calculates an average and ignores hidden cells.

Step 4. To unhide all the data in the table, click the drop-down arrow next to Category in cell C6. In the drop-down menu, check **(Select All)**. Click **OK**.

Step 5. Change the formula in cell E76 to find the **Sum**. Save your work.

On Your Own Solution 11-5   How to Name Cells and a Table

Follow these steps to name cells C3 and C4:

Step 1. Go to cell **C3**. In the name box, type **COMM_CLOTHING** and press **Enter**. The name appears in the name box.

Step 2. Name cell C4 as **COMM_OTHER**.

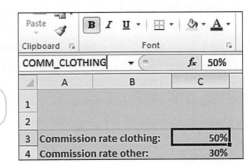

> **Not Working?** Don't forget to press **Enter** after you type the cell name.

To name the table, follow these steps:

Step 1. Click anywhere in the table so the Design tab displays. Click the **Design** tab.

Step 2. In the Table Name field, enter **SalesTable** and press **Enter**.

On Your Own Solution 11-6   How to Use the IF Function to Calculate the Commission Column and the Due to Seller Column

Follow these steps to build the Commission and Due to Seller columns:

Step 1. Enter the following column headings:

Cell	Text
H6	Commission
I6	Due to Seller

Step 2. Select cells H6 and I6 and autofit the column widths.

Step 3. Enter this formula in cell H7 and press **Enter**:

=IF([Category]="CLOTHING", [Sold Price]*COMM_CLOTHING, [Sold Price]*COMM_OTHER)

> **Not Working?** If Excel does not automatically copy the formula into the entire column, the cells in the column are not empty. In this situation, you can manually copy the formula into the entire column.

Step 4. Enter this formula in cell I7 and press **Enter**:

=[Sold Price]-[Commission]

Step 5. The total row is row 76. Click cell **H76**. Click the drop-down arrow next to the cell. Click **Sum** and press **Enter**. Click cell **I76**. Click the drop-down arrow next to the cell. Click **Sum** and press **Enter**. Format these totals as Currency with 2 decimal places.

Step 6. Compare your Sales worksheet with that shown in Figure 11-11 in the chapter and correct any problems you see. Save your work.

On Your Own Solution 11-7   **How to Build the Sellers Worksheet**

To build the Sellers worksheet, follow these steps:

Step 1. Using the ConsignmentShop workbook, name the second worksheet **Sellers**.

Step 2. In cell A1, enter **Seller Information**. Format the cell using the **Title** cell style.

Step 3. On the DVD, locate the **SellerInfoTable** in the Sample Files folder. Double-click the file to open it in Word.

Step 4. To select the entire table, click the selection icon in the upper-left corner of the table.

Step 5. On the Home ribbon, click **Copy** (see Figure S11-3). The table is copied into the Windows Clipboard.

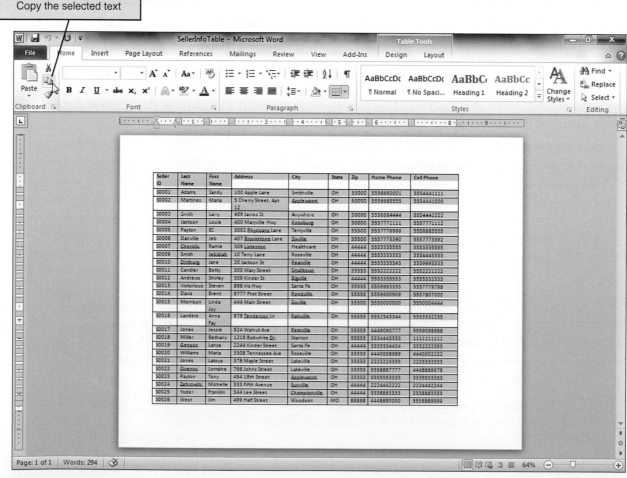

FIGURE S11-3
Copy the entire Word table into the Windows Clipboard.

Step 6. Return to the Excel window. Click cell **A3**. On the Home ribbon, click the down arrow under Paste. In the drop-down menu, click the second Paste icon, which is labeled **Match Destination Formatting**. The data is pasted into the worksheet.

Step 7. Click anywhere in the data. On the Home ribbon, click **Format as Table**. In the list of table styles, select **Table Style Medium 3**. Click **OK**. The table is created.

Step 8. Select cells **H4** through **I28**. Click **Format** on the Home ribbon. Click **Format Cells**. Click **Special**. Click **Phone Number** and click **OK**.

Step 9. Select the entire table. Use **AutoFit Column Width** to adjust the column widths.

Step 10. To name the table, first click anywhere in the table. On the Design ribbon, enter **SellerInfo** in the Table Name box and press **Enter**.

Step 11. Save your work.

On Your Own Solution 11-8   **How to Calculate Sales Totals for One Month**

Follow these steps to enter a title and labels on the Month Summary worksheet:

Step 1. Using the ConsignmentShop workbook, name the third worksheet **Month Summary**.

Step 2. Enter the worksheet title **Monthly Sales Summary** in cell A1 and format the cell using the **Title** cell style.

Step 3. Enter the following text:

Cell	Text
A3	Category
B3	Sold Price
C3	Commission
D3	Due to Seller
A4	CLOTHING
A5	BOOKS
A6	FURNITURE
A7	MEDIA
A8	OTHER

Step 4. Select the column titles and the first column and autofit the column widths.

Use one of the following methods to create the SUMIF function in cell B4.

To use the Formulas ribbon, follow these steps:

Step 1. Go to cell **B4** and click **Insert Function** on the Formulas ribbon. The Insert Function dialog box appears.

Step 2. In the *Search for a function* field, enter **SUMIF** and click **Go**. In the list of functions, click **SUMIF** and click **OK**. The Function Arguments dialog box appears.

Step 3. Enter the Range, Criteria, and Sum_range, as shown in Figure S11-4. Click **OK** to enter the function into cell B4.

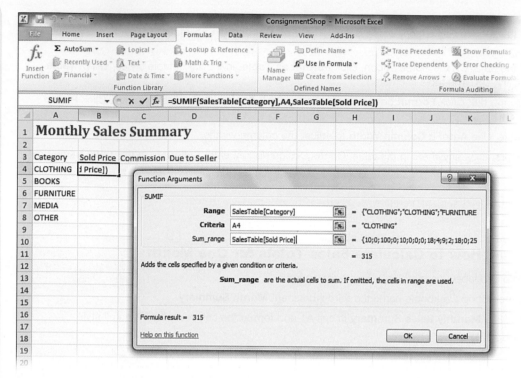

FIGURE S11-4

The SUMIF function has three arguments.

To type the SUMIF function in cell **B4**, follow these steps:

   Step 1. Go to cell B4.

   Step 2. Type the following formula and press **Enter**:

```
=SUMIF(SalesTable[Category],A4,SalesTable[Sold Price])
```

   Step 3. Go to cell B4. Press and drag the grabber handle in the lower-right corner of the selection box down through row 8.

   Step 4. Enter the following formula in cell C4 and copy the formula down through row 8:

```
=SUMIF(SalesTable[Category],A4,SalesTable[Commission])
```

   Step 5. Enter the following formula in cell D4 and copy the formula down through row 8:

```
=SUMIF(SalesTable[Category],A4,SalesTable[Due to Seller])
```

   Step 6. Format cells B4 through D8 using **Number** with **2** decimal places.

   Step 7. To convert the data to a table, first click anywhere in the data. On the Home ribbon, click **Format as Table**. In the list of table styles, select **Table Style Medium 12**. Click **OK**. The table is created.

   Step 8. To enter a total row, click anywhere in the table. On the Design ribbon, check **Total Row**. In the total row, insert a **Sum** in columns B and C. Excel automatically inserted a sum in column D.

   Step 9. Format the sums in row 9 using **Currency** with **2** decimal places.

Follow these steps to verify the totals on the Month Summary worksheet match up with the totals on the Sales worksheet:

Step 1. On the Sales worksheet, click the down arrow next to Category. Uncheck **(Select All)** and check **OTHER**. Click **OK**. The total Sold Price is $180.00. This total matches the value in cell B8 on the Month Summary worksheet.

Step 2. On the Sales worksheet, click the down arrow next to Category. Uncheck **OTHER** and check **FURNITURE**. Click **OK**. The total Due to Seller is $747.60. This total matches the value in cell D6 on the Month Summary worksheet.

Step 3. On the Sales worksheet, clear the filter from Category.

On Your Own Solution 11-9   How to Enter Titles and Seller Name and Address on the Seller Statement

Follow these steps to create the Seller Statement worksheet and add titles at the top:

Step 1. To add a new worksheet to the Consignment Shop workbook, click the **Insert Worksheet** tab at the bottom of the Excel window. A new sheet is added.

Step 2. Right-click the sheet tab, click **Rename**. Name the worksheet **Seller Statement**.

Step 3. Apply the **40% - Accent1** cell style to cells A1 through I8.

Step 4. Enter the following text:

Cell	Text
A1	Gently Used Consignment Shop
A2	300 Main Street
A3	Spring Hill, OH 90099

Step 5. Use the Cell Styles command on the Home ribbon to format cell A1 using the **Title** cell style. Format cells A2 and A3 using the **Heading 4** cell style.

Step 6. Select cells A1 through I1 and click the **Merge & Center** command on the Home ribbon. Also merge and center rows 2 and 3.

Follow these steps to enter the name and address lines for Seller ID S0001:

Step 1. Enter the following formula in cell A5:

```
=CONCATENATE(Sellers!C4," ",Sellers!B4)
```

Step 2. Enter the following formula in cell A6:

```
=Sellers!D4
```

Step 3. Enter the following formula in cell A7:

```
=CONCATENATE(Sellers!E4,", ",Sellers!F4," ",Sellers!G4)
```

Not Working? If you get an error using the CONCATENATE function, pay close attention to the double quotation marks, commas, and spaces. Also make sure you spelled the function correctly.

Step 4. Apply the **Header 4** cell style to cells A5 through A7.

On Your Own Solution 11-10   How to Copy Table Values to the Seller Statement

Follow these steps to put the sales data on the Seller Statement worksheet:

Step 1. On the Sales worksheet, verify that filtering is not applied to any column in the table. To do that, make sure the Filter icon ⌁ does not appear in a column heading. Remove any filters you see.

> **Hint** To remove a filter, click the drop-down arrow next to the column heading, click **Clear Filter From**, and click **OK**.

Step 2. Click the drop-down arrow next to Seller ID. Uncheck **(Select All)**. Check **S0001** and click **OK**. The table displays activity for S0001.

Step 3. Press and drag to select cells A6 through I76. Click **Copy** on the Home ribbon.

Step 4. Go to the **Seller Statement** worksheet. Click cell **A10**. On the Home ribbon, click the down arrow under Paste. Click the third Paste icon under Paste Values. The text and values are copied, but formulas are not copied.

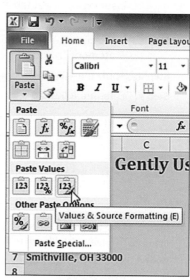

Follow these steps to prepare the worksheet to print on a single page without scaling:

Step 1. Select all cells in the table and autofit the column widths.

Step 2. Click **D** in the column letter bar at the top of the worksheet. The entire column D is selected. On the Home ribbon, click the **Wrap Text** button (see Figure S11-5). Text wraps in the column.

FIGURE S11-5

Text wrap helps to print a worksheet on a single page without scaling the font sizes on the page.

Step 3. Click **10** in the row bar on the left side of the Excel window. The entire row 10 is selected. Click the **Wrap Text** button ≋ on the Home ribbon.

Step 4. To determine if the column widths need to be adjusted, click the **View** tab and click **Page Break Preview**. Dotted lines appear where the page will break when printed. Click **Normal** on the View ribbon to return to normal view.

Step 5. To change the layout to landscape, click the **Page Layout** tab, click **Orientation**, and click **Landscape**. Adjust column widths as necessary so the dotted line is to the right of column I, the last column to print.

On Your Own Solution 11-11   How to Insert a Chart in the Month Summary Worksheet

Follow these steps to insert a chart using the Category and Commission data:

Step 1. Press and drag over cells A4 through A8. Hold down the **Ctrl** key and press and drag over cells C4 through C8. Both columns of data are selected.

Step 2. On the Insert ribbon, click the drop-down arrow next to Pie. Click **Pie in 3-D**, as shown in Figure S11-6.

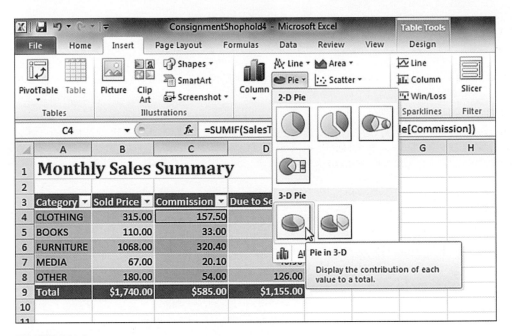

FIGURE S11-6
Select the data and then insert a chart that is built using the selected data.

Step 3. Press and drag an edge of the chart container box to move it to the right of the data. To resize the box, press and drag a corner of the box.

Step 4. With the container box still selected, click the **Layout** tab. Click **Chart Title** and click **Above Chart**. In the text box that appears, change the text to **Commissions for January**.

Step 5. To add labels, select the container box and click **Data Labels** on the Layout ribbon. Then click **Best Fit**. A label is added to each slice.

Step 6. Click the pie to select all the slices. Click the green **FURNITURE** slice to select only it. Press and drag it outward away from the other slices.

Step 7. Save your work.

The solutions in this appendix are for you to use if you get stuck when doing an On Your Own activity in the chapter. To learn how to teach yourself a computer skill, always try the On Your Own activity first before turning to these solutions.

On Your Own Solution 12-1   How to Examine Network Connections and Settings

Follow these steps to examine your network connections and settings:

Step 1. If you don't see the network icon in the taskbar, click the white up arrow ▲ in the taskbar. Click **Customize**. The Notifications Area Icons window opens. Under Network, change the Behaviors to **Show icon and notifications**. Click **OK**.

Step 2. Look at the network icon in the taskbar. The 🖳 icon indicates a wired connection. The ▦ indicates a wireless connection.

Step 3. Click the network icon and then click **Open Network and Sharing Center**. In the Network and Sharing Center window, the connections are listed under *View your active networks*. You might have no, one, or two connections.

Step 4. Look for the location under *View your active networks*. The network location is listed as Home, Work, or Public network.

Step 5. A problem with connectivity is indicated by a red X on this window. Check the top area of the window for this X. If you see the X, click it to fix the problem.

Step 6. Click the Internet icon. 🌐 Internet Explorer launches.

Step 7. Click the This computer icon. 🖳 The Computer window opens.

On Your Own Solution 12-2   How to Connect to a Wireless Hotspot

The details of connecting to a wireless hotspot are given in the chapter and are not repeated here.

On Your Own Solution 12-3   How to Verify Your Wired Network Connection

You can do this activity if your computer is connected to a wired network. Follow these steps:

Step 1. Does your network port have status indicator lights? If so, check the status of these lights. Are the lights lit or blinking?

Step 2. If the indicator lights are not lit, make sure the network cable is solidly connected at both ends. Verify you have network connectivity by using Internet Explorer to surf the web.

Step 3. If you cannot surf the web, open the Network and Sharing Center. Click the red **X** and follow directions onscreen to fix the problem. Make sure you have network connectivity before you proceed to the next step.

Step 4. Unplug the network cable.

Step 5. If your computer is wireless and has a wireless switch, turn off the wireless switch. If your wireless computer has no wireless switch, disconnect from the hotspot. To do that, click the network icon in the taskbar. Click the wireless connection and then click the **Disconnect** button.

Step 6. You should have no network connectivity. Open the Network and Sharing Center. Note that the window reports the problem with a red X.

Step 7. To fix the problem, plug in the network cable, turn on the wireless switch, and make the wireless connection. Connectivity is restored.

Step 8. To verify that Internet access is restored, open Internet Explorer and try to surf the web.

On Your Own Solution 12-4   **How to Install Windows Updates**

Follow these steps to find out what service packs are already installed:

Step 1. Click **Start**. Right-click **Computer**. In the shortcut menu, click **Properties**. The System window appears.

Step 2. Look in the Windows edition area to find any service packs that have been installed.

Follow these steps to install important Windows updates that might be pending:

Step 1. Click **Start**, **All Programs**, and **Windows Update**. The Windows Update window opens. If important updates are pending, they are reported on this window (see Figure S12-1).

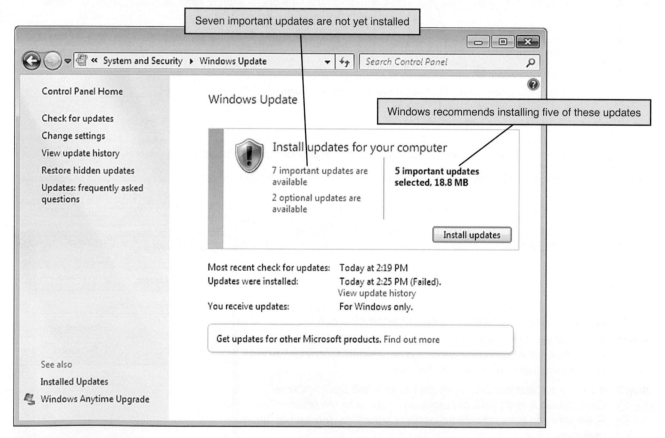

FIGURE S12-1
This computer has seven important updates pending, and five are selected for installation.

Step 2. To view the list of updates, click **important updates are available**. The Select updates to install window appears (see Figure S12-2). On this window, you can check or uncheck updates or leave the selections as Windows recommends. If you see a Windows 7 Service Pack listed, check only updates listed before the service pack and do not check the service pack. It needs to be installed as the only update. Click **OK** to install the selected updates.

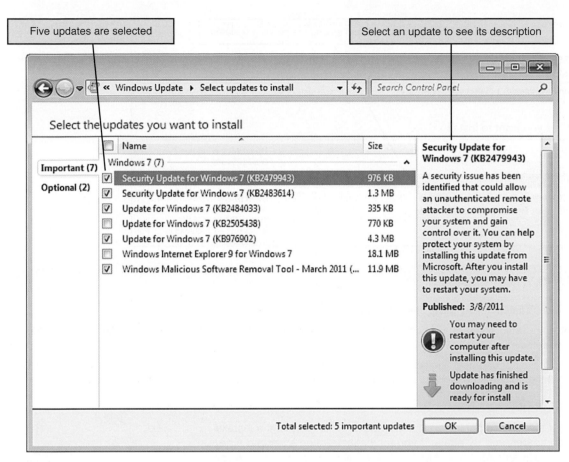

FIGURE S12-2
Windows has selected important updates to be installed.

Step 3. On the Windows Update window, click **Install updates** or **Restart now**, whichever button appears. The updates install.

Step 4. If the computer restarts, log back onto Windows, and the Windows desktop appears. Open the **Windows Updates** window.

> **Not Working?** Sometimes Windows displays a message during an update asking to install additional software, such as the System Update Readiness Tool. If so, you can allow Windows to install the software. If you get an error message you do not understand, you can cancel the update and ask a more experienced technician to finish updating Windows.

Step 5. In the left pane, click **Check for updates**. If more important updates are available, install them now.

Step 6. Return to the **Windows Updates** window and check for more important updates. Keep installing them until all important updates are installed and Windows reports there are no important updates pending.

As you work your way through the updates, the Windows 7 Service Pack 1 appears in the list if it has not already been installed (see Figure S12-3).

12

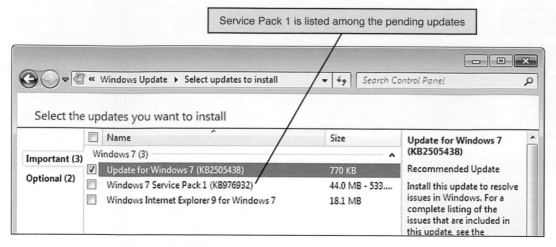

Service Pack 1 is listed among the pending updates

FIGURE S12-3
Select all updates before the service pack.

If you see the service pack listed, follow these steps to install it:

Step 1. If updates are listed before the service pack, select them and do not select the service pack (refer to Figure S12-3). Install the selected updates.

Step 2. Return to the list of updates. The service pack should be listed first. Select it as the only update to install. Click **OK** and install the update. The process takes about 30 minutes. Your computer restarts during that process.

> **Not Working?** If the service pack installation gives an error, cancel the installation, restart your computer, and try again. If you try the installation a second time and still get an error, ask an experienced technician to help you interpret the error message and decide what to do to complete the installation.

Step 3. After the computer restarts, log on to Windows. When the Windows desktop appears, a message box appears saying the service pack is installed. Click **Close** to close the box.

Step 4. Return to the **Windows Updates** window and check for more important updates. Keep installing them until all important updates are installed and Windows reports there are no important updates pending.

On Your Own Solution 12-5 How to Verify or Change Windows Update Settings

Follow these steps to verify or change Windows update settings:

Step 1. If necessary, open the **Windows Update** window. In the left pane, click **Change settings**. The Change settings window appears (see Figure S12-4).

Step 2. In the drop-down list under Important updates, select **Install updates automatically (recommended)**.

Step 3. Under Install new updates, select **Every day**. Select a time of day when you do not expect to be using your computer and the computer is connected to the Internet.

Step 4. Check **Give me recommended updates the same way I receive important updates**.

Step 5. Check **Allow all users to install updates on this computer**.

Step 6. Check **Give me updates for Microsoft products and check for new optional Microsoft software when I update Windows**.

Step 7. Click **OK**.

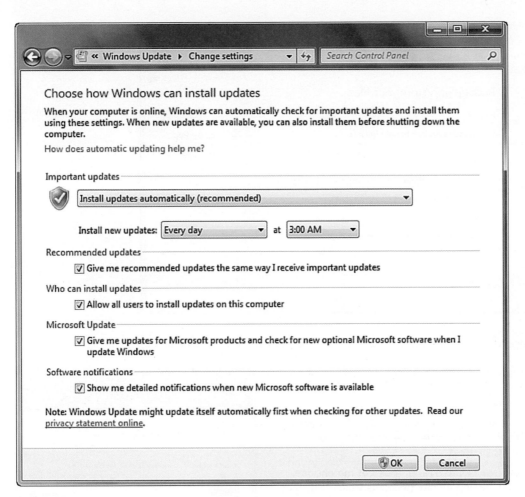

FIGURE S12-4
Control how and when Windows receives and installs updates.

On Your Own Solution 12-6   **How to Use Windows Backup and Restore**

Follow these steps to use Windows Backup and Restore to back up the Documents library on your hard drive:

Step 1. Make sure your backup media is available. For example, you can plug in an external hard drive or USB flash drive, or you can insert a rewriteable CD in the optical drive.

Step 2. To open the Windows Backup and Restore utility, click **Start, All Programs**, **Maintenance**, and **Backup and Restore**. If no backup schedule has been set up on this computer, the window looks like that in Figure S12-5.

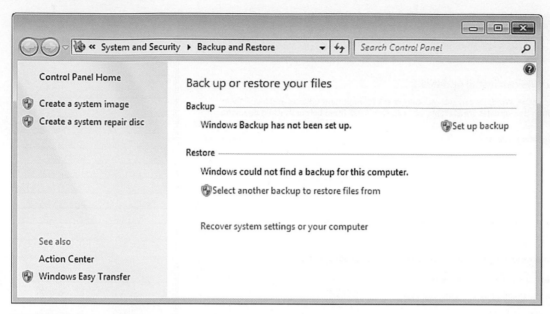

FIGURE S12-5
You can use the Windows Backup and Restore utility to back up data on your hard drive to another storage media.

Step 3. Click **Set up backup**. If you are not logged on using an administrator account, the UAC box appears. Enter the administrator password and click **Yes**.

Step 4. On the next window, select your backup location. For example, in Figure S12-6, a second hard drive is selected. Your window might look different. Click **Next**.

Step 5. On the next window (see Figure S12-7), click **Let me choose**. This option gives you the opportunity to decide which folders or libraries to back up. Click **Next**.

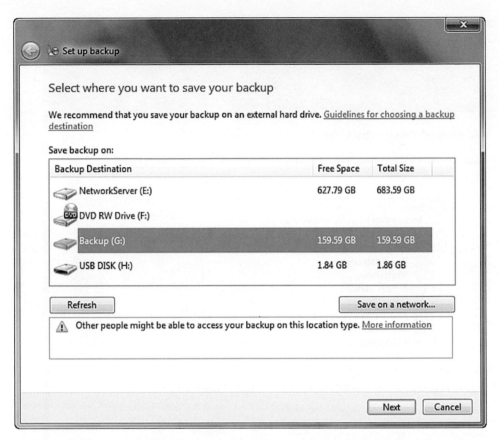

FIGURE S12-6
Select the storage media to receive the backup.

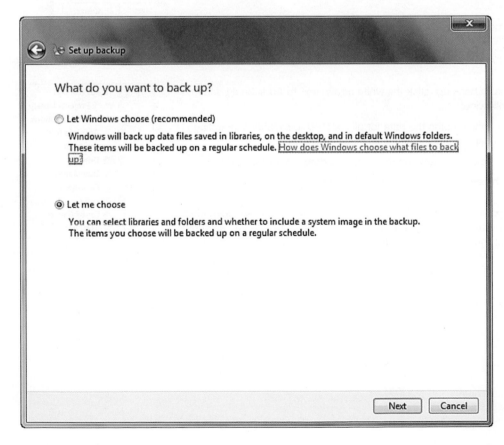

FIGURE S12-7
Choose the option to make your own selections as to what to back up.

Step 6. On the next window, check the libraries and folders to back up. In Figure S12-8, the Documents Library for Jean Andrews is selected.

Documents library is selected for backup

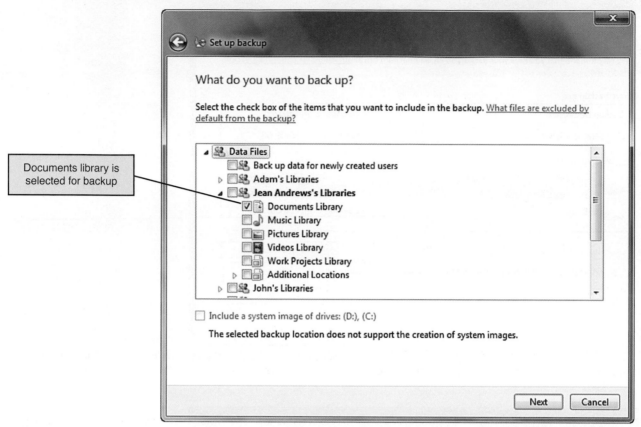

FIGURE S12-8
Select the libraries and folders to back up.

Step 7. To find the other items to back up, click the white arrow next to Additional Locations and then check the following:

▶ **AppData folder**, which holds the data for all installed applications including Outlook for this user

▶ **Desktop**, which holds the items on the Windows desktop for this user

▶ **Favorites**, which holds the IE favorites for this user

Step 8. Click **Next**. On the next window, click **Change schedule**. On the next window, check **Run backup on a schedule (recommended)**. For How often, select **Daily**, as shown in Figure S12-9. Select the time and click **OK**.

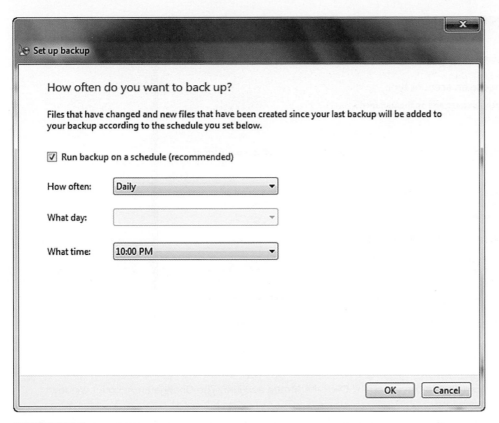

FIGURE S12-9
Set the backup schedule.

> **Step 9.** Check your settings and then click **Save settings and run backup**. The selected items are backed up. Close the **Backup and Restore** window.

On Your Own Solution 12-7   **How to Create a Standard Account**

You need an administrator account and password to do this activity. Follow these steps to create a standard account and explore how the account works:

> **Step 1.** Log on to Windows with an administrator account.
>
> **Step 2.** Click **Start**, **Control Panel**. The Control Panel opens. In the User Accounts and Family Safety group, click **Add or remove user accounts**. The Manage Accounts window opens.
>
> **Step 3.** Click **Create a new account**. In the Create New Account window, name the account **Mattie** (see Figure S12-10). Verify **Standard user** is selected and click **Create Account**.

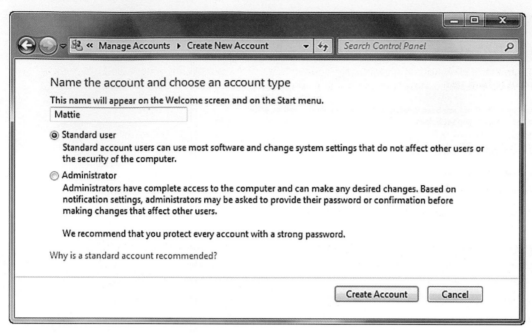

FIGURE S12-10
The name of the standard account is Mattie.

Step 4. The Mattie account is listed among the accounts. Click the **Mattie** account. The Change an Account window opens. Click **Create a password**.

Step 5. Type the password **Matt1E** in each box (see Figure S12-11). Type a password hint, but be careful not to give the password away in the hint because any user can see the hint. Click **Create password**. Close the window.

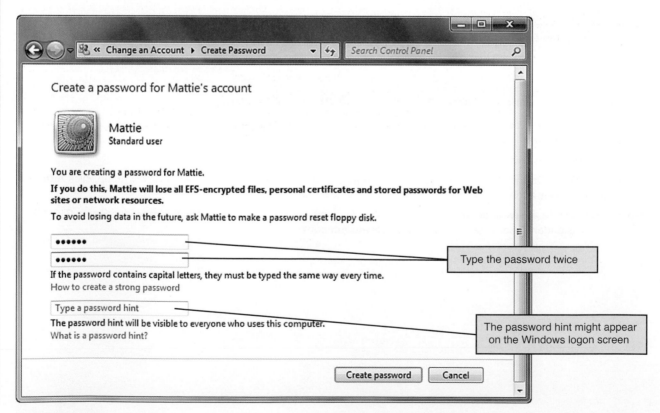

FIGURE S12-11
Type the password twice.

Step 6. Log on to Windows using the Mattie account. The first time a user logs in, Windows prepares the desktop and user folders and libraries.

Step 7. Open Windows Explorer. Verify you can view the contents of Mattie's **Documents** library.

Step 8. Open **Control Panel** and click **Add or remove user accounts**. The UAC box appears. Because Mattie has a standard account, she cannot create a user account without entering the password to an administrator account.

On Your Own Solution 12-8   How to Manage Windows Passwords

Follow these steps to change your password:

Step 1. Log on to your Windows account. Open **Control Panel**. Click **User Accounts and Family Safety**.

Step 2. On the next window, under **User Accounts**, click **Change your Windows password**. On the next window, click **Change your password**.

Step 3. On the next window, type your new password two times. Click **Change password**. Close the window.

Using an administrator account, follow these steps to reset a password for another user:

Step 1. Open **Control Panel**. Click **Add or remove user accounts**.

Step 2. Click the **Mattie** user account. On the next window, click **Change the password**.

Step 3. Type the password **changeme** twice and click **Change password**. Close the window.

On Your Own Solution 12-9   How to Secure a Wireless Network

You can do this activity if you have access to a wireless router in a small home network. Follow these steps to access the router setup program and change the router password:

Step 1. Look in the user guide of the wireless router to find the IP address of the router and the router password assigned by the router manufacturer. Know that this original password might have been changed. It is likely the IP address is 192.168.1.1.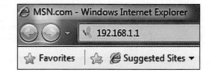

Step 2. Use a computer that has a wired connection to the router. Open **Internet Explorer**. Enter the IP address of the router in the IE address box.

Step 3. In the Windows Security box that appears, enter the password to the router and click **OK**. (The User Name is not required.) The router setup main menu appears. Figure S12-12 shows the main menu window for one router, but yours might look different.

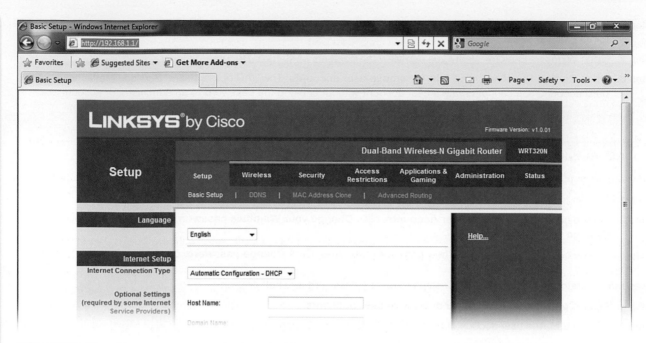

FIGURE S12-12
This main menu window is provided by the wireless router setup program.

Step 4. To change the router password for the Linksys router used in this solution, click the **Administration** tab (see Figure S12-13). Enter the new password and then scroll down to the bottom of the window and click **Save Settings**. Your router setup software might work differently.

FIGURE S12-13
Change the password used to access the router setup software.

Follow these steps to secure the wireless network:

Step 1. Find the window that sets up the wireless security for the router, such as that shown in the chapter in Figure 12-18. To access this window on this particular router, click the **Wireless** tab and then click **Wireless Security**. If you have options for the Security Mode, select **WPA2** as shown in the figure. Enter a strong password to the wireless network. Be sure to write down the password. A good place to write it is in the router user guide.

Step 2. Save your changes and exit the router setup program. Close Internet Explorer.

Step 3. Using a wireless computer, connect to the wireless network. You must enter the wireless network password when you make the connection. If you need help, refer to On Your Own Solution 12-2.

On Your Own Solution 12-10   **How to Use a Homegroup to Share Data**

To do this activity, one of the two computers must be running Windows 7 Home Premium or Windows 7 Professional. Follow these steps on each computer to set up a homegroup:

Step 1. To open the Network and Sharing Center, click the network icon in the taskbar, and click **Network and Sharing Center**. The network location might be set to Home network, Work network, or Public network. If the network location is Home network, the HomeGroup status displays. This HomeGroup status might be Ready to create, Available to join, or Joined.

Step 2. Click the network location. The Set Network Location dialog box appears. Refer to Figure 12-5 in the chapter. Click **Home network**. Another Set Network Location dialog box might appear. If so, click **View or change HomeGroup settings**.

Step 3. The next window allows you to create a homegroup or join an existing homegroup (see Figure S12-14). Check **Pictures**, **Documents**, **Music**, and **Videos** to share these libraries. If you have a printer connected to your computer, check **Printers** to share the printer. Click **Next**.

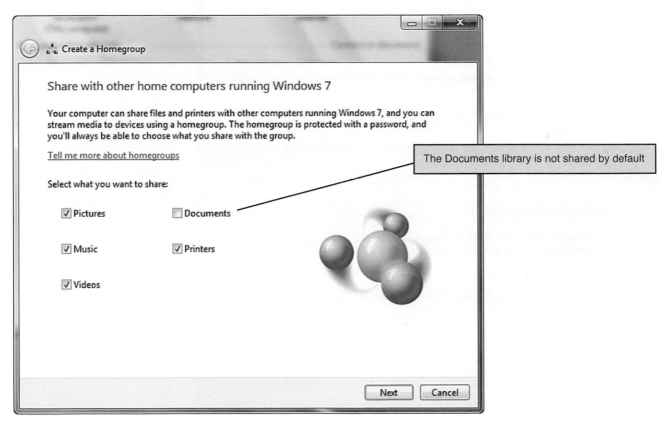

FIGURE S12-14
Decide what to share with the homegroup.

Step 4. The next box suggests a password if you are creating a homegroup or requires you to enter the password if you are joining a homegroup. Figure S12-15 shows the box when creating a homegroup. Write down the password so you can use it on other computers. Figure S12-16 shows the box when joining an existing homegroup. Type the password and click **Next**.

FIGURE S12-15
Windows suggests a strong password for the homegroup.

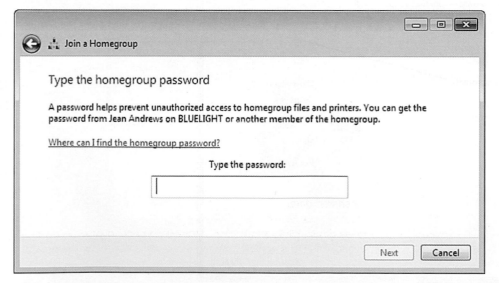

FIGURE S12-16
Enter the homegroup password to join a homegroup.

> **Step 5.** Click **Finish** to create or join the homegroup.

Follow these steps to view homegroup settings:

Step 1. Click **Homegroup** in the left pane of the Network and Sharing Center. The HomeGroup window appears (refer to Figure 12-20 in the chapter).

Step 2. To view the homegroup password, click **View or print the homegroup password**. Close the dialog box.

To complete this part of the activity, you need to be able to write files to the hard drive. Follow these steps to copy a file from one computer to the other:

Step 1. Open **Windows Explorer**. In the left pane, drill down into the **Homegroup** group to see computers in the homegroup and the shared libraries and folders on these computers. Drill down into your partner's computer. Double-click the **Document** library on that computer.

Step 2. In the right pane of Windows Explorer, right-click a file in the Documents library of the other computer (see Figure S12-17). Click **Copy** on the shortcut menu. The file is copied to the Windows Clipboard.

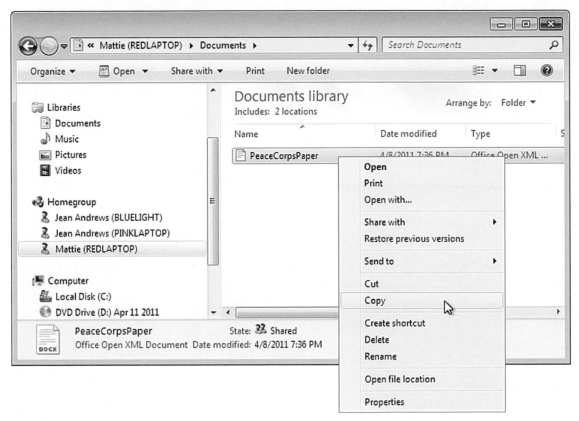

FIGURE S12-17
Drill into the computers listed in the Homegroup group to find shared data.

Step 3. In the left pane of Windows Explorer in the Libraries group, click **Documents**. In the right pane, right-click anywhere in the whitespace. Click **Paste** on the shortcut menu. The file is copied from the other computer to the Documents library of your computer.

CHAPTER 13 SOLUTIONS
Maintaining a Computer and Fixing Computer Problems

The solutions in this appendix are for you to use if you get stuck when doing an On Your Own activity in the chapter. To learn how to teach yourself a computer skill, always try the On Your Own activity first before turning to these solutions.

On Your Own Solution 13-1:   How to Clean Up the Hard Drive

Follow these steps to clean up the hard drive:

Step 1. Right-click the **Recycle Bin** on the Windows desktop. In the shortcut menu, click **Empty Recycle Bin**. Click **Yes** in the dialog box that appears.

Step 2. Open Windows Explorer. Right-click Local Disk (C:) in the left pane and click **Properties** in the shortcut menu. In the Properties box, click **Disk Cleanup**.

Step 3. Click **Clean up system files**. If you are not logged on as an administrator, you must enter the administrator password to continue. The list of files to delete now includes temporary system files.

Step 4. In the Disk Cleanup for (C:) box, check the items that you want to delete under *Files to delete*. Click **OK**. Then click **Delete Files**.

Follow these steps to calculate the percentage of free space on the hard drive:

Step 1. In the drive's Properties box, note the Capacity and Free space. For example, in Figure 13-1 in the chapter, the Capacity of the drive is 98.6GB. The Free space is 14.6GB.

Step 2. Divide the amount of free space by the capacity of the drive. Then convert the fraction to a percentage. In our example, the calculation is $14.6 \div 98.6 = 0.148$. This fraction rounds up to 15%.

Note that steps to verify when defragmenting happens are given in On Your Own 13-1 and are not repeated here.

On Your Own Solution 13-2:   How to Uninstall Software You No Longer Need

Follow these steps to uninstall software:

Step 1. Open Control Panel. Click **Uninstall a program**. The Programs and Features window appears.

Step 2. To uninstall a program, select it and then click **Uninstall** in the menu bar. Follow directions onscreen to uninstall the program.

On Your Own Solution 13-3:   How to Limit Startup Programs Using System Configuration

Follow these steps to use System Configuration:

Step 1. Click **Start**. Type **msconfig** in the *Search programs and files* box and press **Enter**. If you are not logged in with an administrator account, you must enter the administrator password. The System Configuration window opens.

Step 2. Click the **Startup** tab. To better read the lines in each column, you can press and drag the vertical bar in the column heading to widen a column.

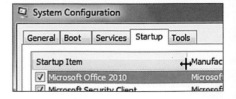

Step 3. To keep a program from launching each time Windows starts, uncheck the program.

Step 4. If you made any changes, click **Apply**. Click **OK**. Restart your computer for the change to take effect.

On Your Own Solution 13-4: **How to Manage Power Settings**

Follow these steps to manage power settings:

Step 1. Open Control Panel. Click **Hardware and Sound**. Click **Power Options**.

Step 2. Note which power plan is selected. To find the power settings for this plan, click **Change plan settings** to the right of the selected plan.

Step 3. To find out what the power button does, click **Choose what the power buttons do**. To find out about a password required at wakeup, click **Require a password on wakeup**.

Step 4. Using a laptop or netbook, to find out what happens when you close the lid, click **Choose what closing the lid does**.

Step 5. When working with the Power Options window, if you made changes, click **Save changes** before you close the window.

On Your Own Solution 13-5: **How to Practice Changing Monitor Settings**

Follow these steps to practice changing the monitor settings:

Step 1. Open a Word document or a web page in your browser so you can see black text on a white background. Resize the window so you can view the window as well as the Windows desktop.

Step 2. To adjust the screen resolution, right-click somewhere on the desktop and select **Screen resolution** from the shortcut menu. Click the down arrow under Resolution. In the drop-down menu, use the sliding scale to select your resolution. Click off the menu, and then click **Apply**. Click **OK** to close the window.

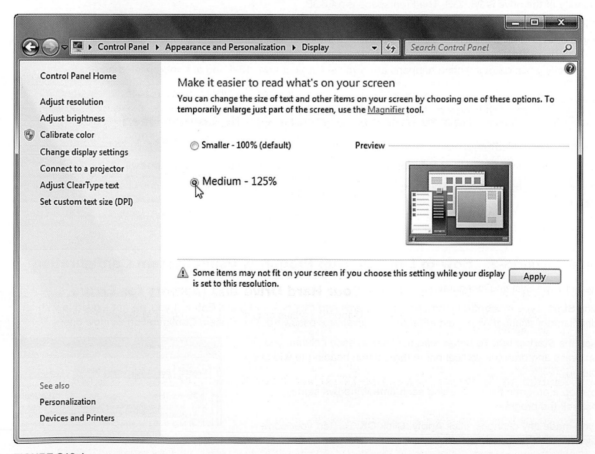

FIGURE S13-1
Adjust display setting to enlarge text so it is easier to read.

Step 3. To adjust text size, right-click on the desktop and select **Personalize** from the shortcut menu. Click **Display** in the Personalization window. The Display window appears. Another way to get to the Display window is to click **Start, Control Panel**. In the Control Panel, click **Appearance and Personalization**, and then click **Display**. In the Display window, select **Medium – 125%** (see Figure S13-1). Click **Apply** and follow directions onscreen to make the change. You must log off Windows and log back on for your changes to take effect.

To adjust the settings on a desktop monitor, do the following:

Step 1. Not all monitor buttons work the same way. In general, press the **Menu** button to open a menu on the monitor screen and then use other buttons to work your way through this menu.

Step 2. Know that most monitors have an Auto or Reset option that you can use to return the monitor to default settings if you have a problem.

On Your Own Solution 13-6: **How to Use Task Manager to Close an Application**

Follow these steps to use Task Manager:

Step 1. Open the Paint application. To open Task Manager, right-click the taskbar and select **Start Task Manager** from the shortcut menu.

Step 2. To close the Paint program, first make sure the Applications tab of Task Manager is selected. Then select the Paint program on the Application tab and click **End Task**. The Paint program closes.

Step 3. Close Task Manager.

On Your Own Solution 13-7: **How to Use the Printer Queue**

Follow these steps to use the printer queue:

Step 1. Turn off your printer. Open a Word document that you want to print. Command Word to print the document. Command Word to print the document a second time. How to print a Word document is covered in Chapter 2, "Finding and Using Information on the Web." Neither printout happens because the printer is turned off.

Step 2. To open the printer window, click **Start, Devices and Printers**. In the Devices and Printer window, double-click the printer icon. The printer window opens.

Step 3. To see the items in the printer queue, click **document(s) in queue**. To delete one of the items, right-click it and click **Cancel** on the shortcut menu. Click **Yes**. The item is deleted from the queue.

Step 4. Turn on the printer. The one document should now print. Watch the printer queue as the document prints and the queue is empty. Close all windows.

On Your Own Solution 13-8: **How to Check Your Hard Drive and Memory for Errors**

Detailed directions for using the Check Disk and Memory Diagnostic utilities are listed in the chapter in the section "Windows Gives Strange Errors" and are not repeated here.

On Your Own Solution 13-9: **How to Decide Whether Your Computer Needs a Memory Upgrade**

Follow these steps to decide whether your computer needs a memory upgrade:

Step 1. Open the System window. There, you can find the edition of Windows (for example, Windows 7 Home Premium), system type (for example, 32-bit operating system), and amount of memory installed (for example, 2GB).

Step 2. Right-click the taskbar and click **Task Manager**. In the Task Manager window, click the **Performance** tab. Click **Resource Monitor**. The Resource Monitor window opens.

Step 3. Click the **Memory** tab. Click the down arrow to the right of Physical Memory.

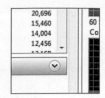

Step 4. Open **Microsoft Word**. Leave the application window open. Open **Internet Explorer** and surf the web.

Step 5. As you work, watch the Resource Monitor bar graph. Free memory is displayed as the light blue area on the right side of the bar graph (refer to Figure 13-24 in the chapter). Did the free memory area of the bar graph disappear as you worked? If so, you can benefit from a memory upgrade.

Follow these guidelines to decide whether you need an upgrade:

▶ A 32-bit operating system benefits from 4GB of memory. If you don't have 4GB of memory, you might improve performance with an upgrade.

▶ A 64-bit operating system benefits from 8GB of memory. If you don't have 8GB of memory, you might improve performance with an upgrade.

On Your Own Solution 13-10: **How to Use Safe Mode**

Follow these steps to use Safe Mode:

Step 1. Close any windows you have open and shut down your computer.

Step 2. Power up your computer. Press and hold down the **F8** key as your system powers up. The Advanced Boot Options menu appears. Use your arrow keys to select **Safe Mode with Networking** and press **Enter**.

Step 3. Log on to Windows. When the Windows desktop appears, open Internet Explorer and surf the web.

Step 4. Restart Windows and log back on. The normal Windows desktop appears.

CHAPTER 14 SOLUTIONS
Buying Your Own Personal Computer

The solutions in this appendix are for you to use if you get stuck when doing an On Your Own activity in the chapter. To learn how to teach yourself a computer skill, always try the On Your Own activity first before turning to these solutions.

On Your Own Solution 14-1 How to Determine What Upgrade Would Improve Your Computer's Performance

Follow these steps to find out what upgrade would improve a computer's performance:

Step 1. Click **Start**, right-click **Computer**, and click **Properties** in the shortcut menu. In the System window, click **Performance Information and Tools**. The Performance Information and Tools window appears as shown in Figure 14-7 in the chapter. The Base score in this window is the index. The expected performance of a computer based on the index is listed in Table 14-1 in the chapter.

Step 2. Look in the Subscore column for the lowest value, which indicates the slowest component. This component might be the processor, memory, graphic or video subsystem, or hard drive on which Windows is installed.

On Your Own Solution 14-2 How to Determine the Value of Your Computer

Follow these steps to collect the information you need to determine the value of your computer:

Step 1. Click **Start**, type **msinfo32** in the *Search programs and files* box, and press **Enter**. The System Information window opens. On this window, locate the System Manufacturer and System Model. If your computer is not a brand-name desktop but a desktop that was built from parts, this information applies to the motherboard. Otherwise, it applies to the computer itself.

Step 2. On this window, locate the Processor information and the amount of memory installed.

Step 3. Open the Computer window. On this window, locate the size of the hard drive.

Step 4. Open the System window. On this window, locate the Windows edition installed.

Step 5. If you are including the applications installed with the computer, click **Start**, **All Programs**, and note the applications installed. You can also find this information in the Programs and Features window of the Control Panel.

You now have the information you need to determine the value. For example, suppose this is the information for your computer:

▶ It is a four-year-old Sony VAIO laptop, model VGN-CR120.

▶ The processor is a Core2 Duo 1.80 GHz, 2 GB of memory is installed, and the hard drive is 140 GB.

▶ Windows 7 Home Premium is installed.

▶ The warranty has expired.

Follow these steps to find the value of this Sony VAIO laptop:

Step 1. Open Internet Explorer and go to **ebay.com**. Search for a laptop for sale. The eBay site allows you to refine your search for a laptop by offering options on the left side of the search window (see Figure S14-1). Check the options to refine your search.

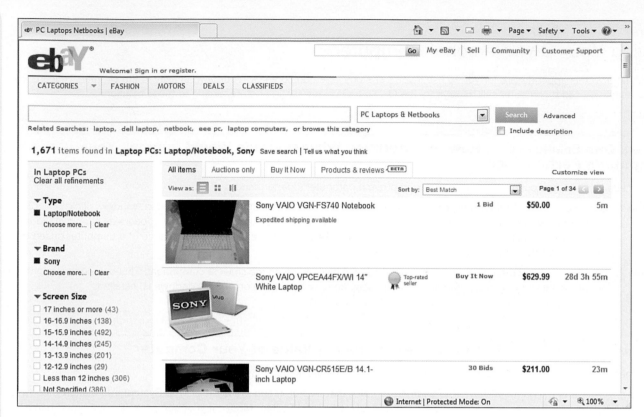

FIGURE S14-1

Use eBay to search for comparable computers.

Step 2. You also can try to enter a description of the computer in the search box on eBay. For example, Figure S14-2 shows a search on "laptop sony core2 duo." Your search might return different results.

Step 3. Go to craigslist.org and search for a comparable computer. For example, Figure S14-3 shows one computer that is similar to the Sony VAIO Core2 Duo.

Step 4. Calculate the average price of all the comparable computers you found to determine the value of your computer. In our example, the calculations are reported in Table S14-1. Your calculations might be different.

TABLE S14-1   Average Price of Comparable Computers

Computer	Price
Sony VAIO VPCEA44 laptop	629.99
Sony VAIO VGN-CR515E/B	211.00
Sony VAIO VGN-CR320E	169.00
Sony VAIO VGN-NR180E	299.99
Dell Latitude D830 Core 2 Duo	550.00
Average price	$372.00

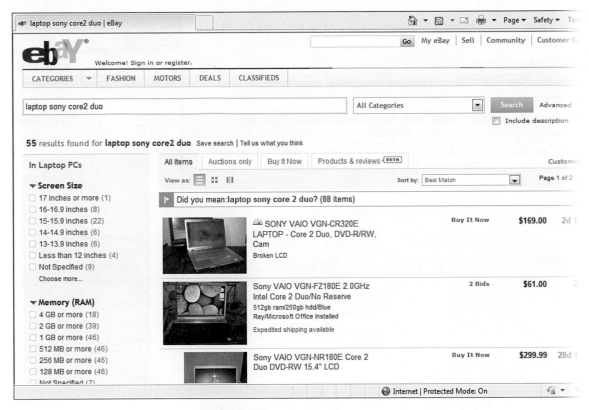

FIGURE S14-2

Try entering a description of the computer in the eBay search box.

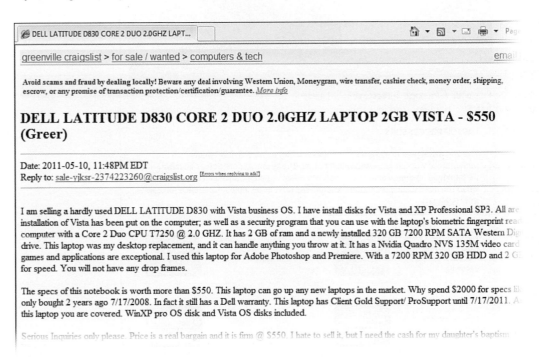

FIGURE S14-3

This Dell Latitude on craigslist.org has the same processor as the Sony VAIO.

On Your Own Solution 14-3 How to Investigate the Latest Intel Processor for Laptops

Do the following to find the latest Intel processor for laptops:

Step 1. Go to **Google.com** and search on **latest Intel processor for laptops**. Find the processor you think is the latest.

Step 2. To verify your findings, go to **intel.com**. Search for products. Then search for processors. Then search for laptop processors.

Step 3. The latest Intel laptop processors are listed. Figure S14-4 shows the latest one is the Core i7 Mobile Processor Extreme Edition. Your search might turn up a newer processor.

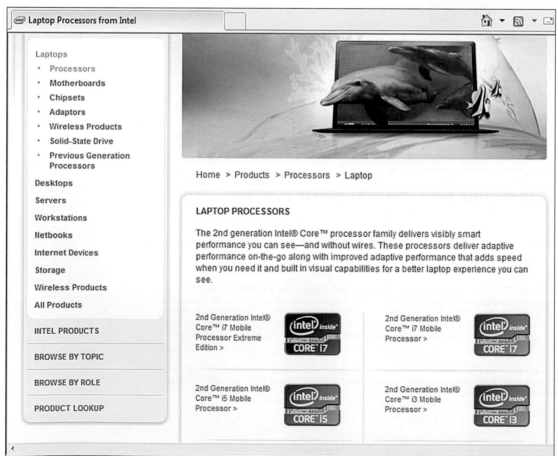

FIGURE S14-4
The latest laptop processors by Intel are in the Core i7 family of processors.

On Your Own Solution 14-4   How to Compare Prices for a Desktop and a Comparable Laptop

Follow these steps to find online a low-priced desktop without extra features:

Step 1.   Open Internet Explorer and go to **compusa.com**. Search for a low-priced desktop computer. One search turned up the HP XZ777UT desktop shown in Figure S14-5. Your search results might be different.

FIGURE S14-5
This HP desktop sells for $369.99.

Step 2.   Find in the ad the specifications for the desktop. For the HP XZ777UT, the information is

- ▶ Brand and model: HP XZ777UT
- ▶ Price: $369.99
- ▶ Processor: Athlon II by AMD
- ▶ Memory: 3 GB
- ▶ Hard drive: 250 GB
- ▶ Optical drive: DVDRW
- ▶ Operating system: Windows 7 Professional 64-bit

Step 3.   Search the compusa.com site for a laptop using the same or similar processor, memory, hard drive, optical drive, and operating system. If you can't find an exact match, try to match at least the brand, processor, and operating system. For example, one search on the compusa.com site turned up the laptop shown in Figure S14-6.

14

FIGURE S14-6
This HP laptop sells for $629.99.

The information for this laptop is

▶ Brand and model: HP WZ225UT

▶ Price: $629.99

▶ Processor: Athlon II Dual Core by AMD

▶ Memory: 3 GB

▶ Hard drive: 320 GB

▶ Optical drive: DVDRW

▶ Operating system: Windows 7 Professional 32-bit

The price of the laptop is $260 more than the desktop. However, when considering the total cost of the system, don't forget you might need to buy a monitor to use with the desktop.

On Your Own Solution 14-5   How to Compare Prices for Windows 7 Editions

The answers to the questions in this activity can be found in Figure S14-7:

Step 1. There is no difference in the cost of a 32-bit version of Windows 7 and a 64-bit version.

Step 2. Windows 7 Home Premium (32-bit or 64-bit) is included in the price. Add $45 for Windows 7 Professional (32-bit or 64-bit). Add $95 for Windows 7 Ultimate (32-bit or 64-bit).

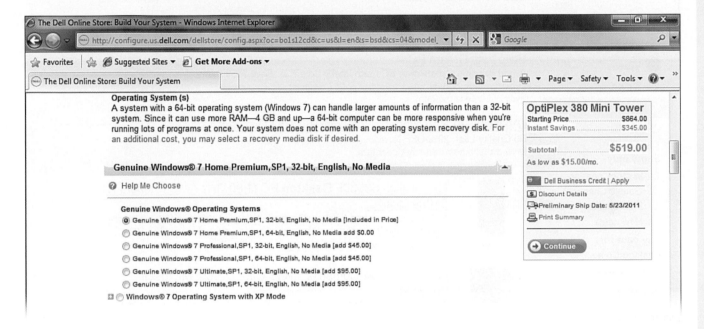

FIGURE S14-7
Dell offers a choice of operating systems for the OptiPlex 380 desktop.

On Your Own Solution 14-6   How to Compare Prices for a Computer with a Blu-ray Burner

Follow these steps to find an inexpensive new computer with a Blu-ray burner:

Step 1. Because desktops are usually less expensive than laptops, let's search for a desktop computer. Go to Google.com and enter **desktop with blu-ray burner** in the search box and click **Shopping** in the menu bar. A list of products and prices appear. Figure S14-8 shows the results of one search, but yours will be different.

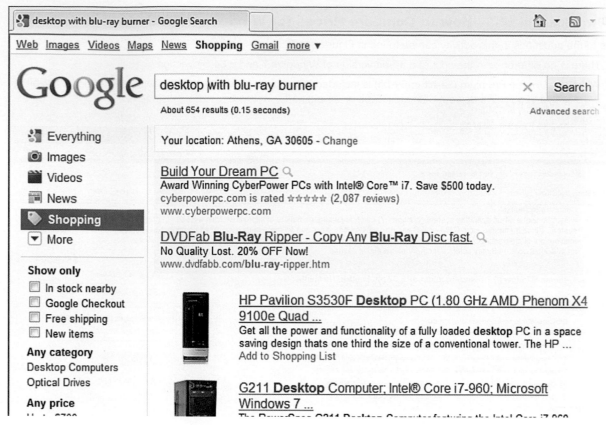

FIGURE S14-8

Search results include desktop computers with a Blu-ray burner.

Step 2. The search results might include stand-alone optical drives. To narrow the search to desktop computers, look for that category in the left pane. For example, in Figure S14-8, click **Desktop Computers** to narrow the search. Notice you can also refine the search to a lower price range.

Step 3. Use the Sort by field on the right side of the window to sort results by **Price: low to high**.

Step 4. Drill down to each computer until you find the least expensive computer with a Blu-ray burner. A computer might appear in the list that has a DVD burner and a Blu-ray player or reader, so you need to verify the details. In this search, the least expensive computer with a Blu-ray burner turned out to be a custom-built desktop shown in Figure S14-9, but your search might give different results. Typically, a custom-built computer costs less than a comparable brand-name computer.

Step 5. A custom-built computer is available only from the source where you found it. However, if you find a brand-name computer, you might want to do a Google search on it to find the best buy. For example, suppose your search turns up the PowerSpec G211 desktop. You can use Google.com to search on **PowerSpec G211** to find the best buy for this particular brand and model.

FIGURE S14-9
This custom-built desktop includes a Blu-ray and DVD burner drive.

On Your Own Solution 14-7   **How to Investigate Computer Manufacturers**

Here are some general tips to help you find a review about a product, customer service, or warranty from each of the computer manufacturers listed in Table 14-5 in the chapter:

▶ Amazon.com publishes customer reviews of its products. For example, find a product by Acer such as the one shown in Figure S14-10 and click **customer reviews**. Take one sentence from one of these reviews.

▶ Do a Google.com search on a product review. For example, the MacBook is a laptop made by Apple. Use Google.com to search on **review of the Apple MacBook**. Find a review and take one sentence from the review.

▶ To find a review about Dell's customer service, do a Google search on **dell customer reviews**.

▶ To find a review about the warranty offered by a company, do a Google search on key words such as **review for warranty with Hewlett Packard**.

▶ Use Google.com to search on **laptop reviews 2012**. The search results should turn up reviews for the top-selling laptops for this year. Most of the manufacturers in Table 14-5 are likely to appear in the reviews.

▶ Do a Google.com search on **best desktops reviews 2012**. Any manufacturers you have not yet found are likely to be in this list.

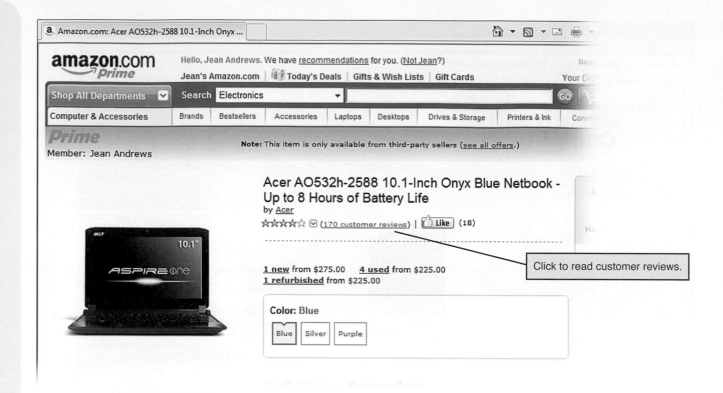

FIGURE S14-10
Amazon.com publishes customer reviews about its products.

On Your Own Solution 14-8   How to Find Laptops with Extra Features

You can find a laptop with specific requirements using one of these methods:

Step 1. Go to Google.com and enter the search string and click **Shopping**. For example, to find a laptop with 3D display, enter **laptop with 3D display** as the search string.

Step 2. In the new laptops that appear, click one to drill down to verify it meets the requirements. Some retail sites don't show all the details you need. If the web page that appears is displayed by a retail site, you might need to go to the website of the laptop manufacturer and search on the product to see the details. One laptop is shown in Figure S14-11.

Step 3. Another method is to go to a manufacturer's retail site and custom build a computer to meet the requirements. For example, the computer shown in Figure S14-12 uses wireless HD video.

Step 4. To find a review about a computer, go to Google.com and search on the word **review** followed by the computer model. For example, to find a review of the Alienware M17x 3D, search on **review Alienware M17x 3D**.

> **Hint** To print or save a web page, see "On Your Own Solution 2-9: How to Print and Save a Web Page" in Chapter 2 Solutions.

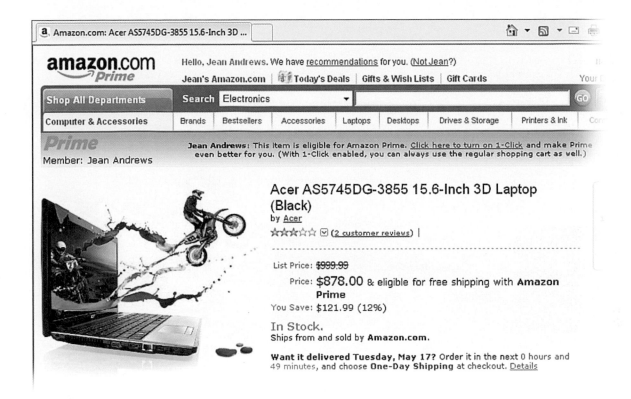

FIGURE S14-11
This Acer laptop has a 15.6-inch screen and supports 3D display.

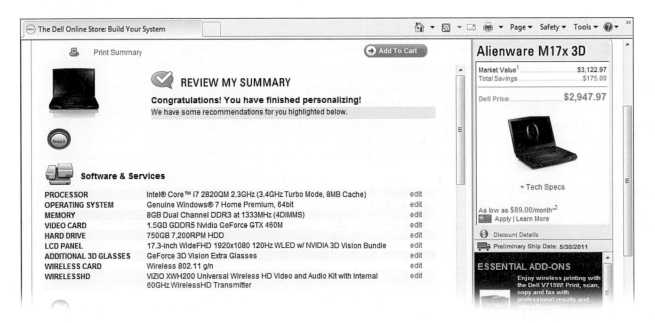

FIGURE S14-12
A customized Dell Alienware laptop uses wireless HD video.

Index

Symbols

A

C

D

G

M

N

S

T

U

X

Y

Z